EXPLORE & APPLY

Students taking their first course in economics face the hurdle of learning a new language that includes many new terms and concepts and a new way of making decisions and analyzing world events. To promote learning and critical thinking rather than memorizing, Collinge and Ayers have created a special section in each chapter entitled *Explore & Apply*. These sections achieve four goals:

1. Grab students' attention by presenting real-world domestic, international, and technology-related issues such as the impact of the war on terrorism on the economy, the role of government in healthcare, and the problems Russia has encountered in transitioning toward a free market system.

A quote and photo capture reader interest.

192   Part 3: Aggregate Supply and Aggregate Demand

8.4 CLASSICAL VERSUS KEYNESIAN—THE GREAT DEBATE

This chapter started with reference to the Great Depression, which was ended by World War II and the massive government spending associated with it. Keynesian analysis was thought to have been proven correct. As President Richard Nixon phrased it in 1972, "We are all Keynesians, now." However, just as Nixon was proclaiming that Keynes had won, the economics profession was focusing in a more classical direction. It began to emphasize its microeconomic foundations, such as incentives facing individuals and firms that can influence the performance of the overall economy.

Economic analysis influences people's politics and vice versa. For example, political liberals often adopt Keynesian policy prescriptions. The reason is presumably not because most liberals have studied the economy in detail and are convinced of the validity of the Keynesian economic model. More likely, political liberals tend to believe that an activist government can be a powerful force for good in the world. Keynesian economics calls for government to be just such a force. It provides justification for a large government, but leaves open specific categories of spending.

A similar analysis applies to political conservatives, who tend to adhere to a classical perspective on the role of government. Conservatives usually distrust big government, preferring instead a more laissez-faire approach. Classical analysis suggests that much government action does more harm than good to the macroeconomy, which is in keeping with the conservative perspective.

While some controversy in macroeconomics is positive, concerning factual issues of cause and effect, most disagreement among macroeconomists is normative. For example, modern Keynesian models incorporate classical analysis of the long run. What makes these economists and their models Keynesian is that they discount the significance of the long run, preferring instead to emphasize practical issues in the workplace that inhibit adjustments to full employment. Thus, the disagreement between modern Keynesians and classical economists often boils down to the degrees to which they are willing to trade off short-and long-run objectives.

EXPLORE & APPLY

8.5 FIGHTING TERRORISM—WHAT PRICE DOES THE ECONOMY PAY?

"The world is not ending."

—New York Mayor Rudy Giuliani after the September 11 terrorist attack

On September 11, 2001, hijackers turned four passenger airliners into terrorist bombs, demolishing the World Trade Center skyscrapers in New York City and destroying a portion of the Pentagon in Washington, D.C. One of the hijacked planes crashed in rural Pennsylvania. About three thousand people lost their lives from these attacks. Immediately, before any more hijackings could be committed, the U.S. Federal Aviation Authority grounded all planes until security could be tightened. It was only when expensive and time-consuming security measures were in place that planes resumed flying. The country prepared for war, the war against terrorism.

No one could know at the time just what would lie ahead. One thing was certain, however, and that was the addition of tighter security throughout the country. The added security measures meant that it became more expensive to do business. The security industry prospered, as demand and prices went up in that line of business. However, numerous other industries suffered as they faced higher costs of production and slower deliveries of their raw materials.

The added costs for security services cause an increase in the real costs of producing the final goods and services recorded in GDP. The economy's limited resources are thus not

2. Encourage students to apply economic concepts to policy issues. The *Explore & Apply* sections apply the concepts of the chapter to real-world policy debates.

Chapter 9: Public Goods, Regulation, and Information   213

SEEING RED OVER SPY-CAMS   *SNAPSHOT*

Often they are nearly invisible. Other times, they are intentionally obvious. Sometimes they're even phony, just there to make us think twice about breaking the law. Increasingly, they are banned, made illegal by an exasperated public. They are the watchful cameras of the highways, carefully positioned to take our pictures as we speed, run red lights, or merely drive along a toll road. We might get those pictures in the mail, along with a bill for the toll or traffic fine we owe. The totals can be staggering. By the start of 2002, for example, Washington, D.C.'s forty-four traffic cameras had caused D.C. drivers to fork over $23 million in fines.

Traffic cameras merely enforce the law, so why would anyone be upset? Perhaps it's the impersonality of it all. Perhaps we don't want to be watched so much. Perhaps it is that the penalties for our traffic violations were set with the idea that we usually don't get caught. In contrast, the modern technology of the traffic cam is coming to mean that we usually cannot escape. ◄

9.4 HEALTHCARE—CAN THE ILLS BE CURED?

EXPLORE & APPLY

Good health is an essential ingredient in the quality of our lives. Yet proper treatment is expensive and it takes specialized skills to know what to do. Healthcare accounts for roughly 14 percent of U.S. spending, compared to about 10 percent in Canada and 7 percent in Japan. A big part of healthcare's high cost lies in what we buy. Over time, healthcare has come to include increasingly sophisticated techniques. Because of healthcare's high and often unpredictable expenses, we typically resort to insurance. Sometimes that insurance is privately provided. Sometimes it is provided by the government through Medicaid for the poor or Medicare for the elderly. Figure 9-8 shows the sources and uses of medical spending in the United States.

For both physicians and patients, health insurance alters incentives. For example, patient might pay *co-insurance*—a percentage of costs over some deductible amount. For example, a patient might pay 20 percent of yearly healthcare expenses after paying a $300 deductible out-of-pocket.

Healthcare is provided by the insurance company in exchange for annual premiums, usually paid for by a person's employer. Because the per-unit price of healthcare is reduced to the patient, patients seek more of it, just as the law of demand would suggest. However, this lower price to patients does not mean the price paid to the health service providers has fallen. The result is the problem of *moral hazard* in which the insurance has led to the over-consumption of healthcare services. Figure 9-9 illustrates how moral hazard leads patients to consume too much medical care.

Examples provided by the fifty-year-old National Health Service in Great Britain offer clear evidence of moral hazard. Healthcare in Great Britain is free at the point of service. For that reason, a large proportion of those who make appointments with their family doctors have no good medical reason to do so, resulting in less care for those who really need it. So-called free medical care also delays treatment, sometimes for years if the ailment is placed in a non-urgent category.

Figure 9-8 also shows another problem in the healthcare market, this one having to do with information. Typically, healthcare providers bill the insurance company for more than contractually agreed-upon rates. This is not usually a problem, as the insurer merely adjusts the charges downward to what is allowable. However, it becomes a problem if for some reason the patient is not covered by insurance. In that case, the patient is surprised with the full charge, labeled in the graph as the price to the uninsured. If this price was known beforehand, patients would have shopped for lower rates or reduced their quantities

Policy issue is highlighted.

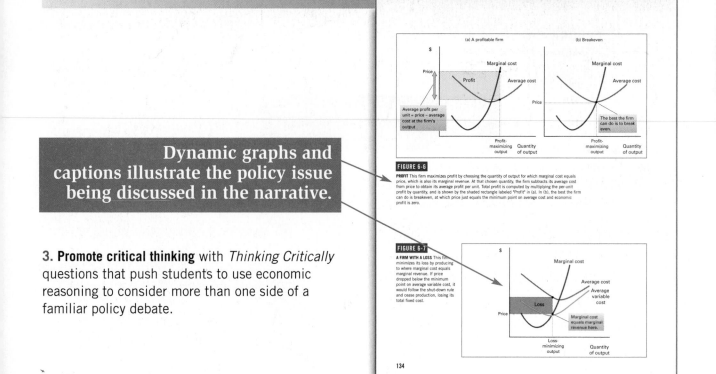

FIGURE 6-6

PROFIT This firm maximizes profit by choosing the quantity of output for which marginal cost equals price, which is also its marginal revenue. At that chosen quantity, the firm subtracts its average cost from price to obtain its average profit per unit. Total profit is computed by multiplying the per-unit profit by quantity, and is shown by the shaded rectangle labeled "Profit" in (a). In (b), the best the firm can do is breakeven, at which price just equals the minimum point on average cost and economic profit is zero.

Dynamic graphs and captions illustrate the policy issue being discussed in the narrative.

3. **Promote critical thinking** with *Thinking Critically* questions that push students to use economic reasoning to consider more than one side of a familiar policy debate.

FIGURE 6-7

A FIRM WITH A LOSS This firm minimizes its loss by producing to where marginal cost equals marginal revenue. If price dropped below the minimum point on average variable cost, it would follow the shut-down rule and cease production, losing its total fixed cost.

134

Chapter 8: A Framework for Macroeconomic Analysis   195

FIGURE 8-10

A DOUBLE DOSE OF INFLATION As shown in (a), demand-side inflation could occur if government spending rises dramatically. Higher government spending could reflect the costs of fighting a war or merely the costs of tax and spending programs intended to prevent or offset an economic downturn. As shown in (b), the demand-side inflation might come in addition to the initial supply-side inflation caused by the higher costs of security and transportation.

1. Identify some additional effects of the war on terrorism that would shift aggregate supply or aggregate demand.

2. What could cause wartime full employment to exceed peacetime full employment? Give some examples from the United States' actual wartime experience.

THINKING CRITICALLY

Visit www.prenhall.com/ayers for updates and web exercises on this Explore & Apply topic.

SUMMARY AND LEARNING OBJECTIVES

1. **Contrast the perspectives of classical economists to those of Keynesians.**
   ■ When the economy's resources are fully employed, the economy has attained full-employment output, also called full-employment GDP. Actual GDP could be at, above, or below the full-employment level of GDP.
   ■ The book *The General Theory of Employment, Interest, and Money* (1936) by John Maynard Keynes revolutionized economics and launched the new field

of macroeconomics. Keynes distinguished between the short run and the long run, observing that "In the long run we are all dead." Keynesian economics takes a short-run perspective. Keynes' goal was to further the understanding of why the economies of the world remained mired in the Great Depression of the 1930s.
   ■ Classical economics emphasizes the long run. It has achieved a resurgence of interest as the Great Depression recedes further into the past.

4. **Expand teaching materials and opportunities.** The book's Companion Web site, **www.prenhall.com/collinge**, includes updates on each *Explore & Apply*. This will save professors many hours of research time finding current topics for their lectures. A custom-filmed video series supports and extends on *Explore & Apply* topics.

Thinking Critically questions push students to use economic reasoning to consider more than one side of a familiar policy debate.

PRENTICE HALL SERIES IN ECONOMICS

ECONOMICS BY DESIGN

SURVEY & ISSUES

ECONOMICS BY DESIGN
SURVEY & ISSUES

THIRD EDITION

ROBERT A. COLLINGE
University of Texas at San Antonio

RONALD M. AYERS
University of Texas at San Antonio

PEARSON

Prentice
Hall

Upper Saddle River, New Jersey 07458

Library of Congress Cataloging-in-Publication Data

Collinge, Robert A.
  Economics by design : survey & issues / Robert A. Collinge, Ronald M.
Ayers.--3rd ed.
    p. cm.
  Includes bibliographical references and index.
  ISBN 0-13-140058-4
  1. Economics. I. Ayers, Ronald M. II. Title.

HB 171.5 .C845 2003
330--dc21

2003056472

Executive Acquisitions Editor: Rod Banister
Editor-in-Chief: P. J. Boardman
Managing Editor (Editorial): Gladys Soto
Project Manager: Marie McHale
Editorial Assistant: Joy Golden
Media Project Manager: Victoria Anderson
Marketing Manager: Kathleen McLellan
Marketing Assistant: Melissa Owens
Managing Editor (Production): Cynthia Regan
Production Editor: Michael Reynolds
Production Assistant: Joe DeProspero
Permissions Supervisor: Suzanne Grappi
Manufacturing Buyer: Diane Peirano
Design Manager: Maria Lange
Designer: Steve Frim
Interior Design: Karen Quigley
Cover Design: Anthony Landi
Cover Illustration/Photo: John Hewle/Corbis
Manager, Print Production: Christy Mahon
Composition/Full-Service Project Management: Carlisle Publishers Services
Printer/Binder: Von Hoffmann Press
Cover Printer: Phoenix

Credits and acknowledgments borrowed from other sources and reproduced, with
permission, in this textbook appear on appropriate page within text (or on page 453).

Pearson Education Ltd.
Pearson Education Singapore, Pte. Ltd
Pearson Education, Canada, Ltd
Pearson Education–Japan

Pearson Education Australia PTY, Limited
Pearson Education North Asia Ltd
Pearson Educación de Mexico, S.A. de C.V.
Pearson Education Malaysia, Pte. Ltd

10 9 8 7 6 5 4 3 2 1
ISBN 0-13-140058-4

ABOUT THE AUTHORS

ROBERT A. COLLINGE

Robert Collinge is Professor of Economics at the University of Texas, San Antonio. Among other courses at the graduate and undergraduate levels, Dr. Collinge has taught micro principles, macro principles, or the combined survey/issues class in each of his 16 years at UTSA. In the last few years, Professor Collinge has twice been awarded his University President's Outstanding Achievement Award, once for overall teaching and once for teaching at the core curriculum level. Most recently, he has received his College's Combined Teaching, Research, and Service Excellence Award. Along with Ronald Ayers, Professor Collinge co-directed his University's Center for Economic Education.

After undergraduate studies at the State University of New York at Buffalo, Bob enrolled at the University of Maryland at College Park, where he went on to receive his B.A., M.A., and Ph.D. degrees. In 1982, he joined the Economics faculty at the University of Louisville. To gain experience outside of academia, Dr. Collinge worked in Washington, D.C., first as a Visiting Economist with the U.S. International Trade Commission, and then as an Economist in the Policy Analysis Department of the American Petroleum Institute.

Professor Collinge's research focuses on the design and analysis of public policies, such as his recent articles in the *Journal of Environmental Economics and Management* and the *Canadian Journal of Economics.* He has contributed to an array of other books and journals, including *The Economic Journal, The Journal of Public Economics,* and *World Development.* Professor Collinge currently serves as a member of the editorial board of *Public Works Management and Policy.* In his free time, Bob enjoys hiking through the woods near his Texas Hill Country home.

RONALD M. AYERS

Ronald Ayers is Associate Professor of Economics and Director of the Teaching and Learning Center at the University of Texas, San Antonio. He teaches principles of microeconomics and macroeconomics, as well as the university's core curriculum course in political economy and various field courses, including labor economics, money and banking, and industrial organization. His classes have ranged from small honors sections to lecture sections of 300.

After receiving Bachelor's and Master's degrees from the University of New Orleans, he subsequently received his Ph.D. in economics from Tulane University. Earlier in his career, Dr. Ayers served as a faculty member at Loyola University (New Orleans), Ohio State University, and Texas A&M University. He has also worked as a consultant for the City of San Antonio and several private consulting firms and attorneys. In recent years he was awarded the President's Distinguished Achievement Award for Core Curriculum Teaching, the College of Business Teaching Award, and the U.T. System Chancellor's Council Teaching Award. He also was named a Senior Fellow, Texas Higher Education Coordinating Board, in 2000. In 2001–2002, Professor Ayers was elected to serve as the Chair of the University's Faculty Senate.

Dr. Ayers has published chapters in *Putting the Invisible Hand to Work: Concepts and Models for Service-Learning in Economics* (University of Michigan Press) and *U.S.-Mexican Economic Relations: Prospects and Problems* (Praeger Publishing Company). In addition, he has published articles in many different journals, including the *National Social Science Journal,* and the *Journal of Urban and Regional Information Systems.* Along with Robert Collinge, Professor Ayers has written *Economics: Explore & Apply.* When he is not pursuing his interest in how people learn, Dr. Ayers enjoys spending time with his dogs, collecting books, and tinkering.

BRIEF CONTENTS

CONTENTS

A BOOK FOR TODAY'S STUDENTS

Taking your first course in economics can be like finding yourself in a foreign country where you do not know the language. You want the freedom to explore various interesting spots, but you cannot read the street signs for direction and you struggle when trying to communicate with the locals. There may be several different, exciting paths you can choose, but you are not sure which is best. To get your bearings in the country and reach your destinations, you need to learn something about the country's language.

Students in a first economics course face many of the same challenges as a wandering traveler. They have registered for the course, but they face the hurdle of learning a new language that includes many new terms and concepts. They also face the challenge of learning how to read and interpret graphs. *Economics by Design: Survey and Issues* was written to help students in one-term courses learn the language of economics. As in the first two editions, substance, access, and interest motivate learning. We engage students with familiar real-world examples and applications that bring economics to life. Our goal is to encourage students to apply the concepts they learn in this book to personal, business, and social issues that will face them long after their economics course is over. We teach students how to analyze events in the world around them and draw their own conclusions. To achieve our goal, we use three key tools:

1. Real-world applications
2. Sound pedagogy
3. Straightforward presentation

The third edition of *Economics by Design* is significantly revised from the second edition. It is now subtitled *Survey and Issues* to emphasize that each chapter surveys fundamental economic concepts and applies the analysis to economic issues. The third edition expands the number of chapters from 14 to 17, which allows for an easier learning pace through core micro and macro material, as well as through the analysis of both market and government failure. Because of the expansion of the book, *Economics by Design* now offers adopters full chapters on market power (Chapter 7), the economics of the environment (Chapter 10), public choice (Chapter 11), and fiscal policy (Chapter 15). All chapters are oriented toward coverage of current issues, an emphasis which is often at the heart of the one-term course. Pedagogical adjustments have been made throughout, such as the more intuitive and expanded graphical presentations in the chapter on supply and demand (Chapter 3) and its applications (Chapter 4).

REAL-WORLD APPLICATIONS

A course in economics is often required for a variety of majors, since its subject matter relates to so many of life's issues: Should I stay in school, or quit and get a full-time job? Which major should I select? Why does it matter if the Federal Reserve increases or decreases interest rates, or if Microsoft is a monopoly? To help students find the answers to such questions and fulfill the purpose of this course, we emphasize both economic tools and the application of those tools.

Explore & Apply

A unique feature of *Economics by Design* has been its issues section that follows the teaching of each chapter's core economic principles. The third edition retains this approach by concluding each chapter with an *Explore & Apply* section that provides an in-depth application of the chapter's analysis to a selected issue. Many of these segments are new or thoroughly updated for this edition. New topics include:

- market incentives in China
- the economy's role in military success
- electricity shortages in California
- business ethics in principle and practice
- the growth of government
- the war on terrorism
- deficits and debt
- technology and the new economy
- energy security

Each *Explore & Apply* includes two *Thinking Critically* questions that promote economic reasoning and encourage students to debate a policy issue. A compass icon, located in the chapter-opening learning objectives and various places in the chapter, identifies material and questions related to the *Explore & Apply* sections. Below are excerpts of narrative, a graph, and questions from the Chapter 3 *Explore & Apply*.

To keep the *Explore & Apply* sections up to date and to strengthen class discussions, we offer two kinds of web support materials at www.prenhall.com/collinge:

1. Updates on each *Explore & Apply* section and supporting exercises.
2. Eight custom-filmed videos that further explore the issues at hand. Current statistical information and interviews with professionals and students highlight the various viewpoints. Tips on how to use these videos appear in the book's Instructor's Manual.

3.4 DEMANDING BETTER SCHOOLS, SUPPLYING BETTER SCHOOLS

Some people know the importance of education because they have it. I know the importance of education because I didn't.

—Frederick Douglass, ex-slave and abolitionist

"Our schools must be improved!" From kindergarten through the twelfth grade, the education of America's youth is a top concern of both the president and parents. There is less concern, however, about improving colleges; the reasons relate to demand and supply.

College students shoulder the high cost of college, with cost playing a major role in college choice. Consistent with the law of demand, the lower the price of a college education, *ceteris paribus*, the greater the number of students who will apply and the more education they will choose. To promote college education, government offers tax deductions, subsidies, and financial aid that in effect lowers its price.

High school seniors choose among a varied assortment of colleges. In lower grades, however, there is normally a powerful financial incentive to choose only the government-provided local public school. The reason is that taxpayer financing makes those schools free to the student.

FIGURE 3-13

EFFECTS OF SCHOOL VOUCHERS Vouchers lower the price of private schooling, which increases the quantity demanded. The effect in the market for public schooling, a substitute, is to decrease demand and enrollments. Vouchers increase competition among schools, providing them with the incentive to provide the best value for money spent on education.

1. Should educational quality be allowed to differ based on family income? Should vouchers be allowed to supplement a tuition payment at a private school, with the result that some childrens' quality of education would differ from other childrens'? Discuss.

2. *Myra:* I think voucher amounts should vary with household income. The more income, the less help—it's only fair.

   Fred: I think education should be free for everyone. Your income shouldn't have anything to do with how much voucher power you have.

   Evaluate Myra's and Fred's ideas. If a voucher plan is to be used, should the voucher amount depend upon a person's income?

THINKING CRITICALLY

Visit www.prenhall.com/ayers for updates and web exercises on this Explore & Apply topic.

PEDAGOGY

Our pedagogical features, dramatically expanded for the third edition, support our goal of helping students learn the language of economics and apply what they have learned.

- **Learning Objectives.** Each chapter opens with a list of objectives that establishes the goals and organization of the chapter. We repeat these learning objectives and use them as an organizational tool for the end-of-chapter summary. The linking of the learning objectives and summary provides students with a helpful and coherent way to review the concepts in each chapter. One learning objective per chapter supports the *Explore & Apply* section.

- **Snapshots.** Students retain economic concepts best when they see how these concepts relate to their immediate world. We include three Snapshots in each chapter to reinforce key concepts that have been presented. ⟶

- **QuickChecks.** Three or more questions with answers interspersed throughout each chapter allow students to check their knowledge of key concepts before moving on. ⟶

- **Margin Definitions.** This running glossary allows students to check their understanding of key terms.

- **Graphs.** Reading and interpreting graphs is central to understanding economic concepts. Colors are used consistently to reinforce key concepts. For example, the supply and aggregate supply curves are red, the demand and aggregate demand curves are blue, and shifts in curves are shown with a different shade. Call-out boxes are inserted into the graphs to help students interpret them. Graph captions are clear and self-contained so that students can understand how and why curves are shifting.

- **Extensive Array of End-of-Chapter Pedagogy.** Each chapter ends with a wide array of summary and self-test materials that appeal to a variety of teaching and learning styles:

  Summary and Learning Objectives summarize the key points of the chapter and tie those points back to the learning objectives that opened the chapter.

  Key Terms List gives students an opportunity to review the concepts they have learned in the chapter. A page reference is included next to each term so that students can easily locate the definitions.

  Test Yourself questions in true/false and multiple-choice formats give students self-assessment opportunities and support the *Explore & Apply* section. Solutions appear at the end of the book.

  Questions and Problems are annotated by topic. The annotation appears before each question and problem so that instructors can easily make assignment choices. Solutions to even-numbered items appear in the back of the book. All solutions appear in the instructor's manual.

  Web Support Materials encourage students to visit www.prenhall.com/collinge to access more self-test quizzes, Exploring the Web exercises, news articles, and much more.

The third edition appears in full color, including a photo to accompany each A Look Ahead, Snapshot, and *Explore & Apply*. Graphs also appear in full color and are fully labeled, with abbreviations avoided.

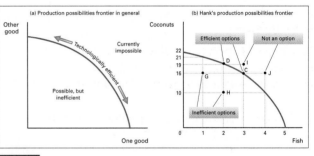

FIGURE 2-3

POSSIBILITIES FOR EFFICIENCY All points on the production possibilities frontier are output combinations that are technologically efficient and feasible, as shown in (a). Points within the production possibilities frontier are also feasible, but are not efficient. Points outside the frontier cannot be reached with current resources and technology.

For example, (b) shows Hank's production possibilities on Castaway Island. On this graph, point *G* represents 16 coconuts and 1 fish. That combination of outputs is possible, but Hank could do better at point *D* by producing 19 coconuts and 2 fish. Likewise, point *C* is more efficient than point *H*. Both *C* and *D* are efficient in a technological sense, meaning that at either point, Hank cannot produce more of one good without giving up some of the other. Hank would like to achieve points *I* or *J*, but does not have the resources and technology to do so.

STRAIGHTFORWARD PRESENTATION

One of the most frequent complaints about many existing textbooks is that they offer more material than can be covered adequately during the term. *Economics by Design* responds to this concern by covering essential concepts without bogging down the reader in too much detail. The book accomplishes this objective by emphasizing the intuition of economics and focusing on those concepts that are at the heart of economic analysis. The result is a 17-chapter book that can easily be read and taught from with an ample but not excessive read amount of material.

ORGANIZATION

Previous users of the book will find much that is familiar, along with that which is new. The third edition, like the first two, presents micro before macro. However, in this edition the macro material has been reorganized and expanded, with aggregate supply and aggregate demand now serving as its framework. Coverage of taxation and Social Security have been integrated into the new fiscal policy chapter. Chapters on economic growth and the international economy have been repositioned to conclude the book, which is consistent with traditional placement of this material.

THE GLOBAL ECONOMY

Whether it be economic incentives in China, the multinational nature of the work force, or treaties on the global environment, international economic issues are integrated throughout the book. Furthermore, they appear in many of the *Explore & Apply* sections, Snapshots, and comparative tables and figures. *Part 6* concludes the book by looking at the global marketplace, including the role of exchange rates and issues of trade policy.

CURRENCY AND ACCURACY

At all times, we strive for currency of content. Graphs and tables include the most recent data available. Throughout the book, we apply economic analysis to genuinely current issues—the ones that appear in headlines today and promise to continue making headlines in years to come. We will also keep the *Explore & Apply* sections current via the book's Web site.

PRINT SUPPLEMENTS

Economics by Design has a comprehensive supplements package that is coordinated with the main text through the numbering system of the headings in each chapter. The major sections of the chapters are numbered (1.1, 1.2, 1.3, and so on), and that numbering system is used consistently in the supplements to make it more convenient and flexible for instructors to develop their course assignments.

Study Guides

The authors have personally prepared the comprehensive study guide that accompany the text. Tied directly to sections of the text, the study guides enhance and reinforce economic concepts for increased student comprehension. Each chapter features the following elements:

- **Chapter Reviews.** A comprehensive summary of the key concepts of the chapter, including the *Explore & Apply* sections.

■ **StudyChecks.** These problems are included throughout the Chapter Review for quick practice with the concepts just covered.

■ **Self Tests.** These sets of true/false/explain, fill in the blanks, and multiple choice questions give students an opportunity to test their knowledge.

■ **Grasping the Graphs.** This section provides students with practice in labeling and analyzing key graphs from the book.

■ **Solutions.** Detailed answers to all study guide questions.

Instructor's Manuals

The Instructor's Manual, written by Rose LaMont of Modesto Junior College, provides the following teaching support materials:

■ **Summaries**

■ **Detailed Chapter Outlines** (available for users' lecture notes) integrating the following:

   Key terminology
   Topics for Class Discussion
   Teaching Tips including suggestions for incorporating the book's Web site into the classroom.

■ **Extended Applications** that help make economics relevant to students.

■ **Experiments and Exercises** to use in the classroom.

■ **Sample Syllabi**

■ **Solutions** to all problems in the book.

Test Banks

The test bank, prepared by Fernando Quijano, includes *over 5,000 questions,* organized by chapter section. Each question is keyed by degree of difficulty as easy, moderate, or difficult. *Easy* questions involve straightforward recall of information in the text. *Moderate* questions require some analysis on the student's part. *Difficult* questions usually entail more complex analysis. To help instructors select questions quickly and efficiently, we have used the skill descriptors of fact, definition, conceptual, and analytical. A question labeled *fact* tests a student's knowledge of factual information presented in the text. A *definition* question asks the student to define an economic term or concept. *Conceptual* questions test a student's understanding of a concept. *Analytical* questions require the student to apply an analytical procedure to answer the question.

The test bank includes questions with tables that provide students with the numbers that they need to use in solving for numerical answers. It also contains questions based on the graphs that appear in the book. The questions ask students to interpret the information presented in the graph. There are also many questions in the test bank that require students to sketch out a graph on their own and interpret curve movements. Test bank questions also support the *Explore & Apply* sections.

INTERNET RESOURCES

Prentice Hall's Internet Resources provide students with a variety of interactive graphing and self-assessment tools. It also supplies numerous current news articles and supporting exercises.

Companion Website

The Companion Website connects students to In the News economics articles, *Explore & Apply* updates, Internet exercises, and Practice Quizzes that include many graphs from the text. The Practice Quizzes were prepared by Fernando Quijano and Yvonn Quijano. These quizzes provide immediate feedback for correct answers, and let students e-mail results to their professors.

For Instructors

- **Syllabus Manager.** This feature allows instructors to enhance their lectures with all the resources available with this text. Instructors can post their own syllabus and link to any of the material on the site.
- **Downloadable Supplements.** These features allow instructors to access the book's PowerPoint presentation, Instructor's Manual, and transparency masters for all figures and tables in the text. Please contact your Prentice Hall sales representative for password information.

Companion Website PLUS for Instructors and Students

Available by using the access code packaged with every new text, Companion Website PLUS uses all of the content of the Companion Website listed previously and the following other interactive resources:

- **Active Graphs.** Forty-two Active Graphs support key graphs in the text. These JAVA applications invite students to change the value of variables and curves and see the effects in the movement of the graph.
- **Smart Graphs.** Twenty-three Smart Graphs ask students to modify graphs based on an economic scenario and questions. Students receive an instant response detailing how they should have changed the graph.
- **Animated Graphing Tutorial with Audio.** Guides the student through a multimedia version of Chapter 1 Appendix: "Working with Graphs and Data."
- **Egraph and Graphing Questions.** This electronic tool allows students to create precise, colorful graphs, using Flash technology. Students can e-mail these graphs to their professor or print and save them. To apply this technology, we have included *Graphing Questions* that require students to analyze information gathered on the Web, then create graphs using the Graphing Tool. Complete answers, with graphs, are included. The *Graphing Questions* were prepared by Leonie L. Stone of the State University of New York at Geneseo.
- **Explore & Apply Video Series.** A series of seven custom-filmed videos support selected *Explore & Apply* sections. The videos dig deeper into the issue presented in each chapter and highlight various viewpoints of the policy issue being discussed. A guide to using the videos is included with the videos and provides summaries, lecture tips, discussion questions, and exercises.

ONLINE COURSE OFFERINGS

To accommodate various teaching styles, we offer a complete range of technology-support materials.

WebCT www.prenhall.com/webct

Developed by educators, WebCT provides faculty with easy-to-use Internet tools to create on-line courses. Prentice Hall provides content and enhanced features to help instructors create a complete online course. Online courses are free when shrinkwrapped with the text and contain the online study guide and all test questions from the test item files. Please visit our Web site at www.prenhall.com/webct for more information or contact your local Prentice Hall sales representative.

Blackboard

Easy to use, Blackboard's simple templates and tools make it easy to create, manage, and use online course materials. Prentice Hall provides content, and instructors can create online courses using the Blackboard tools, which include design, communications, testing, and course management tools. Please visit our Web site at www.prenhall.com/blackboard for more information.

CourseCompass

This customizable, interactive online course-management tool, powered by Blackboard, provides the most intuitive teaching and learning environment available. Instructors can communicate with students, distribute course material, and access student progress online. For further information, please visit our Web site at http://www.prenhall.com/coursecompass or contact your Prentice Hall sales representative.

TECHNOLOGY SUPPLEMENTS FOR THE INSTRUCTOR

The following technology supplements are designed to make teaching and testing easy.

TestGen-EQ Test-Generating Software

The test bank appears in print and electronically in the form of the TestGen-EQ test-generating software. This computerized package allows instructors to customize classroom tests. Instructors may edit, add, or delete questions from the test bank; edit existing graphics and create new graphics, analyze test results, and organize a database of tests and student results. This new software allows for flexibility and ease of use. It provides many options for organizing and displaying tests, along with a search and sort feature. *Economics by Design* is supported by a test-item file with over 5,000 questions. This testbank is described in detail under the "Print Supplements" section of this preface.

PowerPoint Lecture Presentation

The PowerPoint presentation, by Paul Harris of Camden County College, offers summaries and reinforcement of key text material. Many graphs "build" over a sequencing of slides so that students may see the step-by-step process of economic analysis. Instructors can create full-color, professional-looking presentations and customized handouts for students. The PowerPoint presentation is downloadable from www.prenhall.com/collinge.

Explore & Apply *Videos on VHS Cassette*

A series of custom-filmed videos support the *Explore & Apply* sections in the text. The seven videos for *Economics By Design* include School Choice (Chapter 3, Demand and Supply); Business Ethics (Chapter 5, The Firm and Production); U.S. Postal Service (Chapter 7, Market Power); Long Island Sound (Chapter 10, Externalities and Common Property Resources); Paying for Airport Security (Chapter 13, A Framework for Macroeconomic Analysis); The Federal Reserve System (Chapter 14, Money and Monetary Policy); Debt for Dorms (Chapter 15, Fiscal Policy). These video segments are included on the Explore & Apply Video Series produced for our *Economics: Explore & Apply* and are available on the books Web site or packaged on VHS cassette with a video guide.

SUBSCRIPTIONS: *WALL STREET JOURNAL, FINANCIAL TIMES,* AND *ECONOMIST.COM*

Analyzing current events is an important skill for economic students to develop. To sharpen this skill and further support the book's theme of exploration and application, Prentice Hall offers you and your students three *news subscription* offers:

The Wall Street Journal *Print and Interactive Editions Subscription*

Prentice Hall has formed a strategic alliance with the *Wall Street Journal,* the most respected and trusted daily source for information on business and economics. For a small additional charge, Prentice Hall offers your students a ten-week subscription to the *Wall Street Journal* print edition and the *Wall Street Journal* Interactive Edition. Upon adoption of a special book with the subscription package, professors will receive a free one-year subscription of the print and interactive versions as well as weekly subject-specific *Wall Street Journal* educators' lesson plans.

The Financial Times

We are pleased to announce a special partnership with *The Financial Times.* For a small additional charge, Prentice Hall offers your students a fifteen-week subscription to *The Financial Times.* Upon adoption of a special book with the subscription package, professors will receive a free one-year subscription. Please contact your Prentice Hall representative for details and ordering information.

Economist.com

Through a special arrangement with *Economist.com,* Prentice Hall offers your students a twelve-week subscription to *Economist.com* for a small additional charge. Upon adoption of a special book with the subscription package, professors will receive a free six-month subscription. Please contact your Prentice Hall representative for further details and ordering information.

ACKNOWLEDGMENTS

We would like to start by expressing our hearty thanks to Rod Banister, Executive Editor, Lena Buonanno, Senior Developmental Editor, and Gladys Soto, Managing Editor, for their ceaseless commitment to quality. Michael Reynolds, Production Editor, skillfully managed all phases of the production process and ensured a quality product. The extensive print and technology supplements that accompany this book are the result of the dedication of Marie McHale, Assistant Editor; Victoria Anderson, Media Project Manager; and Joy Golden, Editorial Assistant. Kathleen McLellan, Executive Marketing Manager, and David Theisen, National Sales Director for Key Markets, provided recommendations through various phases of the book development and created an innovative marketing strategy. Abby Reip, our photoresearcher, located the dynamic and effective photographs that appear in each chapter. Along with the rest of the team at Prentice Hall, their hard work and vision were instrumental in achieving the finished products we have been discussing in this preface.

In addition to having the expertise of the Prentice Hall staff, we benefited from the expertise of many professors who teach the introductory economics course. We extend our special thanks and appreciation to Mary Lesser of Iona College for her careful attention to the extensive supplement package.

Special thanks also go to the members of our *Accuracy Review Board,* who helped us identify and correct accuracy issues: Paul Comolli, University of Kansas; Barry Kotlove, Edmonds Community College; Matthew Marlin, Duquesne University; and Garvin Smith, Daytona Beach Community College.

We owe a debt of gratitude to our talented and dedicated supplement authors: Paul Harris of Camden County College, and Fernando Quijano and Rose LaMont of Modesto Junior College.

We also owe a great deal to the many reviewers and focus-group participants who assisted us in developing this book. The following professors provided us with thoughtful recommendations and constructive criticism:

Cinda Adams, Chattanooga State Technical Community College

Christie Agioutanti, City University of New York, Baruch

Carlos Aguilar, El Paso Community College

Uzo Agulefo, North Lake College

Ercument G. Aksoy, Los Angeles Valley College

Frank Albritton, Seminole Community College

Newton E. Aldridge, Hinds Community College

Farhad Ameen, SUNY, Westchester Community College

Khalid Al-Hmoud, Texas Tech University

Len Anyanwu, Union County College

Hamid Azari-Rad, State University of New York, New Paltz

Mina N. Baliamoune, University of North Florida

Getachew Begashaw, William Rainey Harper College

Adolfo Benavides, Texas A&M University, Corpus Christi

Victor Brajer, California State University at Fullerton

Fenton L. Broadhead, Brigham Young University, Idaho

Kathleen K. Bromley, Monroe Community College

Jack A. Bucco, Austin Community College

Melvin C. Burton, Jr., J. Sargeant Reynolds Community College

Regina Cassady, Valencia Community College

Chandana Chakraborty, Montclair State University

Marc C. Chopin, Louisiana Tech University

Pam Coates, San Diego Mesa College

John P. Cochran, Metropolitan State College of Denver

Paul Comolli, University of Kansas

Bienvenido S. Cortes, Pittsburgh State University

Chandrea Thomas Crowe-Hopkins, College of Lake County

Rosa Lea Danielson, College of DuPage

Irma T. de Alonso, Florida International University

Amrik Singh Dua, Mount San Antonio College

Rex Edwards, Moorpark College

Michael D. Everett, East Tennessee State University

William George Feipel, Illinois Central College

Clara V. P. Ford, Northern Virginia Community College

Kirk D. Gifford, Ricks College

Michael G. Goode, Central Piedmont Community College

Lynde O. Gilliam, Metropolitan State College of Denver

Richard Gosselin, Houston Community College

John W. Graham, Rutgers University

Julie Granthen, Oakland Community College

Chiara Gratton-Lavoie, California State University at Fullerton

Mehdi Haririan, Bloomsburg University

Paul C. Harris, Jr., Camden County College

Victor Heltzer, Middlesex County College

Michael G. Heslop, Northern Virginia Community College

Rick L. Hirschi, Brigham Young University, Idaho

James H. Holcomb, University of Texas, El Paso

Norman Hollingsworth, Georgia Perimeter College

Jeff Holt, Tulsa Community College

R. Bradley Hoppes, Southwest Missouri State University

Yu Hsing, Southeastern Louisiana University

Safiul Huda, Community College of Rhode Island

Scott Hunt, Columbus State Community College
Paul E. Jorgensen, Linn-Benton Community College
Thomas Kemp, Tarrant County College, Northwest Campus
Jenni Kim, Pasadena City College
Marcelle Anne Kinney, Brevard Community College
Barry Kotlove, Edmonds Community College
Louis H. Kuhn, Edison Community College
Rose LaMont, Modesto Junior College
Phillip Letting, Harrisburg Area Community College
Kenneth E. Long, New River Community College
Kjartan T. Magnusson, Salt Lake Community College
Matthew Marlin, Duquesne University
Pete Mavrokordatos, Tarrant County College
Diana McCoy, Truckee Meadows Community College
Erika Weis McGrath, Golden Gate University
Saul Mekies, Kirkwood Community College
Barbara Moore, University of Central Florida
Francis Mummery, Fullerton College
John Nader, Grand Valley State University
Kelly Noonan, Rider University
Alex Obiya, San Diego City College
Charles C. Okeke, College of Southern Nevada
Shawn Osell, Anoka-Ramsey Community College, Augsburg College
Charles Parker, Wayne State University
Elizabeth Patch, Broome Community College
Michael C. Petrowsky, Glendale Community College

Marilyn Pugh, Prince George's Community College
Fernando Quijano, Dickinson State University
Robert Reichenbach, Miami Dade Community College
Charles A. Reichheld, III, Cuyahoga Community College
Teresa Riley, Youngstown State University
Fred D. Robertson, Hinds Community College
Larry Lynn Ross, University of Alaska, Anchorage
Sara Saderion, Houston Community College
Ramazans Sari, Texas Tech University
Reza Sepassi, McLennan Community College
Peter Mark Shaw, Tidewater Community College
William L. Sherrill, Tidewater Community College
Ken Slaysman, York College of Pennsylvania
Garvin Smith, Daytona Beach Community College
Noel S. Smith, Palm Beach Community College
David Sollars, Auburn University
Leonie L. Stone, State University of New York at Geneseo
James L. Swofford, University of South Alabama
Lea Templer, College of the Canyons
J. Ross Thomas, Albuquerque Technical and Vocational Institute
Donna Thompson, Brookdale Community College
Anthony Uremovic, Joliet Junior College
Abu Wahid, Tennessee State University
Chester G. T. Waters, Durham Technical Community College
Paul R. Watro, Jefferson Community College
Mark W. Wilkening, Blinn College

We also wish to thank our many students at the University of Texas at San Antonio. They have provided us with inspiration and have been a great source of feedback.

We welcome comments about the book. Please write to us c/o Economics Editor, Prentice Hall Higher Education Division, One Lake Street, Upper Saddle River, NJ 07458.

Robert A. Collinge

Ronald M. Ayers

Save a Tree!

Many of the components of the teaching and learning package are available in electronic format. Disk-based and web-based supplements conserve paper and allow you to select and print only the material you plan to use. For more information, please ask your Prentice Hall sales representative.

ALTERNATIVE SEQUENCES

MICRO FIRST	MACRO FIRST
1 The Economic Perspective	1 The Economic Perspective
2 Production and Trade	2 Production and Trade
3 Demand and Supply	3 Demand and Supply
4 The Power of Prices	4 The Power of Prices
5 The Firm	12 Output, Employment, and the Price Level
6 The Price Taker	13 A Framework for Macroeconomic Analysis
7 Market Power	14 Money and Monetary Policy
8 Earnings and Income Distribution	15 Fiscal Policy
9 Public Goods, Regulation, and Information	16 Economic Growth
10 The Environment and Common Property Resources	5 The Firm
11 Public Choice	6 The Price Taker
12 Output, Employment, and the Price Level	7 Market Power
13 A Framework for Macroeconomic Analysis	8 Earnings and Income Distribution
14 Money and Monetary Policy	9 Public Goods, Regulation, and Information
15 Fiscal Policy	10 The Environment and Common Property Resources
16 Economic Growth	11 Public Choice
17 Exchange Rates and International Trade	17 Exchange Rates and International Trade

ECONOMICS BY DESIGN

SURVEY & ISSUES

C H A P T E R 1

THE ECONOMIC PERSPECTIVE

A LOOK AHEAD

Choosing the right mix of government and free enterprise involves questions of economics, philosophy, and politics. Economic incentives can lead to the success or downfall of political systems. As discussed in the Explore & Apply section in this chapter, China's leaders recognized the importance of incentives. They shifted the country's policies away from government directive in order to draw upon the incentives found in a dynamic market economy.

Any country's economic system reflects its choices about how to organize economic activity. Scarce resources and unlimited wants force us to make choices, whether they be the grand choices we make as a nation or the personal choices we make in everyday living. Economics examines how to make choices well. This chapter sweeps across the economic landscape to provide the context for our choices.

LEARNING OBJECTIVES

Understanding Chapter 1 will enable you to:
1. Describe how scarce resources and unlimited wants lead to the study of economics.
2. Distinguish between microeconomics and macroeconomics.
3. Identify three basic questions that all economies must answer.
4. Recognize the strengths of the marketplace and motivations for government involvement.
5. Understand what a model is and why models are best kept simple.
6. Explain why incentives are important for economic prosperity.

EXPLORE & APPLY

*Economics **studies the allocation of limited resources in response to unlimited wants.***

1.1 SCARCE RESOURCES, UNLIMITED WANTS

scarcity a situation in which there are too few resources to meet all human wants.

Economics is about choice. We are forced to choose because of **scarcity,** which means that society does not have enough resources to produce all the goods and services we want to consume. Both individually and as a society, we seek to choose wisely.

Securing the most value from limited resources is the objective of economic choice. At a personal level, we each have our own economy. We have limited income to spend on the many things we want. For this reason, we might forgo the new Porsche automobile we've long dreamed of in order to pay tuition at Highbrow College. Usually, however, resource scarcity does not force us into all-or-nothing decisions. We might be able to purchase a used Dodge Neon and still afford tuition at Home State University.

MAKING DECISIONS AT THE MARGIN

the margin the cutoff point; decision making at the margin refers to deciding on one more or one less of something.

When something is scarce, we must choose. We commonly make choices at **the margin,** meaning incrementally—in small steps. Decision making at the margin is about the choice of a little more of this and a little less of that. It's about weighing and balancing the benefits and costs of alternatives. Table 1-1 provides examples of choices facing a consumer, a business, and a government. Each choice is considered at the margin and is phrased as a question. In the study of economics, questions will often be posed in this manner in order to emphasize the marginal nature of many decisions.

🐦 RESOURCE ALLOCATION AND SCARCITY

It is not a scarcity of money that is at the root of economics. Scarce resources lead to scarce goods, whether or not money is involved. To illustrate that point, consider what would happen if everything were declared to be "free." Supermarkets, department stores, discount stores, and other retailers would quickly be picked bare. People would complain that they did not take home everything they wanted or that they arrived too late to obtain anything at all. This is often what happens during humanitarian relief efforts, in which food and other

TABLE 1-1   EXAMPLES OF CHOICES AT THE MARGIN

Choices Facing a Consumer:
- Should I eat the last slice of pizza?
- What is the best use of the next hour of my time?
- How should I spend the last dollar in my pocket?

Choices Facing a Business:
- Should revenues be used to hire another worker or to upgrade the office computer system?
- Should one more entree be added to a restaurant's menu? Should one be deleted?
- Should the restaurant stay open an hour later, or close an hour earlier?

Choices Facing Government:
- Should we add another freeway exit ramp?
- Should a new elementary school be built?
- How badly does the city need another water treatment plant?

aid is distributed from the back of a truck. The result seen in Somalia and other recipient countries is that the fastest and strongest, rather than the neediest, get the goods. Free distribution is not an economical way to allocate scarce resources and the goods and services they produce.

Resource allocation refers to the uses to which resources are put. How resources are used depends partly upon *technology,* which refers to the techniques of production. When new technologies are created, the results can include new ways of doing things, new product choices, and new uses for resources. For example, the development of the Internet meant that existing television cables could also be used to deliver Web sites to home computers.

When society makes choices about what will be produced, it is also choosing its allocation of resources. The choices can literally be a matter of life and death, such as involving a nation's healthcare system. In wealthier nations, it might seem as if scarcity of resources doesn't apply, and that more and better healthcare could be provided for all, apparently without giving up anything else. But since more healthcare requires a greater number of doctors and nurses, where would they come from? Some people who otherwise would have sought careers in engineering, teaching, business, and other fields would have to obtain their degrees in medicine. As a consequence, there would be less *output* of goods and services elsewhere in the economy. The consequences of resource scarcity cannot be avoided.

STUDENTS OF ECONOMICS—ALWAYS EXPLORING, ALWAYS APPLYING

SNAPSHOT

"Let's explore that mountain pass!" shouts the hiker. "Let's explore the financing options," suggests the car dealer to the customer. "Let's explore the possibility of sending astronauts to Mars," argues the scientist. Like these three, everyone is an explorer. We think through our possibilities in life, and that is exploration.

Exploring can involve web surfing, visiting a bookstore, or mingling with one another. It expands our knowledge and experience, which we can then apply in order to make better choices. For example, our explorations can lead to writing a better term paper, finding a good book, making new friends, or other applications.

Students of economics are most assuredly explorers. As a student, you explore the principles and issues of economics, then apply what you learned from your explorations. You apply economics to choosing a career, a mate, a senator, and what to eat for breakfast. The exploration of economics and its application to life's choices are found throughout this book. The Explore & Apply section that precedes each chapter summary offers the opportunity to dig deeper into an issue. Like Daniel Boone, Ponce de León, and John Glenn, you are now a pioneer on a journey of discovery. ◀

QUICKCHECK

Would $2 million satisfy all of your wants?

Answer: It would be quite difficult to discover someone with $2 million who would decline to accept a third million. Even billionaires would accept another billion, if only to better endow their trust funds. Unless you would actually decline to accept that third million, then $2 million does not satisfy all of your wants. Essentially, your wants are unlimited.

1.2 SURVEYING THE ECONOMIC LANDSCAPE

We have seen that economics applies to a vast expanse of choices. To make progress in the study of economics, it is useful to narrow our field of vision by dividing economics into two broad categories: microeconomics and macroeconomics.

MICROECONOMICS—COMPONENTS OF THE ECONOMY

microeconomics analyzes the individual components of the economy, such as the choices made by people, firms, and industries.

Microeconomics studies the individual parts of the economy. It looks at the choices of individuals in their roles as consumers and as workers. It also includes the choices of businesses—*firms*—which are the companies that produce goods and services as their outputs. Microeconomics also studies the industries within which firms operate, where an *industry* is composed of firms producing similar outputs. For example, the airline industry includes United Airlines, American Airlines, Southwest Airlines, and many other airlines.

Microeconomics revolves around the interaction of consumers and producers in markets. Markets can take physical, electronic, or other forms. The common characteristic of all markets is that they make possible the voluntary exchange of resources, goods, and services. Market prices serve as the signals that guide the allocation of resources. Participants in the economy make choices based upon the *incentives* provided by the prices they face, meaning that these prices motivate their actions.

Microeconomic applications affect our lives each day. Suppose you decide to go on vacation. What will be your destination? Will you use the services of a travel agent? At which hotel will you stay? If you decide to fly, which airline will you choose? Is the fare lower if you purchase tickets in advance? Why do many airlines reduce the fare if you stay over a Saturday night? How are ticket prices related to government regulation of the airlines? Should government regulate airplane noise? If so, how? As you can see, the list of microeconomic questions is long. Answering them requires us to know the prices of the various alternatives.

MACROECONOMICS—THE BIG PICTURE

macroeconomics analyzes economic aggregates, such as aggregate employment, output, growth, and inflation.

Macroeconomics looks at the big picture. It concentrates on the analysis of economic *aggregates*, total values that describe the economy as a whole. The most important aggregate is *gross domestic product (GDP)*, which measures the market value of a country's aggregate output—the market value of the goods and services that a country produces in one year. Macroeconomic issues are often raised in the news. Employment, economic growth, interest rates, inflation, and the federal budget are examples of macroeconomic issues. These issues reflect the macroeconomic goals that each country sets for itself. Widely accepted goals include a high rate of economic growth, low inflation, and high employment.

Macroeconomics was first considered a separate field of study following the 1936 publication of *The General Theory of Employment, Interest, and Money* by British economist John Maynard Keynes [1883–1946]. Keynes suggested macroeconomic answers to the problems of the Great Depression, answers that seemed lacking in the microeconomic mainstream of economic thought. The writings of Keynes and his followers so influenced the economics profession that for three decades after the publication of *The General Theory*, macroeconomics and *Keynesian* economics were virtually one and the same. Today, Keynesian economics is still prominent, but other macro analysis is also held in high regard.

QUICKCHECK

Pose three questions illustrating microeconomic issues and another three questions illustrating macroeconomic issues.

Answer: The micro questions you ask should be related to an individual, firm, or industry. There are many possible questions. Examples are: Why is the price of a Lexus greater than that of a Toyota? Why do some firms advertise? What do I want for lunch? Your macro questions should be related to issues of the whole economy. Examples are: What is the cause of inflation? Why is there unemployment? What causes an economy to grow?

1.3 THREE BASIC QUESTIONS: WHAT, HOW, AND FOR WHOM?

Every economy must answer three basic economic questions:

1. **What?** What goods and services will be produced and offered for sale and in what quantities? The latest fashions, CDs from established pop stars, medical services, fast food, and countless other items are produced by our economy. What is the reason that these goods are produced, while other items, such as vinyl records and 8-track tapes, are not?

2. **How?** How will goods and services be produced? There are numerous production techniques available. Some methods of production use simple hand tools and much labor. Other production methods employ machines or computers in combination with labor. For example, a shirt could be sewn by hand with no more than a needle and thread. However, most shirts are sewn with a sewing machine that saves on the use of labor. How are these decisions made, and what motivates the development of new and better ways of doing things?

3. **For whom?** Who will consume the goods and services that are produced? People who live on Poverty Row consume less than those who live on Park Avenue, so income matters in the distribution of goods and services. But what determines income? If a family's income is small, should income be redistributed from others who are wealthier? What problems does redistribution cause?

When it comes to deciding what, how, and for whom, society must choose among three kinds of *economic systems.* Government might make the decisions. If so, the economy is termed **command and control**. Alternatively, government might stay out of the picture and allow economic choices to be made entirely in the marketplace. In that case, the economy is characterized by laissez-faire free markets, also termed laissez-faire capitalism. *Laissez faire* means "let it be." **Free markets** are free from government intervention and characterized by freedom of choice in both production and consumption. Free markets are associated with capitalism, in which resources are privately owned.

In practice, all countries have **mixed economies,** meaning that they choose a combination of markets and government. Different countries choose different combinations, with some leaning toward command and control, and others toward laissez faire. The exact mix is influenced by custom, tradition, religion, political ideology, and other factors. Figure 1-1 illustrates this spectrum of choice.

command and control government decrees that direct economic activity.

free markets the collective decisions of individual buyers and sellers that, taken together, determine what outputs are produced, how those outputs are produced, and who receives the outputs; free markets depend on private property and free choice.

mixed economies the mixture of free-market and command-and-control methods of resource allocation that characterize modern economies.

THE SPECTRUM OF ECONOMIC SYSTEMS Command and control involves government allocation of resources. Laissez faire is characterized by private resource allocation. In reality, all countries have mixed economies, with the mix varying from country to country.

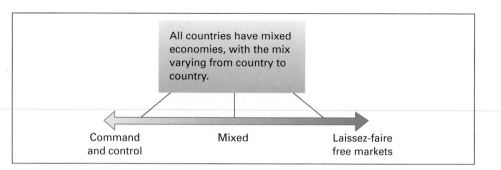

All countries have mixed economies, with the mix varying from country to country.

Command and control   Mixed   Laissez-faire free markets

THE GOALS OF EQUITY AND EFFICIENCY

equity fairness.

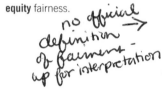

no official definition of fairness - up for interpretation

There are two primary economic objectives to guide countries in choosing how much government to mix with free markets. The first objective is *equity*, which refers to fairness. While we often intuitively sense what is fair, the concept of equity is difficult to pin down. There are commonly accepted principles of equity that apply in certain circumstances, such as in discussions about taxation and government spending. However, equity is ultimately a matter of personal perception. Well-meaning people can reasonably disagree about what is equitable, and their views cannot be proved or disproved.

The second economic objective is *efficiency*, sometimes called economic efficiency, which means that resources are used in ways that provide the most value—that maximize the size of the economic pie. Efficiency means that no one can be made better off without someone else becoming worse off. Efficiency has both a technological and allocative component, defined as follows.

efficiency resources are used in ways that provide the most value; implies that no one can be made better off without someone else becoming worse off.

technological efficiency the greatest quantity of output for given inputs; likewise, for any given output, the least-cost production technique.

allocative efficiency involves choosing the most valuable mix of outputs to produce.

- **Technological efficiency** implies getting the greatest quantity of output from the resources that are being used. Conversely, for any given output, technological efficiency requires that a least-cost production technique must be chosen.
- **Allocative efficiency** involves choosing the most valuable mix of outputs to produce. For example, the economy might be able to produce the largest number of toothpicks from the resources at its disposal. That choice would be technologically efficient. However, if the economy produces nothing but toothpicks, consumers would not be getting the greatest value from the economy's resources. The economy would be allocatively inefficient, because the wrong mix of goods would have been chosen.

There is frequently a tradeoff between efficiency and equity, meaning that more equity may result in less efficiency. Likewise, less equity may result in greater efficiency. For example, many people believe that, for the sake of more equity, tax systems should be something like Robin Hood—taxes should take from the rich and give to the poor. However, as taxes paid by the rich rise, their incentives to work and invest can be expected to fall because the rich get to keep less of their earnings. Thus, the more redistributional the tax system, the less productive the economy is likely to be. The economic pie may be divided more equitably, but its size would be diminished.

To see the difficulty in identifying equity and the tradeoff between efficiency and equity, suppose that on the first day of class your instructor reads the following grade policy: "The final grades of all students who have earned an *A* or *B* will be reduced by enough points to bring each of them down to a *C*. The points taken away from them will be distributed among the students who earn a *D* or *F* so that they also receive a *C*." Your instructor supports the equity of this policy by arguing that it recognizes the many differences in learning abilities and opportunities. Perhaps you would agree that the policy is fair. Perhaps you would disagree. In either case, though, the policy is likely to reduce the number of high grades available for redistribution. In an effort to promote equity, this instructor's policy changes students' incentives to work hard for excellence.

COMMAND AND CONTROL—WHO NEEDS MARKETS?

The marketplace seems cluttered with choices. Wouldn't it be better to do away with seemingly unnecessary variety, skip all the advertising, and just have government direct the economy for the good of us all? Throughout history, many countries have embraced economic systems that promised to eliminate the perceived disorder of the marketplace. Often, these efforts have involved government *central planning* that sets production plans for most goods, which are produced by government-owned state enterprises.

Even the most well-meaning central planners cannot know our desires as well as we can know them ourselves. Moreover, nothing ensures that only the most well-meaning central planners will rise to the top. Even if they do, they face difficulties in motivating actual producers to do their bidding. For example, if the government plan assigns farmers production quotas measured by the ton, farmers will seek to maximize the weight of their crops and ignore their quality. The result of command-and-control methods is often inefficiency, in which resources are squandered on the production of the wrong goods and services or wasted through use of the wrong production techniques.

Centrally planned economies must also match production to consumption. If production fails to match their plans, then the government may be forced to ration goods and services. Government *rationing* occurs when consumers are permitted to buy only limited amounts of the goods they want. Rationing has been adopted in the United States, but on a temporary basis and with mixed results. For example, gasoline, tires, sugar, meat, and other essentials were rationed during World War II. When the war emergency was over, rationing was quickly ended by popular demand.

THE INVISIBLE HAND—WHO NEEDS GOVERNMENT?

Is it not something of a mystery that goods and services are regularly offered for sale in quantities that satisfy the wants of consumers? After all, there is no commander-in-chief ordering an army of workers to bring those goods to market. In the *Wealth of Nations*, published in 1776, Scottish philosopher–economist Adam Smith explained this puzzle. Smith described how the **invisible hand** of the marketplace leads the economy to produce an efficient variety of goods and services, with efficient production methods as well. Guided by this invisible hand, producers acting in their own self-interests provide consumers with greater value than even the most well-intentioned of governments.

invisible hand the idea that self-interest and competition promote economic efficiency without any need for action by government.

The reasoning behind the invisible hand is straightforward. To prosper in the marketplace, producers must provide customers with goods and services that they value. Those producers who are best at doing so thrive. Those who pick the wrong goods and services to produce, or who produce them in an inferior manner, lose out. For this reason, an essential ingredient of the invisible hand is *competition,* which pits rival firms against one another in a contest to win the favor of consumers.

Free markets offer people opportunity—the opportunity to get ahead or to fall behind. The market rewards people who use their abilities to satisfy their fellow citizens, so long as that satisfaction is embodied in a good or service that can be sold in the marketplace. As the saying goes, "Build a better mousetrap, and the world will beat a path to your door."

All participants in a market economy, including consumers, businesses, investors, and workers, make choices on the basis of information conveyed by market prices. The use of prices to answer the three basic questions—what, how, and for whom—characterizes *the price system*. **Prices provide information about scarcity.** For example, you could probably not afford to hire your friend's favorite rock star to perform at her birthday party. The scarce talents of superstars generally command a price that only a very large audience can pay. Responding to this market price, superstars would skip the birthday party in favor of the concert. More generally, **it is the price system that allocates resources in a market economy to their highest-valued uses.**

Price changes lead to changes in both consumer and firm behavior. Following the onset of relatively low gasoline prices in the 1980s, consumers moved up—literally—to gas-guzzling sport-utility vehicles and pickup trucks, with some even sporting monstrous V–10 engines. Light-truck divisions at automakers became profit centers, while companies that relied heavily upon the manufacturing of small cars suffered. However, during times when gasoline prices spike upward to significantly higher levels, just the opposite occurs. Those are the times that small car dealers prosper while the owners of pickups and SUVs are left to their regrets at the gas pump.

Guided by market prices, free-market choices lead the economy toward allocative efficiency. The preferences of consumers dictate answers to the "what" question. Competition provides the incentive for firms to choose least-cost production techniques, thus answering the "how" question. The "for whom" question is answered when people offer their labor and other resources in the marketplace—their incomes reflect the value of these resources to others.

MIXING GOVERNMENT WITH THE MARKETPLACE

For various reasons, markets sometimes fail to achieve efficiency. And when it comes to equity, markets seem amoral—sometimes fair and sometimes not. Markets seem fair in rewarding those who work instead of lying on the beach all day, but can seem unfair in the opportunities presented to one person relative to another. So government steps in to correct the inefficiencies and remedy the inequities that would arise in the laissez-faire marketplace.

Some of the most efficient public policies do not abandon markets. Rather, markets can often be steered back on course with public policies that are minimally disruptive to the workings of the invisible hand, while avoiding the inefficiencies of command and control. For example, government took action against Microsoft in order to increase competition in the marketplace, not to replace it with government planning. Likewise, some of the best pollution-control policies are those that change incentives in the marketplace rather than dictate exactly what firms should do.

The distribution of income in the free marketplace rewards those who provide the most value to others. To some extent this arrangement seems fair. To some extent, it does not. For example, through no fault of their own, some people are incapable of providing much of value in the marketplace. This situation could be due to physical impairment or the lack of opportunity to acquire knowledge and skills. The result is poverty. Government attempts to promote greater equity by redistributing income and by providing social services. For example, welfare programs and public housing are government actions that are rooted in the concerns about equity.

Sorting out when government intervention is helpful and how it might best be done is probably the most challenging task facing a nation and one that different countries answer in different ways. The result is that all economies combine government action and the marketplace. Some economies, such as that of Cuba, lie toward the command-and-control end of the spectrum. Others place greater reliance upon the marketplace, but still retain a role for government.

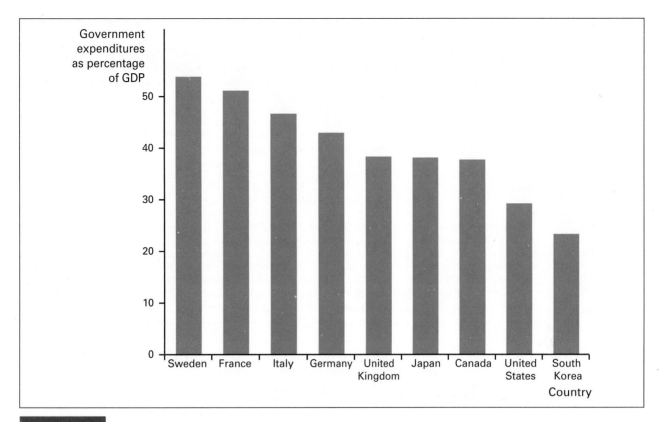

FIGURE 1-2

GOVERNMENT EXPENDITURES AS A PERCENTAGE OF GROSS DOMESTIC PRODUCT (GDP), SELECTED COUNTRIES As evident from the data, countries choose widely varying mixes of government and the market economy. For example, while government expenditures account for more than half of Sweden's GDP, they make up less than a quarter of South Korea's GDP.

Source: 2001 Statistical Abstract of the U.S., Table 1347. Data are for 2000.

Figure 1-2 sheds light on the economic significance of government in selected countries. Specifically, the figure shows the fraction of total economic activity (measured by GDP) directly accounted for by government in each country. In effect, the figure shows the cost of government as a percentage of aggregate output. Government's role in the economy is usually greater when the percentage is higher. The data in the figure understate the economic significance of government to the extent that the costs of complying with government regulations are paid for by firms and individuals rather than government.

Unlike in the nineteenth and early twentieth century, the United States can no longer lay claim to having a nearly pure laissez-faire free-market economy. The transition to a larger, activist government has occurred in response to a public perception that government policy provides the only means for correcting inequities and other problems in the marketplace. At the other extreme, few governments still promote central planning because widespread use of command and control in the formerly communist countries was associated with economic stagnation, leaving their citizens with relatively low living standards. China has been quite successful in creating a vibrant market sector that coexists along with state enterprises. Table 1-2 summarizes briefly the key differences between laissez-faire economies, command-and-control economies, and mixed economies.

TABLE 1-2   A BRIEF COMPARISON OF BASIC ECONOMIC SYSTEMS

	LAISSEZ FAIRE	MIXED ECONOMY	COMMAND AND CONTROL
Key Characteristics	Limited role for government implies a small government with few powers. Low taxes. Private property.	Significant role for government. Taxes take a significant portion of national output. Most production of goods and services occurs in the private sector, but there are many regulations and some government production.	Government ownership of property and government directives control the production of goods and services.
Organizing Principle	Invisible hand guides free markets.	Mix of free markets and command and control. Emphasis upon markets relative to government varies from country to country.	Central planning of the economy by government.
Daily Life	Large degree of personal freedom. Most goods and services provided by the private sector, including such essentials as food and education. Market prices and market wages.	Moderate limits on personal freedom because of government regulation and taxation. A few essential goods (education, for example) provided by government, while others (such as food) provided by the private sector. Market prices, with the possibility of some government price controls. Minimum wage laws and a small degree of other government control of wages.	Severe limits on personal freedom due to government control of the economy. Most goods provided by government. Prices set by government rather than the market. Government-set wages.
Countries Where Applied	None, although the United States, Australia, and some other countries value laissez faire in principle.	All countries, including China, Russia, and other countries in transition away from command and control.	None entirely. Cuba and North Korea come the closest.

SNAPSHOT   ## INTERTWINING ECONOMIC AND POLITICAL PHILOSOPHIES

Bigger or smaller government? An economic stimulus package? Lower taxes? More money for homeland defense? These questions are all answered in the political process. Yet their content is most decidedly economics!

During the eighteenth and nineteenth centuries, economics was called political economy. The term *political economy* makes clear that politics and economics intertwine. Even today, some refer to economics as political economy when they want to emphasize the close ties between economics and public policy. ◄

1.4 ECONOMIC ANALYSIS

The practice of economics involves analysis and problem solving. Sometimes these problems force us to think in terms of value judgments; sometimes they are factual. For example, which of many candidates for liver transplants will receive them? The answer involves a value judgment as to what criteria should be used to allocate scarce transplants. It also involves facts, such as what the possibilities are. Then, we apply logic to solve the problem of how best to meet our objectives with our possibilities.

Care must be taken to avoid faulty reasoning that leads to false conclusions. An example is the *fallacy of composition.* This error in reasoning occurs when it is assumed that what is true at the micro level must also be true at the macro level. In other words, the fallacy of composition involves the observation of a truth about some individual component of the economy accompanied by the assumption that this truth will also apply to the economy at large.

Changes in income can illustrate the fallacy of composition. For example, you would probably consider yourself better off if your income were to double, since that would allow you to purchase twice as much as before. However, to then generalize and think that everyone would be better off if everyone's income doubled would be to commit the fallacy of composition. There would be an important fact missing in that generalization. Specifically, while a change in your personal income would not affect prices, a change in everybody's income would. If prices also doubled, people would be no better off than they had been.

POSITIVE AND NORMATIVE ECONOMICS

Economic pronouncements are in abundant supply from an array of sources. Media commentators, politicians, ordinary citizens, and many economists are often quite eager to share their thoughts. How can we make sense of this mishmash of opinions? Is it truly nothing but opinion?

With some sorting, unsupported opinions can be separated from thoughtful analysis. A good start distinguishes between normative and positive economic statements. **Normative** statements have to do with behavioral norms, which are judgments as to what is good or bad. Examples of normative statements often include "ought" or "should" in them. They imply that something deserves to happen, such as: "The federal government ought to balance its budget."

Positive statements have to do with fact. They may involve current, historical, or even future fact. Positive statements concern what is, was, or will be. The accuracy of positive statements can be checked against facts, although verifying predictions about the future will have to wait until that future arrives. Sometimes it is also hard to judge the accuracy of a statement, although in principle it could be done. For example, "A balanced federal budget will lead to lower interest rates" is a positive statement that would be difficult to verify. Positive economic statements are not necessarily true. However, factual evidence may be introduced to support or refute any positive economic statement. Professional economists generally deal in positive economics, although they might assume some basic normative goals, such as goals of efficiency and equity. Table 1-3 provides examples of positive and normative statements, categorized by whether the subject matter is microeconomics or macroeconomics.

Both positive and normative economics rely upon theory, which is organized thought aimed at answering specific questions. Theories can be tested by logic and, for positive economic theories, by data. Theories are first tested for their internal logic. Does a theory make

normative having to do with behavioral norms, which are judgments as to what is good or bad.

positive having to do with what is, was, or will be.

TABLE 1-3   CATEGORIZING ECONOMIC STATEMENTS

	MACROECONOMICS	MICROECONOMICS
Positive	The unemployment rate is rising.	People are eating so much chicken that I'll lose my job at the beef-packing plant.
	Inflation is lower today than it was twenty-five years ago.	DVD players are cheaper today than when they were first introduced.
Normative	The unemployment rate is too high.	People should eat more chicken.
	There's no need to worry about inflation.	DVD players are too expensive.

sense? Sometimes the testing stops there. When feasible, theories are tested by collecting facts to see whether the facts are consistent with the theory. Testing of theories allows us to judge their value, so that the results become more than mere opinion or idle speculation.

For example, consider an economic problem facing Dr. Joan Parker, president of Carbound College. President Parker has commissioned a survey that reveals that the average Carbound College student spends twenty minutes per day driving around looking for parking spaces. Conversations with students lead President Parker to theorize that students will be willing to pay an additional $30 per year in parking fees to cut their search time down to five minutes. Based on past construction costs, the president also theorizes that the required number of parking places could be added for less than this amount. President Parker's theorizing is positive because it is about fact—the benefits and costs of more parking spaces. Before authorizing new parking lot construction, though, the president might be well advised to collect additional data that might more fully indicate if the theory is correct. In the process, President Parker is practicing economics.

ECONOMIC MODELING: THE ROUTE TO HIGHER-LEVEL UNDERSTANDING

Economics, like other academic fields such as physics, psychology, and political science, makes extensive use of models. A **model** is a simplification of reality that emphasizes features essential to answering the questions we ask of it. A roadmap is a familiar model. A section of a roadmap is seen in Figure 1-3. In this model the wide red lines that designate interstate highways let us know of major high-speed routes. The circles and yellow splotches show us the locations of towns and larger cities. If our goal is high-speed driving, we want the map kept simple, since we need to read it quickly.

Economic models remove unneeded detail, keeping only features that are essential. Similarly, a roadmap eliminates many features of the terrain, such as trees, houses, and hills. That lack of detail would be inappropriate if the map is for surveying or hiking. For driving, though, including those details would reduce the map's usefulness. A good model need not be totally realistic, even in the features it does include. After all, from a helicopter we would not actually find huge red lines connecting black circles and yellow splotches. The roadmap is merely representative, as a good model should be.

models simplified versions of reality that emphasize features central to answering the questions we ask of them.

QUICKCHECK

Categorize the statements below as normative or positive. Explain your reasoning.

a. The federal government collects more tax revenue than any state government.

b. After the tornado hit Central City, Uncle Sam moved too slowly in providing aid.

Answers:

a. Positive. The statement can be checked for its factual accuracy.

b. Normative. The statement implies that the government should have moved more quickly, without telling us what is meant by too slowly. A positive version of the statement might read as follows: "After the tornado hit Central City, it took two weeks for aid to reach the stricken population. Officials predict a quicker response to future disasters."

FIGURE 1-3

A FAMILIAR MODEL A roadmap is a model. The map is a simplification of reality that retains the features of the landscape that are most important to travelers.

Keep in mind a guiding principle when producing a model. This principle is termed *Occam's razor,* formulated by the fourteenth-century English philosopher William of Occam. Occam argued that reasoning is improved by focusing one's thinking on the most essential elements of an issue. He suggested using a figurative razor to cut away the unnecessary elements from analysis. Occam's razor increases the likelihood that modeling will lead to correct conclusions when the principle is applied correctly.

To keep models simple, economists make *assumptions,* meaning that they act as though certain things are true without proving them to in fact be true. One common assumption is termed *ceteris paribus,* which is Latin for holding all else constant. The assumption of *ceteris paribus* allows us to look at one thing at a time. For example, when President Parker was considering whether to add to student parking spaces, the *ceteris paribus* condition in her model might be that student enrollments and driving habits stay unchanged. Effects of changes in student enrollments or driving habits could then be looked at separately.

Economists develop models to explain the choices people make and the consequences of those choices. Economic models may be presented in words, as graphs, or using mathematical equations. If you lack experience in working with graphs you should study the appendix to this chapter, since you will encounter numerous graphical models throughout this book.

MODELS—FROM EINSTEIN'S MIND TO YOURS

SNAPSHOT

The renowned physicist Albert Einstein (1879–1955) was in the business of modeling. The most famous model to come from his mind, summarized in the equation $e = mc^2$, provided key insights that led scientists to the ability to split the atom. It is not only economists and physicists that model, however. Psychologists tell us that all of us walk around with models of life in mind.

Take your model of learning. How do you perceive the learning process? A simple model holds that the job of the instructor is to fill your mind with knowledge. In this model you are a passive recipient of facts, figures, and principles. Students whose internal learning model is similar to this one often fail to prosper academically because some important elements of the learning process have been omitted. Remember, Occam's razor tells us to omit only the nonessential elements from models. As Einstein told us, "Everything should be made as simple as possible, but not simpler."

A more sophisticated learning model allows for the student to interact with the instructor, the material, and other students. Key elements of this model involve setting aside time to reflect on the material, to ask questions, and to work with others. Which model is yours? ◄

1.5 FROM MAO TO NOW—MARKET INCENTIVES TAKE HOLD IN CHINA

For much of the twentieth century, the idea of a command-and-control economy had deep, widespread appeal. Many people believed that the unemployment, inflation, depressions, and other problems faced by mixed economies could be avoided through central planning. Charismatic national leaders came into power offering to implement command-and-control principles. Lenin in Russia, Mussolini in Italy, Hitler in Germany, Mao Tse-Tung in China, and Ho Chi Minh in Vietnam are the best known.

For one reason or another, all these countries have turned away from command and control. Consider China. Chinese civilization is one of the oldest on the planet. Its history is one of extremes, both good and bad. In the mid-to-late twentieth century, that extreme was bad. Faced with grinding poverty and stagnation after the death of Mao, the Chinese leaders decided that a larger role for markets was the only thing that could save their country. Let's look at why China needed to be saved.

Like the former Soviet Union and other communist countries, the People's Republic of China was guided by the philosophy of the controversial nineteenth-century theorist, Karl Marx. Marx had a simple maxim: "From each according to his ability, to each according to his need." This idea was used to justify a strong central government that would allocate resources according to the communist idea of equity. That idea focused on equal outcomes rather than equal opportunities. Equality would be achieved by government ownership of resources and central planning of the economy.

Marx's idea was not easy to put into practice. What does a person need? A chicken in every pot? Rice and beans? A glass of wine and a loaf of bread? We each have different ideas when it comes to fulfilling our personal needs. People want more, and yet make do with little. How is a government to know what people want? The result is that Marxist governments expounded a philosophy of *egalitarianism*, in which everyone would get identical access to everything from soap to medical care.

Unfortunately for an economy, egalitarianism provides little incentive for people to be productive. If a country's government distributes the same amount of goods and services to everyone, its people are not motivated to work their hardest and do their best. In this system, smart people act stupid. There is no incentive to do otherwise. Indeed, the smarter you act, the more that might be expected of you and the more risks you run. Great efforts were made in China under Chairman Mao to submerge individual identity into a collective mentality that always put the needs of the state before the needs of the individual. Egalitarianism went so far as to see that everyone—men, women, and children—wore the same "uniform," which consisted of denim pants and jacket topped with a small-billed denim military-style cap.

With central planners attempting to direct the "what," "how," and "for whom" of production, bad choices were made and resources were squandered. Everyone had a job, but productivity and purchasing power lagged badly behind the West. China, already the most populous nation on earth, faced a population explosion that promised to lead to mass starvation and unrest unless the economy could be made to perform. Thus, the turn to the market. Table 1-4 shows selected key events in the economic transition from command and control to the market, a transition that is still occurring.

TABLE 1-4	SELECTED MILESTONES IN CHINA'S TRANSITION TOWARD A MIXED ECONOMY

YEAR	EVENT
1978	Transition from a planned to a market-oriented economy begins.
1979–1983	Collective farming is replaced by "household responsibility system" of individual farms.
1980	Special economic zones are created to experiment with market reforms.
1986	Foreign investment law is passed.
1988	Enterprise law allows for the existence of privately owned stock companies.
1990	Chinese stock markets are established.
1993	Modern corporate system at state-owned enterprises is introduced.
1994	China allows the exchange value of its currency to be set on world markets, reflecting the common practice of market economies.
1999	China's economy becomes the world's second largest, behind only that of the United States.*
2001	Price controls on key items are lifted as China is admitted as a member of the World Trade Organization.
2003	The highly contagious SARS virus takes hold in Southern China, causing death and slowing economic activity.

*As ranked by the International Monetary Fund's purchasing power parity index.

THE ROLE OF GOVERNMENT IN A MARKET ECONOMY

The advantage of a market economy is that the marketplace rewards those producers best able to offer goods and services of value to others. The better a person is at providing things of value to others, the more will be that person's income. Those who fail to provide value, and their employees, will experience unemployment. In this way, each person has an incentive to develop his or her productive potential to the maximum of his or her abilities. The marketplace rewards ability and industriousness with more income. That seems fair, to some extent.

A problem arises when, through no fault of their own, people do not all have the same potential. Furthermore, people may develop their potentials in ways that seem productive at the time, but turn out not to be. For example, elevator operators found their skills obsolete when the ingenuity of manufacturers created automatic push-button elevators. That example reflects the changing opportunities in society, but hardly seems fair to many of the people whose livelihoods are involved. In other cases people find themselves with disabilities that prevent them from reaching their full potential to provide for others. This situation does not mean that they are worth any less as humans, although they tend to earn less income than people without disabilities. Again, that does not seem fair.

Enter government, with its power to tax. Specifically, government redistributes wealth by imposing taxes that take wealth from those who can afford to give and that give to those in need. Taken to an extreme, this redistribution of wealth would eliminate incentives for individuals to behave more productively and lead to stagnation. Therefore, in taxing, government must weigh the tradeoff between equity and incentives for efficiency. In the case of China this has meant the willingness to keep taxes relatively low and tolerate inequality in income and wealth. While the majority of its citizenry remain poor, other Chinese have been allowed to become millionaires, with all the trappings of wealth. This change has generated great controversy in China, with many older citizens seeking a return to the former ways of the country.

In China, Russia, and other transition economies in Eastern Europe and elsewhere, the urge to impose new government regulations as a response to every problem must be tempting. The invisible hand is just that, invisible. For this reason, it is often not well understood, at least until people have a chance to observe it in action. What the mix of markets and government ultimately chosen by China will look like is anyone's guess. What we can say is that China seems to have learned the value of mixing incentives into the recipe for its economy.

$\mathscr{T}$HINKING $\mathscr{C}$RITICALLY

1. *Jesse:* I like the idea of a strong central government. We need freedom and opportunity within limits, where government keeps us from going too far.
   Lee: When people harm others or take their property, then government needs to intervene. Otherwise, government should keep out, since it's just one group imposing its version of morality on everybody else.
   This exchange illustrates that the mixed economy involves much more than the magnitude of taxes and government regulation. What are some other points of contention in how "free" free markets should be?

2. Some people think that the more democratic a country, the greater reliance it will place upon free markets. Do you think this is true? Explain.

 Visit **www.prenhall.com/collinge** for updates and web exercises on this Explore & Apply topic.

SUMMARY AND LEARNING OBJECTIVES

1. **Describe how scarce resources and unlimited wants lead to the study of economics.**
   - Economics is the study of how to allocate scarce resources to satisfy unlimited wants. Scarcity forces people to make choices, both individually and collectively.
   - Economic choices are often made at the margin, meaning in increments rather than all or nothing. The choices made by individuals, businesses, and government determine the economy's allocation of resources.

2. **Distinguish between microeconomics and macroeconomics.**
   - Economic issues can be classified as falling within microeconomics or macroeconomics. Microeconomics deals with the individual parts of the economy, such as consumers or firms. Macroeconomics looks at the big picture, including gross domestic product, unemployment, inflation, money, and interest rates.

3. **Identify three basic questions that all economies must answer.**
   - The three basic economic questions are what, how, and for whom. The *what* question refers to the choice of goods and services produced. The *how* question is about the choice of production methods. The *for whom* question relates to who receives the output the economy produces.

   - To answer the three questions, countries choose a mix of laissez faire and command and control. The result is that all countries have mixed economies, with the mix varying from country to country.

4. **Recognize the strengths of the marketplace and motivations for government involvement.**
   - In making decisions about the choice of system, countries can be guided by two economic objectives: equity and efficiency. Equity refers to fairness; efficiency to getting the most value from economic resources. Efficiency is of two types: allocative and technological. The first refers to producing the highest-valued mix outputs; the second to producing any particular output in the least-costly way.
   - In a free-market economy, resources are allocated as if, in Adam Smith's famous phrase, by an invisible hand. A laissez-faire or hands-off policy by government means that market prices guide the allocation of resources.
   - When the market fails to achieve efficiency, government tends to take action. Government action is also directed toward equity issues. Such government actions include the government provision of goods and services.

5. Understand what a model is and why models are best kept simple.

- Sound logic is essential to proper economic analysis. Care must be taken to avoid the fallacy of composition, which is the error of assuming that what is true for the part is true for the whole.
- Economic analysis can involve normative or positive statements. Normative economics involves value judgments about whether something is good or bad. Positive economics concerns facts.
- Economic analysis is practiced using models, often expressed with graphs. Occam's razor suggests that models ought to be stripped down to their necessary elements. They should be as simple as possible, while still conveying the essence of an issue.

6. Explain why incentives are important for economic prosperity.

- Egalitarianism was a key feature of the economy in China under Chairman Mao. That economy was also characterized by central planning, which led to the inefficient use of resources. For this reason, China's leaders introduced market incentives. How much government to mix with the private marketplace is a choice that each country must make. Care must be taken that incentives are sufficient to promote productivity.

KEY TERMS

economics, 2
scarcity, 2
the margin, 2
microeconomics, 4
macroeconomics, 4
command and control, 5

free markets, 5
mixed economies, 5
equity, 6
efficiency, 6
technological efficiency, 6
allocative efficiency, 6

invisible hand, 7
normative, 11
positive, 11
models, 12

TEST YOURSELF

TRUE OR FALSE

1. The problem of resource scarcity has been solved in recent years through advances in technology.
2. Industry studies are examples of macroeconomic analysis.
3. The tradeoff between efficiency and equity means that increases in efficiency will often be accompanied by less equity.
4. Adam Smith's concept of the invisible hand is that the free marketplace functions better when the hand of government guides it.
5. Occam's razor is a principle that is used in the drawing of roadmaps.

MULTIPLE CHOICE

6. Economics is primarily the study of
   a. stocks and bonds.
   b. allocating limited resources to meet unlimited wants.
   c. methods to eliminate scarcity.
   d. why consumers want what they do.

7. Making decisions at the margin is about
   a. all-or-nothing choices.
   b. choices involving money.
   c. incremental choices.
   d. normative economics.

8. Macroeconomics looks at
   a. the "big picture."
   b. only the government portion of the economy.
   c. only the business portion of the economy.
   d. the behavior of individuals, but not of firms.

9. Which of the following is the best example of microeconomics?
   a. A study of new automobile prices.
   b. Evaluation of the Federal budget.
   c. A statement about what ought to be.
   d. A history of U.S. inflation.

10. The three basic questions an economy must answer are
    a. why produce; how much to produce; who to produce it?
    b. what to produce; how to produce it; who to consume it?
    c. what to produce; why produce; how to produce?
    d. when to produce; how to produce; what to produce?
11. Command-and-control economies are characterized by
    a. reliance upon free markets.
    b. adherence to the principles of capitalism.
    c. economic freedom.
    d. government decision making.
12. Laissez faire is the term for
    a. the philosophy that hard work is bad for a person.
    b. government command-and-control policies.
    c. let it be.
    d. a partnership between government and business.
13. Which of the following is NOT an advantage of market allocation of resources over central government allocation of resources?
    a. Markets distribute income in the most equitable manner possible.
    b. Market prices allocate resources to their highest-valued uses.
    c. People out for their own self-interest in the marketplace have more incentive to provide products of value to others than would government bureaucrats.
    d. Competition among firms causes products to be produced in the most technologically efficient manner.
14. In a capitalist economy, economic activities are coordinated by
    a. tradition.
    b. prices.
    c. government.
    d. business firms.
15. The concept of a mixed economy refers to a mixture of
    a. positive and normative economics.
    b. microeconomics and macroeconomics.
    c. government and free markets.
    d. command with control.
16. Efficiency means
    a. resources are distributed in a fair manner.
    b. all material wants are satisfied.
    c. no one can be made better off, except at someone else's expense.
    d. technology does not change.
17. The idea that the economy should produce its outputs with the least costly combinations of inputs is known as
    a. allocative efficiency.
    b. technological efficiency.
    c. economic efficiency.
    d. equity.
18. The invisible hand of the marketplace refers to the tendency for
    a. government to control the economy behind the scenes.
    b. pollution and other side effects of market activities to harm the economy.
    c. producers to conspire with each other, so as to get as much money as possible out of consumers' pockets.
    d. sellers out for their own self-interests to provide the most valuable assortment of products at the lowest possible prices.
19. Which of the following is the best example of a positive economic statement?
    a. New York should repeal its income tax.
    b. An increase in the minimum wage is likely to increase unemployment.
    c. It is unfair to subsidize farmers.
    d. The price of gasoline is just fine!
20. In response to the inefficient use of resources in China in the days of Mao Tse-Tung, recent Chinese policy has emphasized
    a. egalitarianism.
    b. central planning.
    c. free Internet access.
    d. market incentives.

QUESTIONS AND PROBLEMS

1. *[scarcity]* Describe how scarcity affects the following decision makers:
   a. the president of the United States.
   b. a business executive.
   c. a city manager.
   d. the mother of a baby.
2. *[the margin]* Think back over all the decisions you have made in the last twenty-four hours. Select a few of the clearest examples of decisions made at the margin.
3. *[resource allocation]* Explain how the economy's resource allocation depends in a small way upon the choices you make. For example, how does your choice of going to college affect the economy's resource allocation?
4. *[microeconomics versus macroeconomics]* Identify each of the following topics and issues according to whether they are more appropriate to the study of microeconomics or macroeconomics.

a. the U.S. unemployment rate
b. electricity prices
c. gross domestic product
d. money
e. advertising by the tobacco industry

5. *[three economic questions]* List and briefly explain the three economic questions that every economy must answer.

6. *[economic systems]* What are the three types of economic systems? Which of these best describes the economic systems of Canada, the United States, and Western Europe? Discuss the characteristics of this type of economic system.

7. *[equity and efficiency]* Each of the following situations describes an aspect of the issues of equity or efficiency. Identify each situation according to whether it relates to equity, technological efficiency, or allocative efficiency. Explain why you chose the answers you did.

   a. Jane, a supervisor at the Built-Rite construction company, is concerned because her company does not offer health insurance to its part-time employees, while full-time employees are covered.

   b. Ted, the owner of Ted's Automotive, a small automobile repair shop, has rearranged the layout of the tools and equipment in the shop in order to service more customers each week.

   c. Juanita, a professor of economics at Home State University, is pondering whether to curve the grades on the last test her students took.

   d. Jason, the president of a medium-sized company producing shoes, has decided to stop producing the model #102 running shoe because of a lack of sales.

   e. Ramiro, the owner–manager of BookMax, a chain of discount book stores, has decided to install a $1,000,000 automated shipping system to more quickly and accurately respond to orders that are placed by customers on the store's web site.

8. *[tradeoffs]* Explain why there could be a tradeoff between efficiency and equity, using taxation as an example.

9. *[role of prices]* During World War II, sugar, gasoline, meat, and other goods were rationed by the U.S. government. Families were issued ration cards that allowed them to buy a government–determined quantity of rationed goods. Why would the government bypass the free market in times of war? Is government rationing, rather than rationing by price, a good idea? How does government rationing affect the allocation of resources?

10. *[role of prices]* If farmers stopped farming or transportation workers quit shipping the food that farmers grow, we might wake up one morning to discover our cupboards bare. Why don't we lose sleep over that possibility? What causes food and other goods to appear in stores?

11. *[mixed economy]* Explain how choices made between government's spending of taxpayer money, or taxpayers spending that money themselves, affect the allocation of society's resources.

12. *[political economy]* Why is economics sometimes called political economy? Explain.

13. *[fallacy of composition]* Ralph the theater manager knows that he can walk from a first row seat to the rear exit in fifteen seconds. When the fire marshal asked Ralph how long it would take his customers to leave the theater in the event of a fire, Ralph responded that it would take fifteen seconds. What flaw in Ralph's reasoning has caused him to commit the fallacy of composition?

14. *[positive versus normative economics]* Why is the statement "Movies today are too violent" a normative statement? Convert the statement into a positive statement. Is your positive statement true? What sort of evidence could be used to establish the truth or falsity of the statement you wrote?

15. *[economic models]* Generally speaking, what is the purpose of an economic model? What guidance does Occam's razor give in creating models? Why do economists make assumptions in developing models? What does the assumption of *ceteris paribus* mean?

16. *[economic models]* Suppose that a college president is developing a model that the administrator hopes will explain how much students will be willing to pay for additional campus parking. Briefly comment on how each of the following might influence student willingness to pay.

   a. Class schedules.
   b. Available bus service.
   c. Students' incomes.

 Visit **www.prenhall.com/collinge** for Exploring the Web exercises and additional self-test quizzes.

A P P E N D I X

1

WORKING WITH GRAPHS AND DATA

Economists draw graphs in order to clarify thoughts and show economic relationships in a way that can be more easily understood than with words alone. Graphs that present factual information are often drawn as line graphs, bar charts, and pie charts, all of which are seen in this book.

Other graphs represent economic models and contain lines that are referred to as curves. As you read this book, you should study each graph and read its caption. The horizontal line is commonly called the X axis and the vertical line the Y axis, with the specific labels of the axes varying from graph to graph, depending on what the graph is modeling. Pay attention to both labels and to what the graph is trying to tell you.

When it comes to graphs of models, you will understand the graph better if you can draw it yourself. If you are able to visualize economic relationships graphically, can put an explanation of the graph into your own words, and can draw the graph, you will greatly increase your understanding of economic concepts.

MODELS: DIRECT VERSUS INVERSE RELATIONSHIPS

Each axis of the graph of a model is labeled with the name of a variable, where a variable refers to the name of anything that can change. For example, the price of a pound of tomatoes is a variable because the price could be any of many different values. The price can change with the passage of time. Likewise, the quantity of tomatoes sold is a variable because the quantity sold can change from one time period to the next.

Within the axes, a relationship between two variables is shown by a curve—a line. Some graphs will have more than one curve in them. Other graphs will only show one curve.

Curves that slope upward to the right show a *direct relationship,* also termed a *positive relationship,* between the variables. Curves that slope downward to the right show an *inverse relationship,* also termed a *negative relationship.*

An example will help. Suppose we are interested in the relationship between the average annual quantity of umbrellas sold and the average annual quantity of rainfall, measured in inches. Hypothetical data for these variables in five communities are given in Figure 1A-1.

The relationship between rainfall and umbrella sales is clearly positive, because increases in rainfall are associated with a greater number of umbrellas sold. In Figure 1A-1, the data on the left are plotted in the graph on the right, with rainfall measured on the horizontal axis (the axis that goes left to right) and umbrella sales on the vertical axis (the axis that goes up and

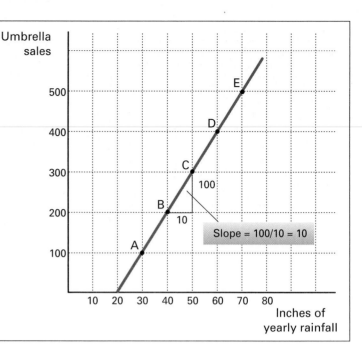

Hypothetical data on yearly rainfall and umbrella sales			
Data point	Community	Yearly rainfall	Umbrella sales
A	Center City	30 inches	100 units
B	Moose Haven	40 inches	200 units
C	Blountville	50 inches	300 units
D	Houckton	60 inches	400 units
E	Echo Ridge	70 inches	500 units

FIGURE 1A-1

A POSITIVE SLOPE A curve that slopes upward to the right illustrates a positive relationship between two variables, also called a direct relationship. The slope of the curve in this figure is positive and constant, equaling 10.

down). A curve is drawn through the plot of data points. The curve slopes upward to the right, again confirming the direct relationship between the two variables.

In contrast, the graph in Figure 1A-2 shows a curve that slopes downward to the right, indicating an inverse relationship between variables. The axes are labeled to show the relationship between the sales of woolen coats, measured on the vertical axis, and the average January temperature, measured on the horizontal axis, in five cities. A greater quantity of coats are sold when temperatures are lower. The data that are plotted in Figure 1A-2 are observable in the table on the left side.

THE SLOPE OF A CURVE

The slope of a curve is measured by the amount of change in the variable on the vertical axis divided by the amount of change in the variable on the horizontal axis. Slope is sometimes referred to as the "rise over the run." In Figure 1A-1, the slope of the curve equals 100 (the rise, or vertical change) divided by 10 (the run, or horizontal change), which equals 10:

Slope = (change in variable on vertical axis)/(change in variable on horizontal axis)
= rise/run
= 100/10 = 10

Applying the definition of slope to Figure 1A-2, the slope of the curve in Figure 1A-2 equals −10, a negative value because the vertical change involves a decrease. Downward sloping curves always have a negative value for their slope.

Straight lines are linear and always have a constant slope. This means that if you know the slope between any two points on the line, you know the slope everywhere on the line. Thus, in Figure 1A-1 the slope equals 10 all along the curve and in Figure 1A-2 the slope equals −10 everywhere on that curve.

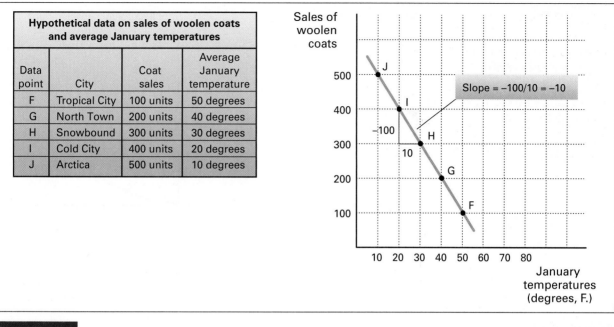

FIGURE 1A-2

A NEGATIVE SLOPE A curve that slopes downward illustrates a negative relationship between two variables, also called an inverse relationship. The slope of the curve shown is negative and constant, equaling −10.

The slope of a nonlinear curve changes from one point to the next on the curve. In Figure 1A-3 graphs (a) and (b) both show curves that have a positive slope. However, the slope becomes decreasingly positive in (a), but increasingly positive in (b). Graphs (c) and (d) show curves with negative slopes. In (c), the slope becomes decreasingly negative, while the slope becomes increasingly negative in (d). Figure 1A-3 illustrates another point about graphs. Notice that these graphs do not have numbers. Graphs of models will often be presented this way when the numbers are less important than the type of relationship between the variables.

Many economic relationships are portrayed as linear. This convention simplifies the analysis, in keeping with the principle of Occam's razor, and allows us to focus our attention on the analysis rather than the shape of the curve. When curves are drawn as nonlinear, the nonlinearity will typically be important to the analysis.

Merely glancing at a curve is often revealing. When the curve slopes upward to the right, you know that it has a positive slope and thus shows a direct relationship between the variables on the axes. Likewise, when the curve slopes downward to the right, it has a negative slope that portrays an inverse relationship between the variables.

The slope of a curve provides information at the margin. The downward sloping curve in Figure 1A-4 shows the incremental spending by the customers of a restaurant in response to additional hours of operation. Note that the slope of the curve equals −25, because incremental customer spending decreases by $25 every additional hour the restaurant remains open. The owners of the restaurant could use this information, in conjunction with data relating to the cost of staying open, to reach a decision about how long to stay open.

SHIFTS AND INTERSECTION POINTS

A change in the relationship between two variables is indicated by a shift in a curve. For example, suppose that umbrellas become a fashion accessory to be carried even when it is

NONLINEAR RELATIONSHIPS The graphs in parts (a) through (d) show nonlinear relationships since the curves in the graphs are not straight lines. The two axes are labeled X and Y, which can represent any two variables. The slopes are:
(a) becoming decreasingly positive as X increases,
(b) becoming increasingly positive as X increases,
(c) becoming decreasingly negative as X increases,
(d) becoming increasingly negative as X increases.

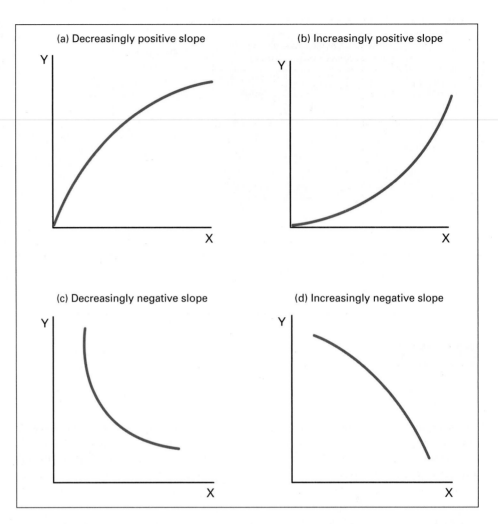

(a) Decreasingly positive slope

(b) Increasingly positive slope

(c) Decreasingly negative slope

(d) Increasingly negative slope

INFORMATION AT THE MARGIN Incremental spending by customers at this restaurant decreases as it stays open longer. The slope shown equals −25, which means that the additional spending by restaurant customers decreases by $25 with each passing hour.

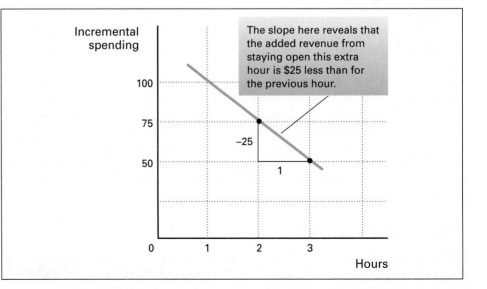

Incremental spending

The slope here reveals that the added revenue from staying open this extra hour is $25 less than for the previous hour.

100

75

−25

50

1

0   1   2   3

Hours

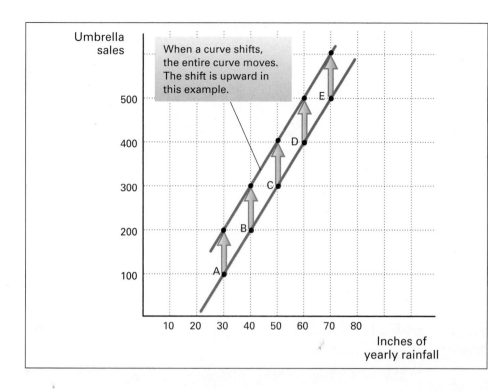

FIGURE 1A-5

A SHIFT IN A CURVE When a curve changes position, we say there has been a shift in the curve. A shift represents a new relationship between the variables. This curve shifts upward because umbrellas have become more popular. The shift indicates that 100 additional umbrellas will be sold for each level of rainfall.

not raining. The curve shown in Figure 1A-5 would shift up. In this example, the sales of umbrellas increase by 100 units in each community. If the popularity of umbrellas fades, the curve would shift back down. The student should also be aware that **there is a difference between a shift in a curve and a movement along a curve.** A change in the amount of rainfall will cause a movement along the curve, as in moving from one point to another in Figure 1A-5. For example, the original curve in Figure 1A-5 shows that umbrella sales would increase from 100 to 200 units if rainfall increased from thirty inches to forty inches a year. That increase in sales is a movement along the curve. The increase in umbrella sales from 100 to 200 units would also occur if rainfall stayed at thirty inches a year, but the curve shifted upward, as shown in Figure 1A-5. This time the increase in sales is associated with a shift in the curve, not a movement along it.

Some graphs show two different relationships between the variables on the axes. Each relationship will be illustrated by its own curve. You have just seen this possibility illustrated by a shift in a curve. However, another case involves two relationships that are independent of each other. An example of this possibility occurs when two curves intersect (cross each other). When two curves intersect, the intersection point will sometimes be of particular interest. **At the intersection point the values of each variable will be identical for both relationships—both curves.** Their values are equal only at that point. For example, Figure 1A-6 shows two curves, one that slopes upward and one that slopes downward. The two curves intersect at a point, labeled *A* in the figure. The figure shows that at the intersection point the *X* value is 2 and is the same on both curves. The *Y* value is 75 and is also the same on both curves.

TIME-SERIES AND CROSS-SECTIONAL DATA

Numerical data are important in economic analysis. Data can be presented in a table or a graph. In general, graphs of data are preferred to tables when the details of the data are less

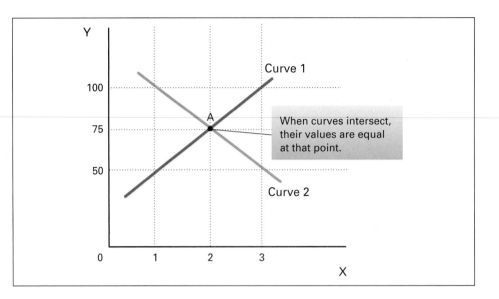

AN INTERSECTION POINT At the intersection point of two curves, their values are identical. Point *A* shows a value of 2 for variable *X* and 75 for variable *Y*. Only at that point does curve 1 equal curve 2.

important than the general pattern, since general patterns are more easily ascertained by looking at a graph than at a table.

Time-series data show the values of a variable as time passes. Economists utilize time-series data when changes in the value of a variable over time are the focus of interest. The number of people employed in the United States for each year between 1979 and 2001 is an example of time-series data, as shown by the line chart in Figure 1A-7. Notice that these data could have been presented in a table, but that a table would require more careful study than the graph. The graph easily reveals that the trend in employment was up, since in most years employment increased. Employment moved down, against the trend, in 1982, 1991, and 2001 because of economic slowdowns in those years.

Cross-sectional data are fixed at a moment in time, but vary in some other way. In other words, cross-sectional data change because of some cause that is unrelated to the passage of time. The 2000 unemployment rate for the United States, Canada, Japan, France, Germany, Italy, and the United Kingdom is an example of cross-sectional data. These data are shown in Figure 1A-8 (see page 28) as a bar chart. The bar chart shown would be useful to an economist studying differences in country unemployment rates in the year cited.

SOURCES OF ECONOMIC DATA

Economic research utilizes data in order to identify problems and issues, and to provide evidence about the causes of economic phenomena. Much of the numerical data economists use is collected by various levels of government. Important nongovernmental sources of data include industry trade associations, the United Nations, the Organization for European Community Development (OECD), the International Monetary Fund (IMF), World Bank, Standard and Poor's, Moody's, and Robert Morris Associates.

A short list of useful sources of data follows:

■ *Economic Report of the President.* Annual. Roughly one-third of the book is a compilation of numerous data tables selected from among those issued by government agencies. The text is written by the President's Council of Economic Advisers, and provides a professional assessment of the performance of the economy. Written to be understood by the

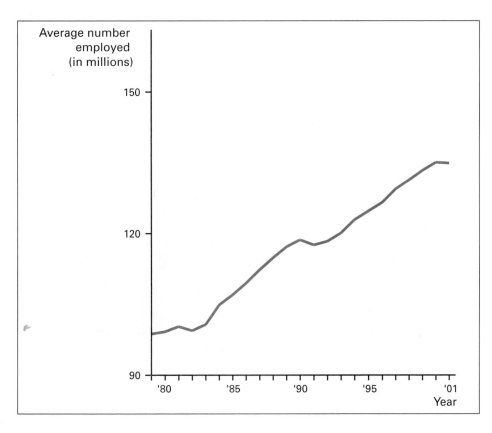

FIGURE 1A-7

TIME-SERIES DATA: NUMBER EMPLOYED The yearly average number of people employed in the United States since 1979 is an example of time-series data. Time-series data show how something changes with time.

Source: Federal Reserve Bank of Dallas online data base.

general public, the Economic Report is probably the best place for both novices and experts to start a general search for data about the U.S. economy.

■ *International Financial Statistics.* Monthly. Published by the International Monetary Fund in English and other languages, the book presents several hundred large pages of finely printed economic data on the world at large, and on specific countries throughout the world. The focus is on the financial side of economic activity, such as inflation, interest rates, government budgets, and exchange rates. There is also data on a variety of nonfinancial features of world economies, such as the composition of exports and imports. To promote easy access, the IMF also provides a CD-ROM version.

■ *Federal Reserve Bulletin.* Monthly. The user will find extensive data on money, banking, interest rates, and finance, along with news relating to the financial environment. Also featured are articles that analyze economic developments. Articles are written to be accessible to the general reader.

■ *Survey of Current Business.* Quarterly. This publication of the U.S. Department of Commerce offers a rich source of data on business conditions.

■ *City and County Data Book.* Annual. What is the population of your hometown? What is the average age of its residents? Average income? This data source provides information about the economies of U.S. cities and counties.

■ *Statistical Abstract of the U.S.* Annual. This source contains hundreds of data tables, packed full of facts about the United States.

■ **The Internet.** The Internet has marked a huge change in the way data are retrieved. There are numerous sites offering economic data. Some data sets are free; others are not. For example, the *Economic Report of the President* is freely available online, as are many other data sets from the federal government.

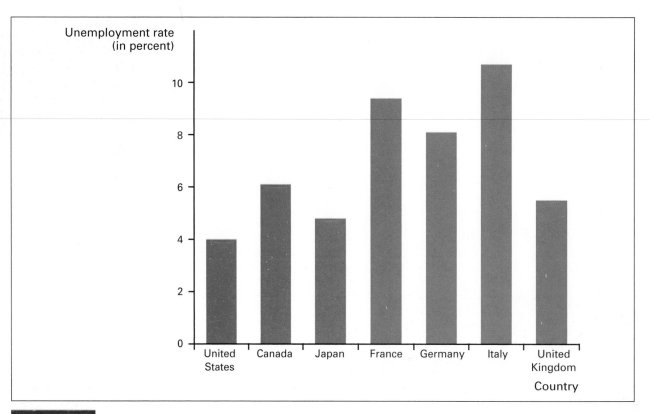

FIGURE 1A-8

CROSS-SECTIONAL DATA: COUNTRY UNEMPLOYMENT RATES The average unemployment rate in each of several countries is an example of cross-sectional data. These data are not time-series data, because they are for a single year, 2000.

Source: 2002 Economic Report of the President, Table B-109. Data for Italy and the United Kingdom are preliminary figures. All figures are for unemployment as a percent of the civilian labor force.

EXERCISES

1. Consider the relationship between a college student's grade in a course and the amount of time spent studying. Draw a graph with the vertical axis labeled "grade" and the horizontal axis labeled "time spent studying" that shows the general relationship you would expect between these variables. Do you think the relationship would necessarily be linear? What factors other than study time would affect the grades of college students? How would changes in these other factors shift the curve in the graph you have drawn?

2. Gross domestic product data for the imaginary country of Janica are as follows: 1998 GDP = $175 billion; 1999 GDP = $145 billion; 2000 GDP = $164 billion; 2001 GDP = $200 billion; 2002 GDP = $215 billion. Plot the GDP data on a graph in which the vertical axis measures GDP and the horizontal axis years. Connect the data plots to create a line graph.

CHAPTER 2

PRODUCTION AND TRADE

A LOOK AHEAD

What does the word *model* bring to mind? A fashion model? A model airplane? A model citizen? In this chapter, we will model the essence of economics—scarcity and choice. While models are designed with different purposes in mind, the economic model shares a common trait with other models. That trait is a studied simplicity that highlights the features of greatest significance.

The basic model of economics developed in this chapter extends from our daily routines as individuals to the grand plans of our society—from our choice of occupations to the rise and fall of nations. For example, the twentieth century has been dubbed "America's century" to reflect the strengths of the U.S. economy in providing for its citizens and in defeating its adversaries. In the Explore & Apply section that concludes this chapter, we will discover how economics helps us better understand those victories. As we journey through the twenty-first century, we will encounter new and sometimes fearsome choices. Economic models can help us to recognize our options so that we will choose well.

LEARNING OBJECTIVES

Understanding Chapter 2 will enable you to:
1. **Analyze tradeoffs facing both individuals and countries.**
2. **Categorize the types of resources an economy possesses.**
3. **Model a country's production possibilities, and how these possibilities respond to technological development.**
4. **Describe how economies can grow faster if they are willing to cut back on current consumption.**
5. **Visualize the flow of goods and services, resources, and money in the economy.**
6. **Explain how people and countries gain from trade by specializing according to comparative advantage.**
7. **Convey how economic strength can lead to victory, sometimes without a fight.**

2.1 SCARCITY AND CHOICE

There is no such thing as a free lunch.

Economics exists because resources are scarce relative to our wants. Scarcity means we have to make choices. Take lunchtime for example. Suppose your school cafeteria holds a Student Appreciation Day and offers a free sandwich buffet between noon and 1:00 next Thursday. Would you go? Your decision depends upon opportunity costs.

OPPORTUNITY COSTS

opportunity costs the value of the best alternative opportunity forgone.

Opportunity costs represent the value of forgone alternatives. Specifically, the opportunity cost of an action is the value of the single most highly valued alternative choice that has been forgone. Perhaps you contemplate how good the cafeteria's sandwiches are, relative to other things you could eat. You might also consider how pleasant the surroundings are, relative to other lunch spots. You would also want to check your calendar—your time may be needed for something of higher priority, such as studying for an exam. If you choose to eat the cafeteria's sandwiches, you must give up the value of the best alternative way to spend that time. While no money is taken, the lunch is in reality far from free.

The money you pay for an item could have alternatively been spent on something else. The value of the best alternative use of that money is an opportunity cost, but not usually the only opportunity cost. The value of forgone alternative uses of time or other nonmonetary resources must also be included. To compute your own opportunity cost of going to college, for example, you must compute what you would be doing if you were not in school. Would you be working? Then the cost of a semester is tuition plus the forgone earnings from the job you would have had. Maybe you would have been spending all of your time at the beach. That, too, has an opportunity cost. Only you can know how high it is, because only you can know what value you receive from lying in the sun and listening to the surf.

SNAPSHOT

"THE GRASS IS ALWAYS GREENER ...

… on the other side of the fence," the saying goes. Take marriage, for example. How many married men and women do not catch themselves envying the freedom of their single friends—freedom to meet new people and do what they want, when they want to do it? How many of those single friends do not look back with envy of their own, seeing the warmth and security of sharing one's life with someone special? Oh, those opportunity costs! We cannot have it all! ◄

RESOURCES

Resources are combined to produce outputs of goods and services. *Inputs* is another name for resources, which are usually divided into the categories of land, labor, capital, and entrepreneurship. We refer to the ability of a resource to produce output as that resource's *productivity.*

land natural resources in their natural states.

Land refers to all natural resources in their natural states. These gifts of nature include such things as minerals, water, and soil. Neither motor oil nor gasoline would fall under the category of land. Rather, they are products that use land as an input. The crude oil from which the motor oil and gasoline were derived is land.

labor the human capacity to work.

human capital acquired skills and abilities embodied within a person.

Labor refers to people's capacity to work. It ignores the increased labor productivity from acquired skills and the development of peoples' abilities, which constitute **human capital.** Human capital is a special case of an economy's third resource, capital.

QUICKCHECK

Just before leaving office in 2001, President Clinton designated as parkland millions of acres of land owned by the federal government. Since the government already owned the land, is it true that there were no opportunity costs to the president's decision?

Answer: No. Although the government did not have to spend money to acquire the land, there were still opportunity costs. For one, national parklands are restricted in terms of their uses. Thus, mineral exploration is curtailed. Ranchers are also not allowed to graze their animals in national parks. By converting the land into a park, the federal government gave up the opportunity of selling it. These opportunity costs are difficult to estimate, but are real nonetheless. The opportunity costs account for the public protests that accompanied the president's action.

Capital is anything that is produced in order to increase productivity in the future. Along with human capital, there is also *physical capital,* which includes buildings, machinery, and other equipment. For example, a college education adds to human capital, and the classroom in which that education was obtained is physical capital. The classroom aids in the production of an education, and the education aids in productivity in the workplace.

capital anything that is produced in order to increase productivity in the future; includes human capital and physical capital.

Caution: The definition of capital used in economics differs from that used in finance. Financial capital refers to financial instruments, such as stocks, bonds, and money.

Entrepreneurship is taking personal initiative to combine resources in productive ways. Rather than accepting jobs where orders are handed down from above, entrepreneurs blaze new trails in the world of commerce. If you start your own business, you are an entrepreneur. Entrepreneurs take risks, but have the potential to become the economy's movers and shakers. Countries tap the creative potential of entrepreneurship in order to improve the value they get from other resources. In the process, the entrepreneurs themselves are sometimes handsomely rewarded.

entrepreneurship personal initiative to combine resources in productive ways; involves risk.

The possibilities for combining an economy's resources depend upon technology. **Technology** refers to possible techniques of production. Technological advances both improve the selection of goods and services and the manner in which we can produce them. As technologies change, the relative values of various resources also change. For example, natural harbors declined in significance in response to the technology of air transportation. While the value of land around harbors diminished, air travel increased the importance of other resources, such as the human capital needed to pilot the planes.

technology possible techniques of production.

2.2 PRODUCTION POSSIBILITIES

Land, labor, capital, and entrepreneurship combine in various ways to produce the output of various goods and services. This section examines the output opportunities these combinations allow and the resulting choices that all economies must make.

MODELING SCARCITY AND CHOICE

Recall that a model is a simplification of reality. Following the principle of keeping a model simple, a good model emphasizes only those features pertinent to solving the problem at hand. This section models the essence of economics, which is scarcity and choice. An economy's scarce resources limit its options, so it must make choices about what to produce. We can model these options, and possibilities for choice among them, with a production possibilities frontier.

production possibilities frontier
a model that shows the various combinations of two goods the economy is capable of producing.

The **production possibilities frontier** illustrates scarcity and choice by assuming that only two goods can be produced. This simplification is appropriate, because understanding choice between any two goods allows the understanding of choice between each good and any other. It is termed a *frontier* because it represents the limits of output possibilities, given current resources and technology. Frontiers of knowledge and capability are made to be expanded, and the production possibilities frontier is no exception. Over time, as people and firms accumulate more resources and learn new production techniques, the production possibilities frontier will expand.

Consider the fictional economy of Castaway Island, inhabited exclusively by a castaway named Hank. Hank has the island to himself, and it provides for all his material needs. Still, he must spend time gathering food to eat. His options are to catch fish or harvest coconuts. He values both of these foods in his diet and can spend up to eight hours a day to obtain them. Figure 2-1 illustrates a production possibilities frontier for Hank's economy.

The graph of production possibilities in Figure 2-1 reveals the same information as the table, but does so in a visual way that can be interpreted at a glance. Each row of the table corresponds to a point on the graph. For example, the combination of three fish and sixteen coconuts can be read from the third line of the table or seen as point C on the graph.

Relationships among data are more readily apparent in the graph than in the table in Figure 2-1. For example, a basic message of the production possibilities frontier is that the more fish Hank catches, the fewer coconuts he can collect. A glance at the graph reveals this relationship. The inverse relationship between fish and coconuts illustrates the opportunity cost of Hank using his limited resource, time.

The opportunity cost of more fish is the number of coconuts forgone. The table in Figure 2-2 shows these opportunity costs. Since we are showing the opportunity cost of more fish, Figure 2-2 rearranges the rows in Figure 2-1 to start with row F, which corresponds to zero fish.

As Hank increases his catch from zero fish (row F in the table) to a maximum of five fish (row A), we see the number of coconuts he collects drop at an increasing rate. In other words, the opportunity cost of the first fish is only one coconut. The opportunity cost of two fish is giving up three coconuts. Then opportunity costs really jump. The opportunity cost of four fish is 12 coconuts, which is quadruple the opportunity cost of two fish. Five fish

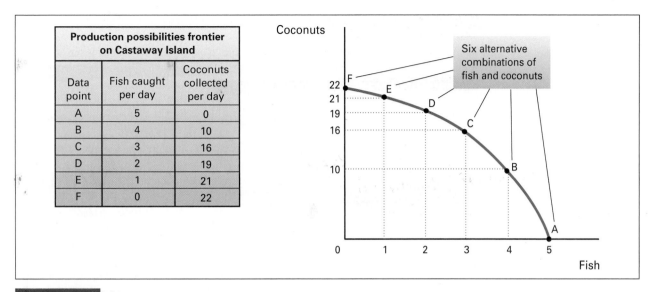

FIGURE 2-1

THE PRODUCTION POSSIBILITIES FRONTIER ON CASTAWAY ISLAND The production possibilities frontier is a curve that illustrates an economy's options from which to choose. If Hank devotes all of his labor to collecting coconuts, he will have 22 coconuts but no fish, as shown by point *F*. Alternatively, he could catch one fish and still have 21 coconuts, as shown by point *E*. Points *A, B, C,* and *D* on the production possibilities frontier illustrate other possible combinations of the two goods.

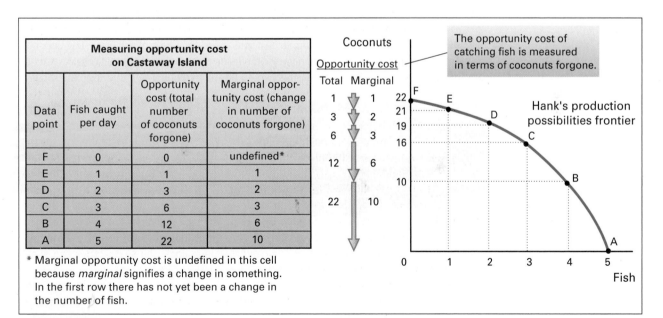

FIGURE 2-2

MEASURING OPPORTUNITY COST ON CASTAWAY ISLAND The opportunity cost of fish can be measured at the margin or in total. The marginal opportunity cost is measured one fish at a time. The first fish costs one coconut, the second costs another two coconuts, and so forth. The total opportunity cost is the sum of the marginal opportunity costs, as shown on the left. For example, the total opportunity cost of two fish is three coconuts.

carry an opportunity cost of 22 coconuts, meaning that Hank must give up all coconuts if he wants to catch five fish.

The final column in Figure 2-2 shows *marginal opportunity cost*, which is the additional opportunity cost from catching one more fish. In economics, marginal means incremental—referring to one additional unit of a good or service. For example, you can see that the marginal opportunity cost of the second fish equals 2, computed as the difference between the opportunity cost of two fish and one fish. Similarly, the marginal opportunity cost of the fifth fish equals 10, which is the difference between the opportunity cost of four fish and five fish. The graph in Figure 2-2 duplicates the graph in Figure 2-1, except that Figure 2-2 shows the marginal and total opportunity costs.

law of increasing cost the rise in the marginal opportunity cost of producing a good as more of that good is produced.

The numbers in Figure 2-2 illustrate a principle known as the **law of increasing cost,** which states that as an economy adds to its production of any one good, the marginal opportunity cost of that good will rise. The reason is that resources are often specialized, being more suitable to producing one output than another output. So to increase the output of a good, the most appropriate resources are used first, followed by resources that are increasingly less appropriate for producing that good.

Because marginal opportunity cost increases as output increases, the production possibilities frontier is bowed outward, meaning that its slope becomes increasingly negative. In contrast, if marginal opportunity cost were constant, the production possibilities frontier would be a straight line with a constant downward slope. To understand the law of increasing cost and why the production possibilities frontier is bowed outward in Hank's case, consider the choices he must make.

Each daylight hour, Hank has to choose between fishing and gathering coconuts. The most productive fishing occurs at certain hours of the day when the fish are biting. While all hours are equally well suited to gathering coconuts, Hank knows that the number of coconuts gathered per hour declines as he spends more hours per day gathering, because he gathers the most accessible coconuts first. Knocking a few hours off of coconut gathering allows Hank to fish when the fishing is best and comes at a cost of relatively few coconuts forgone. Adding more hours to his fishing time leads to less and less incremental productivity in fishing and takes away increasingly more productive hours in gathering. The result is the law of increasing cost.

Like Hank, economies are forced to make choices about how to use scarce resources. In producing any good *X*, an economy first uses resources that are best suited to producing *X*. If the economy keeps adding to the production of good *X*, it uses resources that are increasingly less well suited to *X*, but increasingly better suited to some other good, *Y*. The result is that the production of good *Y* drops at an increasingly rapid rate as *X* production increases. The production possibilities frontier bows outward because resources are not equally suited to the production of different goods.

For instance, classrooms are well suited to producing education, but not to producing automobiles. Resources are often specialized to perform limited tasks: fish hooks are great for fishing, cooktops for cooking, coal mines for mining coal, and so on. They can sometimes be used for other purposes, but will not be as productive in these uses. For example, coal mines are fine places to grow mushrooms and have led to commercial production under such brand names as Moonlight Mushrooms. However, until the coal seams are fully mined, the coal output is likely to be of higher value.

Figure 2-3(a) shows a production possibilities frontier without numbers, since the idea of a production possibilities frontier transcends any particular numbers. If you have trouble with a graph without numbers, however, just put in some illustrative numbers as is done in Figure 2-3(b). All points within or along the production possibilities frontier are feasible combinations of two goods. For the economy to reach that frontier, it must use all of its resources. It must also use these resources efficiently in the technological sense of getting

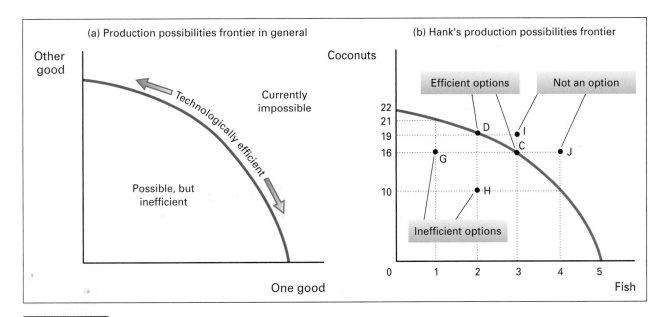

FIGURE 2-3

POSSIBILITIES FOR EFFICIENCY All points on the production possibilities frontier are output combinations that are technologically efficient and feasible, as shown in (a). Points within the production possibilities frontier are also feasible, but are not efficient. Points outside the frontier cannot be reached with current resources and technology.

For example, (b) shows Hank's production possibilities on Castaway Island. On this graph, point *G* represents 16 coconuts and 1 fish. That combination of outputs is possible, but Hank could do better at point *D* by producing 19 coconuts and 2 fish. Likewise, point *C* is more efficient than point *H*. Both *C* and *D* are efficient in a technological sense, meaning that at either point, Hank cannot produce more of one good without giving up some of the other. Hank would like to achieve points *I* or *J*, but does not have the resources and technology to do so.

the most output for given inputs. Otherwise, the economy would be inefficient and at a point inside the frontier. In short, **any point along the production possibilities frontier is a technologically efficient combination of outputs.** Points inside the frontier are inefficient and points outside the frontier are currently unattainable.

Recall from Chapter 1 that, while *technological efficiency* is part of economic efficiency, there is also another part, *allocative efficiency*. Allocative efficiency implies a specific point on the production possibilities frontier that is the most valuable combination of outputs. In general, **there will be only one point on the production possibilities frontier that is allocatively efficient,** and we cannot know what it is by sight. However, the invisible hand of the market economy will tend to lead the economy to that point on the production possibilities frontier that is the allocatively efficient combination of outputs. In Hank's case, his preferences for fish vis à vis coconuts will guide his use of time so that he picks the combination of fish and coconuts that provides him with the most satisfaction.

ECONOMIC GROWTH AND TECHNOLOGICAL CHANGE

Land, labor, capital, and entrepreneurship—these are the resources available to the economy. Production possibilities will depend on how much of each resource the economy has and on the technology that is available to make use of those resources. As resources increase

QUICKCHECK

Are all points along a production possibilities frontier equally efficient? Is an economy indifferent among them?

Answer: All points on the production possibilities frontier are technologically efficient, meaning that it is impossible to produce more of one good without giving up some of the other. However, while technological efficiency is necessary for overall economic efficiency, so too is allocative efficiency, which identifies the specific point on the production possibilities frontier that is the most valuable combination of outputs. Not all points on the production possibilities frontier are allocatively efficient, meaning there is a point that will be preferred over others since it best reflects wants.

economic growth the ability of the economy to produce more or better output.

or technology improves, production possibilities grow and the economy's entire production possibilities frontier shifts outward, as shown in Figure 2-4(a). **When the production possibilities frontier shifts outward, the economy experiences economic growth.** Economic growth occurs when the economy uses expanded production possibilities to produce an output of greater value. In the event of natural disasters, the exhaustion of natural resources, or anything else that causes an economy's resource base to shrink, the country's production possibilities will also shrink, which would lead to negative economic growth. Figure 2-4(b) illustrates negative economic growth as a shift inward of the production possibilities frontier.

Let's return to the economy of Castaway Island for examples of positive and negative growth. Hank might find some netting that has washed ashore that he can use to catch fish or to collect the coconuts as they fall to the ground. The netting is capital that allows him to catch more fish and to collect more coconuts per hour. This shifts Hank's production possi-

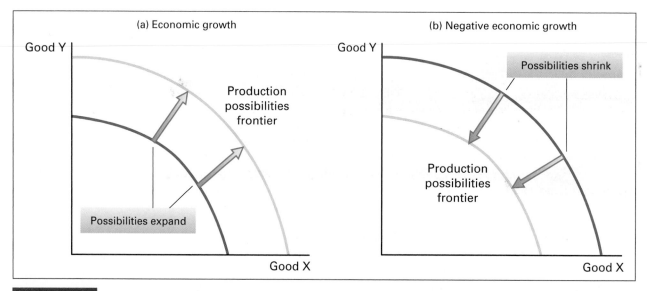

FIGURE 2-4

ECONOMIC GROWTH Economic growth shifts the production possibilities frontier outward, as shown in (a). More resources or improved technology have this effect. Negative economic growth, seen in (b), is associated with a shift inward in the frontier. Negative growth can be caused by the destruction of resources, such as from natural disasters or warfare.

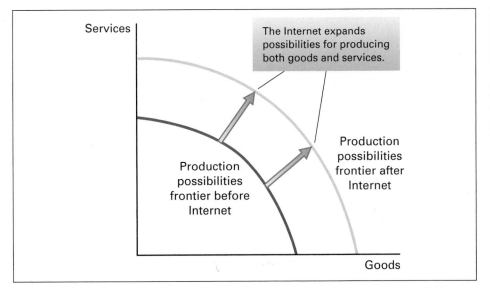

Services

The Internet expands possibilities for producing both goods and services.

Production possibilities frontier after Internet

Production possibilities frontier before Internet

Goods

FIGURE 2-5

ECONOMIC GROWTH FROM THE INTERNET The efficiencies brought about by the Internet shift the production possibilities frontier outward. The equipment that allows this flow is capital, and includes such things as fiber optic cables and personal computers.

bilities frontier outward. Alternatively, were Hank to overfish and a coconut blight to strike, fewer fish and coconuts would be available. His production possibilities frontier would shift inward.

Closer to home, the Internet has improved information flows and allowed more efficient choice. The result is that the economy is able to obtain more output from its scarce resources. The Internet is at least partly capital because it was produced in order to make information flow easier, which can increase the production of other goods and services. It includes such components as the computer and modem from which you connect, the lines upon which the data travel, and the routers and switches that direct that data to the right places. Adding this Internet capital to the economy causes the production possibilities frontier to shift outward, as shown in Figure 2-5.

MODELING GROWTH—IMPOVERISHED COUNTRIES FACE A DIFFICULT TRADEOFF

It takes capital to make use of technological change and increase labor productivity. Since capital represents output that is produced now for the purpose of increasing productivity later, the creation of capital comes at the expense of current consumption. This choice can be illustrated with the production possibilities frontier, as shown in Figure 2-6.

For example, at point *A* the economy is devoting nearly all of its resources to producing goods for current consumption. The result is that the amount of capital it possesses decreases over time, because of equipment wearing out, buildings falling into disrepair, and other forms of *depreciation*. With its economy producing too little new capital to offset depreciation of existing capital, the production possibilities frontier shifts inward. Point *B*, in contrast, trades off some current consumption for significantly more production of capital, more than enough to offset depreciation. The result is that the production possibilities frontier shifts out over time.

When an economy is characterized by widespread poverty, the route to economic growth involves particularly tough tradeoffs. For countries to reduce poverty, they must channel resources into amassing capital. Those resources are taken away from the production of goods that meet current needs, such as food and housing. Yet Bangladesh, Somalia, and other countries that can ill afford to sacrifice current consumption are the ones most in need of the economic growth that such a sacrifice would bring.

FIGURE 2-6

CAPITAL'S ROLE IN GROWTH
Sacrificing current consumption in favor of producing more capital hastens economic growth, but may be painful in the present. For example, choosing point *B* provides the capital needed to expand production possibilities over time. In contrast, choosing point *A* allows for more current consumption, but shrinks the production possibilities frontier over time. This is because not enough new capital is produced to offset the depreciation of existing capital.

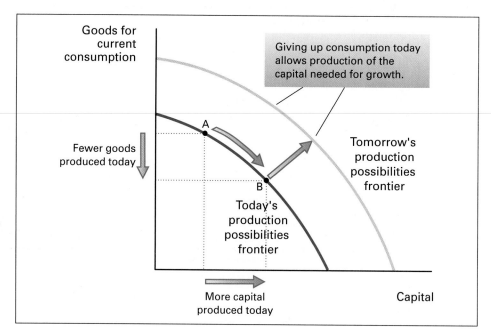

SNAPSHOT

JAPANESE RICE FOR NORTH KOREAN ROCKETS

Was it a test missile or a satellite launch vehicle that North Korea fired in the direction of Japan? Either way, the Japanese were not amused by this unexpected projectile hurtling their way late in the summer of 1998. In response, Japan was quick to cut off its food aid to North Korea. After all, it was the food aid that allowed North Korea the luxury of devoting resources to developing its expertise in rocketry. Food aid from Japan was meant to help the North Koreans survive, not to allow them to reallocate their resources toward financing investment in new, threatening capabilities, now thought to include nuclear weapons. ◄

GENERAL AND SPECIALIZED GROWTH

Technological change can increase productivity across a broad range of industries, as with the better information flows made possible by modern computers and telecommunications. Oftentimes, however, technological change is specific to an industry. For example, an advance in biotechnology might improve cucumber yields but have no effect on the steel industry.

Figure 2-7 illustrates the difference between general growth and specialized growth, where the economy starts from the original production possibilities frontier. In the case of general growth, productivity in both the pretzel and pumpkin industries increases. In the case of specialized growth, productivity increases in only one industry.

The production possibilities frontiers in the graph labeled Specialized Growth in Figure 2-7(b) indicate technological improvement in only the pretzel industry. To see why growth occurred in the pretzel industry but not the pumpkin industry, consider the output of each good separately when none of the other is produced. When no pretzels are produced, the technological change has not affected the production possibility for pumpkins, because the point on the vertical axis is the same as before. However, when no pumpkins are produced, the technological change has allowed an increase in the possible output of pretzels. We know this because the intercept on the horizontal axis has moved to the right. Whatever that maximum quantity of pretzels had been, it is now higher. **Specialized growth thus pivots**

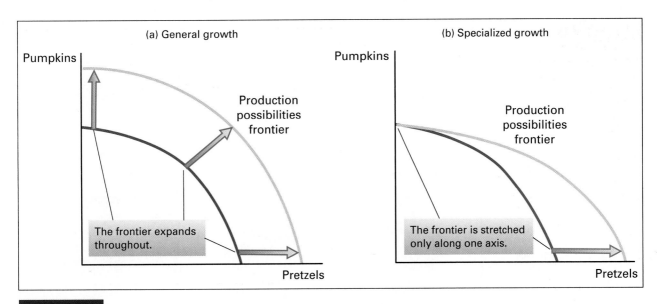

FIGURE 2-7

GENERAL AND SPECIALIZED GROWTH Broad-reaching technological change brings general growth, which shifts the entire production possibilities frontier (ppf) outward as shown in part (a). Specialized technological change brings specialized growth, which causes the production possibilities frontier to expand in the direction of the industry to which the new technology applies. In part (b), that industry is pretzels.

the production possibilities frontier in the direction of more output in the industry affected by the technological change.

In summary:

- The production possibilities frontier shows how much of one good can be produced for any feasible amount of another good.
- If an economy is on its frontier, the opportunity cost of producing more of one good is less of the other good.
- The production possibilities frontier is bowed outward, consistent with the law of increasing cost, which notes the increasing marginal opportunity cost of additional output.
- Every point along the production possibilities frontier is technologically efficient.
- Points inside the frontier imply some unemployed or misallocated resources and are thus inefficient.
- Points outside the frontier are unattainable with current resources and technology.
- Economies grow by acquiring resources or better technology, which shifts the frontier outward.
- If the economy acquires resources that are specialized in the production of a certain good, the production possibilities frontier expands outward in the direction of more of that good.

2.3 THE CIRCULAR FLOW OF ECONOMIC ACTIVITY

Production possibilities frontiers are about *possibilities*. What a market economy will actually choose to produce is decided through the interaction of consumers and businesses. In effect, consumers vote with their money for the assortment of goods and services that is offered. **Money** is a medium of exchange, meaning that it facilitates the exchange of goods and services. Without money, people would be forced to exchange goods directly, a situation

money a medium of exchange that removes the need for barter; also a measure of value and a way to store value over time.

FIGURE 2-8

THE CIRCULAR FLOW OF ECONOMIC ACTIVITY The sale of goods and services by business firms occurs in the output market, while the purchase of resources by firms occurs in the input market. The circular flow model shows that household income depends on the sale of resources, as seen by the arrows that pass through the input market along the bottom of the flow. The arrows through the output market indicate that household spending determines outputs. Taxes, regulations, and other government actions will influence both markets.

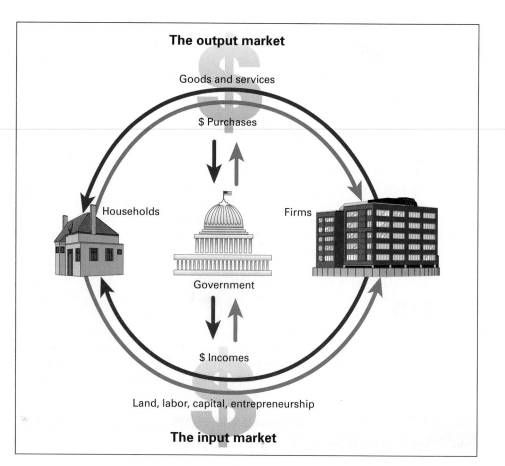

barter the exchange of goods and services directly for one another, without the use of money.

known as **barter.** Barter would be very difficult in a complicated economy. For example, to buy a mystery novel, you would have to provide something the bookseller would want in return. What do you have? Would you offer a chicken? What if the bookseller is in the mood for Buffalo wings? Money comes to the rescue—it greases the wheels of commerce.

Many things have served as money through the years. In prisoner-of-war camps during World War II, cigarettes served as money. Traditionally, gold, silver, and other scarce metals have been considered money, since they are inherently scarce and relatively easy to transport in the form of coins. Paper is even easier to transport, which is why it is the most common form of money in use today. However, for paper or anything else to be used as money, its quantity must be limited, which is why counterfeiting is illegal. Government must also be careful about printing too much currency if it wishes its currency to retain value as money.

circular flow a model of the economy that depicts how the flow of money facilitates a counterflow of resources, goods, and services in the input and output markets.

Figure 2-8 illustrates the **circular flow** of economic activity, a model that depicts how markets use the medium of money to determine what goods and services are produced and who gets to buy them. The top part of the diagram illustrates the **output market** in which businesses sell goods and services to consumers. The actual assortment of goods and services is determined by how much households are willing to pay relative to business firms' production costs.

output market the market where goods and services are bought and sold.

input market the market where resources are bought and sold.

The bottom part of the diagram shows the **input market,** which illustrates that households supply the resources of land, labor, capital, and entrepreneurship. All of these resources are ultimately owned by people, who make up households. The sale of resources to business firms provides the income that households use to buy products. Since people own businesses, business profits also belong to households. For this reason, the circular flow of inputs and outputs is maintained by a counterflow of dollars.

Through taxation, regulation, and production, government influences the mix of goods that is produced and the manner in which resources are used. The circular flow diagram could be expanded to include foreign commerce, banking, or other economic details, but can become complex and difficult to interpret.

2.4 EXPANDING CONSUMPTION POSSIBILITIES THROUGH TRADE

For their own self-interest, economies engage in trade with other economies. This is true for national economies, regional economies, local economies, and even personal economies. For example, we each have our own production possibilities. Yet, if we each had to rely upon our own production possibilities frontier and could not trade, we would be hard-pressed to live as well as Hank the castaway. Instead, we trade with one another. We trade our labor services for income to let us buy what we want. We trade so that we can consume more quantity and variety than we could produce on our own. Cities, states, and countries trade among themselves for the same reasons individuals trade with one another.

People specialize in their jobs according to their interests and opportunities. They then use the income they earn in order to purchase goods and services. Note that this is a two-part decision. First people decide what to produce; then they decide what to consume. The economies of countries engaged in international trade operate the same way.

In order to gain from trade, an economy must *specialize* according to its **comparative advantage. An economy has a comparative advantage in producing a good if it can produce that good at a lower opportunity cost than could other economies.** This means the economy chooses to produce those things it does well relative to other things it could be doing. Contrary to popular belief, trade is not based on **absolute advantage,** which refers to the ability to produce something with fewer resources than could others. **To gain from trade, specialize according to comparative advantage, whether or not you have any absolute advantage.**

> **comparative advantage** the ability to produce a good at a lower opportunity cost (other goods forgone) than others could do.

> **absolute advantage** the ability to produce a good with fewer resources than other producers.

The principle of comparative advantage holds even in our imaginary wanderings through space, as illustrated in the *Star Trek* series that got its start in the 1960s. One of the early mainstays was the pointy-eared science officer named Mr. Spock. With his mental prowess and physical strength, Spock had an absolute advantage in performing a variety of tasks. For example, he might have been a master at quickly cleaning the passageways of the *Starship Enterprise.* However, he did not spend his time mopping the floors because, as Spock would say, "That would be illogical!" It would waste his time.

Logic suggests making the most productive use of our time. We don't have time to do everything, something today's college students know well. College students follow their comparative advantages and specialize when selecting their majors and careers. For example, Michael Jordan selected economics as his major and basketball as his career. With his physical prowess and mental savvy, he could have excelled at other majors or other careers. But he had to make a choice. He chose basketball, where he could dazzle. He tried baseball for a time, but quickly returned to his area of relative strength.

Even if a person cannot do anything well, he or she can still do some things relatively better than other things. It might take Doug longer to mow yards than it would take other people. Yet, if that is what Doug could do best, he would mow yards. Other people would be delighted to hire him because he would charge them less than the opportunity cost of their own time were they to do the mowing themselves. Michael Jordan might hire him. It would be irrelevant whether Michael could mow his own lawn faster. The opportunity cost of his time would be too high.

These lessons apply to any economy, whether the economy is that of an individual or that of a country. Countries gain from trade whether or not they have an absolute advantage in anything. The country can start off rich or poor and still gain from trade.

exports goods and services a country sells to other countries.

imports goods and services a country buys from other countries.

While a country is constrained to produce along or inside its production possibilities frontier, it can exchange some of its own output for the output of other countries. Goods and services a country sells to other countries are termed **exports.** Exports are traded for **imports,** which are goods and services a country buys from other countries. **Through trade, a country can consume a combination of goods and services that lies outside its production possibilities frontier, meaning that the country's consumption possibilities will exceed its production possibilities.**

International trade is more important to small countries than to large countries. This is because the larger the country, the more opportunities there are to specialize internally. For example, the United States produces potatoes in Maine and Idaho for sale throughout the other states. Likewise, Michigan specializes in automobile production, Texas in oil and gas production, and so forth. If the United States were broken into fifty different countries, this trade among states would all be international. As it is, the tremendous diversity of resources found within the United States leads it to have one of the smallest proportions of international trade relative to its output of any country in the world. Figure 2-9 shows the propor-

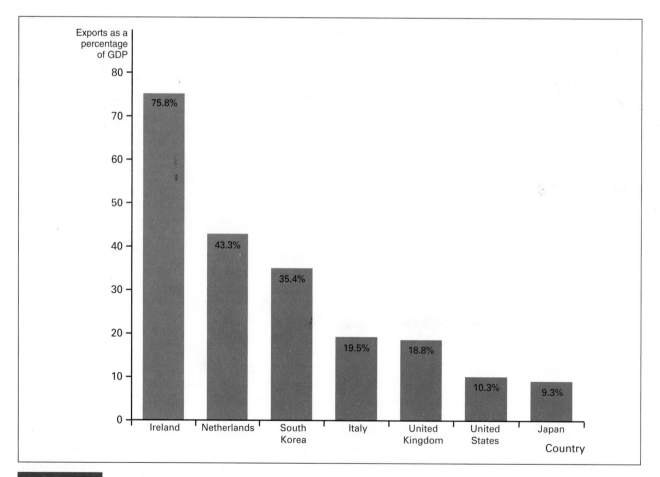

FIGURE 2-9

EXPORTS AS A PERCENTAGE OF GROSS DOMESTIC PRODUCT Countries with larger economies usually export a smaller percentage of their output than do countries with smaller economies. The United States and Japan are two of the world's largest economies and both export a relatively small percentage of their output.

Sources: 2001 Statistical Abstract of the U.S. Percentages compiled from 1999 data in Table Nos. 1340 and 1386. U.S. percentage compiled from Tables B–1 and B–106 in *2002 Economic Report of the President.*

tion of various countries' exports relative to their outputs. The smaller the country, typically, the higher that ratio is, and the more it gains from trade. These gains occur because smaller countries would be hard pressed to produce the variety of goods and services that are available through trade.

Economists rarely compute the goods in which countries have their comparative advantages. Rather, markets do that quite effectively on their own. If a country has a comparative advantage in producing certain goods, it can produce those goods cheaply, relative to the other goods that it could produce. Those goods in which it has a comparative advantage will be the goods it can offer at the best prices in the international marketplace. Thus, without any economic research, economies engaging in international trade naturally tend to export those goods for which they have a comparative advantage and import the rest.

COMPETING WITH COMPARATIVE ADVANTAGE

SNAPSHOT

Many great athletes are multitalented, possessing strength, speed, and muscle coordination that dwarf that of the general population. These qualities are needed for success in a variety of sports, yet few athletes play more than one sport professionally, even though they might be able to do so. Simply look at the sports pages. Venus Williams makes headlines by swinging a tennis racket, while Tiger Woods swings a golf club and Barry Bonds swings a bat. Their choices tell the rest of us about their comparative advantages.

The best teams exploit the comparative advantages of their players. Each player has a job to do and specializes in doing it well. Whatever the sport, owners and fans expect this principle of comparative advantage to be followed and demand coaches who will best exploit the talents of their players. But even the best coaches can err, as when Cleveland Indians' baseball coach Tris Speaker said in 1921, "Babe Ruth made a great mistake when he gave up pitching. Working once a week, he might have lasted a long time and become a great star." ◄

2.5 GUNS AND BUTTER—VICTORY FROM A STRONG ECONOMY

"We will bury you."

—Nikita Khrushchev, Soviet Premier, speaking to the United Nations in 1960

"I pledge allegiance to the flag of the United States of America ...."

—Sergei Khrushchev, son of Nikita Khrushchev, taking oath of citizenship in 1999

On December 7, 1941, the Empire of Japan attacked Pearl Harbor and drew the United States into World War II. As President Roosevelt reported the next day, that attack also caused "severe damage" to American military capabilities. At the time, Japanese military might extended through much of the Far East, and Nazi Germany controlled most of Europe. Yet, the United States was able to quickly convert many civilian industries to military production and play a pivotal role in defeating both the Nazis and the Japanese three and a half years later. The world marveled at the ability of the U.S. economy to accomplish this feat. The United States had not sought war, but nonetheless proved able to win.

Nearly five decades later, the United States economy was again able to defeat a foreign adversary that had engaged it in a "cold war." This time, the adversary was the Union of Soviet Socialist Republics, a country armed to the teeth and openly hostile to the United States. Yet, when the United States decided to strengthen its armed forces in the 1980s, the Soviet Union struggled so hard to keep pace that it impoverished its own people and lost its will to exist. The Soviet Union was formally dissolved in 1991 without a shot being fired, breaking up into several different countries, including Russia. That's the best kind of victory, unlike, in the words of Ronald Reagan, "The bloody futility of two World Wars, Korea, Vietnam and the Persian Gulf."

Now, as we seek to surmount the unfolding terrorist threats of the twenty-first century, the lessons of America's twentieth-century success can help guide our way. How has the United States been able to maintain prosperity during peacetime and yet still have the wherewithal to be victorious in wartime? The secret has been the vibrancy of a strong U.S. economy, meaning that the United States has been able to maintain production possibilities that exceed those of its adversaries.

Figure 2-10(b) depicts the production possibilities frontier for a country with a strong economy, such as the United States in the 1980s, and another production possibilities frontier for an adversary with a weak economy, such as the Soviet Union in the 1980s. The axes of the production possibilities frontier are labeled *guns* and *butter,* where guns represents military output and butter represents output for civilian consumption. In Figure 2-10(a), the Soviet Union is shown to be producing more guns in the 1970s than produced in the United States. However, because of its strong economy, the United States could increase its production of guns to exceed that of the Soviet Union and still have more butter for its civilians. When the Soviets tried to match U.S. spending on guns in the 1980s, their production of butter fell so low that the Soviet people were forced to endure severe hardships. The result is shown in Figure 2-10(b).

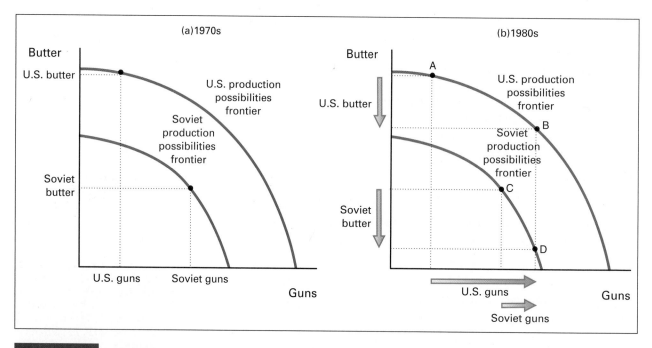

FIGURE 2-10

GUNS AND BUTTER In the 1970s, the Soviets are seen in (a) to devote more resources to their military (guns) than did the United States, even though production possibilities for the Soviets were less. The result was a lower standard of living in the Soviet Union (less butter). In the 1980s, as shown in (b), the Soviets decided to match what was by then a higher U.S. output of guns. This reduced still further the already meager Soviet output of butter, resulting in a standard of living that the Soviet people would not accept. In 1991, the Soviet Union dissolved itself in favor of market-oriented economies that chose fewer guns and more butter.

HOW EFFICIENCY LEADS TO GROWTH

To maintain a strong economy, a country must use its existing resources and technology efficiently. As shown in Figure 2-11, moving from an inefficient economy to an efficient economy allows the production of both more guns and more butter. The economy must use the right people and the right capital to produce the right goods in the right way. By producing more in the present, the economy also has more ability to put aside some current consumption of guns and butter in favor of investing in new capital and better technology that will allow production possibilities to grow over time. In other words, the more efficient an economy is in the present, the more ability it will have to expand its production possibilities for the future, as shown by the long arrow in Figure 2-11.

The United States has been able to use its production possibilities with relative efficiency and achieve significant economic growth over time by relying in large measure upon the marketplace to allocate resources. The lure of profit in the market economy has motivated people and companies to look for the most valuable products to produce, keep costs as low as possible, and invest in new capital that expands the country's production possibilities frontier. These actions constitute the invisible hand of the marketplace that motivates individuals out for their own self-interests to best serve the needs of others.

While there are exceptions in which either markets or government policies have failed to achieve efficiency, it is its reliance upon a market economy that has generally allowed the United States to prosper relative to its adversaries with more centralized economies. In contrast, as former Soviet Premier Mikhail Gorbachev told Columbia University students in March 2002, the Soviets had created an "unreal system" of "pure propaganda." In that system, the ruling politicians "were discussing the problem of toothpaste, the problem of detergent, and they had to create a commission of the Politburo to make sure that women have pantyhose."

The twentieth century has not always brought victory to the United States or other prosperous countries. As the United States learned in Cuba and Vietnam, citizens of impoverished countries can be stubborn adversaries when their patriotic zeal is aroused. Why not peace, with its promise of prosperity?

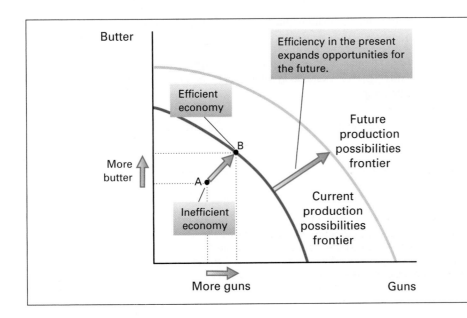

FIGURE 2-11

SHAPING THE FUTURE Today's choices shape future possibilities. Increasing efficiency within the economy, such as moving from point *A* to point *B,* allows the production of both more guns and more butter. In addition, a more efficient economy has more possibilities for growth over time, which would shift the production possibilities frontier outward.

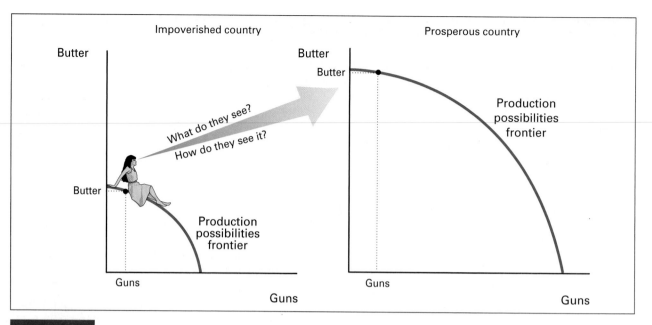

FIGURE 2-12

LOOKING TOWARD PROSPERITY Will impoverished countries choose to emulate prosperous countries and follow their path to success? Such a path would be one of peace and mutual self-interest. Alternatively, the view from below could be one of resentment, providing a spawning ground for ongoing conflict.

Whether the world in the twenty-first century sees economic victory or the impoverishment of warfare might hinge in part upon attitudes. Are people of impoverished nations inspired to replicate for themselves the success of the United States and other developed countries? Or is that prosperity seen as out of reach and the source of resentment and ongoing conflict? While economic analysis can help frame the questions, such as in the manner of Figure 2-12, only time will reveal the answers.

*T*HINKING
*C*RITICALLY

1. While it clearly helped the United States in World War II and in the Cold War against communism, does a strong economy do any good in battling terrorism? Explain.

2. Describe ways in which the U.S. government attempts to be efficient in how it spends money militarily. Give an example in which spending might be inefficient and explain why that might happen.

Visit **www.prenhall.com/collinge** for updates and web exercises on this Explore & Apply topic.

SUMMARY AND LEARNING OBJECTIVES

1. **Analyze tradeoffs facing both individuals and countries.**
   - Opportunity costs, which are the value of forgone alternatives, influence the choices people make.
   - The concept of opportunity cost makes clear that nothing is free. By considering the opportunity cost of an action, both people and countries can make better choices.

2. **Categorize the types of resources an economy possesses.**
   - Resources include land, labor, capital, and entrepreneurship. Land refers to natural resources in their natural states. Labor refers to the human ability to work. Capital is produced to increase future productivity. Physical capital includes buildings, machines, and equipment. Human capital represents acquired skills and abilities. An entrepreneur takes risks by combining resources in productive ways.
   - Human capital is different from physical capital because it is embodied within a person.

3. **Model a country's production possibilities, and how these possibilities respond to technological development.**
   - The production possibilities frontier represents all combinations of two goods that would be technologically efficient.
   - The production possibilities frontier typically has a bowed outward shape. Points outside the frontier are not now attainable. Points inside the frontier are inefficient. Inefficiency arises from unemployment and/or misallocated resources. Only points on the frontier are both attainable and efficient.
   - Opportunity costs are illustrated by the production possibilities frontier. Movement from one point to another on the frontier means that more of one good is produced, but less of the other. The amount by which the production of the other good decreases equals the opportunity cost of the increase in the first good.
   - Economic growth expands the frontier by shifting it outward. Such growth can occur if a country adds more capital or other resources, or experiences technological change that enhances its productivity. Specialized growth pivots the frontier outward in the direction of more output in the industry affected by technological change.

4. **Describe how economies can grow faster if they are willing to cut back on current consumption.**
   - Depreciation shifts the frontier inward because it decreases the amount of capital. The effect of depreciation on the frontier can be overcome by producing new capital, with the amount of that production being at least large enough to offset depreciation.
   - Capital production comes with an opportunity cost since it requires the sacrifice of current consumption.

5. **Visualize the flow of goods and services, resources, and money in the economy.**
   - The circular flow graph shows how economic activity depends upon markets. Flows of goods and services go toward the household sector as households make purchases. Goods and services are sold in the output market. Households earn the incomes needed to make those purchases by selling the resources they own to businesses. Resources are bought and sold in the input market. Money is used to make it easier for market exchanges to take place.

6. **Explain how people and countries gain from trade by specializing according to comparative advantage.**
   - Countries specialize according to their comparative advantage, as do people. A comparative advantage in the production of a good requires that a country have a lower opportunity cost of production than other countries. Trade according to comparative advantage allows countries to consume beyond their production possibilities frontiers, thus benefiting the countries that trade.
   - A country has an absolute advantage if it is able to produce something with fewer resources than other countries. It is not necessary to have an absolute advantage in the production of a good to benefit from specialization and trade.

7. **Convey how economic strength can lead to victory, sometimes without a fight.**
   - A stronger economy can produce more guns and more butter than a weaker economy. A stronger economy's production possibilities frontier will be outside that of a weaker economy. The difference in economic prosperity illustrated by the location of the production possibilities frontiers can lead to envy and resentment of wealthy countries by the citizens of relatively poor ones. Alternatively, poorer countries can aspire to peacefully become prosperous themselves.

KEY TERMS

opportunity costs, 30
land, 30
labor, 30
human capital, 30
capital, 31
entrepreneurship, 31
technology, 31

production possibilities frontier, 32
law of increasing cost, 34
economic growth, 36
money, 39
barter, 40
circular flow, 40
output market, 40

input market, 40
comparative advantage, 41
absolute advantage, 41
exports, 42
imports, 42

TEST YOURSELF

TRUE OR FALSE

1. If you decide to buy a Butterfinger candy bar, instead of an equally priced Almond Joy, the opportunity cost of your purchase is the value you would have received from that Almond Joy.
2. The axes of the production possibilities frontier are labeled price and quantity.
3. Economic growth is represented on a production possibilities frontier as a shift outward of that frontier.
4. The circular flow model of economic activity assumes that resources are owned by businesses.
5. With international trade, a country is able to produce outside its production possibilities frontier.

MULTIPLE CHOICE

6. The opportunity cost of a new city police contract is
   a. the amount of money it takes in order to provide the city with the most highly qualified personnel.
   b. the value of the other goods and services that the city and taxpayers will be forced to give up in order to pay for the contract.
   c. the cost to victims of crimes that the new contract would prevent.
   d. the value of the opportunities that city policemen acquire by accepting it.
7. Which of the following items is the best example of an economic resource?
   a. A stock certificate.
   b. A one-hundred dollar bill.
   c. A tractor.
   d. A plate of spaghetti and meatballs.
8. Which of the following is the best example of earning income from human capital?
   a. Melody takes a job as an interpreter for the hearing impaired.
   b. Josie invests her life savings into her own business, "Jeans by Josephine."

   c. Seth toils all day in the hot summer sun as a common laborer, just to earn enough money to keep food on the table.
   d. J.R. kicks up his heels and watches the royalty checks flow in from his oil fields.
9. A production possibilities frontier shows combinations of
   a. inputs that can produce a specific quantity of output.
   b. outputs that people consume.
   c. outputs that can be achieved as technology improves.
   d. outputs that can be achieved in a given time period with all available resources employed using current technology.
10. If a nation's production possibilities indicate that 1,000,000 battle tanks and 6,000,000 houses could be produced, or alternatively, 750,000 tanks and 8,000,000 houses could also be produced, the opportunity cost of each additional house would be
    a. 250,000 tanks.
    b. 8 tanks.
    c. 0.125 tanks.
    d. 2,000,000 houses.
11. As a nation develops economically, its production possibilities frontier
    a. remains stable.
    b. shifts inward.
    c. shifts outward.
    d. becomes steeper, but does not shift.
12. Suppose an economy produces only gizmos and widgets. If there is a technological advance in the production of widgets, the economy's production possibilities frontier will shift
    a. outward along the widget axis, but not along the gizmo axis.
    b. outward along the gizmo axis, but not along the widget axis.
    c. outward along both axes.
    d. inward along both axes.

13. Of the points listed in Self-Test Figure 2-1, the fastest rate of economic growth would occur at
    a. *A.*
    b. *B.*
    c. *C.*
    d. *D.*

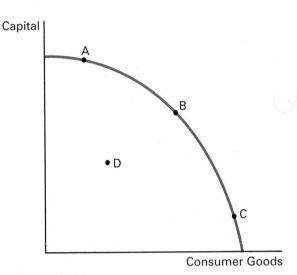

Capital

Consumer Goods

SELF-TEST FIGURE 2-1
PRODUCTION POSSIBILITIES FRONTIER

14. All points along the production possibilities frontier are
    a. technologically efficient.
    b. allocatively efficient.
    c. economically efficient.
    d. equitable.
15. In a circular flow diagram, the output market is where
    a. goods and services are exchanged for money.
    b. resources are exchanged for money.
    c. consumer outlays of dollars are exchanged for wages, rent, interest, and profits.
    d. resources are exchanged for goods and services.

16. Money in the economy today
    a. is needed in order for barter to occur.
    b. is primarily commodity money.
    c. facilitates the circular flow of economic activity.
    d. is an economic resource along with land, labor, capital, and entrepreneurship.
17. In order to gain from trade, it is necessary to
    a. specialize according to comparative advantage.
    b. specialize according to absolute advantage.
    c. find a trading partner with an absolute advantage in something.
    d. find a trading partner without an absolute advantage in anything.
18. When a country can produce a good with fewer resources than any other country, the country has
    a. a comparative advantage.
    b. a resource advantage.
    c. an absolute advantage.
    d. an unfair advantage.
19. A country has a comparative advantage in the production of a good if it can produce that good _____ than can other countries.
    a. with fewer raw materials
    b. at a lower opportunity cost
    c. at a higher quality
    d. with fewer labor-hours
20. By having an efficient economy today, a country's future production possibilities frontier will allow the production of
    a. both more guns and more butter.
    b. more guns, but not more butter.
    c. more butter, but not more guns.
    d. neither more guns nor more butter.

QUESTIONS AND PROBLEMS

1. *[opportunity cost]* Provide plausible opportunity costs for each of the following choices.
   a. Valerie stays home from work to watch an especially interesting episode of the Ricki Lake program.
   b. Frank spends Saturday night watching videos with his friend Erica.
   c. Renee spends Saturday afternoon playing golf with her church singles group.
2. *[entrepreneurship]* Do management skills differ from entrepreneurial skills? Explain.
3. *[resources]* Explain the concept of capital, as it is used in economics. Part of your answer should distinguish between human capital and physical capital.
4. *[production possibilities frontier]* Suppose the country of Baseballia's production possibilities frontier between baseballs and bats is as shown in the table below.

BASEBALLIA'S PRODUCTION POSSIBILITIES FRONTIER

Number of Baseballs Produced per Hour	Number of Baseball Bats Produced per Hour
0	10
5	9
10	7
15	4
20	0

   a. What is the opportunity cost of producing 20 baseballs?
   b. What is the opportunity cost of producing 15 baseballs?
5. *[production possibilities frontier]* What would a straight-line production possibilities frontier between coconuts and fish on Castaway Island say about opportunity costs?
6. *[general growth]* Draw a production possibility graph that shows general growth. Briefly state how the numbers in the production possibilities frontier table in question #4 above would change if the economy of Baseballia experienced general growth.
7. *[production possibilities frontier]* Draw the original production possibilities frontier in Figure 2-7. How does the frontier change when technological change affects only the pumpkin industry?
8. *[money]* What is meant when money is described as a medium of exchange? Is money a part of the circular flow diagram?

9. *[circular flow]* In the circular flow diagram, how do households earn incomes?
10. *[trade]* California and France both produce wine.
    a. Without international trade, U.S. consumers would be unable to consume French wines, but they would still be able to consume California wines. Would this arrangement be better for the United States as a whole? For any particular groups within the United States?
    b. Do you think France imports U.S. wines? Explain.
11. *[trade]* Succinctly evaluate the validity of the following:
    a. "The United States is losing its competitive edge to other countries with more diligent and skilled workers. The problem is that we are becoming increasingly incapable of producing anything that other countries would want to buy. We are fast on our way to becoming a nation of burger flippers."
    b. "The U.S. standard of living has been the envy of the world. Unfortunately, because we have allowed imports from countries where working conditions are dismal and labor is cheap, our own standard of living is rapidly being pulled down to match the competition."
12. *[absolute advantage]* Briefly explain the difference between the concept of absolute advantage and the concept of comparative advantage. Which principle explains how countries specialize?
13. *[comparative advantage]* Since the principle of comparative advantage applies to people as well as economies, identify at least three areas in which you have a comparative advantage relative to your friends.
14. *[consumption possibilities]* Draw a graph of the production possibilities frontier. Then comment on the validity of the following statements, referring to the graph you have drawn:
    a. A country that trades with other countries will produce at a point outside its production possibilities frontier.
    b. A country that trades with other countries will consume at a point on its production possibilities frontier.
15. *[comparative advantage]* Explain the sport your favorite athlete has chosen to play in terms of that person's comparative advantage. How does an athlete's comparative advantage change with age?

 Visit **www.prenhall.com/collinge** for Exploring the Web exercises and additional self-test quizzes.

CHAPTER 3

DEMAND AND SUPPLY

A LOOK AHEAD

"Teach a parrot the terms 'supply and demand' and you have an economist!" That humor from Thomas Carlyle has been handed down for decades in introductory economics courses. While not literally true (we hope), it does point out how central the concepts of supply and demand are to economic analysis.

How are the prices of music CDs, apartment rents, and the prices of other goods and services determined? Why do people build so many homes where hurricanes are known to strike? What do cows eat? The answers? "Squawk, supply and demand!" This chapter fills in the details of these answers and shows how to answer a host of additional questions about the workings of supply and demand that underlie the market economy. The Explore & Apply section that concludes the chapter discusses how public policy might tap into the forces of supply and demand to improve our schools.

LEARNING OBJECTIVES

Understanding Chapter 3 will enable you to:
1. **Distinguish between the general notions of demand and supply used in ordinary conversation and the precise notions employed in the study of economics.**
2. **Explain what it means to shift demand and supply and why shifts might occur.**
3. **Describe how the marketplace settles on the equilibrium price and quantity.**
4. **Specify how demand and supply shifts cause market equilibriums to change.**
5. **Describe how the elasticity of demand determines whether a price change increases, decreases, or does not change total revenue to sellers.**
6. **Discuss how vouchers use competition to improve the quality of schooling.**

EXPLORE & APPLY

Competition provides consumers with alternatives. The competition by producers to satisfy consumer wants underlies markets, which are characterized by demand and supply. Market economies rely upon competition, and thus upon demand and supply, to answer the three basic economic questions: *What? How?* and *For whom?* The economic definitions of demand and supply are more precise than the fuzzy notion that demand is something a person wants or needs and supply is what is available. Rather, demand and supply are both defined as relationships between price and quantity. We start by looking at demand.

3.1 DEMAND

demand relates the quantity of a good that consumers would purchase at each of various possible prices, over some period of time, *ceteris paribus.*

quantity demanded the quantity that consumers would purchase at a given price.

Demand *relates the quantity of a good that consumers would purchase at each of various possible prices, over some period of time,* ceteris paribus.

Demand is a relationship, not a single quantity. For a given price, demand tells us a specific quantity that consumers would actually purchase if given the opportunity. This quantity is termed the **quantity demanded**. In other words, demand relates quantity demanded to price over the range of possible prices. To emphasize that demand is a relationship and not just a single point, demand is also sometimes called a *demand schedule*. A demand schedule is a table that shows possible prices and their quantities demanded. When the numbers in a demand schedule are plotted in a graph, the line that is plotted is called a *demand curve*. In other words, the terms *demand, demand schedule,* and *demand curve* all refer to the same thing.

Demand must be defined for a set period of time. For example, demand for coffee will be quite different if the period in question is one day, one week, or one year. Moreover, anything else that might influence the quantity demanded must be held constant. This is termed the *ceteris paribus* condition. It means that we only look at one relationship at a time, where

ceteris paribus holding all else constant.

ceteris paribus is the Latin for holding all else constant.

Suppose we want to know how an increase in water rates will affect the amount of water people use on their lawns. To avoid mixing up the effects of price and rainfall, for example, we might estimate one demand curve for times of normal rainfall and another for times of drought. This approach allows us to focus exclusively on the relationship between price and quantity demanded.

BY WORD, BY TABLE, BY GRAPH

There are various ways to express relationships between variables. One is to provide a schedule, which is a table showing various values of the variables. Another is to show the data with a graph. For example, the data shown in Figure 3-1 make up a demand schedule. The data can be plotted on a graph to form the demand curve labeled Demand, also shown in the figure. The horizontal axis is labeled Quantity to denote the quantity demanded at each possible price. Since price is measured in dollars, the dollar sign provides the label for the vertical axis.

law of demand as price falls, the quantity demanded increases.

Note how the graph pictures an inverse relationship between price and quantity demanded. As price rises, quantity demanded falls. As price falls, quantity demanded rises. This relationship is termed the **law of demand**. It is an empirical law, meaning that no one enforces it, but buyers almost always adhere to it because it makes sense. When the price of an item falls, consumers not only can afford to buy more, but will also substitute the lower-priced good for higher-priced alternatives.

You've heard the saying "a picture is worth a thousand words." That saying usually applies to supply and demand analysis in general and to the law of demand in particular. While a table of data can be useful for applications calling for numerical calculations, a graph is ordinarily better suited for broader messages, such as the inverse relationship between price and quantity demanded. When the specific data are less important than the

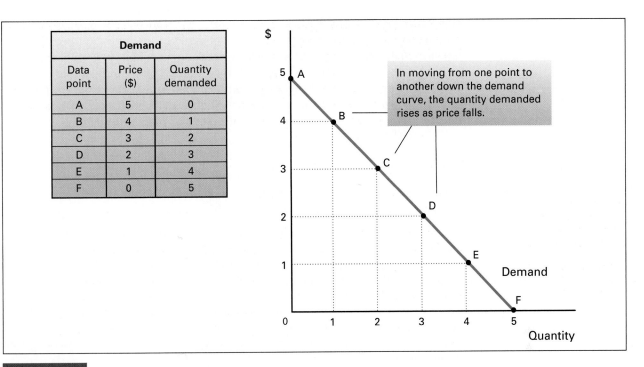

FIGURE 3-1

DEMAND Demand slopes downward, showing that price and quantity demanded are inversely related. For example, as the price drops from $4 to $1, the quantity demanded rises from 1 unit to 4 units. This is seen as a movement from point *B* to point *E* along the demand curve.

QUICKCHECK

What is the minimum quantity demanded and the maximum quantity demanded in Figure 3-1?

Answer: At a price of $5, the quantity demanded is zero units, which is the minimum. At a price of $0, the quantity demanded is 5 units, the maximum. These quantities occur where demand intersects the axes.

general nature of the relationship, it is common to draw a graph without attaching any numbers to that graph, as is done in many of the graphs in this chapter and the rest of this book.

If you are uncomfortable with a graph without numbers, recall the simple solution mentioned in Chapter 2: Add some numbers. Even though the numbers would be artificial, the graphical relationship may then become easier to comprehend. For example, we could have labeled Figure 3-1 with different numbers or with no numbers at all. The graph would still impart the notion that price and quantity vary inversely.

SHIFTING DEMAND VERSUS MOVEMENTS ALONG A DEMAND CURVE

Price is not the only influence on how much people buy. Quantities purchased are also dictated by income, tastes, the prices of other goods, and various other factors. By holding all but price constant, the *ceteris paribus* assumption lets us focus on one thing at a time. This approach provides order to what otherwise might seem like a jumble of simultaneous changes.

What happens to demand when other influences on demand change? Changes in other aspects of the world have the potential to shift the entire demand curve, leading to a new relationship between price and quantity. This is shown by a change in the position of the demand curve—a shift. Anything that causes the curve to shift is termed a *shift factor*. **An *increase in demand* occurs when demand shifts to the right. A *decrease in demand* occurs when demand shifts to the left.** Figure 3-2 summarizes these shifts. Note that a change in the price of the good neither increases nor decreases demand—demand does not shift. Rather, **a price change would change the quantity demanded, which involves** *moving along the demand curve,* **but would not change the demand curve itself.** A lower price results in a movement down the demand curve, while a higher price causes a movement up the demand curve.

Consider an example of demand shifting that is associated with a fast-growing economy. An upward surge in the economy often causes family incomes to rise. With more income at their disposal, some families will decide to buy new homes. That decision increases the demand for new homes. To the extent that higher income causes consumers to

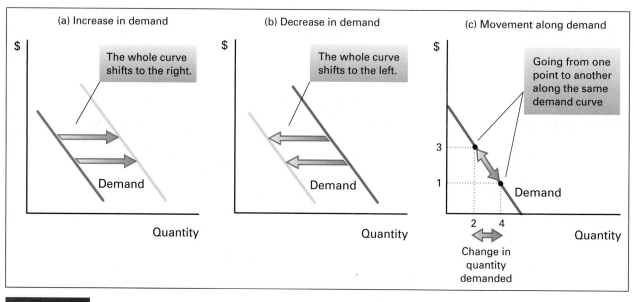

FIGURE 3-2

A SHIFT IN DEMAND VERSUS A MOVEMENT ALONG DEMAND Demand shifts when there is a change in any shift factor. An increase in demand moves the demand curve to the right, as shown in (a). A decrease in demand moves the demand curve to the left, as shown in (b). A change in price does not shift demand. Rather, a price change causes a movement along the demand curve to a new quantity demanded, as shown in (c).

buy more of any good at a particular price, the higher income increases demand, depicted by the rightward-pointing arrow in Figure 3-2(a).

Whether it be a hurricane's pounding surf that washes away expensive beachfront homes, a swollen river that engulfs entire communities along its course, or sliding mud that obliterates whatever stands in its way, the effects of wind and rain cost U.S. citizens billions of dollars annually. Much of this loss is a direct result of expensive structures being built in harm's way. For example, huge amounts of real estate development occur in some of the most at-risk areas, including California hillsides, property fronting the beaches of Florida, and in the flood plains of scenic West Virginia rivers.

Is the large amount of building in risky areas proof of people's shortsighted irrationality? More likely, it is evidence of the law of demand in response to government low-interest loans for rebuilding and other assistance that reduce the cost of disasters to their victims. Specifically, disaster assistance lowers the price of taking the risk to build in disaster-prone locations. The lower price leads people to do more building there. Thus, by the law of demand, the unintended consequence of compensating disaster victims for property losses is that there will be a larger amount of property lost when the next disaster strikes.

To reduce the amount of risk-taking, it is increasingly common for government aid to be contingent upon the recipients rebuilding in safer spots. Even so, disaster aid lowers the expected price of risk-taking for the rest of us. We respond to this lower price by daring to live closer to our country's scenic but dangerous places. ◄

CHANGES IN DEMAND

As listed in Table 3-1, various events are likely to shift demand. **For *normal goods*, an increase in income shifts demand to the right.** However, there are many goods that people buy less of as their incomes rise. These are termed **inferior goods. An increase in income shifts the demand for inferior goods to the left.** Is there anything you would buy less of as your income increases? Perhaps you would eat fewer hot dogs and cans of tuna, and more steak and fresh fish. If so, for you, hot dogs and tuna would be inferior goods, and steak and fresh fish would be normal goods.

Changes in the prices of substitutes and complements also shift demand. A **substitute** is something that takes the place of something else. Different brands of coffee are substitutes. So are coffee and tea. A **complement** is a good that goes with another good, such as ketchup on hot dogs or cream in coffee. The degree to which one good complements or substitutes for another will vary according to each person's tastes and preferences. For example, many coffee drinkers prefer to take their coffee black. For them, coffee and cream are not complements. Likewise, to the extent a consumer is loyal to a particular brand of a product, other brands might not be viewed as acceptable substitutes unless the price difference is dramatic.

What would happen to demand for a good if the price of a substitute changes? To answer questions like this one, it often helps to be specific. For example, consider how much Sparkle Beach laundry detergent shoppers purchase at various possible prices. Those quantities would go up or down depending upon the prices of Tide, Surf, All, and other possible substitutes. If the price of the substitutes rises, *ceteris paribus*, shoppers buy more Sparkle Beach. Their demand for Sparkle Beach shifts out. Likewise, should the substitutes be reduced in price, *ceteris paribus*, shoppers would buy less Sparkle Beach—demand shifts in. Thus, **demand varies directly with a change in the price of a substitute.**

Conversely, **demand varies inversely to a change in the price of a complement.** Since complements are the opposite of substitutes, a change in the price of a complement shifts

normal goods demand for these goods varies directly with income.

inferior goods demand for these goods varies inversely with income.

substitutes something that takes the place of something else, such as one brand of cola for another.

complements goods or services that go well with each other, such as cream with coffee.

TABLE 3-1   CHANGES IN DEMAND

SHIFT FACTORS	DEMAND SHIFTS TO THE LEFT WHEN	DEMAND SHIFTS TO THE RIGHT WHEN	EXAMPLES
Price of substitutes	The price of a substitute decreases.	The price of a substitute increases.	A decrease in the price of butter causes the demand for margarine to decrease. An increase in the price of butter causes the demand for margarine to increase.
Price of complements	The price of a complement increases.	The price of a complement decreases.	An increase in the price of computers decreases the demand for software. A decrease in the price of computers increases the demand for software.
Income, when the good is normal	The good is normal and income decreases.	The good is normal and income increases.	The demand for jewelry decreases when income decreases. The demand for jewelry increases when income increases.
Income, when the good is inferior	The good is inferior and income increases.	The good is inferior and income decreases.	The demand for thrift store clothing decreases when income increases. The demand for thrift store clothing increases when income decreases.
Population	Population decreases.	Population increases.	The demand for shoes decreases when population decreases. The demand for shoes increases when population increases.
Consumer expectations of future prices	Consumers expect the price to decrease in the future.	Consumers expect the price to increase in the future.	Demand for coffee decreases because consumers expect the price of coffee to decrease later. Demand for coffee increases because consumers expect the price of coffee to increase later.
Tastes and preferences	Tastes and preferences turn against the product.	Tastes and preferences turn in favor of the product.	The demand for action movies decreases because consumers prefer less-violent movies. The demand for action movies increases because consumers prefer more-violent movies.

demand in the opposite direction from what would occur if there were a change in the price of a substitute. For example, peanut butter is complementary to jelly. An increase in the price of jelly would decrease consumption of jelly and anything that goes with it. Demand for peanut butter would shift to the left. Likewise, a decrease in the price of jelly would shift demand for peanut butter to the right.

Changes in tastes and preferences will also shift demand. Over time, as some items become more popular, their demand curves shift out. Other items see their popularity fade and their demand curves shift in. Producers often use advertising in an attempt to influence tastes and preferences toward their particular brand of product.

Changes in population, in expectations about future prices, or in many other factors can cause demand to shift. **Demand will increase or decrease to the extent that population increases or decreases. A change in consumer expectations about future prices will shift demand in the present.** For example, if you expect prices to fall in the future, you might put off your purchases now, in effect shifting your current demand curve to the left. You would be treating future purchases as a substitute for current purchases. For some products, other

(a) Leftward shift (decrease) in demand

(b) Rightward shift (increase) in demand

Demand shifts left when:
• Price of a substitute decreases.
• Price of a complement increases.
• Good is normal and income decreases.
• Good is inferior and income increases.
• Population decreases.
• Consumers expect price to fall in the future.
• Tastes and preferences turn against the product.

Demand shifts right when:
• Price of a substitute increases.
• Price of a complement decreases.
• Good is normal and income increases.
• Good is inferior and income decreases.
• Population increases.
• Consumers expect the price to rise in the future.
• Tastes and preferences turn in favor of the product.

FIGURE 3-3

FACTORS THAT SHIFT DEMAND Factors that shift demand to the left are listed in (a), along with a graph showing the leftward shift. Factors that shift demand to the right are shown in (b), along with a graph showing the rightward shift.

factors could be significant, such as conjectures about future technologies that might make products with current technologies obsolete.

Summing up, when consumers buy less of a good at each price, demand shifts to the left. When consumers buy more of a good at each price, demand shifts to the right. Table 3-1 and Figure 3-3 summarize the causes of these shifts. A change in the price of the good causes a change in the quantity demanded, but does not shift demand. Rather, a change in price causes a movement along the demand curve.

NEW COKE? OR OLD COKE IN A NEW BOTTLE?   *SNAPSHOT*

It was either a stroke of marketing genius or just dumb luck. But what it did for demand is one for the record books. The year was 1985 when, losing market share to its arch-rival Pepsi, the Coca-Cola Company tossed aside its secret recipe and ceased making "the real thing." Instead, Coke drinkers were presented with a reformulated New Coke that tasted oh-so-syrupy sweet. It seems that taste tests found consumers favoring the sweeter taste of Pepsi over traditional Coke, but found New Coke beating all. Market research notwithstanding, New Coke was a huge flop.

"Bring back the real thing!" cried Coke customers, and back it came under the name Coca-Cola Classic. Curiously, even though the formula is the same as that of traditional Coke, Coke Classic has proven more popular. Was it the publicity? The near loss of something millions of Coke drinkers took for granted? Was it nostalgia? Whatever the reasons, the demand for Coke shifted to the right and has stayed shifted ever since. In the back of their minds, it's what Coke's owners were hoping to find. ◄

3.2 SUPPLY

supply relates the quantity of a good that will be offered for sale at each of various possible prices, over some period of time, *ceteris paribus.*

Supply *relates the quantity of a good that will be offered for sale at each of various possible prices, over some period of time,* ceteris paribus.

The first thing to note about supply is its symmetry with demand. Supply tells us the quantity that will be offered for sale at various prices. This quantity is termed the **quantity supplied**. Note that supply and quantity supplied are not synonyms. Supply refers to the entire set of data that relates price and quantity and is thus also called a *supply schedule* or *supply curve.* Quantity supplied is the quantity associated with a single point on that schedule. As price changes, quantity supplied changes, but supply does not.

quantity supplied the quantity that will be offered for sale at a given price.

Supply is often referred to as the supply schedule or supply curve in order to emphasize that it is not any single quantity. Like demand, supply must be specified for a set period of time, such as a day, month, or year. The *ceteris paribus* condition makes sure that other things are held constant, so that we can focus clearly on the relationship between price and quantity supplied.

BY WORD, BY TABLE, BY GRAPH

Just as with demand, supply can be presented as a table or as a graph. Figure 3-4 shows an example of supply. In contrast to the downward-sloping demand curve, the supply curve nearly always slopes upward to the right. This direct relationship between price and quantity supplied is known as the **law of supply**. As price rises, the quantity offered for sale by producers increases. The reason is that a higher price means higher revenue per unit sold, which will in turn cover the cost of producing some additional units.

law of supply as price rises, the quantity supplied increases.

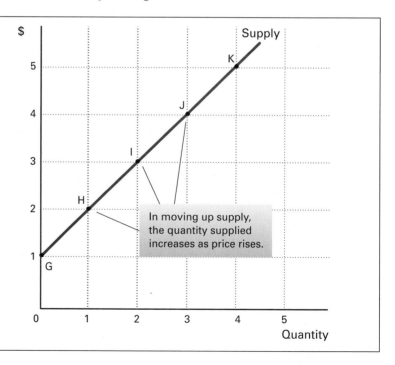

Supply		
Data point	Price ($)	Quantity supplied
G	1	0
H	2	1
I	3	2
J	4	3
K	5	4

In moving up supply, the quantity supplied increases as price rises.

FIGURE 3-4

SUPPLY Supply slopes upward. An increase in price leads to a greater quantity supplied. For example, an increase in price from $3 to $5 would cause the quantity supplied to increase from 2 to 4 units. This result is seen as a movement from point *I* to point *K* along the supply curve. The supply curve itself remains unchanged.

...

CHANGES IN SUPPLY

An *increase in supply* occurs when the entire supply curve shifts to the right, with more quantity supplied at each particular price. Likewise, a *decrease in supply* occurs when the entire supply curve shifts to the left, showing less quantity supplied at any particular price. A change in price does not shift supply, but rather causes a *movement along the supply curve.* Figure 3-5 illustrates these three possibilities.

Supply's most important shift factors differ from those for demand. Remember, for demand, the most important shift factors are income, prices of substitutes and complements, tastes and preferences, and consumer expectations about future prices. When it comes to supply, changes in expectations as to future prices are still important, but it is the expectations by producers, and not by consumers, that matter. The other important supply shift factors are different from the demand shift factors. In addition to producer expectations as to future prices, important shift factors include: (1) the number of firms; (2) prices of inputs; (3) technological change; (4) restrictions in production; (5) prices of substitutes in production; and (6) prices of jointly produced goods.

Why would expectations of future prices be important to a seller? To answer that question, suppose you own an oil field, and that it costs you $1 per barrel to pump your crude oil from the ground. How much oil would you offer for sale if the price were $15? $20? Why would you think twice about pumping your oil field dry if the selling price were $1.50?

For each possible current price, you would ask yourself how likely it would be for the price to go higher in the future. If you thought prices were on their way up, you would put off your pumping until later. If you expect prices to remain flat or to drop in the future, you would pump more now. If your expectations change, your entire supply schedule for pumping oil in the present would shift. For example, if you become convinced that the world is about to run out of oil, your supply curve in the present would shift far to the left, so that

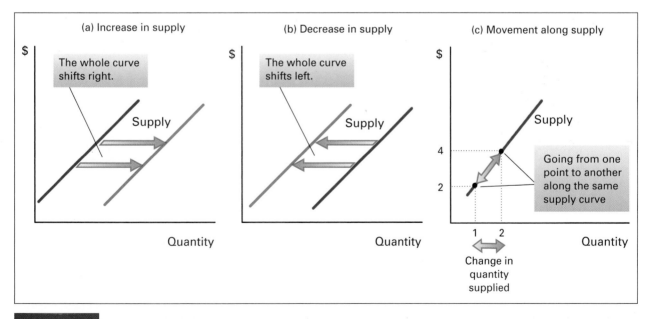

FIGURE 3-5

A SHIFT IN SUPPLY VERSUS A MOVEMENT ALONG SUPPLY Supply shifts when there is a change in any of its shift factors. An increase in supply moves the supply curve to the right, as shown in (a). A decrease in supply moves the supply curve to the left, as shown in (b). A change in price does not shift supply. Rather, a price change causes a movement along the supply curve to a new quantity supplied, as shown in (c).

you would retain plenty of oil to sell at high prices in the future. Thus, **today's supply curve shifts in the opposite direction from changes in expected future prices.**

If the price of labor or other input prices fall, firms see their expenses drop, and are willing to produce more at any given price. Hence, a decline in input prices increases supply, meaning that supply shifts to the right. Were input prices to increase, supply would decrease, meaning that it would shift to the left. In that case, fewer units are offered for sale at any given price. In general, **supply will shift in the opposite direction from changes in input prices.**

Firms adopt technological change in order to produce more output per unit of input. This has the same effect as a decrease in input prices. **Technological change in the production of any good shifts its supply to the right.**

Firms sometimes face restrictions in how they are allowed to do business. **Production restrictions decrease supply.** For example, a contract between a firm and its labor union might restrict the firm's ability to hire, fire, and make work assignments. Such restrictions have the potential to increase per-unit production costs. Likewise, automobile makers must meet exhaust-gas emission standards by installing catalytic converters, which adds to the cost of each car. For any given price, the automakers will offer fewer units for sale because of the increased expense of producing an automobile. This expense shifts the supply curve of automobiles to the left.

Additional shift factors could be important in some applications. For example, the 1990s saw thousands of acres in the South converted from cotton to corn because of the relatively high price of corn. As the price of corn rose, *ceteris paribus,* cotton plantings fell and the cotton supply curve shifted to the left. If the price of corn were to fall, conversely, the cotton supply curve would shift to the right. More generally, **supply varies inversely to the price of a substitute in production.** Be aware that substitutes in production are not the same as the substitutes in consumption that shift demand. After all, would you be willing to trade in your morning corn flakes for a hearty bowl of cotton flakes?

Turning to another agricultural example, some products are produced jointly, such as beef and leather. An increase in the popularity and price of beef would lead to a movement up the supply curve for beef. The greater quantity supplied of beef means that more cattle are raised for slaughter, which has the effect of shifting the supply of leather to the right. In brief, more leather would be offered for sale at each price of leather, in response to people consuming more steak and hamburger. Thus, **supply varies directly with the prices of products that are jointly produced.**

Summing up, when producers offer to sell less of a good at each price, supply decreases. When producers offer to sell more of a good at each price, supply increases. Table 3-2 and Figure 3-6 summarize these shifts. Remember that a change in the price of the good causes a change in the quantity supplied, but does not shift supply. Rather, a change in price causes a movement along the supply curve.

THE LIVESTOCK GOURMET ON A HOT SUMMER DAY

While humans huddle by their air conditioners to escape the sweltering summer sun, life is good for some Iowa pigs and cattle—they enjoy a gourmet feast of tasty wet corn feed. On particularly hot days, farmers in the vicinity of the Cargill corn processing plant in Eddyville, Iowa, can buy this high-quality feed for a very low price. It's not that Cargill pities overheated animals. Rather, it is the availability of electricity that shifts out Cargill's supply of wet feed.

The many air conditioners that run on exceptionally hot days stress the ability of the local electric company to provide power. The ensuing power shortage leads to electricity cutbacks and leaves Cargill with huge piles of perishable wet feed, because there isn't enough electricity to dry and store it. The result is that, although power curtailment is not one of the more common things that shift supply, it's one that leaves some cows very contented. ◀

TABLE 3-2   CHANGES IN SUPPLY

SHIFT FACTORS	SUPPLY SHIFTS TO THE LEFT WHEN	SUPPLY SHIFTS TO THE RIGHT WHEN	EXAMPLES
Number of sellers	The number of sellers decreases.	The number of sellers increases.	The supply of shoes decreases when the number of shoemakers decreases. The supply of shoes increases when the number of shoemakers increases.
The price of labor or other inputs	The price of labor or any other input rises.	The price of labor or any other input falls.	The wages of shoemakers rise, which decreases the supply of shoes. The wages of shoemakers fall, which increases the supply of shoes.
Production restrictions and technology	Government, labor union, or other restrictions on production practices increase cost.	Technological change lowers cost.	The garment workers' labor union negotiates extra holidays for its members, which increases the cost of making clothing, thus decreasing the supply of clothing. Technological improvements in sewing machines lower the cost of making clothing, thus increasing the supply of clothing.
Price of substitutes in production	The price of a substitute in production rises.	The price of a substitute in production falls.	The price of corn rises, causing the supply of wheat to decrease. The price of corn falls, causing the supply of wheat to increase.
Price of jointly produced products	The price of a jointly produced product falls.	The price of a jointly produced product rises.	The price of beef falls, causing the supply of leather to decrease. The price of beef rises, causing the supply of leather to increase.
Producer expectations of future prices	Producers expect prices to rise in the future.	Producers expect prices to decline in the future.	Wheat farmers expect the price of wheat to rise and so withhold wheat from the market, causing the supply of wheat to decrease. Wheat farmers expect the price of wheat to decline, and so rush wheat to the market, causing the supply of wheat to increase.

3.3 EQUILIBRIUM—DEMAND MEETS SUPPLY AND THE MARKET CLEARS

Now that we have taken a close look at demand and supply, let's put them together to see how prices are determined. We will first need to make clear the distinction between demand and supply at the individual level and at the market level.

MARKET DEMAND AND SUPPLY

Demand can be one individual's or the market's as a whole. Likewise, supply can be from one firm or all firms in the market. Most of the time when economists use demand and supply analysis, they have in mind demand and supply for the entire market. When necessary, the terms *market demand* and *market supply* can be used to clarify that demand and supply are for the entire market rather than for a single buyer or seller.

The market is the bringing together of buyers and sellers. While most people think of a market as a physical location, markets usually extend well beyond any single place. Markets can be local, regional, national, or multinational in scale. For example, gold, crude oil, and

(a) Leftward shift (decrease) in supply

(b) Rightward shift (increase) in supply

Supply shifts left when:
• The number of sellers decreases.
• The price of labor or other input rises.
• Producers expect the price to rise in the future.
• Government, labor, or other restrictions on production practices increase cost.
• Price of a jointly produced product falls.
• The price of a substitute in production rises.

Supply shifts right when:
• The number of sellers increases.
• The price of labor or other input falls.
• Producers expect the price to fall in the future.
• Technological change lowers cost.
• Price of a jointly produced product rises.
• The price of a substitute in production falls.

FIGURE 3-6

FACTORS THAT SHIFT SUPPLY Factors that shift supply to the left are listed in (a), along with a graph showing the leftward shift. Factors that shift supply to the right are shown in (b), along with a graph showing the rightward shift.

many other commodities are sold in global markets, with only minor variations in price throughout the world.

Market demand is the sum of all the individuals' demands in that market. Summing individuals' demands is straightforward if you remember to add quantities, not prices. For each price, the quantity demanded in the marketplace is the sum of the quantities demanded by all consumers. On the graph of demand, as we will see in Figure 3-7, **market demand is the horizontal summation of individuals' demand curves.** An example will demonstrate this process.

For simplicity, we will consider a market with only two consumers, Jack and Jill. Jack and Jill are both interested in purchasing—what else?—pails of water. While climbing the hill for pails of water is great aerobic exercise, there is always some danger of tumbling down. So both Jill and Jack are willing to buy pails of water. The quantities they demand depend upon price, as shown by Jill's and Jack's demand curves in Figure 3-7. These demand curves combine into a market demand, as also shown in Figure 3-7. To obtain market demand, Jill's and Jack's quantities demanded are added at each possible price. As always, it is quantities that are added, not prices. Since quantity—the number of pails of water—is measured on the horizontal axis, we say that market demand is the horizontal sum of individual demand curves.

Market supply depicts the total quantity offered for sale in the market at each price. To obtain market supply, merely add the quantities offered for sale by all sellers at each price. Graphically, **market supply is the horizontal summation of each seller's supply curve.** Continuing with the example, Figure 3-8 shows the supplies of two sellers of pails of water— Wally and Wanda—and how their supplies sum to market supply.

Market demand sums the quantities demanded by each buyer			
Price ($)	Jack's quantity demanded	Jill's quantity demanded	Market quantity demanded
5	1	0	1
4	2	1	3
3	3	2	5
2	4	3	7
1	5	4	9
0	6	5	11

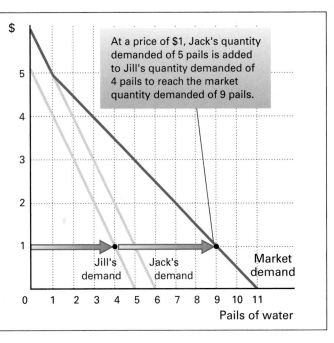

At a price of $1, Jack's quantity demanded of 5 pails is added to Jill's quantity demanded of 4 pails to reach the market quantity demanded of 9 pails.

FIGURE 3-7

MARKET DEMAND Market demand is the horizontal summation of all buyers' demands. At a price of $1, Jill would be willing to purchase 4 pails of water and Jack 5 pails. Added together, the market quantity demanded would be 9 pails of water, as seen on the market demand curve. Likewise, at a price of $4, Jill's quantity demanded would be 1 pail of water and Jack's would be 2 pails. Taken together, the market quantity demanded would be 3 pails of water.

Market supply sums the quantities supplied by each seller			
Price ($)	Wally's quantity supplied	Wanda's quantity supplied	Market quantity supplied
5	4	5	9
4	3	4	7
3	2	3	5
2	1	2	3
1	0	1	1
0	0	0	0

At a price of $4, Wally's quantity supplied of 3 pails is added to Wanda's quantity supplied of 4 pails to reach the market quantity supplied of 7 pails.

FIGURE 3-8

MARKET SUPPLY Market supply is the horizontal summation of all sellers' supplies. At a price of $1, Wally would supply no pails of water and Wanda 1 pail. Adding these quantities, the market quantity supplied at $1 is 1 pail of water. If the price rises to $4, Wally supplies 3 pails and Wanda supplies 4 pails. The market quantity supplied is then 7 pails of water, as shown on the market supply curve.

THE MARKET EQUILIBRIUM

When supply and demand meet in the marketplace, a market price is created. While individual sellers are free to price their products however they wish, **there is only one price that *clears the market,* meaning that the quantity supplied equals the quantity demanded.** The market-clearing price and the resulting quantity traded comprise what is known as the **market equilibrium**, meaning that there is no tendency for either price or quantity to change, *ceteris paribus.*

market equilibrium a situation in which there is no tendency for either price or quantity to change.

Market equilibrium is determined by the intersection of supply and demand, as shown in Figure 3-9. A market equilibrium is associated with an *equilibrium price* and an *equilibrium quantity.* In our example, the market equilibrium occurs at a price of $3 and a quantity of 5 pails.

surplus the excess of quantity supplied over quantity demanded, which occurs when price is above equilibrium.

At any price above the equilibrium price, there would be a **surplus**, representing the excess of quantity supplied over quantity demanded. For example, a price of $4 would be too high, resulting in a surplus of 4 pails. In that case, Wally and Wanda would compete with each other for sales by lowering their prices. More generally, in any market in which a surplus occurs, some sellers would cut their prices slightly in order to be the ones that make the sales. Other suppliers would then be without customers, and would consequently lower their own prices enough to capture customers from their competitors. This leapfrogging process would continue until the quantity demanded and supplied are equal, which occurs at the equilibrium price.

shortage the excess of quantity demanded over quantity supplied, which occurs when price is below equilibrium.

A price that is below the equilibrium price results in a **shortage**, equal to the amount by which quantity demanded exceeds quantity supplied. For example, a price of $2 would be

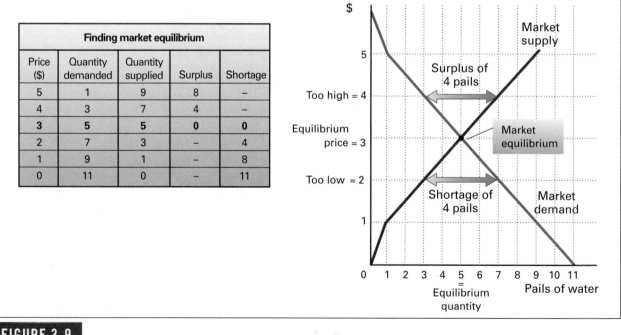

Finding market equilibrium				
Price ($)	Quantity demanded	Quantity supplied	Surplus	Shortage
5	1	9	8	–
4	3	7	4	–
3	5	5	0	0
2	7	3	–	4
1	9	1	–	8
0	11	0	–	11

FIGURE 3-9

MARKET EQUILIBRIUM Market equilibrium occurs where demand and supply intersect. In this example, the equilibrium is at a price of $3 and a quantity of 5 pails. Any price above $3 would lead to a surplus, causing price to fall until the equilibrium is reached. Any price below $3 would lead to a shortage, causing price to rise until the equilibrium is reached.

too low and result in a shortage of 4 pails. Because there is not enough water to meet demand at that price, Jack and Jill would scramble to be the first to buy. More generally, whenever there is a shortage in any market, buyers compete against each other for the limited quantities of the goods that are offered for sale at that price. For sellers, shortages provide an opportunity both to raise prices and to increase sales, a doubly appealing prospect. Price would thus rise to its equilibrium value, the point at which the shortage disappears. Thus, without any guidance, the invisible hand of the market eliminates either surpluses or shortages and leads to the market-clearing equilibrium.

Suppose either supply or demand were to change. For example, suppose an increase in consumer income or a decrease in the price of a complement shifts demand to the right. One of the most common mistakes students make is to think this shift in demand would also shift supply. It would not, because demand is not a shift factor for supply. Rather, the rightward shift in demand leads to a movement up the supply curve and results in a new, higher equilibrium price and quantity. More generally, **a change in supply would cause a movement along demand. Similarly, a change in demand would cause a movement along supply.**

For practice, you might draw the basic supply and demand diagram, and then sketch a few shifts in either demand or supply. Note the effect on the equilibrium price and quantity. Note also that shifting demand does not cause a shift in supply or vice versa.

The market equilibrium will change whenever supply or demand shift. Taken one curve at a time, there are only four shifts possible:

1. An increase in supply, which shifts supply to the right.
2. A decrease in supply, which shifts supply to the left.
3. An increase in demand, which shifts demand to the right.
4. A decrease in demand, which shifts demand to the left.

These shifts and their effects on equilibrium price and quantity are shown and summarized in Figure 3-10. The four rows of the table, labeled case 1 through case 4, match the four graphs in the figure.

QUICKCHECK

In Figure 3-9, how much would be sold if the price is $4? If the price is $2?

Answer: Remember that each sale requires both a buyer and a seller. If the price is $4, then 3 pails of water would be sold, because 3 is the quantity demanded. If the price is $2, it would still be 3 pails of water sold, this time because 3 is the quantity supplied.

3.4 THE ELASTICITY OF DEMAND

The **elasticity of demand** measures the responsiveness of quantity demanded to changes in price. The formula for the elasticity of demand is given by the percentage change in quantity demanded divided by the percentage change in price.

Since price and quantity demanded are inversely related, the computation of the elasticity of demand will always result in a negative value. **For convenience, the elasticity of demand is stated as an absolute value, meaning that the minus sign is dropped.** Otherwise the elasticity of demand would always be a negative value, because price and quantity demanded always change in opposite directions.

elasticity of demand measures the responsiveness of quantity demanded to changes in price; computed as the percentage change in quantity demanded divided by the percentage change in price; expressed as an absolute value.

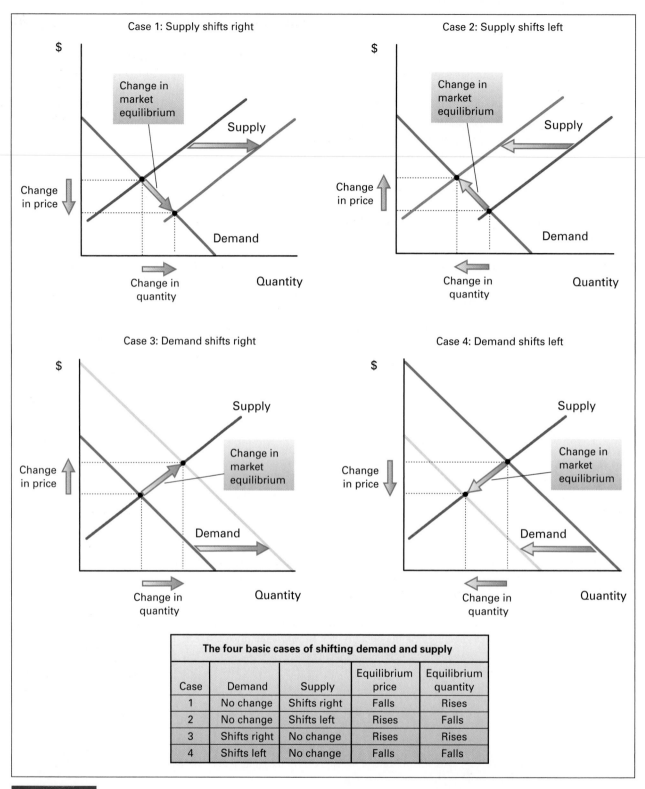

The four basic cases of shifting demand and supply				
Case	Demand	Supply	Equilibrium price	Equilibrium quantity
1	No change	Shifts right	Falls	Rises
2	No change	Shifts left	Rises	Falls
3	Shifts right	No change	Rises	Rises
4	Shifts left	No change	Falls	Falls

FIGURE 3-10

EFFECTS OF SHIFTS IN DEMAND AND SUPPLY A shift in either supply or demand will affect the market equilibrium price and quantity, as seen in cases 1 through 4. When demand and supply shift simultaneously, the result can be found by first analyzing one shift and then the other. That process would involve combining two of the four cases.

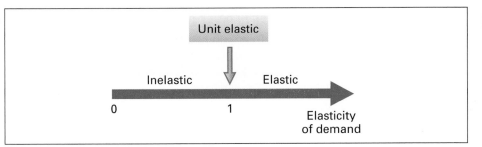

FIGURE 3-11

PRICE ELASTICITY OF DEMAND
This value can range from zero to infinity (in absolute value).

The elasticity of demand is classified as inelastic, unit elastic, or elastic, according to its numerical value.

■ **Inelastic demand:** Elasticity of demand lies between 0 and 1; in this range, the quantity demanded is relatively unresponsive to price. For example, a 2-percent change in price that leads to a 1-percent change in quantity demanded results in an elasticity of demand equal to 0.5.

inelastic demand demand has an elasticity that is less than 1.

■ **Unit elastic demand:** Elasticity of demand equal to 1; in this range, the quantity demanded changes proportionally to changes in price. For example, a 2-percent change in price that leads to a 2-percent change in quantity demanded results in an elasticity equal to 1.

unit elastic demand demand has an elasticity that equals 1.

■ **Elastic demand:** Elasticity of demand is greater than 1; in this range, the quantity demanded is relatively responsive to changes in price. For example, a 2-percent change in price that leads to a 3-percent change in quantity demanded results in an elasticity equal to 1.5.

elastic demand demand has an elasticity that is greater than 1.

The range of numerical values associated with each class of elasticity is portrayed in Figure 3-11.

Consumer spending translates into revenue for sellers. The revenue sellers receive equals the quantity sold multiplied by the price, and is called **total revenue.** In other words,

total revenue price × quantity.

$$\text{Total revenue} = \text{Price} \times \text{Quantity}$$

Total revenue, which is the same as total spending by consumers, can be shown graphically as the rectangular area created when a price and corresponding quantity demanded are multiplied by each other. Figure 3-12 illustrates total revenue graphically.

FIGURE 3-12

TOTAL REVENUE Price multiplied by quantity demanded equals total revenue, as shown by the area of the shaded rectangle. The total revenue is received by sellers. Since it represents spending by consumers, total revenue equals total spending.

TABLE 3-3	THE EFFECT OF A CHANGE IN PRICE ON TOTAL REVENUE
CHANGE IN PRICE	**EFFECT ON TOTAL REVENUE**
Higher Price	If demand is inelastic, total revenue rises.
	If demand is unit elastic, total revenue remains constant.
	If demand is elastic, total revenue falls.
Lower Price	If demand is inelastic, total revenue falls.
	If demand is unit elastic, total revenue remains constant.
	If demand is elastic, total revenue rises.

Many people assume that when the price increases, the sellers of a product earn more revenue. However, this assumption is often not true, because quantity demanded falls any time price rises. An increase in price will bring in more revenue only if demand is inelastic, meaning that the fall in quantity demanded is less significant than the rise in price. In contrast, were demand to be elastic, the quantity demanded would be quite responsive to price. Any increase in price would cause a proportionally greater fall in the quantity sold and thus would lower total revenue. Table 3-3 summarizes the price change effects on total revenue.

Figure 3-13 illustrates the idea that price changes can sometimes lead to increased total revenue and at other times lead to decreased revenue. Part (a) shows elastic demand, meaning that the total revenue rectangle becomes larger when price is lowered. Part (b) depicts a demand that is inelastic in the price range shown. In such cases, a decrease in price decreases the total revenue rectangle, as seen in the figure.

The elasticity of demand will vary along most demand curves. Along a downward-sloping, straight-line demand curve, demand is unit elastic at the midpoint, elastic above the midpoint, and inelastic below the midpoint. The variation in elasticity is shown in Figure 3-14. To remember, observe that the lower the point on a straight-line demand curve, the less its elasticity. The reason is that, when we move down the demand curve, the percentage change in price becomes larger relative to the corresponding percentage change in quantity demanded.

QUICKCHECK

Wally's Water Works sells water. Wally has set the price of water at $5 per pail, but wonders if he should charge less. If Wally faces an elasticity of demand for water equal to 0.3, why would he regret lowering his price? What if the elasticity equals 3?

Answer: An elasticity of demand equal to 0.3 means that demand is inelastic. If Wally lowers his price, the increase in sales will not be enough to make up for the loss of revenue per unit. In other words, keeping the price at $5 per pail means that he sells fewer pails but makes more total revenue than if the price is lower. In contrast, an elasticity of demand equal to 3 would mean that Wally faces an elastic demand for his water. In that case, a price reduction would lead to such a large percentage increase in sales that Wally's revenues would rise.

FIGURE 3-13

ELASTICITY AND TOTAL REVENUE Total revenue is the rectangle formed by multiplying price by quantity sold. In the elastic range of demand, as shown in (a), price and total revenue vary inversely. Decreasing price would cause total revenue to rise. The revenue loss from the lower price per unit is more than off-set by the revenue gain from the larger quantity sold.

  In the inelastic range of demand, as shown in (b), price and total revenue vary directly. Decreasing price would cause total revenue to fall. The additional revenue from increasing the quantity sold does not make up for the revenue loss from the lower price per unit.

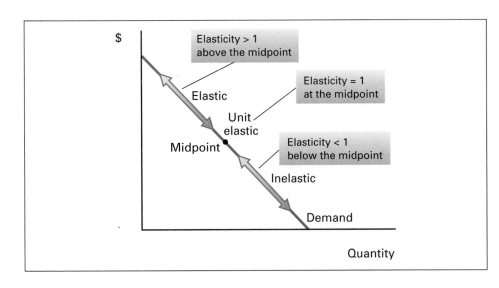

FIGURE 3-14

ELASTICITY ALONG A LINEAR DEMAND CURVE The midpoint of a straight-line demand curve separates the elastic from the inelastic portion. In moving down the linear demand curve, the elasticity of demand declines from elastic to unit elastic to inelastic. The reason stems from elasticity being based upon percentage changes rather than merely upon slope, which remains constant.

To illustrate the importance of elasticity, Figure 3-15 depicts the market for recreational drugs, where the model is deliberately nonspecific as to exactly what sort of drugs these are. The addictive nature of drugs leads to an inelastic demand curve. The market price and quantity of drugs in the free market is determined by the intersection of supply and demand. The drug war shifts that supply by increasing the riskiness and cost of supplying drugs. The result is a higher equilibrium price and lower equilibrium quantity.

FIGURE 3-15

EFFECTS OF THE DRUG WAR
Tougher enforcement of drug laws make it riskier and more costly to supply recreational drugs, which decreases supply. The drug war causes market equilibrium price to be higher and quantity to be lower. Because demand is inelastic, the drug war also increases total revenue in the industry. With more money at stake and no recourse to the law, there is an incentive for violence as suppliers compete for control. The higher prices also lead to more property crime among impoverished addicts seeking money to buy drugs.

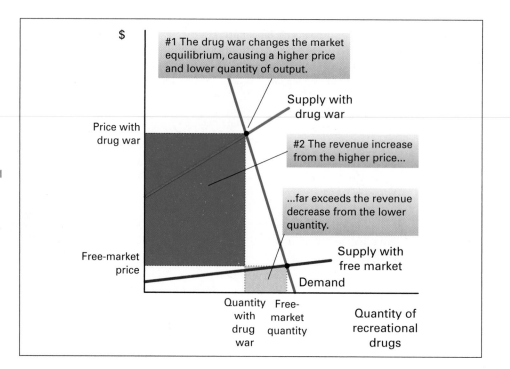

Relative to the outcome under the drug war, the free market would appear to offer both good news and bad news. The good news is that the quantity of spending, given by price multiplied by quantity, would be lower without the drug war. This means less crime to raise money to buy drugs. Since drugs would be sold by legitimate businesses in the free market, the violent territorial crime of the drug rings would also largely disappear. The bad news is that drug use would rise unless demand shifts, since quantity demanded rises as price falls.

3.5 DEMANDING BETTER SCHOOLS, SUPPLYING BETTER SCHOOLS

Some people know the importance of education because they have it. I know the importance of education because I didn't.

—Frederick Douglass, ex-slave and abolitionist

"Our schools must be improved!" From kindergarten through the twelfth grade, the education of America's youth is a top concern of both the president and parents. There is less concern, however, about improving colleges; the reasons relate to demand and supply.

College students shoulder the high cost of college, with cost playing a major role in college choice. Consistent with the law of demand, the lower the price of a college education, *ceteris paribus,* the greater the number of students who will apply and the more education they will choose. To promote college education, government offers tax deductions, subsidies, and financial aid that in effect lowers its price.

High school seniors choose among a varied assortment of colleges. In lower grades, however, there is normally a powerful financial incentive to choose only the government-provided local public school. The reason is that taxpayer financing makes those schools free to the student.

Free public schooling was established in the nineteenth century to promote equal opportunity—an equal start in life. However, public schools are not all the same, and the gap between the best and the worst is not likely to close on its own. Schools in wealthy neigh-borhoods often spend more per pupil than schools in poor ones. Some schools are bureau-cratic, inefficient, and ineffective, while others have strong academic reputations. Inefficient schools are insulated from competitive pressures to reform because even the best private schools find it hard to compete with "free" tuition. In addition, it would take moving to a new school district to enroll in a different public school.

If there were no free public schools, the invisible hand of the marketplace would cause schools to become efficient at responding to the demands of parents. While parents lack for-mal teaching credentials they could be guided by reputation or brand name in much the same way that they are guided in buying the family car and refrigerator. Schools that are most efficient at providing value would gain students, while others would lose them. However, because family incomes differ, the market outcome would not achieve equal edu-cational opportunities for all children. The political outcome has been to sacrifice the effi-ciency of competition for the veneer of equity provided by equal access to free public schools. But is there a way to achieve our goal of equity in a manner that is less costly to the efficiency of free markets? Can we introduce competition to achieve more efficient schools?

Limited competition is provided by *charter schools,* a form of public school. Charter schools are started when a group of parents form or hire a nonprofit organization to set up a new school that meets state specifications. The new school receives a state contract called a charter to operate a school for a limited time, usually five years, after which the charter is renewed if the school meets educational standards. Because charter schools call for parental involvement, they are more accountable to parents than traditional schools. Recently, over 250,000 students were enrolled in about 800 charter schools in thirty-seven states.

INTRODUCTION TO VOUCHERS

Much more competition can be achieved through *vouchers,* which provide money that recip-ients can spend, although spending is restricted to a certain category of goods. The Food Stamp program provides low-income recipients with vouchers—food stamps—that can only be used on food purchases. Food Stamp recipients buy what they want rather than being forced to eat the offerings of a government-run food kitchen. A similar situation holds true when vouchers are applied to education. *School vouchers* provide parents with money that they must spend on schooling their children. With vouchers, the money is received by the school of each parent's choosing rather than being spent directly by the government-run public school.

School vouchers were first proposed in 1955 by Nobel-prize-winning economist Milton Friedman. Today, voucher programs of one sort or another are underway in Ohio, Florida, Texas, and elsewhere. Still, vouchers are poorly understood and controversial.

Figure 3-16 illustrates the effects of school vouchers, where public schools and private schools are substitutes. Vouchers lower the price of private schooling to parents, thus increasing their quantity demanded. Private schools are willing to increase the quantities they supply at each price because of the supplemental payment they receive from vouchers. Figure 3-16(a) shows this effect as a rightward shift in supply to parents who are provided vouchers. The result is a lower price and more children enrolled in private schools. Government-owned public schools, which are substitutes for private schools, offer unlimited enrollment at a price of "free" to parents. Vouchers result in a decrease in demand and enrollments in public schools, as shown in Figure 3-16(b).

With vouchers, the location, design, and operation of schools is driven by parental choice. Such radical change has proven difficult to enact into law. Most proposals for school vouchers retain support for public schools, either by restricting vouchers to apply to public schools only, or by providing vouchers just to students who attend "failing" public schools.

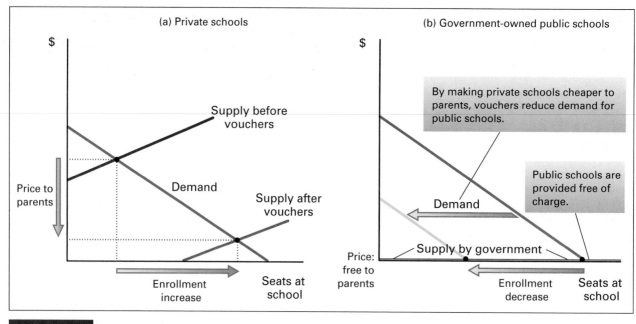

FIGURE 3-16

EFFECTS OF SCHOOL VOUCHERS Vouchers lower the price of private schooling, which increases the quantity demanded. The effect in the market for public schooling, a substitute, is to decrease demand and enrollments. Vouchers increase competition among schools, providing them with the incentive to provide the best value for money spent on education.

A *pure voucher system* would permit children to attend any school, whether church sponsored or not. In the summer of 2002, the U.S. Supreme Court upheld a lower court ruling that allows vouchers so long as their purpose is to promote education, not religion. Similarly, financial aid is available to college students even if they attend a college operated by a religious denomination.

Opponents of vouchers fear that the competition for voucher money would cause schools to shortchange educational objectives and promote popular, but not very worthwhile, activities. For example, schools might de-emphasize academic achievement, while emphasizing football. Schools could also appeal to parents' religious preferences to gain enrollments and the dollars they bring.

Voucher opponents predict that competition would impede learning in other ways. For example, private schools might seek corporate sponsors who would pay for the right to put advertisements in school learning materials, thus possibly distracting students from learning. Voucher critics want to see schooling remain in the hands of educational professionals whose motives they feel would be more focused on learning and less on money.

Another criticism of vouchers relates to funding. Public schools are funded on the size of their enrollments. By reducing enrollments, vouchers would also drain public schools of money and jobs. Less money would cause the public schools to shrink in size. Just like inefficient companies in other sectors of the free market, inefficient public schools would whither and die. So, too, would inefficient private schools. The process might be hard on both the faculty and students.

Perhaps more time and experience with vouchers will clarify the issues. By promoting competition, vouchers offer the promise of improved schools. Would parents demand well for their children or should that choice be left to educational professionals? You be the judge.

1. Should educational quality be allowed to differ based on family income? Should vouchers be allowed to supplement a tuition payment at a private school, with the result that some children's quality of education would differ from other children's? Discuss.

2. *Myra:* I think voucher amounts should vary with household income. The more income, the less help—it's only fair.

   Fred: I think education should be free for everyone. Your income shouldn't have anything to do with how much voucher power you have.

   Evaluate Myra's and Fred's ideas. If a voucher plan is to be used, should the voucher amount depend upon a person's income?

Visit **www.prenhall.com/collinge** for updates and web exercises on this Explore & Apply topic.

SUMMARY AND LEARNING OBJECTIVES

1. **Distinguish between the general notions of demand and supply used in ordinary conversation and the precise notions employed in the study of economics.**
   - Supply and demand analysis captures the essential role of competition in the free marketplace. The what, how, and for whom questions you studied in Chapter 1 are answered by demand and supply in a market economy.
   - Demand is more than merely wanting a good or service. Demand is a relationship between price and quantity. By the law of demand, market demand curves slope downward, indicating an inverse relationship between price and quantity demanded. In other words, at each possible price there is a specific quantity demanded.
   - Like demand, supply is also a relationship between price and quantity. Supply shows the quantity supplied for each possible price. Unlike the demand curve, market supply curves slope upward, reflecting the law of supply. Thus, price and quantity supplied are directly related.

2. **Explain what it means to shift demand and supply and why shifts might occur.**
   - Demand will shift with changes in the price of a substitute or complement, a change in income, a change in population, changes in expectations, and changes in tastes or preferences. An increase in demand shifts the demand curve to the right. A decrease in demand shifts the demand curve to the left.
   - Two goods are substitutes for each other when the goods are similar and serve the same purpose. An increase in the price of a substitute for a good will increase the demand for the good. Two goods are complements to each other when they are used together. An increase in the price of a complement for a good will decrease the demand for the good.
   - An increase in income will increase the demand for a normal good, but reduce the demand for an inferior good.
   - There is a distinction between a change in demand and a change in quantity demanded. A change in demand means the demand curve shifts. A price change causes a movement from one point to another on a demand curve and results in a change in quantity demanded.
   - Supply slopes upward, indicating a direct relationship between price and quantity supplied. A price change causes a change in quantity supplied and is seen as a movement along a supply curve. A change in supply means that the whole supply curve shifts. An increase in supply is seen as a shift to the right in the supply curve, while a decrease in supply occurs when the supply curve shifts to the left.
   - Supply will shift with a change in the prices of substitutes in production, changes in the prices of jointly produced products, changes in union work rules or government regulations that change costs, changes in technology, changes in input prices, and changes in seller expectations.
   - A shift in supply causes a movement along the demand curve, while a shift in demand causes a movement along the supply curve.

3. **Describe how the marketplace settles on the equilibrium price and quantity.**
   - The interaction of supply and demand leads to a market equilibrium price and quantity, from which there is no tendency to change. Market equilibrium occurs at the intersection of demand and supply. At this point, quantity demanded equals quantity supplied.
   - A market price that is less than the market equilibrium price will cause a shortage, in which case the price will adjust upward toward the equilibrium price. The shortage will be gone when the price reaches its equilibrium level. A price that is above the market equilibrium price will cause a surplus. The price will adjust downward toward the market equilibrium price until the surplus is eliminated.

4. **Specify how demand and supply shifts cause market equilibriums to change over time.**
   - Demand and supply usually shift with the passage of time. When the demand or supply of a good shifts, then the good's price and quantity adjust to a new market equilibrium. There are four cases involving a shift in either demand or supply, but not both: an increase in demand, a decrease in demand, an increase in supply, and a decrease in supply.
   - An increase in demand by itself causes an increase in the market equilibrium price and quantity. A decrease in demand by itself causes a decrease in the market equilibrium price and quantity. An increase in supply by itself causes a decrease in equilibrium price, but an increase in equilibrium quantity. A decrease in supply alone increases the equilibrium price and decreases the equilibrium quantity.

5. **Describe how the elasticity of demand determines whether a price change increases, decreases, or does not change total revenue to sellers.**
   - The elasticity of demand is particularly important for its insight into the revenue effects of price changes. Inelastic demand, an elasticity less than one, leads to a change in total revenue in the same direction as the price change. Elastic demand, an elasticity greater than one, leads to a revenue change in the opposite direction from the price change. Unit elastic demand, an elasticity equal to one, leads to no change in total revenue.
   - Along a straight-line demand curve, the elasticity changes from one point to the next. The upper half of the demand curve is the elastic range; the lower half, the inelastic range; and the midpoint is unit elastic.

6. **Discuss how vouchers use competition to improve the quality of schooling.**
   - School vouchers increase competition in the market for education. Vouchers are controversial because of the fear that the public schools would be harmed. However, the efficiency of public schools would likely be increased because of their need to compete with private schools for students and money.

KEY TERMS

demand, 52
quantity demanded, 52
ceteris paribus, 52
law of demand, 52
normal goods, 55
inferior goods, 55
substitutes, 55

complements, 55
supply, 58
quantity supplied, 58
law of supply, 58
market equilibrium, 64
surplus, 64

shortage, 64
elasticity of demand, 65
inelastic demand, 67
unit elastic demand, 67
elastic demand, 67
total revenue, 67

TEST YOURSELF

TRUE OR FALSE

1. If price rises, demand falls.
2. *Ceteris paribus,* if the price of Coca-Cola rises, the quantity sold of Pepsi will fall.
3. If something happens that leads producers to expect the price to rise in the future, supply will initially shift to the left.
4. If the market clears, there is likely to be a shortage.
5. If demand is elastic and price rises, total spending by consumers also rises.

MULTIPLE CHOICE

6. The law of demand states that consumers
   a. must not buy more than they need.
   b. must not waste what they buy.
   c. must pay for what they buy.
   d. will buy more as the price falls.

7. Demand and supply curves are drawn assuming *ceteris paribus,* which means
   a. consumers and producers care only about money.
   b. that product is the only product in existence.
   c. to ignore all assumptions.
   d. that all other things are held constant.

8. Assume that used cars are an inferior good and that new cars are a normal good. If consumer incomes increase, the demand for
   a. used cars will decrease, and the demand for new cars will increase.
   b. used cars will increase, and the demand for new cars will decrease.
   c. both new and used cars will decrease.
   d. both new and used cars will increase.

9. An increase in the price of football tickets would cause the _____ basketball tickets, a substitute, to _____.
   a. demand for; increase.
   b. supply of; increase.
   c. demand for; decrease.
   d. supply of; decrease.

10. Which of the following would be most likely to shift the demand for widgets?
    a. A change in the price of widgets.
    b. Unionization of the widget industry.
    c. Discovery of a valuable use for by-products generated in the production of widgets.
    d. A news report that widget prices are expected to increase in the future.

11. An upward-sloping supply curve means that
    a. consumers will wish to purchase more at higher prices.
    b. consumers will wish to purchase more at lower prices.
    c. business firms will wish to sell more at higher prices.
    d. business firms that lower their prices will desire to sell more.

12. A decrease in supply is illustrated as
    a. a downward shift in the supply curve.
    b. a shift to the left in the supply curve.
    c. an upward movement along the supply curve.
    d. a downward movement along the supply curve.

13. Which event is most likely to result in an increase in the price of a Whopper hamburger at Burger King?
    a. French fries go up in price.
    b. New competing hamburger restaurants open.
    c. Beef prices increase.
    d. Scientists declare that hamburgers are a health hazard.

14. In Self-Test Figure 3-1, which of the following would cause a movement from point *A* to point *B*?
    a. An increase in the cost of inputs.
    b. A decrease in the cost of inputs.
    c. An increase in demand.
    d. A decrease in demand.

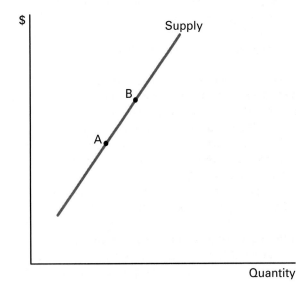

SELF-TEST FIGURE 3-1

15. Suppose a new technique is discovered that is expected to result in cars and houses of the future obtaining all of their energy requirements from roof-mounted solar panels. In the present-day market for oil, it is most likely that
    a. demand would shift to the right.
    b. demand would shift to the left.
    c. supply would shift to the right.
    d. supply would shift to the left.

16. If research reveals that carrot juice cures cancer, it is likely that
    a. the supply of carrot juice will increase, which will increase the quantity demanded.
    b. demand for carrot juice will increase, which will increase the quantity supplied.
    c. neither the demand for carrot juice nor the supply of carrot juice will increase.
    d. both the demand for carrot juice and the supply of carrot juice will increase.

17. Let Jack and Jill be the only two consumers in the market for pails of water. Jack's demand schedule is:

Price	Quantity Demanded
$1	10
$2	5
$3	0

Jill's demand schedule is:

Price	Quantity Demanded
$1	15
$2	10
$3	5
$4	0

Which of the following would be the market demand for pails of water?

a.

Price	Quantity Demanded
$1	12½
$2	7½
$3	2½
$4	0

b.

Price	Quantity Demanded
$1	15
$2	10
$3	5
$4	0

c.

Price	Quantity Demanded
$1	25
$2	15
$3	5
$4	0

d.

Price	Quantity Demanded
$1	15
$3	10
$5	5
$7	0

18. When there is an initial shortage, market prices eventually reach equilibrium because
    a. supply increases.
    b. price decreases.
    c. price increases.
    d. equilibrium output falls.

19. Moving down a downward-sloping straight-line demand curve, elasticity
    a. goes from elastic to unit elastic to inelastic.
    b. goes from elastic to inelastic to unit elastic.
    c. goes from inelastic to unit elastic to elastic.
    d. remains constant at unit elastic throughout.

20. School voucher plans are likely to do all of the following EXCEPT
    a. increase the amount of control that parents have over schools.
    b. threaten the job security of teachers in the public schools.
    c. violate the constitutional separation between church and state.
    d. increase the amount of educational choices available.

QUESTIONS AND PROBLEMS

1. *[demand]* Do price and quantity demanded show an inverse or a direct relationship between each other? Draw a graph showing a plausible demand curve for milk. Be sure to correctly label the axes of your graph.

2. *[individual and market demand]* Draw a single graph indicating someone's demand curve for hot dogs. Be sure to label the axes of your graph appropriately. Label the demand curve with the words Individual's Demand. On this graph, indicate what market demand would be if there were only two people willing to buy hot dogs, and if each had a demand curve identical to the one you just drew. Label this curve Market Demand.

3. *[demand]* Suppose Clare's demand for tomatoes is represented by the figures in the accompanying table. Draw and label the axes of a graph that shows Clare's demand for tomatoes. Scale the axes appropriate to the figures in the table. Plot the price–quantity pairs from the table in your graph, then connect the points plotted and label the resulting curve with the word Demand. Is the demand curve you plotted a straight

line? Why are most of the demand curves in the text drawn as straight lines?

Price per Pound	Quantity Demanded per Week (in pounds)
$1.00	0
75 cents	1/2
50 cents	3/4
25 cents	1
Free	2

4. *[demand]* Why does insurance increase the number of homes that are built in areas prone to hurricane damage? Explain, using a graph of demand.
5. *[substitutes]* List at least five substitutes for your favorite soft drink, in order, starting with the best substitute, second best, and so on. Comment on whether the products on your list are good substitutes. How much would the price of your favorite soft drink have to increase before you would begin to purchase the best substitute?
6. *[complements]* Name at least one other good that would be a complement for each of the following goods: pencil, baseball, personal computer, postage stamp, sugar, and butter. What effect on the demand for each of these goods would there be if the price of a complement for the good were to increase (decrease)?
7. *[inferior goods]* Keeping in mind the economic definition of inferior goods, list several products that would be inferior goods for you personally. Do you think that these would also be inferior goods for most other people?
8. *[normal versus inferior goods]* When Mr. Johnson lost his job, thus cutting his income, his demands for various products changed. The accompanying table lists five normal goods and five inferior goods for Mr. Johnson. However, the goods may not be in the correct column. Bearing in mind the distinction between normal and inferior goods, use your best judgment to rearrange the goods by placing them in the correct column. Will the demand for the normal goods increase or decrease because of Mr. Johnson's income reduction? Will the demand for the inferior goods increase or decrease?

Normal Goods?	Inferior Goods?
Generic paper towels	Antique furniture
Restaurant food	Tickets to pro football games
Tommy Hilfiger clothing	Used cars
Fresh vegetables	Home-brewed coffee
Spam	Ramen noodles

9. *[demand]* As in the chapter, suppose Jack and Jill are the only two consumers in the market for pails of water. However, suppose that their demand curves change over time from the data in the chapter to the following:

Price	Jack's Quantity Demanded	Jill's Quantity Demanded
$1	10	15
2	5	10
3	0	5
4	0	0

  a. Compute market demand.
  b. Compute the quantities purchased in total and by Jack and Jill individually if the price per unit is $2.
  c. Graph Jack's demand and Jill's demand on separate graphs. Note that, if you connect the data points you are given, you are actually inferring additional data. For example, connecting the data points on Jack's demand implies that Jack would be willing to purchase 2.5 pails of water at a price of $2.50 per pail.
10. *[demand versus quantity demanded]* Is there a difference between a *change in demand* and a *change in quantity demanded*? Explain.
11. *[direct or inverse supply curve]* Does a supply curve show a direct or an inverse relationship between price and quantity supplied? Draw a graph showing a plausible market supply curve for spinach. Be sure to correctly label the axes of your graph.
12. *[shift factors for supply]* In each of the situations that follow, state whether supply would increase or decrease. Sketch each shift by drawing a graph for each case.
  a. The price of a substitute in production falls.
  b. The price of a jointly produced product falls.
  c. Sellers expect prices of their output will increase in the future.
  d. The technology of production improves.
13. *[supply versus quantity supplied]* Explain why an increase in *quantity supplied* is NOT the same as an increase in *supply*. Which of these would be associated with a rightward shift in the supply curve? Which would be associated with a movement up the supply curve?
14. *[equilibrium]* Explain what is meant by saying that, at equilibrium, the market clears. Why do markets tend toward equilibrium?
15. *[surplus]* Will a surplus result from a price that is above the equilibrium price or a price below the equilibrium price? Why would a surplus be only temporary?

16. *[shortage]* Will a shortage result from a price that is above the equilibrium price or a price below the equilibrium price? What adjustment will take place so that the shortage eventually disappears?

17. *[surplus, shortage, equilibrium]* Fill in the surplus or shortage in the table below. In each case identify whether the number is a surplus, shortage, or neither. Identify the equilibrium price, and explain why a price above equilibrium would not last.

Price	Quantity Demanded	Quantity Supplied	Surplus or Shortage
$7	12	30	
$6	15	25	
$5	19	19	
$4	23	10	

18. *[adjustment to equilibrium]* Suppose that a market is initially in equilibrium. Now suppose that demand increases. At the initial equilibrium price, will the effect of the increase in demand be to create a surplus or a shortage? What must happen for the market to attain a new equilibrium?

19. *[shifts in demand and supply]* Fill in the missing information in the following table by stating whether equilibrium price and quantity will increase or decrease in each case.

Demand	Supply	Equilibrium Price	Equilibrium Quantity
Shifts to the right	Does not shift		
Shifts to the left	Does not shift		
Does not shift	Shifts to the right		
Does not shift	Shifts to the left		

20. *[elasticity and revenue]* Durango Dan, owner of Durango Danceland, must decide if he should offer half-price dance lessons on Wednesday nights, when business is slow. After counting up his receipts for a few weeks with Wednesday promotions in place, he concludes that revenues rise when his prices fall. Is demand at Durango Danceland elastic on Wednesday nights? Explain.

    Visit **www.prenhall.com/collinge** for Exploring the Web exercises and additional self-test quizzes.

CHAPTER 4

THE POWER OF PRICES

A LOOK AHEAD

The United States shines like no other country, at least when looked at from outer space. Electric power and lighting are taken for granted as inalienable rights. Yet there was a time not long ago when the lights blinked out in California. The consequences were severe in terms of consumer annoyance and lost industry output. As we will see in the Explore & Apply section that concludes this chapter, the culprit was a policy that ignored some basic economic lessons concerning supply, demand, and market price.

Prices are powerful! They guide the marketplace to produce the right things in the right way and distribute them to those who place the most value upon them. Sometimes the results of the market price system seem unfair. But tampering with market prices can be perilous in terms of efficiency. As we will see, sometimes the effect is to harm the very people the policies intend to help.

LEARNING OBJECTIVES

Understanding Chapter 4 will enable you to:
1. **Interpret how demand represents marginal benefit and supply represents marginal cost.**
2. **Explain the concept of social surplus and how it is divided between consumers and producers.**
3. **Demonstrate how both exports and imports increase efficiency while simultaneously harming either consumers or producers.**
4. **Identify inefficiencies associated with price ceilings.**
5. **Show why price supports are unnecessary and potentially counterproductive.**
6. **Pinpoint the economic flaw in California's deregulation of electricity.**

price signals help consumers decide how much to buy and help producers decide how much to sell.

The marketplace depends upon **price signals,** meaning that the market price sends a message to consumers and producers. The price signals to consumers how much of a good they will wish to buy, and signals to producers how much of a good they will wish to sell. When the market equilibrium price rises, consumers respond by buying less of a good and producers respond by offering more for sale. Just the opposite is true when price falls. We start Chapter 4 by examining why these price signals are desirable. We then examine various public policies that are intended to either lower or raise prices from their market equilibrium values.

4.1 PRICE SIGNALS FOR EFFICIENT CHOICE

Consumers buy something because they expect that they will be better off by doing so. The same holds true when producers sell something. Therefore, when a consumer buys a good that a producer sells, both parties are better off. The mutual gains from such market exchanges lead the economy to greater efficiency. This section looks at how gains are measured, how much is gained by consumers and producers, and how market prices can maximize these gains, including when trade occurs internationally. Later chapters examine exceptions, such as possible reasons for restricting international trade.

MARGINAL BENEFIT AND CONSUMER SURPLUS

The demand curve depicts the quantity that would be purchased at each of various prices, *ceteris paribus.* Another way of looking at it is that the demand curve shows the maximum price the consumer would pay for each quantity that might be purchased. This maximum price is the consumer's **marginal benefit**—the incremental value of each additional item consumed. Figure 4-1 illustrates this way of looking at demand.

marginal benefit the incremental value of an additional unit of a good.

Consider Dwight, who is shopping for blue jeans. Dwight won't buy blue jeans if the price is over $20. He'll buy one pair if the price is $20, two pair if the price is $15, or three pair if the price is $10. In other words, the first pair is worth $20 to him, the second pair is worth an extra $15, and the third an extra $10. His marginal benefits from blue jeans, therefore, are $20 for the first pair, $15 for the second, and $10 for the third. Table 4-1 shows how demand translates into marginal benefit and total benefit. Dwight's *total benefit* from his blue

FIGURE 4-1

MARGINAL BENEFIT Demand is the marginal benefit to consumers. Marginal benefit declines as quantity demanded rises. The length of the arrows represents the marginal benefit of the quantities 1, 2, and 3, respectively.

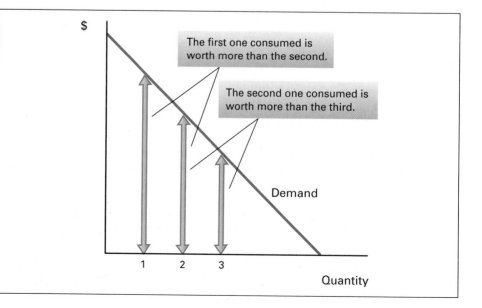

TABLE 4-1	DWIGHT'S DEMAND, MARGINAL BENEFIT, AND TOTAL BENEFIT			
(A) **DWIGHT'S DEMAND FOR BLUE JEANS**		**(B)** **DWIGHT'S BENEFITS FROM BUYING BLUE JEANS**		
PRICE	**QUANTITY**	**QUANTITY**	**MARGINAL BENEFIT**	**TOTAL BENEFIT**
$20	1	1	$20	$20
$15	2	2	$15	$35
$10	3	3	$10	$45

jean purchases is the sum of his marginal benefit from each pair. So, if he buys three pair, the blue jeans would bring Dwight $45 worth of total benefit, where $45 = $20 + $15 + $10.

Since Dwight must pay for the blue jeans he buys, the remaining value to him of his blue jean purchases equals the total benefit from the blue jeans minus what he pays. This value is termed **consumer surplus,** which is the difference between the total benefit and total cost to the consumer. Graphically, it is the demand curve minus price, as shown in Figure 4-2(a). Therefore, if the price of blue jeans is $10, then Dwight would buy three pair at a cost of $30. Subtracting that $30 from his total benefit of $45 would leave him with a consumer surplus of $15, as shown in Figure 4-2(b).

consumer surplus consumers' total benefit minus cost; graphically, demand minus market price.

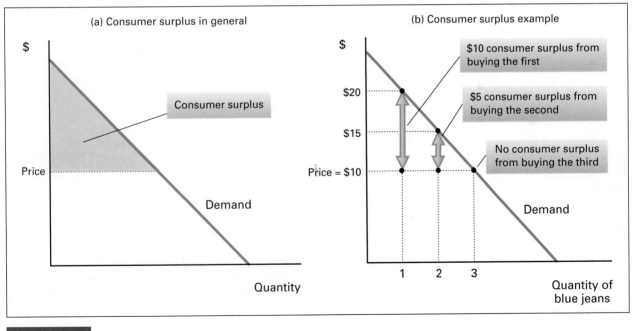

FIGURE 4-2

CONSUMER SURPLUS Consumer surplus is the area under the demand curve and above the market price. It is what consumers gain from their purchases after deducting the cost. The general idea is shown in graph (a).

Graph (b) applies this idea to the example of Dwight. At a price of $10 per pair of jeans, Dwight buys three pair and receives $15 worth of consumer surplus. His consumer surplus equals the sum of the consumer surplus from the first, second, and third pairs, which is $10 + $5 + $0 = $15. If the price were higher, Dwight's consumer surplus would be lower, as shown in Table 4-2.

TABLE 4-2	DWIGHT'S CONSUMER SURPLUS FROM BLUE JEANS				
PRICE	QUANTITY BOUGHT	TOTAL BENEFIT	TOTAL PAID	CONSUMER SURPLUS
$20	1	$20	$20	$0
$15	2	$35	$30	$5
$10	3	$45	$30	$15

Table 4-2 computes Dwight's consumer surplus for three different prices of blue jeans. As you can see in that table, **consumer surplus varies inversely with price.** The greater the price, the less is consumer surplus, and the lower the price the greater is consumer surplus.

MARGINAL COST AND PRODUCER SURPLUS

Supply, like demand, can be viewed in two ways. A supply curve shows the quantity that would be offered for sale at each of various prices, *ceteris paribus.* The supply curve also depicts the minimum price that the producers of a good would be willing to accept for each quantity offered. That minimum price is the producer's *marginal cost,* which is the incremental cost of producing each additional item offered for sale. Figure 4-3 illustrates this way of looking at supply.

Consider Buddy, who sells blue jeans. Buddy won't offer any blue jeans for sale if the price is under $5. He is willing to sell one pair if the price is $5, two pair if the price is $7.50, or three pair at a price of $10. Those prices are also his marginal costs when he produces the first three pair of blue jeans. Table 4-3 shows how supply translates into marginal cost and total cost. Buddy's *total cost* of blue jeans sold is the sum of his marginal cost from selling each pair. So, if he sells three pair of blue jeans, he would incur total costs of $22.50, where $22.50 = $5 + $7.50 + $10.

The value Buddy receives from the sale of his product equals total revenue minus total cost. This value is termed **producer surplus,** which is the excess of revenue to producers over their costs of production. Graphically, it is the market price minus the supply curve, as shown in Figure 4-4(a) on page 84. If the price of blue jeans is $10 in our example, then

producer surplus producers' revenue minus production cost; graphically, market price minus supply.

> ### QUICKCHECK
>
> Suppose coffee costs $1 per cup at Handy Stop Shop and $1.05 per cup at Gas'n N Goin' next door. If you buy coffee at Handy Stop Shop, does this mean your consumer surplus from coffee is only five cents?
>
> Answer: No, consumer surplus does not depend upon alternative prices for the same product. Rather, it asks you what is the most you would be willing to pay to avoid doing without the product altogether and then subtracts the price you actually pay. Thus, whatever your consumer surplus from a cup of coffee may be, it is five cents more if you buy your coffee at Handy Stop Shop than at Gas'n N Goin'.

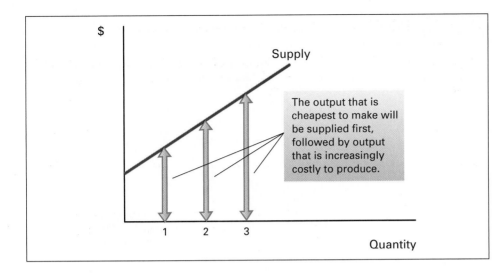

FIGURE 4-3

MARGINAL COST Supply is the marginal cost to producers. Marginal cost increases as quantity produced rises. The length of the arrows represents the marginal cost of the quantities 1, 2, and 3, respectively.

TABLE 4-3   BUDDY'S SUPPLY, MARGINAL COST, AND TOTAL COST

(A) BUDDY'S SUPPLY OF BLUE JEANS		(B) BUDDY'S COSTS OF PRODUCING BLUE JEANS		
PRICE	QUANTITY	QUANTITY	MARGINAL COST	TOTAL COST
$5	1	1	$5	$5
$7.50	2	2	$7.50	$12.50
$10	3	3	$10	$22.50

Buddy would sell three pair for a total revenue of $30, where total revenue is computed by multiplying price by quantity. Subtracting the total cost of $22.50 from the $30 would leave him with a producer surplus of $7.50, as shown in Figure 4-4(b).

Table 4-4 computes producer surplus for three different prices of blue jeans. As seen in that table, **producer surplus varies directly with price.**

TABLE 4-4   BUDDY'S PRODUCER SURPLUS FROM BLUE JEANS

PRICE	QUANTITY SOLD	TOTAL COST	TOTAL REVENUE	PRODUCER SURPLUS
$5	1	$5	$5	$0
$7.50	2	$12.50	$15	$2.50
$10	3	$22.50	$30	$7.50

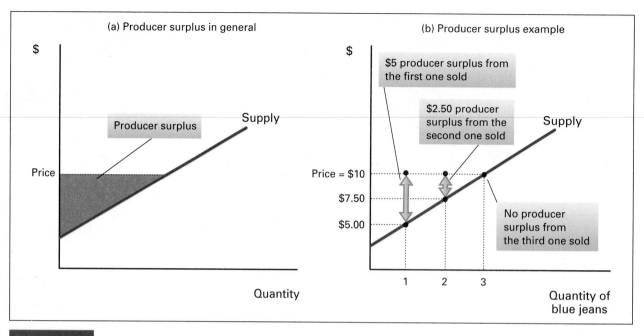

FIGURE 4-4

PRODUCER SURPLUS Producer surplus is the area above the supply curve and under the market price, as shown in (a). It is what producers gain from their sales after deducting their costs.

Graph (b) shows that, at a price of $10 per pair of jeans, Buddy sells three pair and receives $7.50 worth of producer surplus. His producer surplus equals the sum of his producer surplus from the first, second, and third pair, which is $5 + $2.50 + $0 = $7.50.

QUICKCHECK

What is the difference in meaning between the terms *surplus, consumer surplus,* and *producer surplus*?

Answer: A surplus exists when the market price is above the equilibrium price, as discussed in Chapter 3. The surplus equals the quantity supplied minus the quantity demanded at that price. In contrast, consumer surplus refers to the value that a consumer receives in excess of what was paid for the purchase—it equals demand minus the market price. Producer surplus is the value a seller receives in excess of cost—it equals market price minus supply.

THE EFFICIENCY OF THE MARKETPLACE

social surplus the sum of consumer surplus and producer surplus.

Markets are efficient to the extent that they maximize social surplus, which is the sum of consumer and producer surplus. Social surplus is the difference between how much a good is worth and how much it costs to produce. It is the total value the economy gains by having the good produced and consumed. In the blue jeans example, the social surplus at a price of $10 would be $22.50, which equals $15 in consumer surplus for Dwight plus $7.50 in producer surplus for Buddy.

Any time marginal benefit exceeds marginal cost, social surplus would increase if more of the good were to be produced and sold. That is just what the marketplace does.

(a) The market equilibrium price maximizes social surplus

$

Social surplus
= consumer surplus
+ producer surplus

Consumer surplus

Supply

Equilibrium price

Producer surplus

Demand

Efficient quantity

Quantity

(b) Any other price causes a deadweight loss

$

Deadweight loss

Supply

High price

or

Low price

Demand

Quantity decreases

Low quantity   Efficient quantity

Quantity

FIGURE 4-5

EFFICIENCY OF THE EQUILIBRIUM PRICE The market equilibrium price leads to the efficient quantity, as shown in (a). No other quantity would generate a larger total of consumer and producer surplus. Any other price, such as either of the prices shown in (b), would lead to a lower quantity sold. If the price is high, the quantity falls because consumers aren't willing to buy as much. If the price is low, quantity falls because producers aren't willing to sell as much. In either case, there is a triangular area of deadweight loss that shows how much social surplus is forgone relative to the amount at an efficient quantity.

Producers keep on selling until their marginal cost just equals the market price. Likewise, consumers keep on buying until their marginal benefit equals the market price. This means that marginal benefit equals marginal cost at the market equilibrium price and that social surplus is maximized. Any more output would add more cost than benefit. Thus, the *rule of efficiency* states that **the efficient output occurs when society's marginal benefit equals marginal cost.**

The marketplace achieves an efficient output through price adjustments. At the market equilibrium price, marginal benefit equals marginal cost and social surplus is maximized. Figure 4-5(a) illustrates how the market price—also the equilibrium price—signals an efficient quantity that maximizes social surplus. In this figure the intersection of demand and supply establishes the efficient quantity. Since demand represents marginal benefit and supply represents marginal cost, the rule of efficiency is satisfied. Any other price, such as the high price or low price shown in Figure 4-5(b), would lead to less output and a smaller social surplus.

The triangular area of forgone social surplus caused by inefficient pricing is called a **deadweight loss.** The size of the deadweight loss will decrease when the price is closer to the market price, but increase when the price moves farther away from its equilibrium value. Prices that differ from their equilibrium values will not persist because those prices will adjust toward equilibrium. The deadweight loss will in this way eventually disappear.

deadweight loss reduction in social surplus caused by inefficient price; shown graphically as a triangular area.

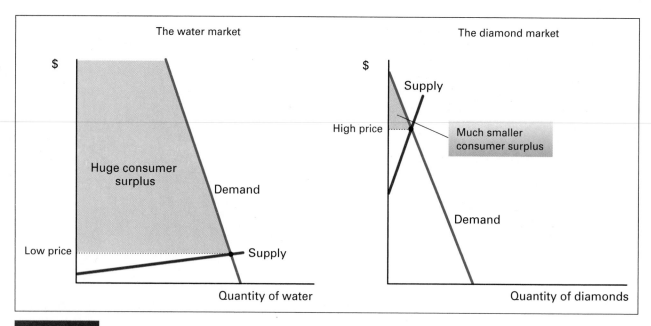

FIGURE 4-6

THE PARADOX OF DIAMONDS AND WATER Price measures the value of consuming one more unit of a good. Consumer surplus measures the total value to consumers from all of their consumption of the good. While the marginal benefit from a glass of water is far less than from a diamond, as revealed by the relatively low price of water, the total benefit from all water as measured by its consumer surplus is immensely larger than it would be for all diamonds.

SNAPSHOT   **THE PARADOX OF DIAMONDS AND WATER**

Some necessities that have a great deal of intrinsic worth are priced lower than luxuries we could easily do without. For example, people pay much more for a diamond than for a glass of water, which seems paradoxical. If we were stranded in Death Valley with neither water nor diamonds, which would seem the better bargain—a diamond for a nickel or a glass of water for a one-hundred-dollar bill?

The paradox disappears when we realize that price merely tells the value of a good at the margin. The last bit of water is not worth much when water is plentiful. It is the scarcity of diamonds that keeps that price high. To understand the total value of a good, though, we must look beyond price to consumer surplus. As shown in Figure 4-6, the consumer surplus from water purchases is vastly greater than the consumer surplus from diamond purchases. It is consumer surplus that truly measures the total value consumers receive from the things they buy. ◄

THE EFFICIENCY OF IMPORTS AND EXPORTS

Questions of efficiency often arise in the context of international trade. If a country chooses not to engage in international trade, the market prices of its goods and services would reflect only the supply and demand within that country. Those prices are called *domestic* prices. Opening an economy to international trade will change market prices in a country by bringing into its markets a world of new consumers and producers. *World prices* of goods and services are determined by the supply and demand from all countries.

Countries that trade buy goods and services from other countries—their *imports*. They also sell goods and services to other countries—their *exports*. Whether a country imports a good or exports a good will depend upon whether the good's world equilibrium market price is below or above what the country's price would otherwise have been—its domestic price.

In other words, **the result of trade is that the price in the domestic market will come to equal the world market price.** If the domestic price rises to meet a higher world price, then the country exports the good. If a lower world price causes the domestic price to drop, then the country imports the good, meaning that it is purchased from producers in other countries. In either case, there are some people within the country who gain and others who lose. However, as we will see, the gains can be expected to exceed the losses.

Figure 4-7 shows the case of a world price of a good that would lead a country to import that good. Domestic consumers will not be willing to pay any more than the world price. Producers will also refuse to sell for less than the world price. Because the domestic quantity supplied is less than the quantity demanded, consumers make up the difference with imports, as shown in Figure 4-7(a).

Adding together consumer surplus and producer surplus, it is apparent by looking at Figure 4-7(b) that the total increases. Specifically, allowing imports increases social surplus by the amount labeled. Although the lower price will cause producer surplus to shrink, the increase in consumer surplus is seen to more than compensate for that loss. Because the gains to consumers more than offset the losses to producers, efficiency calls for allowing imports.

Figure 4-8 is similar to Figure 4-7 except the world price is above the domestic price. In this case, the price difference causes the domestic quantity supplied to be greater than the domestic quantity demanded. This difference between quantity supplied and quantity

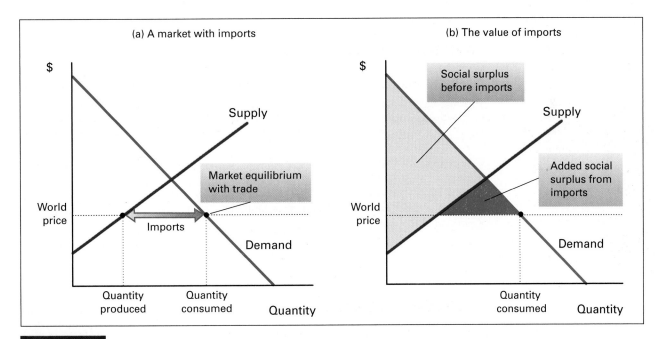

FIGURE 4-7

THE EFFICIENCY OF IMPORTS Imports result from a world price that is below what the country's equilibrium price would have been without trade. The lower world price causes the country's consumption to rise and production to fall, with the difference being the amount imported, as shown in (a).

Trade leads to an efficient quantity consumed because it increases the value of social surplus by the added triangular area shown in (b). However, the gains go disproportionately to consumers. Producer surplus is smaller because of the lower price.

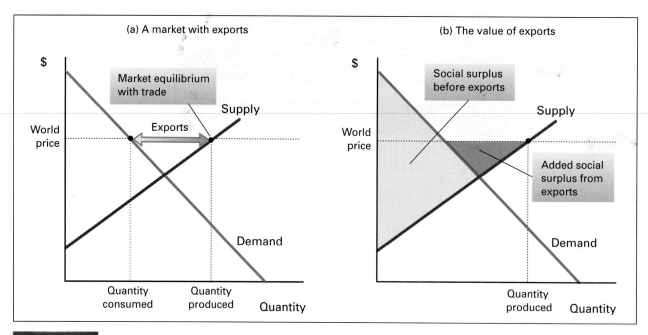

FIGURE 4-8

THE EFFICIENCY OF EXPORTS Exports result from a world price that exceeds what the country's equilibrium price would be without trade. The higher world price causes the country's consumption to fall and production to rise, with the difference being the amount exported, as shown in (a).

Trade leads to an efficient quantity produced because it increases the value of social surplus by the added triangular area shown in (b). However, the gains go disproportionately to producers. Consumer surplus is less because of the higher price.

QUICKCHECK

Since consumers gain from imports, but domestic producers lose, isn't a country just as well off to forgo imports altogether? Similarly, since consumers lose from exports, but domestic producers gain, isn't a country just as well off to do without exports? Explain.

Answer: No, consumers gain more from imports than producers lose. Likewise, producers gain more from exports than consumers lose. Thus, both imports and exports bring net gains to the country.

demanded results in an excess quantity of the product. This excess is exported, as shown in Figure 4-7(a).

Adding together consumer surplus and producer surplus in Figure 4-8(b) shows that the total increases. Specifically, allowing exports increases social surplus by the amount labeled. Although the higher price will cause consumer surplus to shrink, the increase in producer surplus is seen to more than compensate. Because the gains to producers more than offset the losses to consumers, efficiency calls for allowing exports.

In short, consumers come out winners from imports, but producers lose. Producers come out the winners from exports, but consumers lose. In each case, though, the gains exceed the losses. So, whether it be from imports or from exports, the country as a whole comes out the winner.

4.2 PRICE CEILINGS—HOLDING PRICES DOWN

In 1973, the Organization of Petroleum Exporting Countries (OPEC) succeeded in restricting oil supplies to Western countries and achieving a dramatic spike upward in energy prices. In response, Congress enacted temporary gasoline price controls, which capped price increases and cut into the social surplus. This action caused fuel shortages, with drivers losing much time and patience in long lines at the gas pumps. Yet the problem of gasoline shortages and wasteful gas lines has little to do with gasoline and much to do with the economics of a **price ceiling,** which is a law that establishes a maximum price that can be legally charged for a good. As discussed in the following sections, price ceilings arise in various contexts.

price ceiling a maximum price that can legally be charged for a good.

PROMOTING AFFORDABLE HOUSING—ARE RENT CONTROLS THE ANSWER?

With rising populations in competition for scarce land, major cities sometimes choose rent controls as a way to insulate tenants from higher housing costs. **Rent controls** hold the monthly price of rental housing to below its equilibrium level. Price tries to rise, but bumps up against the rent control ceiling. As we will see, the long-term consequences often differ from what proponents have in mind.

rent controls a price ceiling applied to the price of rental housing.

The market for rental housing is like other markets in which demand slopes down and supply slopes up. Demand slopes down because prospective tenants are unwilling to rent as many apartments when prices are high as when they are low. Some people continue living with their parents. Others choose to share rental homes and apartments with roommates. Still others live on their own, but rent smaller and less-desirable quarters than they would have preferred. The supply of rental housing slopes upward as higher rental prices motivate prospective landlords to partition off rental rooms, repair vacant apartments, and in other ways increase the quantity of housing supplied.

Figure 4-9 illustrates a housing market with rent controls in place. **For these rent controls to be meaningful, the ceiling price must be set below the market equilibrium price.** The result is a housing shortage, as shown in Figure 4-9(a), in which less housing is offered for lease, while more housing is demanded.

One effect of rent controls is to transfer wealth from current landlords to current tenants, as shown in Figure 4-9(b). Such **transfer payments,** in which one party's loss is another's gain, are not themselves inefficient since they merely redistribute social surplus. However, when transfer payments are caused by government price controls, there are multiple sources of inefficiency that shrink social surplus. The first inefficiency is the deadweight loss triangle associated with a less-than-efficient overall quantity, such as labeled in Figure 4-9(b).

transfer payments the redistribution of social surplus from one party to another; rent controls create transfer payments from landlords to tenants.

A second source of inefficiency comes from misallocating apartments that are leased. For example, even though Tanisha in Figure 4-9 would get a larger benefit from the apartment than would Candice, the landlord would receive the same payment from either and so might well rent the apartment to Candice. Since any tenant would be constrained to pay the same rent and there are more potential tenants than available apartments, the landlord would find it easy to discriminate, whether on the basis of income, occupation, or anything else the landlord thinks is important. It might be difficult to prove if that discrimination was illegal, such as based on race, color, or creed.

A third inefficiency involves **search costs,** which are the costs of finding an apartment. Since landlords have plenty of prospective tenants for rent-controlled apartments, they do not need to advertise. As a result, some enterprising would-be tenants have taken up such tactics as reading the obituaries or, to get the jump, listening to police radios and checking out emergency rooms. In the absence of rent controls, there would be little or no need for such wasteful behavior.

search costs the costs of finding something; rent controls increase search costs for rental housing.

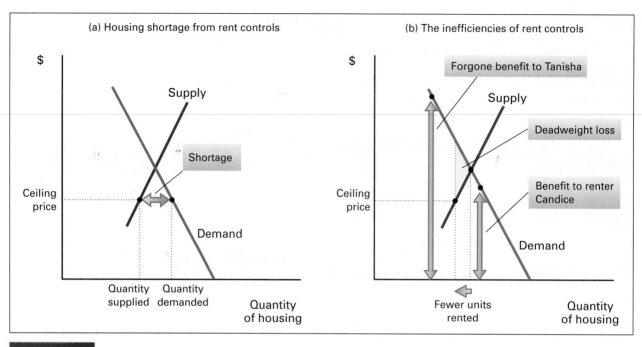

FIGURE 4-9

RENT CONTROLS A rent control law imposes a ceiling price that leads to a shortage of rental housing, as shown in (a). As shown in (b), the inefficiencies of rent controls include a deadweight loss from fewer units rented and an inefficient allocation of apartments among prospective tenants. For example, a landlord might rent an apartment to Candice, since she is willing to pay the ceiling price. However, that might leave Tanisha without an apartment, even though it is worth more to her.

The inefficiencies of rent controls are likely to get worse over time as demand grows with an increasing population while rent-controlled apartments are allowed to deteriorate. For example, New York City and Washington, D.C., have seen rent-controlled housing crumble for decades. A look at some of the aging cities of Europe also reveals deep scars from rent control. Paris has had some rent controls in place for over two hundred years. The rent-controlled apartment houses in Paris have seen little modernization in that time, with few apartment units containing their own plumbing facilities. In the rent-controlled period between 1914 and 1948, almost no new rental housing was constructed in all of France.

While rent controls have problems, there are also problems associated with removing them. The immediate effect of abolishing rent controls is that rents jump to their market equilibrium value. That value could be quite high if rent controls have been in place for a long time and the housing shortage has become severe. Higher rents would eventually shift supply to the right as old apartments are refurbished and new ones are built. However, this process would take time and the only immediate effect would be higher rents.

housing vouchers government grants that recipients can spend only on housing.

There are alternatives to rent controls. One alternative is to identify the needy and assign them housing vouchers. **Housing vouchers** are government grants that the recipient can spend only on housing. Thus, even though the price of rental housing may be high, housing vouchers can bring it within reach of impoverished tenants.

ANTI-GOUGING LAWS

price gouging price increases in response to increased demand related to emergencies.

Rent controls are far from the only time government seeks to keep prices down. For example, local governments have often attempted to protect consumers against **price gouging,**

QUICKCHECK

If rent controls are removed, is there likely to be as much illegal discrimination against apartment applicants?

Answer: No, uncontrolled rents will clear the market, meaning that the shortage of apartments will be eliminated. Landlords will no longer have the luxury of picking from a crowd of applicants all offering the same rent. In competing for tenants, landlords have a financial incentive to avoid discrimination. Those who insist on discriminating on the basis of irrelevant prejudices are by definition accepting less than the most valuable offer. Because the price of discrimination has risen, its quantity will fall.

which is the disparaging term for hiking up prices in response to temporary surges in demand. The idea is to promote equity. The cost is in terms of efficiency, though, because high prices in times of emergency prevent shortages and allocate sought-after goods to those who value them the most.

Profitably high prices also motivate rapid restocking, which means that prices do not stay high for long. For example, when hurricanes move toward the coast, oceanfront homeowners seek out plywood to board up their windows. If stores can raise prices, they have an incentive to send out extra trucks for new supplies. Otherwise, homeowners must scramble to snatch up and hoard supplies before the shelves go bare. If homeowners are lucky, stores might use the occasion to generate goodwill and restock promptly despite the extra costs.

Local governments also often have laws against *ticket scalping*—the practice of buying tickets at the price set by concert promoters and then reselling at whatever the market will bear. Scalping is a form of *arbitrage*, which means buying low and selling high. Arbitrage directs goods to their highest-valued uses, thus efficiently allocating seats at concerts, ball games, and other events. As for equity, however, opinions differ. Good seats get snared quickly by scalpers, many of whom hire stand-ins to buy up blocks of tickets. Those seats are made available to true fans, but the price might be much higher.

SCALPING THE STONES   *SNAPSHOT*

With four decades of touring under their belts, the Rolling Stones know all about how to please a crowd. And their fans know all about the crowd of scalpers that snatch up all the best tickets! Their techniques? One ticket reseller paid $20 each to the brothers of a college fraternity just for standing in the ticket line. That reseller hired over 150 stand-ins for a single Rolling Stones concert. Who could blame Stones' fans for crying that they "can't get no satisfaction"?

Some fans—those willing to spend extra money to avoid the time in line—were glad for the choice and convenience offered by the scalpers, who these days usually put their tickets up for auction at eBay, uBid, or other online auction sites. Others cried that it wasn't fair to fans or promoters, who want to generate excitement with below-market ticket prices. Which should it be? During their 2002–2003 World Tour, the Rolling Stones played in stadiums, arenas, and clubs in cities including Boston, Chicago, and Los Angeles. Concert tickets sold out quickly, leaving many fans with two choices: wait for another tour or pay an above-market price. The price of some tickets on eBay reached $3,000. The fans who didn't pay got to know all too well the words of Mick Jagger, "You can't always get what you want." If you have the money, though, "you can get what you need!" ◄

4.3 PRICE FLOORS—PROPPING PRICES UP

Although consumers are better off when prices are low, producers prefer them high. Both groups often turn to government for help. If politics dictates propping up prices, government can establish a **price floor,** also termed a **price support,** which sets a minimum price that producers are guaranteed to receive. One way to implement a price floor is for government to agree to buy at that floor price. This approach can cause surpluses to pile up at taxpayer expense. Such is the case of agricultural price supports. Note that the term *surplus* in this context refers to a quantity of output, specifically the excess of what is produced over what is consumed, not to the term *social surplus* that is also used in this chapter. We will also look at minimum wage laws, which have no budgetary cost to government but nevertheless do have significant costs to both job applicants and employers.

price floor (price support)
minimum price guaranteed to
producers by the government.

AGRICULTURAL PRICE SUPPORTS

Although only 2 percent of the United States' labor force currently derives a living from agriculture, the political influence of agriculture has been strong enough to maintain agricultural price supports in the United States since the 1920s. These price supports have been justified on two counts. One is that they sustain the lifestyle of the family farm, an American tradition. However, the reality is that family farming has continued to decline, and a disproportionate amount of price support payments have gone to large farms and corporations. The second justification is that they ensure a plentiful supply of food for American consumers. This line of reasoning does not withstand the logic of economic analysis.

Figure 4-10 shows the effects of an agricultural price support, such as for corn or wheat. By holding price above the equilibrium, there is more farm output produced, but less consumed. The result is a surplus, as shown. Such agricultural surpluses have averaged many billion dollars' worth of foodstuffs annually in the United States. Agricultural price supports have increased in recent years, most notably with President Bush's 2002 signing of a farm bill estimated to cost taxpayers $190 billion over ten years. With the Census Bureau estimating the U.S. population to be about 287 million at the time of signing, the $190 billion cost

FIGURE 4-10

PRICE SUPPORTS Price supports cause a surplus because they prompt consumers to reduce consumption even as producers increase production. Applied to the grain market, the support price shown in this graph generates additional production at a cost that is greater than its value, causing a triangular area of deadweight loss. A second triangular area of deadweight loss results from the reduced consumption brought by the artificially higher price. Additional deadweight loss can be expected when government distributes the surplus grain it has purchased.

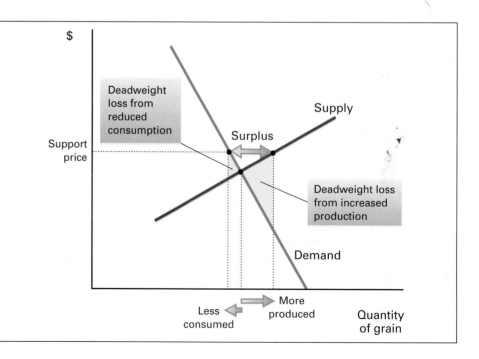

What determines the amount of the surplus when there is a price support? Will there be a surplus if the support price is set below the equilibrium price?

Answer: Other things equal, the higher the support price, the larger will be the surplus. There will be no surplus when the support price is at or below the equilibrium price.

of the legislation translates to an average of $662 apiece from every man, woman, and child in the United States.

The effect of agricultural price supports is to transfer money from both taxpayers and consumers to those in the agriculture industry. Maintaining a high price redistributes social surplus from consumers to producers. There is a deadweight loss associated with both increased production and decreased consumption, as shown in Figure 4-10. Additional deadweight loss can be expected to occur because government must buy and dispose of the surplus quantity, which is nearly impossible to do in an efficient manner. Government cannot merely sell the surplus to the highest bidder, because it must prevent the surplus commodities it buys from being distributed to people who would otherwise purchase that product in the marketplace. To do otherwise would merely mean more of a surplus that government would be forced to buy, because those who received from government would buy less from farmers.

One option is to give the surplus quantity away in a relatively unpalatable form, such as by turning excess milk into powdered milk. Another option is to export the surplus in a manner that does not compete with other agricultural exports. For example, foreign aid to impoverished countries might work, to the extent that the aid does not supplant other food exported from the donor country. However, recipient countries often fear becoming too dependent upon food aid based on unpredictable agricultural surpluses. The dependency arises when farmers in those countries are driven out of business by the low food prices that years of plentiful food aid brings.

There are other options. To rid itself of surplus butter, for example, Denmark offers it for a reduced price if the buyer agrees to export that butter by baking it into Danish butter cookies. Still another common practice is to store surplus commodities until they are no longer edible and then discard them. It's like the fate of leftover food in a refrigerator!

THE MINIMUM WAGE

The **minimum wage,** which is a requirement that employers pay no less than a specified wage rate, has been a cherished American tradition since the Great Depression of the 1930s. We all remember our first jobs. We each remember how hard we worked to find a job and how we deserved no less than that minimum wage for the work we did. For many, the job served as a springboard toward great success in life. Backing for the minimum wage also arises out of American compassion for the downtrodden. Americans cherish the notion that no one should be exploited. On the face of it, the minimum wage seems like a good protection against such exploitation. On closer examination, however, the case is arguable.

minimum wage lowest wage legally allowed to be paid to workers.

People support the minimum wage with the idea of reducing poverty. The minimum wage has the potential to reduce poverty by increasing the wages paid to low-skilled labor. That is also its problem. The higher wage means that more people are willing to work. These extra workers include many college and college-bound students already on the road to success. The lure of a higher minimum wage would detour some short-sighted students away from that path—in other words, the opportunity cost of following it has become greater for them.

The higher wage for low-skilled labor also means that fewer jobs are offered. Fast-food restaurants, car washes, and other businesses "make do" with fewer people, but train and

TABLE 4-5   SELECTED STUDIES ON THE EFFECTS OF THE MINIMUM WAGE

AUTHOR(S)	YEAR PUBLISHED	FINDINGS IN BRIEF
Peterson	1957	The minimum wage reduces employment.
Mincer	1976	Unemployment caused by the minimum wage is concentrated among minority teens.
Hammermesh	1982	The minimum wage reduces teenage employment.
Behrman, Sickles, and Taubman	1983	The minimum wage helps whites and hurts blacks.
Bonilla	1992	Increase in the minimum wage leads to lower incomes for single parents.
Neumark	2002	Cities with local minimum wage laws experience less poverty, but a greater number of unemployed.

Source: The first four studies and many others are referenced in *50 Years of Research on the Minimum Wage,* Joint Economic Committee, 1995.

work them harder. They also may replace some labor with capital, such as automated dish-washers and car-washing equipment. The result is that along with higher wages comes a surplus of labor—or a shortage of jobs, depending upon how you look at it. The least employable—those with poor language, computational, or social skills—are out of luck. They cannot get that first job they need to start climbing the ladder of success. They cannot join the "jobs club"—it has become too exclusive.

Table 4-5 presents the findings from just a few of the many studies conducted over the last fifty years on the effects of the minimum wage. The overwhelming majority of them conclude that whatever help it provides to some recipients, the minimum wage also causes harm among those it is intended to help.

Figure 4-11 shows how minimum wage laws increase the number of people seeking low-skilled work while decreasing the number of jobs available. For example, Tony would not have worked for the equilibrium wage. With a minimum wage, however, Tony might wind up taking Dave's job, even though Dave would have been willing to work for less. Because higher wages are offset by fewer jobs, there is no guarantee that minimum wage laws actually increase the total amount firms spend to employ low-skilled workers.

As was the case with rent controls, minimum wage requirements make it easier to dis-criminate. With numerous applicants for each job opening, employers can pick and choose as they wish. It would be quite difficult to prove if they choose to discriminate on an illegal basis.

There are alternatives to the minimum wage. One alternative is for a so-called *living wage* that would increase the minimum wage so high that a person could live on it, or possibly even support a family on it. A living wage would be attractive to numerous prospective job seekers, but would accentuate the problems with the minimum wage, as previously discussed.

Another alternative is to subsidize the earnings of low-income workers. Such a subsidy is already embedded in the U.S. personal income tax—the earned income tax credit. The drawback is that earnings subsidies come at a high budgetary cost, because they reduce gov-ernment tax collections or involve actual cash payments. Minimum wage laws also have high costs, but these costs are borne by businesses, consumers, and those unable to find a job.

Subsidies to education also serve as an alternative to the minimum wage. Such subsi-dies include free public schooling or government financial assistance to students attending private schools, subsidized student loans for college students, and subsidized tuition at

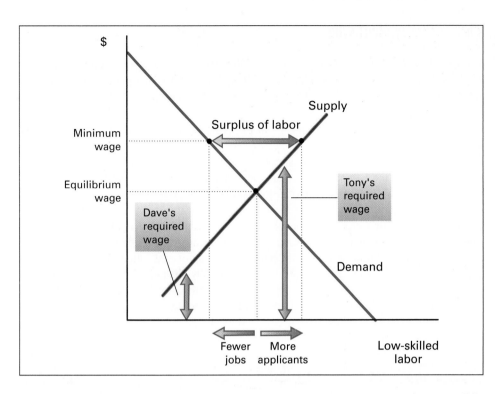

FIGURE 4-11

THE MINIMUM WAGE Minimum wage laws make it tough to find a job, especially for the least-experienced and least-skilled job seekers. The higher wage causes fewer jobs and more applicants. Some of the new applicants (such as Tony) take jobs from others who need the jobs more desperately (such as Dave).

public universities. The more widely available are educational opportunities, the more skills the workforce will acquire. The result is that the supply of low-skilled labor shifts to the left as the opportunity cost of accepting such jobs rises for workers with more human capital that can be applied elsewhere. As shown in Figure 4-12, the leftward shift in supply increases the equilibrium wage for low-skilled labor, which is the purpose of minimum wage laws. The advantage of education subsidies is that they help people develop their skills, leaving the low-skill jobs for those who need them most.

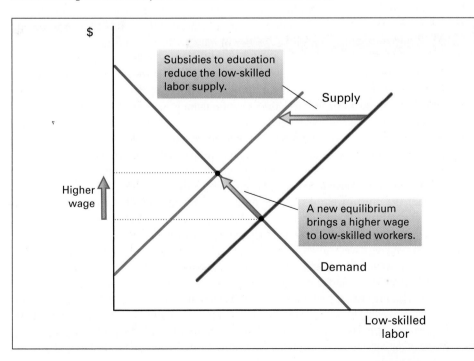

FIGURE 4-12

AN ALTERNATIVE TO THE MINIMUM WAGE Subsidies to education reduce the supply of low-skilled labor, which causes a higher equilibrium wage. Unlike the minimum wage, all workers willing to work at that higher wage will get jobs.

HOMELESS AND WITHOUT A JOB

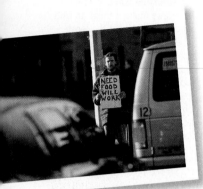

The homeless often carry a disturbing sign—"Will Work for Food." Although the offers are often a sham, advocates for the homeless are quick to point out that many of the homeless are indeed eager to find steady work. More often than not, however, there are no steady jobs offered to them.

Lack of a home is itself an impediment to finding a job. For example, employers may worry about the employee's personal health and hygiene, and about whether or not the employee is a drifter. For these reasons, potential employers are usually unwilling to pay the minimum wage to the homeless. There are too many other applicants with fewer problems. While employers would be willing to offer jobs at lower wages, such job offers are prohibited.

The homeless are thus caught in the grips of a political vise. Minimum wages are one side of this vise while so-called flophouses that offer cheap nightly lodging are on the other side. Many flophouses have closed down, however, because the residents could not afford rent increases that would be needed to pay the expense of renovation. The law demands such renovation to provide accessibility for the physically challenged. It also requires security from hazards such as fires, lead in pipes and paint, and asbestos. Such government policies are intended to add fairness to what is sold in the marketplace. Together with minimum wages, however, those policies block access to those markets for the very people who need it most, the homeless. ◄

4.4 AROUND THE WORLD—BLACK MARKETS AS A SAFETY VALVE

Price controls are practiced throughout the world. In Taiwan, the Statute for Salt Administration applies price controls to salt. The price of oil is also regulated in order to provide Taiwanese companies with stable prices on what is an important input in manufacturing. Venezuela lifted its price controls in 1996 as a condition for receiving foreign aid. Belarus, a country that once was part of the Soviet Union, made a similar pledge. Price support programs have been common in agriculture. Belgium and other countries of Europe have found that attempts to cut price support programs have been met with vociferous protests from farmers.

black market market in which goods are bought and sold illegally; associated with price controls.

Any time government tries to hold prices above or below market equilibrium, it provides profit opportunities to those willing to take advantage of them. **Black market** activity is said to occur when goods are bought and sold illegally. Under rent controls, for example, it is not uncommon to hear of prospective tenants bribing landlords for an apartment. Sometimes this black market may seem somewhat gray, as when the bribes are merely offers of gifts, or agreements by tenants to "fix up the place." There are also many reports of people being hired "off the books" for less than the minimum wage, especially when the unemployment rate is high.

The black market is nothing more than the free market trying to assert itself when government has attempted to influence that market through taxes or regulation. Regulation could take the form of price controls or the outright ban of market activities. In either case, it is hard to keep willing buyers and sellers from negotiating mutually beneficial illegal deals.

Governments often owe a debt of gratitude to black markets that temper destructive policies. For example, Cubans rely heavily on the black market in their country. If they had to depend upon government rations, they could not obtain enough food to survive. Similarly, the shelves were often bare in the government stores when the countries of Eastern Europe were under communism. These countries relied in large measure on the industriousness of black marketers to keep their economies going.

Recognizing the critical role played by the black market in their economy, the centrally planned former Soviet Union legalized private for-profit agricultural production on approximately 3 percent of its arable land. Despite the small acreage involved, this market-driven component of agriculture produced nearly one-third of all Soviet agricultural output.

4.5 THE PRICE OF POWER

It was the winter of 2001 when California flirted with disaster. This was no earthquake or tidal wave. Instead, California felt painful shortages of electricity, the lifeblood of modern commerce. Inadequate electric supplies prompted rolling blackouts that cut off electricity to 670,000 households and businesses for two hours at a time. In San Francisco and elsewhere across the state, traffic snarled and motorists screamed as traffic lights died, elevators ground to a halt, and computer screens abruptly turned black. The rolling blackouts were imposed without warning, so as not to alert burglars and robbers that security systems would fail. Even the technological elite of Silicon Valley were not immune, with Cisco Systems and other industry titans complaining of billions of dollars of lost commerce.

EFFECT OF ELECTRICITY DEREGULATION IN CALIFORNIA

Nature was not to blame for California's fiasco. State government was. In order to increase the efficiency with which electricity was generated and distributed at the wholesale level, California lawmakers deregulated the wholesale electricity market. Deregulation caused the state's wholesale electricity providers to compete for customers.

Competition reduces costs through weeding out inefficiencies. *Ceteris paribus,* greater efficiencies in wholesale electricity production and distribution cause the wholesale electricity supply to shift to the right and the price of electricity in the wholesale market to fall, as shown in Figure 4-13(a). Utilities pay less for the electricity they distribute and these savings are passed along to the utilities' residential and business customers. California lawmakers, therefore, felt comfortable promising California voters that their electricity rates

FIGURE 4-13

CALIFORNIA'S WHOLESALE ELECTRICITY MARKET Increased competition after deregulation was expected to shift supply to the right and lower electricity prices, as shown in (a). However, soaring prices of crude oil, coal, and natural gas—inputs into the production of electricity—more than offset the effects of deregulation. The result was that electricity supply in fact shifted to the left, causing the price to increase as shown in (b).

FIGURE 4-14

CALIFORNIA'S RETAIL ELECTRICITY MARKET Higher wholesale electricity prices caused the supply of retail electricity to shift to the left. Ordinarily, that would cause consumers to face a higher price of electricity. However, with retail electricity prices held down by California law, the result was a shortage as the market moved from point *A* to point *B*. The market would achieve the equilibrium shown at point *C* if controls were lifted and price allowed to rise.

would not go up, at least not very much, and might even go down. Making this promise was a big mistake.

In the real world many things can change at once. In particular, world crude oil prices skyrocketed, more than doubling soon after California's deregulation of wholesale electricity took effect. The prices of natural gas, coal, and other substitutes for crude oil likewise increased. Since oil and other fuels are significant inputs into the production of electricity, rising fuel prices shifted the supply of electricity at the wholesale level significantly to the left. That leftward shift more than offset any rightward shift caused by deregulation. As shown in Figure 4-13(b), the decrease in the supply of wholesale electricity caused the wholesale price of electricity to rise sharply.

Left to itself, the marketplace will not allow a shortage for long. The price of electricity at the retail level will rise in response to a shortage. In turn, consumers will consume less electricity, and producers will provide more, until an equilibrium is reached. However, because of the lawmakers' promise that consumer electricity prices would be held in check, the market was not left to itself. Rather, rates were held down to less than the market equilibrium price. The result in the retail electricity market was a shortage, as shown in Figure 4-14.

There was no incentive for the utilities to provide additional electricity because the controlled price they were allowed to charge their customers was less than what they were paying for the electricity they bought on the wholesale market. Losses among the California utilities climbed to $13 billion (as reported by SoCal Edison and Pacific Gas & Electric) and they were teetering on the brink of bankruptcy before the state fashioned a plan to keep the power on. Under the terms of that plan, California borrowed $10 billion to tide the utilities through, with California taxpayers responsible for repaying this added debt. All in all, the decision by California lawmakers to hold electricity rates below the market equilibrium price turned out to be a very costly proposition for the very customers they sought to protect.

The restructuring of the electricity industry toward more competition is not just a California event. About half of the states are currently active in this effort, with electricity deregulation moving from the planning stage to reality in state after state. The experience of California, one of the first to deregulate, will be remembered and analyzed for what can be learned. The most vivid memory is sure to be of the electricity shortages. We must remember one more thing: price ceilings cause shortages.

1. Californians wound up paying a high "price" because the state held down the price of electricity. Explain.

2. California's tough environmental regulations were a factor in preventing the construction of new power plants in California in the 1990s. The result is that California wound up importing more of its power from elsewhere. Explain how that decision might or might not have been efficient. If the tough regulations were inefficient, why would California have imposed them?

Visit **www.prenhall.com/collinge** for updates and web exercises on this Explore & Apply topic.

SUMMARY AND LEARNING OBJECTIVES

1. **Interpret how demand represents marginal benefit and supply represents marginal cost.**
   - Marginal benefit equals the incremental value associated with the consumption of additional units of a good. The marginal benefit of any unit of a good is measured by how much consumers are willing to pay for it, as shown by their demand curves. The demand curve slopes downward, indicating the marginal benefit of additional consumption decreases.
   - Marginal cost equals the incremental cost associated with producing additional units of a good. The marginal cost is equivalent to the price required to induce a producer to supply a particular quantity. The supply curve slopes upward, depicting the increase in marginal cost that occurs as more units of output are produced.

2. **Explain the concept of social surplus and how it is divided between consumers and producers.**
   - Social surplus is the sum of consumer surplus and producer surplus.
   - Consumer surplus is the difference between the market price and the price that consumers are willing to pay. The total amount of consumer surplus is shown as a triangular area bounded by the market price and the demand curve.
   - Producer surplus is the difference between the market price and the price that producers would be willing to receive in order to sell their goods. Producer surplus is represented by the triangular area bounded by the market price and the supply curve.
   - Because social surplus is the sum of consumer and producer surplus, social surplus is also represented by a triangular area. This area is bounded by the demand curve and the supply curve.

- A price that deviates from the equilibrium price will create a deadweight loss, which represents the loss of social surplus.
- The paradox of diamonds and water is that the price of water, a necessity, is less than the price of diamonds. The paradox is resolved by recognizing that price reveals only marginal benefit. The consumer surplus from water is higher than from diamonds.

3. **Demonstrate how both exports and imports increase efficiency while simultaneously harming either consumers or producers.**
   - Exports occur when a country's domestic price of a good is below the world price of that good.
   - Imports occur when a country's domestic price of a good is above the world price of the good.
   - When a country opens its doors to trade, its domestic prices are replaced by world prices for traded goods.
   - Imports increase a country's social surplus. The bulk of the increase goes to consumers since consumer surplus increases with the consumption of imports, but producer surplus shrinks because of cuts in domestic production.
   - Exports also increase a country's social surplus. The bulk of the increase goes to producers since producer surplus increases with the production of more goods for export. Consumer surplus shrinks because production that is exported cannot be consumed by domestic consumers.

4. **Identify inefficiencies associated with price ceilings.**
   - For the sake of equity, government often seeks to change free-market prices. Unfortunately, because

price signals are basic to how markets operate, changing these signals sacrifices market efficiency.

■ Anti-gouging laws are examples of price ceilings. Price ceilings hold price below the market equilibrium, resulting in shortages. Market quantity will be less than the equilibrium quantity, which is also the efficient quantity. The lower the price ceiling is set by government, the greater the shortage that results.

■ Rent controls are an example of a price ceiling. A number of cities around the world have enacted rent control legislation, although a number of these laws have been repealed in the United States recently. When rent controls are present, the incentive to provide new rental housing is reduced.

■ Housing vouchers are an alternative to rent controls. Housing vouchers avoid the shortages created by rent controls, but require that government set aside money for the vouchers.

5. Show why price supports are unnecessary and potentially counterproductive.

■ When a price is kept higher than the market equilibrium price because of a government price floor, also called a price support, the result is a surplus in which production rises and consumption falls. The higher the price floor, the greater the surplus.

■ Black markets are a response to price ceilings. Black markets are illegal, but arise anyway when price ceilings are present. Goods are sold in black markets at or above their market equilibrium prices.

■ Minimum wage laws are another example of price floors. Minimum wages that are set above the market equilibrium wage decrease the quantity demanded of labor while increasing the quantity supplied of labor. The result is that minimum wage laws create unemployment.

■ Educational subsidies provide many of the same benefits as the minimum wage. Educational opportunities reduce the ranks of low-skilled workers by shifting the supply of low-skilled labor to the left. The shift in supply increases the wages of the remaining low-skilled workers. In this way educational subsidies increase the wages of low-skilled workers without creating unemployment.

■ When surpluses or shortages are present because of price ceilings and supports, markets are not efficient.

6. Pinpoint the economic flaw in California's deregulation of electricity.

■ The flaw involved price ceilings. Rising fuel prices increased the wholesale price of electricity just as California was deregulating the market for wholesale electricity. Rather than being allowed to pass on their price increases, electric utilities serving consumers were forced to hold rates down because of government imposed price controls. The result was shortages of electricity and accompanying power outages.

KEY TERMS

price signals, 80
marginal benefit, 80
consumer surplus, 81
producer surplus, 82
social surplus, 83

deadweight loss, 85
price ceiling, 89
rent controls, 89
transfer payments, 89
search costs, 89

housing vouchers, 90
price gouging, 90
price floor (price support), 92
minimum wage, 93
black market, 96

TEST YOURSELF

TRUE OR FALSE

1. Consumer surplus is greater for diamonds than for water.
2. For an economy to be efficient, it must eliminate producer surplus.
3. A price ceiling set below the market equilibrium price results in a shortage.

4. Rent controls provide a good way to fight discrimination in housing.
5. Consumers in the United States have more food on their tables than they would without agricultural price supports.

MULTIPLE CHOICE

6. If Yvette would be willing to pay up to $10 for one gizmo, up to $8 for a second, and up to $6 for a third, and the price of gizmos is $6 apiece, then Yvette's consumer surplus totals
   a. $24.
   b. $18.
   c. $6.
   d. $4.

7. Efficiency requires that
   a. total consumer surplus equal zero.
   b. market prices be fair.
   c. marginal social benefit equal marginal social cost.
   d. people buy low and sell high.

8. The benefits of price ceilings are received by
   a. consumers able to buy the product.
   b. producers able to sell the product.
   c. all consumers.
   d. all producers.

9. If the government places a price ceiling of $1.20 on a good with an equilibrium price of $1.00, then
   a. there will be a shortage of the good.
   b. there will be a surplus of the good.
   c. neither a surplus nor a shortage will occur.
   d. if demand for the good decreases, the government will not let the price go below $1.00.

10. Over time, rent controls that remain in place lead to
    a. increased renovation of old apartments.
    b. a greater ability for tenants to move to the best apartment for their needs.
    c. increasingly severe housing shortages.
    d. rents that are higher than they would be if the controls were to be removed.

11. Housing vouchers offer an alternative to rent controls by
    a. ensuring that landlords keep their word to keep rents low.
    b. giving prospective tenants the ability to pay higher rents.
    c. setting up detailed standards landlords must adhere to in order to qualify for permits to offer rental units.
    d. constructing new, low-rent public housing on government-owned land.

12. Anti-gouging laws that keep prices of essentials low in times of emergency are likely to
    a. be efficient.
    b. lead to surpluses.
    c. lead to shortages.
    d. distribute the available goods fairly.

13. Ticket scalping is most likely to be
    a. neither efficient nor equitable.
    b. equitable, but not efficient unless online auctioning is banned.
    c. efficient, but of questionable equity.
    d. both efficient and equitable, but very unfair.

14. Of the following, the best example of a black market is
    a. the sale of secondhand furniture at a used-furniture shop.
    b. a mail-order purchase of a computer.
    c. renting an apartment for more than the rent-controlled price.
    d. discriminating against minority applicants for a job opening.

15. A price floor placed on a good is a _____ that will normally result in a _____.
    a. maximum price; shortage
    b. maximum price; surplus
    c. minimum price; shortage
    d. minimum price; surplus

16. Compared to a free-market equilibrium, agricultural price supports have the effect of
    a. increasing both the quantities supplied and demanded.
    b. decreasing both the quantities supplied and demanded.
    c. increasing the quantity supplied and decreasing the quantity demanded.
    d. decreasing the quantity supplied and increasing the quantity demanded.

17. Which of the following is NOT a way that governments dispose of agricultural surpluses?
    a. Let the surpluses rot in storage.
    b. Sell the surpluses to purchasers in the marketplace, without restrictions on the use or resale of the commodities involved.
    c. Give the surpluses away in an unappealing form to the poor.
    d. Give the surpluses to needy countries that are unable to afford enough food.

18. If the minimum wage is set below the equilibrium market wage, the effect will be
    a. a surplus of labor.
    b. neither a surplus nor a shortage of labor.
    c. unemployment of labor.
    d. higher wages.

SELF-TEST FIGURE 4-1

19. In Self-Test Figure 4-1, the two-headed arrow labeled *A* represents the
    a. surplus of labor caused by the minimum wage.
    b. shortage of labor caused by the minimum wage.
    c. inefficiency of the minimum wage.
    d. efficiency of the minimum wage.
20. Minimum wage laws would most likely DECREASE
    a. the number of homeless people without jobs.
    b. opportunities for the least employable to gain job experience.
    c. discrimination in the job market.
    d. wages paid for low-skilled labor.
21. The reason California suffered from a shortage of electricity in 2001 is fundamentally because of
    a. insufficient regulation by the state.
    b. too many people.
    c. antiquated power lines.
    d. price controls on retail electricity.

QUESTIONS AND PROBLEMS

1. *[consumer surplus]* Compute consumer surplus in the market for pails of water, described in Figure 3-9.
2. *[consumer surplus]* Of all the purchases you have made in the last three months, which one has given you the largest amount of consumer surplus? State the amount of consumer surplus by subtracting what you paid for the item from the amount you would have been willing to pay.
3. *[social surplus]* Using a supply and demand graph, illustrate the area of social surplus. Explain how the area of social surplus can be broken down into two parts, the areas of consumer and producer surplus.
4. *[efficient output]* Is the efficient output equal to the equilibrium output? Explain.
5. *[diamonds and water]* Why is water so much cheaper than diamonds, when water is so much more important to human life?
6. *[imports and exports]* When the world price of a good is less than what a country's price would be without trade, will the country import or export the good? Will the country produce any of the good itself? Will it gain from trade? Explain, using a graph as part of your explanation.
7. *[imports and exports]* When the world price of a good is more than what a country's price would be without trade, will the country import or export the good? Will the country produce any of the good itself? Will it gain from trade? Explain, using a graph as part of your explanation.

8. *[price ceiling]* For a ceiling price to have any effect in a competitive market, must it be set above or below the equilibrium price? Explain by drawing two graphs. The first graph should show the ceiling price above the equilibrium price; the second graph should show the ceiling price below the equilibrium price. Each graph should be accompanied by an explanation noting the effects of the price ceiling in that graph.
9. *[efficient quantity; price ceiling]* Using the data provided in the accompanying table, fill in the last column and then provide answers to the following questions.

Price	Quantity Demanded	Quantity Supplied	Surplus (+) or Shortage (−)
$12	7	9	
11	8	8	
10	9	7	
9	10	6	
8	11	5	
7	12	4	

a. What is the efficient quantity?
b. What price results in the efficient quantity?
c. Suppose a price ceiling of $8 is established. Does a surplus or shortage result? What is the amount of the surplus or shortage?
d. Suppose a price ceiling of $7 is established. Describe its effect.

e. Suppose a price ceiling of $11 is established. What is its effect?

f. Suppose a price ceiling of $12 is established. Why does it have no effect?

10. *[efficiency versus equity]* Comment on the efficiency and equity aspects of ticket scalping.

11. *[price ceilings]* Do price ceilings increase or decrease social surplus? Explain.

12. *[rent controls]* Rent controls lower rents for those lucky enough to have apartments. However, there are several problems. List three inefficiencies of rent control.

13. *[price floors]* For a price floor to have any effect in a competitive market, must it be set above or below the equilibrium price? Explain by drawing two graphs. The first graph should show the price support above the equilibrium price; the second graph should show the price support below the equilibrium price. Each graph should be accompanied by an explanation noting the effects of the price support in that graph.

14. *[price floors]* Do price floors increase or decrease consumer surplus? Explain.

15. *[price floor]* Using the data in question #9, what would be the effect of a price floor set at a price of $8? What would be the effect of a price floor set at a price of $11? What would be the effect of a price floor set at a price of $12? Since the goal of a price floor is to increase the income of producers, which price(s) in the data table would logically be chosen as a floor price?

16. *[minimum wage]* Is the minimum wage law an example of a price ceiling or a price floor? Explain.

17. *[minimum wage]* Minimum wage laws are an American tradition. Although the laws seem caring and do raise wages for minimum wage labor, there are many problems. List five problems caused by minimum wage laws and briefly indicate why each occurs. Why are minimum wage laws so popular?

18. *[black markets]* What is a black market? Explain why black markets might arise as a consequence of price controls, but not as a consequence of price supports. What function do black markets perform? Are black markets legal?

 Visit **www.prenhall.com/collinge** for Exploring the Web exercises and additional self-test quizzes.

CHAPTER 5

THE FIRM AND PRODUCTION

A LOOK AHEAD

Bill Gates, Steve Jobs, Sam Walton, John D. Rockefeller, Henry Ford: the names are familiar. So are the companies: Microsoft, Apple, Wal-mart, Exxon, and Ford. Our familiarity with them illustrates the fundamental role of business in the economy and in our lives. Whether familiar or not, all businesses face ethical issues. The economic perspective on business ethics is discussed in the Explore & Apply section at the end of the chapter.

We begin by examining the legal forms a business can take and the choice among methods of financing. We then show two different ways to measure profit. After pointing out some difficulties that a business can encounter when it grows large, we take an in-depth look at production, the building block of business success.

LEARNING OBJECTIVES

Understanding Chapter 5 will enable you to:
1. **Identify the three legal forms of business and the advantages and disadvantages of each.**
2. **Explain the methods of financing a business.**
3. **Distinguish between accounting profit and economic profit.**
4. **Identify difficulties in maximizing profit that are created by the principal–agent problem.**
5. **Relate the key concepts of production, including the law of diminishing returns.**
6. **Recognize and reflect on issues relating to business ethics.**

firm a business that employs inputs to produce output.

Firms take inputs of resources and produce outputs of goods and services to be sold in the marketplace. The desire for profit, to be discussed in this chapter, motivates firms to produce.

5.1 BUSINESS BASICS

Certain elements of business economics are common to all firms. Choosing a legal form, obtaining financing, computing profit or loss, making the best use of personnel, and producing a good or service are universal experiences for firms. We start with choosing a legal form.

LEGAL FORM—PROPRIETORSHIP, PARTNERSHIP, AND CORPORATION

A firm can choose to operate in one of the following three legal forms: sole proprietorship, partnership, or corporation. Which should it be?

Consider the personal implications if you open a small business, such as a medical, legal, or accounting practice. If you start informally, you'll become a *sole proprietorship*—a business with a single owner. You may want to visit City Hall and file a d.b.a. (doing business as), which lets the public know that you are the operator of a business recognizable by the name you select for your firm. Or you might just print business cards and go to work. You can hire employees if you wish, but remember that you'll be legally liable for injuries caused to or by the employees acting in the course of their duties. You'll also be personally liable for all debts and taxes of the business. If your firm doesn't earn enough income from sales, you will have to tap into your personal resources to pay off your creditors and the tax collector. You'll report the business's profits or losses on your personal tax return.

If you can find one or more people with whom to start your business, you can form a *partnership*. Partnerships are similar to proprietorships. Each partner can hire employees. Each partner is also liable for business debts that the business is unable to pay.

To avoid the disadvantages of proprietorships and partnerships, many firms are formed as corporations. A **corporation** is a firm that is a legal entity, a thing separate from the people who own, manage, and otherwise direct its affairs. Corporations tend to be big business. While they account for only about 21 percent of businesses in the United States, they earn over 91 percent of the revenues. Figure 5-1 shows the distribution of U.S. firms and the revenues they earn according to their legal form.

Unlike other forms of business, corporations can issue shares of **stock,** which are shares of ownership in the corporation. In addition to being able to issue stock, two major advantages of the corporate form of business are *limited liability* and *perpetual existence*. Limited liability means that the owners are not personally liable for the debts of the business. If you choose to incorporate and the business fails, then creditors cannot lay claim to your personal assets. For example, when United Airlines declared bankruptcy in December 2002, none of its creditors could seize the houses or cars of its stockholders. Perpetual existence means the corporation can outlive its owners, providing that it avoids dissolution through bankruptcy.

The major disadvantage to the corporate form of business is the need to pay a corporation income tax, which takes up to 39 percent of profits. There are also reporting and procedural requirements that other forms of business do not face. These disadvantages explain why few small businesses choose to incorporate. Table 5-1 summarizes the key advantages and disadvantages of the legal forms of business.

corporation a type of firm that is a legal entity separate from the people who own, manage, and otherwise direct its affairs.

stock shares of ownership in a corporation.

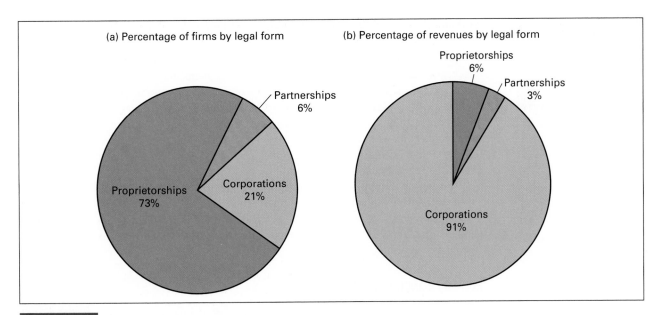

FIGURE 5-1

PERCENTAGE OF FIRMS AND PERCENTAGE OF REVENUES BY LEGAL FORM Although corporations are far out-numbered by proprietorships, corporations receive the lion's share of revenues earned by U.S. firms.

Source: 1997 Economic Census, U.S. Census Bureau. Percentages may not add to 100 because of rounding, as well as the existence of firms whose legal form was unable to be classified, or was in litigation.

TABLE 5-1   COMPARING THE LEGAL FORMS OF BUSINESS

TYPE OF BUSINESS	ADVANTAGES	DISADVANTAGES
Sole Proprietorship	Easy to start; controlled by owner	Owner personally liable for business debts
Partnership	Access to partner's funds	Partners personally liable for all partnership debts
Corporation	Access to funds through issuance of shares of stock; limited liability; perpetual existence	Corporate income tax; corporate reporting and procedural requirements

FRANCHISING—TEAMING SMALL BUSINESSES WITH GIANT CORPORATIONS

You see them everywhere. The names include McDonald's, Best Western, Pizza Hut, Radio Shack, and many others. They are *franchises,* arrangements that let a person or group start a business that uses the name and standards of a parent corporation. The advantage to becoming a franchisee, the holder of a franchise, is the chance to achieve success by putting a well-known name on your business, taking advantage of brand-name advertising, and selling a product mix with a proven track record. Franchise holders also receive training in how to operate their businesses. In return, franchisees pay fees and a percentage of their income or profit to the parent corporation.

Franchising thus pairs the advantages of the corporation with those of the sole proprietor or partnership in the hope of forming a winning team. This teamwork is sometimes contentious, however, as evidenced by the complaints of Subway franchisees, who claimed the parent corporation was franchising so much that franchisees wound up taking each other's customers and profits. ◄

HOW TO FINANCE A BUSINESS

In order to operate, firms must have *financial capital,* the money needed to start or grow a business. Firms can choose one or more of the following four options:

- Use personal funds
- Use retained earnings
- Borrow
- Issue shares of stock

In the case of many small businesses, such as flea market sellers, Amway dealers, and the like, startup financial capital comes from the owners' personal savings. New small businesses often are unable to obtain funds from other sources.

Retained earnings are a firm's savings. Just as the name suggests, retained earnings are monies kept from a business's earnings for the purpose of financing its operations. A business that has never had any earnings, such as a new business, will have no retained earnings. Retained earnings are also called *internal funds.* **Internal funds make up the majority of funds used to finance the operations of U.S. firms.**

Corporations and other firms with established track records and valuable assets are likely to be able to borrow financial capital from banks or other lenders. Only corporations are able to borrow funds by issuing bonds, where a **bond** is a promise to repay borrowed funds at some future date. Businesses that borrow funds must not only repay them, but also pay interest to the lenders, where *interest* is a periodic payment as a percentage of the face value of a bond or loan. While small startups cannot easily borrow from banks, or issue bonds, the owners of these businesses will often borrow funds from friends and relatives. Most firms use a combination of retained earnings and borrowed funds to finance their expansion.

bond a legally binding promise to repay borrowed funds with interest at a specified future date.

Only corporations have the option of issuing shares of stock. The corporation receives revenue from the initial sale of its stock, but not later when the stock "trades" from one owner to another. Stock exchanges, such as the New York Stock Exchange, the so-called "Big Board," are *secondary markets,* meaning that already existing shares of stock are traded there.

A corporation's market value is given by:

Market value of corporation = Number of shares of stock × Market price per share

The market price of a share of stock is determined by demand and supply in the *stock market,* in which shares of stock are bought and sold, often on a stock exchange. Other things equal, the greater the number of shares of stock, the lower the price per share. It is ultimately buyers and sellers of stock who determine its price and the ultimate value of a corporation. The market value changes as often as the market price of its stock changes.

Only newly issued stock provides funds to a corporation. When new shares are issued, they are sold through so-called public offerings. Despite their name, public offerings are ordinarily not open to the general public. Instead, shares from public offerings are typically purchased by large investment firms that specialize in the purchase and later resale of new shares of stock.

When firms look to sources outside themselves for financing, they are said to be seeking *external funds.* Stocks, bonds, and loans provide external funds. Historically, loans have provided about 60 percent of external funds for U.S. businesses, with bonds providing about 30 percent and stocks about 2 percent. (Other sources of external funds, such as the government, provided the remainder.) External funds are not, however, the primary source of funds for firms. All the external sources of funds—including stocks, bonds, and loans—provide only about 25 percent of the funds that firms use. Thus, as stated earlier, retained earnings provide most financing for firms.

U.S. firms, especially corporations, are not restricted to this country in their search for external funds. Financial markets today are global in scope as financial capital flows relatively freely across international borders. Large pools of savings have developed in other industrial countries—money that can flow to any firm anywhere that offers the greatest expected rewards. Banks also take advantage of opportunities to raise financial capital overseas. The flow of money is a two-way street. Just as U.S. firms and banks can look overseas for financial capital, so too can firms in other countries look outside their borders for funds.

FIVE FOR A DIME   *SNAPSHOT*

Little square hamburgers with five holes, onions, and soft buns are the unlikely hero of a classic American success story. The first White Castle opened in Wichita, Kansas, in 1921 with the help of a $700 loan. Selling for a nickel each, the little White Castle hamburger sandwich was popular enough to prompt partners Walter Anderson and "Billy" Ingram to open a second restaurant in 1924. Thus began a steady expansion, creating America's first restaurant chain in the process.

White Castle pioneered fast food. The first fast-food newspaper coupons, in 1932, offered five White Castles for 10 cents! Over the next 70 years, many other innovations followed. One of the most recent was the popular frozen White Castles sold in supermarkets. Today, White Castle has a cult following around the world, often in places far from the chain's few hundred restaurants, which are mostly found in the American Midwest. The firm has never gone public, remaining in the hands of the Ingram family all these years later. The company long ago repaid its $700 loan and today steadfastly avoids the perils of debt. ◄

5.2 THE GOAL OF MAXIMUM PROFIT

profit (economic profit) total revenue minus total cost; unlike accounting profit, economic profit defines cost to include implicit opportunity costs.

Profit, also called **economic profit,** is the difference between total revenue and total cost:

$$\text{Profit} = \text{Total revenue} - \text{Total cost}$$

total revenue price × quantity.

Total revenue is the sum of income received by a firm. For a firm selling a single product at a single price, total revenue equals the quantity sold multiplied by its price:

$$\text{Total revenue} = \text{Price} \times \text{Quantity}$$

total cost the sum of the firm's expenses.

Total cost, which must be subtracted from total revenue to compute profit, is the sum of the firm's expenses.

To say that a firm maximizes profit means that it earns the greatest amount of total profit that it is capable of earning. **The economic analysis of firms usually assumes the goal of profit maximization.** This assumption enhances our understanding of why a firm chooses its specific quantity of output to produce. As we study the behavior of firms in future chapters, we will assume that they maximize profit. We now turn our attention to clarifying economic profit, which will require us to consider total costs in greater depth.

DISTINGUISHING AMONG NORMAL PROFIT, ECONOMIC PROFIT, AND ACCOUNTING PROFIT

Normal profit is that rate of minimum profit which a firm must earn in order to survive in the market.

—Alfred Marshall, British economist (1842–1924)

Firms employ accountants to measure profit for reporting to the government and shareholders. However, the accounting measures do not explain the behavior of firms. For example, firms sometimes pull out of a particular business or operation even when it is profitable according to accounting data. If a firm spends a million dollars to earn one dollar in profit, as reported by its accountants, the owners of that firm would consider themselves to have lost money. They could do better by putting their money in the bank or into other investments.

explicit costs costs accountants aim to measure.

To explain the behaviors of firms, we must distinguish between two components of total cost. All of the costs accountants aim to measure are termed **explicit costs,** no matter what the accountants call them. Explicit costs are all internal to the firm, in the sense that they depend upon decisions that the firm makes. Examples of explicit costs include the cost of labor, raw materials, shipping, insurance, rent, and utilities.

implicit opportunity costs (implicit costs) the value that the firm's capital and the entrepreneur's time would have in their best alternative uses.

Consider Ali's King-of-Ribs restaurant. The napkins, eating utensils, food, salaries of cooks and servers, and the cost of the ingredients in the dinners served are all explicit costs. However, there are other costs that accountants do not measure. These are **implicit opportunity costs,** or **implicit costs** for short, that are associated with nonpurchased inputs. These costs are the value that the firm's capital and entrepreneur's time would have in their best alternative uses.

Implicit costs vary with forces external to the firm, in the sense that the firm has no control over them. Examples include interest rates from alternative investments and the opportunity cost of the entrepreneur's time. Accountants do not try to measure these costs, because they vary in unforeseeable ways over time and among entrepreneurs. A firm that is profitable when John Doe is in charge would probably be unprofitable with Bill Gates at the helm because Bill Gates' time is worth too much elsewhere. Accountants cannot know just what his opportunities are, nor their value. Because the value of alternatives cannot be known, accountants ignore implicit opportunity costs when calculating profit:

$$\textit{Accounting profit} = \text{Total revenue} - \text{Explicit costs}$$

To explain the behavior of firms, however, economists include implicit costs in their calculation of profit.

$$\text{Economic profit} = \text{Accounting profit} - \text{Implicit opportunity costs}$$

Normal profit represents the portion of accounting profit that just covers implicit opportunity costs. **From an economic perspective, normal profit is a cost. It is the accounting profit needed to keep the firm in business.** For this reason, normal profit is the same as a firm's implicit costs. A firm must earn at least a normal profit for its resources to continue to be employed in their current use. If a normal profit is not present or expected in the future, the owners of the firm would make plans to eventually go out of business and *liquidate*—sell off—the firm's assets. Substituting for implicit cost in the equation for economic profit, we have:

$$\text{Economic profit} = \text{Accounting profit} - \text{Normal profit}$$

Figure 5-2 illustrates the relationship between economic profit, accounting profit, and normal profit.

Successful companies are well aware of their implicit costs and the notion of normal profit, even if they cannot know its exact amount. The owners invest their time and money expecting to do at least as well with them as they could elsewhere. For example, Ali had other investment opportunities for the funds he invested in his restaurant. If the best alternative use of his money would have paid a return of $1,000 per month, that is the implicit cost of Ali's investment. Let's take a more detailed look at the King-of-Ribs restaurant's revenue and costs.

Suppose that Ali's restaurant sells an average of 5,000 of its honey-glazed baby back rib dinners each month. Customers pay $10 for each dinner, which is the only item sold at the restaurant. Ali thus earns an average of $50,000 ($10 × 5,000 = $50,000) per month in total revenue. The restaurant incurs two explicit costs, the expenses for food and supplies, and for hired labor. Ali's implicit costs are the opportunity cost of his entrepreneurship (he could try his hand at a different business), the opportunity cost of his own labor hours, and the return on alternative investments. The implicit opportunity costs represent real costs of using Ali's resources of entrepreneurship, labor, and capital in the King-of-Ribs restaurant instead of elsewhere.

Table 5-2 shows the computation of profit for the King-of-Ribs restaurant. In Ali's case, accounting profit equals $10,000, but economic profit equals only $4,000. **Because implicit**

normal profit the portion of accounting profit that equals implicit opportunity costs.

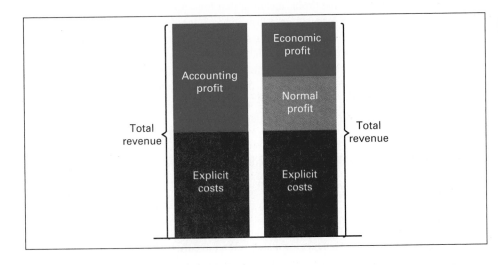

FIGURE 5-2

ACCOUNTING PROFIT VERSUS ECONOMIC PROFIT Accounting profit will be greater than economic profit by the amount of normal profit, which is the portion of accounting profit necessary to keep the firm in business. Normal profit consists of implicit costs that are beyond the scope of the firm, including the opportunity cost of the owners' time and the rate of return on alternative investments. If normal profit is not achieved or expected, profit-maximizing owners will plan to go out of business.

TABLE 5-2   MONTHLY ECONOMIC PROFIT AT ALI'S KING-OF-RIBS RESTAURANT

Total revenue		$50,000
Minus explicit costs:		
Raw food and supplies	−$27,000	
Hired labor	−$13,000	
Accounting profit		$10,000
Minus implicit costs:		
Value of Ali's entrepreneurship in alternative business venture	−$3,000	
Value of Ali's labor at a different job	−$2,000	
Value of alternative investments that Ali could have made	−$1,000	
Economic profit		$ 4,000

costs are subtracted from accounting profit to obtain economic profit, economic profit will always be less than accounting profit.

Let's suppose that food and labor costs—excluding Ali's own labor, for which he is not explicitly paid—at Ali's King-of-Ribs restaurant increase by exactly $4,000. Assuming all other data stay the same, then economic profit at Ali's drops to zero. Will Ali close his restaurant? No, because while he has no economic profit, total revenue does cover his implicit costs. Thus, the King-of-Ribs restaurant earns a normal profit. That normal profit is sufficient to keep all the resources of the restaurant in their current use.

There are three possible outcomes when economic profit is computed:

excess profit economic profit; the accounting profit in excess of normal profit.

- The firm can earn a positive profit, also called **excess profit,** meaning that total revenue exceeds total cost. For the King-of-Ribs restaurant, the profit is $4,000.

loss occurs when economic profit is negative.

- The firm can earn a negative profit, meaning that total revenue is less than total cost. A negative profit is called a **loss.** When a firm incurs a loss, it may be able to continue in business for awhile. However, if it continues to incur losses, its resources will eventually be put to different uses and the firm will be out of business.

breakeven occurs when economic profit is zero.

- The firm can earn zero profit, meaning that total revenue equals total cost. Zero profit is also called **breakeven,** meaning that the firm earns just enough revenue to provide it with a normal profit, but no more. While a firm would prefer to earn a positive profit, breakeven alone is enough to keep it in business.

THE PRINCIPAL–AGENT PROBLEM—AN ISSUE OF INCENTIVES

If you want something done right, do it yourself.

—Old saying

While the owners of a firm may seek to maximize profit, not all of the firm's employees are likely to share that goal. Managers and staff often have their own personal agendas. This

How could a firm that earns an accounting profit have an economic loss at the same time?

Answer: The implicit opportunity costs of the owner's time and capital are not considered in computing accounting profit. When these costs are deducted from total revenue, it could be that economic profit is negative, meaning that the firm incurs a loss even though the accounting profits remain positive. For example, if a firm's total revenue equals $10,000, explicit costs equal $9,000, and implicit costs equal $2,000, then the firm earns $1,000 of accounting profit. Subtracting the implicit costs leaves the firm with an economic loss of $1,000.

brings about a **principal–agent problem,** which refers to the difficulties of making employees, who are called agents, act in accordance with the will of the owners, who are called principals. As readers of the comic strip *Dilbert* know all too well, managers may use the firm's resources in ways that contribute little to the revenue of the business. Also, employees are often guilty of *shirking,* which is usually known on the job as "goofing off." The bigger the company, the more distance there is between the owners and the employees and the more pronounced the principal–agent problem is likely to be.

> **principal–agent problem** the difficulty of making agents, such as employees, act in the interests of principals, such as owners.

One way of facing up to the principal–agent problem is to provide employees with economic incentives to maximize the firm's profits. These incentives are sometimes highly personal, as in the case of sales commissions. More often, they depend on the performance of the company as a whole and also of the division of the company in which the employee works. These incentives can take a variety of forms, including:

- *Stock-option plans* in which employees are provided the option to buy stock at a fixed price, irrespective of what the market price of the stock might become. Employees thus have the collective incentive to increase the profitability of the company so that its stock price will go up.
- *Incentive pay* systems that let employees share in the profitability of the firm. An example of incentive pay is the traditional holiday bonus, the value of which depends upon how well the company has done.

When employees are rewarded based upon the company's performance, they have more incentive to work diligently. Perhaps even more importantly, they also have an incentive to keep an eye on one another to ensure that everyone is working hard. Shirking would not be cool!

Sometimes designing a proper system of incentives is problematic and can itself pit the interests of agents against principals. For example, the executives of many companies have been accused by shareholders of devising stock option plans that are too generous to themselves. Also, if your businesses faced the task of devising a scheme of incentive pay as a reward for exemplary performance, how would you measure such performance? If sales doubled in the previous year, would your managers deserve bonuses? Not if your competitors' sales tripled! Only with carefully selected benchmarks is it possible to interpret performance. For example, Enron, Adelphia Communications, Worldcom, and a number of other companies have been accused of misleading their investors into driving up the value of company stock, with the result that insiders could cash out lucrative stock options.

GIVING AWAY OTHER PEOPLE'S MONEY

Whether it be to fund public broadcasting or the local cultural museum, firms are often sought out for charitable contributions. Firms, in turn, look for good publicity in making such donations. Should they be charitable when it detracts from profits?

Remember that management is the agent of the owners and is employed to follow the wishes of owners. The owners usually prefer to make their own charitable decisions based on their personal preferences and financial circumstances. Witness Bill and Melinda Gates' decision to set up their own family-controlled foundation for charitable giving, a foundation that started with a net worth of about $24 billion. One of the foundation's objectives has been to vaccinate children in the world's poorest countries, a cause toward which it has already contributed about $850 million. Through this charity, Bill Gates gave away his own money, not the money of shareholders in Microsoft Corporation. Corporate officers must think twice before giving away that which is not theirs to give! For this reason, firms encourage employees to give to the United Way campaign or to make other individual charitable donations out of the employees' own money. ◄

5.3 PRODUCING THE PRODUCT

In order to earn a profit, a firm must have something to sell. It must produce a good or service using labor, capital, and perhaps other inputs. The relationship between the amounts of inputs and the quantities of output a firm produces is called its **production function.**

THE LONG RUN AND THE SHORT RUN

Production decisions are made by firms in either a long-run or a short-run context. The **long run** is a time period sufficiently long that all inputs are *variable,* meaning that their quantities can be changed. For this reason, the long run is sometimes called the *planning horizon.* Actual production occurs in the **short run,** a time period where at least one input is fixed. The quantity of a *fixed* input cannot be changed.

While firms employ numerous inputs, our model of the firm simplifies matters by assuming only two inputs. Specifically, assume that labor is a variable input and that capital is a fixed input in the short run. It may be helpful to think of a unit of labor as an hour of work, and a unit of capital as an hour's use of machinery.

Modeling production with only two inputs highlights the distinction between variable and fixed inputs. The implications pertaining to labor apply in the real world to any variable input, including variable capital inputs such as pencils and lightbulbs. Likewise, the analysis of capital applies to any fixed input, including long-term employment contracts.

Short-run decision making by the firm focuses only on the variable input. For instance, in your favorite supermarket, another cashier can quickly be put to work when long lines build up, assuming an idle cash register is available. The number of cashiers to put on duty is an example of a short-run decision about a variable input.

While the number of cash registers is fixed in the short run, the long run offers a supermarket enough time to add checkout lanes or even build a larger store. Hence, in the long run, both labor and capital are variable for a supermarket, factory, or any other firm.

PRODUCT—TOTAL, MARGINAL, AND AVERAGE

In the short run, when capital is fixed, the amount of output depends on the amount of labor. The output produced is said to be the *product* of labor, since nothing is produced without workers. **Total product** refers to the total quantity of output produced. We will thus use the terms *total product* and *total output* interchangeably. The additional total product from additional units of labor is termed the *marginal product of labor,* or **marginal product** for short:

production function the relationship between the amounts of inputs and the quantities of output a firm produces.

long run period of time sufficiently long that all inputs are variable.

short run period of time in which at least one input is fixed.

total product the firm's total quantity of output.

marginal product additional output produced by the addition of one more unit of labor; change in output ÷ change in labor.

$$\text{Marginal product} = \frac{\text{Change in total product}}{\text{Change in labor}}$$

In contrast, **average product** is the quantity of output per worker:

$$\text{Average product} = \frac{\text{Total product}}{\text{Total labor}}$$

average product total quantity of output ÷ total quantity of labor.

For example, consider a firm that increases its employment of labor from 100 units of labor to 101 units of labor, and experiences an increase in total product from 50,000 units to 51,000 units. The marginal product of the 101st unit of labor is 1,000 units of output. Average product for 100 units of labor is $\frac{50,000}{100}$, which equals 500 units, and for 101 units of labor is $\frac{51,000}{101}$, which equals approximately 505 units of output.

Notice that average product increased in the preceding example. **Average product will increase when marginal product is greater than the initial average product, decrease when marginal product is less than average product, and remain constant when marginal product is equal to average product.**

The relationship between averages and marginals is more general than just average and marginal product. For instance, consider Joyce, who has an average grade of 82 in her economics course after having taken the first two tests. When she takes the next test—the marginal test—her average grade will increase if her grade is greater than 82, or decrease if it is less than 82. Her average remains the same if she gets exactly 82 on that third test. So, in general, a marginal above average pulls the average up; a marginal below average pulls the average down; and a marginal equal to average will not change the average. That rule applies no matter what the marginals and averages are in reference to.

Marginal product is subject to the **law of diminishing returns,** which states that, **when additional units of labor or any other variable input are added to a fixed input, the marginal product of the variable input must eventually decrease.**

Once a firm reaches the point of diminishing returns, each successive unit of labor will add less and less to total product. This is shown in the shape of total product, as seen in Figure 5-3, where diminishing returns set in at the point so labeled.

law of diminishing returns states that when additional units of labor or any other variable input are added in the short run, the marginal product of the variable input must eventually decrease.

FIGURE 5-3

THE TOTAL PRODUCT OF LABOR CURVE The total product of labor is a short-run relationship between the quantity of output produced and the amount of labor employed. Marginal product is the slope of total product. The law of diminishing returns causes marginal product to decrease at some point, as shown. Marginal product can even become negative, which occurs when total product turns downward. In the long run, the firm could vary its capital, which would change total product.

Marginal product equals the slope of total product. To understand why, recall the definition of marginal product, which is: the change in total product divided by the change in labor. Also recall that the slope of a curve is found by "rise over run." The "rise" is the change in the variable on the vertical axis—the change in total product in Figure 5-3. The "run" is the change in the variable on the horizontal axis—the change in labor. "Rise over run," the slope of total product, is thus equivalent to marginal product. In the figure, the slope of total product decreases after the point of diminishing returns. When the slope of total product is decreasing, marginal product must be decreasing as well.

The law of diminishing returns assumes that all labor is of equal quality, which signifies that diminishing returns occur for reasons other than those relating to differences in labor quality. For example, although the 101st unit of labor in the earlier example had a marginal product equal to 1,000 units of output, the 102nd unit of labor will exhibit a marginal product of less than 1,000 units if the firm is past the point of diminishing returns.

The explanation for the law of diminishing returns is found in the commonsense proposition that adding more and more labor to a fixed amount of capital reduces the amount of capital each unit of labor has to work with. Eventually, the effect of less capital per worker reveals itself in the form of diminishing returns. **Because there is a fixed input, the law of diminishing returns applies only in the short run.**

The principle of diminishing returns applies to all types of businesses. For example, Figure 5-4 illustrates marginal and average product for Ali's King-of-Ribs Restaurant.

Ali has a relatively small building. At first, marginal product rises because his employees can specialize. In Ali's case, the major specializations would be the tasks of taking orders, cooking, and cleaning up. After the third worker, the need for specialization is less

Total, marginal, and average products of labor			
Units of labor	Total product (Quantity of meals per hour)	Marginal product (Change in total product ÷ change in labor)	Average product (Total product ÷ total labor)
0	0	undefined	undefined
1	3	3	3
2	10	7	5
3	20	10	6.7
4	27	7	6.75
5	31	4	6.2
6	32	1	5.3
7	30	−2	4.3

FIGURE 5-4

THE MARGINAL AND AVERAGE PRODUCTS OF LABOR The table shows the calculation of marginal product, which is shown in the graph. For example, when labor increases from 3 to 4 units, total product increases from 20 to 27. This 7 unit increase in total product is the value of marginal product between 3 and 4 units of labor. Note that marginal product becomes a negative value when 7 units of labor are employed. The table also shows the calculation of average product, which is plotted in the graph. For example, average product at 2 units of labor equals 5 because total product ÷ labor equals 10 ÷ 2 = 5. When marginal product is greater than average product, average product will increase. When marginal product is less than average product, average product will decrease.

Explain how a student faces the law of diminishing returns.

Answer: A student combines ability—an input that is fixed in the short run—with the variable input of time. The output is knowledge as measured by an examination grade. When studying, a point is reached at which each succeeding minute of study time adds less and less to the student's knowledge. Sometimes students press their studying beyond diminishing returns and into negative returns, which start when an additional minute of continuous studying begins to result in mental confusion. Such a student will lament: "I studied too much for the exam."

clear-cut, which puts Ali's restaurant into the region of diminishing returns. For example, the next three workers might "float," relieving the cashier of tending the drive-through window, helping with cleanup, or doing whatever other tasks seem most important at the time. These workers increase Ali's total production, as shown in the total product column, but the marginal product column shows that the increments to output decline.

There is a danger from hiring too many employees. "Too many cooks spoil the ribs," Ali always says, as he imagines excess employees with little to do, chatting and getting in each other's way instead of attending to customers. Suppose Ali mistakenly continues to increase employment to seven workers while keeping his capital constant. In that event, he will reach *negative returns*, in which marginal product is negative. Because output is higher with fewer employees, firms seek to avoid negative returns.

In Figure 5-4, observe that **marginal product intersects average product at the maximum point on average product but in the declining portion of marginal product.** This is because average product is pulled up when marginal product lies above it, and pulled down when marginal product lies below it. **Diminishing returns are associated with the downward-sloping part of marginal product;** negative returns are illustrated by the portion of marginal product that lies below the horizontal axis.

5.4 BUSINESS—ETHICAL IN PRINCIPLE, NOT ALWAYS IN PRACTICE

He intends only his own gain, and he is in this, as in many other cases, led by an invisible hand to promote an end which was no part of his intention. . . . By pursuing his own interest he frequently promotes that of the society more effectually than when he really intends to promote it.

—*Adam Smith, The Wealth of Nations, 1776*

The invisible hand Adam Smith describes above is a fundamental concept in economics, which explains how self-interest can be in the public interest. Yet Adam Smith was no advocate of unbridled greed, and had even authored an earlier work, entitled *The Theory of Moral Sentiments* (1759), about morality and virtue. In his renowned *The Wealth of Nations* (1776), Adam Smith made it clear that competition is the key to reining in business self-interest and making sure that the public gets the most for its money. Without competition, Smith thought that firms would join together in a "conspiracy against the public interest." Perhaps he could also have warned us of conspiracies against stockholders' interests by business management and Wall Street insiders.

News of insider trading, misreported profits, bogus stock "buy" recommendations from stockbrokers who were busy selling the stocks they were recommending, excessive salaries, overabundant stock options, and much more has highlighted issues of *business ethics*, the fairness and honesty of business. Unfortunately, the invisible hand is often not present to keep unfairness and dishonesty in check.

In a particularly glaring case, the misrepresentation of Enron Corporation's accounts by its auditors camouflaged its deteriorating financial condition, as well as its impending bankruptcy. The indictment and conviction of the auditors, the accounting firm of Arthur Anderson, for obstruction of justice followed within months. The fact that Enron executives were paid $680 million in the year prior to the firm's bankruptcy raised additional ethical and legal issues.

If we cannot rely upon people and businesses to voluntarily act ethically, then at least we can, by the threat of punishment, discourage certain actions by making them illegal. This was the idea behind the legislation to create a new corporate fraud chapter in the federal criminal code, legislation that was unanimously passed by the Senate in July 2002. That legislation, plus additional proposed legislation to stiffen criminal penalties for white-collar crimes, occurred in response to the Enron and other corporate scandals. To put teeth in the new legislation, proposals were made to increase funding for the Securities and Exchange Commission (SEC), the government's watchdog over the stock market.

In spite of regulation of the stock market by the SEC, investors sometimes take it on the chin, even from their brokers. For example, a number of stock brokers increased their profits on "playing the spread" between the bid and ask prices by colluding to keep this spread artificially high. In effect, they were rigging the rules in their favor. When confronted with a class action lawsuit over these practices, these dealers agreed in 1997 to stop colluding and to pay over $1 billion into a settlement fund that would cover the costs of the lawsuit and finance payments to investors who had been harmed.

Laws also protect consumers. Consumer protection laws limit the fraudulent misrepresentation of products by sellers. Consumer safety laws are designed to make sure that the products that we buy do not threaten our safety. Truth-in-lending laws punish lenders who act dishonestly in their dealings with borrowers. Lemon laws are designed to force manufacturers to produce a product that performs the functions it was designed to perform. The antitrust laws govern the behavior of businesses toward their competitors, seeking to ensure that even the little fish can swim with the big sharks of the business world and still survive.

Laws are not always necessary. For example, a few years ago, the owners of some vehicles produced by Ford began to see the paint on their vehicles peeling, which occurred after their warranties had expired. Ford had no legal obligation to assist the owners, who were forced to spend hundreds of dollars each to have their vehicles repainted. Nonetheless, on a case-by-case basis, Ford paid the costs. On the face of it, Ford cut its profit by the amount of the expenses it incurred on behalf of the car owners. However, by having a defect fixed at its own expense, Ford may have been ensuring itself a greater future profit.

A good *reputation* can be critical for the long-term profitability of a firm. Johnson & Johnson, the maker of Tylenol, ensured its good reputation by its actions when someone poisoned bottles of Tylenol that had been sitting on store shelves in 1982 and 1986, resulting in several deaths. The company, at a huge cost, immediately recalled all bottles of Tylenol. The company was praised for its quick action, and Tylenol is as popular today as ever. In contrast, Ford's reputation suffered badly when, in 2001, Ford Explorers were discovered to be equipped with blow-out-prone tires that caused deadly accidents. Although Ford responded to the problem by offering to replace the tires, public opinion had turned against Ford, and the maker of the tires, Bridgestone-Firestone. Ford's chief executive officer, who took the lead in Ford's response to the problem, was subsequently fired.

ACTING ETHICALLY

It is easy to act ethically when doing so contributes to greater profitability, but what about the issues of business ethics that crop up day-to-day? For example, since monitoring within the firm is imperfect, it is often up to employees to be ethical enough to not take credit for other people's work. Other ethical challenges encompass laws and regulations that can sometimes be eluded. Examples include the illicit dumping of toxic wastes, industrial espionage (in which firms steal ideas from one another), and sexual harrassment in the workplace.

How well firms face up to these challenges is a matter of ethics, which are often a part of company policies. Even Enron, in a July 1, 2000 memo to all employees from Ken Lay, Enron's top executive, stated, ". . . We are responsible for conducting the business affairs of the Company in accordance with all applicable laws and in a moral and honest manner." Enron also published a sixty-four-page "Code of Ethics" booklet that was distributed to all employees. Detailed codes of ethics are found in many large businesses, as well as in professional societies, such as the American Accounting Association. Business schools also require their students to study ethics. With business ethics front and center in the business world, the ethical lapses that surface prove all the more disturbing.

Despite all the ethical challenges within business, **the basic nature of business is highly ethical. Rather than being a** *zero-sum game* **in which the winner wins only what the loser loses, business is a** *positive-sum game* **that can bring benefits to all involved.** The reward of profit goes to the owners of firms that are best at responding to consumer wishes. The reward of a high standard of living goes to us all.

*T*HINKING
*C*RITICALLY

1. In your opinion, what is the greatest ethical problem faced by business people today? What advice could you offer to business people that might promote ethical behavior on their part?

2. Should ethics in the business world be a matter of law or of individual conscience? Would your answer be the same if the question pertained to personal ethics? Explain.

Visit **www.prenhall.com/collinge** for updates and web exercises on this Explore & Apply topic.

SUMMARY AND LEARNING OBJECTIVES

1. **Identify the three legal forms of business and the advantages and disadvantages of each.**
   - A firm will exist in one of the following legal forms: sole proprietorship, partnership, or corporation. The corporation offers the advantages of limited liability and perpetual existence.
   - Sole proprietorships are easy to start, but saddle their owners with unlimited liability. Partnerships provide access to a partner's funds, but like the proprietorship suffer from the disadvantage of unlimited liability. The corporation has disadvantages, too, in the form of the corporate income tax, and various reporting and procedural requirements not faced by proprietorships and partnerships.

2. **Explain the methods of financing a business.**
   - Financial capital includes personal funds, retained earnings, borrowed funds, and funds raised by issuing stock. Retained earnings, a firm's internal funds, are saved from profits earned by a business. External funds are obtained from investors who buy the firm's new shares of stock, or by borrowing. Borrowing includes funds borrowed from banks and funds raised by issuing bonds.
   - Existing shares of stock in corporations are bought and sold on stock exchanges. The stock exchanges are secondary markets, meaning that only existing shares of stock are traded there. New issues of stock are sold through public offerings.

3. **Distinguish between accounting profit and economic profit.**
   - Economists assume the goal of the firm is to maximize profit. Total economic profit equals total revenue minus total cost, where total cost includes both explicit and implicit opportunity costs.
   - Accounting profit subtracts only explicit costs from total revenue. Because accounting profit ignores implicit cost, accounting profit will always be greater than economic profit.
   - A firm that maximizes profit may in fact be able to earn an economic profit. Economic profit means that total revenue is greater than total cost. If total revenue is less than total cost, the firm incurs a loss.

- A firm that earns a normal profit but no economic profit receives just enough revenue to cover its implicit opportunity costs. A normal profit ensures that the resources of the firm will stay in their present use. Firms that break even earn zero economic profit, but their revenue is sufficient to provide a normal profit.

- A firm that incurs a loss will eventually go out of business if the losses continue. The reason is that revenue is not enough to cover the amount of implicit costs. In other words, a firm with a loss is not earning a normal profit.

4. **Identify difficulties in maximizing profit that are created by the principal–agent problem.**

- The principal–agent problem exists because employees' goals are not necessarily the same as those of the owners of the firm. Employees and managers may take actions that benefit them at the expense of the firm's profit. Various incentive methods, including bonuses, are used to try to solve the principal–agent problem. Sometimes these incentive methods cause incentive problems of their own.

5. **Relate the key concepts of production, including the law of diminishing returns.**

- A firm's production function relates the amount of inputs used to the amount of output produced. To simplify the study of production, it is assumed that only two inputs, capital and labor, are used in production.

- Production occurs in a short-run and a long-run context. In the short run, at least one input is fixed in quantity. Generally, the fixed input is assumed to be capital. However, in the long run the quantity of capital can vary. Thus, in the long run all inputs are assumed to be variable.

- Total product is the firm's total production. A total product curve shows the amount of output for each amount of the variable input.

- Marginal product is the change in output resulting from a change in input. The marginal product of labor equals the change in total product divided by the change in the quantity of labor.

- Average product is output per unit of input. The average product of labor equals total product divided by the quantity of labor. An average product curve will always be intersected at its maximum point by the marginal product curve.

- The law of diminishing returns states that the marginal product of labor will eventually decrease as more labor is used.

6. **Recognize and reflect on issues relating to business ethics.**

- Ethical dilemmas occur in the day-to-day operations of a business. Ethical lapses have proven common, as exemplified by the scandals associated with Enron and stock brokers. Many businesses attempt to promote ethical behavior through ethics codes. Professional associations and business schools also promote ethics. The nature of business is ethical since it benefits both consumers and business owners.

KEY TERMS

firm, 106
corporation, 106
stock, 106
bond, 108
profit (economic profit), 110
total revenue, 110
total cost, 110
explicit costs, 110

implicit opportunity costs (implicit costs), 110
normal profit, 111
excess profit, 112
loss, 112
breakeven, 112
principal–agent problem, 113
production function, 114

long run, 114
short run, 114
total product, 114
marginal product, 114
average product, 115
law of diminishing returns, 115

TEST YOURSELF

TRUE OR FALSE

1. Partnerships obtain financing by issuing shares of stock.
2. External funds are a larger source of funds than internal funds for U.S. firms.
3. The value that a firm's capital would have in alternative uses is called an explicit cost.
4. Economists usually assume the goal of a firm is to maximize profits.
5. In the short run, all inputs are variable.

MULTIPLE CHOICE

6. Which of the following is NOT a legal form of business?
   a. Sole proprietorship.
   b. Partnership.
   c. Corporation.
   d. Limited liability.

7. Which of the following types of firms offers its owners protection from personal liability for business debts?
   a. Sole proprietorship.
   b. Partnership.
   c. Corporation.
   d. Limited liability.

8. Startup financing for most small businesses comes from
   a. bank loans.
   b. sale of stock.
   c. issuance of bonds.
   d. personal savings and the savings of family and friends.

9. The stock exchanges are an example of a
   a. primary market.
   b. secondary market.
   c. sole proprietorship.
   d. mutual fund.

10. Explicit costs are
    a. wages and profits.
    b. costs brought on by negative returns in production.
    c. costs that accountants can measure.
    d. costs associated with wasted resources.

11. Suppose a firm earns a return on investment of 5 percent. If investments elsewhere are available paying 8 percent, the firm is
    a. profitable in both an accounting and economic sense.
    b. unprofitable in both an accounting and economic sense.
    c. earning economic profits but not accounting profits.
    d. earning accounting profits but not economic profits.

12. Economic profit equals _____, where normal profit is considered as _____.
    a. total revenue minus total cost; a cost
    b. marginal revenue minus marginal cost; a cost
    c. total revenue minus total cost; revenue
    d. marginal revenue minus marginal cost; revenue

13. When Desico, a producer of drill bits for the oil industry, is said to earn a normal profit, then the firm
    a. earns an economic profit.
    b. incurs an economic loss.
    c. earns just enough to cover its opportunity costs.
    d. will exit the industry.

14. The principal–agent problem occurs when
    a. there is industrial espionage.
    b. a business owner chooses to have no employees but herself.

c. the interests of owners and employees are different.
d. government regulates the stock market.

15. The short run is the
    a. time period in which all inputs are variable.
    b. time period in which all inputs are fixed.
    c. time period in which at least one, but not all, inputs are fixed.
    d. planning horizon.

16. In the long run,
    a. all inputs are fixed.
    b. all inputs are variable.
    c. at least one input is fixed.
    d. one input is variable, while the others are fixed.

17. A firm's total product appears as follows:

Labor	Output
1	2
2	12
3	18
4	20
5	20

Diminishing returns set in with the _____ unit of labor.
    a. second
    b. third
    c. fourth
    d. fifth

18. In Self-Test Figure 5-1, marginal product is positive but decreasing in region
    a. *A.*
    b. *B.*
    c. *C.*
    d. *D.*

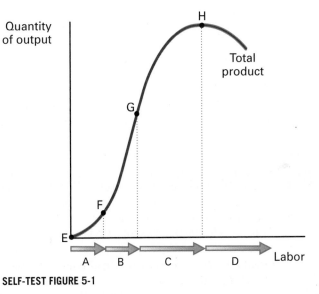

SELF-TEST FIGURE 5-1

19. In Self-Test Figure 5-1, the point of diminishing returns is
    a. *E.*
    b. *F.*
    c. *G.*
    d. *H.*

20. A zero-sum game is one in which
    a. all participants are winners.
    b. all participants are losers.
    c. there are winners and losers and what the losers lose, the winners win.
    d. everyone will refuse to participate since the expected gain is zero.

QUESTIONS AND PROBLEMS

1. *[legal form]* In light of the advantages that corporations possess, why do you think the proprietorship and partnership forms still exist? In your answer, consider the costs and benefits of each form, including the means of financing.

2. *[methods of finance]* List the four methods that a business can use to finance itself. State the advantages and disadvantages of each.

3. *[legal form and finance]* Suppose you wish to start a small lawn care business. Develop a short business plan that states the legal form your business will take and why. Estimate the equipment you will need to start the business and the amount of money each item of equipment will cost. Finally, state in your plan what sources of finance you will pursue to get your business going.

4. *[methods of finance]* What is the difference between internal and external financing? Which type of financing is most commonly used by businesses?

5. *[stock market]* What is a share of stock? Do all corporations issue shares of stock? Do partnerships issue stock? Do sole proprietorships issue stock? Explain.

6. *[stock market]* What is a secondary market? Why is it important to recognize that stock exchanges are secondary markets?

7. *[bond market]* Do all corporations issue bonds? When bonds are issued, what obligations does the issuer take on?

8. *[profit]* State the general definition of profit. What assumption do economists commonly make regarding the firm's behavior toward profit?

9. *[economic profit]* How are implicit costs treated in the calculation of economic profit?

10. *[economic versus accounting profit]* Write two equations where the first equation states accounting profit and the second states economic profit. Why do economists define profit differently from accountants?

11. *[economic profit equation]* Consider the following equation: Economic profit = Total revenue − Total explicit cost − Total implicit opportunity cost = 0. This equation describes a firm that earns no economic profit. Is this firm earning a normal profit? Explain.

12. *[implicit opportunity costs]* Provide examples of plausible opportunity costs in each of the following instances:
    a. $10,000 cash invested in a firm by its owner.
    b. An extra 15 hours of work per week performed for no monetary payment by a business owner.
    c. A business owner's personal automobile used for business purposes.

13. *[normal profit]* When a business earns a normal profit, what is the likelihood that the business will go out of business? Explain.

14. *[principal–agent problem]* What is the principal–agent problem? What does this problem imply about profit maximization?

15. *[inputs]* When economists model production, they assume the firm uses only two inputs. Why do they make this assumption and what are the two inputs?

16. *[long run versus short run]* What is the difference between the long run and the short run? In which of these is there a fixed input? What is the fixed input? Which of these is identified with the planning horizon?

17. *[marginal product]* Is marginal product calculated for the fixed input or the variable input? Why?

18. *[marginal product]* State the definition of marginal product. How does this definition differ from the definition of average product? To which of these does the law of diminishing returns refer?

19. *[diminishing returns]* Suppose you are presented with the three sequences of total product numbers as follows:
    a. 20, 15, 5, 12, 15
    b. 20, 15, 12, 5, 1
    c. 1, 5, 12, 15, 17
    Which illustrates diminishing returns? Why?

20. *[average and marginal product curves]* Graph a typical average product curve and marginal product curve.

Be sure to label the axes of your graph. In the context of marginal product, why does an average product curve rise? In the context of marginal product, why does an average product curve eventually fall? Your graph should show the marginal product and average product curves intersecting at one point. Where is that point?

 Visit www.prenhall.com/collinge for Exploring the Web exercises and additional self-test quizzes.

CHAPTER 6

THE PRICE TAKER

A LOOK AHEAD

Imagine your work and your lifestyle are so intertwined that you cannot separate them no matter how hard you try. You are on the job twenty-four hours a day, seven days a week, working at your own business. Surely this business would pay you well for your dedication. But no, in spite of your best efforts and numerous hardships, you are quite likely to incur losses. Should you quit? This is the dilemma faced by numerous farmers and their families, a dilemma that you will examine in the Explore & Apply section that concludes this chapter.

This chapter is about much more than farming, although farming exemplifies most aspects of running a business. To maximize profit, both farmers and any other business manager must think in terms of costs and revenues. We open the chapter with a detailed look at short-run costs, and then proceed to the principles of profit maximization. We go on to discuss the model of pure competition, one of four market models.

LEARNING OBJECTIVES

Understanding Chapter 6 will enable you to:
1. **Describe the firm's short-run costs.**
2. **Discuss profit maximization within the context of profit, loss, and shut down.**
3. **Name four market types and describe the characteristics of pure competition.**
4. **Illustrate how market demand and supply determine the competitive firm's demand curve.**
5. **Identify the competitive firm's short-run supply curve and its long-run equilibrium.**
6. **Describe the factors that motivate U.S. farm policy.**

EXPLORE
&
APPLY

Firms must know their costs of production in order to produce the profit-maximizing quantity of output. As we study cost and profit maximization, the costs you will see will be the economic costs you studied in the previous chapter. As you learned, economic costs include both explicit costs and implicit opportunity costs.

6.1 SHORT-RUN COSTS

To maximize profit, each firm must select its quantity of output. That decision involves considering both costs and revenues. To understand how much output a firm will produce, we first look at short-run costs.

FIXED AND VARIABLE COSTS

fixed cost a cost that does not vary with changes in output.

Fixed inputs are those resources used by a firm that remain constant in amount in the short run. In contrast, the amount of *variable inputs* can change. Firms that produce output incur both fixed and variable costs in the short run, with a **fixed cost** being the expense associated with the use of the firm's fixed inputs. Examples of fixed costs include property taxes, property insurance, rental and lease payments, and executive salaries. These fixed costs exist because the firm uses inputs of real estate, other real property (possibly including office equipment and factory machinery), and executive labor, all of which cannot be increased or decreased in quantity in the short run.

Total fixed cost, the sum of all fixed expenses, remains constant in the short run regardless of the quantity of production. For example, a firm that pays annual expenses of $10,000 in property taxes, $5,000 in property insurance, $15,000 in rent and lease payments, and $175,000 in executive salaries will incur a total fixed cost of $205,000 (= $10,000 + $5,000 + $15,000 + $175,000). Neither increases nor decreases in the firm's quantity of output will change the $205,000 since this expense is unrelated to the firm's quantity of production.

variable cost a cost that varies in the same direction as output.

Variable cost increases as the quantity of output rises and declines as output falls, because a firm's use of variable inputs varies directly with production. Raw materials costs, the wages of hourly labor, and shipping expenses are examples of variable costs. For example, when Dell computes the variable cost of producing a desktop computer, suppose the processor and other components amount to $500, the labor to assemble the computer an additional $100, and the cost of shipping the computer to a buyer another $75. The variable cost of the computer is then the sum of these costs, which equals $675. The more computers Dell sells, the greater the total variable cost. The total variable cost of 100 computers would equal $67,500 (= $675 × 100), but the total variable cost of 1,000 computers would increase to $675,000 (= $675 × 1,000).

Total cost includes *total fixed cost* and *total variable cost,* as follows:

$$\text{Total cost} = \text{Total fixed cost} + \text{Total variable cost}$$

Total cost, like total variable cost, will vary directly with output in the short run. To simplify, we will assume from this point onward that labor is the only variable input and capital the only fixed input. Thus, variable costs are exclusively related to the use of labor (workers) and fixed costs are exclusively related to the use of capital (machines). The principles we will arrive at apply in the more complicated "real world" in which there are many variable and fixed inputs.

RELATING TOTAL PRODUCT TO TOTAL COST

In the short run, with capital fixed in quantity and labor variable, the firm must ask itself how much output to produce and thus how much labor to employ. The answer will depend

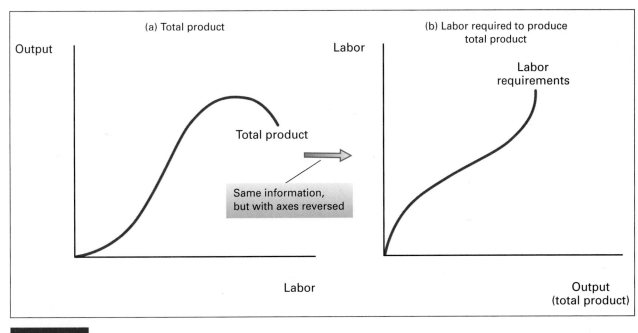

(a) Total product

Output

Total product

Same information,
but with axes reversed

Labor

(b) Labor required to produce
total product

Labor

Labor
requirements

Output
(total product)

FIGURE 6-1

LABOR REQUIREMENTS CURVE Total labor requirements for each level of output are revealed by looking at the total product curve from a different perspective. The same information is contained in both the total product curve shown in (a) and the labor requirements curve shown in (b). The declining portion of total product is not relevant to labor requirements, because the firm will not hire workers who reduce total output.

in part on costs, with costs in turn depending on both the quantity of labor and the *wage rate*, which is the price per unit of that labor.

To make the decision as to how much labor to employ, the first step is to construct a *labor requirements curve*, which shows the amount of labor needed to produce any given quantity of output. The labor requirements curve is nothing more than the total product curve you studied in the previous chapter with the axes interchanged, as shown in Figure 6-1, minus the portion for which marginal product would be negative. Otherwise, the relationship between labor and output in these two graphs is identical.

A firm's total variable cost of output will equal the labor requirement for that output multiplied by the wage rate:

$$\text{Total variable cost} = \text{Wage rate} \times \text{Labor}$$

This equation shows that total variable cost equals the cost of labor employed because we assume that labor is the only variable input. Likewise, with capital as the only fixed input, we have:

$$\text{Total fixed cost} = \text{Per unit cost of capital} \times \text{Amount of capital employed}$$

As seen in Figure 6-2, the shape of total variable cost is identical to that of the labor requirements curve in the prior figure. The only difference is that the vertical axis is now denominated in dollars, rather than units of labor.

Figure 6-2 also shows total cost and total fixed cost. Total fixed cost is constant at all outputs. Thus, the total fixed cost curve is flat, with a slope equal to zero. When total fixed cost and total variable cost are added to obtain total cost, the total cost curve appears with the same shape as the total variable cost curve. This means that the slopes

FIGURE 6-2

TOTAL COST AND ITS COMPONENTS Total variable cost equals the wage rate × labor requirements, and so has the same shape as the labor requirements curve. So does total cost, which is the sum of total variable cost and total fixed cost. Since fixed costs do not change with output, total fixed cost appears as a flat line. Marginal cost is the slope of the total cost curve or, equivalently, the slope of the total variable cost curve. Marginal cost is minimized where this slope is least, as shown.

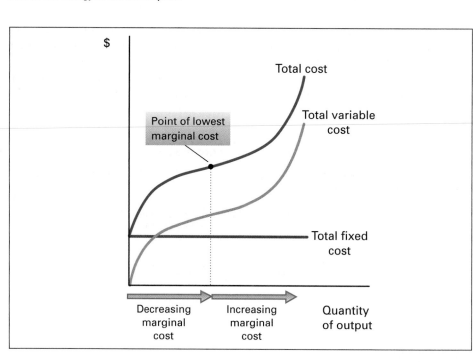

of both total cost and total variable cost are identical. The total variable cost curve starts at the origin, while the total cost curve starts at the point where the total fixed cost curve intersects the vertical axis.

MARGINAL COST AND AVERAGE COST

marginal cost the change in total cost that occurs when there is a one-unit change in output.

Marginal cost is the added cost of an additional unit of output, computed by taking the change in total cost and dividing it by the change in the quantity of output. Marginal cost is also called *incremental cost* because it measures the additions to total cost of one-unit increments in output. To take a simple example, if a bakery's total cost of producing 100 cinnamon rolls is $100 and the total cost of producing 101 cinnamon rolls is $101, then the marginal cost of the additional roll is $1. To continue the example, suppose that pushing the production of cinnamon rolls from 101 rolls to 201 rolls pushes total cost up from $101 to $251. In this case output has increased by 100 units. Since total cost has increased by $150, each additional unit of output costs $1.50 (= $150 ÷ 100). Thus, the marginal cost equals $1.50 in the range of output between 101 and 201 rolls.

Marginal cost is also equal to the slope of the total cost curve, as shown in Figure 6-2. This interpretation of marginal cost requires you to recall that a slope is the "rise over the run." In other words, the slope of a curve is the change in the variable on the vertical axis divided by the change in the variable on the horizontal axis. Since a graph of total cost measures total cost on the vertical axis and the quantity of output on the horizontal axis, the change in total cost divided by the change in quantity is the slope of the total cost curve. It is also the definition of marginal cost, which you can confirm by taking another look at the definition of marginal cost in the first sentence in this section.

Each of the following is a different way to express marginal cost:

- Change in total cost ÷ Change in quantity of output
- Change in total variable cost ÷ Change in quantity of output
- Slope of total cost
- Slope of total variable cost

The change in total cost is identical to the change in total variable cost because the only other component of total cost is total fixed cost, and that does not vary with output. For the same reason, the slope of total cost and the slope of total variable cost are equal.

In addition to presenting costs in total or at the margin, costs are often stated per unit, meaning on average. Specifically, **average cost** equals total cost divided by the quantity of output:

$$\text{Average cost} = \frac{\text{Total cost}}{\text{Quantity of output}}$$

average cost per-unit cost; total cost divided by the quantity of output; also called average total cost.

Average cost is also called *average total cost* because it is the total of both the fixed and variable components of average costs:

$$\text{Average cost} = \text{Average fixed cost} + \text{Average variable cost}$$

where

$$\text{Average fixed cost} = \frac{\text{Total fixed cost}}{\text{Quantity of output}}$$

and

$$\textbf{Average variable cost} = \frac{\text{Total variable cost}}{\text{Quantity of output}}$$

average variable cost variable cost per unit; total variable cost divided by the quantity of output.

Figure 6-3 shows typical marginal cost, average cost, and average variable cost curves. Marginal cost first falls, and then rises, as labeled in Figure 6-3. **Marginal cost intersects both average cost and average variable cost at their respective minimum points.** The difference between the average variable cost and the average cost curves is average fixed cost.

Average cost, like average variable cost, decreases before reaching a minimum and then increases. Notice that average variable cost begins to increase before average cost. Average cost includes the effect of average fixed cost, which is constantly declining as output increases. Ultimately, the downward pull of average fixed cost is offset enough by the upward pull of average variable cost so that average cost begins to increase.

FIGURE 6-3

MARGINAL AND AVERAGE COSTS
Typical shapes of marginal cost, average cost, and average variable cost are as shown. Average fixed cost is the difference between average cost and average variable cost at each quantity. Marginal cost intersects the minimum points of both the average variable cost and average cost curves.

COMPUTING COSTS

Observe the cost calculations performed by Wendy Webster, owner of WW Wholesale Flour, and presented in the table in Figure 6-4. The first column of the table shows various quantities of output, stopping at seven tons of flour. In the second column, Wendy has calculated her firm's total fixed cost and found that it equals $200. The third column shows her computation of total variable cost. When output equals zero, total variable cost also equals zero. As output increases, so does total variable cost. In the fourth column total fixed cost and total variable cost have been added to obtain total cost. Notice that when output equals

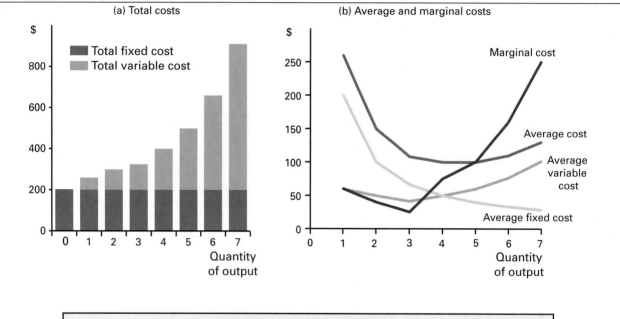

Short-run Costs for WW Wholesale Flour							
(a) Quantity of output	(b) Total fixed cost	(c) Total variable cost	(d) Total cost= (b) + (c)	(e) Marginal cost= change in (d) ÷ change in (a)	(f) Average fixed cost= (b) ÷ (a)	(g) Average variable cost= (c) ÷ (a)	(h) Average cost= (d) ÷ (a)
0	$200	$0	$200	undefined	undefined	undefined	undefined
1	$200	$60	$260	$60	$200	$60	$260
2	$200	$100	$300	$40	$100	$50	$150
3	$200	$125	$325	$25	$66.67	$41.67	$108.33
4	$200	$200	$400	$75	$50	$50	$100
5	$200	$300	$500	$100	$40	$60	$100
6	$200	$460	$660	$160	$33.33	$76.67	$110
7	$200	$710	$910	$250	$28.57	$101.43	$130

FIGURE 6-4

SHORT-RUN COSTS FOR WW WHOLESALE FLOUR The table shows the components of cost for this sample firm. Part (a) shows how total cost is divided into total fixed cost and total variable cost. Note that, at a quantity of 0, total fixed cost is the only component of total cost. Part (b) shows how the data from the table translates into marginal and average cost curves.

zero, total cost equals $200, which is the amount of total fixed cost. Total cost and total fixed cost are always the same when quantity equals zero because total variable cost equals zero at that quantity. Like total variable cost, total cost increases as output increases. Part (a) of Figure 6-4 is a graph that shows the three total cost concepts in the form of a bar chart. Observe that the total fixed cost in each bar is the same height, indicating that total fixed cost does not change.

Column (e) in the table in Figure 6-4 shows the computation of marginal cost. Note that marginal cost initially decreases as output increases. Marginal cost reaches a minimum of $25 before starting to increase. The last three columns in the Figure 6-4 table show the three kinds of average cost. The first is average fixed cost, which will decrease as quantity increases. The decrease in average fixed cost occurs because the constant amount of total fixed cost is divided by larger quantities of output. In contrast, average variable cost first decreases, reaches a minimum, then increases. Average cost also initially decreases before it reaches a minimum, and then increases. Part (b) of Figure 6-4 is a graph that shows the marginal and average cost data in the table plotted as cost curves.

6.2 MEETING THE GOAL OF MAXIMUM PROFIT

Firms produce to earn profit, which is equal to total revenue minus total cost. What quantity of production will maximize profit? The answer lies in comparing costs and revenues.

PROFIT MAXIMIZATION—MAKING DECISIONS AT THE MARGIN

Many firms have no choice but to sell their output for the going market price. For example, if you were to plant a field of soybeans, you would know that the marketplace determines the price. You could charge more than the market price, but you would not sell any soybeans. You could charge less than the market price, but there would be no reason to forgo the extra revenue. In other words, the price you receive would be at the mercy of the marketplace and you would be called a **price taker.**

For price takers, every additional unit of output adds an amount of revenue equal to the market price of the output. This additional income is termed **marginal revenue.**

$$\text{Marginal revenue} = \frac{\text{Change in total revenue}}{\text{Change in quantity of output}}$$

and for price-taking firms:

$$\text{Marginal revenue} = \text{Market price}$$

If an increase in output comes with higher marginal revenue than marginal cost, the firm should produce more. If marginal cost exceeds marginal revenue, the firm should produce less. The only time it should be satisfied is when the two are equal. If no equality is possible, the rule is to keep producing more as long as marginal cost does not exceed marginal revenue. This leads to the rule of profit maximization, as follows:

> ### Rule of profit maximization
> Produce to the point at which marginal revenue equals marginal cost.

The rule of profit maximization reveals the most preferred output at any firm, whether a price taker or not and along whatever dimension output might take. For example, it determines what items are on the menu at Ali's King-of-Ribs Restaurant. Remember Ali from the

price taker a firm that must sell its output at the market price.

marginal revenue the change in total revenue that occurs when there is a one-unit change in output.

rule of profit maximization produce to the point where marginal revenue equals marginal cost.

last chapter? Ali will do anything he can think of for which marginal revenue exceeds marginal cost, and cease doing anything for which marginal cost exceeds marginal revenue. If Ali thinks that offering diners barbecued chicken will add more to total revenue than it adds to total cost, he will offer it. He will adjust the thermostat until his expected marginal cost equals marginal revenue in terms of the temperature of his restaurant. Ali will even provide heated, moist after-dinner napkins if he thinks that the marginal revenue from doing so would exceed the marginal cost. When he is finished, Ali will find that, to a close approximation, marginal revenue will equal marginal cost along all dimensions of his output.

As noted at the start of this section, marginal revenue to a price-taking firm equals the market price. Because price and marginal revenue are equal for a price taker, we can restate the rule of profit maximization accordingly:

> **Rule of profit maximization for a price taker**
> Produce to the point where price equals marginal cost.

The general case of profit maximization by a price taker is illustrated in Figure 6-5. Marginal revenue is shown in the figure by the horizontal line that also portrays the market price. Equating the market price to marginal cost leads to a profit-maximizing quantity, as indicated in the figure. If average cost at this quantity is less than average revenue, given by the market price, the firm will be earning a profit. If average cost at the profit-maximizing output exceeds price, the firm will incur a loss. Because Figure 6-5 shows that price exceeds average cost at the profit-maximizing output, this firm is earning a profit. In the next section we will compare the profitable firm to a firm incurring a loss.

QUICKCHECK

Would a firm change its output if its marginal revenue exceeds marginal cost? Explain.

Answer: The firm would produce additional output until it gets to the quantity for which marginal revenue equals marginal cost. Until it reaches that quantity, additional output would add more to revenue than to cost and would thus increase profit.

FIGURE 6-5

PROFIT MAXIMIZATION The profit-maximizing output occurs when marginal cost equals marginal revenue. For a price-taking firm, marginal revenue is identical to the market price. This firm is profitable, because price exceeds average cost at the profit-maximizing output.

"Crime doesn't pay!" Law enforcement officials everywhere seek to drill that message into the heads of potential criminals. Yes, criminals do think about such things. For example, like businesses in search of profit, thieves plan to keep on stealing only so long as their expected marginal revenue exceeds their expected marginal cost. If punishment becomes more certain or more severe, the expected marginal cost of burglary rises and fewer burglaries are likely to occur.

The difference between legitimate business and thievery is quite simply that businesses do not rob you (some popular complaints notwithstanding). Businesses can only get your money if you offer it voluntarily in exchange for something of value to you. Thieves ignore that nicely. ◄

PROFIT, LOSS, AND SHUT DOWN

When a firm sells all of its output at a single price, that price is the firm's revenue per unit of that output, otherwise known as *average revenue.*

$$\text{Average revenue} = \frac{\text{Total revenue}}{\text{Quantity of output}} = \text{Price}$$

Multiplying average revenue by the quantity of output equals total revenue. By the same token, multiplying average cost by the quantity of output would yield total cost. Thus, a firm's total profit can be expressed as:

$$\text{Profit} = \text{Quantity of output} \times (\text{Average revenue} - \text{Average cost})$$

or, equivalently,

$$\text{Profit} = \text{Quantity} \times (\text{Price} - \text{Average cost})$$

Figure 6-6(a) illustrates a profitable firm. It produces the profit-maximizing output, given by the intersection of marginal cost and marginal revenue (price). The vertical difference between price and average cost at the quantity of output the firm produces is the *average profit* per unit of output. When average profit is multiplied by the quantity produced, the result equals total profit, as shown by the area of the shaded rectangle. This computation applies the length times width formula for the area of a rectangle.

Figure 6-6(b) shows a market price that just equals the firm's minimum point on average cost, which would imply that total revenue and total cost would be equal at that point. Such a situation is called *breakeven* and results in zero economic profits. Because total revenue is enough to pay implicit costs, the firm earns a *normal profit.*

If the price were to fall below the breakeven level, the firm would incur losses. **A firm will experience a loss when the price falls below the minimum value of average cost. When a firm operates at a loss, it will seek to minimize the loss.** The *rule of loss minimization* is the same as the rule of profit maximization:

> ### Rule of loss minimization
> Produce to the point where marginal revenue equals marginal cost.

Figure 6-7 depicts the same firm as in Figure 6-6. The only difference is that the firm is now facing a loss because of a drop in the market price below the price shown in Figure 6-6(b). While the firm still produces the quantity for which marginal cost equals marginal revenue, that quantity is now smaller than it was when the market price was higher. The firm has minimized its loss, the area of the shaded rectangle in Figure 6-7. This area is

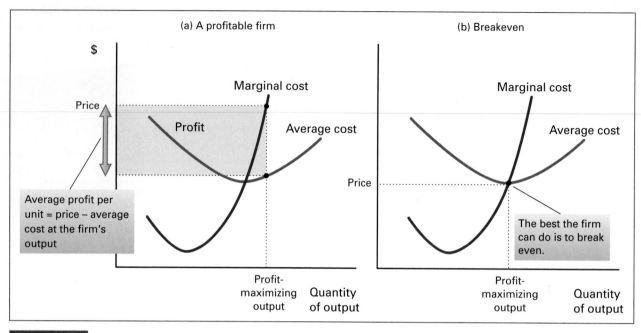

FIGURE 6-6

PROFIT This firm maximizes profit by choosing the quantity of output for which marginal cost equals price, which is also its marginal revenue. At that chosen quantity, the firm subtracts its average cost from price to obtain its average profit per unit. Total profit is computed by multiplying the per-unit profit by quantity, and is shown by the shaded rectangle labeled "Profit" in (a). In (b), the best the firm can do is breakeven, at which price just equals the minimum point on average cost and economic profit is zero.

FIGURE 6-7

A FIRM WITH A LOSS This firm minimizes its loss by producing to where marginal cost equals marginal revenue. If price dropped below the minimum point on average variable cost, it would follow the shut-down rule and cease production, losing its total fixed cost.

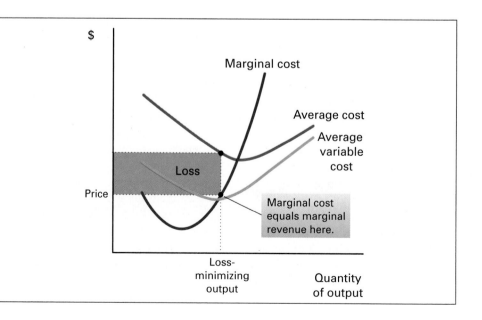

computed similarly to the area of the shaded rectangle in Figure 6-6 except that the market price is shown as less than average cost in Figure 6-7.

$$\text{Loss} = \text{Quantity} \times (\text{Price} - \text{Average cost})$$

A profit-maximizing firm will never lose more than the amount of its total fixed cost. Whether the firm is profitable or operates at a loss, it will determine its quantity of output by equating marginal revenue to marginal cost. However, **when price drops so low that revenues are insufficient to pay variable costs, the firm can avoid those costs by ceasing production altogether.** If the firm ceases producing output but retains the capital that would allow it to resume production later, the firm is said to be **shut down.** Since fixed costs must be paid even if the firm produces nothing, **shutdown results in a loss that is equal to the firm's fixed cost.** The *shutdown rule* is as follows:

shut down when a firm produces no output in order to minimize its loss, which equals total fixed cost; occurs in the short run.

> ### Shutdown rule
> Shut down if total revenue is less than total variable cost.

By dividing both total revenue and total variable cost by the quantity of output, the shutdown rule can equivalently be stated in terms of average revenue and average variable cost. For a firm that charges a single price, this shutdown rule thus becomes:

> ### Shutdown rule in terms of price
> Shut down if price is less than average variable cost.

When price falls that low, shutting down minimizes the loss, which is limited to fixed cost, which still must be paid.

The shutdown rule identifies the only exception to the rule of equating marginal cost to marginal revenue. **Shutdown occurs in the short run.** If a firm foresees continuing losses over the long run, it will **exit** the industry, meaning that it will go out of business or change its line of business. This action is the opposite to the **entry** of new firms, which would occur if the industry appears profitable. **Entry and exit occur in the long run.**

exit when a firm goes out of business or changes its line of business; occurs in the long run.

Table 6-1 summarizes the revenue and cost conditions that lead a profit-maximizing firm to make the output decisions it does. The revenue and cost comparisons in the table are

entry when a firm first opens for business; occurs in the long run.

QUICKCHECK

Suppose a price-taking firm produces 10 units of output. The market price of its output equals $100 per unit. At 10 units of output, average cost equals $105 and average variable cost equals $101. How much profit (or loss) does this firm make? Is the firm maximizing profit (or minimizing loss)?

Answer: Total revenue equals price (average revenue) multiplied by quantity, which is $1,000 in this case. Total cost equals average cost multiplied by quantity, which is $1,050. The firm loses $50. This firm is NOT minimizing its loss, because price is less than average variable cost. By shutting down, the firm would lose the amount of total fixed cost, which is $40. Total fixed cost is computed by first taking the difference between average cost and average variable cost in order to obtain average fixed cost. This computation shows average fixed cost equals $4 ($105 − $101 = $4). When average fixed cost is multiplied by quantity, total fixed cost is obtained ($4 × 10 = $40). This firm should shut down to minimize its loss.

TABLE 6-1   FOUR OUTCOMES OF SHORT-RUN PROFIT MAXIMIZATION

COMPARISON OF REVENUE AND COST	SET MARGINAL REVENUE = MARGINAL COST AND PRODUCE?	OUTCOME
Price > Average cost or Total revenue > Total cost	Yes	Profit, maximized
Price < Average cost, and Price > Average variable cost or Total revenue < Total cost, and Total revenue > Total variable cost	Yes	Loss, minimized
Price = Average cost or Total revenue = Total cost	Yes	Breakeven (normal profit)
Price < Average variable cost or Total revenue < Total variable cost	No, shutdown	Loss, minimized (equal to total fixed cost)

first stated in terms of price and the relevant average cost. By multiplying both the price and the cost by the quantity of output, each comparison is restated in terms of total revenue and the relevant total cost.

6.3 TYPES OF MARKETS

It is clear that there are different types of markets. These different markets are commonly called *industries*. Think about how the municipal water, grocery, and shampoo industries differ. When we buy water we typically face just one seller. When we shop for groceries, there might be several supermarkets in our neighborhood to pick from. Once inside the supermarket, there may be dozens of shampoos from which to choose. Thus, each of these markets is different from the others in terms of the number of sellers.

Markets also differ according to whether the product is homogeneous or differentiated. **Homogeneous products** are identical no matter which firm produces them, and are often called *commodities*. For example, the #2 grade yellow corn produced by farmers is homogeneous. Additional examples include cattle, gold, coal, copper, steel, aluminum, and lumber.

In contrast, **differentiated products** will vary from one producer to the next. One grocery store differs from another, for example, just as the products within also differ from brand to brand. Computers are another example of a differentiated product, varying by brand name and features. These differences lead to four basic **market structures,** which are models of the way markets work. They are:

- **Monopoly**—a market with only one seller of a good without close substitutes. For example, a municipal sewage treatment service or water supply is a monopoly. A monopoly firm maintains a significant amount of control over the price of its product, as will be discussed further in the next chapter.
- **Oligopoly**—a market with more than one seller, where at least one of those sellers can significantly influence price. Oligopoly is usually characterized by just a few significant sellers of a product that can be either homogeneous or differentiated. Passenger airlines and crude oil are both provided in oligopoly markets.

homogeneous products products that are identical, no matter which firms in the industry produce the commodities.

differentiated products products that vary from one producer to another within the same industry.

market structures models of the way markets work.

monopoly a market with only one seller of a good without close substitutes.

oligopoly a market with more than one seller, where at least one seller can significantly influence price.

- **Monopolistic competition**—a market with numerous firms selling a differentiated product and with only a slight ability to control price. Retailers such as dry cleaners, music stores, and restaurants are examples. Both oligopoly and monopolistic competition are discussed after the chapter on monopoly.
- **Pure competition**—a market in which there are many buyers and sellers of a homogeneous product. Farmers are an example. The model of pure competition underlies the supply and demand analysis in Chapters 3 and 4.

monopolistic competition a market with many firms, each with slight market power.

pure competition a market in which there are numerous firms, all of which are price takers. The product is homogeneous and there are no barriers to entry.

Figure 6-8(a) shows a grid of market structures according to the number of firms and differentiation of the product among them. Figure 6-8(b) shows the four market structures arranged according to the amount of **market power**—influence over price by the individual firm. Purely competitive firms have no market power. Monopolistically competitive firms have slight market power. Oligopolistic firms may exhibit a significant degree of market power, while monopoly firms usually have more market power than any other type of firm. Market power arises from *barriers to entry*, which are obstacles to joining an industry, and which include anything that makes producing and selling output more difficult for a new firm than for an existing firm. The next chapter looks more closely at these topics. In pure competition, market power does not exist.

market power when individual firms have at least a bit of control over the prices of their outputs; arises from barriers to entry.

Chapters 3 and 4 introduced supply and demand analysis. Implicitly, that analysis used the model of pure competition. As shown in Chapter 4, **the competitive market equilibrium produces an allocatively efficient amount of output. Competition also forces firms to keep costs in check, thus inducing technological efficiency as well.** For these reasons, the model of pure competition is often used as the standard of efficiency by which other market structures are judged.

ANTIQUARIAN BOOKS IN A DOTCOM WORLD

SNAPSHOT

The Internet has brought buyers and sellers together like never before. Consider the purchase of hard-to-find old books. Well, maybe not so hard to find . . . not any more! Where once the local shopkeeper would do the searching and set the price, now book collectors themselves search the World Wide Web. Booksellers have a huge new market. They also have huge new competition. It is this competition, and not individual sellers, that sets the prices today.

Yes, there are many Mark Twain first editions, and you can find their prices with ease. Those priced too high will not sell. Those priced too low will be sold quickly. The result is that there will tend to be a single market price for any book. Booksellers in the modern world have little ability to control price in what has become a single global market. For as technology changes, so too does market structure! ◀

6.4 PURE COMPETITION

Now that we have a brief overview of the four types of market structure, let's focus on pure competition, which is characterized by the following:

- **Numerous buyers and sellers.** As a result, **each firm and consumer is a price taker,** with firms selling their output at the market price and consumers paying that same market price.
- **A homogeneous product.** The market prices of these items are widely available in newspapers and other media reports. Because products are identical, individual firms reap no benefits from advertising: **firms do not advertise in pure competition.**

	Homogeneous product	Differentiated product
One firm	Monopoly (example: city drinking water)	Not applicable
Few firms	Oligopoly (example: gasoline refineries)	Oligopoly (example: automakers)
Many firms	Pure competition (example: farmers)	Monopolistic competition (example: restaurants)

(a) Market structure by product and number of firms

(b) Market structure arranged according to market power

Increasing market power and barriers to entry

0 →

Pure competition   Monopolistic competition   Oligopoly   Monopoly

FIGURE 6-8

MARKET STRUCTURES Market structures differ depending upon how many firms are in the industry and whether their products are homogeneous or differentiated, as shown in (a). Market structure is associated with market power and its associated barriers to entry. As shown in (b), firms in pure competition have no market power. They have some market power in monopolistic competition, more in oligopoly, and the most in monopoly.

■ **Costless entry and exit of firms.** In the long run, it is easy for firms to start up, called entering an industry, or to leave an industry, which is called exit. Firms might leave an industry by going out of business or by shifting the use of their resources to another industry. For example, Farmer Brown might plant barley instead of corn.

The central implication of pure competition is that firms are price takers. Each firm must decide how much to produce based upon the market price, over which it has no control. Market price is set by the intersection of supply and demand in the marketplace.

THE FIRM'S DEMAND

Figure 6-9 shows how the equilibrium market price becomes the firm's demand curve. **Although market demand slopes downward to the right, as shown in part (a) the demand facing each firm is horizontal (perfectly elastic) at the market price** as shown in part (b). The horizontal demand means that the firm is able to sell as much as it wishes at the market price. It has no reason to sell for less than the market price because its horizontal demand curve means that it can sell as much as it wishes at that price. Also, it cannot sell anything if it charges more than the market price. Thus, **a price taker always sells at the market price.**

The individual firm chooses the quantity of output it produces based upon its demand and its supply. To maximize profit, recall that the firm produces at the point where marginal

QUICKCHECK

If you owned a gold coin of known weight and purity, but without collector value, how would you learn what price to ask for if you were selling it?

Answer: You would be a price taker who would sell at the going market price for gold. This price changes often as supply and demand shift. The price at any given moment is determined by supply and demand in the commodity exchanges, such as the Chicago Mercantile Exchange, and can be accessed through various online quote services.

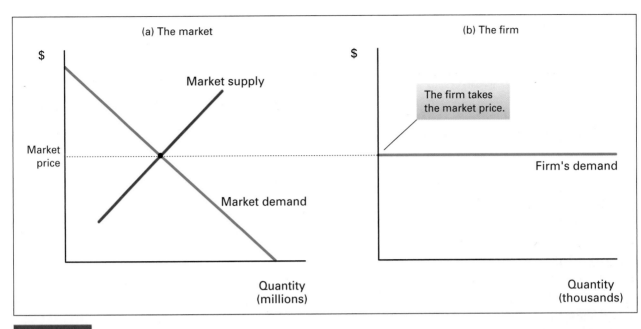

FIGURE 6-9

DEMAND IN PURE COMPETITION The intersection of market demand and market supply sets market price, as shown in part (a). The firm in pure competition faces a demand that is horizontal at the market price, because each firm is a price taker, as shown in part (b). Anything that changes that market equilibrium would lead to a change in price and a corresponding shift up or down in the firm's demand.

revenue equals marginal cost. Recall also that market price equals the price-taking firm's marginal revenue. Here you have seen that the market price equals the firm's demand curve, too. That makes the firm's demand curve its marginal revenue curve. In the next section we show you that the firm's marginal cost curve is also its short-run supply curve. Thus, the rule of profit maximization, which is to produce at the point where marginal revenue equals marginal cost, is equivalent to producing at the point where the firm's demand and supply curves intersect.

SHORT-RUN SUPPLY

At any price above the shutdown price, the profit-maximizing price-taking firm equates marginal revenue and marginal cost. Because the price-taking firm's marginal revenue equals the market price, the firm produces the quantity associated with its marginal cost curve at that price. For this reason, the *firm's short-run supply curve* **is that part of its marginal cost curve that lies above average variable cost.** This supply curve shows the quantity that the firm will offer for sale at each of various possible prices.

Consider the supply curve for WW Wholesale Flour, a purely competitive price-taking firm, is seen in Figure 6-10(a). At a market price of $160, the marginal revenue curve, which is also the firm's demand curve, intersects the firm's supply curve at 6 tons of output. If the market price rises, WW sells more. In the graph, a price of $250 indicates the firm's demand curve intersects its supply curve at 7 tons of output. That quantity makes marginal revenue (equal to price and to the firm's demand) equal to marginal cost (the firm's supply curve). Also shown in the graph is a typical average variable cost curve, which reaches its minimum where intersected by marginal cost. If the market price falls below the minimum point of its average variable cost curve, WW Wholesale Flour will shut down and offer no flour for sale. This shutdown price is shown in Figure 6-10.

FIGURE 6-10

SUPPLY IN PURE COMPETITION The firm's supply is part of the market supply. The firm's supply is that portion of its marginal cost curve that exceeds average variable cost. Market supply adds together the quantities supplied by all firms at each of the various possible prices. For example, if all firms were identical to the firm shown in (a) and if the market had 1,000 firms, the result would be the market supply shown in (b).

Market supply sums the quantities offered by each firm at each price. For example, if there were 999 price takers in addition to WW in the wholesale flour market, each producing 6 tons of flour, the total quantity supplied to the market would equal 6,000 tons (6 tons multiplied by 1,000 firms). Similarly, at a price of $250, the quantity supplied to the market would equal 7,000 tons if the firms were all identical to one another. The market supply curve is shown in Figure 6-10(b).

ENTRY AND EXIT

In the short run, the market price could be sufficiently high that the firm earns profits, or it could be so low that the firm loses money. However, the **long-run equilibrium market price results in the expectation of zero profit for a firm that is considering entry into the industry.** Recall that zero profit, as economists use the term, means that the firm is earning a normal profit measured in accounting terms (normal profit is the accounting profit necessary to keep the firm in business).

Figure 6-11 illustrates long-run equilibrium. The market supply curve in (a) will shift until the market price is just sufficient to cover average cost, shown in (b). When price equals average cost, firms will earn a normal profit and no more shifting will occur. This outcome is indicated graphically in the figure by the firm's demand curve being tangent to its average cost curve at the minimum point of average cost.

The free entry and exit that characterize pure competition explains why long-run equilibrium occurs. Figure 6-12 illustrates how entry and exit affect market supply. The story behind entry and the achievement of long-run equilibrium is quite simple. The expectation of short-run profit attracts new entrants. Their output shifts the market supply to the right. Entry would continue to occur, increasing market supply and driving market price down, until the expected profit falls to zero.

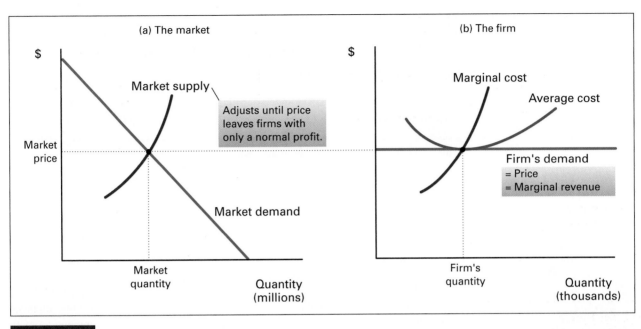

FIGURE 6-11

LONG-RUN EQUILIBRIUM IN PURE COMPETITION The long-run equilibrium in pure competition occurs when the last firm to enter the market earns zero profits, as shown by the firm's average cost curve just tangent to its demand. There would be no reason for a new firm to enter and no reason for an existing firm to exit.

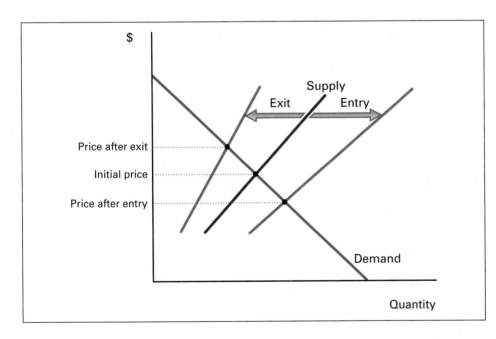

FIGURE 6-12

ENTRY AND EXIT The lure of profit attracts new entrants, which lowers the price until entry stops. Alternatively, losses cause firms to exit the industry, which raises the price until exit stops. This process stops when price achieves its long-run equilibrium, as shown in Figure 6-11.

Likewise, the anticipation of long-run losses would prompt the exit of firms. Exit shifts the market supply curve to the left. The decrease in market supply would continue until the price rises to the level of zero expected profit for firms contemplating entry or exit. Even so, some existing firms will remain profitable in the long run, such as farms with exceptionally fertile and tillable soil.

QUICKCHECK

When will entry occur? What effect will entry have on market supply and price? Once entry is started, when will it stop?

Answer: Entry occurs only when new firms, the entrants, expect to earn a profit. By entering, market supply increases, shown graphically as a shift to the right. The increase in supply causes the market price to drop. Once the market price drops to the point where it equals an entrant's average cost of production, entry will stop.

SNAPSHOT   **OLD MCDONALD FARMS AGAIN!**

Old McDonald had a farm, but losses drove him out of business. Exit was painful and distressing. Still, it was also easy, given the well-developed markets for land and farm equipment. Now he wants to give it a second try. Fortunately for McDonald, entry is also easy. Entry merely takes land, equipment, and skill. Although the inputs are expensive, this is not much of a barrier to entry in today's world. Farmers have access to loans or other financial aid, including funds for education. They are also able to lease land and equipment. So, with the easy entry and exit of pure competition, Old McDonald might once more start ahollerin' "Ee-yi-ee-yi-oh!" ◄

6.5 ADJUSTING TO TECHNOLOGY—FEWER FARMERS, MORE FOOD

EXPLORE & APPLY

The country, indeed much of the world, is fed by crops grown on American farms. You might think that farmers would be handsomely rewarded for keeping the rest of us from starvation, and some are. They are the survivors, though. The financial hardships of farming the land have caused the farm population to dwindle from 30 percent of the U.S. population in 1920 to less than 2 percent today.

The problem facing farmers is one of abundance and changing technology. Technology has increased the productivity of farm labor and capital, making much of both obsolete in the process. For example, it was once the faithful mule that pulled the tillers that prepared soil for planting. Today, there are tractors and many different kinds of specialized mechanical planting and harvesting equipment. The intervening time has served as the long run in economic terms, moving us through a series of short runs characterized by different ways of farming. The technological change over this time has also included the development of new crop varieties, fertilizers, and techniques of production.

In farming, all firms must sell at the same market price, despite some of them having cost advantages over others. For example, some farms spread across wide, flat expanses, while others are nestled in river valleys. The result of differences in the physical characteristics of farms is that technological change increases the profit of some farmers while harming others—farmers who cannot adapt to these changes but nevertheless experience the consequent declines in farm output prices. Farmers who are unable to sell their crops at the market price without suffering economic losses will be forced to leave their farms in the long run.

For example, farmers in the choppy hills of Tennessee are at a disadvantage to their counterparts in the Kansas plains when it comes to employing the modern technology of huge combines and other types of farm equipment. Yet, if they grow the same crop, they must sell it for the same price. As technological change takes hold and supply increases, that crop's price drops. Farmers must adopt the changes or exit the industry.

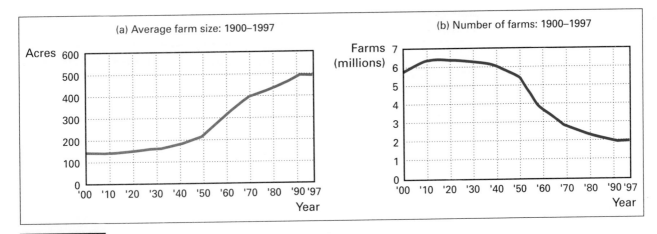

FIGURE 6-13

TRENDS IN FARMING Over time, farm sizes have been increasing and the number of farms shrinking.

Source: Trends in Agriculture, USDA, June 7, 2002.

The average number of acres per farm has been increasing, while the number of farms has been shrinking, as seen in Figure 6-13.

Table 6-2 provides additional data that can help you understand the farm problem. We see in the table the ups and downs in farm income. These fluctuations make it difficult for small farms to keep going. Also note the surge in prices paid by farmers for seed, equipment, fertilizer, and so forth, relative to the prices they receive when they sell their crops. The numbers tell us that farmers are caught in a price squeeze. We also see in the table shrinking employment opportunities in farming for most of the last century.

Even though farms disappear, farmland is usually not abandoned. Rather, it becomes part of someone else's farm. When one farmer loses money working a particular piece of acreage, why should another farmer be able to take it over and earn a profit?

An important reason is economies of scale in farming, such as those associated with the use of large-scale equipment, which causes the average cost of farm output to decrease as farms grow larger. For example, farmers waste less time maneuvering their combines when their fields are large. This means that a bushel of corn, wheat, or other commodity can be produced at a lower cost per unit on large farms. Economies of scale are identified with the downward-sloping part of the U-shaped long-run average cost curve. Economies of scale do have limits, though. Since bringing in the crop and equipment uses time and fuel, fields that extend too far can lead to diseconomies of scale, in which average costs rise.

AGRICULTURAL PRICE SUPPORTS

Government programs to help farmers have attempted to drive up prices through supply restrictions and price supports, which were discussed in Chapter 4. The price supports are maintained through *deficiency payments* that compensate farmers for the difference between the support price and any lower market price. The result has been that some farmers have become wealthy while others cannot scrape out a living.

To use agricultural price supports to keep every farmer in business would require a price of output that would provide even the highest-cost producer with at least a normal profit. Consider the three graphs in Figure 6-14. Farmer A is the low-cost producer, farmer B the medium-cost producer, and farmer C the high-cost producer. Don't forget that each cost curve includes an allowance for the farmer's implicit opportunity cost (normal profit).

Farmer C may be the high-cost producer because he or she has higher explicit costs arising from poorer quality of land or poor management skills. Farmer C might also have

TABLE 6-2   FARM INCOME, EMPLOYMENT, AND PRICES

YEAR	NET FARM INCOME (BILLIONS OF DOLLARS)	FARM EMPLOYMENT (THOUSANDS)	PRICES RECEIVED BY FARMERS	PRICES PAID BY FARMERS
1979	$27.4	3,765	94	66
1980	16.1	3,699	98	75
1981	26.9	3,582	100	82
1982	23.8	3,466	94	86
1983	14.2	3,349	98	86
1984	26.0	3,233	101	89
1985	28.6	3,116	91	86
1986	30.9	2,912	87	85
1987	37.4	2,897	89	87
1988	38.0	2,954	99	91
1989	45.3	2,863	104	96
1990	44.6	2,891	104	99
1991	38.5	2,877	100	100
1992	47.8	2,810	98	101
1993	44.7	2,800	101	104
1994	48.9	2,767	100	106
1995	36.9	2,836	102	109
1996	54.8	2,842	112	115
1997	48.5	2,867	107	118
1998	42.9	2,827	102	115

Source: 2002 Economic Report of the President, Tables B-97, B-100, and B-101. The price values in the table are index numbers, with 1990–1992 equal to 100.

excellent opportunities for earning income off the farm. In that case, farmer C's higher costs result from higher implicit opportunity costs. To keep farmer C farming, the government would have to manipulate prices so that all of farmer C's costs are covered by price. In the process, farmers A and B would grow wealthy on excess profits.

There are several objections to crop prices that keep all farmers farming. For one thing, consumers have to pay the higher prices. Since food is a necessity, high food prices hit the poor the hardest. Another problem concerns where to draw the line at government efforts to help people whose incomes are not enough to keep them in their present line of work. For example, teachers sometimes find it difficult to support a family on their earnings. Should the government eliminate free public schooling and charge students tuition like private schools do so that teachers can be paid more? In general, the incomes of any group cannot be raised without imposing costs on others.

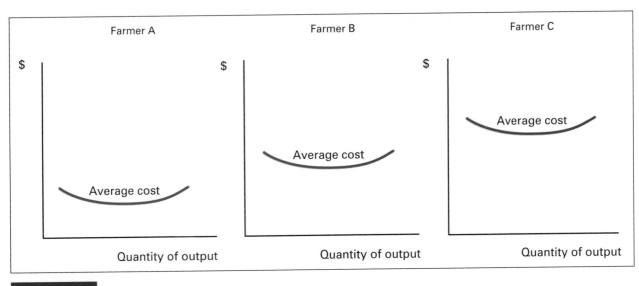

FIGURE 6-14

LOW-, MEDIUM-, AND HIGH-COST FARMS All three farmers face the same price of output, but the high-cost farmers struggle while the low-cost farmers prosper.

Over six decades of price supports failed to stop the exodus from the farm. For this, we should be grateful. If 30 percent of Americans were still to live on farms, as was true in 1920, many goods and services that we enjoy consuming would simply not be available. People would be growing food instead of, for example, assembling cars, building houses, and making movies.

In farm policy, Washington has tough choices to make. Farming has changed, but how much aid should the government provide to farmers in trying to ease the pain experienced by those who are adversely affected by that change? That question can only be answered by consideration of both economics and politics.

THINKING CRITICALLY

1. Identify some technological advances that have changed the face of farming. Were these good for farmers? Why did they adopt them? Explain.

2. Do you view the government's long-term efforts to help farmers as more of a failure or more of a success? What policies toward farming would be best? Should these policies be applied to other occupations also? Explain.

Visit **www.prenhall.com/collinge** for updates and web exercises on this Explore & Apply topic.

SUMMARY AND LEARNING OBJECTIVES

1. **Describe the firm's short-run costs.**
   - In the short run there are both fixed and variable inputs. Thus, short-run costs include fixed and variable costs. Total cost is the sum of total fixed cost and total variable cost. Total fixed cost does not change as the quantity of output changes. Total variable cost increases as output increases, as does total cost.
   - Marginal cost is the change in total cost divided by the change in the quantity of output. Since only variable costs change, marginal cost also equals the

   change in total variable cost divided by the change in the quantity of output. Marginal cost measures the increment to total cost when there is a one-unit change in the quantity of output. Marginal cost is especially important in profit maximization.
   - Three types of average cost are found by dividing the appropriate total cost by the quantity of output. Average fixed cost equals total fixed cost divided by the quantity of output. Average variable cost equals total variable cost divided by the quantity of output.

Average total cost equals total cost divided by the quantity of output.

- Marginal revenue equals the change in total revenue divided by the change in the quantity of output. For a price taker, marginal revenue equals price. Marginal revenue is also the incremental revenue from the production and sale of one more unit of output.

2. Discuss profit maximization within the context of profit, loss, and shut down.

- The rule of profit maximization is to produce output up to the point where marginal revenue equals marginal cost. For a price taker, the rule can be restated as produce to the point where price equals marginal cost.
- If price is so low that a firm cannot cover its average cost, it will incur a loss. The rule of profit maximization in this case is to minimize the loss. If the firm produces at all, it will produce the amount for which marginal revenue equals marginal cost.
- Producing according to the rule of profit maximization leads to three possible outcomes: (1) the firm earns an economic profit; (2) the firm breaks even; and (3) the firm incurs an economic loss. When the firm earns a profit, price is greater than average cost. Breakeven occurs when price equals average cost. Loss involves a price that is less than average cost.
- Graphically, profit is represented by the area of a rectangle. The area of the profit rectangle is found by the following: Profit = Quantity × (Price − Average cost). Loss is also represented graphically by the area of a rectangle. Since price will be less than average cost, the computation of loss results in a negative value.
- A firm will not produce (quantity will be set equal to zero) when the firm follows the shutdown rule. This rule says to shut down when price is less than average variable cost. An alternative statement of the rule says to shut down when total revenue is less than total variable cost. Shutting down keeps the loss from exceeding the firm's total fixed cost. Shut down should be distinguished from exit. In shutting down, the firm retains the use of its capital inputs in hopes of putting them to use again in the future.

3. Name four market types and describe the characteristics of pure competition.

- Market structures refers to types of markets. The four types of markets are: pure competition, monopolistic competition, oligopoly, and monopoly. In pure competition there is a single market price, determined by demand and supply. Firms in purely competitive industries are price takers, selling their output at the market price.

- Monopoly firms exert a significant amount of influence on the price of their output. Oligopoly firms also influence their prices. Monopolistically competitive firms have only slight influence on their prices. Firms in these three industries are not price takers, since influence over price is inconsistent with price taking.
- The characteristics of a purely competitive market are: (1) numerous buyers and sellers; (2) a homogeneous product; and (3) free entry and exit. Homogeneous goods are identical across firms in the industry. Free entry means there are no impediments to any firm that wants to produce in the industry. Free exit means there are no impediments to leaving the industry, such as in going out of business, or producing a different output.

4. Illustrate how market demand and supply determine the competitive firm's demand curve.

- Price-taking firms are found in pure competition. Price taking is exemplified by firms in the commodities industries. An individual price-taking firm has no control over its price, which is determined by demand and supply in the market.
- Market demand is downward sloping. Market demand together with market supply determine the market price of the purely competitive industry's output. Unlike market demand, the purely competitive firm's demand curve is perfectly elastic (horizontal) at the market price.

5. Identify the competitive firm's short-run supply curve and its long-run equilibrium.

- The purely competitive firm's supply curve is the segment of its marginal cost curve that lies above its average variable cost curve. When price is below average variable cost, the firm supplies zero output because it will shut down. When price is above average variable cost, the firm maximizes profit by supplying the quantity of output indicated by the intersection of price with marginal cost.
- The long run in a purely competitive market is characterized by zero profit for the firm considering entering or exiting. This outcome is indicated graphically when the firm's demand curve is tangent to the average cost curve. Because entry and exit are free of barriers in pure competition, in the long run, firms will enter or exit until there is no expectation of either a profit or loss.

6. Describe the factors that motivate U.S. farm policy.

- Technological change and economies of scale have changed farming by reducing the number of farmers. Government policy has aimed to increase the income of farmers who have had difficulty in adjusting to changed conditions. Nonetheless, the exodus from the family farm has continued.

KEY TERMS

fixed cost, 126
variable cost, 126
marginal cost, 128
average cost, 129
average variable cost, 129
price taker, 131
marginal revenue, 131

rule of profit maximization, 131
shut down, 135
exit, 135
entry, 135
homogeneous products, 136
differentiated products, 136

market structures, 136
monopoly, 136
oligopoly, 136
monopolistic competition, 137
pure competition, 137
market power, 137

TEST YOURSELF

TRUE OR FALSE

1. Total fixed cost equals zero when output equals zero.
2. Marginal cost measures the change in cost that results from a change in output.
3. To maximize profit in the short run, a firm must always minimize average costs.
4. Both purely competitive and monopolistically competitive markets are characterized by firms that are called price takers.
5. The short-run supply curve for a purely competitive firm is the portion of its marginal cost curve that lies above its average variable cost.

MULTIPLE CHOICE

6. Marginal revenue equals the _____ divided by the _____.
   a. change in total cost; change in output
   b. change in total revenue; change in output
   c. change in total revenue; price
   d. price; output
7. In Self-Test Table 6-1, the marginal cost of the fifth bag of peanuts equals
   a. $90.
   b. $30.
   c. $18.
   d. $13.

8. In Self-Test Table 6-1, the average cost of the second bag of peanuts equals
   a. $32.
   b. $16.
   c. $3.50.
   d. $2.00.
9. In Self-Test Table 6-1, total fixed cost equals
   a. $25.
   b. $10.
   c. $5.
   d. $2.
10. In Self-Test Table 6-1, if Odetta sells peanuts at the market price of $15 per unit, her profit-maximizing quantity of output is
    a. 1 bag of peanuts.
    b. 2 bags of peanuts.
    c. 3 bags of peanuts.
    d. 4 bags of peanuts.
11. A price-taking firm with a loss will
    a. always shut down.
    b. produce to where the price equals marginal cost, unless the price is below average variable cost.
    c. produce to where price equals average cost.
    d. raise its price until it reaches profitability.
12. To maximize profit, the price-taking firm shown in Self-Test Figure 6-1 will produce the quantity associated with point
    a. *A.*
    b. *B.*
    c. *C.*
    d. *D.*

SELF-TEST TABLE 6-1   ODETTA'S WHOLESALE PEANUTS (20-POUND BAGS)

Output (Quantity per Day)	Total Cost
0	$25
1	30
2	32
3	40
4	60
5	90

SELF-TEST FIGURE 6-1

SELF-TEST FIGURE 6-2

13. If it attempts to maximize profit, the firm shown in Self-Test Figure 6-1 will
    a. be profitable.
    b. show losses.
    c. have zero profit.
    d. need more information before determining if a profit potential exists.

14. Market power refers to the ability of a firm to influence its _____. Market power is _____ for price-taking firms.
    a. output; significant
    b. cost; slight
    c. owners; slight
    d. price; zero

15. In pure competition the firm's demand curve will be
    a. upward sloping.
    b. downward sloping.
    c. hump shaped.
    d. horizontal.

16. Which statement best describes the long-run equilib-.rium in a purely competitive market?
    a. The firm's demand curve is downward sloping.
    b. The market will shrink as firms exit.
    c. The number of firms will be stable because there is no incentive for entry or exit.
    d. In the long run, the market will slowly become a monopoly.

17. If Self-Test Figure 6-2 represents a typical firm in the purely competitive widget industry, the market price of widgets will
    a. increase over time.
    b. decrease over time.
    c. remain constant over time.
    d. increase at first, but return later to the original price.

18. Exit shifts
    a. supply to the left.
    b. supply to the right.
    c. average cost upward.
    d. average cost downward.

19. Pure competition is
    a. inefficient, because too much output is produced.
    b. inefficient, because too little output is produced.
    c. inefficient, because firms waste resources by competing with one another.
    d. efficient.

20. Which economic concept provides the most likely explanation for the decline in the number of farms in the United States?
    a. Limited liability.
    b. Perpetual existence.
    c. Diminishing returns.
    d. Economies of scale.

QUESTIONS AND PROBLEMS

1. *[fixed versus variable cost]* Categorize each of the following expenses incurred by Alonzo's Big Time Chocolate Factory as either a fixed cost or a variable cost:
   a. The monthly payment Alonzo makes to the local telephone company.
   b. Payments to his insurance company for automobile insurance on the company car.
   c. Payments to the local utility for electricity to operate the candy-mixing machines.
   d. Alonzo's salary as chief executive officer of the company.
   e. Payroll expenses.

2. *[marginal cost]* RM Motors has the following schedule for total cost:

Quantity	Total Cost
0	$100
1	150
2	175
3	205
4	245
5	290

   a. What is the marginal cost of a fourth vehicle? Of a fifth vehicle?
   b. How will the marginal cost behave? Why?

3. *[total product and labor requirements]* Sketch a total product curve, identifying the region of increasing returns, diminishing returns, and negative returns (review diminishing returns in the previous chapter, if necessary). Be sure to label the axes. Then draw a graph with the axes reversed from that of total product. Sketch a labor requirements curve. What does the curve show? What two cost curves have a shape similar to that of the labor requirements curve?

4. *[computing costs]* Using the data below on output and total variable cost, compute total cost, average fixed cost, average variable cost, average cost, and marginal cost for each output. Total fixed cost is $100.

Output	Total Variable Cost
0	$0
1	50
2	90
3	140
4	200
5	300
6	500

5. *[cost curves]* Draw two graphs. In the first graph, sketch a typical total fixed cost curve, a total variable cost curve, and a total cost curve. In the second graph, sketch a marginal cost curve, an average variable cost curve, and an average total cost curve. Be sure to label the axes on both graphs. Answer the following questions using your graphs.
   a. Which cost curve has a slope equal to zero?
   b. Which cost curve starts at the origin and then slopes upward?
   c. The slopes of which two cost curves are equal to marginal cost?
   d. Which cost curve starts at total fixed cost and then slopes upward?
   e. Which cost curve has a *J* shape?
   f. Which two cost curves have a *U* shape?
   g. Which cost curve intersects average total cost? At what point does that intersection take place?
   h. Which cost curve intersects average variable cost? At what point does that intersection take place?

6. *[price taker]* Explain why it would make no sense for a price taker to set a selling price that differs from the market price.

7. *[profit maximization]* A price-taking firm, Moo-town Wholesale Milk and Butterfat, is currently producing 1,000 gallons of milk and butterfat per day. The market price of this output equals $1.50 per unit. Its total fixed cost equals $200 per day, while its total variable cost is $150 per day.
   a. Is this firm earning a profit? Show the calculations that led to your answer.
   b. If it is earning a profit, is it maximizing its profit? Explain.

8. *[profit maximization]* What is the rule of profit maximization? How can this rule be restated when the firm is a price taker?

9. *[profit maximization]* Sketch a graph that shows a firm's marginal revenue, marginal cost, and average cost curves. Indicate the profit-maximizing quantity on the graph and label it Q^*. Then explain why the quantity you indicated maximizes profit. Include as part of your explanation why producing $Q^* + 1$ units of output would provide the firm with less profit than producing Q^*. Also, explain why producing $Q^* - 1$ units of output would also provide less profit than Q^*.

10. *[profit maximization]* Suppose a price-taking firm has a total fixed cost equal to $1 and marginal cost as indicated in the following table. Since total variable cost can be calculated by adding the given marginal cost

values, fill in the missing values for total variable cost. Then fill in the missing values for total cost. Compute the values for total revenue assuming a market price of $4.25. What output will maximize profit? How much will the profit be? Will output increase when price goes up to $4.50? To $5.25? Explain.

Quantity of Output per Day	Total Revenue	Marginal Cost	Total Variable Cost	Total Cost
0	$0	—	$0	$1
1		$1		
2		0.50		
3		1	2.50	
4		2		
5		3		
6		4		
7		5		
8		6		

11. *[breakeven]* Draw a graph showing a price-taking firm maximizing profit, but breaking even. Your graph should contain market price, marginal revenue, marginal cost, and average cost curves. Indicate the quantity of output the firm would produce. Be sure to label the axes.

12. *[profit graph]* Draw the axes for a graph with the vertical axis labeled $ and the horizontal axis labeled Quantity. Sketch an average cost curve and an accompanying marginal cost curve. Select a price such that the firm earns an economic profit. Show the profit-maximizing quantity by drawing a dotted line from the intersection of marginal revenue and marginal cost to the horizontal axis. Show profit as the area of a rectangle.

13. *[loss graph]* Draw a graph similar to the one in the preceding problem except adjust the price so that the firm incurs a loss. Illustrate the loss as the area of a rectangle.

14. *[shut down]* The owners of Happy Spud Potato Farms have recently seen their firm incur losses because of a downturn in the market price of potatoes. They are trying to decide whether to shut down and take jobs in a factory in a nearby town until the price of potatoes goes up in the future. Here is the information they have accumulated to help them make their decision:
    - Monthly quantity of potatoes sold: 10,000 bushels
    - Price of potatoes: $3 a bushel
    - Happy Spud's marginal cost of growing potatoes: $3 a bushel

- Total fixed cost (mortgage on farm and other fixed expenses): $6,000
- Total variable cost of producing 10,000 bushels of potatoes (potato slips, labor, and so on): $29,900

Will the loss at Happy Spud be minimized by shutting down or by continuing to operate? Explain.

15. *[shutdown graph]* Draw a graph that illustrates the shutdown rule. Label each curve in your graph and explain how the graph illustrates shutdown.

16. *[market structure]* List the four forms of market structure and briefly describe their characteristics. For each type of market provide an example of an industry or firm that reflects the characteristics of that market.

17. *[market power]* What is market power? In which market structure is market power by firms absent? When market power by firms is absent, what are the firms called?

18. *[homogeneous product and price taking]* Define the term homogeneous product. Explain why price taking occurs when products are homogeneous.

19. *[market versus firm demand]* If a firm has a horizontal demand curve for its output, will the industry demand curve also be horizontal? Explain.

20. *[graph of firm's short-run supply curve]* Draw a firm's marginal cost and average variable cost curves. Label the axes appropriately. Indicate on your graph the short-run supply curve. State the rule of profit maximization and interpret the rule as it relates to the supply curve in your graph.

21. *[firm's short-run supply curve]* Suppose the minimum average variable cost of producing an ounce of gold at Shiny Yellow Gold Mine is $200 an ounce. That minimum value occurs at a quantity of 5 tons of gold per month. Further suppose that the marginal cost of producing each ounce of gold is:

Quantity of Gold (tons per month)	Marginal Cost per Ounce of Gold
0	---
1	$50
2	25
3	75
4	125
5	200
6	275
7	350
8	435
9	525
10	750

Fill in the following table with the supply data for Shiny Yellow Gold Mine.

When the Price per Ounce of Gold Is:	Shiny Yellow Gold Mine Will Produce:
$100	
150	
200	
250	
300	
350	
400	
450	
500	
550	
600	

Does your computation of supply show that higher prices are associated with a greater quantity supplied? Is this result consistent with the usual depiction of supply? Explain.

22. *[market supply curve]* Suppose a purely competitive industry is composed of 1,000 identical firms each producing according to the table below. Fill in the missing market supply numbers in the last column of the table.

Price	Single Firm's Quantity Supplied	Market Supply
$1	10	
2	12	
3	14	
4	16	
5	18	

 Visit **www.prenhall.com/collinge** for Exploring the Web exercises and additional self-test quizzes.

CHAPTER 7

MARKET POWER

A LOOK AHEAD

Most of us can look forward to a visitor every day of the week except Sunday. This visitor sometimes comes bearing gifts, other times bills. The visitor, the U.S. Postal Service letter carrier, is a representative of the country's oldest monopoly. The Postal Service is unique in having its monopoly status mentioned in the U.S. Constitution. This chapter's Explore & Apply section sheds light on technological changes and market shifts that could impact the monopoly status of the Postal Service.

Why should we be concerned with monopolies at all? The model of an unregulated profit-maximizing monopoly shows that a monopoly cuts output and raises price relative to what price and output would be in pure competition.

Oligopolists have quite a bit of control over prices but not so much as to give any one of them a monopoly of its industry. Firms without much market power often compete by providing consumers with a different product or service than the similar products offered by competitors. Firms in these industries are monopolistically competitive, producing products ranging from physical fitness to family-room furniture.

LEARNING OBJECTIVES

Understanding Chapter 7 will enable you to:
1. **Describe how barriers to entry create market power.**
2. **Discuss the profit-maximizing process for a monopolist.**
3. **Explain the inefficiencies of monopoly.**
4. **Name and briefly discuss major U.S. antitrust laws and policies toward monopoly.**
5. **Define product differentiation and state its implications.**
6. **Relate how and why firms charge some consumers more than others for the same products.**
7. **Assess the merits of protecting the U.S. Postal Service from competition.**

The previous chapter introduced the four market structures, arranged according to *market power,* which is the ability to set prices. This chapter starts by examining the market structure of monopoly, in which one firm supplies the entire market. The chapter then proceeds to consider the models of oligopoly and monopolistic competition, in which market power is less pronounced.

7.1 SOURCES OF MONOPOLY

monopoly when a single firm sells an output for which there are no close substitutes.

A monopoly is characterized by a single firm selling an output for which there are no close substitutes. Goods substitute for one another when they fill the same need. For example, if there is only one seller of a good, is the seller a monopolist? Not if another good serves the same purpose. In that case, consumers who are dissatisfied with the price or quality of one good can stop buying it and obtain equivalent satisfaction by purchasing the other.

Whether there are close substitutes for a good or service is often not obvious. Consider your local cable television provider. Usually only one cable company provides service in an area. However, if satellite dishes, network television, theaters, and other recreation are good substitutes, then local cable companies are not truly monopolies.

BARRIERS TO ENTRY

barriers to entry when investors or entrepreneurs find obstacles to joining a profitable industry.

Monopoly is caused by very high **barriers to entry,** which exist when investors or entrepreneurs find obstacles to joining a profitable industry. Barriers to entry include anything that makes producing and selling output more difficult for a new firm than for an existing firm. Monopoly represents the ultimate barrier to entry—one so high that only one firm makes up the entire industry. The cause could be any of the following:

monopoly by law (legal monopoly) when legal barriers restrict the supply of a good to one firm, and when there are no close substitutes for that good.

- **Monopoly by law**—also called **legal monopoly**—when one firm is protected by law from competition, and there are no close substitutes for the good. First-class mail is an example, where the U.S. Postal Statutes make it illegal for equivalent services to be offered by any other provider. Patents, such as for Cipro, AZT, and other pharmaceutical drugs, could also form the basis for a monopoly by law. Typically, however, the barriers to entry that are formed by patents, trademarks, copyrights, and similar legal protections fall short of those needed for monopoly. The reason is that there are nearly always substitutes for the product.

monopoly by possession when a single firm owns a resource needed in the production of a good for which there are no close substitutes.

- **Monopoly by possession**—when one firm is the only owner of a resource needed to produce a good, and there are no close substitutes for the resource or for the good. Diamonds are an example, with De Beers Consolidated Mines, Ltd. producing a good that is like no other. De Beers has been accumulating diamond mines since 1888 and is easily the largest diamond mining company in the world. Its twenty mines in South Africa, Botswana, Namibia, and Tanzania produce about 40 percent of the world's gem-quality diamonds. It has additional production agreements with the owners of another 40 percent of the world's diamond supply. That 80 percent control of output in the diamond market makes De Beers about as close as reality gets to monopoly by possession.

natural monopoly when one firm can supply the entire market at a lower per-unit cost than could two or more separate firms.

- **Natural monopoly**—when it is cheaper for one firm to produce the entire industry's output than it would be for two or more firms to produce the same output. Again, there must be no close substitutes for the good. Natural monopoly might be called monopoly by technology, as technological advances can sometimes replace it with competition. Natural monopoly will be discussed further in the next section.

Barriers to entry bring about market power. This market power reveals itself in the slope of the firm's demand curve. If the demand curve slopes down only slightly, it is probably because there are many close substitutes for the firm's product, which leaves the firm with

FIGURE 7-1

THE EFFECT OF INCREASING MARKET POWER Market power increases as demand steepens. If the firm's demand is horizontal, the firm is a price taker and has no market power. When demand slopes down, the firm has market power. Monopoly is the extreme case in which demand facing the firm slopes down as steeply as market demand—the two are one and the same.

only a little ability to control price. Holding units of measurement constant, **the steeper the demand curve, the more market power the firm has and the greater its ability to determine price.**

Figure 7-1 shows three possible demand curves facing the firm. If the firm's demand is horizontal, it is a price taker with no market power. The firm would have market power if its demand curve slopes down. **Monopoly represents the most market power, in which case the firm's demand is identical to market demand.** The monopolist's demand would slope down relatively steeply, as shown in the figure.

No firm's market power is absolute, because no firm can raise prices without reducing the quantity demanded. Even a monopoly will find that if it raises the price enough, it will reach the point where the demand curve intersects the price axis. At that point, the quantity demanded equals zero. The firm would never want to raise the price nearly that high. Rather, it seeks the price that will sell its profit-maximizing quantity. For this reason, a firm with market power is called a **price maker,** in contrast to the price taker found in pure competition.

price maker a firm that faces a downward-sloping demand curve.

IS THE AMERICAN MEDICAL ASSOCIATION HAZARDOUS TO YOUR HEALTH?

SNAPSHOT

The American Medical Association (AMA) is not a government agency. Nevertheless, this professional association has much to say about the availability of healthcare. Not only does it have power over the standards for licensing physicians, but it also has considerable input into setting standards for medical schools. For better or for worse, these standards form barriers to entry.

Some critics of the current U.S. healthcare system accuse the AMA of setting unnecessarily high standards, which serve to heighten market power within the medical profession. Critics contend that the motivation is more income for physicians—physician self-interest would point that way. The AMA responds that there is merely a coincidence of self-interest and public interest, and that it is the public interest that guides their actions. They point out that medicine is a life or death proposition, and that the public is best served by allowing only the best physicians to do the serving. ◄

NATURAL MONOPOLY

Natural monopoly occurs when one firm can supply the entire market at a lower per unit cost than could two or more separate firms. This means that natural monopoly will occur any time that the minimum point on long-run average cost occurs near or to the right of market demand, as illustrated in Figure 7-2(a) and (b), respectively. **Natural monopoly occurs when there are substantial economies of scale.** A potential entrant will think twice about challenging a natural monopolist. To realize economies of scale, the entrant would need to start large, so large that the entrant and the established firm could not both survive. Few investors would be willing to finance such a challenge.

For example, imagine three or four water suppliers each burying water mains along a street and competing for the business of the nearby residents. A single firm could eliminate this wasteful duplication of effort and in the process lower the average costs of providing service. Water companies and local gas and electric companies are examples of *public utili-*

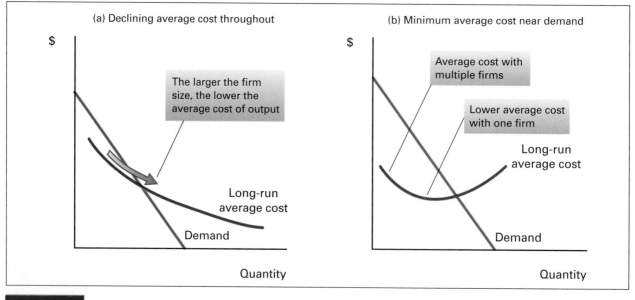

FIGURE 7-2

NATURAL MONOPOLY Natural monopoly occurs whenever one firm can supply the entire market at a lower average cost than could any combination of firms. Graph (a) illustrates a natural monopoly in which long-run average cost declines throughout the relevant range of output. Graph (b) shows a natural monopoly in which long-run average cost reaches its minimum point before intersecting the demand curve, but near enough to demand that one firm could still profitably underprice any combination of two or more firms.

ties, which have distribution lines of pipes, wires, and cables that have traditionally made them natural monopolies.

In recent years, advances in technology have eliminated or scaled back what were once thought to be natural monopolies. For example, local telephone service was a common example of a natural monopoly until near the end of the twentieth century. Today, however, advances in technology for billing and call switching allow customers in many cities to choose among alternative providers of local phone service over the telephone lines. A city's telephone lines have remained owned by one provider, typically, but that isn't a natural monopoly, either. Telephone customers these days have a choice of competing transmission methods, including cable and wireless. More and more people are choosing to rely on their cellular phones or Internet connections for basic telephone service. The result is that telephone service has left the realm of natural monopoly altogether.

Electric service has been another common example of natural monopoly. In this industry, technology has scaled back the natural monopoly portion of the business to only the transmission lines, themselves. As customers in many states already know, it is possible to choose electric power from competing companies, which then feed the electricity into the same power grid for transmission to the customer. Local power lines remain a natural monopoly, since technology has not yet come up with any viable alternatives. That's not to say there have not been attempts. Many dream of solar-powered homes, for example. So far, though, solar collectors on rooftops have proven either too expensive or not feasible. Likewise, septic tanks are usually not a practical substitute for city sewage disposal services, another natural monopoly.

7.2 THE PROFIT-MAXIMIZING MONOPOLY

In competition, firms are price takers and have only to find the intersection between the market price and their marginal cost curves in order to maximize profit. In the long run, competitive firms will have no expectation of profit by entering or exiting an industry. In contrast, monopoly firms must set the price and could potentially earn large and lasting profit. This section examines both the process of profit maximization and the results for the firm and for society.

FINDING THE PROFIT MAXIMUM

Recall from the elasticity chapter that total revenue is maximized when the elasticity of demand equals one, which occurs at the midpoint of a straight-line demand curve. Since the market demand is the demand facing the monopoly firm, it, too, would maximize its revenue when elasticity equals one. Even if production costs were zero, the monopoly would not produce any more than the revenue-maximizing output, since to do so would lower its total revenue, and thus its profit. With a positive marginal cost of production, the monopoly firm will produce less than the revenue-maximizing output. This means that **the monopoly firm always chooses to produce in the elastic range of demand.**

The rule of profit maximization for a monopoly is the same as for all other firms: **produce at the point where marginal revenue equals marginal cost.** Marginal revenue is the slope of total revenue, as shown in Figure 7-3. Marginal revenue equals zero when total revenue is at a maximum, since the slope of total revenue equals zero at its maximum. Maximum total revenue occurs at the same quantity associated with the midpoint of a straight-line demand curve. The midpoint is also the point of unit elasticity, as shown in the figure and discussed previously in the elasticity chapter. Observe that, for this and any straight-line demand curve, marginal revenue slopes down twice as fast as demand, intersecting the horizontal axis under the midpoint of demand.

FIGURE 7-3

MONOPOLY REVENUE Marginal revenue is the slope of total revenue. When total revenue is maximized, marginal revenue equals zero. This outcome occurs at the point for which the elasticity of demand is one. The monopolist will avoid producing so much output that marginal revenue is negative.

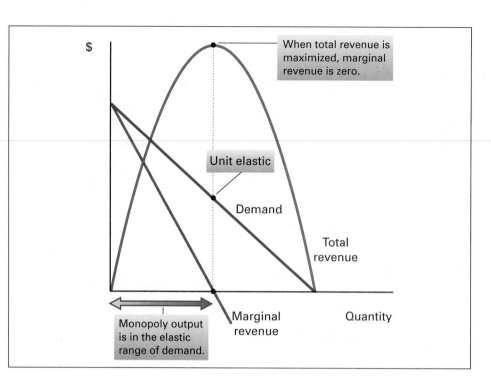

FIGURE 7-4

MARGINAL REVENUE LESS THAN PRICE To increase sales of its output, the monopolist must lower the price of that output. The lower price applies to not only the last unit of output that the monopolist sells, but also to all the other units of output. So while the last unit of output adds its price to total revenue, it also subtracts a little bit from the price of all of the other units of output the monopolist had already been selling. This logic explains why the monopolist's marginal revenue is less than its price.

For monopoly, and other firms with downward-sloping demand curves that charge a single price, marginal revenue is less than that price. The intuition is that, if such a firm wants another sale, it will have to offer potential buyers a lower price. The lower price would then apply to every unit of output that it offers for sale, as shown in Figure 7-4. The result is that the marginal revenue from an extra unit of output would equal the price of that unit minus the price reduction on every other unit sold. For this reason, **a downward-sloping demand curve is associated with a marginal revenue curve that slopes down even more steeply.**

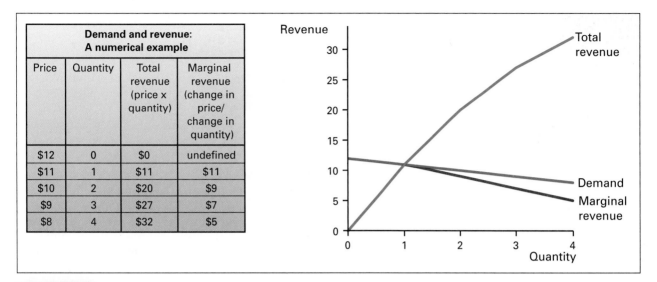

Demand and revenue: A numerical example			
Price	Quantity	Total revenue (price x quantity)	Marginal revenue (change in price/ change in quantity)
$12	0	$0	undefined
$11	1	$11	$11
$10	2	$20	$9
$9	3	$27	$7
$8	4	$32	$5

FIGURE 7-5

DEMAND AND REVENUE—A NUMERICAL EXAMPLE The data in the table are plotted to show demand, total revenue, and marginal revenue for a monopoly. Note that the data confirm that marginal revenue has a steeper slope than demand.

Let's now turn to a numerical example. Consider the monopoly shown in Figure 7-5. The firm must reduce its price in order to sell more output. Total revenue, equal to price multiplied by quantity, is shown in the third column. Marginal revenue, the change in total revenue divided by the change in quantity, is computed in the last column. As before, marginal revenue decreases more rapidly than price as quantity increases.

To see why marginal revenue decreases more rapidly than price, consider the price reduction from $10 to $9. This price cut allows the firm to sell 3 units of output, but also causes the revenue from the sale of the first 2 units, which would have been $20 at the $10 price, to drop to $18. This drop of $2 means that total revenue will rise by less than the $9 price of the third unit. Specifically, total revenue rises from $20 to $27, an increase of $7, which equals the price of $9 minus the decrease of $2 on the first two units.

To find its profit-maximizing price and quantity, the monopoly firm will calculate its marginal revenue at various quantities. It will then compare marginal revenue to marginal cost at each quantity. At some point the two must be equal, because marginal revenue declines as more output is produced and sold, while marginal cost rises because of the law of diminishing returns. Once the profit-maximizing quantity is determined, the firm will charge the highest price possible that allows it to sell that amount of output. This price is given by the point on the demand curve that corresponds to the output that the firm has chosen. This two-step process—first determine output, then price—is shown in Figure 7-6. Note that the price is higher than either marginal cost or marginal revenue at that output.

PROFIT, BREAKEVEN, OR LOSS

Figure 7-7 shows graphically a profit-maximizing monopoly. The profit-maximizing quantity in the figure occurs at the point where marginal revenue equals marginal cost. The profit-maximizing price is set at the corresponding point on the demand curve. The profit is shown as a rectangle, created when the average profit per unit sold is multiplied by the number of

FIGURE 7-6

MONOPOLY OUTPUT AND PRICE
The unregulated monopoly firm selects output and price in two steps. First, the monopolist produces until marginal cost equals marginal revenue. Second, the monopolist charges the highest price that will sell that output.

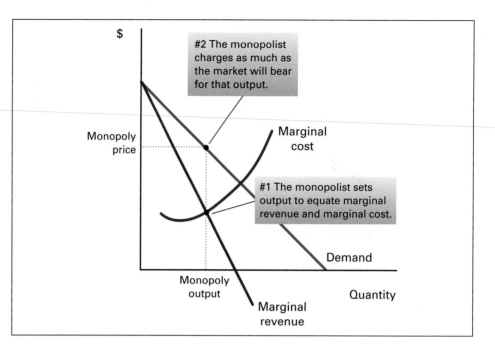

FIGURE 7-7

MONOPOLY PROFIT Total profit equals profit per unit (price - average cost) multiplied by the quantity produced. Profit is shown as the shaded area.

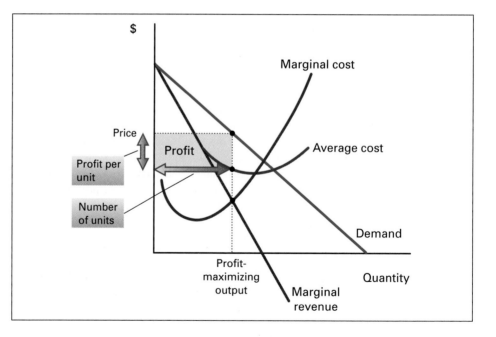

units sold. The average profit per unit is the difference between price and average cost at the profit-maximizing quantity.

Monopolies can sometimes be quite profitable, since there are no other competitors to undercut their prices. However, merely because a firm is a monopoly does not mean it has a profit. A monopoly firm might find that the best it can do is to breakeven or even to lose money, as shown in Figure 7-8. One reason might be that the monopoly's product is no longer as necessary as it once was. For example, telegraph lines fell into disrepair as telegraph services were displaced by the telephone and, later, the Internet.

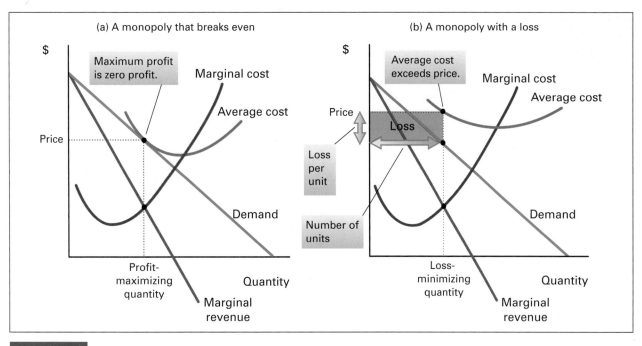

FIGURE 7-8

MONOPOLY BREAKEVEN AND LOSS A profit-maximizing monopolist might find that the best it can do is to break even. As shown in (a), such a firm finds that producing to the point where marginal cost equals marginal revenue allows it to charge a price that merely covers its costs. This result is shown on the graph as average cost just tangent to demand.

If average cost at that point is more than demand, as shown in (b), the firm loses money and would exit the industry in the long run. The loss would equal the loss per unit (average cost - price) multiplied by the quantity produced. Loss is shown as the shaded area.

QUICKCHECK

Suppose a profit-maximizing monopoly firm is incurring a loss. In what way would a graph showing this concept differ from one showing a profit-maximizing monopolist with a profit?

Answer: The difference would be that the average cost curve for the firm with the loss would lie everywhere above the demand curve, causing average cost to be above price at the profit-maximizing (loss-minimizing) output. In both cases, the output will correspond to the intersection of marginal revenue and marginal cost. Also, rather than a rectangle showing profit, there will be a rectangle showing loss. The two situations are depicted in Figures 7-7 and 7-8(b), respectively.

7.3 ANTITRUST AND REGULATION

Allocative efficiency requires that each good be produced up to the point at which its marginal cost of production just equals the marginal benefit from its consumption. Yet firms produce to the point where marginal cost equals marginal revenue. It is only because the market price is identical to marginal revenue for price-taking firms that pure competition is efficient.

In contrast, at any given point in time, monopoly is allocatively inefficient because the quantity that equates marginal cost and marginal revenue falls short of the quantity that equates marginal cost and demand. The result is that the profit-maximizing quantity is less than the efficient quantity. Figure 7-9 shows these differing quantities and the inefficiency caused by the monopolist's choice. The shaded triangular area is the inefficiency, called **deadweight loss,** which shows the benefits that consumers would have received from the additional output minus the cost the firm would have incurred to produce it. In short, deadweight loss is the value of efficiency that is not achieved.

Although an unregulated monopoly will not normally produce an efficient quantity at each point in time, it does have the potential to generate profits that it could invest in research and development to enhance its monopoly status. Competitive firms have neither the incentive nor financial ability to pursue research and development. In addition, the lure of monopoly profit is a powerful motivating force for investment. For these reasons, the overall efficiency of monopoly is a matter of debate. While producing too little and charging too much in the short run, monopoly profits might bring about new and better products in the long run.

There are various ways in which public policy can address the inefficiencies of monopoly and try to protect consumers from unfairly high prices. For example, government might appoint itself as owner of the monopoly. That raises problems of incentives within government, however. Alternatively, as we will see below, laws or regulations can be designed to address the problem of excessive market power without discarding the advantages of a market economy.

ANTITRUST POLICY

Toward the late nineteenth century, large businesses, called *trusts,* began to dominate and even monopolize various industries. By 1890, public outrage over various alleged abuses of the marketplace by the trusts led to calls for action. Congress responded by passing the *Sherman Act* by the overwhelming vote of 52 to 1 in the Senate and 242 to 0 in the House. This act is the foundation of **antitrust law**—public policies designed to limit the abuse of market power by monopolies—and is enforced by the Justice Department. The focus of the act is on the conduct of a business, although specific illegal actions are not spelled out. In general, it prohibits contracts, combinations, and conspiracies in restraint of trade. It also forbids attempts to monopolize markets, but does not make monopoly itself illegal.

deadweight loss value of efficiency that is not achieved.

antitrust law public policies designed to limit the abuse of market power by monopolies.

FIGURE 7-9

THE INEFFICIENCY OF MONOPOLY
Allocative efficiency calls for more output at any given time than monopoly chooses. The inefficiency is the benefits consumers would have received from the additional output minus the costs to produce it. It is referred to as the triangle of deadweight loss.

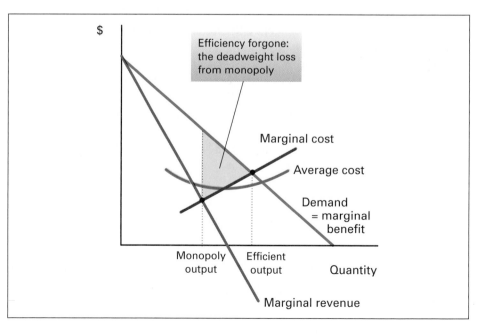

TABLE 7-1 KEY FEATURES OF THE MAJOR ANTITRUST LAWS

LEGISLATION	SUMMARY OF FEATURES
Sherman Act of 1890	Bans monopolization and price-fixing agreements. Provides for criminal and civil penalties.
Clayton Antitrust Act of 1914	Bans certain specific actions that reduce competition.
Federal Trade Commission Act of 1914	Created the Federal Trade Commission, a government agency that investigates allegations of unfair trade practices.

Because of the failure of Congress to write specific provisions into the Sherman Act, it initially proved ineffective at curbing the power of the trusts. Thus, additional legislation was drafted, aimed at spelling out particular anti-competitive behaviors and making them illegal. The *Federal Trade Commission Act* and the *Clayton Act* were signed into law in 1914, thus completing the job of laying the foundation for today's antitrust enforcement. The Clayton Act supplements the Sherman Act by listing specific illegal actions, such as acquiring stock in a competing firm when that action would lessen competition. The Federal Trade Commission (FTC) was created to oversee markets, with the goal of eliminating unfair trade practices. Other antitrust legislation has augmented these laws by preventing firms from taking anti-competitive actions that would give them excessive market power.

Table 7-1 summarizes the key features of the antitrust laws. Note that both the government and competing firms can file antitrust complaints. A violator of the antitrust laws can be forced to pay up to three times the damages it inflicts on other firms. It can also be fined, broken into competing parts, and its employees imprisoned. Sometimes accused firms will sign a consent decree, in which they agree to change their behavior without admitting guilt.

The antitrust laws neither make monopoly illegal nor apply only to monopoly. Rather, they are intended to curb abuses of market power, of which monopolists have the most. They limit the manner in which firms can compete to what is efficient for society and fair to consumers and potential competitors. In considering what constitutes a violation of the law, the Federal Trade Commission will consider the practices listed in Table 7-2. These

TABLE 7-2 POTENTIALLY PUNISHABLE PRACTICES: A GLOSSARY OF ANTITRUST TERMS

Exclusive dealing	A firm prohibits its distributors from selling competitors' products.
Exclusive territories	A firm assigns a geographic area to a distributor and prohibits other distributors from operating in that territory.
Predatory pricing	A firm prices a product below the marginal cost of producing it to drive rivals out of business.
Price discrimination	A firm charges different customers different prices for the same product.
Refusals to deal	A firm prohibits rivals from purchasing/using scarce resources (called essential facilities) that are needed to stay in business.
Resale price maintenance	A manufacturer sets a minimum retail price for its product.
Tie-in sales	A firm conditions the purchase of one product upon the purchase of another.

Source: "Does Big Business Need Taming? The Role of Economics in Antitrust Law," *The Regional Economist,* Federal Reserve Bank of Saint Louis, July 1998.

practices, including the price discrimination we discussed in the previous section, are not intrinsically illegal. Rather, the behavior becomes illegal when competition is lessened in a significant way, without having overriding business justifications. This judgment is made in court and is known as *the rule of reason.*

SNAPSHOT — FINDING MONOPOLY—MICROSOFT YES, DUPONT NO

Imagine America's wealthiest man and his company pitted against government attorneys. The setting was the courtroom of Judge Thomas Penfield Jackson. The verdict? Microsoft Corporation was found to have a monopoly with its Windows personal-computer operating system. Few computer users could realistically avoid using that operating system. Moreover, Microsoft had abused its monopoly power to thwart potential rivals to its other products, thereby violating the antitrust laws. For example, Microsoft's Internet Explorer was so tied in to Windows that rival Netscape, with its Netscape Navigator and Communicator, could not profitably compete. There was just no good substitute for the Windows operating system, which Microsoft was using as leverage to muscle out competitors to its other software products. So ruled Judge Jackson in 2000. His remedy? Break Microsoft into two companies. That draconian punishment was later overturned by a federal appeals court, with Microsoft being allowed to remain a single company, but one agreeing to curb its monopoly ways.

The government does not always win its antitrust cases. For example, it lost its 1956 case against DuPont, producer of nearly all cellophane, a clear packaging material. In this case, the court reasoned that cellophane was one of many packaging materials produced by a number of firms. The availability of plastic wrap, wax paper, and other substitutes meant that cellophane had a relatively low market share in the market for packaging materials. Since the court reasoned that the market was for packaging materials, not just cellophane, Dupont was found by the Supreme Court to have no monopoly. ◄

RATE-OF-RETURN REGULATION

rate-of-return regulation (average-cost pricing) restricts the monopoly from earning more than a normal profit; shown by the intersection of the average-cost curve and demand.

If a monopoly is a natural monopoly, the government will typically either own it or regulate it with **rate-of-return regulation** that restricts the monopolist from charging more than average cost. For this reason, rate-of-return regulation is also known as **average-cost pricing.** While it is marginal cost that is used to determine efficiency, average cost is often a close approximation and does at least guarantee that the firm will neither earn excessive profit nor go out of business. For example, the firm in Figure 7-10 will produce less than the efficient quantity, but not nearly as much less than if its price were unrestricted.

The regulation of industry by the federal government, undertaken to ensure "fair prices," has a long history. The Interstate Commerce Commission (ICC), eliminated in the 1970s, was created by Congress in 1887 to regulate the railroads, the primary means of transporting many kinds of goods at the time. In the 1920s and 1930s, as trucking took a larger share of the transportation market, it seemed natural to extend regulation to that industry as well. Airline regulation was also established as regularly scheduled passenger service took hold in the 1930s. Note that regulation was instituted even though these industries were not characterized by monopoly.

A problem with rate-of-return regulation is that the regulated monopolist has little incentive to control costs or to provide innovative services. Thus, over time, regulation can impede change in production techniques and in the development of new products. For this reason, rate-of-return regulation can cause technological inefficiencies even as it corrects allocative inefficiencies. Regulation can also have the effect of stifling new competition, favoring existing firms at the expense of potential competitors. For example, during the more than thirty-year period that the airlines were regulated, startups of new airlines were few.

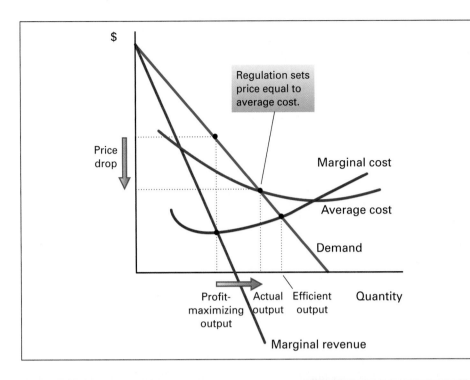

FIGURE 7-10

AVERAGE-COST PRICING In the case of public utilities, regulators commonly attempt to limit monopoly pricing to no more than average cost. The resulting quantity produced more closely approximates the efficient quantity and ensures the firm a normal profit. On the downside, regulators may tend to overestimate the monopolist's costs because they do not know all of the ways that the monopoly could economize and because the regulated monopoly has no incentive to reveal these cost-saving possibilities.

QUICKCHECK

Rate-of-return regulation is intended to restrict a monopolist's price to equal its average production costs. Is this price efficient? If so, why? If not, why not and why use rate-of-return regulation?

Answer: Efficiency requires that the monopolist produce to the point where marginal cost equals demand, not where average cost equals demand as under rate-of-return regulation. Thus, unless marginal cost equals average cost at that point, it would appear that such regulation is not efficient. Still, regulators choose this solution because it is likely to be more efficient than unregulated monopoly and will lead the firm to only a normal profit, meaning zero profit as economists define the term. With zero profit, the firm avoids needing government subsidies to stay in business.

So far, we have looked at market extremes. We started at the extreme of pure competition, in which firms produce a homogeneous product and cannot price discriminate. We then leapt to the extreme of monopoly, in which there is only one firm in the entire industry. Those models allow us to understand many of the essential characteristics of markets. The following section adds to that understanding by examining the models of oligopoly and monopolistic competition, which depict markets between pure competition and monopoly.

7.4 OLIGOPOLY AND MONOPOLISTIC COMPETITION

Oligopoly is characterized by multiple firms, one or more of which will produce a significant portion of industry output. Many oligopoly markets consist of just a few firms. Oligopoly firms are the only firms that are **mutually interdependent,** with the actions taken by one firm influencing actions taken by other firms in the market. Thus, strategy and counterstrategy is the norm in oligopolistic markets.

oligopoly market with multiple firms, at least one of which produces a significant portion of industry output.

mutually interdependent when actions by one firm influence actions taken by other firms in the market.

Mutual interdependence frequently revolves around pricing decisions. For example, the price at which the local cable company offers broadband Internet access will depend in large part upon the price of the substitute DSL broadband access from the local telephone company. Mutual interdependence can also involve product design. For instance, the exploding popularity of sport utility vehicles (SUVs) led small-car maker Saturn to add its first SUV, a 2003 model called the Saturn VUE, to its product lineup. By offering an SUV, Saturn can better compete with its rivals.

differentiated products goods and services that differ among producers.

Oligopoly products may be differentiated or homogeneous. Automobile manufacturing is an oligopoly industry that produces **differentiated products**—products that are similar, but nevertheless differ from one producer to the next. Each vehicle differs from competing models. Styling, colors offered, horsepower, and interior design are just a few of the ways that cars are differentiated. The output of oligopolies is not always differentiated, however. Steel, aluminum, and copper are homogeneous commodities produced by oligopolistic firms.

monopolistic competition a market structure with many firms selling differentiated products and relatively easy entry of new firms.

Monopolistic competition is a market structure with many firms, product differentiation, and relatively easy entry of new firms. Many retailers operate in monopolistically competitive markets. In addition, many of the products they sell are also produced by firms in monopolistic competition.

Monopolistically competitive firms face demand curves that slope downward slightly, because although they are the only providers of their version of the product, other firms offer close substitutes. The result is that firms have only a limited ability to affect prices. For example, Pizza Hut does not just compete with Domino's and other pizza parlors. In addition, it competes with Burger King, Long John Silver's, Taco Bell, and all the other choices for lunch and dinner. Yet nobody else has quite the same products. For this reason, the model of price and output determination under monopolistic competition is akin to that of pure monopoly, but with two exceptions. Specifically, each firm faces a demand curve that is:

- Highly elastic, which gives it a relatively flat appearance.
- Influenced by the firm's own actions and the actions of competitors.

For example, the firm has the incentive to advertise and vary its product as a way of increasing its demand at the expense of its competitors.

Figure 7-11 illustrates price and quantity determination by the monopolistically competitive firm. Like all profit-maximizing firms, the firm we see here produces where marginal cost equals marginal revenue, indicated by the label "Profit-maximizing quantity" in the figure. The firm chooses the price on its demand curve that corresponds to the profit-maximizing quantity. Because demand is highly elastic, marginal revenue slopes down only slightly, too. One consequence is that, like monopoly, the firm does not produce the efficient output (given by the intersection of marginal cost and demand). Unlike monopoly, however, the monopolistically competitive firm chooses a quantity that is very nearly efficient in the short run. What's more, competition among firms also leads them to develop valuable variations on the product over time. They are constantly looking to "build a better mousetrap."

ADVERTISING AND PRODUCT DIFFERENTIATION

The firm's demand is always defined under the condition of *ceteris paribus,* meaning that everything except the firm's price is held constant. In oligopoly marekts, each firm's demand will shift when its competitors change their prices and products. Likewise, the demand facing a firm in monopolistic competition will be affected by the availability of the many substitute products from other firms in the industry. Unlike the firm in pure competition, however, the oligopolistic or monopolistically competitive firm is not a helpless victim of market circumstances. Rather, in these market structures, the firm can actively seek to change its own demand curve through the use of product differentiation and advertising.

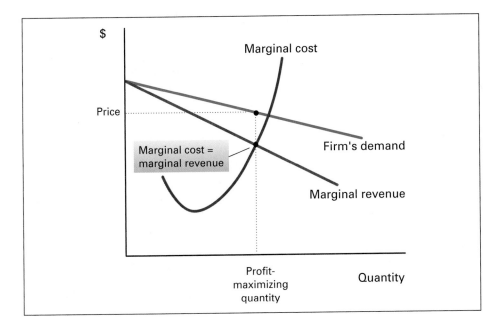

FIGURE 7-11

FIRM'S OUTPUT AND PRICE IN MONOPOLISTIC COMPETITION
Output and price determination under monopolistic competition are the same as under monopoly, except that demand is much more elastic. As a result, the profit-maximizing output occurs close to the efficient output, given by the intersection of marginal cost and the firm's demand.

The key to riches in monopolistic competition is successful product differentiation in such things as style, taste, shape, size, color, texture, quality, location, packaging, advertising, and service. For example, the powerful lure of the trademarked golden arches is one of the features differentiating McDonald's from its competitors. Likewise the thirty-one flavors help differentiate Baskin-Robbins from other sellers of ice cream.

The differentiated nature of products in monopolistic competition and many oligopolies makes it likely that firms will advertise. Some ads focus on facts, such as Yellow Page ads with addresses, phone numbers, and hours of operation. However, much advertising is designed to work on consumers' imaginations and stick in their memories. Advertising slogans permeate our language. Successful advertising, slogans, and sales promotions increase the demand for a firm's version of the industry's output. In addition, advertising that creates customer loyalty for existing firms and their well-known brands forms a barrier to the entry of new firms.

When advertising or otherwise differentiating its product, the profit-maximizing firm is still guided by the same principle that guides its choice of quantity of output: marginal cost equals marginal revenue. **If the marginal revenue generated by advertising exceeds the**

QUICKCHECK

Under what circumstances would a firm decrease the effectiveness of its advertising or vary its product in such a way that consumers like it less? Provide an example.

Answer: These actions might be either deliberate or unintentional. Firms would deliberately decrease the effectiveness of advertising or make a less-desirable product if the money they save in doing so exceeds the revenue they lose from consumers buying less product. An example would be when a firm reduces the size of its ad in the Yellow Pages, knowing that a smaller ad will save money, but mean fewer customers. Alternatively, firms might launch an advertising campaign or a product variation that is unsuccessful. An example would be a restaurant that plays its background music too loud.

marginal cost of that advertising, advertising raises profits. Otherwise it does not. Similarly, the profit-maximizing firm will adjust its hours of operation, selection of merchandise, and every other aspect of product differentiation with this same principle in mind. For example, if a store's marginal revenue from staying open an extra hour in the evening exceeds the marginal cost of staying open the extra hour, the store will choose to stay open that extra hour.

PRICE DISCRIMINATION

price discrimination charging different prices for different units of output, where the differences do not depend on differences in production costs.

You and your roommate are both flying home on the same airline and to the same city, but your roommate paid $200 more than you did . . . is there something wrong with your ticket? More likely, you bought your ticket further in advance and are the beneficiary of **price discrimination,** which is the selling of a good or service at different prices when such differences are not caused by differences in production costs. Price discrimination under monopoly was discussed earlier in this chapter. Examples under monopolistic competition and oligopoly include discounts for senior citizens and students. Coupons that give those who redeem them lower prices also represent price discrimination.

Price discrimination is feasible when different prices can be charged to different market segments. Segments with the highest elasticities of demand usually see the lowest prices, because those consumers are the most price sensitive. For example, it costs no less to screen a movie in a theater filled with children than to show it to adults. Yet adult ticket prices are usually twice those of children's, because adults are less deterred by higher prices—demand for adult tickets is less elastic than demand for children's tickets.

A firm cannot practice price discrimination if buyers who are offered goods at a low price can resell those goods to other buyers at a higher price, a practice called *arbitrage.* For example, pricing adult movie tickets higher than children's would accomplish nothing if adults could see a movie with a child's ticket. The only tickets that a theater could sell would be the child's tickets, purchased by children and then profitably resold to adults at a price less than the regular adult price.

There are various ways to implement price discrimination. For example, when airlines require Saturday night stays and advance purchases for flyers to get the lowest rates, much of the reason has to do with price discriminating between the leisure traveler with a relatively elastic demand and the business traveler whose demand is relatively inelastic. Airlines know that business travelers often must make plans at the last minute and rarely want to spend the weekend away from home. Therefore, requiring advance purchases and Saturday night stays is a good way of identifying that traveler. Merely asking at the counter if a person is a business traveler would not work, not when the penalty for a correct answer is to pay more—typically a lot more!

QUICKCHECK

Differences between in-state and out-of-state tuition at public colleges and universities are usually substantial. Is this price discrimination? How can it be justified?

Answer: It is no more costly to serve a student from one location than from another. Therefore, the custom of charging higher tuition to out-of-state students fits the definition of price discrimination. It is justified by the logic that those whose tax dollars have built the schools deserve a lower price. Thus, this price discrimination is intended to satisfy the goal of equity.

A QUARTER FOR A COKE WHEN YOU'RE COLD

On a hot summer day, an ice-cold Coke might sound oh-so-good. But on a cold winter day? The Coca-Cola Company pondered that situation in the fall of 1999 and came up with a solution: Coke machines that set their price in response to the weather and expected demand. Instead of having delivery van drivers twiddling their thumbs while listening to the winter winds, wouldn't it be better to cut the price at Coke vending machines until sales in cold weather rival those when the summer sun sears? And what about those blazing hot days when the delivery people cannot keep the vending machines from running out? Shouldn't price rise to avoid a shortage and give the Cokes to those who value them the most?

With this logic in mind, the Coca-Cola Company made plans to develop smart vending machines that would charge more when demand is high and less when it is low. The strategy of price discrimination seemed efficient and would have involved both price increases some times and decreases other times. But the idea of being charged more when you are the most thirsty just didn't sit well with the Coke-drinking public. In fact, the press coverage was so intensely negative that Coca-Cola was forced to publicly renounce this latest form of price discrimination. ◄

7.5 THE UNITED STATES POSTAL SERVICE—A MONOPOLY IN THE PUBLIC INTEREST?

Neither snow, nor rain, nor heat, nor gloom of night stays these couriers from the swift completion of their appointed rounds.

—Inscription on Manhattan Post Office, adapted from "The Histories of Herodotus"

No Madison Avenue advertising agency could think up a better slogan for the Post Office than the motto adapted from the centuries-old Greek scripts of Herodotus. . . . The mail must go through. That principle has inspired the Post Office ever since it was established on September 26, 1789. What is probably the oldest monopoly in America is rich in tradition. For instance, the first Postmaster General was Benjamin Franklin, who was given the title by the Continental Congress in 1775, even before the creation of the Post Office itself.

For more than two centuries the Post Office has grown along with the country. The Postal Reorganization Act of July 1, 1971 established the U.S. Postal Service from what had formerly been the Department of the Post Office. The Postal Service is overseen by a Board of Governors appointed by the president and approved by the Senate. It is intended to be self-supporting. In 2001, the Postal Service had 776,000 career employees and earned $65.9 billion in total revenue. If it were a private-sector company, that revenue would have placed it as the twelfth largest on the *Fortune 500* list of the largest U.S. companies. Unfortunately, that revenue was not enough to offset expenses of $67.6 billion, of which 78 percent were wages and benefits associated with some of the most sought-after blue-collar jobs in the government. The result is that the Postal Office lost $1.68 billion.

To try to make up for that loss, the Postal Service hired FedEx to handle its overnight deliveries and increased the basic rate for mailing a letter from 34 cents to 37 cents. In addition to rate increases to enhance revenues, the Postal Service periodically brings up the possibility of eliminating Saturday delivery as a way to cut down costs. Less controversial plans to keep costs down include developing and installing new automated equipment. Additional challenges include:

- the growing popularity of e-mail, which has kept postal volume flat even as the number of new postal addresses grows by about 1.7 million each year.
- the costs of protecting employees and customers from the threat of anthrax or other dangerous substances, including the costs of irradiating mail.

The result has been debated in the Senate as to whether first-class mail delivery should remain exclusively in the hands of the U.S. Postal Service. New Zealand (since 1998) and Sweden (since 1994) have abolished their postal monopolies, with Germany scheduled to follow suit. Even though the trend is toward greater competition in postal services, entrusting delivery of the mail to a governmental postal monopoly is still the norm in countries around the globe.

The U.S. Postal Service is such a monopoly, guaranteed by the postal monopoly statutes and, according to some interpretations, even by the U.S. Constitution. Rivals such as UPS and FedEx are allowed to deliver packages and urgent correspondence, but not other mail. Thus, the law is a barrier to entry that prohibits the rise of competition in postal services. The postal monopoly includes at least two elements of law that act as barriers:

- control over household mailboxes, and
- exclusive rights to delivering first-class mail, which includes personal correspondence, post cards, and many business transactions.

These restrictions explain why private companies do not deliver to household mailboxes, nor do they deliver your bills, or your letters from friends and family.

Even if the postal monopoly laws did not provide a measure of protection to the Postal Service through barriers to entry, it would still have a leg up on its competitors. Specifically, the Postal Service pays no federal income taxes, no state income taxes, and no property taxes. It can also violate certain government regulations with impunity. For example, delivery drivers know that on the busy urban streets with few parking places, traffic cops will walk right past the double-parked Postal Service truck to issue tickets to the similarly double-parked truck of the UPS or other private-delivery service. The reason is the Post Office is exempt from paying traffic fines.

PONDERING PRIVATIZATION

Privatization of the Postal Service would be one option that might increase efficiency in mail delivery. With *privitization,* firms could then compete on an equal footing against one another to capture their share of the first-class mail business, just as they do for parcel delivery. Firms that pay their workers an excessive amount or hire on the basis of politics, cronyism, or anything other than productivity would lose out. Firms that offer poor quality delivery, high prices, and poor hours would also lose. The winners would be those firms that figure out what customers think is worth paying for. Competition would force firms to seek to understand and follow the wishes of postal customers, and provide those services at a low cost.

Privatization of first-class mail delivery would have many hurdles to overcome. One of the first effects of privatization might be confusion, as a jumble of companies competed against each other for customers. Companies would find themselves on overlapping routes, and realize that combining operations would be more efficient by eliminating that overlap. If the postal services are a natural monopoly, only the one most efficient company would survive. However, we see more than one survivor in the package delivery business, so perhaps two or more companies might be able to profitably coexist. Which companies would they be?

Another hurdle is that the Postal Service is committed to *universal access,* in which mail service is offered at equal rates to everyone, despite some addresses being more expensive to serve than others. In this way, local urban delivery of first-class mail subsidizes delivery of first-class mail across greater distances and to rural areas. A more competitive marketplace would price on the basis of cost and eliminate this *cross subsidization,* in which the revenue from some services helps to pay for other services. Competitors would lower prices of the more profitable services and raise the prices of the others.

Dozens of government-provided goods and services have been turned over to the private sector in one place or another. Private-sector provision of services such as garbage collection, tree trimming along city streets, housekeeping and custodial services, forest management, police protection, education, social services, family planning, and many more provide ample evidence of the widespread acceptance of privatization. Yet, there is often resistance to privatization.

Privitization that increases the efficiency of delivery might involve layoffs, which the postal workers' unions would oppose. Competition might lead to nonunion workers being hired, which would also be opposed by the unions. For these reasons and because of the public's high regard for letter carriers, Congress would find itself embroiled in controversy if it were to pass legislation to privatize postal services. With unrestricted privatization, prices of each type of service would tend toward the marginal cost of that service. Prices would be more efficient, but whether they would seem fair might depend on the personal impact of the price changes.

*T*HINKING *C*RITICALLY

1. Do you believe that universal access is a core mandate of the Postal Service? Should the rural population pay the full cost of providing service to those in remote areas?

2. If the Post Office is privatized, how should the government go about picking a new owner? What conditions, if any, do you think should be placed on ownership? Would you prefer to see a privately owned, regulated Postal Service? If so, why? If not, why not?

Visit **www.prenhall.com/collinge** for updates and web exercises on this Explore & Apply topic.

SUMMARY AND LEARNING OBJECTIVES

1. **Describe how barriers to entry create market power.**
   - Barriers to entry reduce competition. When there are no barriers to entry, as in the case of pure competition, the firm's demand curve is perfectly elastic (horizontal). Barriers to entry steepen the firm's demand curve and are the root cause of monopoly.

2. **Discuss the profit-maximizing process for a monopolist.**
   - Monopoly occurs when there is a single seller of an output that has no close substitutes.
   - Monopoly firms are price makers—they have some control over their price. As a consequence their demand curves are downward sloping. The monopoly demand curve equals the market demand curve.

- Monopoly firms include natural monopolies, such as the public utilities. Natural monopoly is created by economies of scale in which the long-run average cost curve is downwardly sloping throughout or nearly throughout the range of demand. One firm is able to supply the entire market at a lower per unit cost than could two or more firms because of the economies of scale.

- A monopoly firm maximizes profit at the point where marginal revenue equals marginal cost. The marginal revenue curve for a monopoly firm will slope downward more steeply than demand. When demand is linear, the marginal revenue curve will be a straight line that is twice as steep as demand.

- The profit-maximizing monopoly will first select its output where marginal revenue equals marginal cost. As a price maker, it will then identify the point on its demand curve associated with the amount of output produced. The appropriate point on the demand curve indicates the price the monopolist will set.
- Graphically, total economic profit earned by a monopoly firm is shown by the area of a rectangle. Total profit equals output multiplied by per-unit profit.

3. Explain the inefficiencies of monopoly.

- The short-run profit-maximizing output for a monopoly firm will be inefficiently small, while the price will be inefficiently high. The unregulated monopolist produces at the point where marginal revenue equals marginal cost, while the efficient output occurs where demand and marginal cost intersect.

4. Name and briefly discuss major U.S. antitrust laws and policies toward monopoly.

- Major U.S. antitrust laws include the Sherman Act (1890), Clayton Act (1914), and Federal Trade Commission Act (1914). These laws aim to curb anti-competitive actions by firms.
- Potentially punishable practices include exclusive dealing, exclusive territories, predatory pricing, price discrimination, refusals to deal, resale price maintenance, and tie-in sales. These practices are not always illegal, but can be illegal when they reduce competition.
- Monopolies are commonly either owned or regulated by government. Rate-of-return regulation by government aims to bring down the monopoly price. Graphically, price is set by the regulators at the intersection of demand and long-run average cost.
- An unprofitable monopoly industry might be subsidized by government. In this case, the government pays the monopolist the amount of its operating losses. Public transit companies are a possible example. Two-part pricing is sometimes an alternative to

subsidies. The price paid by each consumer will consist of a flat monthly fee plus charges for the amount used. Water companies are a possible example.

5. Define product differentiation and state its implications.

- Product differentiation is sometimes present in oligopoly markets, but always present in monopolistic competition. Product differentiation occurs when firms attempt to distinguish their product or service from that of competitors. Product differentiation is intended to increase demand.
- Advertising is a means of achieving product differentiation. Successful advertising by a firm increases its share of the market.

6. Relate how and why firms charge some consumers more than others for the same products.

- Some firms may be able to practice price discrimination. They charge different customers different prices for the same product when there are no cost differences to justify the price differences. Price discrimination is motivated by the desire for greater profit. It requires that the firm be able to segment the market into categories, such as children and adult customers.

7. Assess the merits of protecting the U.S. Postal Service from competition.

- The delivery of mail is characterized by legal monopoly. In the case of first-class mail, the U.S. Postal Service is guaranteed a monopoly by the U.S. Constitution and other law. Private-sector competition in some aspects of mail delivery is allowed. Other competition faced by the Postal Service comes from technological change such as e-mail. Cross-subsidization in Postal Services means that the revenue from some services helps to pay for other services. An alternative to the current Postal Service would privatize the delivery of mail.

KEY TERMS

monopoly, 154
barriers to entry, 154
monopoly by law (legal monopoly), 154
monopoly by possession, 154
natural monopoly, 154

price maker, 155
deadweight loss, 162
antitrust law, 162
rate-of-return regulation (average-cost pricing), 164
oligopoly, 165

mutually interdependent, 165
differentiated products, 166
monopolistic competition, 166
price discrimination, 168

TEST YOURSELF

TRUE OR FALSE

1. One of the best examples of natural monopoly is a taxi-cab company.
2. A firm facing a demand curve that slopes downward to the right has market power.
3. Fair-rate-of-return regulation of monopoly is designed to provide a monopolist with a normal profit.
4. The price charged by an unregulated monopolist will equal the monopolist's marginal cost.
5. Price discrimination occurs when a firm charges different customers different prices because there is a difference in the cost of serving those customers.

MULTIPLE CHOICE

6. Barriers to entry
   a. increase the number of firms in an industry.
   b. decrease the number of firms in an industry.
   c. have no effect on the number of firms in an industry.
   d. have unpredictable effects on the number of firms in an industry.
7. A natural monopoly occurs when
   a. government grants a patent to a firm.
   b. government prohibits the entry of new competitor firms.
   c. one firm can produce at lower average cost than can any combination of two or more firms.
   d. the product that is monopolized pertains to natural resources.
8. The best example of a natural monopoly is
   a. a local electric utility.
   b. the U.S. Postal Service.
   c. an airline.
   d. a public school.
9. A natural monopoly is characterized by
   a. perfectly elastic demand.
   b. an upward-sloping long-run average-cost curve throughout.
   c. a flat long-run average-cost curve.
   d. a demand curve that intersects long-run average cost near or to the left of the minimum point of the long-run average-cost curve.
10. *Ceteris paribus*, a steeper demand curve indicates
    a. the firm is a price taker.
    b. less market power.
    c. more market power.
    d. the firm is not a monopolist.

11. A marginal revenue curve for a monopoly firm will
    a. be shaped like the letter *J*.
    b. lie below the demand curve.
    c. lie above the demand curve.
    d. be identical to the demand curve.
12. To maximize profit, the firm shown in Self-Test Figure 7-1 will produce the output associated with quantity
    a. *A.*
    b. *B.*
    c. *C.*
    d. *D.*

SELF-TEST FIGURE 7-1

13. If it produces at point *B*, the firm in Self-Test Figure 7-1 will achieve a profit per unit equal to the length of arrow(s)
    a. *E.*
    b. *F.*
    c. *G.*
    d. *E + F.*
14. In Self-Test Figure 7-1, the efficient output occurs at quantity
    a. *A.*
    b. *B.*
    c. *C.*
    d. *D.*

SELF-TEST FIGURE 7-2

15. Referring to Self-Test Figure 7-2, rate-of-return regulation leads to the price given by
    a. *A*.
    b. *B*.
    c. *C*.
    d. *D*.
16. In which market structure do firms ALWAYS produce differentiated products?
    a. Pure competition.
    b. Monopoly.
    c. Monopolistic competition.
    d. Oligopoly.

17. Unlike firms in _____, firms in _____ are likely to advertise their products.
    a. pure competition; monopolistic competition
    b. monopoly; pure competition
    c. oligopoly; pure competition
    d. monopolistic competition; pure competition
18. Monopolistically competitive firms
    a. produce homogeneous products.
    b. are also called price leaders.
    c. maximize profit by setting marginal revenue equal to marginal cost.
    d. are few in number.
19. When a firm practices price discrimination it will charge a higher price in the market segment with
    a. unit elastic demand.
    b. the least elastic demand.
    c. the most elastic demand.
    d. the largest number of buyers.
20. Which of the following best describes a service that is offered at an equal price to everyone, despite some people being more expensive to serve than others?
    a. Antitrust.
    b. Universal access.
    c. Barriers to entry.
    d. Privatization.

QUESTIONS AND PROBLEMS

1. *[barriers to entry]* Provide some examples of barriers to entry. When barriers to entry in an industry are high, is market power more or less? Explain.
2. *[market power]* When a firm has no market power, how does its demand curve appear? As market power increases, how does the appearance of a firm's demand curve change?
3. *[definition of monopoly]* What roles do substitutes play in the definition of monopoly? If there is only one seller in the market, but the firm's product has many good substitutes, is the firm a monopoly? Explain.
4. *[natural monopoly]* How is natural monopoly related to economies of scale? Give an example of a firm that is a natural monopolist.

5. *[price maker]* What is meant when a monopoly firm is described as a price maker? How is a price maker different from a price taker? Is a monopoly ever a price taker?
6. *[monopoly demand]* How is the demand curve of a monopoly firm related to the market demand curve? How will a monopoly demand curve appear graphically?
7. *[monopoly marginal revenue]* Why is marginal revenue less than price for a monopoly? Illustrate by drawing a graph with a monopoly demand curve and the corresponding marginal revenue curve. Be sure to label the axes and the curves.

8. *[monopoly and profit]* Does the mere fact of monopoly guarantee that a firm will earn economic profit? Explain.

9. *[monopoly profit maximization]* State the rule of profit maximization for a monopoly firm. Illustrate graphically a monopoly firm that is maximizing profit.

10. *[monopoly profit maximization]* Change the graph you drew in the previous problem to show the monopoly firm incurring a loss. What rule will the monopolist apply in order to select the quantity that minimizes the loss?

11. *[monopoly price and profit maximization]* Comment on the following statement: A purely competitive firm will maximize profit at the point where price equals marginal cost, but a monopolist that behaves this way will earn less than the maximum profit.

12. *[monopoly and efficiency]* Draw a graph that shows the output produced by a monopoly and compare it to the efficient output. At the efficient output, to what is price equal?

13. *[rate-of-return regulation]* What is the goal of rate-of-return regulation? What price will be set by regulators?

14. *[product differentiation]* Product differentiation is found in oligopoly and monopolistic competition. What purpose does product differentiation serve from a firm's perspective? From society's perspective?

15. *[product differentiation and advertising]* Suppose a fruit grower has developed a new type of grape that tastes somewhat like a peach. The grape is yellow in color. How would you advertise this differentiated grape to consumers?

16. *[demand curve in monopolistic competition]* Is the firm's demand curve in monopolistic competition perfectly elastic as in pure competition? Explain.

17. *[profit maximization in monopolistic competition]* Explain, using a graph, the process of short-run profit maximization in monopolistic competition.

18. *[price discrimination]* Discuss the market conditions required for price discrimination to occur. Generally speaking, is price discrimination illegal? Provide at least one example of price discrimination not mentioned in the text.

Visit www.prenhall.com/collinge for Exploring the Web exercises and additional self-test quizzes.

CHAPTER 8

EARNINGS AND INCOME DISTRIBUTION

A LOOK AHEAD

How would you react if your employer forced you to speak a foreign language at work? The French company Alcatel does by requiring its employees to speak in English. Would you be willing to work for a foreign employer, if you could work from home? Computer programmers in India work from home for U.S. companies. New possibilities are presenting themselves to us every day as the internationalization of the workplace proceeds, as explained in the Explore & Apply section that concludes this chapter.

The market for labor affects us all. For most of us, it is our job—our participation in the labor market—that provides our income. People receive incomes in the form of wages from labor, rent, interest, and profit. In this chapter you will find answers to the question of why wages differ from person to person. You will also read about poverty, analyze wage differentials between groups such as men and women, and whites and African-Americans, and see how the famous reap earnings from economic rent, savers from interest, and entrepreneurs from profit.

LEARNING OBJECTIVES

Understanding Chapter 8 will enable you to:
1. **Relate the importance of wages and salaries.**
2. **Analyze why higher wages can lead an individual to prefer either more or fewer work hours.**
3. **List and explain the many causes of earnings differentials among workers.**
4. **Assess the extent and significance of poverty and earnings differentials in the U.S. economy.**
5. **Discuss significant differences between the types of income—wages, rent, interest, and profit.**
6. **Explain why the employment of labor has become increasingly global in scope.**

Explore & Apply

In the preceding two chapters we examined the markets for output. Here we look at the incomes that people receive from producing that output.

8.1 MEASURING INCOMES

What are the sources of your family's income? Wages from a job, interest from a bank account, and perhaps profit from a business put money into the pockets of many American families. Figure 8-1 shows the relative importance in the United States of the primary sources of national income. In that pie chart we see that wages and salaries provide 72 percent of U.S. national income. Businesses provide another 18 percent in the form of corporate profits plus the income from proprietorships. Interest earnings provide another 8 percent, while rents received by landlords provide 2 percent.

Figure 8-1 does not accurately reflect the meaning of wages as economists use the term. This shortcoming of the data arises because some fraction of proprietor's income is in reality wages, while another part of proprietor's income is profit. Likewise, some wage income is a return to labor; other such income is a return to human capital. Even profit in the figure is based on the accounting definition rather than the economic definition. Despite these data shortcomings, Figure 8-1 clearly shows the importance of wages and salaries as a source of income.

Wages are the incomes that workers earn from their jobs. The size of their incomes depends on two variables: the quantity of labor they supply and the amount they are paid. The quantity of labor supplied is usually measured in hours. The price of labor is the *wage rate*—the amount an individual is paid per hour. When the wage rate is multiplied by hours worked, the result is *earnings*, the income from labor. For example, in May 2002, average hourly earnings of production workers were $14.70, which when multiplied by their average weekly hours of 34.2 resulted in average weekly earnings of $502.74.

Most hourly wage workers who work more than 40 hours a week receive time-and-a-half pay for all hours over 40. Hours in excess of 40 are called *overtime* hours. Overtime wage rates are 50 percent greater than the *straight-time* rate that a worker receives for the first 40 hours worked. The Department of Labor enforces these rules, which arise from the *Fair Labor Standards Act,* enacted by Congress in 1938.

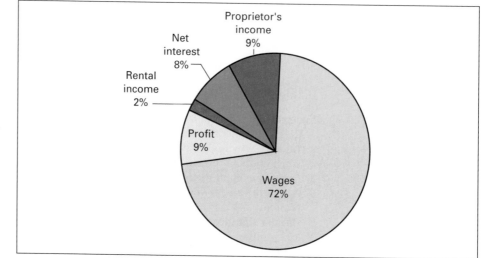

FIGURE 8-1

U.S. NATIONAL INCOME The pie chart shows sources of income in the United States. Wages are by far the largest source of income.

Source: Bureau of Economic Analysis, *National Income and Product Account Tables.* Data are for 2001.

Workers who are paid a *salary* receive a fixed amount of income, no matter how many hours they work. Employers expect salaried employees to work a minimum number of hours per week, typically corresponding to the regular operating hours of the business. If such employees work additional hours, they are not paid for those hours. Labor Department rules govern what types of jobs pay salaries versus hourly wages.

An employer's *total labor costs* are the sum of wages and salaries plus fringe benefits. Some benefits are voluntarily offered by employers; others are required by government. Benefits received by workers include paid vacations, sick leave, and employer contributions to Social Security. *Workers' compensation* coverage (which provides workers who are injured on the job with a stipend while they recuperate from their injuries), paid time off for lunch, and health benefits round out the list of typical benefits. For typical U.S. employers, benefits account for about 28 percent of labor costs. These labor costs for employers are incomes for the workers who receive them.

8.2 INDIVIDUAL LABOR SUPPLY

Labor force participation reflects the decisions of individuals to offer their services in the labor market. To be counted as a member of the labor force, a person must either have paid employment or be actively looking for it. Examples of nonparticipants include full-time students and retirees.

Individual preferences play a key role in explaining labor force participation, and hence earnings. These preferences are reflected in the individual's labor supply curve. Figure 8-2 illustrates an individual's labor supply curve. Below the **reservation wage,** individuals "reserve" their labor—they choose not to work at all. Note that, unlike supply curves for other things, the individual's supply curve of labor services has a *backward-bending* portion. This shape can be understood by considering the substitution effect and the income effect of increasing wage rates.

As wage rates rise at first, the **substitution effect** of the change in wage rates causes individuals to work more—they substitute away from leisure, because the opportunity cost of leisure becomes higher as wage rates rise. The result is that people offer more hours in response to higher wages, causing the supply curve to slope upward. In place of leisure, workers consume goods and services with their increased earnings.

reservation wage the lowest wage offer an individual will accept.

substitution effect when the wage rate increases, individuals recognize that the opportunity cost of leisure has risen, choose to substitute labor for leisure, and thus offer to work more hours.

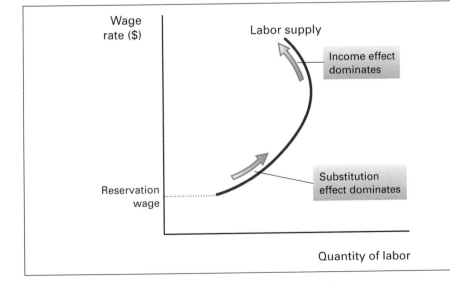

Wage rate ($)

Labor supply

Income effect dominates

Substitution effect dominates

Reservation wage

Quantity of labor

FIGURE 8-2

AN INDIVIDUAL'S BACKWARD-BENDING SUPPLY OF LABOR The backward-bending supply curve of an individual's labor services is explained by the tug of war between the income and substitution effects of a wage change. The income effect is such that, as the wage rate rises, it causes higher income and a desire to take more vacation time to enjoy it. The substitution effect is the response to increase one's labor because it becomes relatively more expensive to take that time off.

income effect when the wage rate rises, individuals offer to work fewer hours because their higher incomes increase their demands for normal goods, including leisure.

As wage rates rise, eventually the **income effect** of the wage change tugs the worker in the opposite direction from the substitution effect. Higher wages bring higher incomes, which prompt workers to demand more of all normal goods. *Leisure*—time away from work—is a normal good. To "buy" more leisure, workers pay the opportunity cost of giving up the income that could have been earned by working. The result is that, as wage rates rise, the income effect prompts workers to offer fewer hours of work.

The supply curve bends backward when the income effect outweighs the substitution effect. This accounts for the huge decline in yearly hours of work for the average American worker over the last 100 years. The standard eight-hour workday and annual paid vacations have permitted workers to enjoy more leisure as real incomes have risen. Self-employed workers, such as physicians and accountants with private practices, can increase their vacation time to enjoy their substantial income. As seen in Figure 8-2, the substitution effect tends to be stronger at lower wage rates, and the income effect tends to be stronger at higher wage rates. The result is a supply curve that first slopes upward and then bends backward.

Individuals' labor supply curves will vary depending on whether they are *primary workers,* the main source of income in households, or *secondary workers,* whose incomes are not as critical to their households' well-being. The labor supply curves of primary workers are nearly vertical, meaning that they will choose to work about the same number of hours, no matter the wages they are able to receive. The quantity of labor supplied by a primary worker is typically in the range of 35 to 45 hours per week. In contrast, secondary workers have a much more pronounced upward slope and backward bend to their supply curves. Secondary workers are more likely to hold part-time jobs than primary workers.

As an example of an individual's labor supply decisions, consider Elena, a full-time college student. Earning good grades is her priority. The $7 an hour paid by the Burger Barn is below her reservation wage. She could earn $8 an hour by modeling hair styles for Hair Trends, but that amount is not enough to induce her to work, either.

If an employer were willing to pay Elena $10 an hour, she would go to work part-time, but not for a penny less—$10 is her reservation wage. Elena would work more hours if she were offered an even higher wage rate. If she were offered $20 an hour, every hour of leisure time would cost her $20 in lost earnings. She would then be willing to work 25 hours a week.

Because of her commitment to school, Elena would not work more than 25 hours. That is the point where her labor supply curve bends back. For example, if she could earn $30 per hour, she would reduce her hours of work below 25 hours because at $30 an hour her income effect would outweigh her substitution effect.

Elena's reservation wage could change. If she needed money for books, she might lower her reservation wage and apply for a job at the Burger Barn. When she graduates, her reservation wage is likely to go up because the value of her labor is greater. If she doesn't receive a job offer that meets her higher reservation wage, she might eventually lower it. Reservation wages can change when people can't find a job.

Labor supply curves may shift. Many persons receive *nonlabor income* from investments, pension funds, government transfer payments, interest on bank deposits, gifts from relatives, and other sources. The amount of nonlabor income received can affect labor market choices. Generally, **a greater amount of nonlabor income will reduce the labor a worker supplies, while a smaller amount would increase the quantity of labor supplied.** If Elena did not receive income from home, it is likely that her labor supply curve would shift to the right and her reservation wage would decline. Figure 8-3 illustrates the effect of a decrease in nonlabor income.

The *market labor supply* sums the quantity of labor supplied at various wage rates for all the individuals in a labor market. Market supply curves of labor are upward sloping in the range of income that is usually relevant to employers.

An *industry labor supply* sums the quantity of labor supplied to a particular industry at various wage rates. Because higher wage rates in one industry attract workers from other industries, any particular industry supply curve of labor is nearly always upward sloping. It

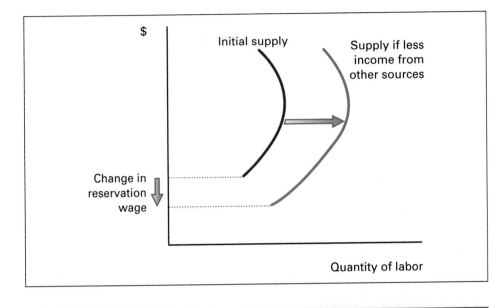

FIGURE 8-3

EFFECT OF A DECREASE IN NONLABOR INCOME A decrease in nonlabor income shifts the labor supply curve to the right and decreases the reservation wage. With less income from other sources, people increase the amount of labor supplied at any wage rate.

QUICKCHECK

Compare the outcome of an increase in the wage rate if Judy's labor supply curve is: (a) upward-sloping; (b) backward-bending; and (c) vertical.

Answer: If Judy's labor supply curve slopes upward, an increase in the wage rate will increase her quantity of labor supplied. If the wage rate intersects the backward-bending portion of her labor supply curve, an increase in the wage rate will decrease her quantity of labor supplied. With a vertical labor supply curve, Judy's quantity of labor supplied would not change.

is also usually quite elastic, meaning that a small increase in the wage rate would result in a large increase in the quantity of labor supplied. For example, as wages rise in the trucking industry, some truckers might work less because of the income effect. However, it is likely that the reduction in work time by individual truckers will be more than offset by an inflow of would-be truckers from other occupations.

TOO RICH TO WORK? OR TOO POOR TO RETIRE?   *SNAPSHOT*

In the easy money days of the late 1990s, many workers saw their accumulated wealth double and double again. They asked themselves, "Why work?" and commenced with planning for early retirement. Then, in the face of an estimated $7.8 trillion worth of stock market declines in the early 2000s, some of these same people were forced to ask themselves the opposite question. Could they afford to retire?

The riches they had amassed had vanished just as quickly as they had appeared. Lavish spending patterns based on that transitory wealth led many to take on debt. Whether it be to credit card companies or home mortgage lenders, that debt must be repaid. To do so takes an income, and an income once more means work. After being teased with thoughts of early retirement, the cold reality for many people is that they cannot reach that life of leisure even as soon as they originally planned. It all goes to show that labor supply is not just about how many hours of work to offer at any given wage. It's also about whether to work at all! ◄

8.3 SOURCES OF EARNINGS DIFFERENTIALS

Wage differentials among workers sometimes seem intuitive. We expect a heart surgeon to earn more than a janitor. Many wage differentials are not so easy to understand, however. Why should physicians earn more than teachers? Why should star athletes earn more than physicians? Individual earnings differ because of a combination of factors, which we will examine next.

OCCUPATIONAL CHOICE AND COMPENSATING WAGE DIFFERENTIALS

Numerous occupations exist. Over 700 basic occupations are cataloged on the Internet database *Occupational Information Network,* also known as *O*NET,* which was created by the U.S. Department of Labor. Occupational choice plays a significant role in earnings power. Generally, the highest-paying occupations are those that require the greatest skills, and the lowest paying are the occupations of the unskilled.

> **compensating wage differentials** additional pay offered by employers to offset undesirable job characteristics.

Different jobs have their own advantages and disadvantages. Most people would rather work at safe jobs in climate-controlled comfort than at dangerous jobs outside in the extremes of weather. Higher pay in the latter jobs can equalize their attractiveness relative to the former jobs. Such increases in pay are termed **compensating wage differentials.**

Sanitation workers, coal miners, and many others have unpleasant or dangerous jobs. To induce workers to take those jobs, employers must pay a compensating differential. Note that even with compensating differentials included, the pay in such jobs may still be relatively low, because skill requirements in many of these jobs are low.

People choose jobs on the basis of numerous job characteristics. Pay, the *pecuniary* attribute, is the most important for some. For others, job security, status, the likelihood of advancement, safe working conditions, interest in the work, or the flexibility of employers in matters of dress or hours is most important. Job features unrelated to pay are called the *nonpecuniary* attributes. Positive nonpecuniary features can offset low pay.

LABOR UNIONS

Workers join labor unions to improve their pay and work environments. At the peak of union membership in 1953, 36 percent of U.S. workers belonged to a union. In 2001 that figure stood at 16.3 million members out of the civilian labor force of 142 million, or about 11.5 percent of the labor force.

The decline in overall union membership masks the concentration of membership in several key industries. Indeed, government employee unionism has reached record levels, with 7 million government workers, equal to about 37.5 percent of such workers, belonging to unions. Table 8-1 shows the percentage of workers belonging to a union. In part (A) we see that over one-third of government workers belong to unions, but less than 2 percent of workers in agriculture do. In part (B) we see that union members are concentrated in the blue-collar occupations.

Possibly the most important factor behind the low percentage of union workers in the economy is more global competition in industries where unions have historically been strong. Fewer U.S. workers in these industries mean fewer union members. Examples include the steel and auto industries. Also contributing to the decline in unionism has been the increasing importance of white-collar jobs, in which the appeal of unions is relatively weak. Nonetheless, a recent nationwide survey of workers showed one-third of those surveyed who were not union members would like to be.

In order to reverse the long-term decline in membership, unions reach out for new members. Union efforts to "organize" an employer—have the right to represent its workers—culminate in a secret ballot representation election, under the supervision of the federal

TABLE 8-1	PERCENTAGE OF WORKERS BELONGING TO A UNION

(A) BY MAJOR INDUSTRY	
INDUSTRY	**PERCENT**
Private wage and salary workers	9.0
Agriculture	1.6
Mining	12.3
Construction	18.4
Manufacturing	14.6
Transportation and public utilities	23.5
Wholesale and retail trade	4.7
Finance, insurance, and real estate	2.1
Services	5.9
Government workers	37.5

(B) BY OCCUPATION	
OCCUPATION	**PERCENT**
Managerial and professional specialty	12.8
Technical, sales, and administrative support	8.9
Service occupations	13.3
Precision production, craft, and repair	21.3
Operators, fabricators, and laborers	19.9
Farming, forestry, and fishing	4.6

Source: *Union Membership*, USDL, Bureau of Labor Statistics, Table 3. The data are from 2001.

government's National Labor Relations Board (NLRB). When more than half of a firm's employees vote in favor of a union, the NLRB certifies the union as the bargaining agent for the workers. Once certified, a union engages in **collective bargaining,** negotiations with employers aimed at improving working conditions, pay, and benefits. Legally, employers must bargain with a union, but are not obligated to reach agreement.

collective bargaining negotiations between an employer and a labor union.

When firms balk at union demands, which side will prevail? **Union *bargaining power* refers to the ability of a union to win an agreement with greater wages and benefits for its members. The primary weapon providing bargaining power to unions is the *strike*, or work stoppage.** The ability to shut down an employer is a powerful weapon, although strikers have the incentive to settle a strike because they are not paid wages while on strike. Generally, a strike will be preceded by negotiations. Thus, a strike indicates the failure of negotiations. However, there are *wildcat strikes*, work stoppages that occur spontaneously because of workers' grievances against their employers. When an employer faces a strike, its most powerful source of bargaining power is the right to hire permanent replacements for

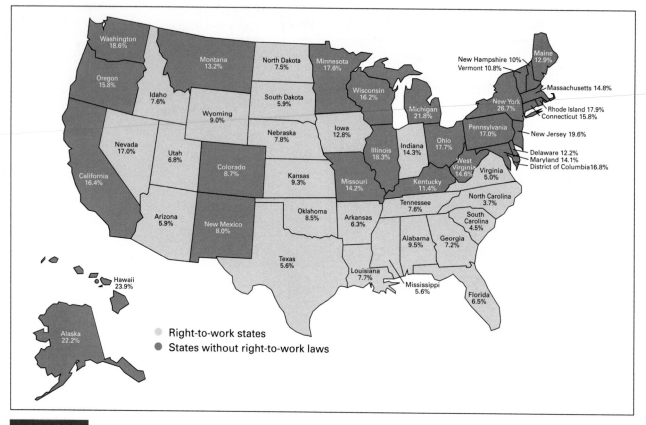

FIGURE 8-4

UNION MEMBERSHIP BY STATE The map shows the percent of employed workers in each state that belong to a labor union. There is wide variation in union membership from state to state. The highest percentage of union members is found in New York, while the lowest is in North Carolina. In general, right-to-work states have a lower percent of union members than do other states.

Source: Union Membership, USDL, Bureau of Labor Statistics, Table 5. The percentages are from 2001. The right-to-work information is also from the USDL, and includes laws and constitutional amendments in effect as of January 1, 2002. Indiana's right-to-work statute applies only to school employees.

striking workers. However, firms often do not exercise that right for fear of violence toward their property or replacement employees.

Union bargaining power is reduced in the 23 states with some form of a *right-to-work law,* which permits a unionized firm's workers the option of not joining the union. In these states, union and nonunion workers may work side-by-side on the job. Hence, workers in right-to-work states are less likely to present a united front when labor disputes arise, a situation that decreases union bargaining power. Figure 8-4 shows the percent of employed workers in each state that belong to a union. Union membership is the highest in New York, and the lowest in North Carolina.

Another union weapon is the *boycott,* a campaign to persuade union members and the public to refrain from purchasing the output of a firm with which the union has a disagreement. Boycotts often go hand-in-hand with strikes.

Given the weapons unions have, it should not be surprising that union wages are high. Median weekly earnings for union members in 2001 were $718, approximately 25 percent higher than the $575 for those not represented by unions.

Higher pay means fewer jobs offered by unionized employers, which increases the supply of labor to similar jobs at nonunion employers, and drives down nonunion wages. Furthermore, the kinds of jobs held by union members differ from the kinds held by other workers. Some of the higher pay in union jobs is likely to be compensating differentials, which would be paid even in the absence of unions. The consensus of research on union wages is that, after taking account of all other factors affecting wages, **unions raise wages for their members. However, estimates of the increase vary too widely to know its magnitude with certainty.**

HUMAN CAPITAL AND SIGNALING

Human capital is another important determinant of earnings differentials. Human capital is the knowledge, skills, and other productivity-enhancing attributes embodied within individual workers. Attending college is a prime example of how to increase one's human capital. Sources of human capital include formal schooling, on-the-job training, and classroom-skills training.

It is costly to build a stock of human capital. There are out-of-pocket, explicit costs, as well as the opportunity costs of forgone earnings. For many college students, opportunity costs far exceed the explicit costs. Is a college degree worth the investment? College graduates are less likely to be unemployed than high-school graduates, and earn higher incomes over their adult lives. The $786 median weekly salary in 2001 for college graduates exceeded the median of $474 for high-school graduates by about 66 percent. The statistics must be interpreted with caution, however, since those going to college may differ in other respects from those who do not. For example, college students might be smarter and more motivated than workers who do not go to college, in which case they would earn more than other people, even without college.

Several studies indicate that the returns to the investment in a college diploma probably increased over the last twenty years, which helps explain why an increasing fraction of high-school graduates attend college. As discussed in Chapter 2, international trade has limited the return to labor in the United States, although it has increased the return to capital, including human capital. There are various other influences, too, such as:

1. The decline in the power of unions to raise wages above competitive levels for their mostly high-school-educated membership.
2. The flow of relatively unskilled immigrants into the United States, many of whom compete for jobs against high-school graduates.
3. The increased desire of employers to hire college graduates for jobs that have not historically required advanced education.
4. The high-tech economy, which places a premium on education.

The **signaling** hypothesis provides an additional explanation for the greater earnings of college graduates. In this view, education provides information to employers about the characteristics of job applicants. Employers believe that more education signals that one is easily trained and reliable.

signaling the view that education provides information to employers about the characteristics of job applicants.

DISCRIMINATION AND EARNINGS

Wage discrimination occurs when a worker who is as productive as other workers doing the same job is paid less because of race, gender, color, religion, or national origin. This discrimination is illegal in the United States. It is difficult to ascertain what part of wage differences between workers occurs as a result of wage discrimination and what part occurs because of productivity differences. Productivity differences among workers often result from differences in human capital, which may reflect differing amounts and quality of schooling. Good schooling requires access to quality schools, which is lacking in many inner-city neighborhoods. It also requires an investment of time and money, which is hard to come by for poor youths whose earnings may be needed within their families.

To the extent that a group experiences systematic discrimination prior to entering the labor market, the outcome is less human capital and lower earnings. For example, blacks may earn less than whites because of such *pre-market discrimination,* in which access to good schooling is denied, and racial stereotyping of black youths occurs. This situation can also harm blacks with higher-than-average human capital to the extent that employers lack essential information about individual job applicants and resort to *statistical discrimination,* which is to judge applicants by the average characteristics of their racial or ethnic group.

Evidence indicates that wage discrimination by employers typically accounts for only a part of wage differentials among racial and gender groups. An individual's age, ability, health, education, marital status, occupation, and number of years of work experience affect his or her productivity and hence earnings. A good part of the lower earnings of minorities and women can be attributed to differences in these attributes.

LUCK AND OTHER INFLUENCES

Wage differentials exist even among individuals who are identical in all measurable attributes that may affect earnings, including race and gender. Such wage differences reflect the effect of difficult-to-measure factors on earnings. Being in the right place at the right time and other forms of luck can play a significant role in wage differences.

Other possible factors creating wage differences include disparities in looks, height, social skills, ambition, selection of a marriage partner, and other tangible and intangible attributes. For example, experiments have shown that good-looking people have an advantage in the labor market. When two people with identical credentials have been sent to the same job interview, the good-looking applicant is usually offered the job while the average-looking one is not. Thus, the greater demand by employers for physical attractiveness will translate into higher earnings for persons possessing such traits.

Wages tend to be related to the cost of living. In localities where the cost of living is high, wages also tend to be high. For example, the cost of living is much higher in New York City than in Mississippi, and so wages tend to be higher in New York City than in Mississippi. Wages also tend to be higher in urban areas than in surrounding rural areas, possibly reflecting a lower cost of living in rural areas. Because of differences in the cost of living, the purchasing power of a particular wage can vary enormously. A wage that barely allows a person to subsist in New York City might allow a comfortable existence in Mississippi. Thus, higher wages do not always mean that the recipients of those wages are better off.

8.4 INCOME INEQUALITY

Income inequality refers to differences in earnings. Here we examine the amount of income inequality. We start with the problem of poverty.

POVERTY

Low wages or lack of a job can create poverty. Poverty is associated with deprivation, which motivates government transfer programs to aid the poor. Some of these transfers are "cash," such as the well-known welfare check. About two-thirds of government transfers to the poor provide *in-kind benefits,* meaning that valuable services are provided instead of money. In-kind benefits include healthcare, food stamps, subsidized housing, and subsidized school lunches. These programs seek to preserve a minimum standard of living for the poor and are commonly referred to as the *social safety net.*

Most households in poverty are very close to the government-set **poverty line.** This income threshold varies by household size and composition. From 1959 to 1973, the number of persons falling below the poverty line decreased from 22 percent to 11 percent of the population, then stayed within the range of 11 to 15 percent over the following years. The poverty rate in 2001 was 11.7 percent. Poverty rates vary by family status, age, and race. For example, about 26.4 percent of families with a female household head and no husband present fell below the poverty line in 2000. With the safety net provided by Social Security, poverty among the elderly has fallen to 10.1 percent of people over 65, down from 35 percent in 1959. Poverty rates are about 3 times higher among blacks than whites. Poverty also varies among the states. Louisiana and New Mexico often are among the states with the highest poverty rates each year, while New Hampshire and Minnesota are usually among the states with the lowest rates.

poverty line a government-set income threshold that varies by household size and composition.

"CUT MY SALARY. PLEASE!"   *S N A P S H O T*

Incentives are changed by the existence of government transfer programs. It is not always easy to predict how people will respond to such incentives. For example, some years ago a professor asked his university's administrators to lower his annual salary by a few hundred dollars. His request was not frivolous. Its purpose was to make his children eligible for subsidized school lunches. The savings from subsidized lunches would have more than made up for his salary reduction. The moral is, those whose earnings are low may have an incentive to reduce their work effort in order to further lower their incomes and qualify for government assistance. ◄

EARNINGS OF WOMEN AND MINORITIES—A WAGE GAP REMAINS

Earnings differentials exist between groups of people. Here we look at earning differences between males and females, and whites and blacks. Even though a substantial fraction of earnings differences are explained by factors other than labor market discrimination, these differences have important social implications. Let's look at women first.

The typical full-time female worker in the United States earns about 74 cents for every dollar earned by the typical male. This figure is up from 59 cents in 1978. The closing of the earnings gap is explained by female workers developing specialized job skills, thereby allowing women to move into professional and managerial jobs. According to the Census Bureau, 7.4 million American women held executive, administrative, or managerial positions in 2001, and that number has been steadily increasing.

Although less so now than in earlier decades, women's earnings and rank are negatively affected by *discontinuous labor force participation,* which occurs when a person leaves and later reenters the labor force. Many women leave their jobs after childbirth and do not return to work for several years in order to care for their children. This in-and-out pattern of labor force participation causes women's human capital to depreciate and reduces their years of labor-market experience relative to men. The result is lower earnings. As increasing numbers of women have stayed in the labor force throughout their lives, their earnings as a group have risen relative to those of men and are expected to rise even more in the future.

Explanations for the remaining earnings gap focus on women's occupational choices. Many occupations are dominated by females. Table 8-2 compares the percentage of males in a select group of traditionally male occupations with the percentage of females in another group containing several traditionally female occupations. Many of these female-dominated occupations pay less than the male-dominated ones that involve comparable education and responsibility.

TABLE 8-2   SELECTED MALE-DOMINATED AND FEMALE-DOMINATED OCCUPATIONS

MALE-DOMINATED OCCUPATIONS (PERCENTAGE OF WORKERS WHO ARE MALES)		FEMALE-DOMINATED OCCUPATIONS (PERCENTAGE OF WORKERS WHO ARE FEMALES)	
Automobile mechanics	98.8	Dental hygienists	98.5
Carpenters	98.3	Prekindergarten and kindergarten teachers	98.4
Firefighters	97.0	Child care workers	97.5
Airplane pilots and navigators	96.3	Receptionists	96.7
Truck drivers	95.3	Cleaners and servants	94.8
Surveyors	92.6	Secretaries	94.6
Engineers	90.1	Bookkeepers and accounting clerks	92.2

Source: 2001 Statistical Abstract of the U.S., Table No. 593.

occupational segregation the concentration of female workers in a limited number of occupations.

Occupational segregation, the concentration of female workers in certain jobs, such as nursing and teaching, is often cited as evidence that women are discriminated against in hiring. The reasoning is that women are forced into these jobs because other jobs are not open to them. However, many economists deem this view simplistic, whether or not some aptitudes correlate with gender. Interruptions in women's careers because of childbearing, child rearing, and the need to change jobs because of a husband's job transfer may motivate women to select occupations in which interruptions in labor force participation will be least harmful to their careers. The skills required in these traditionally female occupations are easily transferred from one employer to another and become obsolete only very slowly.

There are other possible explanations for occupational segregation. Gender-based differences in interests may be one factor. In addition, there might be discrimination against women by the educational system, such as school guidance that channels women away from subjects that lead to employment in traditionally male jobs. Employer discrimination in hiring women for some higher-paying jobs is also sometimes pointed to. These explanations are not mutually exclusive, meaning that some combination of them could apply.

The wage gap based upon gender is a worldwide phenomena, not confined just to the United States. According to the latest data from the Organization for Economic Cooperation and Development (OECD), women workers in the United Kingdom earn 76 percent of what men earn; in France, 87 percent; Spain, 71 percent; Japan, 61 percent; and in Sweden, 83 percent.

Table 8-3 compares the earnings of men and women in the United States. The earnings data are provided by race and they include only full-time, year-round workers. Time-series data are provided in order to show the progress that women and blacks have made in closing the wage gap with white males.

Turning to black–white differences, the data show a significant earnings gap between black and white males, with the median black male earning about 76 percent of the amount earned by the median white male in 2000. While narrowing over time, this gap continues to be a source of concern. In contrast, black women earned 86 percent of the earnings of white women in 1997. African-American women show a greater attachment to the labor force than do white women, which increases the earnings of black women relative to white women. On average, black women stay in the job market longer than white women because the proportion of households headed by women is greater among black households than among white households.

TABLE 8-3   MEDIAN EARNINGS OF YEAR-ROUND, FULL-TIME WORKERS BY RACE AND GENDER

YEAR	EARNINGS OF WHITE MALES	EARNINGS OF BLACK MALES	EARNINGS OF BLACK MALES AS PERCENT OF WHITE MALE EARNINGS	EARNINGS OF WHITE FEMALES	EARNINGS OF WHITE FEMALES AS PERCENT OF WHITE MALE EARNINGS	EARNINGS OF BLACK FEMALES	EARNINGS OF BLACK FEMALES AS PERCENT OF WHITE MALE EARNINGS
1982	$38,209	$27,138	71%	$23,798	62%	$21,270	56%
1985	39,430	27,580	70	25,294	64	22,391	57
1988	39,769	29,150	73	26,487	67	23,734	60
1991	38,338	28,027	73	26,698	70	23,699	62
1994	37,339	28,090	75	27,502	74	23,743	64
1997	38,645	28,779	74	28,322	73	24,357	63
2000	40,350	30,886	76	29,661	74	25,736	64

Source: *2002 Economic Report of the President,* Table B-33. Data are adjusted for inflation and expressed in 2000 dollars.

QUICKCHECK

What effects do discontinuous labor force participation and occupational segregation have on women's earnings?

Answer: Both reduce the earnings of women. Discontinuous participation, which is dropping out of the labor force temporarily, allows women's human capital to depreciate. Occupational segregation concentrates women in certain careers, often those that pay relatively poorly.

SNAPSHOT

HOMESPUN—PROMOTING FAMILY VALUES?

Is working at home right for you? You can earn an income, be your own boss, eliminate commuting and daycare expenses, and spend time with your children. There is one problem, however: legal barriers. The Fair Labor Standards Act of 1938 outlaws commercial *piecework* sale of women's garments sewn at home. Who would know if child labor laws were violated? What if your hourly earnings fell below the minimum wage? Society has an interest in preventing the abuse of labor, but it also has an interest in promoting family cohesiveness. Sometimes laws promote some values over others. ◄

8.5 OTHER INCOMES

Up to this point we have focused on earnings in the labor market since that source of income is by far the most important economically. Now, we look at the three other sources of income: rent, interest, and profit.

RENT—WHEN INPUTS ARE IN FIXED SUPPLY

economic rent earnings in excess of opportunity cost when an input is unique.

Economic rent describes earnings in excess of opportunity costs for a unique input—one that is in fixed supply. For example, raw land is always unique because each parcel has a unique location. Numerous inputs can be unique. For example, there is only one Tiger Woods with his unique set of golfing skills and persona.

There is no data to report on economic rent in isolation. For example, the rental income to landlords that was identified in Figure 8-1 includes economic rent, but also includes a return for what is built on the land. Furthermore, economic rent applies to much more than just land.

Movie stars, top corporate executives, and well-known people in law, academia, and other professions can attribute their high incomes in large part to economic rents. When such people have talents and abilities that are exceptionally scarce and valued in the marketplace, they often find themselves earning much more than they could from their next best alternative. The combination of fixed supply and high demand for the talents of superstars results in sky-high earnings. Yet their opportunity cost, their best earnings opportunity outside their current employment, is usually not nearly so spectacular.

Wage determination and economic rent for a superstar with unique talents are illustrated in Figure 8-5. The fixed supply of superstar-quality talents results in a vertical supply curve of labor with that talent. A higher wage will not induce a greater quantity supplied, as would be the case if the supply curve were upward sloping, but not vertical. The position of the demand curve for the superstar's talents determines earnings. When demand is large relative to supply, high earnings are the outcome. The portion of earnings representing economic rent is indicated by the blue shaded area in the figure.

This model applies to a spectrum of workers. Success in many fields requires exceptional skills. The most successful heart surgeons, stockbrokers, economists, attorneys, and business executives, among others, earn economic rents.

Not everyone, even those with unique talents, is able to earn significant economic rents. Your favorite local singers possess talent that is in fixed supply, because nobody else sings just like they do. Nonetheless, without sufficiently large public demand for that talent, they

FIGURE 8-5

ECONOMIC RENT Economic rent is determined by demand. When demand is large relative to the fixed supply, earnings can be far above opportunity costs.

QUICKCHECK

Does everyone with a unique talent that is in fixed supply earn economic rent?

Answer: No, because there must be a market demand for that talent. For example, the winners of spelling bees, pig-calling contests, and county fair cook-offs exhibit unique, interesting talents, but are rarely able to earn income from those talents.

will never get rich by singing. Similarly, many minor league athletes are close to major league quality in their talents, but the public is willing to pay high ticket prices only for major leaguers. Hence, a minor leaguer with 95 percent of the talent of a major leaguer may earn only 1 percent or less of the earnings of the major leaguer. These examples have led to what is sometimes called a superstar economy, with a winner-take-all reward system.

INTEREST—KEEPING WEALTH PRODUCTIVE

Interest is the price paid for the use of money. In the United States in 2001, interest income represented 8 percent of the total income received. The payment of interest is made by borrowers, while lenders receive interest payments. Often, a *financial intermediary,* such as a bank, credit union, or savings and loan, attracts deposits from savers and lends these savings to borrowers. The government also pays interest to the owners of government *bonds,* which are IOUs of the government. Interest is usually expressed in terms of a percentage, the **interest rate.** A bank that offers savers a 3 percent interest rate will pay $3 in interest per year for each $100 saved.

> **interest** payment made by a borrower to compensate a lender for the use of money.

Interest rates have sometimes been a source of controversy, with some countries and religions over the centuries questioning whether charging money for the use of money should be allowed. However, while those with substantial wealth certainly gain by being able to "live on interest," the economy gains as well. The reason is twofold:

> **interest rate** price of borrowed money, expressed as a percentage.

- The payment of interest to lenders promotes savings that are used to pay for investments in physical and human capital that improve standards of living.
- The requirement that borrowers pay interest makes sure that the money available for investment is used where it will be most productive. Investments should be productive enough to at least be able to cover interest payments.

PROFIT—MOTIVATING THE ENTREPRENEUR

Profit motivates entrepreneurs, who perform the following functions:

- Combining resources—organizing land, labor, and capital into productive uses;
- Innovation—implementing new production methods and creating new products; and
- Taking risks—entrepreneurs face the risk of failure.

These entrepreneurial functions separate the entrepreneur from the hired manager, whose job is to carry out the vision of the entrepreneur.

Entrepreneurs face the possibility of losses as well as profits. Losses can result from a variety of causes, including faulty decision making, bad luck, or stiff competition from other firms. For this reason, some people perceive entrepreneurship as risky business. Even though nearly all workers will receive their paychecks, and nearly all bondholders and bank depositors will receive their interest income, the hard-working entrepreneur runs the risk of reaping no reward. Thus, entrepreneurship is not for everyone. In some countries the lack of entrepreneurs hurts the ability of the country to develop economically.

Economic profit can also be more than just a reward for the successful practice of entrepreneurial skills. Barriers to entry create monopoly and other market structures in which economic profits arise from lack of competition. Perhaps the most surprising aspect of profit is that profit accounts for such a small fraction of national income. Recall from the beginning of this chapter that accounting profit and proprietorship income make up just 18 percent of total national income. From this slice of income comes a significant part of the funds used to push the economy along to greater prosperity, as profits are in effect recyled into additional productive investments.

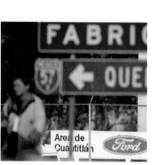

8.6 INTERNATIONALIZING THE WORK FORCE

Where were your shoes made? Your pen? Any other item you own? It is easy to know because by law the country where something is made must be indicated somewhere on the product if the product has been imported into the United States. A portion of U.S. imports are made by foreign firms employing foreign workers, but some of these imports are made by foreign workers in factories owned by U.S.-based *multinational firms.* For example, many U.S. clothing makers operate factories in other countries because of cheaper foreign labor and less regulation than they would face in the United States.

Not all U.S. multinational firms export their overseas production to the United States. For example, both Ford Motor Company and General Motors are multinational firms that operate automobile assembly plants and other manufacturing facilities in many countries around the globe. Most of the goods produced in those plants stay in the countries where they are made.

The home base of their employers is of no consequence to the workers who produce the cars. Since multinationals must abide by the labor laws where they operate, and typically follow local employment practices and customs, it doesn't matter to the workers where their employers live.

While the United States is known as the home base for many multinationals, numerous multinationals are also based elsewhere. German car maker BMW, Mexican food producer Bimbo, and Japanese electronics giant Sony are but a few examples. Whatever its home base, a multinational will have facilities and employ workers in multiple countries. For this reason, multinational firms face an international work force, made up of workers who are protected by different labor laws, speak different languages, have different work ethics, and possess varying educations. Sometimes the firm will require that its work force learn a common language to use in internal communications. Sometimes that language is not even native to the country the company calls its home. In the case of the French telecommunications giant Alcatel, for example, employees were told to learn English because that language dominates the telecommunications world.

WORKPLACE DIVERSITY

Workplace diversity is the norm in many countries. Employers are comfortable hiring the foreign born. To some extent this is because the foreign born help plug skill gaps in the work force. Whether it be a statistics professor from China, a computer systems analyst from India, or a soccer-style NFL field goal kicker from Europe, foreign-born workers are allowed to work in the United States when an employer can demonstrate that no American-born worker is available to fill the job. Table 8-4 shows the number of immigrants admitted to the United States for employment reasons. For the years shown, the total number is over a million immigrants, about 10 percent of all immigrants allowed into the country. These immigrants were allowed in because their employers certified that American workers to fill those jobs could not be found.

TABLE 8-4 U.S. EMPLOYMENT-BASED IMMIGRATION

YEAR	NUMBER OF IMMIGRANTS
1990	58,192
1991	59,525
1992	116,198
1993	147,012
1994	123,291
1995	85,336
1996	117,499
1997	90,607
1998	77,517
1999	56,817
2000	107,024

Source: 2000 U.S. Immigration and Naturalization Service Yearbook. These immigrants are classified into the following subcategories: priority workers, professionals with advanced degrees or aliens with exceptional abilities, skilled workers, professionals, other workers, special immigrants, and employment creation.

There can be a downside to employing these workers, such as for U.S. citizens who lose out on the field goal kicking and other jobs taken by the foreign workers. For the foreign workers, language barriers intrude, as does the paperwork required by the Immigration and Naturalization Service required to legally employ them. This situation sometimes leads to workplace and social stresses that were never envisioned.

Some employers claim they hire the foreign born because they will do the jobs that American workers will not do. These jobs include low-prestige jobs like janitorial work, physically demanding jobs like picking crops, and other low-paying jobs. This claim is controversial. Some of these jobs are filled by workers who are in the United States working illegally. Their employers are violating the law and subject to criminal penalties if caught, and also subject to seeing their workers deported. The result is that these workers often receive less than the minimum wage.

Some countries, such as Japan, make it virtually impossible for foreigners to work. However, the internationalization of the work force that characterizes the United States today also applies in many other countries. In England, for instance, workers from the countries that were part of the old British empire are commonly employed because the laws make it easy for that to happen.

Self-employed entrepreneurs who are foreign born add another dimension to the internationalizing of the work force. Take one 22-year-old American, Ally Svenson, for example. When she and her husband moved to London, England, where he had accepted employment with a multinational firm, she found herself wanting a latte of the kind she had enjoyed back in Seattle. Much to her dismay, there was not a latte to be found anywhere in England, a country best known for its tea drinkers. Her response? She founded the Seattle Coffee Company, a chain of coffee shops that she and her partners subsequently sold to Starbucks for $100 million. Her entrepreneurial impulse helped popularize coffee in

England. Thousands of foreign-born entrepreneurs have similarly changed the preferences of U.S. consumers, whether it be for foreign cuisine, kung fu lessons, or other previously exotic products.

The Internet and new communications technologies that are arising around the Internet are internationalizing the work force in another way. Many employers are exploiting the potential of the World Wide Web to internationalize their operations. Thus, jobs that in the past would have required American firms to fill them with American workers can now be filled with foreign workers who *stay in their home country.* For example, work on computer applications coordinated from the United States can be accomplished with programmers who live in India or most anyplace else in the world. By communicating over the Internet, work can progress simultaneously in each location. Computer software development is currently the most prominent of the jobs that can be done in this way, but employers are finding other applications. Workers in Ireland, for example, now provide many of the back-office services required by U.S. banks.

The Internet is fundamentally changing the way that labor is employed. For this reason, a worker faces competition for jobs not only from fellow citizens, but from labor in other countries. By the same token, a worker in the United States might draw a paycheck from a foreign firm. But change in the labor market is nothing new. Throughout world history, the employment of labor and other inputs has adjusted to change. The U.S. economy, and America's workers, have proven resilient enough to accommodate these changes, with more workers finding employment in the last decade than at any other time in U.S. history.

*T*HINKING
*C*RITICALLY

1. What problems relating to cultural differences might be created for American workers when foreign firms locate in the United States? Do these problems seem serious enough to justify a policy that would limit the ability of foreign firms to open for business in the United States?

2. Write a short paper reflecting upon whether U.S. employers ought to give preference to job applicants born in the United States. Take a position on this issue and justify that position.

Visit **www.prenhall.com/collinge** for updates and web exercises on this Explore & Apply topic.

SUMMARY AND LEARNING OBJECTIVES

1. **Relate the importance of wages and salaries.**
   - Wages and salaries represent over 70 percent of U.S. national income. Corporate profit, interest, proprietor's income, and rental income make up the rest of national income.
   - The price of labor is the wage rate. Earnings from labor are equal to the wage rate multiplied by hours worked. The Fair Labor Standards Act requires employers who hire labor on an hourly basis to pay overtime wage rates for hours of work in excess of 40 each week. Some workers are salaried, meaning they receive a certain amount of pay no matter how many hours they work.
   - Wages and salaries are augmented by fringe benefits to arrive at total labor costs. Fringe benefits account for about 28 percent of labor costs.

   - A person's reservation wage is the lowest acceptable wage. When the market wage rate offered by an employer to someone is less than the individual's reservation wage, a person will choose not to work. Only a wage offer above the reservation wage will be accepted.

2. **Analyze why higher wages can lead an individual to prefer either more or fewer work hours.**
   - The backward-bending individual labor supply curve shows that once the wage rate reaches a high enough level, workers may begin cutting back their quantity of labor supplied.
   - The behavior of an individual's labor supply is determined by the strength of the income and substitution effects. The substitution effect of a wage increase pro-

motes an increase in the quantity of labor supplied because a higher wage increases the opportunity cost of refraining from working. The income effect of a wage increase promotes a reduction in a person's quantity of labor supplied because a higher wage increases the demand for leisure. A personal labor supply curve bends back when the income effect is stronger than the substitution effect.

- Market labor supply curves are upward sloping, implying that higher wages lead to an increase in the quantity of labor supplied. This assertion is true even if individual labor supply curves bend backward.

3. List and explain the many causes of earnings differentials among workers.

- Important factors determining earnings are the choice of occupation, compensating wage differentials, unions, and differences in the amount of human capital. Luck, the cost of living, discrimination, and even a person's looks can affect earnings.
- Wage discrimination against blacks creates a wage differential between blacks and whites. Such discrimination is illegal. However, blacks may earn less than whites because of pre-market discrimination, in which the access of blacks to human capital is reduced. Individual blacks may also be subject to statistical discrimination, in which an employer judges each member of a group according to the group average.

4. Assess the extent and significance of poverty and earnings differentials in the U.S. economy.

- The government sets a minimum income called the poverty line, based on family size. The poverty rate is the percentage of people or families that receive less income than specified by the poverty line. The overall U.S. poverty rate has stayed within 11 to 15 percent in the last 20 years.
- The poverty problem is one example of problems associated with wage differentials. The wage gap between men and women and between whites and blacks is another. One reason for lower earnings for women is occupational segregation.

5. Discuss significant differences between the types of income—wages, rent, interest, and profit.

- Earnings in excess of opportunity cost are called economic rent. Income in the form of economic rent is received when an input is in fixed supply and the demand for the input is strong enough. Superstars in entertainment and other fields receive economic rents.
- Interest is the price paid for the use of money. An interest rate is an expression of interest in percentage terms. Interest helps to ensure that borrowed money is put to good use.
- Profit is the reward for the successful application of entrepreneurship.

6. Explain why the employment of labor has become increasingly global in scope.

- The employment of labor in the United States is affected by competition from workers abroad and by technological change. Foreign labor, both inside and outside the United States, is employed to produce goods and services for companies inside the United States. The Internet is making it possible to spread work around to take advantage of available labor in other countries.

KEY TERMS

reservation wage, 179	collective bargaining, 183	economic rent, 190
substitution effect, 179	signaling, 185	interest, 191
income effect, 180	poverty line, 187	interest rate, 191
compensating wage differentials, 182	occupational segregation, 188	

TEST YOURSELF

TRUE OR FALSE

1. Market labor supply curves are typically backward bending.
2. Evidence is clear that labor union membership has no effect on a person's earnings.
3. Statistical discrimination involves a careful effort to judge each person's characteristics before hiring that person.
4. The poverty line is defined as the earnings provided by full-time, year-round work while earning the minimum wage.

5. Discontinuous labor force participation is one cause of the wage gap between women and men.

MULTIPLE CHOICE

6. An individual's labor supply curve will start at the point called the
   a. backward-bending part.
   b. reservation wage.
   c. amount of nonlabor income.
   d. income effect.

7. In the labor supply curve shown in Self-Test Figure 8-1, which of the following points occurs where the income effect dominates the substitution effect?
   a. *A*.
   b. *B*.
   c. *C*.
   d. Either *A, B,* or *C,* depending upon where labor demand intersects the curve.

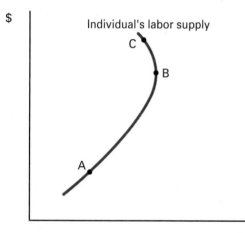

$

Individual's labor supply

C
B

A

Quantity of labor

SELF-TEST FIGURE 8-1

8. The job most likely to offer a significant compensating wage differential is
   a. baker.
   b. accountant.
   c. computer repair person.
   d. police officer.

9. Labor unions in the United States represent about ____ percent of workers.
   a. 44.
   b. 33.
   c. 22.
   d. 11.

10. A right-to-work law
    a. has no effect on union bargaining power.
    b. increases union bargaining power.
    c. decreases union bargaining power.
    d. has unpredictable effects on union bargaining power.

11. From a signaling viewpoint, earning a college degree will
    a. have no effect on earnings.
    b. decrease earnings.
    c. increase earnings because college increases human capital.
    d. increase earnings because a college degree is associated with personal characteristics employers value.

12. For blacks to have lower earnings than whites,
    a. employers must practice wage discrimination.
    b. statistical discrimination cannot be practiced by employers.
    c. pre-market discrimination could be the cause.
    d. blacks must be more productive than whites.

13. The percentage of American families falling below the poverty line in the last two decades has ranged between
    a. 4 to 8 percent of the population.
    b. 11 to 15 percent of the population.
    c. 18 to 22 percent of the population.
    d. 25 to 30 percent of the population.

14. Women earn about what percentage of mens' earnings?
    a. 53 percent.
    b. 61 percent.
    c. 74 percent.
    d. 89 percent.

15. Discontinuous labor force participation is associated with
    a. teenage workers.
    b. women workers.
    c. men workers.
    d. black workers.

16. Occupational segregation is often cited as an explanation for
    a. how people choose their life's work.
    b. the concentration of women workers in certain jobs.
    c. jobs that used to be performed in the United States that are now performed abroad.
    d. child labor.

17. A characteristic of the model illustrating economic rent is a supply curve that
    a. slopes upward.
    b. slopes downward.
    c. is horizontal.
    d. is vertical.

18. A large portion of actress Julia Roberts's earnings from starring in movies is
    a. wages.
    b. rent.
    c. interest.
    d. profit.
19. Profit is primarily associated with which input?
    a. Land.
    b. Labor.
    c. Capital.
    d. Entrepreneurship.

20. The percentage of immigrants admitted into the United States for employment reasons in the last decade was equal to approximately _____ percent.
    a. 10
    b. 30
    c. 70
    d. 90

QUESTIONS AND PROBLEMS

1. *[incomes]* Use common sense to speculate on why wages and salaries make up such a large fraction of total income, while profit makes up such a relatively small portion. As a matter of fact, the fraction representing wages and salaries remains relatively stable in the long run. Why do you think this is so? Speculate as to what the world would be like if the percentages were flipped, with wages making up 9 percent of the total and profit accounting for 72 percent.

2. *[total labor costs]* Why are total labor costs more than just wages? Explain by using examples of other labor costs beside wages.

3. *[wages]* Why do some employers offer fringe benefits that exceed those required by government? Why do other employers choose not to offer such fringe benefits? Evaluate and state the advantage to an employer who offers the following fringe benefits:
    a. Free day care.
    b. Flextime—within limits, employees pick their own starting and quitting times.
    c. Employee lunchroom with lunches provided to employees at cost.
    d. 2 weeks paid vacation.

4. *[reservation wage]* What is your reservation wage today? What will it be when you graduate from college? What could cause your reservation wage to change over the course of your life?

5. *[backward-bending labor supply curve]* Draw a graph that shows a backward-bending labor supply curve. Does this model apply to your behavior? If so, at what income would your personal labor supply curve start to bend backward?

6. *[income and substitution effects]* Discuss the income and substitution effects within the context of the backward-bending labor supply curve. Must a person's labor supply curve bend backward? Explain.

7. *[earnings differentials]* Some employees automatically pay workers according to seniority—how long they have worked for the employer. Others pay according to a person's productivity—merit. Evaluate the following statements.
    a. "Basing pay raises on seniority rewards mediocrity."
    b. "Merit pay plans allow bosses to reward their favorites and punish those they dislike."

8. *[compensating differentials]* Discuss the notion of compensating differentials for the following occupations:
    a. Nurses.
    b. Forest rangers.
    c. Movie and TV actors.
    d. The occupation that you would like to pursue.

9. *[union wages]* What is the most powerful weapon that unions wield in order to win higher wages for their members? Are unions actually successful at winning higher wages? What is the tradeoff for unions?

10. *[unions]* Americans hold strong opinions about unions, with some favoring unions and others opposed to them. Write a short essay that focuses on your personal views toward unions. Justify your views with information from the chapter and from other sources about the role and effectiveness of unions.

11. *[returns to college]* State and briefly discuss the causes that economists have identified as contributing to the increased return to a college education.

12. *[signaling]* Discuss the merits of the signaling hypothesis. Provide at least three positive characteristics that an employer might reasonably believe a college graduate would possess.

13. *[wage gap]* What factors other than discrimination might explain why women earn less than men? If there were no discrimination against women, would women earn the same as men? Why or why not?

14. *[discrimination]* Is it fair to allow firms to pay more productive workers higher wages, even though productivity differences might be caused by forces beyond a person's control. Explain.

15. *[economic rent]* Do economists use the term "rent" in the same way as the general public? Explain.

16. *[economic rent]* Using a supply and demand graph, illustrate the concept of economic rent. Be sure that your graph shows the opportunity cost, hourly earnings, and area of economic rent. Are all of the earnings in your graph economic rent or just a portion? Explain.

17. *[economic rent]* Is it fair for some people to earn huge economic rents? Should those rents be taxed away? Would taxing rents cause superstars to withhold their talents from the marketplace? Explain.

 Visit www.prenhall.com/collinge for Exploring the Web exercises and additional self-test quizzes.

CHAPTER 9

PUBLIC GOODS, REGULATION, AND INFORMATION

A LOOK AHEAD

The healthcare industry is huge and growing. It also stands at the center of a debate over how much government should do in a market economy. Like food, shelter, clothing, and water, healthcare is crucial to a good standard of living. It is also subject to imperfect information and can be very expensive, with inefficient pricing incentives under health insurance distorting market choices. Government efforts to widen healthcare coverage while reining in costs may solve some problems but can make others worse. The market failures of healthcare and government's role in influencing healthcare outcomes are examined in this chapter's Explore & Apply section.

Healthcare is hardly unique in being a target for government action. The United States contains over 80,000 separate governments, ranging from education, sewer, and water districts through municipal, county, and state governments, on up to the federal government. Government regulations apply to nearly all elements of the economy. Why is there so much government involvement in what is basically a market economy? Using the perspective of economic efficiency, this chapter examines the rationales.

LEARNING OBJECTIVES

Understanding Chapter 9 will enable you to:
1. **Distinguish among private goods, public goods, externalities, and common property resources.**
2. **Explain why the private marketplace fails to offer public goods in efficient quantities.**
3. **Identify an optimal amount of highway congestion and policies to achieve that amount.**
4. **Describe why government enacts regulations and what principles can guide it toward efficiency.**
5. **Explain the concept of asymmetric information and how it influences market outcomes.**
6. **Apply the analysis of marginal costs and marginal benefits to explain criminal behavior.**
7. **Identify major issues in healthcare and alternative ways of addressing them.**

Explore & Apply

Technology tells us what can be done. Economics tells us what should be done. Politics tells us what will be done.

This old saying sums up the dilemma facing economists. They are caught in the middle, neither producing goods nor controlling public policy. Rather, economic analysis reveals how the intertwining actions of government and markets can offer citizens the best value. Economics seeks to identify when public policy is needed to meet economic goals, and the types of government actions that are appropriate. Sometimes the action is for the government to produce directly, while at other times government uses regulation to influence production in the private sector.

9.1 IDENTIFYING MARKET FAILURES

The invisible hand of the marketplace leads profit-seeking producers to offer consumers an efficient variety of goods and services. Competition ensures that these goods and services are produced at least cost and in efficient quantities. Efficiency is the market's great success and the reason that market economies have been able to improve living standards over time. However, there are also instances of **market failure,** in which markets do not bring about economic efficiency.

market failure when markets fail to achieve efficiency, as in the case of public goods, externalities, and common property resources.

SOURCES OF MARKET FAILURE

There are two sources of market failure. The first is a lack of competition, which you learned about in the chapter on monopoly. The second source is a good that is not purely private. **Private goods** are *excludable* and *rival,* meaning that people can be excluded from consuming the good and any one person's consumption diminishes the amount that is available for everyone else. For example, your bottle of Arizona Iced Tea would be a private good, because each swig that you offer your friend leaves that much less for you. Most goods are private goods.

private goods goods consumed by one person only—excludable and rival; most goods and services are private.

At the opposite extreme from private goods lie **public goods,** which are *nonexcludable* and *nonrival,* meaning that people cannot be kept from consuming the good, nor does their consumption reduce the amount available for others. The nonrival nature of a public good means that the marginal cost of providing service to additional consumers is zero. The nonexcludable nature of the public good means that, although different people value it differently, we have no choice but to each consume the same amount. National defense provides the best example of a public good. Whether a country's citizens are pacifists, hawks, rich, or poor, and no matter their race, gender, or ethnicity, all consume the same amount of national defense.

public goods goods that are nonexcludable and nonrival, meaning that a person's consumption of the good does not reduce its quantity for others.

Pure public goods are completely nonexcludable and nonrival. To some extent, almost all public goods are impure. An *impure public good* is not consumed with complete equality. Even national defense, the purest of the public goods, is likely to protect people who live in some cities better than the residents of others. But impurities are much more pronounced for many other public goods. Libraries can exclude prospective borrowers. Police patrols provide greater security in some neighborhoods than in others. A fire station provides less protection per house as more houses are built.

An Internet site represents an impure public good. To some degree it is nonrival and nonexcludable. Additional viewers normally add no costs—in other words, the marginal cost is zero. However, it is possible to exclude users who do not register. The fixed cost of providing content and hosting services can be covered by registration fees, or alternatively by advertising. In a similar manner, a national park might charge an entrance fee to cover maintanence, even though the park itself is a public good to the extent that many can use it simultaneously.

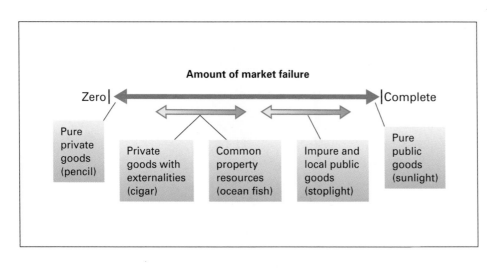

Amount of market failure

Zero | ← Complete

Pure private goods (pencil)

Private goods with externalities (cigar)

Common property resources (ocean fish)

Impure and local public goods (stoplight)

Pure public goods (sunlight)

FIGURE 9-1

THE SPECTRUM OF MARKET FAILURE Market failure depends on the degree of rivalry and excludability. Private goods are completely rival and excludable, while public goods are completely nonrival and nonexcludable. Externalities and common property resources generally fall closer to the private goods end of the spectrum, while local public goods are closer to the pure public goods end of the spectrum. Examples of each good are noted in parentheses.

Impurities in public goods often involve **congestion,** which occurs when the addition of one more user reduces the availability of the good for all other users. **Congestion violates the assumption of nonrivalry needed for a pure public good.** For example, although Internet surfers rarely slow each other down, a particular site can become congested. National parks also become congested. Fees can serve to reduce congestion, as we will discover later in this chapter.

Public goods can extend over a wide or limited area. A city's air quality is an example of a **local public good.** Local public goods provide an economic justification for local and regional governments. For instance, it is better to have local streets and highways under the control of municipal and state governments, respectively, rather than to have Congress decide which potholes get repaired and where street lights are to be installed. The same would hold true for the many other public goods that are primarily local or regional in nature.

In between pure public and pure private goods are common property resources and private goods with externalities. Sometimes the ownership of something is common property, meaning that it is shared. Shared ownership occurs most frequently with natural resources, thus leading to the term **common property resource.** For example, an oilfield could straddle two separate properties, with each property owner having the right to pump as much oil as the owner desires. A common property resource generates contention over who gets to use it.

Other times, the production or consumption of private goods leads to costs or benefits to third parties—people or businesses who were not party to the transaction. Such spillover effects onto third parties are termed **externalities.** Externalities can be either negative or positive. Pollution is an example of a negative externality. Negative externalities impose **external costs** on others. For example, to the extent that air pollution causes health problems or decreases people's enjoyment of outdoor activities, the pollution has imposed external costs on its victims. Conversely, positive externalities confer **external benefits.** For example, when a neighbor kills all the mosquitoes on her property and it results in fewer in your own backyard, you receive the external benefits of greater enjoyment of your backyard and savings on pest control. Figure 9-1 summarizes the range of goods and resources from the extreme of pure private goods to the other extreme of pure public goods. We will put aside a detailed examination of externalities and common property resource issues until the next chapter, focusing in this chapter on public goods, regulation, and information.

congestion when adding an additional consumer of a public good detracts from its value to other consumers.

local public good a public good that affects a particular region, such as a city.

common property resource a jointly owned resource, such as groundwater; people have little incentive to conserve common property resources, but rather seek to capture them for their own private use.

externality side effect of production or consumption that affects third parties who have no say in the matter.

external costs when an externality takes the form of costs, such as from pollution.

external benefits when an externality takes the form of benefits, such as from a neighbor maintaining an attractive yard.

THE PRODUCTION OF PUBLIC GOODS

Private goods are consumed and paid for by the individual. Public goods, however, are consumed simultaneously by everyone regardless of who pays. We share national defense, fresh

FIGURE 9-2

THE VALUE OF A PUBLIC GOOD
The value of a public good is the sum of its value to each person, because everyone consumes the same amount.

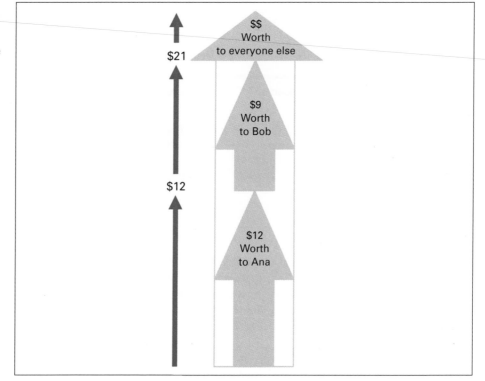

air, and even access to radio signals. Adding more consumers does not diminish the enjoyment we each get from these goods. This arrangement has repercussions on demand that prevent the marketplace from offering an efficient quantity.

Unlike a private good, each unit of a public good is simultaneously consumed by everyone. **The value of a public good is thus the sum of its values to all consumers.** Figure 9-2 illustrates this idea, where the public good is worth $12 to Ana, $9 to Bob, and so forth. It would be efficient to provide this good only if total benefits exceed total costs.

In most applications, the quantity of a public good can vary, which means we must compare the increment to costs with the increment to benefits from producing more of it. In other words, we must consider not only total benefits and costs, but also marginal benefits and marginal costs.

The efficient quantity of a public good is achieved when marginal cost equals marginal benefit, as shown in Figure 9-3. That quantity maximizes social surplus, which is the difference between total benefit and total cost. Maximum social surplus is shown as the shaded area in Figure 9-3.

For private goods, you receive something in exchange for your money. With public goods, the amount you consume seems unaffected by how much you spend. Whether you offer to pay a year's wages or nothing at all makes no discernible difference. You can still consume just as much of the public good as everyone else. The result is a **free-rider problem,** in which everyone has the incentive to let others pay the costs of providing the public good.

free-rider problem the incentive to avoid paying for a public good, because no one person's payment will have any appreciable effect on the quantity of the public good.

The laws of supply and demand apply as much to public goods as to private goods. The lower price of a public good, the less producers are willing to sell and the more consumers are willing to buy. Unfortunately, because public goods are nonexcludable, they are free to use. You don't need to pay a thing. While we value public goods collectively, we do not volunteer to pay for them individually. Therefore, public goods will not be produced unless the government gets involved.

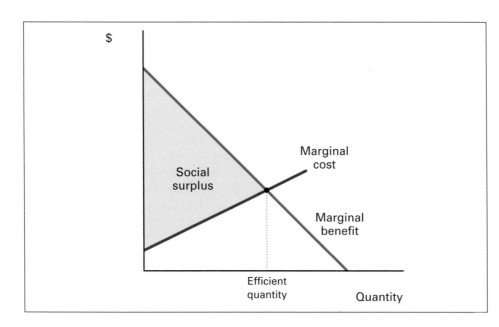

FIGURE 9-3

THE EFFICIENT QUANTITY OF A PUBLIC GOOD Just as for a private good, the efficient quantity of a public good occurs when the marginal benefit of another unit just equals its marginal cost. The shaded area is the social surplus from this quantity.

The solution to the free-rider problem involves taxation. Government compels everyone to contribute, since everyone shares in consuming public goods. How much money people are forced to contribute is then at the discretion of government rather than the consumer directly. Thus, nearly everyone would prefer either more or less government spending on any particular public good.

Sometimes, private entrepreneurs find ways to tie public goods to private goods that individuals or firms are willing to buy. For example, radio and television stations bundle their broadcasts with commercials. Because broadcasts are accessible to all, they are public goods and thus cannot be sold directly. However, commercials are private goods from the standpoint of advertisers. The more valuable the public good aspect of programming, the more stations can charge advertisers for air time. In this and many other cases, there is at least some private provision of public goods. Unfortunately, there is nothing that compels private markets to produce the most efficient quantity or variety of these goods.

The private marketplace also sometimes offers private alternatives to public goods. For example, if all police forces were to be eliminated, there would be a dramatic increase in the sales of firearms, alarm systems, and security guard services. Even so, public safety is likely to be maintained more efficiently through the provision of community-wide police services, a public good.

QUICKCHECK

Much of the content on the Internet is free to use, and yet it costs content providers money to construct and maintain their sites. Explain.

Answer: The free Internet content is offered as a public good in conjunction with advertisements, which hope to induce the web surfer to buy the advertised private goods. Other times, free sites are samples of higher quality restricted sites that the web surfer can access only by paying a fee. The public good is provided because it is tied to private goods.

"WHAT'S A LITTLE SNOW?"

Every year or two, a blizzard will paralyze Washington, D.C., yet work goes on in Buffalo, New York. As one of the snowiest spots in the United States, the people of Buffalo are used to the white stuff. "So what's another foot or two?" they ask as they slog to their jobs, listening to the news reports of prolonged federal government shutdowns and other snow emergencies elsewhere.

True, Buffalonians are battle-hardened veterans of many a' winter campaign. But there is more to the story. What's missing is the part about the efficient choice of a local public good—snow removal. Officials in Buffalo know it's going to snow hard, nearly every year. It is thus efficient for them to spend heavily on snow plows and other capital equipment. With snowfalls much less frequent in other parts of the country, officials there find it more efficient to devote that money to other needs. The result is that when the infrequent blizzard does strike, the Buffalonians drive to work while the Washingtonians wait for a warm, sunny day. ◄

9.2 POLICY OPTIONS

In cases of pure public goods, government has little recourse but to produce the goods itself or provide government payment to private companies who in turn would produce the goods. However, as we move along the spectrum of market failure away from pure public goods, it becomes possible for government to use regulations or price incentives to guide the marketplace toward efficiency.

For example, highways are impure public goods that the government usually constructs by way of contracts with private companies. Once those highways are built, their use is regulated with drivers' licenses and speed limits. In addition, the government might charge for the use of particular highways through the assessment of *user fees,* known more familiarly in this application as tolls. In short, for impure public goods, the government's policy alternatives are of three general sorts:

- **Government can price the good.** For example, tolls can discourage driving when roads are congested.
- **Government can produce the good.** For example, most highways are built by government contractors and subcontractors.
- **Government can regulate the good.** For example, certain highway lanes are reserved for busses or other high-occupancy vehicles—HOV lanes—so as to encourage carpooling or the use of mass transit.

PRICE INCENTIVES—THE CASE OF CONGESTION PRICING

Continuing with the example of highways, we now examine price incentives. Highways are subject to congestion, which you will recall is a frequent trait of impure public goods. Congestion is a special case of externality in which adding another user reduces the benefits received by other users. In the case of highways, additional drivers slow each other down.

Figure 9-4(a) illustrates how an existing highway becomes congested during peak hours. For example, a road that flows smoothly during most hours of the day might become a slow moving sea of vehicles during rush-hour traffic jams. In Figure 9-4(a), the marginal cost of highway usage is assumed to be zero until the point at which congestion sets in. That assumption is largely true for passenger cars, as almost all wear and tear on highways comes from weather and heavy trucks. After the point of congestion, however, adding more vehi-

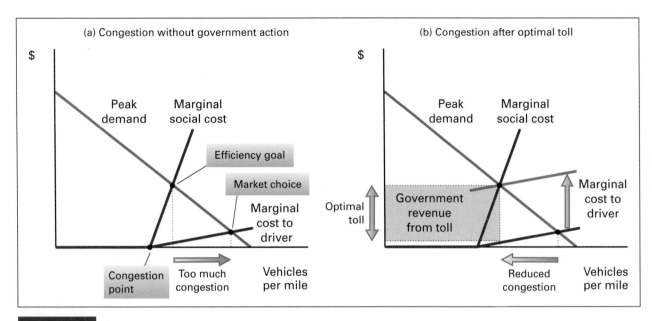

FIGURE 9-4

CONGESTION ON THE HIGHWAY A highway is nonrival until congestion sets in. During off-peak hours, the highway is a public good. However, during times of peak demand, adding another car to the highway slows everybody down. The driver entering the highway considers marginal private cost, which includes how much time that driver loses as a result of congestion. However, the individual driver does not worry about slowing everybody else down, and so does not perceive the full marginal social cost of getting on the highway. The result is too many cars on the highway during peak hours, as shown in (a).

Government can reduce highway usage to an efficient amount by assessing a toll on each driver during times of peak demand, as shown in (b). The optimal toll would increase marginal cost until it intersects demand at the efficient quantity, where the efficient quantity is given by the intersection of demand and marginal social cost. Revenue from the toll is the area of the shaded rectangle, which is obtained by multiplying the number of vehicles subject to the toll by the amount of the toll per vehicle.

cles of any sort slows everybody down, which is costly in terms of time, fuel consumption, pollution, vehicle depreciation, and general annoyance.

The individual driver is motivated to avoid these congested roads only to the extent that it affects that driver personally—marginal private cost. However, there are additional costs to society—marginal social cost—because that driver's presence on the highway makes the problems of congestion worse for everybody else. The result is too much congestion as drivers make their decisions without reference to their own impact on the traffic jam. For this reason, a worker might wait a few minutes to avoid the peak of the evening rush hour, but could care less if his or her entry into the stream of traffic delays others.

Figure 9-4(b) shows how a toll could be used to achieve the efficient amount of congestion by raising the marginal cost perceived by the entering driver. Imposing a toll is becoming increasingly feasible for cities as surveillance technology advances, a reality to which drivers from Houston, Paris, London, Singapore, and numerous other cities can attest. For example, Singapore installed its electronic toll system in 1998, and now adjusts its toll to reflect the time of day and congestion. In 2002, London announced plans to use vehicle monitoring by satellite. No tollbooths needed!

Many drivers prefer the inefficient highway congestion to the toll. The reason is that, although achieving efficiency means that society has more to go around, the drivers themselves could be worse off because the toll would collect a large amount of money from them.

The total toll revenue is shown as the shaded area in Figure 9-4(b). Even if the money collected from drivers is used for good social purposes, the individual toll-payers no longer have it to spend for their own private purposes. In other words, along with the benefit of less congestion comes an income transfer away from the drivers paying the tolls.

GOVERNMENT PRODUCTION—THE ROLE OF COST-BENEFIT ANALYSIS

cost-benefit analysis the process of estimating the costs and benefits of alternative policy choices.

The previous section discussed how government can use price incentives to make efficient use of an existing highway that is sometimes congested. What if the highway is usually congested—should a new one be built? For the answer to that question and a myriad more, government turns to cost-benefit analysis. Government uses **cost-benefit analysis** to estimate and compare the costs and benefits of alternative policy choices.

Cost-benefit analysis is often complex. For example, to analyze costs and benefits of public actions requires that dollar values be assigned to both monetary and nonmonetary costs and benefits. Consider the seemingly simple matter of speed limits. We can save lives by reducing the speed limit on expressways to ten miles per hour. However, since we value our time as well as our safety, we prefer to go faster. But how much faster? Choosing the best speed limit requires the comparison of *intangibles,* which have no market price. Even so, researchers can often infer the value we implicitly place on intangibles, including the intangibles of safety and time.

For example, consider the value of a *statistical life,* which is the expectation of a life saved or lost as a result of a government action, when no one knows exactly whose life it will be. Raising speed limits costs statistical lives. Likewise, adding police officers saves statistical lives. We do not set speed limits at zero, nor do we spend all of our money on traffic patrols. So implicitly, we place a value on life in a statistical sort of way. Getting a handle on how much a statistical life is worth to us might involve looking at pay differentials between risky and nonrisky jobs, such as how much more pay construction workers receive to work on high-rise buildings where their lives are more at risk.

Another intangible is that, unlike private firms, the government cannot observe the prices at which its products sell in the marketplace because the market for its products does not exist. For example, what is the value of saving a wetland? No one offers to purchase public goods of this sort. Some of the best techniques to reveal the benefits of intangibles involve observing other market prices that relate to the good in question. For example, the cost of noise pollution from airplanes can be estimated by observing market prices for homes under takeoff and landing flight paths, and comparing those to market prices of similar homes in quieter locations.

There are many other techniques that policymakers use, depending on the specific types of intangibles that need measuring. Attaching dollar values provides a common measuring rod by which to measure things that are otherwise seemingly incomparable. Because the economy has scarce resources, such choices must be made.

QUICKCHECK

How can we estimate in dollars the damages from airplane noise?

Answer: Damages from airplane noise can be estimated by comparing the market value of land that is subject to plane noise to the market value of comparable land that is not. The difference in these market prices provides an estimate of the cost of noise.

REGULATION AND THE SPECIFICITY PRINCIPLE—
AVOIDING UNINTENDED CONSEQUENCES

Regulation occurs whenever government acts to influence the specifications of goods and services or the manner in which they are produced. Speed limits, smoking bans, seat belt requirements, product standards, and workplace safety laws are a few of the many regulations that affect our daily lives. The extent to which various facets of our economy should or should not be regulated is one of the most controversial topics around.

regulation occurs whenever the government acts to influence the specifications of goods and services or the manner in which they are produced.

> ### A Few of the Many Things Regulated
>
> #### Regulations apply to:
> Labeling requirements for food
> Electricity consumption of air conditioners
> Width of doorways in the workplace
> Emission controls in cars
> Use of hard hats at construction sites
> Safety of children's toys
> Rest requirements for truckers and pilots
> Dimensions of wood sold as a 2 × 4
> Qualifications of professional wrestlers

In determining the type and amount of regulations to apply, policymakers should be aware of the regulations' *administrative and compliance costs.* To achieve efficiency, regulations should only be imposed to the extent that their benefits outweigh their costs, including costs of administration of compliance. **The marginal benefit of additional regulation should equal its marginal cost.** While it is often hard to quantify these benefits and costs, there is often a suspicion that regulation has gone overboard. For example, the paperwork and consulting fees spent on compliance with the myriad of government regulations is a daunting hurdle for new and growing businesses.

To ensure efficiency in regulation, it helps to "hit the nail on the head," a concept that is more formally known as the specificity principle. The **specificity principle** says to target the problem in as precise and narrow a manner as possible. Using the specificity principle, the best solution to a market failure is often not to abandon markets altogether by resorting to government command and control, but rather to correct only the problem within the market that is keeping it from being a success. By following the specificity principle, undesirable side effects of policy actions are kept to a minimum.

specificity principle the idea that policies should be targeted as narrowly and directly at a problem as possible.

APPLYING THE SPECIFICITY PRINCIPLE—
RESOLVING URBAN WATER SHORTAGES

The specificity principle can be used to resolve urban water crises, those situations that periodically occur in cities around the country and around the world in which it might seem like a city's reservoirs are inadequate to meet demand. The reasons might be drought, the unexpected contamination of a reservoir, or earthquake damage to water distribution systems. In most cases, the reaction of urban water authorities is to make rules and regulations that govern how water can be used. The authorities might take it on themselves to declare what are essential uses and what are nonessential uses of water. They might set times for watering yards. They might require low-flow plumbing fixtures. They might assess surcharges for excessive water use. However, **the specific problem is not the specifics of water usage, but rather the lack of a market-clearing price.** Fix that underlying problem and the other problems fix themselves.

The complication is that municipal water distribution is a natural monopoly, and thus a legitimate candidate for regulation. In most major American cities, local government either controls the water supply or regulates the price charged by a protected monopoly franchise. Traditionally, as discussed in the chapter on monopoly, regulation takes the form of average-cost pricing, in which the authorities set the price so as to allow the firm only a normal profit. Unlike other cases of regulated monopoly, though, the quantity of water available at any given time is not easily adjustable. The government cannot make it rain. Unfortunately, aiming price to achieve a revenue objective does not allow it to also target the objective of allocative efficiency. That would require that price be set by the intersection of marginal cost and demand—*marginal-cost pricing*—which might be quite a bit higher in some regions.

Figure 9-5 illustrates the regulatory dilemma in the municipal water market, which is that one price cannot hit two targets. For simplicity, marginal cost is shown as vertical in the figure, as though there is zero marginal cost of using current sources up to the sustainable quantity, and no short-run possibilities of supplementing water supplies. Average cost would then be composed of only average fixed cost, and might be quite low as noted in the figure. In times of peak demand, such as in the dry days of a hot summer, there could be a wide gap between the average-cost price and the marginal-cost price. The result is the possible crisis of a water shortage, in which water reserves are drawn down in a manner that cannot be sustained. For example, it has been reported that the fast-growing city of Atlanta might already be using the maximum sustainable capacity of its reservoirs.

Alternatively, local governments frequently price discriminate, with some customers paying a much higher price than is paid by others. For example, authorities might raise the rates to punish large-volume users, and use the extra revenues to lower rates for everybody else. Unfortunately, the result still does not clear the market and is inefficient in that some customers value the last unit consumed more than other customers do.

There are often political reasons that run counter to the specificity principle. Most commonly, local government authorities might aim to keep prices low for the poor to avoid being accused of imposing what might be called a "water tax." If those authorities were to specify the public interest more fundamentally, though, it would be that their actions should not cause additional impoverishment. Therefore, there are really two goals: (1) to avoid a

FIGURE 9-5

APPLYING THE SPECIFICITY PRINCIPLE TO AVOID WATER SHORTAGES A marginal-cost price clears the market, which avoids persistent water shortages. However, many cities choose to set the price of tap water on the basis of average cost in order to avoid revenue in excess of that needed to cover costs. A single price cannot satisfy both objectives.

QUICKCHECK

If there is a water shortage, why shouldn't the government just figure out who most needs the available water and allocate it to those people?

Answer: People are the best judges of their own water-use possibilities. Market price matches the product—water—to those for whom it is most valuable, meaning that those who buy it are willing to pay the most for it.

water shortage; and (2) to avoid hurting the poor. Price can only meet one of them. Since there are two goals, the specificity principle would suggest two separate policies, such as:

- A single market-clearing price that adjusts as needed to prevent shortages.
- Financial aid on the basis of income needs.

This second policy would not concern itself with water usage, except in the unlikely event that essential water needs would cost so much that they would affect the amount of income needed to escape poverty.

HEAR YE! MESSAGE YE!—AIRWAVES AT AUCTION

SNAPSHOT

The big news? It's about how you get to hear the news, or read the news, or message the news. The news is that government regulation of communication bandwidths now lets the market decide the details of which bandwidths are used for Internet access, cellular phones, paging, instant messaging, personal communication devices, or other modes of service. The Federal Communications Commission used to assign airwave frequencies to potential broadcasters, with all details spelled out. Now, in conformance with the specificity principle, the FCC tries to avoid regulating when the market does not fail. The result is that bandwidth rights are now sold at auction to the highest bidder in the free market. Let the invisible hand rule!

As the airwaves grow increasingly congested with cellular and wireless applications, the FCC has found further market-based avenues toward the public interest. To ensure that the available frequencies are used to their fullest and most valuable extent, the FCC no longer requires each bandwidth owner to obtain a government license for its use. Instead, the FCC now allows bandwidth owners to lease that bandwidth to others. Such efficient exchanges are ho-hum, everyday events in the marketplace. But ensuring that public policy does not tread on market efficiency? That's news! ◄

9.3 IMPERFECT INFORMATION

Everyone makes mistakes and, we hope, learns from those mistakes. We cannot know that we don't like the new flavor of yogurt until we try it. We cannot know if the shoe truly fits until we wear it. We do things that, with better information, we would have done differently. This is the problem of imperfect information, a problem that can lead to market failure. **Imperfect information** occurs when we do not fully understand the choices available to us, or the consequences of those choices.

In the laissez-faire marketplace, there will always be the unscrupulous willing to take advantage of the naive. There will be those who fall victim to scams and frauds because information is not fully shared. While government might step in and seek to help, it must recognize its own imperfections—it is neither all knowing, nor are its actions costless. While recognizing that it cannot solve all of the information problems in the marketplace, government nevertheless can and does look for ways to help.

imperfect information occurs when we do not fully understand the choices available to us, or the consequences of those choices.

For example, investors in Enron Corporation learned firsthand about the implications of imperfect information. At the start of 2001, Enron Corporation had a market value that placed it within the top ten of all U.S. corporations. Yet by the end of that year, Enron was bankrupt. The investors who had bid the price of Enron stock so high had been deceived by complicated and shady accounting practices that they did not understand. The market had made a mistake.

As a result of the Enron debacle, investors and analysts pored over the accounting statements of other companies very, very carefully. Investors had an incentive to do so because their own savings were on the line. This scrutiny caused investors to reallocate their money away from companies with suspect accounting practices, a process that increased both information flow and the efficiency of the market. The government also had a role to play. In 2002, the Securities and Exchange Commission took action to reevaluate the information that public companies were required by law to report to shareholders and when they were required to report it, and Congress enacted new laws governing corporate accountability.

ASYMMETRIC INFORMATION

asymmetric information when one person has access to more information than another on a subject of mutual interest.

When one person has access to more information than another on a subject of mutual interest, he or she is said to possess **asymmetric information.** Asymmetric information is responsible for several puzzling facets of modern life. For example, the value of an automobile drops by a couple thousand dollars as soon as it is first sold. The reason is that prospective buyers of a used car are aware that the seller knows more about the car—the shoppers are aware of what they don't know. They figure that they are not told all of the reasons why the car is being sold and expect the car to have problems that will only become apparent over time.

Asymmetric information may be important to the value of the college degree you seek. If you are studying at one of the top ten universities in the country, for example, you are likely to find that your degree will be worth a great deal more in the job market than degrees held by people who have acquired an equal amount of knowledge at lesser-known schools. This is the problem of *credentialism,* in which people's skills and abilities are judged by the reputation of their degrees or other credentials. Employers use credentials as a way to ensure that their employees are intelligent and well trained. Since grading standards vary from school to school, and since the job interview process cannot hope to uncover all of an applicant's skills and abilities, employers pay more for degrees from schools they have heard of and trust. It often seems inequitable, but it can be efficient.

Asymmetric information provides at least part of the explanation for another phenomenon—*cronyism.* Cronyism occurs when employers hire friends, relatives, fellow church members, and so forth. That may be a profitable business practice if these employees are more reliable than strangers. While it seems unfair to applicants outside the group of cronies, cronyism probably does serve to reduce job turnover and minimize false credentials. Fair or not, cronyism offers a way to circumvent asymmetric information.

PROTECTING LIFE AND LIMB—GOVERNMENT'S ROLE IN WORKPLACE SAFETY

The search for profit motivates firms to implement numerous safety measures, even when no regulation forces them to do so. The rationale is that unsafe working conditions lead to various costs, such as those associated with interruptions in production. A dangerous firm must also offer higher wages and better benefits to attract workers. It would be forced to pay higher insurance premiums to cover healthcare expenses and liability. If these costs exceed the cost of the safety measures, a profit-maximizing firm will undertake the safety measures.

Figure 9-6 shows, in principle, how to choose an efficient amount of safety. The idea is to keep adding safety measures so long as the marginal benefit exceeds the marginal cost. While

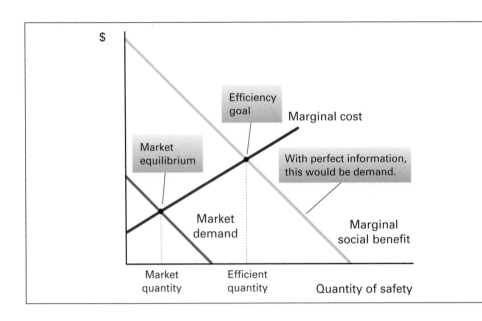

FIGURE 9-6

WORKPLACE SAFETY The efficient quantity of safety at the workplace occurs where marginal cost equals marginal benefit. The quantity chosen in the free market would be less than the efficient quantity if workers underestimate the value of safety measures.

the search for profit motivates the firm to implement safety measures, not all of the benefits from safety improvements might affect profit. If the safety measures don't, firms will not choose to be safe enough. This situation might occur if workers have insufficient information about the value of safety improvements. For example, the workers might not realize how risky a job actually is and thus be unwilling to sacrifice much pay or other benefits in order to receive extra safety. As a result of their workers' imperfect information, the firm perceives less than the true marginal benefits from safety and implements too few safety measures.

If firms do not undertake an efficient number of safety measures, there is a role for government regulators. Specifically, government regulators might estimate the efficient amount of safety and force firms to achieve that amount. However, it is difficult to estimate these marginal costs and benefits of extra safety, especially since different workers have different preferences when it comes to how much risk they are willing to accept in exchange for extra income.

It is impractical for government safety regulations to be tailored to the wants of different groups of workers. The result is that both firms and workers often complain about rigid work rules and safety measures. Some argue that the government should cut back its regulation of workplace safety. In that case, the government could still make information on workplace safety available to workers so that they could choose more efficiently. On the other hand, backers of government safety regulation point out that there are economies of scale in evaluating information about safety. From that perspective, it seems sensible to let experts in government evaluate the information and make more-informed choices than most workers could do themselves.

PUBLIC SAFETY—CRIME AND PUNISHMENT

Imperfect information is at the heart of criminal activity and the fight against it. Criminals constantly seek to hide their activities, while authorities seek to uncover them. In the United States, there are about 100,000 reported crimes per day (the exact number of actual crimes is unknown because many crimes go unreported).

Technology can provide information that assists in uncovering crime, but can also help the criminals themselves. For example, some parents use so-called nanny cams to monitor activities in the house while they are away. These nanny cams often include wireless connections to the telephone or the Internet. Parents can dial up the proper connection and see for

FIGURE 9-7

ECONOMICS OF CRIME Criminals compare their expected marginal benefits to expected marginal costs in deciding how much crime to commit, ignoring the costs to the victims of crime. Increasing the costs and/or lowering the benefits facing the criminal would reduce the amount of crime.

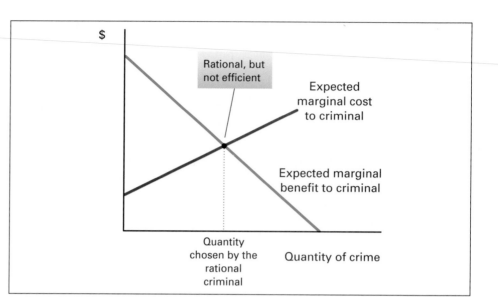

themselves what the camera sees. Unfortunately, high-tech criminals often can do the same thing, using the same signals that are meant to safeguard the house and its occupants. In this manner, criminals can find out when the parents are gone or when someone is home alone.

The costs of crime and crime prevention take many forms. People lose life and property. They pay higher taxes to support the police and criminal justice system. They also pay for deadbolts, alarm systems, guard dogs, and much more. Some flee to the suburbs or small towns. Others hide behind the walls of security-gated subdivisions in the hopes of escaping crime. Hidden costs include psychic costs associated with the fear of becoming a victim, and the loss of freedom when that fear limits activities.

What makes an individual turn to a life of crime? From an economic perspective, a criminal would consider the relative monetary and nonmonetary returns and weigh them against expected costs. These considerations are illustrated in Figure 9-7. **Because there is uncertainty attached to the outcome of criminal activity, the economic model of crime posits that criminals make decisions based on the *expected marginal benefits* and *expected marginal costs* of criminal activity.** On the cost side, the prospective criminal considers the uncertain expected punishment, where the

$$\text{Expected punishment} = \text{Punishment for the crime} \times$$
$$\text{Probability of being caught and convicted}$$

The uncertainties of catching and convicting criminals mean that, for the punishments to serve as effective deterrents, they often seem harsh relative to the actual crime that the person committed.

QUICKCHECK

If a thief steals a dollar, does economic analysis say that the punishment should be $1 plus costs of apprehension and prosecution, and no more?

Answer: No, in addition to considering the amount of damage caused by that one criminal incident, it is also important to consider that the thief faces only a small chance of being caught and convicted. For this reason, the punishment might be more severe than the crime.

SEEING RED OVER SPY-CAMS   *S N A P S H O T*

Often they are nearly invisible. Other times, they are intentionally obvious. Sometimes they're even phony, just there to make us think twice about breaking the law. Increasingly, they are banned, made illegal by an exasperated public. They are the watchful cameras of the highways, carefully positioned to take our pictures as we speed, run red lights, or merely drive along a toll road. We might get those pictures in the mail, along with a bill for the toll or traffic fine we owe. The totals can be staggering. By the start of 2002, for example, Washington, D.C.'s forty-four traffic cameras had caused D.C. drivers to fork over $23 million in fines.

Traffic cameras merely enforce the law, so why would anyone be upset? Perhaps it's the impersonality of it all. Perhaps we don't want to be watched so much. Perhaps it is that the penalties for our traffic violations were set with the idea that we usually don't get caught. In contrast, the modern technology of the traffic cam is coming to mean that we usually cannot escape. ◄

9.4 HEALTHCARE—CAN THE ILLS BE CURED?

Good health is an essential ingredient in the quality of our lives. Yet proper treatment is expensive and it takes specialized skills to know what to do. Healthcare accounts for roughly 14 percent of U.S. spending, compared to about 10 percent in Canada and 7 percent in Japan. A big part of healthcare's high cost lies in what we buy. Over time, healthcare has come to include increasingly sophisticated techniques. Because of healthcare's high and often unpredictable expenses, we typically resort to insurance. Sometimes that insurance is privately provided. Sometimes it is provided by the government through Medicaid for the poor or Medicare for the elderly. Figure 9-8 shows the sources and uses of medical spending in the United States.

For both physicians and patients, health insurance alters incentives. For example, a patient might pay *co-insurance*—a percentage of costs over some deductible amount. For example, a patient might pay 20 percent of yearly healthcare expenses after paying a $300 deductible out-of-pocket.

Healthcare is provided by the insurance company in exchange for annual premiums, usually paid for by a person's employer. Because the per-unit price of healthcare is reduced to the patient, patients seek more of it, just as the law of demand would suggest. However, this lower price to patients does not mean the price paid to the health service providers has fallen. The result is the problem of *moral hazard* in which the insurance has led to the over-consumption of healthcare services. Figure 9-9 illustrates how moral hazard leads patients to consume too much medical care.

Examples provided by the fifty-year-old National Health Service in Great Britain offer clear evidence of moral hazard. Healthcare in Great Britain is free at the point of service. For that reason, a large proportion of those who make appointments with their family doctors have no good medical reason to do so, resulting in less care for those who really need it. So-called free medical care also delays treatment, sometimes for years if the ailment is placed in a non-urgent category.

Figure 9-9 also shows another problem in the healthcare market, this one having to do with information. Typically, healthcare providers bill the insurance company for more than contractually agreed-upon rates. This is not usually a problem, as the insurer merely adjusts the charges downward to what is allowable. However, it becomes a problem if for some reason the patient is not covered by insurance. In that case, the patient is surprised with the full charge, labeled in the graph as the price to the uninsured. If this price was known beforehand, patients would have shopped for lower rates or reduced their quantities

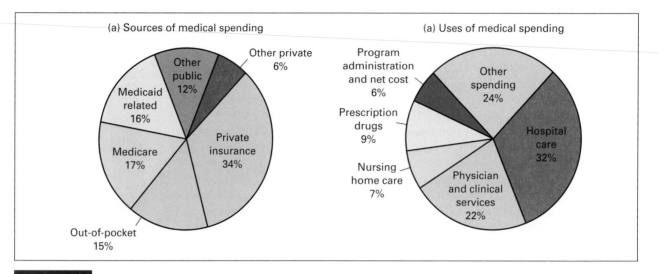

FIGURE 9-8

SOURCES AND USES OF MEDICAL SPENDING IN THE UNITED STATES Chart (a) shows the sources of medical spending in the United States for the year 2000. Chart (b) shows the uses of that spending.

Source: Centers for Medicare & Medicaid Services, Office of the Actuary, National Health Statistics Group.

demanded. The higher price to the uninsured is a way for hospitals, physicians, and other healthcare providers to supplement the low rates paid under government and private insurance plans, rates that cover variable costs but not always fixed costs. The problem revolves around the fairness of this practice to the patient and the efficiency of patient choices in the absence of complete information.

The price of buying insurance is also high for individuals. To understand why, consider the incentives facing insurance companies. These companies are in business to provide a positive return to their investors, not to give away services that cost more than the value of

FIGURE 9-9

MORAL HAZARD AND PRICE SURPRISES Moral hazard results when insurance lowers the price of healthcare for the recipient, thus causing an increase in the quantity of services demanded beyond what is efficient. Additional inefficiency results when insurance does not cover a charge and the patient is faced with a price surprise—a charge that exceeds what insurers would have paid.

the premiums they receive. Consequently, they try to distinguish between ex ante (before the fact) and ex post (after the fact) conditions. The laws of probability allow insurers to cover conditions ex ante.

For example, suppose you have the same chance as everybody else of coming down with some medical condition. By covering many people, most of whom will have no cause to file claims, the insurer can profitably offer you coverage at a fraction of treatment costs. Ex post is another story altogether. If you already have a condition, the insurance company could make money only if they charged you at least the full cost of treatment. That would be no insurance at all! In other words, once you come down with a condition, you lose your option of initiating insurance coverage at an affordable rate.

Even if you do not have any particular medical problems, you still cannot get an individual policy at a price approaching that of a group insurance plan. For example, if you attempt to purchase insurance with coverage identical to that offered by employers, you would be charged a great deal more. The reason revolves around asymmetric information. Even if you do not have any particular condition yet, you probably know much better than the insurance company which conditions you would be most susceptible to. Asymmetric information leads to the problem of *adverse selection*—those who seek out insurance coverage are the most likely to need it.

Because of adverse selection, the expected cost to the insurance company of writing an individual policy is much higher than the expected cost per person under a group policy. Insurance companies that survive in the marketplace must know this, and thus charge individuals a higher price to reflect the higher costs. The lowest rates go to groups that cannot easily be joined just for the insurance, which explains why most people receive health insurance coverage through their employers.

UNIVERSAL HEALTHCARE

Healthcare expenses can vary dramatically and unpredictably from person to person. This uncertainty motivates us to want insurance. We want others to be covered, too, including the sick and injured who cannot help themselves. This is a motivation for *universal coverage*—equal access to healthcare for everyone—which requires government action to achieve.

Universal coverage would overcome the problem of adverse selection because we would all be in the same group. By forcing everyone to participate, universal coverage would also avoid the free-rider problem, which occurs when people figure that some safety-net level of coverage will be available to them whether they contribute insurance premiums or not. However, universal coverage raises a new set of issues. For example, if everyone is to be covered, what should that coverage consist of? Should we eliminate all choice? Who should pay? What about malpractice? Indeed, by expanding the use of the healthcare system and bureaucracy within that system, universal coverage would probably make the problem of moral hazard worse.

In 1993, President Clinton submitted to Congress a sweeping 1,342 page proposal that called for all Americans to be provided with national health insurance, giving citizens complete freedom to choose their own doctors. However, all doctors would have been forced to charge the same "community standard" price, a form of price control. That prospect frightened many people, and led to the proposal's resounding defeat.

There was good reason for concern. Under community standard pricing, doctors with the best reputations would be flooded with potential patients. The competitive response would have these superior doctors turn many patients away and keep others waiting. There would be long waits prior to scheduled appointments, and then long waits in the office before patients would be seen. The patients wind up paying extra, but the payments are in time, not money. Likewise, doctors with good reputations cannot be expected to spend time on tricky cases when they could process the easy ones much faster for more money. The result would be inefficiency. The best doctors would take the easy cases, leaving the tough ones for the less highly skilled. Even though price controls under universal coverage would not work well, the issue of costly care demands attention. Unfortunately, the solutions remain elusive.

$\mathscr{T}$HINKING $\mathscr{C}$RITICALLY

1. Suppose the government were to enact universal coverage with $2,500 deductibles. What problems would that policy solve? What problems would it cause?

2. One of the most significant costs of modern medicine involves malpractice insurance. Should the government limit the amounts that juries are allowed to award victims of medical malpractice, so as to reduce malpractice insurance premiums and thereby lower healthcare costs? Explain.

 Visit www.prenhall.com/collinge for updates and web exercises on this Explore & Apply topic.

SUMMARY AND LEARNING OBJECTIVES

1. **Distinguish among private goods, public goods, externalities, and common property resources.**
   - Market failure occurs when markets fail to achieve efficiency.
   - A good is said to be excludable when someone can be prevented from consuming the good. A good is said to be rival when one person's consumption of the good subtracts from the consumption of another person.
   - Pure private goods are excludable and rival. The goods we buy from retail sellers are almost always private goods.
   - A pure public good, such as national defense, is nonexcludable and nonrival. Pure public goods are consumed equally by everyone. National defense is the best example.
   - Public goods are usually impure, combining to some degree the qualities of a pure public good and a private good. Impure public goods are thus somewhat excludable and rival. Congestion occurs when one user of an impure public good reduces the consumption of another.
   - Between the extremes of pure private goods and pure public goods lie common property resources and private goods with externalities. Common property resources involve shared ownership of natural resources.
   - Private goods sometimes generate externalities. Externalities can be either positive, conferring benefits on third parties, or negative, which impose costs on third parties.

2. **Explain why the private marketplace fails to offer public goods in efficient quantities.**
   - The value of a public good is the sum of the values placed on the good by all the individuals who consume it.

   - The efficient quantity of a public good occurs at the point where marginal benefit equals marginal cost. Social surplus, the area under marginal benefit and above marginal cost, is maximized at this point.
   - The free-rider problem occurs when people seek to consume a public good without having to pay for it. Taxation forces those who would otherwise be free-riders to pay part of the cost of providing a public good. Were the private sector to provide public goods, free-riding could not be eliminated because private-sector firms have no power to tax.

3. **Identify an optimal amount of highway congestion and policies to achieve that amount.**
   - Highway congestion provides an example of why highways are an impure public good. When another vehicle enters a congested highway, the already slow flow of traffic is further impeded. Each additional vehicle slows down traffic even more. The marginal cost of more vehicles rises accordingly.
   - The efficient number of cars on a congested highway will be less than the actual number.
   - Government policy alternatives that would promote efficiency are of three kinds. First, the government could impose a toll for the use of a highway. Second, the government can produce more highways. Third, use of the highway can be regulated, such as through HOV lanes on a freeway.
   - Cost-benefit analysis is used to make decisions about how much of a public good to produce. Intangibles are things that have no market price. They make cost-benefit analysis complex, since it is difficult to put a value on an intangible. Nonetheless, to be accurate, a cost-benefit analysis must estimate the dollar values of intangibles.

4. **Describe why government enacts regulations and what principles can guide it toward efficiency.**

   - Government regulation specifies product characteristics or production methods. Examples include automobile seatbelt requirements and workplace safety laws.

   - Regulation by the government contributes to greater efficiency only if the benefits outweigh the costs associated with regulation. Costs include both administrative and compliance costs. Regulation is controversial, with concerns over the costs of overregulation at the forefront of the controversy.

   - To enhance economic efficiency, additional regulation should only be carried to the point where the marginal cost and marginal benefit are equal. However, government actions may cause undesirable side effects if not targeted precisely. Precise targeting is an application of the specificity principle.

   - Water shortages exemplify what can happen when the specificity principle is not used. Municipal water markets are characterized by monopoly providers of tap water. Price can be used to avoid shortages if set on the basis of marginal cost. However, price is often targeted for a different objective, such as to limit revenue. One policy instrument cannot meet both goals simultaneously.

5. **Explain the concept of asymmetric information and how it influences market outcomes.**

   - Imperfect information is a problem for people because better information makes for better decisions. Imperfect information can be the basis for government action, but the private marketplace can also help.

   - Asymmetric information describes a situation where one party to a transaction has information that the other does not have. Used-car buyers and sellers negotiate a sale on the basis of asymmetric information, with the seller having more information than the buyer. Credentialism is one outcome of asymmetric information. Cronyism is another.

   - Lack of information can cause the workplace to be unsafe. Specifically, if workers have imperfect information about job-related risks to their health, they will demand less safety of their employers than they would if they had perfect information. Government health and safety regulations can force employers toward the social optimum, the point where marginal social benefit equals marginal cost.

6. **Apply the analysis of marginal costs and marginal benefits to explain criminal behavior.**

   - Potential criminals make decisions based on the expected marginal benefits and the expected marginal costs of an action. The cost that a criminal would consider is the expected punishment, which is the punishment multiplied by the probability of being caught and convicted.

   - The rational quantity of criminal acts is the quantity associated with the point where the expected marginal benefit equals the expected marginal cost.

7. **Identify major issues in healthcare and alternative ways of addressing them.**

   - Insurance creates the problem of moral hazard. Moral hazard lowers the price of healthcare for patients and thus causes the quantity demanded of healthcare to exceed the efficient quantity. Asymmetric information creates the problem of adverse selection for insurance companies, in which those most in need of insurance are the most likely to seek it. Universal coverage would overcome the adverse selection problem, but not the problem of moral hazard.

KEY TERMS

market failure, 200
private goods, 200
public goods, 200
congestion, 201
local public good, 201

common property resource, 201
externality, 201
external costs, 201
external benefits, 201
free-rider problem, 202

cost-benefit analysis, 206
regulation, 207
specificity principle, 207
imperfect information, 209
asymmetric information, 210

TEST YOURSELF

TRUE OR FALSE

1. Excludable and rival describe pure public goods.
2. Private goods are never pure because of the existence of externalities.
3. An efficient quantity can be identified for a private good, but not for a public good.
4. The free-rider problem is addressed through taxation.
5. Government should establish regulations whenever there is imperfect information.

MULTIPLE CHOICE

6. The distinction between impure and pure public goods is that impure public goods
   a. are rival but not excludable.
   b. are excludable but not rival.
   c. are sometimes either excludable or rival.
   d. must be paid for through taxation, while pure public goods cost nothing.
7. The value of a public good
   a. is indicated by its demand curve.
   b. cannot be known, even in principle.
   c. is the sum of its values to all consumers.
   d. equals the sum of all taxes paid that are spent on the good.
8. The efficient quantity of a good is identified by
   a. public opinion polls.
   b. its market-equilibrium price.
   c. the point where the good's marginal benefit equals its marginal cost.
   d. the government's Office of Equity and Efficiency (OEE).
9. The free-rider problem is associated with
   a. downtown bus terminals.
   b. pure private goods.
   c. the poverty problem.
   d. public goods.
10. In Self-Test Figure 9-1, congestion sets in at quantity
    a. *A.*
    b. *B.*
    c. *C.*
    d. *D.*
11. In Self-Test Figure 9-1, what tax would achieve an efficient result?
    a. *E − F.*
    b. *F − C.*
    c. *E − C.*
    d. *G − D.*

12. What technique does the government use to decide how much of a public good to provide?
    a. Specificity analysis.
    b. Cost-benefit analysis.
    c. Public opinion polls and surveys.
    d. None, since politics settle the matter.
13. Intangibles
    a. are easily measured.
    b. is another name for the free-rider problem.
    c. are irrelevant to decision making.
    d. are included in cost-benefit analysis.
14. In assessing costs and benefits, the value of a statistical life is
    a. ignored.
    b. assumed to be zero.
    c. infinite.
    d. based on people's willingness to accept risk.
15. In determining the efficient type and amount of regulation to apply, policymakers should follow the rule that
    a. total benefit = total cost.
    b. marginal benefit = marginal cost.
    c. average cost = average benefit.
    d. marginal revenue = marginal cost.

SELF-TEST FIGURE 9-1

SELF-TEST FIGURE 9-2

16. In the municipal water market shown in Self-Test Figure 9-2, the two-headed arrow represents the water
    a. shortage when price is based on average cost.
    b. shortage when price is based on marginal cost.
    c. surplus when price is based on average cost.
    d. surplus when price is based on marginal cost.
17. If policymakers have the objectives of both efficiency and a low burden on the poor, the specificity principle suggests that they should set the price of tap water to equal
    a. zero, because water is a public good.
    b. average cost, because average-cost pricing is both efficient and fair.
    c. average cost and use other policies to address the issue of poverty.
    d. marginal cost and use other policies to address the issue of poverty.

18. Of the following, the most likely explanation for cronyism is
    a. asymmetric information.
    b. the free-rider problem.
    c. common-property resources.
    d. the specificity principle.
19. The expected punishment for committing a crime equals
    a. the punishment for the crime.
    b. the probability of being caught and convicted.
    c. the punishment for the crime plus the probability of being caught and convicted.
    d. the punishment for the crime multiplied by the probability of being caught and convicted.
20. Referring to Self-Test Figure 9-3, moral hazard is most likely to lead to the change shown by arrow
    a. *A.*
    b. *B.*
    c. *C.*
    d. *D.*

SELF-TEST FIGURE 9-3

QUESTIONS AND PROBLEMS

1. *[public goods]* Define and give several examples of public goods. Categorize each of your examples as a pure public good or an impure public good.
2. *[pure public goods]* Describe the nature of a pure public good and contrast it to an impure public good. Are most public goods pure or impure?
3. *[public goods]* List at least five public goods that are valuable to you personally. Are these public goods provided by the government or the private sector? For the public goods provided by the government, could these public goods also be provided by the private sector? Explain.
4. *[value of a public good]* Suppose that there is a public good consumed by Marsha, Marshall, and Maybell. Marsha values her consumption of this good at $3. Marshall values his consumption of the good at $7.

Maybell values her consumption of the good at $1. Assume this public good is a pure public good as you answer the following questions.

a. Will Maybell consume the good? Why or why not?

b. Will Marshall consume more, less, or the same amount of this good as Marsha?

c. What is the value of this public good, assuming that Marsha, Marshall, and Maybell are its only consumers?

5. *[excludability]* Describe what is meant when a good is said to be excludable. Why is the term "rival" also applied to excludable goods?

6. *[market failure]* Is market failure most often associated with purely private goods or with public goods? Explain.

7. *[graphing the efficient quantity of a public good]* Illustrate the efficient quantity of a public good with a graph. Be sure to label the axes, the curves drawn, and the efficient quantity. Write a short paragraph explaining the reasoning behind the efficient quantity.

8. *[free-rider problem]* Explain how the free-rider problem causes private markets to provide too little of a public good.

9. *[highway congestion]* Construct a graph that models the problem of highway congestion. After drawing the axes and labeling them, draw the downward-sloping demand curve for highway use. Then identify the congestion point on the horizontal axis. Add the average cost and marginal cost curves to your graph. Finish the graph by showing the efficient quantity and the actual quantity of vehicles per mile of highway.

Use this graph to discuss the most congested highway or street that you know. Your discussion should include the following points:

a. Approximately how many hours per weekday is the highway congested?

b. Is the highway equally congested on weekends?

c. Provide an estimate of the congestion point for this highway.

d. Estimate the cost to a driver of the average amount of congestion on the highway.

e. Do you think that some drivers try to stay off the highway at times of peak congestion? What alternatives are available to them that would make that possible?

f. Would it be feasible to reduce congestion on this highway by use of a toll? How large do you think the toll would need to be if it were feasible?

g. What other alternatives might be implemented to reduce congestion on this highway?

10. *[cost-benefit analysis]* The presence of intangibles makes it much more difficult to estimate costs and benefits for public-sector projects than for private-sector projects. Give an example of an intangible that might need to be measured in a public-sector cost-benefit analysis, and suggest how the estimation might be performed.

11. *[regulation]* It is difficult to get a handle on the costs to firms of identifying and complying with regulations. For this reason, such costs are often ignored. Explain why the costs are difficult to compute and what problems arise when they are ignored.

12. *[specificity principle]* Apply the specificity principle to the problem of homelessness by writing five debatable arguments that embody the specificity principle and that could be raised during a discussion about the homeless at a city council meeting.

13. *[specificity principle]* "Water is a necessity and thus should be provided by government to everyone at very low prices." Comment on the assertion that water is a necessity. Does it follow that necessities should be provided cheaply by government? Explain.

14. *[workplace safety]* Should all available safety devices be provided to employees by their employer? Explain your answer in terms of the efficient quantity of safety.

15. *[crime]* Does the economic approach to crime assume that criminals are rational? Explain.

 Visit **www.prenhall.com/collinge** for Exploring the Web exercises and additional self-test quizzes.

CHAPTER

EXTERNALITIES AND COMMON PROPERTY RESOURCES

A LOOK AHEAD

Picture yourself driving down the highway, enjoying the view of rolling green fields of corn or a striking city skyline. These are positive externalities that add to your driving pleasure. And then there are those external costs, you realize, as a car in the other lane cuts you off in order to avoid the mangled tire tread lying in the roadway. To offset your adrenaline surge, you roll down the window for some fresh air. Instead you find yourself engulfed in foul-smelling fumes from other vehicles. You have just experienced a few of the many externalities in life, ones that cause markets to be less than efficient.

If your journey takes you to public land, such as a forest or beach, do you have enough incentive to conserve it for others? Do they have enough incentive to conserve it for you? The common property nature of the resource suggests not, as we shall see.

Government can step into the picture to make us all more concerned with our effects upon one another. But what should government aim for, and what are the best ways to achieve those aims? This chapter focuses on the market failures of pollution and common property resources in identifying the problems and appropriate policies. The Explore & Apply section at the end of the chapter examines what governments can do when externalities extend across countries' borders.

LEARNING OBJECTIVES

Understanding Chapter 10 will enable you to:
1. **Identify examples of externalities and common property resources.**
2. **Analyze the effects of externalities on efficiency.**
3. **Explain why common property resources are likely to be overused.**
4. **Discuss the policy instruments that government can use to promote a better environment.**
5. **Identify the efficient amount of pollution and the policies to achieve it.**
6. **Discuss the issue of transborder pollution and the difficulties in finding solutions.**

In the previous chapter we saw how market failure could lead to inefficiencies. This chapter looks more closely at two of those sources of inefficiency. We then examine alternative policy actions that are intended to help.

10.1 EXTERNALITIES AND COMMON PROPERTY RESOURCES

externalities side effects of production or consumption that affect third parties who have no say in the matter.

common property resource a jointly owned resource, such as groundwater.

Recall that **externalities** occur when the production or consumption of private goods leads to costs or benefits to third parties, meaning people or businesses who are not party to the transaction. Recall that market failure also occurs when the ownership of property is shared, meaning that it is *common property.* Shared ownership occurs most frequently in connection with natural resources such as air and water, thus leading to the term **common property resource.** As shown in the sections that follow, the analyses of externalities and common property resources have much in common.

EXTERNALITIES—WHEN SHOULD THERE BE ACTION?

external costs or benefits value lost to (or gained by) third parties who are not represented by market supply and demand.

Externalities can be either negative or positive. Pollution is an example of a negative externality. Negative externalities impose **external costs** on others. For example, to the extent that air pollution causes health problems or decreases people's enjoyment of outdoor activities, the pollution has imposed external costs on its victims. Conversely, positive externalities confer **external benefits,** such as when a neighbor kills all the mosquitos on her property, which leaves fewer to fly into your own backyard. A few of the many examples of externalities are listed in Table 10-1.

private costs or benefits costs or benefits that are borne by the decision maker, such as a buyer or seller.

social costs or benefits the sum of all costs or all benefits to all members of society; includes both private and external costs and benefits.

Externalities in the form of external benefits or external costs are all around us, although frequently they are of minor significance. Externalities occur when the **private costs or benefits** of an action—those borne by the ones taking the action—differ from social costs or benefits. **Social costs or benefits** are defined to equal all costs or benefits within the economy, including both private and external costs and benefits, as follows:

$$\text{Social cost} = \text{Private cost} + \text{External cost}$$

and

$$\text{Social benefit} = \text{Private benefit} + \text{External benefit}$$

By the same token, consider the costs and benefits associated with each additional unit of output, as follows:

$$\text{Marginal social cost} = \text{Marginal private cost} + \text{Marginal external cost}$$

and

$$\text{Marginal social benefit} = \text{Marginal private benefit} + \text{Marginal external benefit}$$

marginal external costs or benefits externalities that cause market outcomes to be inefficient.

It is externalities that occur at the margin—**marginal external costs** and **marginal external benefits**—that are of most interest in economics, because these externalities at the margin cause market outcomes to differ from what is efficient.

Significant external benefits are not as widespread as significant external costs, but do exist. For example, constructing a beautiful new house in a shabby neighborhood will increase the value of other homes in that neighborhood. Likewise, people who successfully pull themselves out of poverty or other difficult situations serve as valuable role models for others seeking to escape similar situations.

In the case of an external benefit as shown in Figure 10-1, market demand does not include all social benefits. External benefits might arise from education, perhaps because an

TABLE 10-1   EXTERNALITIES ALL AROUND US

SAMPLE ACTIVITIES WITH EXTERNAL BENEFITS	SAMPLE ACTIVITIES WITH EXTERNAL COSTS
Answering questions in class	Allowing your cell phone to ring in class
Looking your best	Being distracted by your cell phone while driving
Having your car washed	Driving a vehicle that emits exhaust gas
Getting immunized against disease	Using river water to remove industrial waste
Inspiring others with your ideas and actions	Burning coal to generate electricity

educated person makes better choices in the voting booth. While of value to others, there is no payment to the individual to motivate him or her to choose the socially efficient amount. For that reason, **when marginal external benefits are present, the free market produces too little—output falls short of the quantity that would be efficient.**

The most obvious external cost is from environmental pollution. For example, fumes from the tailpipe of a diesel bus do not bother either the passengers or the bus company. Rather, the cost is external—the fumes bother the drivers behind. Would you wish to follow a gravel truck that drops sand and pebbles that threaten to damage your vehicle? The cost of chipped paint on your PT Cruiser is of no concern to The Pits Gravel Company unless, perhaps, it fears a lawsuit or government reprisal.

Because external costs or benefits are not felt by the person or firm causing the externality, the free-market price signal fails to generate efficient outputs. For example, Figure 10-2 shows the supply and demand for a product that has an external cost. The supply curve represents marginal private cost, but fails to reflect full marginal social cost. Thus, **when marginal external costs are present, the free market produces too much—output exceeds the quantity that would be efficient.**

Marginal external cost is shown to be rising with output, meaning that the difference between supply and marginal social cost rises with increasing output. This is a typical

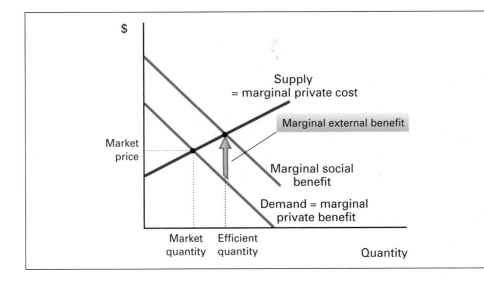

FIGURE 10-1

EXTERNAL BENEFITS—TOO LITTLE PRODUCED The intersection of market demand and supply determine market quantity. Even if we cannot measure what it is exactly, we can still infer that the existence of any marginal external benefits at this quantity would mean that the market produces less than would be efficient, as shown.

FIGURE 10-2

EXTERNAL COSTS—TOO MUCH PRODUCED When external costs are present, supply lies below marginal social cost and the free market produces more than would be efficient.

result, because the usual external cost comes from pollution and results in a degradation in environmental quality. Environmental quality is a public good, with a demand curve that is downwardly sloping, as discussed in the previous chapter. Pollution reduces the quantity of environmental quality, as shown in Figure 10-3(a). The external cost of smoke from a factory, for example, is the reduction in environmental quality as that smoke disperses. The

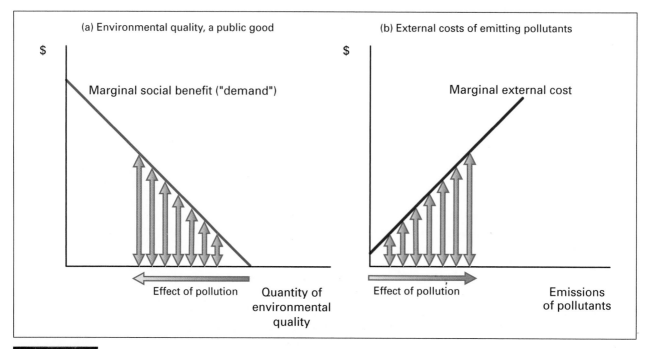

FIGURE 10-3

THE LINK BETWEEN ENVIRONMENTAL QUALITY AND EXTERNAL COSTS Environmental quality is a public good. Pollution reduces the amount of environmental quality, as shown in (a). The marginal external cost curve shown in (b) is a mirror image of the lower part of the "demand" for public goods. It shows the marginal cost of forgoing environmental quality. The curve starts above zero, because there is some environmental degradation that occurs naturally, such as when lightning starts a forest fire.

marginal external costs of pollution are nothing more than the marginal benefits of environmental quality forgone, as shown in Figure 10-3(b). Observe that the marginal external cost curve intersects the vertical axis above zero. The reason is that there are some natural sources of pollution, such as from forest fires started by lightning.

The presence of external costs does not imply that the externality-generating activity should cease. It is efficient to have some pollution, for example. In the course of a day's living, we are each responsible for pollution, such as from the tailpipe of the vehicles that take us where we want to go. Additional pollution is generated in producing the products we buy.

Are manufacturers evil people, who pollute so that we will be miserable? Actually, pollution results from firms using air or water to remove the wastes that are generated by their production of goods and services. The principle of mass balance, a physical law, implies that some waste will always occur when inputs are transformed into outputs. This waste must go somewhere, and water and air provide handy waste removal services.

Lacking government action, polluters pollute too much. The reason is that there is no market for many environmental services. "No market" means just that. The discharge of pollutants into the air, or into lakes, rivers, streams, aquifers, or the ocean can be carried out free of charge because the air and water are publicly owned. There are no sellers of air and flowing water in the marketplace to collect the revenue for their use. The outcome when there is no market is a price of zero.

However, there is a market for some environmental waste-removal services. For instance, firms economize on the solid wastes they generate when they must pay the trash collector to have these wastes disposed of. That's because someone owns the landfill where trash is dumped. In contrast, in the case of liquid and gaseous waste, firms have no incentive to cut back on the production of these pollutants if they can use the publicly owned environment—air and water—to remove these wastes for free.

WHEN MARKETS ARE MISSING

If environmental services provided by common-property water and air were priced, as they would be if sold in a market, firms would economize and pollute less. They would compute how valuable pollution is to them in terms of the extra output it allows. They would also look for alternate ways to produce their output with less pollution. The upshot is that firms would pollute only when the value of their pollution exceeds its environmental costs. That would be efficient.

Occasionally, firms compete on the basis of how environmentally friendly—how "green"—their products are. For example, consumers may pay extra for recycled paper or nontoxic antifreeze. However, consumers rarely seek information on how much pollution is generated in the production of the products they buy, and are rarely willing to pay much of a premium for green products.

Typically, then, competition forces firms to be environmentally neglectful unless there are public policy incentives to be otherwise. Were a firm to go to the expense of cutting back its pollution, that firm would be at a disadvantage in competing against other firms in its industry. Only the heaviest polluters would survive. This is why pollution externalities represent a market failure, one calling for government action to change the rules of the game. The Clean Air Act was one such action. This Act, amended in 1970, has caused the emission of major air pollutants to fall dramatically, as shown in Figure 10-4.

While reliance on public policy is commonplace, it is not the only means to resolve externalities. An alternative would rely on legal safeguards against damage to the property of others. If pollution damages your property, sue for damages! Polluters will seek to avoid damages if they have to pay.

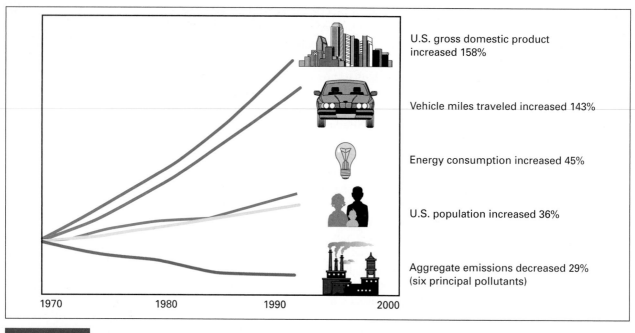

FIGURE 10-4

COMPARISON OF GROWTH AREAS AND EMISSION TRENDS Between 1970 and 2000, gross domestic product increased 158 percent, energy consumption increased 45 percent, vehicle miles traveled increased 143 percent, and U.S. population increased 36 percent. At the same time, total emissions of the six principal air pollutants decreased 29 percent.

Source: Environmental Protection Agency, *Six Principle Pollutants.*

Coase theorem theory that holds parties to an externality would voluntarily negotiate an efficient outcome without government involvement when property rights are clearly defined.

This idea leads to the **Coase theorem,** named after Nobel Laureate Sir Ronald Coase, which holds that parties to an externality would voluntarily negotiate an efficient outcome without government involvement. Government need merely clearly define and enforce property rights. For example, if the value of changing the amount of an externality exceeds its cost, a mutually beneficial agreement would be struck to accomplish this change. That would be efficient. If the value of change is less than the cost, an agreement would not be reached. That would also be efficient.

Few people believe the Coase theorem offers a general solution to externality problems. For example, imagine your neighbor playing his classic Iron Butterfly album at top volume at 2 A.M. Are you likely to ask how much money that experience is worth to him, and compare the amount with your own willingness to pay to avoid hearing it? Would you offer to pay him enough to get him to turn the volume down? You're a reasonable person, aren't you? "Not at 2 o'clock in the morning!" you say?

Anyway, if you pay once, you'll wind up paying again, even if your neighbor decides that he no longer likes listening. He likes the money. That exemplifies the problem of *strategic behavior,* which interferes with the practical application of the Coase theorem. That problem becomes significantly worse when the effects of the externality are widespread. In addition, identifying specific culprits and bringing together victims becomes quite difficult

transaction costs the expense of coordinating market exchanges.

when many parties are involved. **Transaction costs,** the expense of coordinating market exchanges, would be high. Thus, the Coase theorem applies only in the absence of transaction costs and strategic behavior. In practice, this means we either resort to public policy to remedy the externality or ignore the problem and let the market fail.

QUICKCHECK

How can it be efficient to ignore the problem of externality?

Answer: Sometimes legal and policy cures are worse than the disease. Many externalities are minor, such as those caused by other people's attire, cleanliness, and mannerisms. Imagine the problems of trying to measure these externalities and reward or punish them through either public policy or private lawsuit!

BACK IN TIME TO BAKER STREET

SNAPSHOT

Wouldn't you sometimes like to do away with those stinking internal combustion engines and return to the pristine past of horses and carriages? You wouldn't have to deal with smog and ozone alerts.

Dream on, for the reality of life prior to the horseless carriage was anything but pollution free. Witness nineteenth-century London in the days of Sherlock Holmes. Well before the invention of motor cars, the streets of London were beset with acid rain and choking air pollution.

The skies over London were black with smoke from the many coal- and wood-burning fireplaces throughout the city. Now, more than a century later and several million people larger, London offers more breathable air and clearer skies.

Yes, London still has pollution: it is a by-product of generating goods and services ranging from heat to transportation. The difference today is better pollution-control technology spurred on by public policy. Compared with the good old days, then, population and production are up and pollution is down. ◄

COMMON PROPERTY RESOURCES—NO INCENTIVES FOR CONSERVATION

Common property resources are owned jointly, including groundwater, public lands, wild animals, and fish in the oceans, lakes, and rivers. Unless government sets up policies to prevent it, anyone can hunt, fish, pump water, and in other ways capture the common property to make it that person's private property.

Common property resources lead to too much production in the present with insufficient regard for the future. The problem is that, when many people own the same resource, no one has any personal incentive to conserve it. Owners have rights to take or use the resource, but have no way of ensuring its preservation. A common property resource generates a race among its owners to exploit the resource as quickly as possible, before others can get to it. Owners ignore the opportunity cost in terms of future value forgone from using something up today.

For example, imagine sharing a very large joint checking account with all other students at your college. How much money would be left in the account by the end of the day? Most likely, each student would figure that others would quickly raid the account. The bank would see a stampede of students, each seeking to be the first to transfer the entire balance to a private account. Common property resources face much the same problem.

A classic article entitled "Tragedy of the Commons" illustrates this problem with reference to the old English commons.* The common pastureland accessible to all quickly turned

---

* Garrett Hardin, "Tragedy of the Commons," *Science,* 1968.

into a desolate expanse of dirt and mud, while private land nearby was lush and green. Grasses on the commons disappeared because shepherds allowed their sheep to overgraze. Shepherds had no reason to graze their flocks lightly, because the grass they saved would in all likelihood get eaten by someone else's flock. In contrast, on private land nearby, owners sought to conserve some grass to provide for future growth. The sheep were herded to fresh pastures before the grass was munched so short as to become endangered.

The common property resource problem is not a thing of the past. For example, over-fishing along the coast of Maine and in many other ocean fisheries has caused catches to decline dramatically. Another concern is depletion of the ozone layer in the earth's upper atmosphere, as manufacturers in countries around the globe have little incentive to design ozone-friendly products. Likewise, farmers who irrigate their land and cities and towns that tap into groundwater and river water resources have little incentive to practice conservation that would help each other out.

Not only do common property owners have no stake in preserving the resource for future use, but they also do not care if they get in the way of one another's efforts. For example, in fishing or shrimping grounds along the Gulf coast, each additional boat is likely to reduce the amount caught by other boats. Unless all the boats are owned jointly, though, this effect is ignored by the fishermen and shrimpers. Likewise, overfishing today means fewer fish will be available in the future.

Government can solve common property resource problems by selling the common property to a single owner. Most often, however, complete transfers would be impractical or politically unacceptable. For example, few would advocate selling rivers, lakes, and oceans to any single owner. The alternative is for the government to act as the owners' agent and apportion use of the common property so that overuse is avoided. This is the rationale behind fishing and hunting permits, regulation of mesh size on fishing nets, mandated water-saving toilets, and various other restrictions and **user fees**—charges for use of a publicly owned resource.

user fees charges for use of a publicly owned good, service, or resource.

10.2 POLICY TOOLS

Some policy approaches to conservation are more promising than others. This section highlights some prominent policy options for the control of externalities and allocation of common property resources. Although several applications will be mentioned, the focus will be upon pollution and water policy. This focus is warranted because pollution is the most prominent externality, and allocation of common-property water promises to become increasingly significant as the population grows.

MORAL SUASION

"Turn down that thermostat—Don't waste energy!" "Be water tight!" "Don't be a Litter Bug!"
"Only YOU can prevent forest fires!"

From U.S. presidents to Smokey the Bear, we are exhorted to do the right thing. These appeals to our social conscience—called **moral suasion**—are the easiest and most high-profile form of public policy available to fight problems associated with externalities and common property resources. Moral suasion makes it clear to the public that the government is taking action. Unfortunately, moral suasion is rarely adequate to the task and often has undesirable side effects.

moral suasion exhortations to do the right thing, as defined by public policymakers.

A fundamental drawback to moral suasion is that it has no way of achieving any particular target, efficient or otherwise. Also, moral suasion imposes all costs of cutbacks on the "moral." A third and perhaps most troubling problem is that moral suasion can lead to a self-righteous intrusion on personal privacy. Even Nathaniel Hawthorne was troubled by moral suasion, as evidenced by his classic novel *The Scarlet Letter* in which the humiliation of public exposure was used as the deterrent against adultery. These days, moral suasion is most likely to take the form of ad campaigns aimed at the public.

STANDARDS AND TECHNOLOGY MANDATES

Technology mandates occur when government instructs producers as to the exact technology to install as a remedy for some public problem. Low-flow showerheads and low-flush toilets are examples of technology mandates designed to avoid wasting water. Catalytic converters on automobiles are mandated to reduce air pollution. Technology mandates are usually chosen because they are easy to observe and enforce, and seem like a very straightforward solution to the problem.

technology mandates government rules that instruct producers as to the exact technology to use in a product or its production.

Sometimes the mandates are indirect, as with smoke-filtering scrubbers on powerplant smokestacks, and other specific pollution control strategies. Here, the Environmental Protection Agency (EPA) specifies emission *standards* that must be met and suggests technologies that will meet these standards. Producers are free to use other technologies, but would be subject to serious penalties if their approaches fail. In contrast, if the EPA's suggested technologies fail, the producers avoid liability. There is thus much risk and little incentive to experiment with potentially better ways of pollution control.

Technology mandates are often much more expensive and annoying than other policy options. For instance, it is a waste of money and an annoyance to require high-tech, low-flush toilets in regions where water is plentiful. If external costs can be added directly to the prices of products, the higher prices would induce conservation in ways that regulators might be unable to mandate. A price of municipal water that fully reflected its opportunity costs would cause customers to seek out an efficient array of plumbing fixtures, without the need for government mandates. By the same token, there would be no need to mandate irrigation techniques in agriculture if farmers always pay the opportunity cost of the water they use. Using prices avoids the inefficiencies caused by the broad brush of technology mandates.

Economic studies on pollution control estimate that market-based alternatives to technology mandates and standards can achieve the same amounts of emission cutbacks at roughly one-third the cost. For example, the EPA's *bubble plan* allows a firm to increase its emissions from some sources if it offsets those increases by decreasing its emissions from other sources within its plant. One Ohio utility plant responded by periodically hosing down its piles of coal to prevent wind-blown coal dust, rather than install expensive smokestack technology. The firm's particulate emissions dropped, while the cost of pollution control dropped even more. The EPA's *offsets plan* extends this flexible concept across firms to capture even more cost savings.

Government planners cannot be expected to foresee all of the options for pollution control. For example, what planner could have mandated that workers reduce pollution and congestion by abandoning their daily auto commute? Could planners in the 1970s have imagined the option of replacing commuters' automobiles with telecommunications? Yet, the recently available technologies of networked home computers and the Internet have led many people to do just that by working at home. Allowing the market to choose this and other less costly strategies of pollution control means that we can have a cleaner environment at a lower cost.

POLLUTION TAXES—ENVIRONMENTAL USER FEES

As an alternative to technology mandates, pollution taxes can reduce pollution without creating the problems associated with technology mandates. Economists often advocate this action, which is referred to as *internalizing* the cost of an externality directly into prices. How would such a tax work? If an activity generates damages, the value of those damages would be estimated, and a tax would be imposed equal to the amount of the marginal external cost at the efficient level of output. In this way, the tax causes perpetrators of the external cost to pay the full marginal social cost of their activities. This means that externalities become part of the decisions of those who cause them, and efficient choices will be made in the marketplace. For example, if smoking a pack of cigarettes causes an average of $1 in health damages to others, then a tax of $1 per pack would represent those damages.

Figure 10-5 illustrates that a corrective tax on cigarettes shifts the supply curve up by the amount of that tax, since sellers now have to collect that extra payment and pass it along to the government. The price would rise and the quantity fall, as the market equilibrium changes. Note that the price rise of 80 cents in this example is less than the tax of $1. Most of the tax is passed on to consumers, because demand is inelastic relative to supply, as discussed in the elasticity chapter. The rest is absorbed by producers in what is now a smaller industry.

Using fees to remedy externalities often encounters difficulties. For example, external damages may depend upon time and place. Smoking at home does not impose the same externality as smoking in a restroom that many people must use. It is not possible to allow

FIGURE 10-5

THE EFFICIENT TAX A tax can internalize an external cost. Efficiency requires that the tax rate be set equal to marginal external cost at the efficient quantity of output.

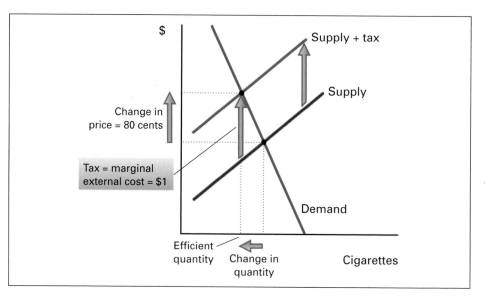

for this difference in imposing cigarette taxes. In other applications, such as taxes on water pollution from industrial waste, fees could vary depending on such factors as the season and time of day.

Measurement of pollution is another hurdle in the way of applying pollution taxes. For example, it may be difficult to constantly monitor the emission of pollutants, especially for autos and other mobile sources. For stationary sources like factories, one can imagine a system of periodic checks and penalties that would punish cheating. Of greater concern, however, is political support for taxing pollution and providing effective penalties to ensure compliance.

Politicians often seek new revenue sources. In contrast to most taxes, those designed to remedy externalities actually promote economic efficiency. Yet, pollution taxes have proven to have little political support. On the one hand, some well-meaning environmentalists will not accept that the environment is an economic resource. They claim that pollution taxes are merely passed along to consumers, and that pollution is not reduced. This line of reasoning ignores the law of demand. It also ignores the role of competition. Competition forces firms to substitute cheaper inputs for the newly taxed use of environmental services.

On the other hand, producers usually oppose pollution taxes. The reason is that those taxes result in significant transfers of revenues from polluters to the government, revenues that pay for the firms' ongoing emissions of pollutants. This revenue transfer is in addition to money spent directly on pollution control. Thus, pollution taxes lack powerful constituencies.

To overcome political barriers to pollution taxes, policymakers sometimes resort to paying for pollution abatement instead. For example, municipal wastewater treatment plants receive significant federal **subsidies,** which are payments from the federal government meant to encourage actions with external benefits or that reduce external costs. Unfortunately, subsidies for reducing pollution have two undesirable side effects, which are:

subsidies payments to promote actions with external benefits or that reduce external costs.

- Subsidies drain government revenues.
- Subsidies reward polluters and, for this reason, can lead to too many polluting firms.

SMOKING WHILE EATING AND PHONING WHILE DRIVING

SNAPSHOT

Anti-smoking laws have cropped up all around the country. Bans on talking on the phone while driving a car are likewise becoming increasingly prevalent. Since both activities are taxed, could not those taxes be set to internalize any externalities so that no heavy-handed prohibitions are needed?

The problem with this proposal is that externalities vary by time and place. A flat tax on cigarettes does not adjust for whether the smoking occurs in a crowded restaurant or in the privacy of one's home. Likewise, talking on a cell phone is not dangerous to other motorists when the talker is not driving on the highway. Since taxes cannot know where the smoking or talking will occur, an alternative is to just ban the activity in situations where the potential for externality is highest.

Bans are not without their costs, however. Smokers value their after-dinner cigarettes just as car callers value the time they save. Therefore, policymakers must weigh the costs and benefits of alternative policies. Sometimes, in fact, the most efficient policy is no policy at all. For example, with no bans on smoking in restaurants some restaurants will differentiate themselves by being smoke-free, some by allowing smoking everywhere, and probably most by having separate sections for smokers and nonsmokers. In the case of smoking while you eat, therefore, the market has a solution. In the case of phoning while you drive, with everyone sharing the same public highways, no market solution is apparent. ◄

MARKETABLE PERMITS—WHOSE PROPERTY?

marketable permits property rights to a specified amount of an activity, such as groundwater pumping or air pollution, where those property rights can be bought and sold; can efficiently achieve quantity targets set by the government.

Marketable permits offer the same economic advantages as taxes, but in a way that has much more political appeal. In application to pollution, **marketable permits** represent property rights to a certain amount of pollutant emissions. The government sets the overall quantity, and then divides up that quantity into a limited number of permits for the various polluters. While these permits could be auctioned, politics causes them more typically to be given away to preexisting polluters without charge.

Because the overall quantity of pollution is controlled directly, environmentalists are usually willing to acknowledge that marketable permits limit total pollution. Polluters prefer this approach to taxes because permits usually require no payment to the government. However, polluters do sometimes worry that the government might take away those rights or impose supplemental charges in the future.

Marketable permits are valuable property rights. The term *marketable* means that those rights can be bought and sold. This feature has appeal not only to producers, but also to economists. If pollution rights are traded, buyers would be firms with high costs of pollution abatement. Likewise, sellers would be firms with low costs of cutting back emissions. This means that emission reductions are undertaken by firms able to do so at least cost.

Trading in emission rights has mushroomed in recent years, so much so that it has formed an industry of its own. Markets for some pollutants are formal and well developed. For example, power plants and other emitters can buy and sell rights for sulfur dioxide emissions on the Chicago Board of Trade. Other pollutants have *thin markets*, where trades are few. When markets are thin, environmental consultants facilitate trading by keeping track of firms willing to sell their permits.

Marketable permits also provide a promising alternative in the allocation of common property resources. Here, a central authority determines how much of the resource can be used now, and still leave enough for the future. For example, the authority might estimate how much water can be pumped from a river without irreparable harm to the river's ecosystem. Pumping rights are then distributed among river users, perhaps in proportion to the users' historical levels of pumping. These rights are then good for each period into the indefinite future. Fluctuations in the river's ability to support pumping might cause the same percentage variations in the quantity allowed per permit.

By allowing permits to be marketable, those valuing water most highly would be the ones that would buy or retain the permits. This outcome is just what economic efficiency prescribes. The main issues are distributional. For example, how are the permits to be initially distributed? Should we compensate feed store owners who lose their livelihoods when local farmers and ranchers sell their water rights to big cities? Political questions of this sort have been the largest obstacles to more widespread use of permits.

APPLYING POLICY DIRECTLY TO POLLUTION

Efficient pollution control can be achieved through either taxes or marketable permits, as discussed in the previous two sections. Since most pollution comes from production rather than from consumption, it is usually best to apply a tax or permit approach directly to pollution rather than to outputs. Sometimes this is difficult or impossible to do. For example, it would take an army of government agents to follow around potential smokers to collect a smoke emissions tax when they light up. In that case, it is far easier to monitor and tax cigarette sales.

When pollution control policy is applied to output, however, pollution is reduced only to the extent that output falls. In contrast, when pollution is taxed directly, polluters also have the incentive to reduce the amount of pollution per unit of that output. It is

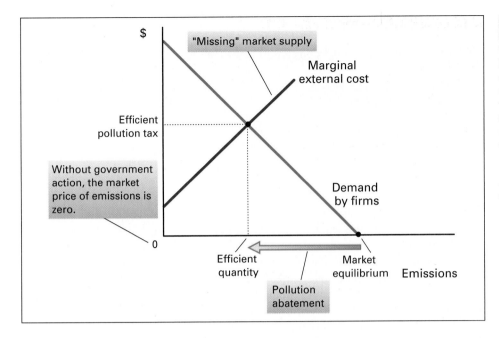

FIGURE 10-6

THE MISSING MARKET FOR POLLUTION To correct problems of pollution externalities in production, the government must first estimate marginal external cost, which is the "missing" market supply curve. The efficient quantity of pollution can be achieved by marketable permits summing to that quantity or through a tax equal to what would be the market-clearing price of a unit of emissions. The result of either policy would be a reduction in pollution to the efficient quantity.

often feasible to tax pollution directly in cases of stationary-source polluters, such as factories. Such taxes require that the government be able to monitor the quantity of pollution that is emitted.

Firms do not pollute for their own sake. Rather, they use the environment to remove waste products, with pollution being the result. For this reason, firms have a demand for the right to emit pollution into the environment. In other words, firms are willing to pay because using the environment to remove wastes is a valuable service to them, just like the services of labor. Firms value this service because consumers value the output that the firms produce. Thus, the benefit of pollution is really the extra value that consumers receive because producers pollute. These benefits are captured in the demand for emission rights, shown in Figure 10-6, the curve that represents firms' willingness to pay for incremental rights to pollute.

Since environmental services are not priced, there is no one in the free market to charge firms for environmental services, because no one owns the environment. For this reason, in the absence of government action, firms are free to pollute as much as they want. In Figure 10-6, the amount that firms pollute in the absence of government action is given by the intersection of demand with the horizontal axis, which is the quantity demanded at a price of zero. In effect, there is a missing market. If a market were to exist, the market supply curve should correspond to marginal external cost, and the market equilibrium would be an efficient quantity. The equilibrium price would equal the efficient tax shown in the figure.

To substitute for the missing efficient market price, the government could charge firms a fee per unit of emissions, where that fee is shown in Figure 10-6 as the efficient pollution tax. **To remedy an externality with a tax, the tax rate must be set equal to marginal external cost at the efficient level of pollution.** Polluters would be forced to pay that price for their emissions in the same manner that they must pay for their other inputs. In this case, it is in effect the government selling them the input of environmental services.

Alternatively, regulators could issue an efficient quantity of marketable permits, which would have the effect of limiting emissions to no more than that amount. The value of the marginal unit of emissions would be the same as the efficient tax, so that competition for emission rights in the marketplace would set a price on those rights just as though there had been an emissions tax.

QUICKCHECK

Why are marketable permits more efficient than technology mandates?

Answer: Technology mandates are inflexible, which can lead to some firms spending much more than others for the same amount of pollution reduction. Marketable permits can achieve overall pollution reduction much more cheaply because the firms that can cut back emissions at least cost will be the ones to do so. In addition, unlike technology mandates, marketable permits make it profitable to improve pollution control technology over time.

While the tax solution brings in revenue to the government for every unit of emissions, a marketable permit system will typically bring little or no revenue to the government. The reason is that emission permits are usually given free of charge to firms in a region, with those firms then free to sell the emission rights as they see fit. The reason for this manner of distribution is mainly political, since firms in a polluting industry lobby hard to avoid massive payments to the government for polluting activities for which they have historically not been charged. Since either the tax or permit approach allows regulators to create a market that allocates emission rights efficiently, marketable permits have become the policy instrument of choice.

10.3 CARING FOR THE GLOBAL ENVIRONMENT

Policies to control pollution or preserve common property resources require a government to administer them. Yet, oftentimes, these market failures go beyond the confines of any single country. In these situations, the best solutions often involve international cooperation. For example, the world's oceans are common property resources, which leads to the overharvesting of whales and other marine life. They can be exploited without restriction, absent international agreements to the contrary.

Another common property resource, one that countries of the world all share, is the earth's atmosphere. This atmosphere filters out many harmful rays of the sun, protecting us from skin cancer and providing the environment to which humans and other species have adapted over the centuries. The burning of carbon-based fuels, the use of certain aerosol propellants, and other actions of a modern industrial society have the potential to harm this shared resource.

Unfortunately, because of the complexity of the world's environment, it is hard to know just exactly what role mankind has in affecting it. For example, scientists have been unable to prove with certainty that the burning of fossil fuels causes global warming, given historical evidence that the earth has experienced numerous periods of general warming and cooling over the centuries. Even so, just because it is nearly impossible to prove does not mean that it is not occurring, which is why the issue of global warming remains contentious.

It sounds like a good idea for countries of the world to somehow get together and protect the common property resources that we all share. Indeed, countries have gotten together to agree upon such matters as *the law of the sea,* including allowing countries to claim up to 200 miles from shorelines as the countries' own territories. The problem is that agreements are often difficult to reach. For example, President Bush reiterated in 2002 that the United States would not abide by the multilateral *Kyoto Accords* on global warming. This is an agreement signed by representatives of many of the world's countries, requiring them to take actions that would protect the world's environment. The United States would have faced much of the cost of this agreement, including changes in lifestyles and ways of production. While that was fine with the large majority of countries in the world, the United States thought otherwise.

Economists identify pollution as a market failure, because firms and consumers ignore the external costs of their actions. In addition, it is important to recognize that many countries' governments have been responsible for the world's pollution. The environmental legacy of the Soviet Union and its European allies provides a tragic illustration. Environmental devastation there ranged from the ecological death of rivers and lakes to radioactive contamination spread over hundreds of square miles by the 1986 explosion at the Chernobyl nuclear power plant. Secretive, bureaucratic governments cannot be expected to be responsive to their citizens' environmental concerns.

KILLER BEES, FIRE ANTS, HUNGRY RABBITS, AND WALKING FISH

SNAPSHOT

Never underestimate the ability of humans to inflict environmental disaster. Take the case of Australia's rabbits, which do significant damage to crops on the island continent. Rabbits are not native to the country, but were introduced when an immigrant youngster's pregnant pet rabbit escaped into the wilds where no natural predators existed. Then there are the fire ants and "killer bees" spreading throughout the United States, threatening people, pets, crops, and the relatively gentle native ants and bees. The ants arrived on boats from South America and found a hospitable climate free of predators. The immigrant bees are the result of a scientific experiment in breeding that went awry when thousands of the pesky critters escaped into the wilds of Brazil and then decided to move north.

Most recently, it is the voracious appetites of the Chinese snakehead "walking" fish that has residents of several states worried. Set free in a Crofton, Maryland, pond when they outgrew their owner's aquarium, these fish found the American environment to be to their liking, free from the predators they had learned to fear in China. Growing up to three feet long and able to travel out of water for three days, these fearsome "Frankenfish" quickly became the predators of frogs, birds, small mammals, and other fish. The situation has prompted the poisoning of ponds and a massive fishhunt to keep them from spreading further. On the bright side, the ugly snakehead fish are reportedly quite tasty! ◄

10.4 BORDERLANDS OF THE SOUTHWEST—WHOSE POLLUTION? WHOSE SOLUTION?

Explore & Apply

Wide open spaces, broad vistas, a freshening breeze—our vision of America's Southwest is one of expansiveness and freedom. It is a place to do and be as we please. The Southwest is part of our psyche; it's a state of mind. It's also a real place with real problems. As ever more people live in the Southwest, unlimited personal freedom comes into conflict with preservation of the environment that attracts them there. The environment of the Southwest is ill-suited to accommodate unrestricted pollution.

As in other parts of the country, citizens of the Southwest must abide by U.S. environmental laws, which means driving cars or operating factories with emission controls in place. The special problem of the Southwest, though, is that those controls apply to only a fraction of the sources of pollution. Much of the air and water pollution has its source in Mexico, an industrializing country with a rapidly growing population and less stringent control over pollutants.

Exemplifying the problem of border air pollution, the city of El Paso, Texas, is in noncompliance with guidelines set by the U.S. Environmental Protection Agency (EPA).

However, the EPA allows this noncompliance to continue without penalty. There is a reason.

If you were to fly into El Paso and look out the airplane window as you approach the city, you may have a good idea as to why the EPA makes exceptions for El Paso. On the south side of the Rio Grande you are likely to see a polluted haze that greatly restricts visibility. The haze on the north side is much lighter. El Paso is on the north side and its twin, Ciudad Juárez, is on the south side. Ciudad Juárez has nearly triple the population and generates proportionally much more pollution than does El Paso. Unfortunately for El Paso, pollution knows no borders.

Transborder pollution is a problem of growing magnitude around the world. The problems are worsening for two reasons. On the one hand, economic growth in the less-developed countries does not emphasize pollution control. Of greater concern to those countries are such tangibles as food, clothing, and shelter. On the other hand, the increased wealth of the developed countries has allowed them the luxury to focus beyond immediate necessities toward the quality and long-term sustainability of lifestyles. Environmental quality is important to both of those lifestyle goals.

Transborder pollution problems come in many forms. Some are global in nature, such as concerns that emissions of chlorofluorocarbons are depleting the earth's ozone layer. The pollution problem of most concern in America's Southwest is more local in nature. Here we have two countries, each of which feels the effects of the other's pollution. What trouble does this cause?

The problem of localized transborder pollution centers on incentives. There is much more incentive to control pollution that affects your own residents than there is incentive to control pollution absorbed elsewhere. For instance, cities along rivers routinely locate sewage treatment plants downstream and city dumps downwind from the city itself. When cities are all governed by one state or country, there are limits to how much pollution exporting is allowed. For example, while sewage from U.S. cities may be discharged down river, at least U.S. law requires that it be treated. Given an absence of a world government, is there some other incentive for neighboring countries to be sensitive to each other's concerns?

POLLUTION CONTROL POLICIES

It would be very difficult for the United States to apply any particular pollution control strategy to firms in Mexico. Options that work well within a jurisdiction don't work as well across jurisdictions. For example, one option long advocated by economists is for the government to impose a tax on emissions of pollutants, such that the external costs of pollution are internalized into the production process. The idea is to make firms pay for environmental services. In other words, firms would be forced to pay for the waste-removal services of the air above or the river next door in the same way they pay for other types of services. In that case, you can rest assured firms would find ways to economize on smoke emissions and discharges into waterways.

A *second-best*, less-desirable alternative would be to tax the output of the firm. This approach would not give firms any incentive to reduce the amount of pollution per unit of output, but it would at least drive up the price of that output. Higher prices would mean fewer sales and thus less pollution. Could we apply either of these tax ideas to transborder pollution?

The answer is the United States probably could not effectively impose pollution taxes on Mexican polluters. The United States could not tax pollution emissions effectively, because it lacks the authority to monitor pollution in Mexico and lacks the authority to impose taxes even if it could monitor that pollution. In principle, the United States could levy a pollution tax on output crossing the border. However, that tax could not effectively differentiate where in Mexico that output was produced. Furthermore, that tax would be politically unpalatable and violate international treaties. Other policy instruments, such as pollution permits or mandated pollution control technologies, would also be infeasible for the same reasons taxes would not work. Where does that leave us?

The best solution may be voluntary cooperation between the United States and Mexico based on mutual self-interest. While both the United States and Mexico gain from trade between the two countries, the gains to Mexico are proportionally larger because it is the smaller country. This cooperative spirit is attested to by the 1994 implementation of the North American Free Trade Agreement (NAFTA), which incorporated Mexico into a revised and expanded free-trade agreement between the United States and Canada.

NAFTA broke new ground in international trade by writing environmental safeguards directly into the treaty and side accords. For example, NAFTA signatories are obligated to maintain effective enforcement of their own environmental laws, even when the affected pollutants spill over the border. While NAFTA does not itself solve the problems of border pollution, it does provide a framework for cooperation.

What kind of cooperation can the United States legitimately expect from Mexico? Should Mexico maintain environmental standards equal to those in the United States? If so, beware of environmental imperialism. The United States cannot expect the world to follow its standards, at least not without granting the rest of the world's citizens voting rights in U.S. elections. Moreover, uniform environmental standards would not make sense across all countries. After all, maintaining those standards is expensive, and incomes in some countries are much lower than incomes in the United States.

Mexico's per-capita income is less than $6,000 per year. Specifically, in 2001, per-capita income in Mexico was only $5,540, compared to $34,870 per-capita income in the United States. Relative to the average U.S. citizen, the average citizen in Mexico thus consumes less in the way of high-quality food, clothing, shelter, medical care, and so forth. For Mexico to upgrade its control of pollution to match that in the United States would require further reductions in outputs of those goods.

One of the best ways for the United States to see greater control of pollution in Mexico is to see greater per-capita income in Mexico. The reason is that environmental quality is a normal good, meaning that people want more as their incomes rise. The growth in income has been occurring in recent years and will be spurred along as NAFTA continues to be phased in. We are already seeing an increased interest in environmental improvement in Mexico. Over time, we can expect this interest to translate into concrete policy action.

In the meantime, there remain pollution problems along the U.S.-Mexican border. For example, sources of air pollution in the El Paso–Juárez air shed include the burning of tires to fuel brick kilns, dusty unpaved streets, and open-air spray painting of automobiles. The citizens of El Paso want action to clean this up sooner rather than later. So too do citizens of Juárez. Is effective action possible?

Along the border, local governments have an incentive to cooperate in order to address the common pollution problem jointly. That is exactly what El Paso and Juárez have done. Specifically, those governments have formed a single international air quality management district for their region. This district is empowered with the authority to set air quality goals and employ market mechanisms to meet those goals.

Unfortunately, much pollution is left over from the past, especially when it comes to toxins on the land and in the water. Therefore, controlling the flow of new pollutants is not enough; there is the stock of old pollutants to clean up. Who will pay for that cleanup? Part of the answer may be found in the *North American Development Bank,* financed by the governments of Mexico and the United States to fund border cleanup projects. In other words the hands of government and the pockets of taxpayers are likely to be major parts of any final resolution to the transborder pollution problems of the American Southwest.

THINKING CRITICALLY

1. The production of many of the goods the United States imports from Mexico causes pollution within Mexico. Is this extra pollution fair to the Mexican people?

2. When firms in Mexico cause pollution that crosses the border, U.S. residents along the border are damaged. That pollution is an external cost, since the U.S. residents have no way to extract payment for damages from the Mexican polluters. What policies should the United States pursue to reduce this pollution?

Visit **www.prenhall.com/collinge** for updates and web exercises on this Explore & Apply topic.

SUMMARY AND LEARNING OBJECTIVES

1. **Identify examples of externalities and common property resources.**
   - When market failure occurs, the level of market production is inefficient. Examples of market failure include externalities and common property resources. Externalities involve third parties who are not directly involved in either the production or consumption of a good or service.
   - Externalities can be either positive, conferring benefits upon third parties, or negative, which impose costs upon third parties. Pollution is an example of a significant negative externality. Many externalities do not warrant government action, such as most of those that involve personal attire.
   - Common property resources are defined by shared ownership. Lakes, rivers, and streams are usually common property resources.

2. **Analyze the effects of externalities on efficiency.**
   - Production creates both social costs and social benefits. If there are no externalities, then social costs are equal to private costs. Likewise, social benefits are equal to private benefits in the absence of externalities. However, when there are externalities arising from production or consumption, then social costs will also include the external costs and social benefits will include the external benefits. The following equations characterize social costs and benefits when externalities are present: Social cost = Private cost + External cost; and Social benefit = Private benefit + External benefit.
   - To analyze market efficiency, you must consider marginal social cost, which is represented by the following equation: Marginal social cost = Marginal private cost + Marginal external cost; and Marginal social benefit = Marginal private benefit + Marginal external benefit. These equations are analogous to the equations for social cost and social benefit, except for the addition of the word *marginal* in each term.

   - Demand represents marginal private benefit. When there are external benefits, marginal social benefits exceed demand because marginal social benefits include both private and external components. Graphically, the marginal social benefit curve lies above the demand curve.
   - Market output occurs at the quantity below the intersection of demand and supply. This quantity of output is less than the efficient quantity when external benefits are present. Thus, the market underproduces goods that confer external benefits.
   - The supply curve of a good is equivalent to the marginal private cost of producing the good. The marginal social cost curve will lie above the supply curve whenever there are external costs present.
   - When external costs are present, the efficient quantity of a good is less than the market quantity of the good.
   - The Coase theorem states than an efficient outcome can be negotiated between the parties involved when externalities exist. Private negotiations between the perpetrators of an externality and those harmed by it occur in lieu of government regulation. Based on the Coase theorem, the role of government is limited to the enforcement of property rights. Two features of reality limit the applicability of the Coase theorem. These features are transaction costs and strategic behavior. Transaction costs make negotiations impractical, while strategic behavior involves the repetition of actions for financial gain.

3. **Explain why common property resources are likely to be overused.**
   - Because common property resources are jointly owned, the incentive to conserve them is lacking. People will try to get their share of the resource before others, thus depleting the resource. Overfishing is an example of the misuse of a common property resource.

- Users of a common property resource ignore that their use of the resource decreases the amount that others can use in the future.

4. **Discuss the policy instruments that government can use to promote a better environment.**
   - Government can choose among various regulatory policy approaches, each of which has different characteristics and implications. Among these policy options are moral suasion, technology mandates, pollution taxes, and marketable permits.
   - Moral suasion attempts to persuade people to voluntarily change their behavior.
   - Technology mandates require the installation of a specified technology.
   - Pollution taxes are a form of environmental user fees. A pollution tax is said to internalize an externality, meaning that the perpetrator of the externality pays for the external cost in the form of the tax. The tax shifts the supply curve upward by the amount of the tax, and thus reduces the amount of the taxed activity.
   - Marketable permits allow firms to pollute, but only up to the permitted amount. Firms have the incentive to reduce their pollution below the allowed amount because they can sell unneeded permits to other polluters.

5. **Identify the efficient amount of pollution and the policies to achieve it.**
   - When pollution can be monitored, taxes or marketable permits can be by far the most efficient policies to control pollution or allocate common property. Since most pollution comes from production and not consumption, taxes or permits can be applied directly to pollution rather than the outputs that are associated with that pollution.
   - Producers demand the use of the environment for waste disposal, but no one but the government has the authority to sell most environmental services. Since the market supply curve is missing, the government must estimate the marginal external cost, which is the missing market supply, and determine the efficient quantity of pollution.

6. **Discuss the issue of transborder pollution and the difficulties in finding solutions.**
   - Transborder pollution crosses national borders. Countries must and do work together to solve such problems. The NAFTA agreement specifically addresses the problem of transborder pollution, offering a framework for cooperation between the United States and Mexico for reducing pollution.

KEY TERMS

externalities, 222
common property resource, 222
external costs or benefits, 222
private costs or benefits, 222
social costs or benefits, 222

marginal external costs or benefits, 222
Coase theorem, 226
transaction costs, 226
user fees, 228

moral suasion, 229
technology mandates, 229
subsidies, 231
marketable permits, 232

TEST YOURSELF

TRUE OR FALSE
1. External costs are associated with positive externalities.
2. Social benefits are the sum of private benefits and external costs.
3. Environmental quality is a public good that is reduced by pollution.
4. The Coase theorem states that carefully crafted government mandates are necessary in order to deal with problems of externalities.
5. Technology mandates are the most cost-effective way to control pollution when pollution is easy to monitor.

MULTIPLE CHOICE
6. The costs associated with a person's actions that the person actually bears are called
   a. social costs.
   b. external costs.
   c. private costs.
   d. private costs + external costs.
7. Spillover costs to third parties are also called
   a. private costs.
   b. marginal costs.
   c. external costs.
   d. internal costs.

8. People who serve as role models to inspire others
   a. impose social costs.
   b. confer private benefits only.
   c. confer external benefits.
   d. are not the cause of any externalities.

9. In Self-Test Figure 10-1, the marginal social cost curve slopes up more steeply than supply because
   a. the demand for environmental quality slopes down.
   b. marginal private cost slopes down.
   c. there are external benefits from larger outputs.
   d. a system of marketable permits is in place.

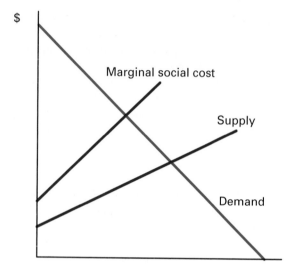

$

Marginal social cost

Supply

Demand

Quantity

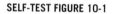

SELF-TEST FIGURE 10-1

10. In Self-Test Figure 10-1, supply represents
    a. marginal private benefit.
    b. marginal social benefit.
    c. marginal external benefit.
    d. marginal private cost.

11. Does the free market ever produce too much?
    a. No.
    b. Yes, when there are external benefits present.
    c. Yes, when there are external costs present.
    d. Yes, when social costs equal private costs.

12. Which of the following is the best example of a common property resource?
    a. A gum ball machine in a barbershop.
    b. The fish in the sea.
    c. A towel for sale at Neiman Marcus.
    d. The movies you rented last week at Blockbuster.

13. The basic reason that overfishing occurs is that
    a. there are no laws against it.
    b. there are laws against it, but they need to be strengthened.

    c. no one person owns the fish before they are caught.
    d. the "fin rights" movement is too disorganized to protect the rights of fish.

14. Common property resource users ignore
    a. taxes, and so use more of the resource than they otherwise would.
    b. taxes, and so use less of the resource than they otherwise would.
    c. the value of conserving the resource for the future.
    d. all of the social costs.

15. Moral suasion is
    a. another name for a pollution tax.
    b. the cost of purchasing a marketable permit.
    c. the process of implementing technology mandates.
    d. an effort to change harmful behavior through appeals to conscience.

16. A pollution tax shifts the
    a. supply curve upward.
    b. supply curve downward.
    c. demand curve to the right.
    d. demand curve to the left.

17. A pollution tax that leads to the efficient quantity must be set equal to
    a. double the market price of the output.
    b. the marginal external cost at the efficient quantity of output.
    c. one-half of the market price of the output.
    d. the cost of a government mandate that would lead to the efficient quantity.

18. Making permits marketable among firms
    a. would increase the total amount of pollution.
    b. would decrease the total amount of pollution.
    c. would have no effect on the total amount of pollution.
    d. can only be applied to a few special types of pollution and so is not worthy of discussion when real-world problems are considered.

19. The efficient quantity of pollution caused by the production of output
    a. must be zero.
    b. is determined by the intersection of market supply and demand.
    c. occurs where the demand for the right to pollute equals the marginal external cost.
    d. is the quantity for which firms would be willing to pay government the most money.

20. The North American Free Trade Agreement (NAFTA)
    a. ignores problems of transborder pollution.
    b. outlaws transborder pollution.
    c. neither ignores nor outlaws transborder pollution, but calls for cooperation to control such pollution.
    d. creates a special police force to find and fine polluters.

QUESTIONS AND PROBLEMS

1. *[externalities]* Explain why externalities can be either positive or negative. Which type of externality is associated with a cost? Which is associated with a benefit?

2. *[external benefits]* Discuss any actions that you, a friend, or someone in your family might have taken in the last month that conferred external benefits on a third party. Also discuss any situations within the last month where you or a family member or friend received an external benefit.

3. *[external benefits]* When there are external benefits to an action, does the market produce too much or too little? What policies should the government follow in this case?

4. *[external costs]* Have your neighbors ever imposed an external cost on you or your family? Describe the nature of the external cost. How was the situation resolved?

5. *[external costs]* When there are external costs to an action, does the market produce too much or too little? Should government policy encourage more production or less? Explain.

6. *[pollution and efficient quantity]* "The only acceptable level of pollution is zero pollution." Evaluate this statement using economic principles.

7. *[efficiency and external costs]* Using a graph, illustrate the market equilibrium quantity of a good. Assume that production causes an external cost. Modify your graph to show the marginal social cost and the efficient quantity.

8. *[efficient quantity]* State the equation that must be satisfied for the quantity to be efficient when there are external costs present.

9. *[external costs; Coase theorem]* Stinkigunco, Inc., has a factory located upstream from a small community that uses the river water for drinking. The plant's emissions of pollutants into the water forces the downstream community to treat the water in order for it to be drinkable. Describe the Coasian solution to this problem of externality and comment on its practicality.

10. *[Coase theorem]* Nineteenth-century farmers sometimes had their crops destroyed when steam locomotives traveling the tracks threw off sparks that set fire to their fields. Write a brief essay discussing the merits of the Coasian solution versus government regulation in this instance. Does the Coasian solution make allowances for any government role? (Note: At the time, there was no government regulation that dealt with this problem.)

11. *[policy tools]* Explain why, when pollution or common property resource use can be monitored and measured, taxes or marketable permits are preferable to technology mandates and moral suasion.

12. *[moral suasion]* Suppose your hometown holds a contest offering an award for the best essay on how to cut down on the amount of trash thrown out at City Park. Write a brief essay arguing that moral suasion is the best policy. In your essay, include a slogan designed to achieve the desired purpose.

13. *[pollution taxes]* Every time you drive your car it emits some amount of air pollution. Does this mean that a pollution tax should be placed on the sale of new vehicles? Explain.

14. *[pollution taxes]* Illustrate graphically how a pollution tax can lead to an efficient quantity.

15. *[marketable permits]* Using a specific example, explain how to create an efficient marketable permit system to control a measurable pollutant. What problem would arise if the government were to distribute permits free of charge each year based upon how much pollution each firm was responsible for the previous year?

16. *[the market to pollute]* In Figure 10-6, notice that a tax on pollution is one way to reduce the amount of pollution to the efficient quantity. Use the graph in this figure to explain how a system of marketable permits could achieve the same result. Be sure to state what quantity of permits would have to be issued and what price they would command in the permits market.

 Visit **www.prenhall.com/collinge** for Exploring the Web exercises and additional self-test quizzes.

CHAPTER 11

PUBLIC CHOICE

A LOOK AHEAD

Big government—we say we don't want it, but we choose to have it. From Franklin D. Roosevelt to John F. Kennedy to Ronald Reagan to Bill Clinton, U.S. presidents have claimed to seek a smaller government. Yet they have not succeeded. Could it be that we really don't want them to? Or does government of the people, by the people, and for the people not reflect the wishes of the people? These questions are addressed in this chapter's Explore & Apply section.

Markets fail when the invisible hand does not guide them well, such as in response to externalities or public goods. In contrast, government has no invisible hand to guide it at all. The result is that the processes of government are often inefficient, with a general tilt toward overspending, as we will see. This chapter examines incentives facing voters on election day, incentives facing our elected representatives in Congress, and incentives facing public servants in government's many administrative agencies.

LEARNING OBJECTIVES

Understanding Chapter 11 will enable you to:
1. **Explain why democracy is imperfect, but still likely to be the best political system.**
2. **Point out why it is reasonable to accept some inefficiencies within government.**
3. **Identify the median voter and explain why that voter holds the key to political outcomes.**
4. **Discuss why legislators engage in vote trading that leads to excessive government spending.**
5. **Describe rent seeking and how it can lead to inefficiency in the political process.**
6. **Explain how both self-interest and the public interest motivate excessive spending within administrative agencies.**
7. **Resolve the apparent contradiction between the public's desire for a smaller government and the data showing increasing government spending over time.**

EXPLORE
&
APPLY

government failure the inefficiency of government processes.

public choice the study of economic incentives within government, including those that face voters, politicians, and the administrators of government programs.

The prior two chapters have examined market failure, which can lead to government action to correct inefficiencies. In addition to market failure, however, there is also **government failure,** which involves inefficiencies within government itself. These inefficiencies are not unexpected, since there would be no reason to have markets at all if government could do everything itself. The field of **public choice** looks at economic incentives within government, including those that face voters, politicians, and the administrators of government programs.

11.1 CHOOSING A POLITICAL SYSTEM

There is no realistic way to get rid of government failure, at least not entirely. But it can help to imagine what such a government might be like, which is where we start.

THE IDEA OF A BENEVOLENT DICTATOR

Economists define a *benevolent dictatorship* as a form of government in which well-meaning and well-informed officials make all of the best choices. Obviously, there is no such thing in practice anywhere in the world. Nor will there ever be, since people make up government, and people have their own views and incentives. A benevolent dictatorship is an abstract form of government that implements the people's wishes without costly political processes and without worrying about providing public servants with incentives.

Dictatorships do not look so benevolent when found in the real world. Although a dictatorship might at first seem like an efficient form of government because it avoids wasting money on political campaigns and political rivalries, there are other inefficiencies that are far more significant. Dictatorships have little incentive to follow the wishes of the public or to avoid waste in government actions. For example, few would argue that the former Taliban religious dictatorship in Afghanistan acted in the best interests of its country. Rather than economic improvement, there was repression, violence, and severe poverty. More generally, prosperous countries of the world are not characterized by dictatorships.

The moral here is that a dictatorship cannot be expected to act in a benevolent manner. This provides justification for a more complicated form of government, one that provides incentives for the government to respond to the wishes of the people.

DEMOCRACY—A MESSY PROCESS TOWARD EFFICIENCY

Democracy is the worst form of government . . . except for all the others.

—*Winston Churchill*

Democracy is an answer to the inefficiencies of dictatorship. It provides for a representative government that responds to the wishes of the public. The processes of democracy are costly and messy, however, leading to tremendous expenditures of time and money for political campaigns, as well as to seemingly endless political bickering. Despite these costs, democracies lead the world in standards of living. But all democracies are not created equal in terms of how well they function. One of the challenges in economics is to understand and offer guidance on how to improve incentives within the democratic process.

Economic incentives appear in every aspect of government. Voters face economic incentives in determining whether and how to vote. Legislators face economic incentives in determining which policies to enact and which taxes to levy. Public servants also face economic incentives in determining the level and type of service to provide.

cycling when the order of political choices determines the outcome.

The political process does not provide definitively efficient answers. For example, there is the problem of **cycling,** in which the order of political choices determines the outcome.

TABLE 11-1 PREFERENCES OF SUBCOMMITTEE MEMBERS

OPTION	RANKING BY AGNES	RANKING BY BIFF	RANKING BY CHRISTINA
Increased defense spending	1	3	2
Tax rebates to the poor	2	1	3
Across-the-board tax cut	3	2	1

Let's take the example of a congressional subcommittee with three members voting on which of three alternative ways of stimulating the economy they will recommend to Congress. The alternatives are to increase spending on national security, to send tax rebate checks to the poor, or to cut tax rates across the board.

Table 11-1 uses this example to show how cycling can occur. The first representative, Agnes, prefers increasing spending to cutting taxes, but prefers a tax rebate to the poor over an across-the-board tax cut. The second representative, Biff, prefers cutting taxes to new spending, but would prefer that the tax cut be directed to the poor rather than across the board. The third representative, Christina, prefers an across-the-board tax cut and strongly opposes sending out rebate checks. Christina views increased defense spending as preferable to sending out rebate checks, but not as desirable as an across-the-board tax cut. Table 11-1 summarizes the preferences of Agnes, Biff, and Christina.

Table 11-2 shows that the recommendation of the subcommittee will depend on the order in which members consider the alternatives. For example, the subcommittee might first vote on whether to increase defense spending or offer tax rebates to the poor. Two of the subcommittee members would vote for increased defense. However, comparing increased defense with an across-the-board tax cut, two of the three members would vote for an across-the-board tax cut. The subcommittee would therefore recommend an across-the-board tax cut. However, if they were to compare an across-the-board tax cut against tax rebates to the poor, the subcommittee would prefer tax rebates to the poor. This process

TABLE 11-2 THE SUBCOMMITTEE'S RECOMMENDATION
The recommendation will depend on the order in which the subcommittee considers the choices.

CHOICES	AGNES'S VOTE	BIFF'S VOTE	CHRISTINA'S VOTE	THE SUBCOMMITTEE'S CHOICE BETWEEN THE TWO ALTERNATIVES
Tax rebates to the poor or Increased defense spending	for defense	for rebates	for defense	increased defense spending
Increased defense spending or Across-the-board tax cut	for defense	for tax cut	for tax cut	across-the-board tax cut
Across-the-board tax cut or Tax rebates to the poor	for rebates	for rebates	for tax cut	tax rebates to the poor

could go on infinitely, which is why it is called cycling. Whoever sets the *agenda* of which alternatives will be considered first also winds up in effect choosing the alternatives that they will recommend to Congress.

The possibility for cycling illustrates how important it can be to set the agenda. Cycling also illustrates a certain irrationality within the collective choice process. It serves to emphasize that, while democracy is likely to be the best public choice process available, it can sometimes lead to inefficient or even random outcomes.

FEDERALISM—EXPERIMENTING WITH MULTIPLE WAYS

Democracy in the United States is characterized by *federalism*, meaning that there are multiple layers of government. This arrangement has an economic basis: It allows those citizens to vote who are most directly affected by the consequences of the choice. For example, residents of a school district pick members of the board controlling schools within that district. Urban residents vote on the size of their city's police budget, since they are the ones who will be protected by the resulting police force. **Fiscal federalism** examines the design of a federal system of government from an economic standpoint. It suggests that decisions should be made by the level of government most directly affected by those decisions.

fiscal federalism the study of the design of a federal system of government from an economic standpoint.

Many issues are national in scope and thus appropriate to consider at the federal level, meaning at the level of government that presides over all of the other governments. Certainly national defense is one such issue. Another is income redistribution. If income redistribution is left to state-owned localities, little of it can occur. The reason is that only the federal government can effectively take from the rich and give to the poor. If such income redistribution is tried by states and cities on their own, the rich wind up moving out and the poor wind up moving in. The result, as New York City discovered in the 1970s, is that there are too few rich people to tax to pay for aid to the burgeoning population of poor people. In New York City's case, many of the rich moved to Connecticut or New Jersey, both well within commuting distance.

Even when the federal government does not directly control policies at the state and local levels, it often influences these policies through financial incentives. For example, the federal government will withhold transportation aid that goes to highway construction and repair if states do not enforce speed limits and other safety measures that comply with federal guidelines.

Having multiple layers of government has the added benefit of allowing policies to be tried out on a small scale before they are enacted on a large scale. Four of the last five American presidents—George W. Bush, Bill Clinton, Ronald Reagan, and Jimmy Carter—often referred back to their experiences at the state level for guidance on what would work at the national level. Apparently voters recognize the value of this experience, or they would not have voted these former governors into the office of the presidency.

There is sometimes a conflict between the federal governments and states over which government should be the final authority. For example, Oregon legalized medically assisted suicide for terminally ill elderly patients who are capable of making such a choice. The federal government recognizes no such right and promised to prosecute doctors who assist in such suicides. In a similar vein, some localities have legalized the medical use of marijuana. However, under federal law, no medical use of marijuana is allowed. As these examples suggest, the issue of allowing states leeway to try different ways of doing things is fraught with contention.

CHOOSING A PRESIDENT, FLORIDA STYLE   *SNAPSHOT*

It was deep into the night of the presidential election of 2000. The world watched with humor and amazement as bleary-eyed poll workers stared intently at machine-readable ballots, trying to determine voter intent. The world got to learn the meaning of *chad*, those little pieces intended to be punched out of computer-readable cards. The problem was that sometimes the chad was not fully punched—resulting in a dimpled chad. Alas that we would need to learn about such things!

The true lesson is one of federalism, in which different states and even different localities conduct elections in different manners. In hindsight, some states and localities obviously used better methods than others. It was a learning process. But why even have the election determined on a state-by-state basis? Wouldn't it be enough to tally the popular votes across the country and just see who wins the majority?

The answers again revolve around federalism. Tallying votes according to each state and then having the states elect the president through an electoral college makes sure that candidates do not ignore portions of the country altogether. It certainly does influence where time and money will be spent on the campaign trail. ◄

11.2 CHOICES BY THE VOTERS

Because we delegate decisions collectively, none of us gets exactly what we want. Moreover, each candidate for public office represents a **bundled good,** meaning that the voter cannot pick and choose which items on a candidate's agenda to support and which to oppose—one vote buys all. The result is a compromise that is not fully satisfying to anyone. In the case of public goods, such as national defense, the quantity that is chosen by public officials must then be consumed by everyone, no matter their personal preferences. However, the culprit is not the public officials, but the nature of the public good itself—public goods are consumed jointly. Where possible, people prefer to make choices for themselves.

A second source of concern over government action has to do with the **principal–agent problem.** Over 19 million workers in this country are employed by government as public servants. Public servants range from teachers to Marines to, until recently, an official tea taster. No matter the job, they are all *agents* of the public (the *principal*). However, because the public is so large, no individual has direct control. For example, we do not advise informing the traffic officer preparing to give you a ticket that he or she is your servant and should follow your orders. This generalized accountability provides a great deal of leeway on the part of the agents to do as they please.

bundled good in the context of voting, occurs when voters must take the whole package, including elements they don't want; candidates represent bundled goods.

principal–agent problem the difficulty of making agents, such as public servants, act in the interests of principals, such as voters.

QUICKCHECK

When the size of government grows, public dissatisfaction with government can also be expected to grow. Why?

Answer: When choices are made collectively, almost no one gets exactly what he or she wants. Therefore, one explanation for dissatisfaction with bigger government is that growth in the size of the government budget comes at the expense of individuals' abilities to make their own decisions. In addition, the larger the size of the government budget, the larger the size and visibility of inefficiencies within the public sector, such as those caused by the principal–agent problem.

THE MEDIAN VOTER MODEL

A funny thing happens on the road to public office. In U.S. presidential campaigns, for example, Democratic and Republican candidates for president often sound much farther apart on the issues in the primaries than they do when it comes time for the general election. For an explanation of this and other aspects of election outcomes, we can turn to the median voter model.

median voter model predicts that in two-candidate races, the winner will be chosen by the median voter—50 percent of the other voters prefer further to the right and 50 percent prefer further to the left.

The **median voter model** says that candidates will seek the support of the decisive swing voter that can tilt the balance from one candidate to the other. This median voter will be quite different in the general election than the median voter in either the Democratic or Republican primaries. The median voter model thus predicts that successful politicians will seek to always follow that median to wherever it moves.

The median voter model is applicable when voters—those who actually vote—can be lined up along a spectrum from left to right. Maybe the spectrum is political, ranging from the left wing to the right wing. Perhaps the spectrum is budgetary, ranging from a lower budget to a higher budget. In any case, the *median voter* is the one for whom 50 percent of the other voters prefer further to the right on the spectrum and 50 percent prefer further to the left. In an election in which all voters pick between two candidates, the candidate chosen by the median voter will win by garnering a minimum of just over 50 percent of the vote. Note that voters are considered to be those people who do indeed vote.

Figure 11-1 illustrates the importance of the median voter in two-candidate elections. In this figure, nine voters and four candidates are lined up along the political or budgetary spectrum. Each voter is numbered. Candidates are labeled by the names Ann, Buck, Carlos, and Darlene. Which candidate would defeat any opponent in a two-person race? The median voter holds the answer.

Voter 5 is the median voter and would vote for Buck against any opponent. If the opponent was to the left of Buck, Buck would also be preferred by voters 6 through 9 and thereby win with a majority of the vote. Likewise, if the opponent was to the right of Buck, voters 1 through 4 would side with the median voter to grant Buck the majority.

Suppose we divide voters into Democrats and Republicans and then hold primary elections to determine each party's candidate. For simplicity, we'll assign voters 1 through 5 and candidates Ann and Buck to the Democrats. Voters 6 through 9 and candidates Carlos and Darlene go to the Republicans. In the Democratic primary, voter 3 now becomes the median

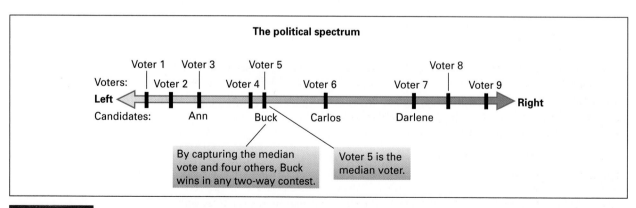

FIGURE 11-1

THE MEDIAN VOTER MODEL The median voter model helps explain the outcome of the political process. Voter 5 is the median voter, because there are an equal number of voters on either side. This voter's preference for candidate Buck would cause Buck to win if running against any single one of the other candidates.

voter and would vote for Ann. In the Republican primary, voters 7 and 8 tie for median voter honors. Their votes would go to Darlene. That means the general election would come down to a race between Ann and Darlene.

Voter 5 has not been forgotten. Between the primaries and the general election, the candidates turn their attentions toward the overall median voter, voter 5. They start sounding more and more alike. The candidate best able to shift to the positions of voter 5 is thus most likely to win the election.

RATIONAL IGNORANCE

Democracy is first and foremost of the people. Yet in most elections below the level of presidential elections, considerably less than half of registered voters bother to vote. Even when registered voters do vote, they often have little idea of what they are voting on. There are many choices on the typical ballot, so many in fact that voters do not have time enough to research all of the candidates and propositions seen on the ballot. Even people who want to be involved find themselves with insufficient time to prepare as well as they would like for the voting process. The result is **rational ignorance** on the part of the voters, meaning that they make a rational choice to remain uninformed on many public issues.

rational ignorance when voters make the rational choice to remain uninformed on many public issues.

Most voting choices are for people rather than specific policy actions. A voter will vote for a candidate based on that candidate's reputation and positions on certain issues. The voter relies on the candidate to address other issues in a similar way. Therefore, voters delegate authority to politicians, who in turn delegate to the administrative bureaucracy. The amount of detail involved in governing the country is too overwhelming to do otherwise. If voters were asked to vote on every issue directly, the amount of rational ignorance would be much greater than it is under the system of voting for candidates.

Political parties are, in part, a response to the rational ignorance of voters. Instead of having to figure it all out for themselves, voters can select political parties according to their philosophical preferences. In this way, voters rely on the political parties to do much of the detailed research into the issues and into the candidates that are running for office. "Voting the party line" can be a reasonable way to address the problem of rational ignorance. If voters pay too little attention, though, political parties and the politicians they produce might too closely align themselves with special interests that do pay attention.

11.3 CANDIDATES AND COALITIONS

To achieve the results constituents expect, the holder of a political office will often find it necessary to compromise and bargain with other elected representatives. In addition, voters' rational ignorance means that politicians and bureaucrats can often safely follow their own personal agendas, even when those agendas conflict with what the public would want them to do. In politics, appearance matters, too.

STAYING IN OFFICE

Most elected officials want to remain in office. Incumbent politicians routinely get reelected, even though *term limitations*—laws that restrict the number of sequential times a politician can hold one public office—are quite popular. Achieving reelection can be accomplished through **logrolling**—vote trading—in order to obtain projects of direct benefit to constituents. Logrolling unfortunately results in massive spending packages that contain numerous local spending projects of questionable merit. These projects (often called *pork*) and

logrolling when politicians trade votes in order to obtain projects of direct benefit to constituents in their districts.

other accomplishments are then reported back to constituents through a newsletter. Left out is any focus on cost, however, even though the pork does not come cheaply.

Remember, to obtain projects for their districts, legislators must vote for all of the other costly items in the legislation, including those of no benefit to their constituents. When voters focus on visible benefits from projects and ignore the less-obvious costs, they are said to suffer from **fiscal illusion,** which tends to bring about excessive spending.

fiscal illusion when voters focus on visible benefits from projects and ignore the less-obvious costs.

Even if the costs of logrolling are considered, they are still likely to be of little concern to the electorate. After all, the costs are in terms of other districts' wasteful projects that are included in an appropriations bill. However, if a majority of other legislators are signing onto the bill, you don't want your district left out. In other words, if you are going to be paying for other districts' pork, you want pork of your own. Thus, constituents rarely hold pork-barrel politics against their own legislators, even though they may disapprove of the practice in general.

There is good reason to disapprove. *Pork-barrel politics* leads to excessive government spending, as the cost of the myriad of relatively small projects gets lost in the general budget. For example, the constituents in most districts would be delighted to accept federally funded projects, such as for highways or drainage. It does not matter whether the project's benefits exceed its costs, because the costs are spread across the country, while the benefits are concentrated in that district. They are grateful to their elected representatives. For voters in other districts, the project is too small to focus on and has no bearing on the reelection of their own representatives. The result is too much government spending.

line-item veto power that allows a governor to veto parts of appropriations bills, rather than having to accept or reject the bills in their entireties.

One check on logrolling is the line-item veto powers of many state governors. The **line-item veto** allows a governor to veto parts of appropriations bills, rather than having to accept or reject the bills in their entireties. If the governor were to be a Democrat, for instance, he or she could veto all of the Republicans' pet projects, except projects of Republicans who support the governor's agenda. In turn, because Republicans would know their projects would not survive, they would not go along with voting for the Democrats' pet projects. The result would be much less pork. The governors of forty-three states have some form of line-item veto authority. Although Congress voted in 1996 to grant the president line-item veto power, the Supreme Court subsequently ruled this application of line-item veto authority to be unconstitutional. The Justices reasoned that it violated the separation of powers between the president and Congress.

Not all vote trading is inefficient. For example, a worthy project might serve only a portion of the country. Consider levees along a river that benefit the residents of only a few states. Without vote trading, the project would not be passed by Congress, since a majority of states would perceive no benefits. Such projects could still be undertaken, however, if the affected states join forces and proceed on their own. Payment for the project would then come from the residents of those states instead of from general tax revenues.

QUICKCHECK

Would line-item veto authority for the president stop logrolling in the federal government?

Answer: Logrolling would probably be reduced but not eliminated. For example, friends of the president would not have their pet projects vetoed. However, the president's friends would have a more difficult time lining up support for those projects in Congress, especially if the president routinely vetoes the pet projects of other legislators.

11.5 ADDRESSING GOVERNMENT FAILURES

Is there anything citizens can do to counter all the incentives within government to spend too much? The options are limited. For example, limiting the number of years legislators can serve might keep representatives more in touch with the voters. However, such term limits deprive the government of experienced legislators, and also run the danger of focusing legislators' attentions on personal profit opportunities once they leave office.

There is no easy way to provide the proper incentives for efficiency within government. That should come as little surprise. After all, if the government were efficient, there would be little reason to adopt competitive free markets. We turn to government when markets fail. We must merely keep in mind that market failure does not imply government success.

11.6 GROWING THE GOVERNMENT

That government is best which governs least.

—Thomas Jefferson

The size of government and its proper role have been debated in the United States from the days of its founding. President Ronald Reagan, for example, was well known for trying to slow the growth of government. In 1996, even President Clinton proclaimed, "The era of big government is over." On the flip side, Treasury Secretary Alexander Hamilton, pictured on the $10 bill, favored change that would strengthen the power of the federal government. He offered strong arguments favoring the creation of a Bank of the United States, an early version of what we now refer to as a government central bank. More recently, in leading the fight against terrorism, President George W. Bush pushed through significant increases in government spending and powers.

U.S. history shows that the balance of power shifted back and forth between those favoring a bigger government and others who disagreed. Figure 11-3 shows the growth in federal government spending as a percentage of GDP since 1929. This growth is attributable to the growth in transfer payments, as shown in the figure. *Transfer payments,* such as for income redistribution and Social Security, refer to government spending that isn't for goods, services, or investments.

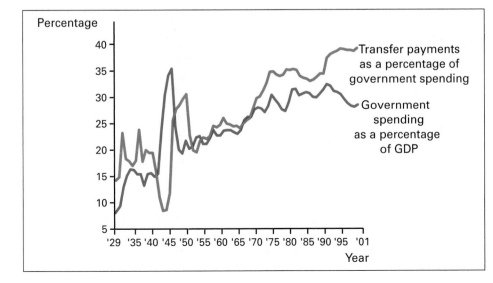

FIGURE 11-3

GROWTH OF AMERICAN GOVERNMENT SINCE 1929
Government spending as a fraction of GDP is today more than three times its value in 1929. Transfer payments as a fraction of government spending rose to historic highs in the 1990s.

Source: Bureau of Economic Analysis, *National Income and Product Account Tables.*

What led the country down the path to bigger government? The U.S. Constitution says that government is obligated to "promote the general welfare." The welfare of the country covers a lot. Earliest efforts by the government to promote a growing economy focused on filling the transportation needs of a young nation. From building roads and canals at first, and then later railroads, government provided the resources needed to build a transportation system that would tie the states together and promote commerce. But government was always limited in what it could do because it had no way to raise the money to fund the cost of a "big government," even if there had been agreement that government ought to be bigger.

Following the expansion of government power and influence that necessarily accompanied the Civil War and the Reconstruction era, the federal government continued to take on more responsibilities. To regulate commerce, the Interstate Commerce Commission was created in 1887. The first antitrust law, the Sherman Act, designed to halt the growth of monopoly power, was enacted in 1890. Then came a major event that allowed an unprecedented expansion in the size of the federal government. The federal income tax was enacted into law in 1913, which led to a dramatic increase in federal revenues. All these new laws, agencies, and obligations of government were controversial because they expanded government power and influence. Yet by 1929, the eve of the Great Depression, government's share of aggregate spending was still only a small fraction of its current share.

President Franklin D. Roosevelt promised the nation a New Deal to overcome the misery of the Great Depression. The Supreme Court soon declared a number of these policies unconstitutional, thus acting as a brake on the expansion of government. Not even the popular FDR could bring the American people along in support of his plan to "pack" the Court with new justices who would support all his proposals.

WHY THE ROLE OF GOVERNMENT GREW

After World War II ended in 1945, an explosion of American prosperity enriched consumers as never before. U.S. prosperity ultimately spread to the war-shattered countries of Western Europe and Japan, as the United States served as the engine of growth and these countries got pulled along for the ride. While the government had not been particularly successful in ending the depression in the 1930s, the government proved in the 1940s that it could successfully wage war. Americans were united in their support of their government's war effort and it was natural that these good feelings toward government would continue following the war.

The expansion of government reached its pinnacle with President Lyndon Johnson's Great Society, which added about 500 social programs between 1965 and 1968. Some programs, such as Medicare, have become familiar standbys. Others, such as Model Cities, have long since been forgotten. These programs aimed to meet nearly all of the social issues of the time, and more. They included programs to solve the problems of hunger, homelessness, discrimination, and excess immigration. Great Society programs provided higher minimum wages, vocational training, agricultural subsidies, truth in labeling, clean highways, and on and on.

The big-government expansion of the 1960s seemed too much for many citizens by the end of the 1970s. In 1980, Americans elected Ronald Reagan as their thirty-sixth president. Reagan promised to "get the government off the backs of the American people." As president, Mr. Reagan spoke of the need for less government regulation, saying, "Millions of individuals making their own decisions in the marketplace will always allocate resources better than any centralized government planning process." The American people adopted

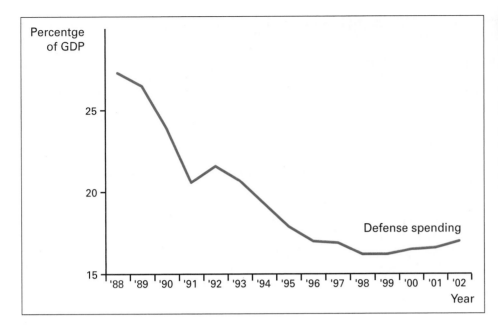

FIGURE 11-4

SPENDING ON NATIONAL DEFENSE
After a defense buildup in the
1980s, the economy reaped a
"peace dividend" in which it
reduced spending on defense.
That trend toward lower defense
spending appears to have now
ended.

Source: Department of Defense,
*National Defense Budget Estimates,
FY 2003,* Table 7-7.

his view that government should be smaller. As Reagan put it, "Government's view of the economy could be summed up in a few short phrases: If it moves, tax it. If it keeps moving, regulate it. And if it stops moving, subsidize it." More pointedly, Reagan stated "There is a threat posed to human freedom by the enormous power of the modern state. History teaches the dangers of government that overreaches—political control taking precedence over free economic growth—secret police, mindless bureaucracy, all combining to stifle individual excellence and personal freedom."

Reagan did oversee a buildup in military spending, but one that was directed at convincing the Soviet Union that it could not afford to maintain its adversarial stance. With the demise of the Soviet Union, the United States in the 1990s was able to reap a so-called peace dividend of lower defense spending needs. As shown in Figure 11-4, military spending was cut dramatically during the administrations of George H. W. Bush and Bill Clinton in the 1990s. In light of terrorist threats and a perception that cuts in the 1990s were too deep, the military spending trend has turned once more to the upside under President George W. Bush, as has spending on farm subsidies and other programs. Time will tell the extent to which George W. Bush oversees another federal government expansion.

1. In the 2000 campaign for the presidency, neither candidate Al Gore nor candidate George W. Bush proposed to significantly change the size of government. Discuss plausible economic events that would have to occur in the future to prompt a president to again declare that "the era of big government is over."

2. Why do the citizens of some countries seem to prefer big government, while the citizens of other countries prefer a smaller government? What factors might prompt the citizens of countries with big governments to change their preferences in the direction of smaller government?

*T*HINKING
*C*RITICALLY

Visit **www.prenhall.com/collinge** for updates and web exercises on this Explore & Apply topic.

SUMMARY AND LEARNING OBJECTIVES

1. **Explain why democracy is imperfect, but still likely to be the best political system.**
   - A benevolent dictatorship is a form of government in which well-meaning and well-informed officials make the best choices. Real-world dictatorships are not of this type, since dictators have little incentive to follow the wishes of the public.
   - Democracy provides for representative government, responding to the wishes of the public, but is still subject to inefficiencies.
   - One problem that can sometimes arise is called cycling, which means that outcomes are determined by the order in which choices are considered. In this case, whoever sets the agenda also determines the outcome. Cycling indicates an irrationality within the collective choice process.
   - Federalism, multiple layers of government, characterizes democracy in the United States. Fiscal federalism looks at the design of a federal system of government from an economic standpoint. From this perspective, decisions should be made by the level of government most directly affected by any decision. Issues that are national in scope are appropriate for consideration by the federal government. National defense is an example.
   - The federal government influences decisions by states and localities through financial incentives, even when it does not make those decisions itself.

2. **Point out why it is reasonable to accept some inefficiencies within government.**
   - Government failure refers to inefficiencies in government itself. The principal–agent problem, rational ignorance, logrolling, and fiscal illusion all contribute to government failure. Pork-barrel politics leads to excessive government spending.
   - Rational ignorance on the part of the public allows politicians to follow their own agendas on many issues. It is rational for the public to remain unaware of much of what their elected servants do because of the public's lack of time to stay fully informed.

3. **Identify the median voter and explain why that voter holds the key to political outcomes.**
   - The median voter model explains why candidates often take similar positions in general elections. The candidate best able to attract the vote of the median voter is most likely to win the election.
   - The median voter is in the middle position regarding issues. Half of the remaining voters will be on one side of the median voter and the other half will be on the other side. Politicians will pitch their appeals to the median voter since that voter will tilt an election result to the candidate receiving the vote cast by the median voter.

4. **Discuss why legislators engage in vote trading that leads to excessive government spending.**
   - Logrolling involves politicians in vote trading. A legislator agrees to support another legislator's bill in exchange for that legislator's support for his or her bill. In this way projects are approved that benefit the voters back home and help the legislator get reelected. Much of the spending that results from logrolling is wasteful and is often referred to as pork. Politicians who bring home the pork often find themselves being repeatedly reelected.
   - Fiscal illusion occurs when voters remember the benefits of government spending but forget about the less-obvious costs. When voters suffer from fiscal illusion, legislators are likely to respond by spending too much relative to taxation.
   - The line-item veto, available to forty-three state governors, allows a governor to veto parts of appropriation bills. The line-item veto is thus a weapon against logrolling and pork-barrel spending. A line-item veto for the president was approved by Congress in 1996, but subsequently ruled unconstitutional by the Supreme Court.

5. **Describe rent seeking and how it can lead to inefficiency in the political process.**
   - Special-interest groups and their lobbyists influence government spending. Lobbyists are commonly able to prevent an action that they oppose when the benefits of the action are spread broadly and the costs are concentrated.
   - Lobbying can be efficient when it provides legislators with information that promotes informed actions. Lobbying often involves wasteful rent seeking, in which the special-interest groups' aims are to increase the size of their slice of the economic pie, even if the pie itself is made smaller.

6. **Explain how both self-interest and the public interest motivate excessive spending within administrative agencies.**
   - Government agencies have the incentive to expand their budget beyond the efficient amount. Graphically, a budget that is efficient is identified by the

point where the marginal net benefit of the agency is zero. A budget that is too big pushes the value of the marginal net benefit of additional budget allocations into negative values.

■ Government agencies employ various strategies to obtain funds. While an agency might be aware of ways to save money, there is no incentive to reveal that information to anyone else. This case is an example of the problem of asymmetric information, in which one party has information that another party lacks, but would find useful.

■ Another method to maintain agency budgets is a response to "use it or lose it" rules. If an agency fails to spend all of its budget in one year, then its budget for the next year will possibly be cut by the amount unspent. Hence, agencies facing the end of the year with unspent monies in their budgets tend to find things to purchase with these funds, regardless of whether this spending is efficient.

■ Another method to keep an agency's budget up is the Washington Monument strategy. When an agency is threatened by budget cuts, it responds by proposing to eliminate or reduce its most popular programs rather than try to cut the fat out of its spending. Often, protests by the public are enough to restore the threatened agency's funding.

7. Resolve the apparent contradiction between the public's desire for a smaller government and the data showing increasing government spending over time.

■ Controversy over the size and role of government has existed throughout U.S. history. Various events, including wars and the Great Depression, led to an increased role for the federal government. Although defense spending declined during the 1990s, that trend has reversed course under President George W. Bush.

KEY TERMS

government failure, 244
public choice, 244
cycling, 244
fiscal federalism, 246
bundled good, 247

principal–agent problem, 247
median voter model, 248
rational ignorance, 249
logrolling, 249
fiscal illusion, 250

line-item veto, 250
lobbyists, 251
rent seeking, 251
block grants, 252
Washington Monument strategy, 254

TEST YOURSELF

TRUE OR FALSE

1. The field of public choice is concerned with economic incentives within government.
2. The median voter model predicts that in general elections politicians will ignore the positions of the median voter.
3. Fiscal illusion refers to the tendency of voters to ignore the benefits of government projects due to their concern over the costs.
4. The president of the United States, like the governors of most states, have line-item veto authority.
5. A government budget that is efficient exhibits a net marginal benefit of zero.

MULTIPLE CHOICE

6. Public choice economics suggests that
   a. markets always fail from the public's viewpoint.
   b. opportunities to correct market failure should be evaluated in light of possibilities for government failure.
   c. the public's choices are equitable, while government choices are efficient.
   d. incentives within government are usually more efficient than those in the marketplace.
7. If members of a congressional committee have preferences that would lead to cycling, then the most powerful person on that committee would be the one
   a. with the most endurance.
   b. with the longest tenure on the committee.
   c. who controls the committee's agenda.
   d. who is the last to vote.

8. Looking at the design of a federal system of government from an economic standpoint is called
   a. fiscal federalism.
   b. rational ignorance.
   c. a benevolent dictatorship.
   d. the median voter model.

9. In Self-Test Figure 11-1, the median voter is
   a. Voter 3.
   b. Voter 4.
   c. Voter 5.
   d. Voter 6.

The political spectrum

SELF-TEST FIGURE 11-1

10. Under the assumptions of the median voter model, the candidate who receives the vote cast by the median voter will
    a. win the election, with a majority of votes.
    b. lose the election.
    c. receive campaign funds from the government.
    d. receive less than half the votes, but win the election anyway.

11. Rational ignorance occurs when _____ do not have time to fully research candidates.
    a. political parties
    b. bureaucrats
    c. the public
    d. lobbyists

12. Term limits are laws that seek to control government spending by
    a. restricting how much time lobbyists are allowed to spend with a legislator.
    b. outlawing vote trading.
    c. giving each government agency a specific amount of time to spend various items in its budget before losing that budgetary allocation.
    d. limiting the number of times an elected official can serve in a particular position.

13. The line-item veto provides a check on
    a. the median voter.
    b. fiscal illusion.
    c. a benevolent dictator.
    d. logrolling.

14. Pork-barrel politics
    a. increases government spending.
    b. decreases government spending.
    c. has no effect on overall government spending, but impacts specific parts of the budget.
    d. leaves overall government spending and each part of the budget unchanged.

15. Rent-seeking behavior involves
    a. real estate transactions.
    b. illegal government corruption.
    c. measuring the benefits from public housing.
    d. seeking favors from the government.

16. Block grants from the federal government to the states
    a. increase the influence of Washington lobbyists.
    b. decrease the influence of Washington lobbyists.
    c. have no effect on the influence of Washington lobbyists.
    d. grant legislators in the House and Senate the right to travel at the expense of lobbyists in blocks of up to fifteen members of Congress.

17. A government agency has spent too much when the marginal net benefit of its spending is
    a. zero.
    b. any positive value.
    c. a positive value between zero and one.
    d. a negative value.

18. The Washington Monument strategy is
    a. used by budget cutters to reduce government spending.
    b. used by tax cutters to make the case for reduced taxation.
    c. employed by government agencies threatened with budget cuts.
    d. used by government architects to obtain funding for memorials and monuments.

19. Unfunded mandates
    a. provide a means to implement public policy without more government spending.
    b. are illegal, having been declared unconstitutional by the Supreme Court.
    c. are favored by the median voter and voters to the right of the median voter, but not by voters to the left of the median voter.
    d. appear as an item on the federal budget.

20. Of the following, the American president most known for expanding government is
    a. Thomas Jefferson.
    b. Lyndon Johnson.
    c. Ronald Reagan.
    d. Bill Clinton.

QUESTIONS AND PROBLEMS

1. *[government failure]* Explain how the typical taxpayer is made worse off by government failure. In your explanation, provide examples of government failure you have observed. Is government failure likely to be a greater problem when government is big or when it is small? Defend your answer by applying logical reasoning as well as opinion in your answer.

2. *[benevolent dictatorship]* Describe the idea of a benevolent dictatorship. In what respect would a benevolent dictatorship be more efficient than democracy? Why are there no benevolent dictatorships in reality?

3. *[fiscal federalism]* Describe the concept of fiscal federalism and how it provides a rationale for the many layers of government found in the United States.

4. *[principal–agent problem]* State briefly how the principal–agent problem contributes to government failure. Include in your answer whether government failure leads to overspending or underspending, and why.

5. *[bundled good]* Since every elected official can be viewed as a bundled good, why not change the government to allow the public to vote on every issue instead of electing a representative to make choices for them?

6. *[bundled good; government failure]* It is increasingly popular among the states to allow the public to place various propositions on the ballot. When more than 50 percent of votes cast are in favor of a proposition, it is approved and becomes law unless it is held up in the courts. For example, proposals relating to tax cuts, gay rights, and other contentious issues have been on the ballot in various states in recent years. Does the increasing popularity of this method relate to elected officials being bundled goods? Does this popularity also suggest that the public is responding to government failure? Explain.

7. *[voting]* We allow people to buy and sell most of what they own, so should we also allow voters to buy and sell their votes? Alternatively, since most potential voters do not vote, should we eliminate voting and replace it with surveys that measure public opinions? Explain.

8. *[median voter model]* Illustrate graphically a voting scenario in which eleven people will vote in an election that has two candidates. One of the candidates favors tax cuts, while the other candidate favors the status quo. Opinion polls show that five voters generally favor tax cuts, although the intensity of their preferences for tax cuts varies among them. Opinion polls also show that five other voters generally favor the status quo,

although the intensity of their preferences also varies. One of the voters is undecided about the wisdom of tax cuts. Answer the following questions after you have drawn your graph.
   a. Where on your graph is the median voter located? Explain.
   b. Is the undecided voter the median voter? Explain.
   c. Why would it be worthwhile for the candidates to aim their campaign advertising and promotions at the undecided voter? Explain.

9. *[rational ignorance]* How does "voting the party line" relate to the problem of rational ignorance? Does it cure the problem? Explain.

10. *[rational ignorance]* How does rational ignorance on the part of voters give elected officials freedoms they would not have if the public became more knowledgeable about government?

11. *[logrolling]* Explain how logrolling can lead to excessive government spending. Would eliminating logrolling cause too little spending?

12. *[pork-barrel politics]* Are you aware of a pork-barrel project in your area? If not, do the research that will allow you to identify such a project. Are local officials and the public proud or ashamed of the elected official who delivered the pork?

13. *[incentives within government]* Illustrate graphically the model that identifies the efficient budget for a government agency. Suppose the actual budget is larger than the efficient budget. Identify such a budget on your graph and shade in the loss of net benefits for the budget you select. Write a brief explanation of why the larger budget is more likely to be allocated to the agency than the efficient budget. In your explanation be sure to state the names of specific strategies that could lead to this outcome.

14. *[incentives within government]* If you are in charge of rebuilding roads, why might your personal self-interest suggest that you not devote your budget to fixing the worst portions of the roads first? If you leave obvious examples of roads in need of repair, what strategy are you following? Is there a danger to this strategy? Explain.

15. *[term limits]* Many governments have term limits to prevent so-called empire building by holders of public office. For example, the president of the United States can serve only two four-year terms. Is this a good idea? Should the idea be extended to other levels of government? What problems are likely to arise?

CHAPTER 12

MEASURING OUTPUT, INFLATION, AND UNEMPLOYMENT

A LOOK AHEAD

If we as a society are to achieve our macroeconomic goals, we'd best have ways of measuring our successes and failures. Government collects and makes available to anyone who is interested a vast amount of statistical information about our economy. This chapter starts with the measurement of the nation's aggregate output, then discusses inflation, unemployment, and the business cycle.

Accurate statistics can help paint a clear picture of the economy—where it's been, where it's at now, and where it's going. Statistics on the aggregate economy also guide decision makers in government as they allocate funds to education, defense, healthcare, and other government programs. It turns out that the data used by Congress are often wrong, and wrong in a way that is obvious to its members. The Explore & Apply section at the end of this chapter discusses how the use of the wrong numbers by Congress can make sense.

LEARNING OBJECTIVES

Understanding Chapter 12 will enable you to:
1. **Present three widely accepted goals for the economy.**
2. **Define gross domestic product (GDP) and discuss its components.**
3. **Interpret and apply a price index.**
4. **Distinguish the four types of unemployment.**
5. **Track the stages of the business cycle.**
6. **Identify the advantages and disadvantages of static and dynamic scoring.**

Explore & Apply

Macroeconomics deals with the economy as a whole. The millions of individual microeconomic decisions of people, businesses, and government in their totality represent the nation's economy. Everyone thus influences the economy at least a little bit, and the performance of the economy likewise affects everyone.

12.1 MACROECONOMIC GOALS

Economic growth, low inflation, and high employment are the three primary goals of macro policy. Economic growth occurs when the economy's total output of goods and services increases. Higher living standards are a by-product of economic growth. In effect, growth enlarges the economic pie, allowing many people bigger slices. Table 12-1 shows a handful of the many ways in which the United States standard of living has improved. Economic growth in the United States has promoted changes in our living standards that range from greater computer ownership to greater life expectancy. Because the wealth of our nation increases as a consequence of economic growth, more of us are able to own our homes, go to college, and access the Internet.

An economy grows because of increases in available resources and improvements in technology. Economists usually believe that the economy can sustain a long-term growth rate of about 2.5 percent per year. Strong economic growth in the late 1990s offered hope that the U.S. economy is capable of growing faster than previously believed possible. Because of that strong growth, some optimists argue that a sustained growth rate of as much as 5 percent is possible. Over the long run, differences in the economy's growth rate can make a large difference in living standards. It would take about 29 years for aggregate output to double at a 2.5 percent growth rate, but only half that time in the more optimistic case of 5 percent annual growth.

Doubling times, such as that for aggregate output, can be estimated using the *rule of seventy-two*. Whatever the percentage growth rate of a variable is, dividing that number into 72 will reveal the approximate doubling time. For example, a 5 percent growth rate means that output doubles about every 14.4 years, because 72/5 equals 14.4.

In reality, economic growth does not occur smoothly. The economy surges and stumbles at periodic intervals. These ups and downs in the growth of output sometimes put the economy above, and other times below, its long-run sustainable growth rate.

High employment is a major goal of public policy. When economic growth falls short, unemployment is usually the result. Concerns over unemployment motivate economists to develop macro models designed to help us better understand its causes and identify policies to achieve full employment.

inflation a sustained increase in the price level.

price level prices of goods and services in the aggregate.

inflation rate the annual percentage increase in the price level.

Inflation is a sustained rise in the **price level,** which refers to the prices of goods and services in the aggregate. Inflation is usually expressed in terms of the **inflation rate,** the annual percentage increase in the price level. Policymakers in government seek to preserve the value of money by keeping the inflation rate low. In practice, the economy has experienced some inflation every year since 1955. Annual inflation reached a peak of 13.5 percent in 1980 before declining sharply after that. By 2001, the inflation rate had fallen to slightly less than 3 percent. When the inflation rate is low and stable, history shows that public concern over inflation subsides. However, even a seemingly low inflation rate, such as 3 percent, would cause the price level to double in about 24 years. If inflation were to reach 10 percent today, and stay at that rate permanently, it would take a little more than 7 years for the price level to double. Seven more years after that, the price level would have doubled again, and so forth. Such behavior of the price level explains why increases in the inflation rate merit concern, especially for people living on fixed incomes.

| TABLE 12-1 | EFFECTS OF GROWTH: SELECTED CHANGES IN THE U.S. STANDARD OF LIVING |

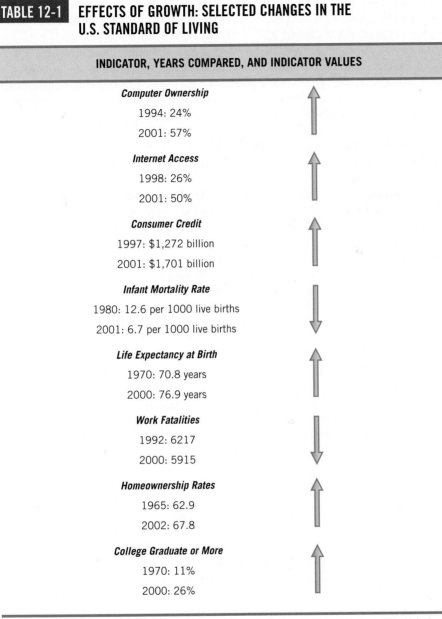

INDICATOR, YEARS COMPARED, AND INDICATOR VALUES

Computer Ownership
1994: 24%
2001: 57%

Internet Access
1998: 26%
2001: 50%

Consumer Credit
1997: $1,272 billion
2001: $1,701 billion

Infant Mortality Rate
1980: 12.6 per 1000 live births
2001: 6.7 per 1000 live births

Life Expectancy at Birth
1970: 70.8 years
2000: 76.9 years

Work Fatalities
1992: 6217
2000: 5915

Homeownership Rates
1965: 62.9
2002: 67.8

College Graduate or More
1970: 11%
2000: 26%

Sources: Various publications of U.S. government agencies, including the *Statistical Abstract of the United States.*

12.2 MEASURING NATIONAL OUTPUT

From the earliest days of American history, the government has kept statistical records. As the economy has grown larger and more complex, the importance of keeping track of the economy has increased. Policymakers rely on government data to design policies that will improve economic performance and help achieve the macro goals of economic growth, full employment, and low inflation.

The value of goods and services produced is the single most important measure of the nation's output. According to the circular flow of income, the value of national output must be identical to the value of national income. This equality occurs because every dollar that buyers spend on output represents income to the sellers of that output as depicted in the circular flow model shown in Chapter 2.

The economy's output of goods and services is diverse, running the gamut from A to Z, including the proverbial kitchen sink. One way to measure output is to classify the goods and services produced according to who is purchasing the output. To this end, purchases are classified by dividing the economy into four sectors, each identified with a different type of purchaser. These are the household, business, government, and foreign sectors. Each unit of output eventually finds its way to one of these sectors. The output is valued at *market value,* which is measured by market prices (the prices paid by the purchasers). Apples, oranges, the kitchen sink, and all other goods and services are valued by the common dollar-denominated yardstick of market prices.

Output is measured by tallying the market value of *final goods and services*—those that are sold to their final owners. The most widely reported measure of the economy's output is **gross domestic product (GDP),** the market value of the final goods and services produced in the economy within some time period, usually one quarter or one year. Spending on *intermediate goods*—goods used to make other goods—is not included in GDP so as to avoid counting the same output twice. For instance, a new Ford Focus purchased by a consumer includes a new battery and tires as standard equipment. Since the total value of the Focus includes the value of these and other input components, the values of the new Focus and its inputs should not be counted separately. While the value of the Focus is included in GDP, the values of the battery, tires, and other intermediate goods are not included in GDP. On the other hand, replacement batteries and tires are counted because they are purchased by their final users. For this reason, GDP includes expenditures by car owners who replace their old tires and batteries with new ones from Sears, Wal-Mart, AutoZone, and other retailers.

In order to track spending in different parts of the economy, GDP is measured as the sum of spending on output by households, businesses, government, and the rest of the world. Thus, we turn our attention now to consumption spending, investment, government purchases, and the effect of foreign commerce on GDP.

gross domestic product (GDP) the market value of the final goods and services produced in the economy within some time period, usually one quarter or one year.

CONSUMPTION

consumption spending purchasing by households; makes up the majority of GDP spending.

Purchasing by households comprises **consumption spending**. Household spending makes up the majority of spending in the U.S. economy, generally close to 70 percent of total spending. This spending may be on services or on consumer durable or nondurable goods. Nondurable goods are consumed quickly, by definition in one year or less. Food is an example. Durable goods have an expected life span of more than one year, such as automobiles. Note that the purchases of new houses by consumers are included in investment spending, as explained below.

INVESTMENT

investment spending now in order to increase output or productivity later; includes spending on capital, new housing, and changes in business inventories.

Investment—spending now in order to increase output or productivity later—is the most variable component of GDP over time. Although there are many forms of investment, such as a college student's investment in the human capital provided by an education, GDP statistics record only three measurable types:

- Purchases by firms of **capital,** such as new factories and machines.
- Consumers' purchases of **new housing,** a form of consumer capital.
- The market value of the **change in business inventories** of unsold goods.

Purchases of capital allow firms the opportunity to increase their future outputs of goods and services. As such, a pickup truck purchased by a firm is counted as an investment. If that same truck had been purchased by you for your personal use, it would have been included in consumption. New homes are included under investment because they provide an ongoing stream of housing services over many years. In that sense the purchase of a new house is an investment.

To see why the change in business inventories is included as an investment, consider an increase in inventories. Inventories increase when firms deliberately produce more than they can immediately sell. Inventories also increase when demand falls short of firms' estimates, as when the economy slows down. Inventory investment is different from investment in capital in that an increase in inventories may be unintended. Nonetheless, accumulations of inventory represent investment because they allow for increased sales in the future. When goods in inventory are sold, inventory investment shows a decrease and other spending an equivalent increase.

Investment may be measured as either gross or net. **Gross investment** is the total amount of investment that takes place. Gross investment by private sector firms, *gross private domestic investment,* is the measure of investment used to compute GDP. It usually amounts to between 15 and 18 percent of GDP. **Net investment** is gross investment minus depreciation. Because plants and machines wear out or become technologically obsolete, net investment will be less than gross investment. A positive value for net investment measures the increase in the economy's productive capacity. A negative value for net investment means that depreciation exceeded the total amount of investment, which implies that the productive capacity of the economy declines. When the focus is on net investment, **net domestic product (NDP)** is a more appropriate measure than GDP. NDP equals GDP minus depreciation.

gross investment the total amount of investment.

net investment gross investment minus depreciation.

net domestic product (NDP) gross domestic product minus depreciation.

SNAPSHOT

ARE DISASTERS GOOD FOR THE ECONOMY?

Hurricanes, floods, and earthquakes are good for the economy, right? After all, they force people to spend more, which increases output. Isn't an increase in output a reason to rejoice?

Clearly, something is amiss with this reasoning. What is the key to understanding this faulty logic? Spending on additions to our stock of goods and services increases living standards. However, spending that follows natural disasters merely replaces goods in order to bring living standards back to some semblance of their former levels. ◀

GOVERNMENT PURCHASES

Governments at the federal, state, and local levels accounted for about 18 percent of the total purchasing of goods and services in the U.S. economy in 2001. Although estimates are imprecise, perhaps one-tenth of government purchasing could be classified as investment.

QUICKCHECK

What would a value of net investment equal to zero say about the economy's ability to produce goods and services?

Answer: Net investment equal to zero implies that the economy's productive capacity did not grow. The investment that occurred merely replaced depreciated capital. For example, if 100 machines wore out during the year, net investment equal to zero means that the 100 machines were replaced, and the total number of working machines remained constant.

Examples of government investment include new highways and other infrastructure, such as government-owned buildings, including schools, offices, and airports. Government also pays for social services provided by teachers, social workers, parole officers, and others. These are civilian goods and services. Defense goods, such as tanks, missiles, and the services of military personnel, are also purchased.

Government *transfer payments,* such as Social Security and unemployment benefits, are received by individuals who do not provide goods and services in return. **Government purchases and investment should be distinguished from government transfer payments. The latter are not included in the computation of GDP.** In Figure 12-1, transfer payments are contrasted to government expenditures that count toward GDP. The figure shows that transfer payments have become increasingly important over time. To the extent that transfer payments are used by the households that receive them to buy goods and services, they are counted as consumption spending. Through this backdoor route, the dollars received as transfers do ultimately contribute to GDP.

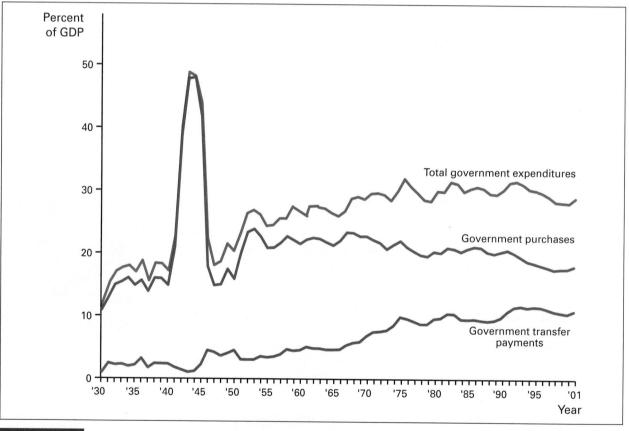

FIGURE 12-1

GOVERNMENT PURCHASES VERSUS GOVERNMENT TRANSFER PAYMENTS Government expenditures take two forms: purchases and transfer payments. When the government purchases goods and services GDP increases. However, transfer payments do not represent payments for production, and are not counted toward GDP. As a percentage of GDP, transfer payments have risen significantly over time, while government purchases are back to what they were at the start of the 1950s. The spike seen in the 1940s was caused by World War II.

Source: Computed from National Income and Product Accounts data.

NET EXPORTS

Some of the output produced by the economy is purchased by foreigners in the form of exports. Exports should be included when GDP is computed because they represent goods and services produced. However, consideration of the role of foreign commerce on GDP must not stop there. Because a portion of spending by U.S. consumers, businesses, and government is on imports, it is necessary to subtract imports from exports in order to compute GDP. In other words, a part of consumption spending, investment, and government purchases is on goods not produced in the United States. The value of these imports should not be counted in GDP.

Exports minus imports defines *net exports*. It is the value of net exports that goes into GDP. A negative value for net exports means that spending on imports is greater than spending on exports; a positive figure means that spending on imports is less than spending on exports. The value of net exports varies from year to year, but has been negative for many years. For example, in 2001, exports equaled $1.03 trillion, about 10.2 percent of GDP. Imports equaled $1.38 trillion, about 13.7 percent of GDP. Net exports were thus equal to −$0.35 trillion, about −3.5 percent of GDP.

net exports exports minus imports.

12.3 GROSS DOMESTIC PRODUCT—A CLOSER LOOK

GDP is shown below as an equation, with data from 2001 and the percentage each component contributes shown in parentheses. The percentages shown are rounded, which is why they do not sum to 100 percent. Figure 12-2 illustrates the components of GDP graphically. Figure 12-3 shows their behavior over time.

GDP = Consumption spending + Gross investment + Government purchases + Net exports
$10.1   + $6.99   + $1.59   + $1.86   − $0.35
              (69%)   (16%)   (18%)   (−3.5%)

Note that net exports enters the equation with a minus sign because exports were less than imports.

Per capita GDP is GDP per person. The total U.S. GDP is seen to be $10.1 trillion ($10,082,200,000,000—a trillion is a million millions or a one followed by twelve zeros). This number is more easily placed into perspective when divided by the U.S. population that year of 284,796,887 people. Performing that division, we see that per capita GDP comes to $35,401. This is the amount of output produced that each person would receive if output were divided equally among every person living in the United States, whether adult or child.

Until 1992, the chief measure of the economy's output was *gross national product (GNP)*. GNP differs from GDP in that the value added to production by resources located outside the United States, but owned by U.S. citizens, is counted in GNP. Unlike GDP, GNP excludes value added within the United States by foreign-owned resources. Typically, U.S. GDP and GNP differ by less than 1 percent, so that either can be used to evaluate the performance of the economy.

GDP AS VALUE ADDED

As an alternative to the expenditures approach, **GDP may also be viewed as the sum of values added in the economy.** Each firm takes inputs of materials and intermediate goods and increases their value through the firm's production process. **Value added** equals the revenue from the sale of output minus the cost of purchased inputs.

value added the difference between revenue and the cost of purchased inputs.

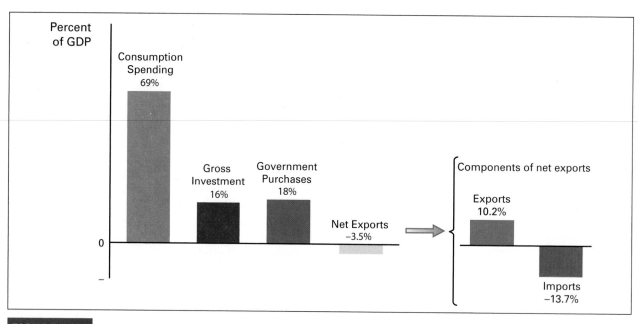

FIGURE 12-2

THE FOUR COMPONENTS OF GDP GDP equals the sum of the four categories of spending. Net exports equals the value of exports minus the value of imports. Net exports have a negative value because the value of imports outweighs the value of exports, as shown.

Source: Bureau of Economic Analysis, *National Income and Product Account Tables,* Table 1.1.

Let's examine the computation of value added by looking at the steps in the production of a single jar of dill pickles. A seed company produces cucumber seeds that are sold to a farmer. Suppose it takes 30 cents worth of seeds to grow the cucumbers in a jar of dill pickles. Assuming the seed company buys no intermediate goods, this initial step generates 30 cents of value added by the seed company. The farmer who purchases the 30 cents worth of seeds subsequently sells the resulting cucumber crop to a pickle maker for $1.00. The farmer has added value equal to 70 cents. The pickle maker sells the pickles it produces to a supermarket for $1.50, and in so doing contributes another 50 cents in value added. When the supermarket sells the pickles to shoppers for $2.25 a jar, which is the market value of a jar of pickles, an additional 75 cents is contributed toward value added.

The $2.25 market value of the jar of pickles represents the value of the production of a final good, since that is the sum of money spent by consumers who will eat the dill pickles in question. The spending of the $2.25 on each jar of pickles is spending on a final good that increases GDP by that amount. This $2.25 worth of GDP can be computed by summing the values added at each step of production:

Increase in GDP from production of a jar of pickles = $0.30 + $0.70 + $0.50 + $0.75 = $2.25

Figure 12-4 illustrates the computation of value added for this example.

INTERPRETING GDP—THE UNDERGROUND ECONOMY, HOUSEHOLD PRODUCTION, AND INTANGIBLES

underground economy market transactions that go unreported to government.

The value of many of the goods and services produced in our economy goes unreported in the GDP statistics. Market transactions that go unreported make up the **underground economy.** Some of these goods and services are illegal. For example, while a drugstore's

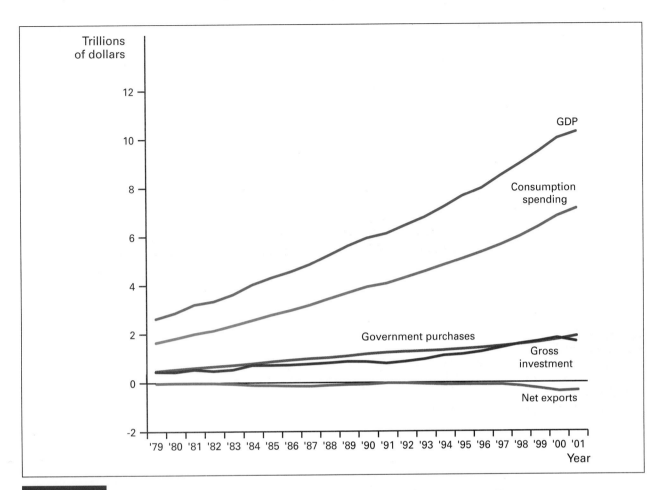

FIGURE 12-3

TRACKING GDP AND ITS COMPONENTS OVER TIME GDP is the sum of the four components shown in the figure: consumption spending, gross investment, government purchases, and net exports.

Source: 2002 Economic Report of the President, Table B-1; and Bureau of Labor Statistics, *National Income and Product Accounts Tables,* Table 1.1. Data are nominal values, meaning they have not been adjusted for price changes.

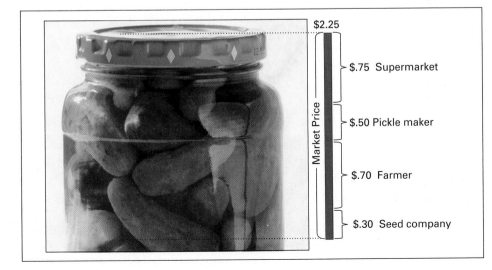

FIGURE 12-4

VALUE ADDED Value added is the firm's revenue minus the cost of the inputs it purchases from other firms. Jars of pickles sell for their market value, $2.25. Since pickles are a final good, GDP increases by $2.25 for each jar of pickles produced. Of the $2.25 in total value added, the seed company contributed 30 cents for supplying the seeds, the farmer 70 cents for growing the cucumbers, the pickle maker 50 cents for making the pickles, and the supermarket 75 cents for selling the pickles.

sales of prescription medications are included in GDP, the crack cocaine sales of a drug dealer are not. The underground economy includes other goods and services that, while not illegal, are not reported to government so that their producers can avoid paying taxes. In sum, the existence of an underground economy means that GDP understates the economy's true output.

The government's statisticians ignore some output deliberately, because they don't know how to place a value on it. For example, GDP does not include the value of *household production*, which is the production of goods and services for use within the household. So, if you cook your own dinner tonight, the value of that service does not appear in GDP. But if you eat out, the value does. That's because there is a market price for a restaurant meal but not for a home-cooked meal. As a result, if all married couples were to divorce and pay one another for their household services, GDP would skyrocket despite the economy not actually producing any more than it had before.

GDP is often used as a proxy for our well-being. This practice is convenient, but can also be misleading. For example, just looking at GDP, it might be hard to fathom how anyone could be nostalgic for the past. After all, GDP is up, and so is the variety of goods and services we can buy. Yet, there is more to life, including *intangibles* that cannot be measured easily. Unmeasured intangibles of value include simplicity, love, freedom, harmony, neighborliness, and many other qualities. On the downside, intangibles include pollution, loneliness, and traffic congestion.

Then there are the things that are measured, but that do not actually indicate that the people are better off. For example, increases in military spending increase GDP, but might be associated with a lower standard of living if the spending is in response to heightened dangers in the world. Likewise, increased spending on cigarettes adds to GDP in the same way as increased spending on healthcare made necessary by previous smoking.

SNAPSHOT

SHHH! WANT A ROLEX? HOW ABOUT A "HONEY DO"?

While it is obviously difficult to measure illegal activity, estimates place the underground economy at from 3 percent to 15 percent of total economic activity in the United States. Other countries see even higher percentages. As a general rule, the more burdensome a country's taxes and regulations, the larger its underground economy.

Most people think that the underground economy consists of prohibited goods and services, such as drugs and prostitution, along with stolen or counterfeit items. Yes, that Rolex watch being hawked on the street corner is probably fake or stolen. But there is much more. A significant portion of the underground economy consists of legal goods that are sold off the record in order to avoid taxes or regulatory requirements.

Examples of this type of underground activity include toxic wastes illegally dumped, workers illegally employed, goods sold without the collection of sales taxes, and services sold without required paperwork. Yes, the underground economy may even include that friendly handyman willing to take on the "honey-do-this, honey-do-that" odd jobs—no license inspected, no credit cards accepted, and no tax collected. ◀

12.4   MEASURING INFLATION

Recall that inflation is a persistent increase in the price level. Thus, inflation is not the same as a one-time increase in the prices of a few products. Rather, inflation involves widespread price increases, affecting the prices of many goods and services. The inflation rate is the annual percentage increase in the price level.

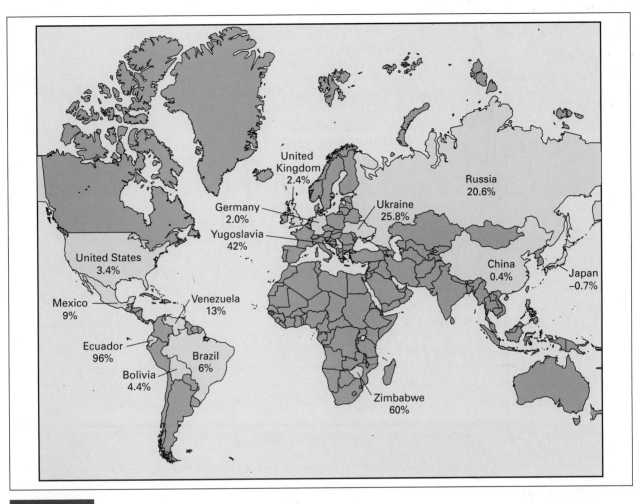

FIGURE 12-5

INFLATION RATES IN SELECTED COUNTRIES Inflation rates vary significantly from country to country. Developing countries tend to have higher inflation rates than do developed countries.

Source: Central Intelligence Agency, *The World Factbook, 2001.* All data are for 2000, except Yugoslavia, which is for 1999. Except for the United States, Brazil, and Venezuela, the data are estimated values. The inflation rates are for consumer prices.

The Central Intelligence Agency (CIA) estimates that the average inflation rate in the world in 2000 was 25 percent. Throughout recent history, inflation has been most severe in developing nations, ones facing a variety of economic and social problems. The CIA estimates that developing countries had inflation rates between 5 percent and 60 percent in 2000, which is markedly higher than the typical 1 percent to 3 percent inflation rate in developed countries. Figure 12-5 shows recent inflation rates for selected countries.

When the inflation rate is negative, *deflation* is said to occur. That would happen if the price level declined from one year to the next. For example, Figure 12-5 shows that Japan has recently seen mild deflation. Severe, persistent deflation has yet to occur in modern U.S. history, although the economy showed slight deflation in 1949 and 1955, which you can see in Figure 12-6.

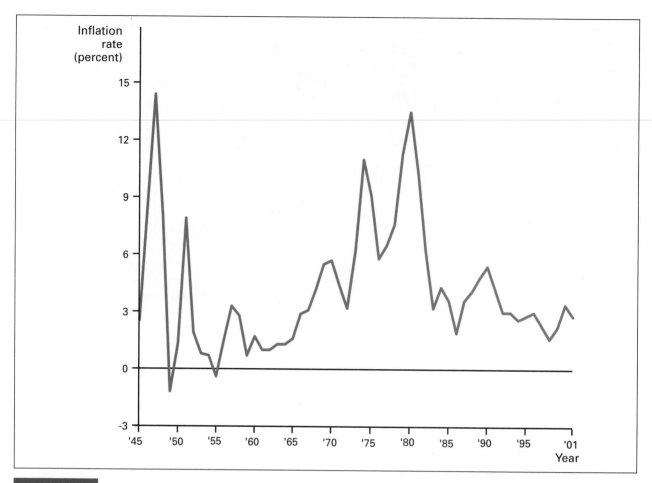

FIGURE 12-6

THE U.S. INFLATION RATE SINCE 1945 The annual inflation rate changes from year to year. The relatively high inflation rates in some years tell us that the goal of low inflation is sometimes elusive.

Source: 2002 Economic Report of the President, Table B-64. The inflation rates shown are based on the Consumer Price Index.

QUICKCHECK

What is the price level? How is the inflation rate related to the price level?

Answer: The price level refers to the prices of goods and services in the aggregate. An inflation rate is expressed as an annual percentage increase in the price level.

consumer price index (CPI) measures prices of a market basket of purchases made by consumers living in urban areas.

GDP chained price index (GDP price index) a price index used to compute real GDP by linking together successive years of data.

A *price index* measures the average level of prices in the economy. There are several price indexes, each created for a specific purpose, with a different set of prices measured. Two of the most widely referenced are:

■ The **consumer price index (CPI),** the best-known price index among the public, which measures prices of typical purchases made by consumers living in urban areas.
■ The **GDP chained price index,** called the **GDP** price index for short, which is the most broadly based price index because it includes prices across the spectrum of GDP.

Let's look at the CPI first since it is the most-used price index.

THE CONSUMER PRICE INDEX

To understand the CPI, let's start with the concept of the *base period.* **The base period is an arbitrarily selected initial time period against which other time periods are compared.** The CPI is assigned a value of 100 during the base period. For instance, the base period for the CPI is presently 1982 to 1984, and the CPI has been assigned an average value of 100 over that period of time.

Table 12-2 reproduces values of the CPI for selected years. The table shows, for example, that the CPI for 1951 equals 26. That value means that a dollar's worth of consumer purchases in the base period would have cost 26 cents in 1951. The table also shows that the CPI for 2001 equals 177.1. On average, a consumer would have needed $1.77 to pay for the purchases that cost a dollar during the base period. Notice that the CPI for years before the base period exhibits values less than 100 because prices were lower than in the base period.

We can use the CPI data to compute the inflation rate. The inflation rate is calculated by taking the percentage change in the CPI as follows:

$$\text{Inflation rate} = \frac{\text{Change in price index}}{\text{Initial price index}} \times 100$$

For example, from Table 12-2, the CPI equaled 177.1 in 2001 and 172.2 in 2000. The change in the CPI between 2000 and 2001 was 4.9 units, equal to 177.1 minus 172.2. When 4.9 is divided by 172.2 and the result multiplied by 100, the annual rate of inflation is seen to be 2.8 percent:

$$\text{Inflation rate in 2001} = \frac{4.9}{172.2} \times 100 = .028 \times 100 = 2.8 \text{ percent}$$

What prices are measured by the CPI? If it were possible to count all the consumer prices in the economy, the number of different prices would likely be in the millions. It is unrealistic to expect so many prices to be used in the computation of a price index. The calculation of the CPI is based upon the prices of selected goods and services that consumers typically purchase. **The collection of goods and services used in the calculation of the CPI is called the *market basket.*** The market basket represents a sampling of the items that consumers buy that make up a significant part of their budgets. The market basket is based on extensive surveys of consumer purchases. There are around 200 specific categories of goods and services in the market basket, ranging from apples to women's dresses. Each item in the market basket is assigned a *weight* that reflects its importance in consumers' budgets. For example, personal care items such as shampoo have a smaller weight than gasoline. The Bureau of Labor Statistics (BLS) computes the CPI for the market basket every month. This effort requires BLS employees in eighty-seven urban areas to collect a total of 80,000 different prices.

The 200 or so specific categories of goods in the CPI market basket are divided into eight broad expenditure categories, as shown in Figure 12-7. All goods and services in the market basket belong to one of these categories. The weight on each category, which reflects the relative importance of the categories to consumers, is also shown in the figure. The relative importance is stated as a percentage of total spending by the average consumer. For example, housing expenditures are the largest component of the expenditure categories, amounting to 40.9 percent of expenditures by average consumers. The weights are so important in contributing to the accuracy of the CPI that they are now updated every two years, rather than every ten years, as in the past. Current weights help to ensure that the CPI reflects how people are spending their money.

In an effort to provide even more accurate inflation data, another type of CPI was introduced in August 2002. This CPI is called the C-CPI, with the first C standing for chained. A *chained price index* uses continuously updated expenditure weights. While the CPI weights are updated every two years, the new C-CPI is chained monthly. In effect, the weights for the C-CPI are updated continuously.

TABLE 12-2 THE CONSUMER PRICE INDEX, SELECTED YEARS

The CPI typically rises year to year, as is seen here. The average value of the CPI for 1982, 1983, and 1984 equals 100 because the 1982–1984 period is the base period.

YEAR	CONSUMER PRICE INDEX
1951	26
1961	29.9
1971	40.6
1979	72.6
1980	82.4
1981	90.9
1982	96.5
1983	99.6
1984	103.9
1985	107.6
1986	109.6
1987	113.6
1988	118.3
1989	124.0
1990	130.7
1991	136.2
1992	140.3
1993	144.5
1994	148.2
1995	152.4
1996	156.9
1997	160.5
1998	163.0
1999	166.6
2000	172.2
2001	177.1

Averages to 100, the base-period value

Source: 2002 Economic Report of the President, Table B-60.

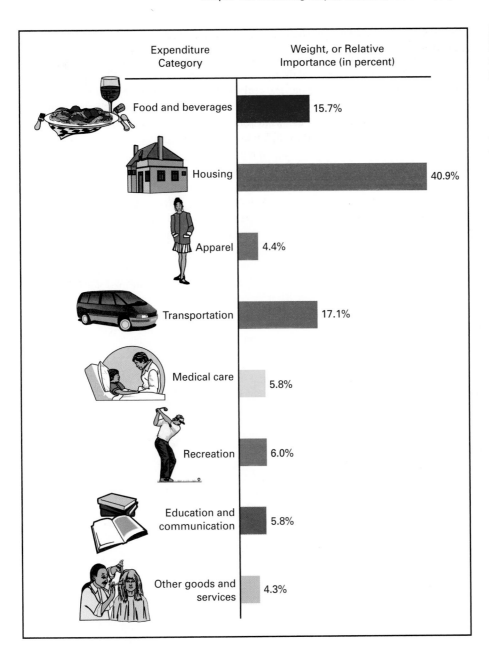

Expenditure Category	Weight, or Relative Importance (in percent)
Food and beverages	15.7%
Housing	40.9%
Apparel	4.4%
Transportation	17.1%
Medical care	5.8%
Recreation	6.0%
Education and communication	5.8%
Other goods and services	4.3%

FIGURE 12-7

CPI MARKET BASKET EXPENDITURE CATEGORIES

Source: Bureau of Labor Statistics, *Relative Importance of Components in the Consumer Price Indexes: U.S. City Average, December 2001.* The weights are for 1999–2000, and are obtained by surveys of consumers.

QUICKCHECK

What is the significance of the base period for the CPI? How is the base period selected?

Answer: The base period provides a point of reference to which the current price level can be compared. The CPI is set to a value of 100 during the base period. The selection of the base period is arbitrary.

USING A PRICE INDEX: NOMINAL VALUES VERSUS REAL VALUES

nominal value a value that is not adjusted for inflation.

real value a value that results from adjusting a nominal value for inflation.

nominal GDP GDP that is stated without adjusting for inflation.

real GDP the value of GDP after nominal GDP is adjusted for inflation.

An increase in GDP due solely to price increases does not increase economic well-being. We can use a price index to adjust economic measures for the effects of inflation. The **nominal value** of a variable is not adjusted for inflation. The **real value** of a variable adjusts for inflation.

Specifically, **nominal GDP** is the value of GDP expressed in current dollar terms. The nominal value may be thought of as "what you see is what you get." By contrast, **real GDP** adjusts the nominal value of GDP for inflation. Real GDP expresses GDP in terms of a constant value of money—dollars with the same purchasing power.

The real value is expressed in terms of the value of the dollar during a selected base period. The time period chosen as the base period is not very important. What is important is that each year's measuring units be the same—dollars with the same purchasing power.

The distinction between real and nominal values is important not only to the study of macroeconomics, but also to individuals. Consider a worker whose weekly pay increases from $100 to $110. That worker has experienced a 10 percent increase in nominal income. If the price level remains constant, the worker's real income is also 10 percent greater. However, if the price level increases by 10 percent, the $110 of current income will purchase only as much as $100 purchased in the past. That means that the real income has not changed.

The following formula shows how to use a price index to compute a real value:

$$\text{Real value} = \frac{\text{Nominal value}}{\text{Price index}} \times 100$$

For example, suppose Jason earned nominal incomes of $39,000 a year in the base period and $40,500 in the current year, a 3.8 percent increase over the base period. Is Jason better off in the current year than in the base period? If the price index in the current year equals 105, then:

$$\text{Jason's real income} = \left(\frac{\$40,500}{105}\right) \times 100 = \$38,571.43$$

Jason's real income, which measures his purchasing power, has fallen since the base period. In terms of his real income he is not better off.

Applying the formula for a real value, we compute real GDP, as follows:

$$\text{Real GDP} = \frac{\text{Nominal GDP}}{\text{GDP price index}} \times 100$$

12.5 MEASURING UNEMPLOYMENT

An economy with unemployment is wasting resources and producing at a point inside its production possibilities frontier. The concept of unemployment applies to any resource that lies idle. In common usage, however, unemployment refers to idle labor.

THE LABOR FORCE AND UNEMPLOYMENT

labor force individuals age 16 and over, excluding those in the military, who are either employed or actively looking for work.

unemployment rate the ratio of the number of unemployed persons to the number of persons in the labor force.

The U.S. *civilian labor force*—the **labor force**—is composed of individuals age 16 and over, excluding those in the military, who are either employed or actively looking for work. The labor force typically expands as the adult population increases. The labor force also expands as job opportunities improve, which causes some of the people not previously in the labor force to look for work.

The labor force can be divided into two parts, consisting of the employed and the unemployed. The employed are those who work for pay, and the unemployed are those who do not work, but are seeking jobs. The **unemployment rate** is the fraction of the labor force who are unemployed, expressed in percentage terms:

$$\text{Unemployment rate} = \frac{\text{Number of unemployed}}{\text{Labor force}} \times 100$$

Separating the employed from the unemployed would seem easy, but there are many details to consider. For example:

- Are you employed if your job is not full time? Yes, people are counted as employed regardless of how many hours they work, just so long as it's one hour a week or more for pay.
- Can someone who works without pay be counted as employed? Again, yes, just so long as that person is working in a family business for at least fifteen hours a week.
- Does going to school count as having a job? No. For students, school may seem to be a full-time job, but it's not considered that way by government statisticians. Neither are students counted among the unemployed, unless they are looking for jobs.

In the United States the BLS estimates the number of employed and unemployed, and hence the unemployment rate. The estimates are based on a monthly survey of households and employers, and a tally of unemployment insurance claims. Figure 12-8 shows yearly unemployment rates since 1947.

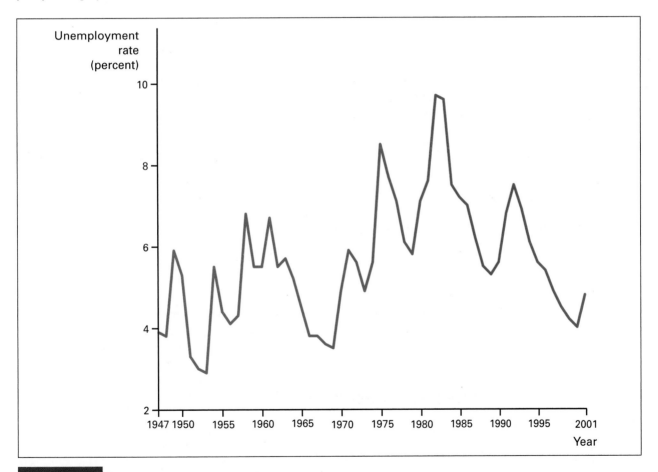

FIGURE 12-8

HISTORY OF THE U.S. UNEMPLOYMENT RATE The U.S. unemployment rate changes frequently. When the economy slows down, the unemployment rate rises. Faster economic growth promotes a lower unemployment rate. The unemployment rate fell significantly during the 1990s, but bounced upward in 2001 as the economy slowed.

Source: 2002 Economic Report of the President, Table B-35.

The unemployment rate, while useful, does not tell us all that we would like to know about the labor market. Some workers who have part-time jobs would like to have full-time jobs. Those workers are *underemployed.* Other workers would like to have a job, but have tried unsuccessfully to find one in the past and have given up looking. Because they have stopped looking, they are not counted in the unemployment statistics. Such would-be workers are called **discouraged workers.** Government estimates put the number of discouraged workers at 317,000 in mid-2002. **The presence of discouraged workers would cause the reported unemployment rate to understate true unemployment because discouraged workers are not in the labor force.** Concerns over the accuracy and meaning of the unemployment rate have led some economists to coin a saying about it: "The unemployment rate is like a hot dog. It's hard to tell what's in it."

discouraged workers people who would like to have a job, but have given up looking; not counted as unemployed because they are not included in the labor force.

People are unemployed for a variety of reasons, with some reasons of more concern than others. For example, some people are unemployed because they have voluntarily left their jobs. These unemployed persons are of less concern than the unemployed who have been involuntarily laid off. Some other people who are unemployed are actually earning incomes in the underground economy. **The underground economy causes the reported unemployment rate to overstate true unemployment.**

TYPES OF UNEMPLOYMENT

Unemployment can be divided into the following four types:

frictional unemployment unemployment associated with entering the labor market or switching jobs.

seasonal unemployment unemployment that can be predicted to recur periodically, according to the time of year.

structural unemployment unemployment caused by a mismatch between a person's human capital and that needed in the workplace.

cyclical unemployment unemployment from a downturn in the business cycle that affects workers simultaneously in many different industries.

- **Frictional Unemployment**—occurs when someone enters the labor market or switches jobs.
- **Seasonal Unemployment**—recurs periodically, according to the time of year.
- **Structural Unemployment**—caused by a mismatch between a person's human capital and that needed in the workplace. This mismatch can be caused by an evolving structure of the economy as some industries rise and others fall. It can also be caused by minimum wage laws or other structural *rigidities* that inhibit job creation or the movement of workers into new jobs.
- **Cyclical Unemployment**—results from a downturn in the business cycle and affects workers simultaneously in many different industries.

Structural and cyclical unemployment are usually of most concern, because they represent *involuntary unemployment,* meaning that employees have little choice in the matter. In contrast, frictional and seasonal unemployment frequently represent *voluntary unemployment,* which can be planned for and more easily overcome.

SEASONAL AND FRICTIONAL—WAITING FOR THE OLD OR SWITCHING TO THE NEW   Seasonal unemployment affects workers in agriculture, many tourism-related occupations, education, tax accounting, professional sports, and some other industries. There is usually little concern over this unemployment, because it can be planned for—it is part of the job. Workers are not even counted as unemployed if they have labor contracts that restart after the off-season, such as often occurs in teaching and professional sports.

Frictional unemployment occurs when people are between jobs, either because they were fired and have yet to line up new jobs or have quit voluntarily, such as in preparation for moving somewhere else or trying something new. Either way, their stay on the unemployment roles is likely to be brief. Frictional unemployment also includes many young people entering the labor market for the first time and older workers reentering the work force after an absence to raise children.

Changing jobs does not imply frictional unemployment. Most voluntary job switching is done without it; people line up new jobs before leaving their old ones. However, involuntary job changes, such as in response to layoffs and firings, commonly do result in frictional unemployment. In the case of involuntary frictional unemployment, publicly provided unemployment compensation acts as a safety net. It allows the job seeker to hold out longer in search of the best job opportunity.

STRUCTURAL—HUMAN CAPITAL MISMATCHES AND LABOR MARKET RIGIDITIES   Changes in the structure of the economy can give rise to structural unemployment, as demands for some types of goods and services give way to demands for others. This change in structure arises from such factors as technological change, international trade, and changing ways of doing business. For example, computers and telecommunications have opened doors to many types of jobs, but have cost many types of jobs, too.

Former telegraph operators exemplify structural unemployment. Once a valuable skill, the ability to speedily send coded messages over telegraph lines now has no market. Telegraph operators who were displaced by the technology of telephones could not easily find other employment at comparable wages. Their skills were not in demand. Until they retrained or found new jobs (usually at much lower wages), the ex–telegraph operators were structurally unemployed.

Human capital is often specific to a particular firm or kind of job—**specific human capital**—and does not apply readily to other firms or other jobs. As telegraph operators learned the hard way, workers with specific human capital are most prone to structural unemployment. It is a risk that people take voluntarily, since the best-paying jobs usually involve specific human capital. In contrast, **general human capital** involves such skills as language and math. General human capital is easily transferred from job to job. Those who possess it are less likely to be structurally unemployed.

> **specific human capital** human capital that is specific to a particular firm or kind of job.

> **general human capital** skills such as language and math that are easily transferred from job to job.

For most students, an undergraduate economics education represents general human capital. Economics majors are qualified to hold a variety of jobs in business and government. However, graduate training in economics is more specialized, and thus represents specific human capital. Students who earn a doctoral degree in economics usually build a career as a business or government economist, or as a college teacher of economics.

Structural unemployment is a necessary part of economic evolution. Without structural unemployment, there would be no progress—no industrial revolution, no railroad, no automobile, no computer. Those skilled workers who lose their jobs often find the transition to new jobs difficult, since economic change has depreciated the human capital that supported their incomes. They are usually forced to evaluate their alternatives, and either take a job with lower pay or drop out of the labor force to retire or learn new skills.

The government sometimes offers job-training programs to cushion the blows of structural unemployment. The question arises, though, as to the form of that training. For example, should the government train people to be hair stylists? That would take the jobs of other hair stylists or force them to work at lower wages. Such human capital is also so specific that it would not be pertinent for many of the structurally unemployed. The 50-year-old steelworker would probably not enroll.

CYCLICAL—A SYSTEMIC DISORDER   A troublesome form of unemployment is caused by downturns in the business cycle, *panics* as they were called in the nineteenth century. In these periodic downturns, which we refer to as recessions today, people in numerous sectors of the economy lose their jobs simultaneously. There just does not seem to be enough spending to go around, at least for awhile. Cyclical unemployment is thus a *systemic disorder*—a problem felt throughout the entire economy. The increase in U.S. unemployment in 1991 and 1992, and again in 2001 and 2002, exemplifies cyclical unemployment since those increases were associated with the mild recessions that occurred at those times.

Cyclical unemployment is a temporary phenomena because recessions are temporary. As the economy pulls out of a recession, job creation leads the cyclically unemployed to return to their old jobs or find new ones. In this way cyclical unemployment diminishes and eventually disappears.

SNAPSHOT   ## A WORLD WITHOUT CHANGE

Change is distressing. It disrupts our lives and makes us scramble to adapt to it. It causes stress in our lives, especially when it causes us to lose our jobs. Just ask the bank tellers who lost their jobs to automatic teller machines. Or the typewriter repair people who just never learned about computer keyboards. Or the many others whose skills became obsolete when technology or tastes changed against the industries or occupations in which they worked. They are the structurally unemployed.

When spending patterns change, so do the available jobs. The only way to avoid such disruption and the structural unemployment it brings would be to freeze ourselves in time. For example, if change had been forbidden since the 1950s, we'd still watch "I Love Lucy" on black and white TV. Our cars would be huge and our cell phones nowhere to be found. ◄

12.5 THE BUSINESS CYCLE—THE UPS AND DOWNS IN ECONOMIC ACTIVITY

Cycles in economic activity have been a feature of economies throughout history. In the twentieth century, the Great Depression of the 1930s stands out as an economic collapse of historic proportions in the United States and other countries around the world. Although most downturns in the economy are mild and short-lived, we still worry about the cyclical nature of our economy.

STAGES OF THE BUSINESS CYCLE

business cycle the uneven sequence of trough, expansion, peak, and recession that the economy follows over time.

recession a sustained decrease in real GDP.

The term **business cycle** refers to the expansions and contractions in economic activity that take place over time. Figure 12-9 shows the stages of a business cycle as a smooth curve. The low point in economic activity is called the *trough*. Following the trough is the *expansion* stage. When the expansion is ready to end, the economy reaches its *peak*, and then falls into **recession** in which real GDP decreases. An especially severe recession is termed a *depression*. Subsequently, another trough will mark the point where the process begins repeating itself.

The economic fluctuations represented by the business cycle are an example of *short-run* features in the economy. The business cycle occurs around an upward trend in real GDP. Economic trends describe persistent features in the economy. Thus, trends describe the *long-run* features of the economy.

In the real world, the ups and downs in the economy do not occur in such a smooth fashion. Expansions typically last much longer and are much stronger than recessions. Thus, the business cycle occurs within the context of a rising trend in real GDP. Figure 12-10 reveals the upward course of GDP over time. It also shows that, since the Great Depression of the 1930s, recessions in the United States have been infrequent, mild, and short lived. None of the post-war recessions has come close to matching the Great Depression in length or magnitude.

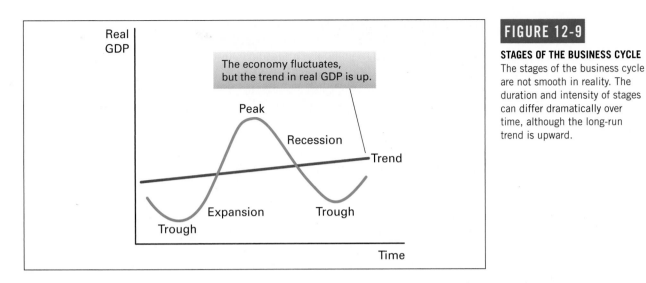

FIGURE 12-9

STAGES OF THE BUSINESS CYCLE
The stages of the business cycle are not smooth in reality. The duration and intensity of stages can differ dramatically over time, although the long-run trend is upward.

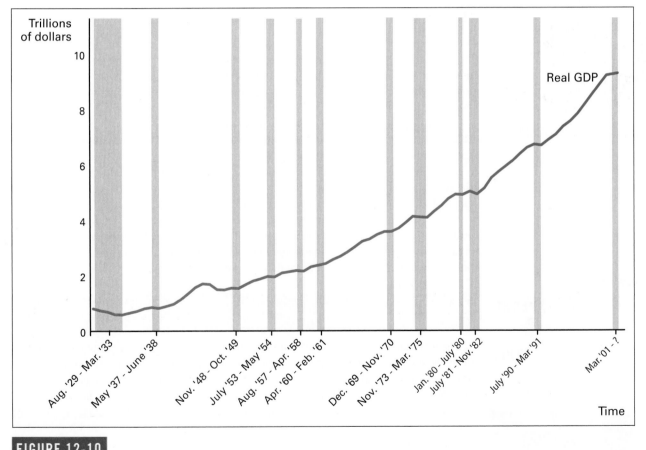

FIGURE 12-10

REAL GDP SINCE 1929 People living during the Great Depression of the 1930s would have found it difficult to agree with the idea that the trend in GDP was upward. In contrast, the ten recessions since the end of World War II in 1945 have been relatively short and mild, thus reducing public fear that another Great Depression might occur. Recessions are identified in the graph by the shaded vertical bars.

Source: Bureau of Economic Analysis, *National Accounts Data,* and National Bureau of Economic Research, *Business Cycle Expansions and Contractions.*

Who decides when the economy leaves one stage of the business cycle and enters the next stage? In the United States, that job is not left to government economists, whose judgment might be swayed by political considerations. Instead, an independent organization, the National Bureau of Economic Research (NBER), is entrusted with the dating of business cycle turning points. To accomplish this task, the NBER considers the depth and duration of the downturn, along with the dispersion of its effects throughout the economy.

Because important indicators of the economy, such as GDP, employment, and industrial production, sometimes move opposite to each other, the job of the NBER is a difficult one. In many instances, the NBER will not announce the onset of a recession until it has observed the indicators for months. There are also often delays in dating the beginning of expansions.

There are hundreds of economic indicators capable of illuminating various aspects of the economy. History has shown that some of these indicators, called **leading economic indicators**, will usually change direction before the economy does. Examples include the index of building permits, housing starts, and manufacturers' new orders for durable goods. These data series and several others are combined to form a composite *index of leading economic indicators,* which can help predict which way the economy will go.

leading economic indicators statistics that are expected to change direction before the economy at large does, thereby indicating where the economy is headed.

SEASONAL ADJUSTMENTS—HELPING TO ISOLATE CYCLICAL EFFECTS

Many economic variables move either up or down at the same time each year. For example, construction activity slows down during the winter because of bad weather and picks up during the warmer months. Retail sales increase during the Christmas season. Agriculture follows seasonal patterns. Thus, downswings in economic activity do not always indicate recession, just as upswings do not always signal expansion.

These seasonal effects make it difficult to disentangle actual growth in economic variables from changes in them due to seasonal volatility. That is why most published economic data are seasonally adjusted, using statistical models. Seasonal adjustments to data help reveal the underlying trends. For example, when construction activity drops off in January, the seasonally adjusted data can tell us whether the decline is merely the usual winter slowdown or whether construction is stronger or weaker than usual for that time of year.

Seasonal adjustments can reveal unusual strength or weakness in the economy. For example, if the seasonal adjustment shows that the January decline in construction activity is not as sharp as usual, and many other economic measures are also above their seasonal norms, we have compelling evidence that the economy is expanding.

𝒺 XPLORE & 𝒜 PPLY

12.7 ASSESSING ECONOMIC PERFORMANCE— DARE WE PREDICT THE FUTURE?

The federal government must have answers, even if they are not the ultimate answers. It must know whether there are macroeconomic problems. If there are problems, it must know how serious those problems are. Otherwise, government cannot know which actions to take, or even whether to take action at all. Thus, it turns to economic statistics.

Some economists would say that government should ignore the aggregate economy, and just focus on prudent budgetary practices. If the government follows sensible rules, they say, the economy will take care of itself. However, whether or not the government's best macro policy strategy is active or passive, it is still necessary to track economic performance. The reason is that government policies affect the rest of the economy, which in turn affects government revenues and expenses. Without knowing revenues and expenses, government cannot budget effectively.

Of course, just knowing economic data does not mean that government will choose to budget sensibly. The federal budget deficit—a shortfall of federal revenues below

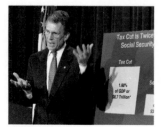

expenses—is evidence. Until the surpluses of 1998–2001, the federal government incurred a budget deficit every year between 1960 and 1997. With an estimated $165 billion deficit in 2002, deficits are expected to continue. In response to citizen outrage over the earlier deficits, Congress revised its budgetary practices. As we will see, the result has been to give economic statistics a more central role than ever before.

In 1985, in an attempt to lead the federal budget into balance, Congress passed the Gramm–Rudman–Hollings Act. This legislation set specific deficit-reduction targets. Each time targets were not met, the act called for across-the-board budget cuts that would bring spending into line with those targets. According to the Gramm–Rudman–Hollings targets, the federal deficit was to be eliminated by 1991.

When 1991 rolled around, the federal budget deficit was $215 billion dollars, higher than it had ever been before. What happened? Well before 1991, Congress had modified and then abandoned the Gramm–Rudman–Hollings approach. The across-the-board budget axe was not used. It fell victim to special interests, especially the interests of Social Security recipients. Too much spending was exempted from cuts.

Congress instead instituted a different set of budgetary procedures to add integrity to the budget process. Specifically, in the Budget Enforcement Act of 1990 that expired in 2002, Congress legislated that policy changes should not increase the budget deficit. Thus, policy changes that would add to the budget deficit must be balanced by other changes that would offset that effect. Doing so sounds reasonable, but brings back that basic statistical problem—measuring the effects on government revenues and expenses of alternative public policies. As we will see, these statistics are not immune from politics.

DO LUXURY TAXES WORK?

Is government able to forecast the effects of policy changes? In 1990 Congress imposed a surcharge on luxuries including, among other things, new yachts and other luxury boats. Immediately after the so-called luxury tax took effect, orders for new yachts all but disappeared. Although the tax rate was higher, government revenue from boat sales was much lower. Overall the luxury tax did bring in more money, but the amount was about $13 million by 1993, rather than the $76 million over that period that was designated in the Congressional budget.

Although the revenue effect of the luxury tax could have been predicted with much greater accuracy, the Budget Enforcement Act did not allow Congress to do so in its budgetary calculations. Thus, the luxury tax surcharge was assumed to bring in $76 million of extra revenue, which then allowed Congress to pass an additional $76 million of new spending programs.

This traditional manner of computing the effects of federal actions is known as *static scoring*. Static scoring assumes no general change in macroeconomic behavior as a result of government policy changes. Hence, the effect of the luxury tax on the demand for luxury goods was ignored. The alternative is called *dynamic scoring*, which does allow for consideration of all behavioral changes over time caused by changes in government policy.

Static scoring has led to other serious problems. Prior to the final passage of the internationally negotiated revisions to the General Agreement on Tariffs and Trade (GATT) in 1994, for example, Congress was nearly forced to abandon the agreement. Negotiations over the GATT had dragged on for over seven years, as countries around the world sought to retain their special trade protections. The final agreement dramatically lowered trade barriers, which had been America's objective all along. The problem was those static scoring rules.

Although the entire purpose of reducing trade barriers was to promote trade, static scoring rules assumed that the volume of trade would remain constant. Thus, any tariff cut was automatically scored as a revenue-loser by the same percentage that the tariffs were cut.

Budget rules meant that tariffs could not be cut without other policy changes that would add revenues or cut expenditures in other areas to offset the purported revenue loss. It was only through an extraordinary act of juggling other elements of the budget that the congressional budgetary rules were finally satisfied.

Static scoring is stupid, you might say. Washington policymakers know that taxes can change our behavior. Static scoring has been a budgetary mainstay because it provides an obvious baseline estimate, the baseline being the status quo. Analysts may know that behavior will change, but are unlikely to agree on exactly what forms the changes will take or how significant will be their effects. Because of such disagreement, dynamic scoring must inevitably lead to controversy.

Everyone in the budget process knows that static scoring gives wrong answers. Still, as the saying goes, the devil you know is better than the devil you don't know. If the government were to follow a dynamic scoring standard, who could tell what controversies would lie buried beneath the surface?

Consider the possibilities. There was hot debate over President George Bush's recently enacted tax cuts when, on May 16, 2002, the Congressional Joint Committee on Taxation (JCT) issued a report urging Congress to modify its budget rules in order to allow dynamic scoring. The Committee pointed to economic studies suggesting that, while cutting tax rates would reduce the amount of tax revenue per dollar earned, a significant portion of that revenue loss would be offset by revenues gained from an increase in aggregate economic activity. Senate Majority Leader Tom Daschle objected. In a public letter to House Speaker Dennis Hastert on June 25, 2002, Daschle declared, "Having JCT include the macroeconomic effects into its cost estimates would subject the committee's work to huge potential errors and would only serve to undermine its credibility."

The problem of budgetary discipline also arises on the spending side. For example, advocates of social programs often find themselves attracted to the dynamic standard, arguing that cutting back spending on social programs could cause tax revenues to decline over time. The idea is that money spent on social programs helps to develop productive, taxpaying citizens who pay back many times more than they received. Thus, they sometimes argue, cutting social spending would threaten to increase rather than decrease budget deficits.

The issue of static versus dynamic scoring underscores the old adage that politics makes strange bedfellows. Conservatives seeking to cut taxes find themselves allied with liberals seeking to expand government spending on social programs. Both support dynamic scoring. On the other side are conservatives and liberals who fear political manipulation of the budget process. Whatever the immediate outcome of this tug-of-war, the issue will remain with us.

Is it better to continue with static scoring that we know gives wrong answers or to allow our elected officials the leeway to use their best judgments as to which forecasts to accept? Do we trust them to think well? Is it better to analyze and maybe get it wrong than not to analyze at all? Those are the questions.

Thinking Critically

1. Senate Majority Leader Tom Daschle was quoted in this Explore & Apply as declaring, "Having JCT include the macroeconomic effects into its cost estimates would subject the committee's work to huge potential errors and would only serve to undermine its credibility." Using your own words, explain what he meant and why others might disagree.

2. As a taxpayer, do you support static or dynamic scoring? Which do you think is more likely to lead to lower taxes? To higher taxes? Explain your answers.

Visit **www.prenhall.com/collinge** for updates and web exercises on this Explore & Apply topic.

SUMMARY AND LEARNING OBJECTIVES

1. **Present three widely accepted goals for the economy.**
   - The three goals for the economy are economic growth, full employment, and low inflation.
   - An annual growth rate of 2.5 percent is usually considered sustainable. Evidence from the late 1990s suggests a possible sustainable growth rate of up to 5 percent.
   - The rule of seventy-two can be used to compute doubling times. For example, at a 2.5 percent rate of growth, the economy's output would double in approximately 29 years. A growth rate of 5 percent would cut this doubling time in half.
   - In order to know whether the nation is meeting its macro goals, government collects data that measure the aggregate economy.

2. **Define gross domestic product (GDP) and discuss its components.**
   - Gross domestic product (GDP) is the most widely reported measure of the aggregate economy. It measures the value of final goods and services produced by an economy within some time period. Intermediate goods are used to make other goods. To avoid double counting, GDP does not count the production of intermediate goods, since their value is included in the value of final goods.
   - GDP equals the sum of consumption, investment, government purchases, and net exports. Per capita GDP is GDP per person, computed by dividing GDP by the population. GDP is an imperfect measure of a nation's well-being, because it does not count the value of goods and services produced in the underground economy and at home.
   - The largest component of total spending in the United States is consumption spending, which includes most spending by consumers.
   - Total spending also includes investment, government purchases, and net exports. Investment is the sum of three items: spending on capital by businesses, spending on new housing by consumers, and the change in business inventories.
   - Government spending is the sum of spending on purchases of goods and services by governments at the local, state, and national levels. Government transfer payments are not directly included in the computation of GDP.
   - Net exports equal the value of exports minus the value of imports. Net exports have been negative in the recent past.

   - Gross national product (GNP) is computed by first adding income received from the rest of the world to GDP, and then subtracting income payments to the rest of the world. GNP and GDP typically differ by a relatively small amount.
   - The value of production that occurs at home is not counted in GDP. Neither is the value of goods and services produced for the underground economy. Thus, GDP is an imperfect measure of a nation's well-being.

3. **Interpret and apply a price index.**
   - Several price indexes, including the consumer price index (CPI) and the GDP price index, can be used to measure inflation. The CPI is the price index that is used most commonly.
   - The base period for a price index is an initial time period, currently 1982 to 1984 for the CPI, to which prices in other time periods are compared. The base period is selected arbitrarily. By convention, the value of a price index equals 100 during the base period.
   - As the price level rises, the value of the CPI increases. The CPI for 2001 equals 177.1, which is interpreted to mean that the price level in 2001 is 77.1 percent higher than in the base period. Alternatively, it would take $1.77 to purchase what $1.00 purchased in the base period.
   - The CPI is calculated using items that urban consumers typically purchase, the so-called market basket of goods and services. There are about 200 categories of goods and services in the CPI, grouped into eight major expenditure categories. The relative importance of an expenditure category is used as a weight in the computation of the CPI. Currently, the CPI is computed using weights that are updated every two years.
   - A recent alternative to the CPI is the C-CPI, which is a chained price index with weights that are updated every month.
   - Price indexes are used to compute a real value from a nominal value. With knowledge of the nominal value of a variable and the value of a price index it is possible to compute the real value of the variable. Real values are useful to know. For example, the real value of the minimum wage over time shows us that the purchasing power of the minimum wage has varied significantly.
   - Nominal GDP, when divided by the GDP price index and multiplied by 100, equals real GDP. Real GDP pro-

vides a more accurate measure of the economy's actual output over time than does nominal GDP. Nominal GDP will rise whenever production increases, but also because of inflation. Real GDP will only rise when production increases.

4. **Distinquish the four types of unemployment.**
   - The civilian labor force equals the number of persons age 16 and over who have a job or are looking for one. The unemployment rate equals the number of unemployed persons divided by the civilian labor force, multiplied by 100.
   - The unemployment rate must be interpreted carefully, because of the existence of discouraged workers. Discouraged workers are not counted in the labor force because they have given up looking for work. If they were counted, the reported unemployment rate would rise.
   - The reported unemployment rate is higher than the true unemployment rate because of the underground economy. Note that the underground economy biases the reported unemployment rate in the opposite direction from discouraged workers.
   - Unemployment of labor comes in four basic types: seasonal, frictional, structural, and cyclical.
   - Seasonal unemployment is related to the time of year. Examples include the department store Santa Claus without a job after Christmas, and the farm worker who becomes unemployed after the crop is harvested.
   - Frictional unemployment is associated with job switching and entry into the labor force. Frictional unemployment cannot be eliminated since, even though most job switches occur without unemployment time, there will always be some new jobs that cannot be lined up prior to departure from the old. Even when there is time between jobs, the frictionally

unemployed typically do not stay unemployed for long.
   - Structural unemployment occurs when job skills become obsolete. Without skills that are in demand in the labor market, the structurally unemployed will remain unemployed for an extended time. Job training programs can reduce structural unemployment.
   - Cyclical unemployment is associated with the business cycle. During recessions, workers are laid off and the unemployment rate rises accordingly.

5. **Track the stages of the business cycle.**
   - The business cycle refers to the expansions and contractions in economic activity that take place over time. In the expansion phase, real GDP rises. Real GDP reaches its maximum at the peak of any business cycle. During the recession phase, economic activity declines. Real GDP reaches its lowest level at the trough of the business cycle.
   - The leading economic indicators are various data series that are supposed to predict turning points in the business cycle. Since they do not always predict accurately, anyone using them to make decisions must proceed with caution.

6. **Identify the advantages and disadvantages of static and dynamic scoring.**
   - Static scoring and its opposite, dynamic scoring, are alternative methods for gauging the effects of a policy action taken by government. In contrast to dynamic scoring, static scoring assumes that policy changes have no macroeconomic effects. Dynamic scoring is potentially more accurate than static scoring, but also allows for more opportunities to manipulate predicted outcomes to match political preferences.

KEY TERMS

inflation, 264
price level, 264
inflation rate, 264
gross domestic product (GDP), 266
consumption spending, 266
investment, 266
gross investment, 267
net investment, 267
net domestic product (NDP), 267
net exports, 269
value added, 269

underground economy, 270
consumer price index (CPI), 274
GDP chained price index (GDP price index), 274
nominal value, 277
real value, 277
nominal GDP, 277
real GDP, 277
labor force, 278
unemployment rate, 278
discouraged workers, 279

frictional unemployment, 280
seasonal unemployment, 280
structural unemployment, 280
cyclical unemployment, 280
specific human capital, 281
general human capital, 281
business cycle, 282
recession, 282
leading economic indicators, 284

TEST YOURSELF

TRUE OR FALSE

1. Low unemployment is a widely accepted goal of macro policy.
2. The investment component of GDP includes spending on human capital.
3. Net exports equal about 5 percent of GDP.
4. A chained price index links quantities in one year to the next.
5. When real GDP decreases during the business cycle, the lowest point is called the peak.

MULTIPLE CHOICE

6. Applying the rule of seventy-two, it would take _____ years for GDP to double at a steady growth rate of 3 percent in GDP.
   a. 216
   b. 72
   c. 24
   d. 3
7. A loaf of french bread is used by a bakery to cut into croutons that are sold to Bridgette. The value of the loaf of french bread is not counted in GDP because it is a(n) _____ good. The value of the croutons are counted in GDP because they are a(n) _____ good.
   a. final; intermediate
   b. intermediate; final
   c. consumption; investment
   d. investment; consumption
8. The consumption spending portion of GDP includes
   a. durable goods, nondurable goods, and services.
   b. goods, services, and new houses.
   c. intermediate goods, but not final goods.
   d. about 90 percent of all production that occurs in the economy.
9. Gross investment equals
   a. net investment plus depreciation.
   b. investment adjusted for the effects of inflation.
   c. a negative component of GDP.
   d. the change in business inventories.
10. Net exports are computed as
    a. exports minus depreciation.
    b. exports minus imports.
    c. exports minus GDP.
    d. imports minus exports.
11. U.S. gross national product (GNP)
    a. is another name for gross domestic product (GDP).
    b. excludes net exports, since its purpose is to compute national consumption and investment.
    c. includes production by U.S. firms in other countries and excludes production by foreign firms in the United States.
    d. is no longer computed, having been replaced by GDP.
12. Per capita GDP is
    a. GDP minus net exports.
    b. GDP adjusted for inflation.
    c. GDP per person.
    d. computed by taking the legal output and the illegal output of the economy and adding them together.
13. How is the output of goods in the underground economy treated in the computation of GDP?
    a. They are difficult to measure accurately, but the government estimates their value and adjusts GDP to reflect that value.
    b. They are included in GDP as one of the components of investment.
    c. Government produces goods for the underground economy and, thus, they are included in the government purchases component of GDP.
    d. They are not counted.
14. The goods and services included in the computation of the consumer price index (CPI) are referred to as the _____
    a. base period.
    b. fixed weights.
    c. market basket.
    d. price level.
15. How is an inflation rate computed?
    a. The inflation rate equals the value of a price index.
    b. The inflation rate equals the change in the value of a price index.
    c. By the following computation: (change in price index/initial value of price index) multiplied by 100.
    d. By the following computation: change in price index multiplied by the initial value of the price index.
16. Using a price index, a real value is computed by
    a. multiplying a nominal value by the price index, and then dividing by 100.
    b. dividing a nominal value by the price index, and then multiplying by 100.
    c. averaging two nominal values.
    d. dividing the current nominal value by the base period nominal value.

17. Which type of unemployment is associated with technological change?
    a. Frictional.
    b. Seasonal.
    c. Structural.
    d. Cyclical.
18. Which type of unemployment is typically long term?
    a. Frictional.
    b. Seasonal.
    c. Structural.
    d. Cyclical.
19. If the real value of GDP decreases from one year to the next, it is most likely that
    a. inflation is a problem in the economy.
    b. real GNP is up.

c. consumption spending is down while government purchases are up.
d. the economy is in a recession.
20. The primary difference between static and dynamic scoring is that
    a. static scoring is legal but dynamic scoring is illegal.
    b. static scoring considers real values of variables, but dynamic scoring considers nominal values.
    c. static scoring is favored by Congress, but dynamic scoring is favored by the president.
    d. static scoring assumes that behavior does not change when policies change, but dynamic scoring allows for the possibility of behavioral changes.

QUESTIONS AND PROBLEMS

1. *[macro goals]* List the three primary macroeconomic goals and briefly discuss why the achievement of these goals is desirable.
2. *[macro goals]* After obtaining the most recent edition of the *Economic Report of the President* from your library or the Internet, compare the discussion of macroeconomic goals in this chapter with those discussed in the *Report*. Are all the goals mentioned in the chapter also in the *Report*?
3. *[final versus intermediate goods]* Explain why GDP excludes the value of intermediate goods, while including the value of final goods and services.
4. *[components of GDP]* Explain each of the four components of GDP. Include in your explanation answers to the following: (a) Is investment measured as gross or net? (b) Does the government component include transfer payments? (c) Which component has a negative value?
5. *[computing GDP]* Suppose you have the following information available to compute the GDP of the country of Traczania: Consumption spending = $150; Gross investment = $55; Net investment = $50; Government purchases = $75; Government transfer payments = $30; Imports = $25; Exports = $20. Compute Traczania's GDP.
6. *[GDP and the underground economy]* What is meant by the underground economy? Is the output of the underground economy counted in measuring GDP?

7. *[value added]* Jay Jones runs a small business out of his home, making bird houses from scrap lumber that he finds in dumpsters. Last year Jay sold $8,000 worth of his birdhouses to happy birdwatchers. How much value added did Jim contribute to GDP last year? Is the value added equal to spending by consumers on his birdhouses? Explain.
8. *[CPI base period]* Why does an understanding of the CPI require you to understand the base period concept?
9. *[CPI market basket]* Why does an understanding of the CPI require you to understand the concept of the market basket?
10. *[CPI]* Suppose that the CPI in year 5 equals 123 and in year 6 equals 130. What was the inflation rate in year 6?
11. *[real versus nominal values]* Three years ago Johnson earned $100 a week. Today he earns $125 a week. He would like to know whether his real income is higher today than it was three years ago. If the consumer price index increased from 150 to 175, has Johnson's real income risen, fallen, or remained the same? Explain.
12. *[labor force]* Can you think of a logical reason for excluding persons under the age of 16 from the labor force statistics, but not excluding persons over age 65 or even age 70 from the statistics? Explain.
13. *[unemployment rate]* How is the unemployment rate calculated? Are discouraged workers included?
14. *[types of unemployment]* List three instances when you or someone you know has been unemployed. For

each, explain the type of unemployment, such as frictional, seasonal, structural, or cyclical.

15. *[structural unemployment]* Explain the role of human capital in the ability of an individual to find and keep a job.

16. *[business cycle]* Illustrate graphically the stages of the business cycle. Be sure to include appropriate labels on the axes and on the curve you draw.

 Visit **www.prenhall.com/ayers** for Exploring the Web exercises and additional self-test quizzes.

CHAPTER 13

A FRAMEWORK FOR MACROECONOMIC ANALYSIS

A LOOK AHEAD

The twentieth century ended with a string of prosperous years for the United States economy. Productivity surged and unemployment fell to record lows. Because of its success, the economy faded into the background of our collective consciousness. Then, as the twenty-first century unfolded, productivity sagged and unemployment reared its ugly head. Business profits were slim, bankruptcies were up, and stock prices were down. People with their jobs on the line or their savings decimated by stock-market declines demanded action from the federal government. In response they got tax rebates and interest-rate cuts, but nothing seemed to help.

Then came the terrorist attacks of September 11, 2001. A war on terrorism was declared. Immediately, the stock market plunged and 100,000 people were laid off in the airline industry alone. The monthly unemployment rate jumped by ½ percent, the largest one-month leap in twenty-one years. Some urged the government to take action to shore up the economy. Others said it would be best to wait and let the economy take care of itself. This chapter frames these choices and the tradeoffs involved. The Explore & Apply section that concludes this chapter pays particular attention to the macroeconomic consequences of the war against terrorism.

LEARNING OBJECTIVES

Understanding Chapter 13 will enable you to:
1. **Contrast the perspectives of classical economists to those of Keynesians.**
2. **Describe how full-employment output can change.**
3. **Explain why the price level does not matter in the long run.**
4. **Interpret and apply the aggregate demand–aggregate supply model.**
5. **Relate the difference between demand-side and supply-side inflation in the long run.**
6. **Interpret how the war against terrorism can cause both inflation and lower output, and ways in which these effects might be countered.**

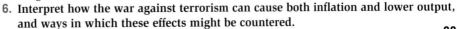

"Prior to 1929, kids had too much of everything. Then after the crash, they didn't have enough of anything. So they became too much concerned with economic problems. We began to think too much about sharing the wealth, instead of creating it. Youth should create something, and it should have something to create."

—*Perry Mason, by Earl Stanley Gardner, The Case of the Drowning Duck, 1942*

The above passage was written as America was preparing to enter World War II. Having endured a lingering depression for over a decade, the state of the U.S. economy was high on people's minds. Then World War II brought forth a massive civilian and military mobilization that brought with it a new resolve and new spending. After the war, the economic crisis was over and America prospered like never before. Unemployment fell from the 14.6 percent in 1940 (before the war) to 3.9 percent in 1946 (after the war had ended). The one and only Great Depression of the twentieth century was over.

In late summer of 2001, Americans were again troubled by a declining economy. Unemployment was under 5 percent, but up from its lows of under 4 percent. Stock prices had been in a jagged slide since March of the previous year. Business profits were squeezed and layoffs announced. Having lived comfortably for decades, U.S. citizens were not used to worrying about the overall economy, but that started to change.

Then came terrorist attacks that killed thousands of Americans. The Dow-Jones Industrial Average of stock prices reacted by falling nearly 15 percent in a single week, exceeded only by the 15.5 percent drop in 1933 during the depths of the Great Depression. Consumers held tight to their money and business investment was at a standstill. During October 2001, businesses cut their payrolls by 415,000 jobs, the largest one-month decline in over two decades. All at once, it seemed, everybody wanted to know what was to become of the economy. How did it work? What could be done?

13.1 KEYNESIAN SHORT-RUN AND CLASSICAL LONG-RUN PERSPECTIVES

long run involves underlying economic forces that make themselves felt over time.

short run a period of time during which the economy transitions to the long run.

Answering sweeping macroeconomic questions about employment, output, and inflation requires providing near-term events with a long-term perspective and context. This context is called the **long run,** which involves underlying economic forces that make themselves felt over time. For example, economic growth is a long-run consideration. In contrast, the **short run** represents more immediate and transitory economic developments, such as the increased unemployment in the months following the September 11 attacks. Much of the difference of opinion within the economics profession concerns how much weight to attach to short-run versus long-run outcomes. The issues are especially contentious when the policies that are best for long-run economic health come at the price of short-run problems.

KEYNESIAN AND CLASSICAL SCHOOLS OF THOUGHT

During the Great Depression of the 1930s, the biggest short-run problem was unemployment. It was against this backdrop that, in 1936, John Maynard Keynes authored *The General Theory of Employment, Interest, and Money.* In this path-breaking work, Keynes took issue with the mainstream of economic thinking at the time. Instead of accepting that government should sit back and wait for the economy to pull itself out of recession, he proposed ways in which government could actively manage the economy toward prosperity. Keynesian theory came to define the field of macroeconomics for nearly half a century. Before it, the field of macroeconomics did not even exist.

After the work of Keynes and the economic recovery seemingly brought about by the government spending of World War II, it appeared that government had a duty to shepherd the economy through times of economic distress. In the United States, that duty was embodied in the Employment Act of 1946. When the problem was too little spending and too few people employed, the government could go far toward solving the problem through spending more itself and giving its citizens incentives to do likewise. At the time, there seemed to be no macroeconomic tradeoffs in this course of action. As time progressed, however, efforts by the government to keep unemployment low started to cause the unwanted side effect of inflation in the 1960s and 1970s.

As a result, the emphasis in economics shifted away from short-run cures and toward looking for policies that would facilitate smooth long-run economic growth without significant inflation. From this perspective, government should not adjust its policies in order to promote spending when unemployment rises, but should rather provide the stability that allows the economy to adjust on its own.

Macroeconomic theory can be placed within either of two broad categories, depending on whether the emphasis is on short-run or long-run processes. These schools of thought are:

- **Keynesian,** which suggests that government action is an appropriate response to short-run macroeconomic problems.
- **Classical,** which suggests that a steady policy aimed at the long run best allows the economy to take care of itself.

Keynes himself was emphatic about the difference between these perspectives. He vigorously argued that the short run should be our focus because, as he put it, "In the long run we are all dead." Economists today commonly tap into both schools of thought, with their emphasis depending on the severity of short-run problems encountered. Later in this chapter, we will see how to use the models of aggregate demand and aggregate supply to provide the long-run framework of analysis. In the next few chapters, we will see how the framework can be developed to address short-run issues as well.

Keynesian a macroeconomic school of thought that emphasizes the short run and the importance of fiscal policy.

classical a macroeconomic school of thought that emphasizes the long run and reliance upon market forces to achieve full employment.

THE PHILLIPS CURVE—A MATTER OF INFLATIONARY EXPECTATIONS

Aggregate supply and aggregate demand analysis was motivated by the Phillips curve, named after British economist A.W. Phillips who first identified it. The **Phillips curve** is a graphical representation of data that, from the 1960s in the United States, depicted a distinct curvilinear tradeoff between low unemployment and low inflation, as seen in Figure 13-1. The evidence seemed so convincing that many economists at the time hailed the Phillips curve as a newly revealed fundamental truth.

By the end of the 1960s, the Phillips curve relationship was falling apart, as seen by the later data points in Figure 13-1. Data beyond the decade of the 1960s showed no systematic relationship between unemployment and inflation. The Phillips curve is now viewed as a

Phillips curve a graphical representation of data from the 1960s in the United States that shows a curvilinear tradeoff between low unemployment and low inflation.

QUICKCHECK

What is the essential difference between the Keynesian view and the classical view of the economy?

Answer: Keynesians emphasize the importance of the short run, while classical economists emphasize the importance of the long run.

FIGURE 13-1

THE PHILLIPS CURVE The Phillips curve showed a tight, inverse relationship between inflation and unemployment in U.S. data from the 1960s. In later decades, though, the relationship no longer held true.

Source: 2002 Economic Report of the President, Tables B-42 and B-43.

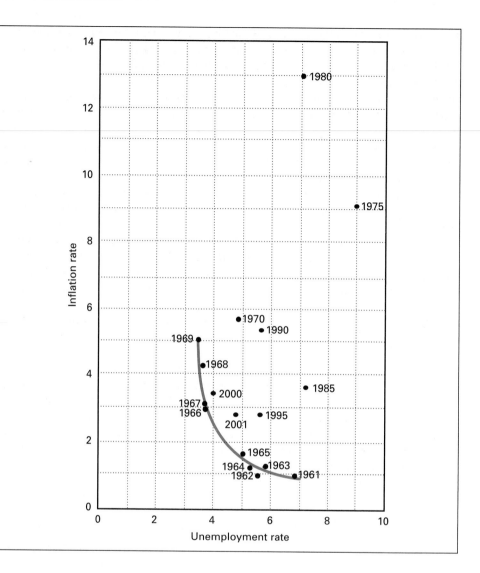

inflationary expectations predictions about future inflation that people factor into their current behavior.

adaptive expectations when people form expectations as to future prices according to what their experiences have been in the past.

short-run phenomenon that did not hold up in the long run. The reason is thought to revolve around how people form their expectations.

Whether we are particularly conscious of it or not, we each have **inflationary expectations,** meaning expectations about how much higher or lower prices will be in the future. For example, if we think that we are going to be paying less for everything later on, we might be willing to accept a wage cut. If we think we will be paying more for everything later on, however, we might demand a wage increase.

There are two ways for people to form their inflationary expectations. One way is through **adaptive expectations,** where we form our expectations about future prices according to our past experiences. So if the price level goes up at a rate of 2 percent per year, we would expect inflation of 2 percent to continue on into the future. If prices rise or fall in a manner inconsistent with the past, adaptive expectations could lead to our being fooled and slow to adjust our wage demands.

For example, a big new government spending program might add to both GDP and inflationary pressures in the short run before people catch on. In the 1960s, government spending in the United States did increase significantly in response to the Vietnam War and President Lyndon Johnson's Great Society social programs. The prolonged period of time in which the public was apparently tricked by unexpectedly high inflation suggests that the public was basing its expectations on what it had previously experienced rather than forming its opinions based on current policy actions. With a U.S. economy characterized by adaptive expectations in the 1960s, increased government spending would cause lower unemployment and higher inflation, exactly what was shown by the Phillips curve of the time.

By the 1970s, people and businesses had learned to factor the effects of inflation into their personal and business plans. Government could no longer inflate its way to lower unemployment. This limitation on government's ability to manage the economy was shown by the combination of high inflation and unemployment—**stagflation**—experienced in that decade. People had learned to predict more accurately the impacts of public policy.

stagflation the combination of high inflation and unemployment.

These days, public policy is unlikely to succeed if it depends on assuming that government knows more than participants in the marketplace. With the instant communications of the modern world, people are more likely to have **rational expectations** in which they correctly predict the implications of government policy action and thus cannot be systematically tricked. With rational expectations, we keep up with the news analyses and base our expectations on the best information available to us. Public policies that have been debated in Congress, commented on by the media, and passed into law are not likely to surprise us.

rational expectations when we base our expectations upon the best information available to us.

The rise of rational expectations explains the demise of the Phillips curve relationship of the 1960s. In those years, government actions that caused inflation also caused people to work more because they didn't recognize that inflation. People at the time were tricked by higher wages into working more. They later came to understand that the higher wages were only in nominal terms, not in real terms, because prices were rising to match. From then on, it became standard practice for workers to compare wage increases to their expected cost-of-living increases. The more experience they had with being surprised, the more attention they paid to inflation predictions in the media.

If people have rational expectations, government policy that is intended to stimulate the economy will have no predictable effect. In other words, the best guess is that policy actions will not change the economy much in either direction. The idea of rational expectations provides support to the classical argument that government should step back and let the macroeconomy take care of itself.

BUDDY, CAN YOU SPARE A THEORY?   *SNAPSHOT*

"Buddy, can you spare a dime?" The mood of the Great Depression was somehow captured in that poignant refrain. There just didn't seem to be enough spending to keep everyone working. So thought Keynes when, at the height of the Depression, he came out with what became known as the Keynesian theory. In short, if people weren't spending enough, the government should bridge the gap with spending of its own. So spend on the Civilian Conservation Corps, spend on the Works Progress Administration, spend on just about anything, and help beat the Depression!

Classical economists disagree, contending that it was time and not government spending that spelled the demise of the Great Depression in the 1940s. Some might say, "Something worked so why argue about it now?" The answer is not for the sake of the past, but is for the future. Hashing out how best to keep the economy humming and out of depression is what macroeconomic theory is all about. It's about not having to ask a stranger for a dime. ◄

13.2 MODELING THE LONG RUN WITH AGGREGATE SUPPLY AND AGGREGATE DEMAND

full-employment output (full-employment GDP) the real GDP the economy produces when it fully employs its resources.

A fundamental goal for the economy is to achieve **full-employment output,** also termed **full-employment GDP,** which is the real GDP the economy produces when it fully employs its resources. At any given point in time, actual output can be either above or below the amount associated with the full-employment amount. For example, in times of unemployment, actual output would fall short of full-employment output.

THE NATURAL RATE OF UNEMPLOYMENT

In countries around the globe, unemployment rates average significantly closer to zero than to 100 percent. This is no coincidence. People look for ways to work because work puts food on the table. Even in the Great Depression of the 1930s, unemployment in the United States never exceeded 25 percent of the work force, and was as high as 20 percent for only four years, 1932–1935. Given that income is critical to living, however, it does not take many percentage points of unemployment to cause severe human trauma. The Great Depression was proof of the misery that high unemployment can bring.

Over time, the unemployment rate does not tend toward zero, exactly. Rather, the tendency is for unemployment to settle at a few percentage points above zero, due to the inevitable presence of seasonal, frictional, and structural unemployment. The minimum sustainable level of unemployment is termed the **natural rate of unemployment,** and is thought to be around 5 percent of the U.S. work force today.

natural rate of unemployment the minimum sustainable level of unemployment; associated with zero cyclical unemployment.

The economy would tend toward a lower natural rate in the absence of unemployment insurance and other social *safety net* programs, such as Medicaid, food stamps, and additional programs designed to cushion the impact of unemployment or poverty. Without the safety net, the unemployed would be subject to greater misery, and a correspondingly greater incentive to grasp at any job offer, without regard to its long-term consequences for their future prospects. From an employer's perspective, minimum wage laws, liability laws, and many other policies discourage job formation because of the cost of complying with them. Other government policies, such as employment-related tax breaks for businesses, can have the opposite effect. Thus, government policies can and do affect the level of employment. Because of government actions, it is likely that the natural rate of unemployment has risen from a little over 2 percent a century ago to somewhere in the vicinity of 5 percent today.

full employment 100 percent minus the natural rate of unemployment.

The flip side of the natural rate of unemployment is **full employment,** which equals 100 percent minus the natural rate of unemployment. Because the natural rate of unemployment exceeds zero, full employment occurs when the employment rate is less than 100 percent. In short, economies will always have people who are looking for jobs.

QUICKCHECK

What are some reasons that the natural rate of unemployment is higher today than it was a century ago?

Answer: Unlike a century ago, the out-of-work today need not fear starvation or resort to private charity. Unemployment compensation, food stamps, and other programs provide a safety net that removes some of the urgency about finding a job right away. Another reason is structural unemployment caused by minimum wage laws, laws that did not exist a century ago.

The economy can temporarily exceed full-employment output if workers accept over-time, work more than one job, or find new jobs exceptionally quickly. Whether actual GDP is above or below full-employment GDP, **the existence of a natural rate of unemployment implies that the long-run tendency is toward full-employment GDP.**

For most of its history, the U.S. economy has been successful at living up to its poten-tial. In other words, actual GDP has been in the vicinity of *potential GDP*, which is the amount that we can expect the economy to achieve at full employment. This history is shown in Figure 13-2.

Periods of unemployment in which actual GDP falls short of potential GDP represent transition times in a market economy—the time markets take to adjust to their market-clearing equilibriums. During these times, there is a surplus of workers in the labor market. As they compete for jobs, workers drive down wages until the labor surplus is absorbed. In response to lower labor costs, competition forces output prices to fall, too. These wage and price adjustments reflect supply and demand in action in the many markets that make up the economy as a whole. These adjustments can take time, however, the significance of which forms the crux of the debate between classical and Keynesian economists.

LONG-RUN AGGREGATE SUPPLY

The economy supplies full-employment output in the long run, no matter the price level, as shown by the **long-run aggregate supply** in Figure 13-3(a). Because the price level is irrel-evant to the potential for full-employment output, **long-run aggregate supply is always vertical.** The logic is the same as the logic behind the natural rate of unemployment. Specifically, **in the long run, the desire of people to receive income pushes unemploy-ment down toward its natural rate and leads to full-employment output.**

The vertical long-run aggregate supply curve means that the same quantity of real GDP will be produced whether the price level is low, high, or in-between. In other words, the price level does not make a difference in determining the full-employment level of GDP. As evidence that the price level does not matter in the long run, consider that the price level today is quadruple that of the late 1960s. However, market wages have also adjusted upward. Other than requiring that we earn and spend about four times as much to obtain the same goods and services, the rise in wages and prices has had little long-run significance for the aggregate economy.

Over time, long-run aggregate supply shifts in response to changes in the amount of resources available to the economy and in the technology available to use these resources. For example, warfare or natural disasters could destroy resources, which would reduce full-employment output and shift aggregate supply to the left, as shown in Figure 13-3(a).

More commonly, economies add resources and improve technology over time. The result is economic growth that increases full-employment output and thus shifts long-run aggregate supply to the right, as shown in Figure 13-3(b).

AGGREGATE DEMAND

Aggregate supply reveals how much real GDP the economy has to offer, whatever the price level. To understand what the price level will be requires that we look beyond the supply side of the economy. Therefore, we examine the demand side, using the concept of **aggregate demand,** which tells us how much real GDP consumers, businesses, and govern-ment would purchase at each price level.

In the microeconomy, a demand curve reveals the quantity of a good or service that would be purchased at each of various possible prices. For example, as the price of Pepsi rises, the quantity demanded falls because consumers substitute Coca-Cola and other

long-run aggregate supply the idea that, in the long run, the price level does not affect the amount of GDP the economy produces; graphically, long-run aggregate supply is vertical at full-employment GDP.

aggregate demand relates how much real GDP consumers, businesses, and government will purchase at each price level; graphically, aggregate demand slopes downward.

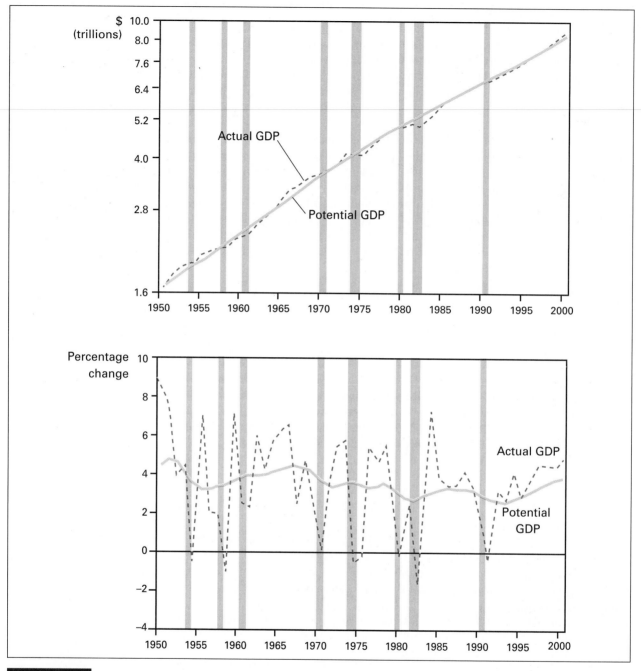

FIGURE 13-2

ACTUAL AND POTENTIAL GDP Over time and with some short-run zigs and zags, actual real GDP in the United States has generally been close to the economy's full-employment potential. The upper graph shows actual and potential GDP in trillions of dollars. The lower graph shows the percentage change in both. Actual GDP is seen to be more volatile than potential GDP.

Source: Congressional Budget Office, 2001, using data from the Department of Commerce, Bureau of Economic Analysis.

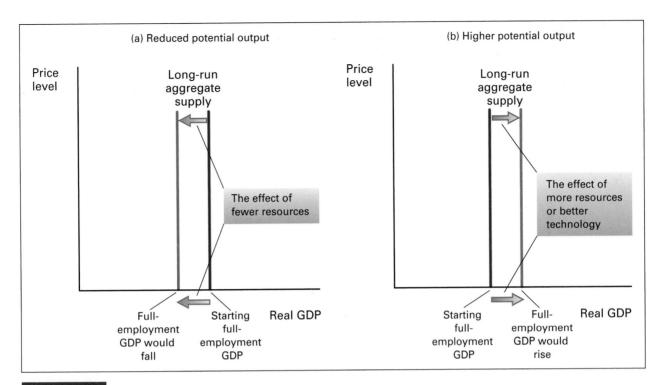

FIGURE 13-3

LONG-RUN AGGREGATE SUPPLY Long-run aggregate supply is graphed as a vertical line at full-employment GDP, which implies that the price level does not affect an economy's potential output in the long run. As shown in (a), a loss of resources reduces full-employment output and shifts aggregate demand to the left. Conversely, as shown in (b), long-run aggregate supply shifts to the right over time as the economy acquires greater resources and better technology that increase the amount of output produced at full employment.

QUICKCHECK

What would be the effect on long-run aggregate supply of an earthquake that destroys an economy's productive capacity? Why?

Answer: The long-run aggregate supply would shift to the left. This movement shows that, even if the country's work force is fully employed, there would be less output.

beverages. In the event of a general inflation in the prices of all goods and services, though, consumers can no longer merely substitute away from products whose prices have risen. Yet consumers can no longer buy as much as before either, because the inflation has eroded their wealth and the purchasing power of their income. So, in the overall economy, an increase in the price level will also cut back the aggregate quantities that consumers purchase.

Likewise, a decrease in the price level will increase aggregate purchases. The reason is twofold. First, at a lower price level, money buys more goods and services. In other words, even if all of us continue to spend the same amount of money, a lower price level causes the real GDP we purchase to be greater. Second, a lower price level increases the inflation-adjusted value of money and personal savings. When people think that they have more wealth, they spend more of their current income.

FIGURE 13-4

AGGREGATE DEMAND Aggregate demand slopes downward, which illustrates that a lower price level increases both the purchasing power of current income and the value of savings.

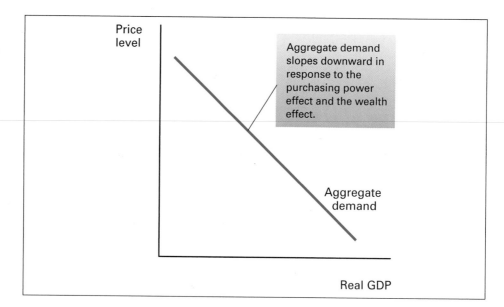

The two effects of a price level change are summed up as follows:

purchasing power effect the effect of the price level on consumers' ability to buy goods and services.

wealth effect the change in the fraction of current income spent caused by a price-level change affecting the real value of savings.

- **Purchasing power effect:** A lower price level allows consumers to receive more goods and services for any given number of dollars they spend. A higher price level means consumers receive fewer goods and services for any given number of dollars they spend.
- **Wealth effect:** A lower price level causes consumers to spend more of their current incomes because the lower price level increases the value of their savings. Conversely, a higher price level would reduce the real value of savings and lead consumers to spend less out of current income.

Both the purchasing power effect and the wealth effect cause an inverse relationship between the price level and the quantity of GDP demanded. Thus, **aggregate demand slopes down** as shown in Figure 13-4.

THE FULL-EMPLOYMENT EQUILIBRIUM

full-employment equilibrium the long-run macroeconomic equilibrium that occurs at a full-employment output.

Figure 13-5 shows a downward-sloping aggregate demand curve, along with a vertical long-run aggregate supply. The intersection of these two curves represents a long-run macroeconomic equilibrium, termed the **full-employment equilibrium** because it occurs at the full-

QUICKCHECK

The lower the price of movies, the more movies you choose to see, according to the law of demand. Would this behavior be different if prices were to fall in the same proportion throughout the economy?

Answer: When the price of movies drops but other prices remain constant, consumers substitute movies for other forms of entertainment. That substitution effect of a price change would not occur if all prices dropped simultaneously. However, if the general price level falls, the purchasing power of your income increases and so you might watch more movies because of the purchasing power effect. You also feel wealthier and so might watch more movies on account of the wealth effect.

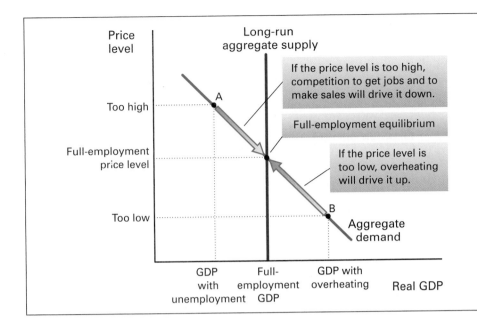

Price level

Long-run aggregate supply

If the price level is too high, competition to get jobs and to make sales will drive it down.

Too high — A

Full-employment equilibrium

Full-employment price level

If the price level is too low, overheating will drive it up.

Too low — B

Aggregate demand

GDP with unemployment   Full-employment GDP   GDP with overheating   Real GDP

FIGURE 13-5

THE LONG-RUN MACRO EQUILIBRIUM The long-run macroeconomic equilibrium occurs where aggregate demand intersects long-run aggregate supply. Competition prevents the price level from remaining either too high or too low, resulting in a movement along the aggregate demand curve until full employment is reached.

For example, the high price level at point *A* on aggregate demand is associated with unemployment. As workers compete to get jobs, they drive down wages and production costs. Competition then forces down prices. In contrast, at point *B*, there are not enough workers to produce all the output people want to buy. Competition drives up wages and prices, a condition known as overheating.

employment output. The figure labels both the full-employment equilibrium and the price level that supports it.

At any price level above the full-employment price level, aggregate spending will be insufficient to support full-employment output. Unemployed workers will compete for jobs, which will drive down wages. Competition in the output market will force firms to lower prices in response to these lower wages. The lower price level that results means that spending will buy more output and thus lead to greater employment. The process continues until the economy reaches full employment and the corresponding full-employment GDP, as shown in Figure 13-5.

If the actual price level were below the equilibrium shown in Figure 13-5, the economy would "overheat," with aggregate purchasing power exceeding the economy's ability to produce. Firms would compete for workers, thus driving their wages up. Competitive firms would pass on these higher wages to consumers by raising their prices. The resulting increase in the price level would soak up the excess purchasing power, thus leading the economy back to its long-run equilibrium.

A STORY TOLD IN A MILLION WAYS   *SNAPSHOT*

If products linger on the shopkeeper's shelf, the prices eventually get lowered to clear the inventory. If you can't find a job with the skills you have, you eventually acquire new ones. If no one will pay you what you ask, you eventually lower your salary expectations. However, if the headhunters are beating at your door with salary offers that you just can't pass up, then you demand a higher salary where you are or switch jobs.

These are stories told over and over for millions of people and products all across the land. Put together, it is nothing more than the economy heading toward full-employment output at an equilibrium price level. But the stories of how to get there are told in ways that are unique to the circumstances of the individuals and firms involved. Each and every story is significant—they are the micro behind the macro of economics. ◀

13.3 ROOT CAUSES OF INFLATION

To fight or prevent inflation, policymakers must identify the source. This section shows how the model of aggregate supply and aggregate demand can help by distinguishing between demand-side and supply-side causes of inflation. This distinction also has implications in regard to full-employment output.

demand-side inflation occurs when aggregate demand shifts to the right. The result is a movement up the long-run aggregate supply curve to a higher price level, but no change in full-employment output.

demand-side deflation occurs when aggregate demand shifts to the left. The result is a movement down the long-run aggregate supply curve to a lower price level, but no change in full-employment output.

DEMAND-SIDE INFLATION AND DEFLATION

Aggregate demand tends to increase—shift to the right—over time. This shift occurs in response to general growth in purchasing power as consumer spending increases, government spending increases, or, most generally, as more money circulates throughout the economy. The effect of an outward shift in aggregate demand is shown in Figure 13-6(a). *Ceteris paribus,* in the long run, the effect is to keep output the same and increase the price level. This effect is known as **demand-side inflation.**

Alternatively, if aggregate demand were to shift to the left, the effect would be **demand-side deflation** as shown in Figure 13-6(b). Demand-side deflation is not common, but can have significant disruptive effects when it happens. Many economists point to the difficulties of adjusting to a lower price level as being a root cause of the Great Depression.

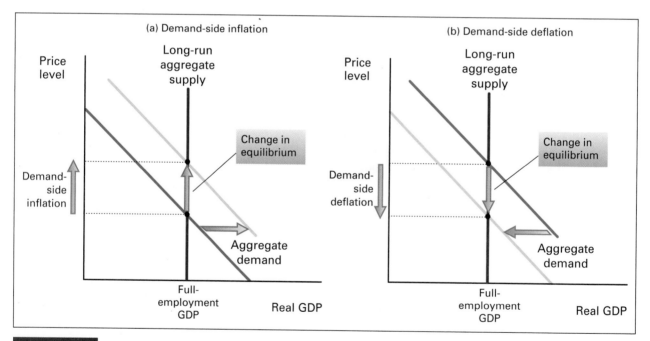

FIGURE 13-6

DEMAND-SIDE INFLATION AND DEFLATION Aggregate demand shifts to the right in response to increased government spending or increased spending by consumers, as shown in (a). The equilibrium price level increases, a result known as demand-side inflation. Spending might increase in response to an increase in the amount of money circulating in the economy.

Aggregate demand shifts to the left when there is less money circulating, such as when the government collects more tax revenue or when consumers are fearful and inclined to hoard cash. The leftward shift in aggregate demand pushes the price level down, resulting in demand-side deflation as shown in (b).

QUICKCHECK

Would the economy be better off if the government were to declare that all incomes shall henceforth be doubled? Use aggregate supply and aggregate demand analysis to support your answer.

Answer: If the economy is working up to its potential, then doubling everyone's income could not increase output, but would rather cause demand-side inflation that increases prices to offset the increased wages. With everyone having more money to spend, aggregate demand would shift to the right. The economy would move to a new long-run equilibrium at the same output and a higher price level.

SUPPLY-SIDE INFLATION AND DEFLATION

Changes on the supply side of the economy can also cause either inflation or deflation. If long-run aggregate supply were to shift to the left, we would see **supply-side inflation** in which the same amount of spending is able to buy fewer goods at higher prices. Supply-side inflation is shown in Figure 13-7(a). Note that full-employment GDP decreases as long-run aggregate supply shifts to the left.

supply-side inflation occurs when long-run aggregate supply shifts to the left. The result is a movement up the aggregate demand curve to a higher price level and lower full-employment output.

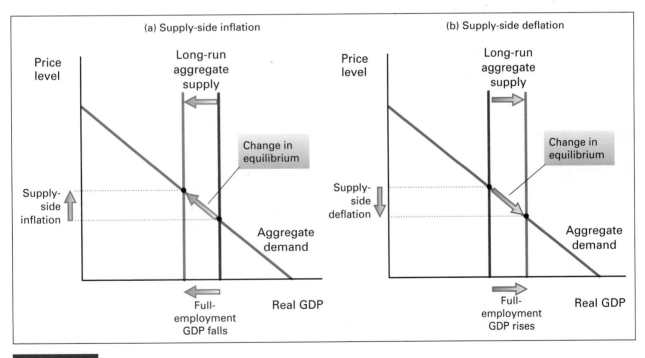

FIGURE 13-7

SUPPLY-SIDE INFLATION AND DEFLATION IN THE LONG RUN A leftward shift in long-run aggregate supply causes supply-side inflation, as shown in (a). Although unemployment remains unchanged, output falls and the price level rises. Explanations for this shift could include the destruction of resources in warfare or government restrictions on business practices.

In contrast, technological change or additional resources would shift aggregate supply to the right, resulting in supply-side deflation. In that case, without changing employment, output would rise and the price level would fall as shown in (b).

supply shock an unexpected event that is major enough to affect the overall economy; shifts aggregate supply.

real business cycle when GDP rises or falls in response to major events that cannot be foreseen.

One possible source of supply-side inflation is a **supply shock,** which is an unexpected event that is major enough to affect the overall economy. Supply shocks, such as caused by wars or natural disasters, cause real changes in productive capacity. The terrorist attacks of September 11 caused a supply shock, the economic effects of which are discussed in this chapter's Explore & Apply section. Supply shocks are behind what is called the **real business cycle,** in which GDP rises or falls in response to major events that cannot be foreseen. Although we don't know what the shocks will be, we can be pretty sure that additional shocks will occur.

Aggregate supply might alternatively shift to the left in response to a change in the laws governing business practices within a country. Recent years have witnessed a number of laws and lawsuits that have changed the way firms can operate. Most notably, firms have seen their production costs increase in response to higher indirect employee costs, higher costs of complying with government regulations, and higher legal costs. Ongoing technological improvements that increase productivity can mask these effects.

supply-side deflation occurs when long-run aggregate supply shifts to the right. The result is a movement down the aggregate demand curve to a lower price level and higher full-employment output.

On the bright side, technological change or an increase in resources increases the output associated with full employment. The result is a rightward shift in long-run aggregate supply. For example, the advent of e-commerce opened up possibilities for on-line shopping that have increased competition. It has also opened up possibilities for on-line payment methods that have reduced the costs of making transactions. As aggregate supply shifts to the right, the economy moves down the aggregate demand curve to a lower equilibrium price level. This process is called **supply-side deflation,** and is associated with an increase in full-employment GDP, as shown in Figure 13-7(b).

SNAPSHOT   ## THE REAL BUSINESS CYCLE—SOME SHOCKING SURPRISES

Cars, wars, oil cartels, computers, and earthquakes may not seem to have much in common, but they do. They have all shocked the economy in one way or another. How could ordinary citizens have foreseen the potential of the auto or the carnage of World War II? We did not know of the oil crisis of the 1970s before it happened, and we did not know that it would disappear in the 1980s. Nor can we know the extent to which technology will alter our lifestyles or when the next big earthquake will strike.

All of these things and more jolt the economy, either to make it more productive or to knock it back a notch. They represent real changes in aggregate supply to which businesses and individuals must adjust. Policymakers can predict these events no better than the rest of us, and so can do little to avert these disruptions to the smooth path of economic growth. When it comes to the real business cycle, then, it is best to expect the unexpected! ◄

13.4 CLASSICAL VERSUS KEYNESIAN—THE GREAT DEBATE

This chapter started with reference to the Great Depression, which was ended by World War II and the massive government spending associated with it. Keynesian analysis was thought to have been proven correct. As President Richard Nixon phrased it in 1972, "We are all Keynesians, now." However, just as Nixon was proclaiming that Keynes had won, the economics profession was focusing in a more classical direction. It began to emphasize its microeconomic foundations, such as incentives facing individuals and firms that can influence the performance of the overall economy.

Economic analysis influences people's politics and vice versa. For example, political liberals often adopt Keynesian policy prescriptions. The reason is presumably not because most liberals have studied the economy in detail and are convinced of the validity of the

Keynesian economic model. More likely, political liberals tend to believe that an activist government can be a powerful force for good in the world. Keynesian economics calls for government to be just such a force. It provides justification for a large government, but leaves open specific categories of spending.

A similar analysis applies to political conservatives, who tend to adhere to a classical perspective on the role of government. Conservatives usually distrust big government, preferring instead a more laissez-faire approach. Classical analysis suggests that much government action does more harm than good to the macroeconomy, which is in keeping with the conservative perspective.

While some controversy in macroeconomics is positive, concerning factual issues of cause and effect, most disagreement among macroeconomists is normative. For example, modern Keynesian models incorporate classical analysis of the long run. What makes these economists and their models Keynesian is that they discount the significance of the long run, preferring instead to emphasize practical issues in the workplace that inhibit adjustments to full employment. Thus, the disagreement between modern Keynesians and classical economists often boils down to the degrees to which they are willing to trade off short- and long-run objectives.

13.5 FIGHTING TERRORISM—WHAT PRICE DOES THE ECONOMY PAY?

"The world is not ending."

—New York Mayor Rudy Giuliani after the September 11 terrorist attack

On September 11, 2001, hijackers turned four passenger airliners into terrorist bombs, demolishing the World Trade Center skyscrapers in New York City and destroying a portion of the Pentagon in Washington, D.C. One of the hijacked planes crashed in rural Pennsylvania. About three thousand people lost their lives from these attacks. Immediately, before any more hijackings could be committed, the U.S. Federal Aviation Authority grounded all planes until security could be tightened. It was only when expensive and time-consuming security measures were in place that planes resumed flying. The country prepared for war, the war against terrorism.

No one could know at the time just what would lie ahead. One thing was certain, however, and that was the addition of tighter security throughout the country. The added security measures meant that it became more expensive to do business. The security industry prospered, as demand and prices went up in that line of business. However, numerous other industries suffered as they faced higher costs of production and slower deliveries of their raw materials.

The added costs for security services cause an increase in the real costs of producing the final goods and services recorded in GDP. The economy's limited resources are thus not capable of producing as much final output, meaning that full-employment output falls. Note that full employment itself remains the same, but the output associated with it is less. The result is a shift to the left in the long-run aggregate supply curve, as shown in Figure 13-8, which leads to a new full-employment equilibrium at a higher price level and a lower level of output.

This shift can be moderated or even completely offset by advances in technology that increase productivity. For example, advances in monitoring and scanning cameras can reduce the need for security personnel, freeing them up to be productive in other ways. More generally, technology is applied to the workplace in order to increase productivity. To the extent it does so, the effect is to increase full-employment output and shift aggregate supply to the right, which is exactly opposite to the changes shown in Figure 13-8.

FIGURE 13-8

SUPPLY-SIDE EFFECTS OF TERRORISM The war on terrorism causes firms to spend more on security, which takes resources that could otherwise produce final goods and services. For this reason, the output associated with full employment decreases and shifts long-run aggregate supply to the left. The macroequilibrium adjusts from A to B, reflecting a higher price level and less output. Either an increase in full employment during wartime or the adoption of improved technologies holds the potential to offset these effects.

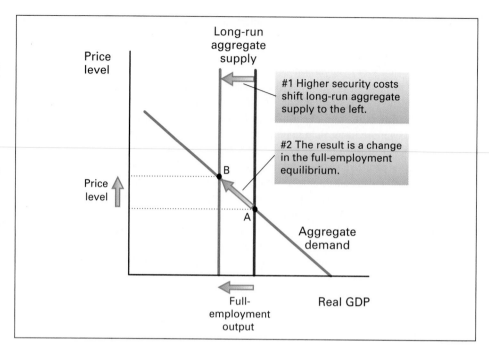

Other influences might also shift aggregate supply to the right. Looking back to World War II, we find that patriotism led to far more hours of work from the general population than was the norm either before or after the war. In effect, wartime full employment was higher than peacetime full employment. Taken by itself, the result was an increase in long-run aggregate supply.

HOW TERRORISM AFFECTS DEMAND

The 2001 terrorist attacks also had a significant effect on the demand side of the economy. The shock and uncertainty caused businesses to postpone new investment and consumers to postpone new purchases. For a while, it seemed everyone was hanging tight to their money and not allowing it to circulate as rapidly as it previously had. Airlines, hotels, amusement parks, and cruise ships all begged for customers. Some went bankrupt. Hundreds of thousands of Americans lost their jobs and millions more worried about their job security. The result was a leftward shift in aggregate demand. In other words, for any given price level, less output was demanded, as shown in Figure 13-9.

Taken by itself, this leftward shift in aggregate demand would have the effect of pushing prices lower, as shown. Before the price level would have a chance to adjust downward, output would fall and unemployment would rise. Were aggregate demand and aggregate supply both shifting left simultaneously, however, their influences would tend to offset each other in regard to price. Therefore, only output would fall.

There was considerable question following the September 2001 attacks as to how long it would take for consumers to resume their former patterns of spending. The answer was significant in terms of what the government should do. In particular, the government was not only spending additional money to combat the terrorists, but was also taking actions to lower borrowing costs and increase the amount of money circulating in the economy. The idea was to offset any drop in aggregate demand.

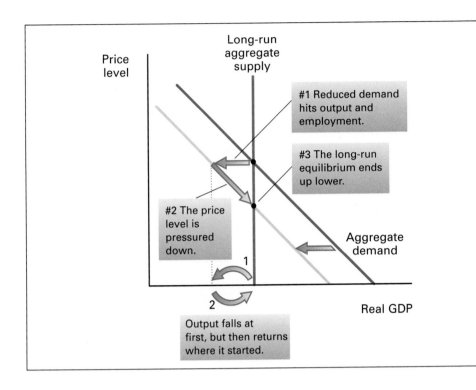

Price level

Long-run aggregate supply

#1 Reduced demand hits output and employment.

#3 The long-run equilibrium ends up lower.

#2 The price level is pressured down.

1

Aggregate demand

2

Real GDP

Output falls at first, but then returns where it started.

FIGURE 13-9

DEMAND-SIDE EFFECTS OF TERRORISM If the threat of terror makes people more cautious about spending, aggregate demand would shift to the left. The result would be:
#1 Firms throughout the economy would be unable to sell all of their output. Unemployment would rise and output would fall at first.
#2 To sell unsold output, firms would lower prices and the price level would fall.
#3 Output would return to the full-employment output once the price level adjusts to a new equilibrium.

The aggregate demand shift would be avoided if government's extra wartime spending exactly offsets the spending slowdown in the private sector, or as people return to their previous spending habits.

While intended to merely offset a drop in aggregate demand, such government actions ran the risk of going too far and actually increasing aggregate demand above what it had been before, particularly once the initial fears subsided and people returned to more normal spending patterns. If aggregate demand were to increase, demand-side inflation would be the result, as shown in Figure 13-10(a). Figure 13-10(b) shows how the situation could easily get out of hand, with demand-side inflation adding to supply-side inflation, causing the economy to move from point A to point B, and on to point C in the figure. This situation is stagflation, in which output falls even as prices rise.

In response to the war against terrorism, there are also additional real and important macroeconomic consequences that lie hidden beneath the surface of the aggregate demand/aggregate supply model. For example, for the purposes of this model, it does not matter whether GDP is composed of military spending that we wish was unnecessary or spending on consumer goods and services that would be the alternative in peacetime. It matters to our standard of living, but we do not see these things in the aggregate economic analysis.

1. Identify some additional effects of the war on terrorism that would shift aggregate supply or aggregate demand.

2. What could cause wartime full employment to exceed peacetime full employment? Give some examples from the United States' actual wartime experience.

Visit **www.prenhall.com/collinge** for updates and web exercises on this Explore & Apply topic.

*T*HINKING
*C*RITICALLY

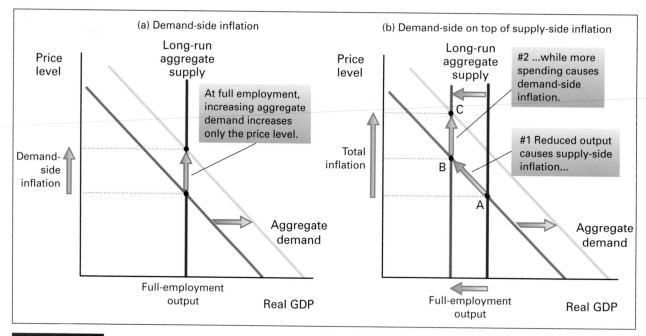

FIGURE 13-10

A DOUBLE DOSE OF INFLATION Graph (a) shows the demand-side inflation that could occur if government spending rises dramatically while the economy is already at full employment. The macro equilibrium would rise as shown. The higher government spending might reflect the costs of fighting a war, or merely the costs of tax and spending programs intended to offset an economic downturn.

The demand-side inflation might follow an initial supply-side inflation from higher costs of security and transportation. In graph (b), the leftward shift in long-run aggregate supply causes supply-side inflation. Because the economy is unable to produce as much output as previously, it moves up the aggregate demand curve from point *A* to point *B*. Then, if government steps in with additional purchases that increase aggregate demand, the economy experiences further inflation as it moves up the long-run aggregate supply curve from point *B* to point *C*. The combined effect is a double dose of inflation.

SUMMARY AND LEARNING OBJECTIVES

1. **Contrast the perspectives of classical economists to those of Keynesians.**

   ■ When the economy's resources are fully employed, the economy has attained full-employment output, also called full-employment GDP. Actual GDP could be at, above, or below the full-employment level of GDP.

   ■ The book *The General Theory of Employment, Interest, and Money* (1936) by John Maynard Keynes revolutionized economics and launched the new field of macroeconomics. Keynes distinguished between the short run and the long run, observing that "In the long run we are all dead." Keynesian economics takes a short-run perspective. Keynes's goal was to further the understanding of why the economies of the world remained mired in the Great Depression of the 1930s.

   ■ Classical economics emphasizes the long run. The long-run tendency in the marketplace is toward the

   natural rate of unemployment and its associated output. That is the classical focus, but the process takes time. The reason for this tendency is rooted in the desire of people to receive income.

2. **Describe how full-employment output can change.**

   ■ Full-employment output changes each time the long-run aggregate supply curve shifts.

   ■ Long-run aggregate supply shifts in response to changes in the amount of resources and in the technology available to use these resources. Warfare or natural disasters could destroy resources, which would reduce full-employment output and shift aggregate supply to the left. More commonly, economies add resources and improve technology over time. The result is economic growth that increases full-employment output.

3. **Explain why the price level does not matter in the long run.**

   ■ As evidence that the price level does not matter in the long run, consider that the price level today is quadruple that of the late 1960s. However, market wages have also adjusted upward. Other than requiring that we earn and spend about four times as much to obtain the same goods and services, the rise in wages and prices has had little long-run significance for the aggregate economy.

4. **Interpret and apply the aggregate demand–aggregate supply model.**

   ■ The determination of real output, inflation, and employment is shown with the model of aggregate demand and aggregate supply.

   ■ The long-run aggregate supply curve is vertical at full employment. It will only shift as the economy's productive capacity changes. That shift will be outward as productive capacity increases.

   ■ The aggregate demand curve is downward sloping because a lower price level will increase the purchasing power of money and prompt people to spend more, the so-called purchasing power effect. The aggregate demand curve also slopes downward to the right because of the wealth effect. The wealth effect is the increase in the real value of savings that accompanies a lower price level.

   ■ The long-run macroeconomic equilibrium is termed the full-employment equilibrium. It occurs at the point where the aggregate demand curve intersects the long-run aggregate supply curve. This equilibrium involves both full-employment output and a full-employment price level.

   ■ When the price level is higher than the full-employment price level, the economy will experience unemployment and actual GDP will be less than full-employment GDP. The economy's tendency to adjust to full employment requires that the price level drop.

   ■ When the price level is lower than the full-employment price level, the economy will overheat. Aggregate demand will be greater than long-run aggregate supply and actual GDP will exceed the full-employment level. Overheating causes the price level to adjust upward. Along with a higher price level will come a decrease in actual GDP back to its full-employment level.

5. **Relate the difference between demand-side and supply-side inflation in the long run.**

   ■ Increases in aggregate spending, such as those caused by additional consumer and government spending, shift aggregate demand outward and lead to demand-side inflation. Demand-side deflation would accompany a leftward shift in aggregate demand.

   ■ Inflation and deflation can also arise from shifts in the long-run aggregate supply curve. An outward shift in long-run aggregate supply leads to supply-side deflation. A leftward shift in long-run aggregate supply leads to supply-side inflation.

   ■ Structural changes in the economy influence inflation and deflation. An increase in the natural rate of unemployment will occur when legislation and other forces make it more difficult for employers to hire workers and for workers to switch jobs. Supply-side inflation is the outcome.

6. **Interpret how the war against terrorism can cause both inflation and lower output, and ways in which these effects might be countered.**

   ■ The war on terrorism will cause the macroeconomic equilibrium to change. Aggregate supply will shift to the left because of the need to devote resources to increase the country's security, causing the price level to rise. Aggregate demand will also shift to the left to the extent that uncertainty inhibits consumer spending, causing the price level to fall. Government spending can offset the drop in consumer spending. If aggregate demand rebounds strongly, the economy could see a combination of supply-side and demand-side inflation pushing the price level upward.

KEY TERMS

TEST YOURSELF

TRUE OR FALSE

1. Both classical and Keynesian economists agree that the economy is most usefully characterized through a long-run perspective.
2. The long-run aggregate supply curve illustrates that full-employment GDP is independent of the price level.
3. One explanation for the downward slope of aggregate demand is the savings effect, which states that people save more as they earn more.
4. Supply-side inflation occurs when there is a decrease in aggregate supply.
5. The aggregate demand and aggregate supply model can explain inflation but not deflation.

MULTIPLE CHOICE

6. "In the long run we are all dead" is a statement that best expresses
   a. Keynesian economics.
   b. classical economics.
   c. both Keynesian and classical economics.
   d. neither Keynesian nor classical economics.
7. The Phillips curve shows an inverse relationship between _____ and _____ .
   a. inflation; unemployment
   b. GDP; price level
   c. supply-side inflation; demand-side inflation
   d. aggregate demand; aggregate supply
8. The natural rate of unemployment
   a. remains constant over time.
   b. is higher today than a century ago.
   c. is lower today than a century ago.
   d. changes every day, so that it is sometimes higher than in the 1970s, but sometimes lower than then.
9. Full employment
   a. occurs only when 100 percent of the labor force is employed.
   b. equals 100 minus the natural rate of unemployment.
   c. is achieved when no one is frictionally unemployed.
   d. is a concept that is useful in the abstract, but never actually occurs in reality.
10. A graph of long-run aggregate supply would show the curve to be
    a. upward sloping to the right.
    b. downward sloping to the right.
    c. vertical.
    d. horizontal.
11. In Self-Test Figure 13-1, point A represents
    a. total unemployment.
    b. an increase in unemployment.

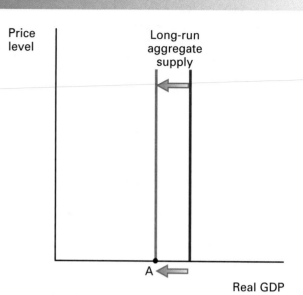

SELF-TEST FIGURE 13-1

   c. a decrease in aggregate demand.
   d. a smaller output associated with full employment.
12. Which of the following is most likely to cause the shift in aggregate supply shown in Self-Test Figure 13-1?
    a. An increase in aggregate demand.
    b. A decrease in aggregate demand.
    c. A decrease in consumer spending.
    d. The destruction of resources in warfare.
13. The aggregate demand curve is
    a. upward sloping to the right.
    b. downward sloping to the right.
    c. vertical.
    d. horizontal.
14. An aggregate demand curve
    a. shows the quantity of a good or service that will be purchased at each of various possible prices.
    b. reveals how much real GDP consumers, businesses, and government will purchase at each price level.
    c. portrays how much real GDP the economy will produce at various price levels.
    d. shows the relationship between interest rates and spending in the economy.
15. Graphically, a long-run macro equilibrium occurs
    a. anywhere along an aggregate demand curve.
    b. anywhere along the long-run aggregate supply curve.
    c. at the intersection of an aggregate demand curve and the long-run aggregate supply curve.
    d. at any value of real GDP so long as the long-run aggregate supply curve and an aggregate demand curve do not intersect.

16. If the economy starts at point *A* in Self-Test Figure 13-2, it is likely to see
    a. the price level increase over time.
    b. the price level decrease over time.
    c. unemployment rise over time.
    d. full-employment output fall over time.

Price level

Long-run aggregate supply

A

Aggregate demand

Real GDP

SELF-TEST FIGURE 13-2

17. Demand-side inflation occurs when
    a. the long-run aggregate supply curve shifts to the left.
    b. inflation causes the aggregate demand curve to shift to the left.
    c. the aggregate demand curve shifts to the right.
    d. inflation rises above 3 percent per year.

18. Supply-side deflation is a phenomena associated with
    a. more government rules and regulations.
    b. decreased consumer spending.
    c. an aggregate demand curve that shifts to the right.
    d. improved technology.

19. The supply shock of a natural disaster is associated with a _____ shift in long-run aggregate supply and a _____ price level.
    a. leftward; lower
    b. leftward; higher
    c. rightward; lower
    d. rightward; higher

20. The war on terrorism could shift aggregate supply to the left and aggregate demand to the right as a consequence of increased government spending. The result would be
    a. demand-side inflation only.
    b. supply-side deflation only.
    c. a combination of demand-side inflation and supply-side inflation.
    d. a combination of demand-side deflation and supply-side deflation.

QUESTIONS AND PROBLEMS

1. *[classical versus Keynesian]* State the essential difference between the classical and Keynesian schools of thought. If you were a public policymaker and received conflicting advice from a classical and a Keynesian economist, how would you choose? Explain.

2. *[Phillips curve]* According to the Phillips curve, what characterizes the relationship between inflation and unemployment? Draw a Phillips curve, making sure to label the axes. Does evidence accumulated after the 1960s support those conclusions?

3. *[inflationary expectations]* What do you expect the inflation rate to be over the next year?
    a. Did you arrive at an answer to this question by adaptive expectations?
    b. What are rational expectations? Are rational expectations or adaptive expectations more likely to be accurate?

4. *[full-employment GDP]* Must actual GDP always be equal to full-employment GDP? Explain.

5. *[full-employment GDP]* Explain how it is possible for actual GDP to temporarily exceed full-employment GDP.

6. *[natural rate of unemployment]* Why do economists reject the notion that the natural rate of unemployment equals zero? Why is the natural rate stated to be in the vicinity of 5 percent instead of an exact number?

7. *[natural rate of unemployment]* Explain how the natural rate of unemployment relates to long-run aggregate supply.

8. *[long-run aggregate supply]* Explain why the long-run aggregate supply curve is drawn as a vertical line. At what point on the horizontal axis is the long-run aggregate supply curve located? Why would the long-run aggregate supply curve shift outward?

9. *[long-run aggregate supply]* Why does the price level not make a difference to full-employment output in the long run? Illustrate your answer by drawing a long-run aggregate supply curve and explaining the implications of the vertical nature of the curve.

10. *[aggregate demand]* Define aggregate demand. Draw a graph of aggregate demand. What are the two effects that explain the slope of the aggregate demand curve?

11. *[long-run macro equilibrium]* Illustrate graphically and explain the long-run macro equilibrium.

12. *[aggregate demand/aggregate supply model]* Draw a graph that shows the long-run aggregate supply curve and an aggregate demand curve. Be sure to label the axes and the point on the horizontal axis that represents full-employment GDP. Illustrate on your graph an economy with unemployment. What is the cause of unemployment? Describe how the economy will adjust toward full employment.

13. *[aggregate demand/aggregate supply model]* Redraw the aggregate demand/aggregate supply graph you created in the preceding question. Illustrate on your graph an economy that is overheating. What is the cause of overheating? How will the economy adjust toward full employment?

14. *[inflation]* On separate graphs, show demand-side and supply-side inflation, labeling the axes, curves, and changes in output and the price level. Explain how the two might occur together.

15. *[deflation]* On separate graphs, show demand-side and supply-side deflation, labeling the axes, curves, and changes in output and the price level. Explain how the two might occur together.

16. *[Classical versus Keynesian]* Which group, political liberals or conservatives, is more likely to take Keynesian positions on the economy? Explain.

Visit **www.prenhall.com/collinge** for Exploring the Web exercises and additional self-test quizzes.

CHAPTER 14

MONEY AND MONETARY POLICY

A LOOK AHEAD

The Federal Reserve (the Fed) is the U.S. *central bank*, a special kind of bank charged with regulating money and commercial banks. The 1977 amendment to the Federal Reserve Act of 1913 spells out the objective of monetary policy: to "promote effectively the goals of maximum employment, stable prices, and moderate long-term interest rates." The Fed was created to be independent and free to act without interference from the president, Congress, big business, or big labor. The Fed would not be beholden to any branch of government, nor to any special-interest group. The Explore & Apply section in this chapter looks at the issue of Federal Reserve independence, and how it promotes a healthy, stable economy.

Commercial banks are the banks we find on Main Street. Together, the commercial banks and the Federal Reserve make up the U.S. banking system, which plays an instrumental role in shaping the quantity of money. Money, in turn, is itself at the heart of the macroeconomy. This chapter begins by examining money, its functions, and how it is measured. A discussion of banking, the Fed, and monetary policy completes the chapter.

LEARNING OBJECTIVES

Understanding Chapter 14 will enable you to:
1. **Identify the types, functions, and liquidity of various money measures.**
2. **Describe key elements of the banking industry.**
3. **Discuss how banks create money.**
4. **Describe the structure, functions, and policy tools of the Federal Reserve.**
5. **Work through the process of monetary expansion using the deposit multiplier.**
6. **Explain the equation of exchange and its role in monetary policy.**
7. **Address the importance of central banks staying independent of political pressures.**

$\mathscr{E}$XPLORE
&
$\mathscr{A}$PPLY

Meeting the macro goals of high employment, low inflation, and economic growth is made easier by the existence of money and banks, including a central bank. In previous chapters money has stayed in the background, but here it comes front and center, along with banks and the Federal Reserve.

14.1 MONEY

money what is used to buy and sell things.

barter exchange of one good for another.

Money is whatever is commonly used in an economy to buy and sell things. To put money into perspective, imagine a world in which it did not exist. To fulfill our wants, we would have to either swap one good for another—**barter**—or produce on our own all the goods and services we consume. Both alternatives are inefficient. Money provides us with higher living standards; that's why money is no fad and never goes out of style. In one form or another, money has been in continuous use from the earliest days of civilization. Among the important qualities of money are *portability* and *divisibility*. Money should be easy to carry around, and divisible to make it convenient to spend and receive change.

THE CHARACTERISTICS OF MONEY

Everyone knows what money is. It's the rectangular pieces of paper with pictures of presidents and the shiny metallic coins that we carry with us when we go shopping, right? Not quite. If it has value, is portable, and doesn't turn to mush, it has probably served as money somewhere. Among Native Americans, wampum (seashells) was used as money. Livestock, produce, tobacco, colonial currency, foreign currency, and furs were money at various times in the early days of America.

Gold was money for thousands of years. Given the long history of monetary gold, it may surprise you that gold is not used as money in the United States today. What, then, performs the role of money? Government-issued currency and coins are money, but they are most assuredly *not* the largest part of the money that we own. The electronic notations of bankers representing checking account money hold that distinction, as we'll see in the next section.

Money performs the following functions:

medium of exchange the purchasing function of money.

store of value the function of money related to holding wealth.

unit of account a use of money that occurs when the value of one item is compared with the value of another in terms of monetary units.

fiat money money not backed by a commodity; money by decree of law.

- **Medium of exchange.** Money is used to make purchases. Money must be acceptable to sellers, who will find it so only if they believe that others will, too.
- **Store of value.** Money is a means of holding wealth, but by no means the only one. Real estate, jewelry crafted of precious stones and metals, and stocks and bonds also serve as stores of value, because they are not perishable. Conversely, food and clothing are not used as money.
- **Unit of account.** The market values of goods and services are expressed as prices, which are stated in terms of money. The monetary unit varies from one nation to another. These monetary values are used for a variety of purposes, including measuring GDP and comparing goods.

Fiat money is money because the law says it is. Paper currency and current U.S. coins are examples. Because the government accepts fiat money, individuals and businesses do as well. Look at your paper money and see this reminder that our money is fiat money: "This note is legal tender for all debts, public and private." Gold and silver coins, once a commonplace form of money in the United States, are examples of *commodity money*. Commodity money is made from precious metals. In contrast, coins today are made from cheaper metals. The silver dimes that once filled change drawers in store cash registers have been replaced by dimes made of cheaper metals. Paper currency in the United States is not backed by gold, silver, or any other precious metal. As fiat money it does not need to be.

Unfortunately, commodity money is subject to **Gresham's law**—bad money drives out good. In other words, people have the incentive to nick, shave, or otherwise reduce the metallic content of coins. A little bit of gold shaved from the edges of enough coins can add up to a nice little nest egg. When the shaved coins are spent, they will be accepted by sellers who do not examine them closely. If they notice later, anyone possessing such an altered coin tries to spend it first and hoard the better, unaltered ones that contain more precious metal. This practice forces recipients of commodity money to examine it carefully, weigh it, and even bite it. People do not wish to examine their money this closely, and thus turn to fiat money instead. Of course, fiat money must be designed so that it is not easily counterfeited.

Gresham's law bad money drives good money out of circulation.

The governments of virtually all nations today hold a monopoly on the production of fiat money. The profit from the difference between the value of money and the cost of producing it is called *seigniorage*. For example, the U.S. Mint has reported that the cost of making 1,000 pennies, with a face value of $10, was $8.21 in 2000. The difference between the face value and the cost, equal to $1.79, is an example of seigniorage. Seigniorage is much greater for higher denomination coins and paper money.

DEBIT OR CREDIT?   *SNAPSHOT*

That plastic card that you swipe through the reader at your local Home Depot could be a traditional credit card, like those used for more than fifty years, but it is increasingly likely to be a more recent invention, the debit card. What is the difference? The debit card immediately transfers the amount of your purchase out of your checking account and into the store's deposit account. In effect, it saves you the trouble of writing a check, and eliminates the possibility of bouncing a check. You can't use a debit card to make a purchase unless you have the amount of your purchase in your account.

In contrast, a credit card provides you with a loan in the amount of the purchase. When you receive your monthly statement you must repay at least part of the loan. The debit card came much later than the credit card because debit cards would not be practical without high-speed computer networks. Debit cards make it easier for consumers to spend their checking account money. Like credit cards, debit cards are not money. Even if every bank depositor were issued a debit card tomorrow, the amount of money that exists would not change. It would just be easier to spend. ◄

LIQUIDITY: M1, M2, AND M3

When paper money and coins are deposited in banks, money changes form. Deposits into checking accounts create **demand deposits,** also termed *checkable deposits*. More money is held in the form of checkable deposits than in any other form. These deposits are money because checks—

demand deposits checking account deposits at commercial banks.

orders to a bank to make payment—are generally accepted by sellers. Traveler's checks are also generally accepted by sellers of goods and services. In addition, currency may be transformed into any of several "near monies," such as balances in savings accounts.

liquidity how easily and quickly an item can be turned into a spendable form.

Liquidity refers to how easily and quickly something of value can be converted into spendable form. An item is highly liquid if it is spendable without delay. Money is highly liquid, but some types of money are more liquid than others. Three definitions of money, termed the *monetary aggregates,* categorize various types of money according to how liquid they are. The monetary aggregates include M1, M2, and M3. M1 is the most liquid of these and totaled $1.2 trillion in 2001. M2 is slightly less liquid and totaled $5.5 trillion that year, while M3, which is much less liquid, totaled $8.0 trillion. The specific components of each category are as follows:

M1 most liquid measure of money; currency plus demand deposits, traveler's checks, and other checkable deposits.

- **M1:** The sum of currency and coins in the hands of the public, demand deposits, other checkable deposits, and traveler's checks. These forms of money are the most easily and immediately spendable. **Currency stored in bank vaults is not counted in the money supply because it is not available to make purchases.**

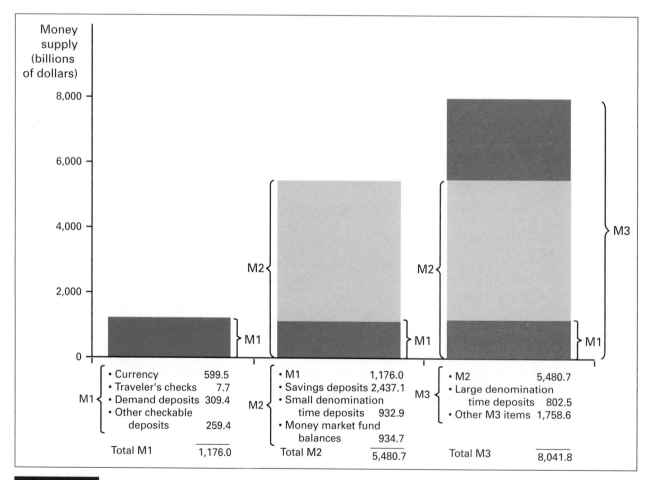

FIGURE 14-1

THE COMPONENTS OF M1, M2, AND M3 The M1 measure of the money supply includes only the most liquid items. Less-liquid items are added to arrive at M2 and M3. The bars rise in height when the additional components of the M2 and M3 money supply are added. Values are in billions of dollars.

Source: Money Stock Measures, June 13, 2002. The data shown are for April 2002. The values in the figure vary slightly from those in the source because of rounding.

- **M2:** M1 plus the balances in savings deposits, "small" time deposits, and balances in money market mutual funds. *Time deposits* are certificates of deposit (CDs), which can be withdrawn without penalty only after some period of time, such as one or five years. The Fed considers CDs small if they are less than $100,000!

- **M3:** M2 plus large time deposits (at least $100,000), and several other near monies. These additional components of M3 are even less likely to be spent than the items in M2.

M2 obtained by adding savings deposits, small time deposits, and money market fund balances to M1.

M3 expands M2 by adding large time deposits and several other near monies.

Figure 14-1 illustrates how the M2 and M3 measures of the quantity of money build on the M1 measure.

Because currency and coins are immediately spendable, they are completely liquid. Demand deposits are only slightly less liquid, because businesses often require check writers to present some form of identification before the check is accepted. Savings account deposits are slightly less liquid than demand deposits, but can be converted into demand deposits or currency with a trip to the bank.

THE EURO—OUT WITH THE OLD AND IN WITH THE NEW   *SNAPSHOT*

U.S. residents take it for granted that the same dollar bills are just as spendable in New York as New Orleans. Europeans, on the other hand, have historically had to contend with changes in currency and coins even for short trips that cross borders between countries. That has recently changed.

January 1, 1999 marked an historic moment in monetary history. The three-year transition to a new monetary unit began in eleven of the countries making up the European Monetary Union. The German mark, the French franc, the Italian lire, and the other familiar currencies issued by many European countries began to disappear in 2002, replaced by the euro. More countries may also make the jump to the euro as time passes. The Monetary Union also requires a new European Central Bank to conduct monetary policy, which was once the job of central banks in individual countries.

Why would countries risk confusion by dropping their familiar currencies, not to mention the loss of control over their own money? These changes are all part of a long-term effort to integrate the economies of Europe to make them more competitive with the United States and Japan in the global marketplace. A common currency will also ease the burdens on harried travelers who would rather worry about the price of lodging in the night's ski chalet than about having the right currency to pay that price! ◄

QUICKCHECK

State the effect on the money supply in each of the following instances:
   a. **Check printing companies print more blank checks.**
   b. **An individual deposits $9,000 in currency into a checking account in the bank.**
   c. **An individual moves $500 from a savings account to a checking account.**

Answer: (a) The printing of more blank checks does not change the money supply since it is the balances in demand deposit accounts that are measured by M1. (b) Depositing currency into a checking account leaves the money supply the same. (c) Moving balances from a savings account to a checking account leaves the M2 money supply the same. The M1 money supply increases because this move increases demand deposits.

14.2 MONEY AND BANKING IN THE UNITED STATES

As Americans moved westward during the first 100 years of the country's existence, new banks were needed to facilitate commerce whenever towns grew up. For the most part, banking regulation was weak, and so banks were easy to start. The legacy of that frontier history lives on, as the United States today has more banks than any other country. Currently, about 8,500 U.S. commercial banks accept deposits and make loans.

THE BANKING SYSTEM

Since the mid-1980s the number of banks in the United States has plummeted because of bank failures and bank mergers. More specifically, the number of banks fell an astonishing 41 percent between 1986 and 2000. During this period the United States has seen the rise of megabanks—large banks that do business in many locations. Megabanks thrive in today's climate of *interstate banking* as legal barriers against branching across state lines have fallen. On-line banking from home or work using the Internet has become common, allowing people to check their account balances, pay bills, or transfer funds among accounts. The fact is that banks are becoming ever more national, and even international, institutions in terms of their reach.

Banks are regulated by both state and federal governments. Bank regulation is designed to protect against unsound banking practices that could bankrupt both depositors and government insurance funds. Bank regulation is controversial. Since regulations inhibit banks from responding to the demands of their customers, regulations can lead to inefficiencies in the financial system.

To understand how our banking system operates, it is useful to consider a simplified *balance sheet* showing the assets and liabilities of a bank, as seen in Table 14-1. The assets are things that a bank owns, and reveal how banks use funds. In a balance sheet, assets are always listed on the left side. The liabilities are what the bank owes, and reveal how a bank raises funds. Liabilities are listed on the right side.

Take a look at bank assets first. The two most liquid assets, vault cash and deposits held by the Federal Reserve, are normally lumped together to form what are called cash assets. Bank deposits at the Fed are cash assets for banks because banks can cash in their deposits at the Fed in the same way that you can go to your bank and withdraw cash from your checking or savings accounts. The sum of vault cash plus deposits with the Fed is called **bank reserves.** Bank reserves are highly liquid and so are available immediately to meet depositor withdrawals. This liquidity provides banks with a margin of safety should depositor withdrawals unexpectedly increase.

bank reserves vault cash plus deposits held by the Fed.

TABLE 14-1 A BALANCE SHEET—MAJOR ASSETS AND LIABILITIES OF BANKS

ASSETS	LIABILITIES
Vault cash (part 1 of bank reserves)	Customer deposits
Deposits held by the Federal Reserve (part 2 of bank reserves)	Federal funds
Loans	Discount loans
Securities	
Other	

Banks hold some fraction of their deposits on reserve to meet the cash needs of their customers. Individual banks are also required by law to meet the *reserve requirements* imposed by the Fed. The current reserve requirement of approximately 10 percent for demand deposits means that banks must hold at least $10 in reserves for every $100 of customer deposits. Reserves in excess of **required reserves** are called **excess reserves.** Hence, total reserves equal required reserves plus excess reserves.

Bank reserves are a non-income-producing asset. This characteristic motivates banks to minimize the amount of bank reserves held so long as the banks are meeting the reserve requirement and are satisfied with the margin of safety provided by the quantity of reserves held. If bank reserves provide banks with no income, how then do they earn revenues? Loans and securities provide the answer.

The next asset in Table 14-1 is loans, which represent promises by borrowers to repay borrowed funds. Bank loans go to both the household and business sectors. Banks lend to borrowers in order to earn income in the form of **interest**. Bank loans are extended to borrowers for many purposes, such as to finance a business, a car, home improvements, and college tuition. An **interest rate** is the price of borrowed money expressed as a percentage. Interest rates that borrowers pay on a bank loan vary, mainly depending on the purpose of the loan, and the risk to the bank that the loan will not be repaid in full. One interest rate on bank loans that is widely known to the public is the *bank prime lending rate.* This interest rate applies to short-term business loans. When there are changes in interest rates, the prime rate is usually singled out by the news media to represent interest rates in general.

Interest payments on investments purchased by banks also provide banks with income. *Securities,* in the form of **bonds,** are interest-paying investments. The government issues bonds when it borrows money from investors in order to pay the expenses of government that are not covered by tax collections. Large business firms also issue bonds in order to borrow money. Investors that purchase bonds include individuals, banks, and other financial institutions. Many people are familiar with U.S. Savings Bonds, which provide a safe investment vehicle for small savers. Banks do not invest in these bonds. Neither do they invest in bonds issued by business firms. Instead, they mostly purchase federally issued short-term bonds called *T-bills*, which is short for *Treasury bills.* T-bills are an attractive investment because their owners can easily convert them to cash. T-bills come in large denominations of $10,000 each. To the federal government, T-bills and other Treasury bonds are debt because they represent money the government borrows.

Although banks are prohibited by law from investing in risky securities, loans to borrowers do carry a risk of non-repayment. Sometimes loans go sour when borrowers are unable to repay them. It is normal for a small fraction of loans to be uncollectible. The expenses generated by bad loans raises the cost of borrowing and reduces the profits earned by banks. If the amount of bad loans goes beyond norms, banks might not be able to pay off their depositors. That possibility is why the *Federal Deposit Insurance Corporation (FDIC)* insures deposit accounts up to $100,000. This insurance reduces the likelihood of bank runs, in which numerous depositors simultaneously seek to withdraw funds because of fears about the financial soundness of a bank. The tradeoff is that FDIC insurance allows banks to make riskier loans without scaring away their depositors. These depositors know that their funds are secure no matter how many unsound loans a bank may make.

Banks also own other assets, such as their buildings, equipment, and fixtures. These assets are needed in order to do business with the public.

Now take a look at the liabilities in Table 14-1. Bank deposits are liabilities because they are funds owed to depositors. Banks also raise funds by borrowing, both from each other and from the Federal Reserve. Funds borrowed from other banks are called *federal funds.* The interest rate that banks charge on loans to other banks is called the **federal funds rate.** The federal funds rate is determined by the supply and demand in the marketplace for federal funds. Most of the funds borrowed in the federal funds market are repaid the next day.

required reserves bank reserves held to meet the Fed's reserve requirement; expressed as a percentage of deposits.

excess reserves the amount of bank reserves that exceed the amount needed to meet the reserve requirement.

Interest payment made by a borrower to compensate a lender for the use of money.

Interest rate price of borrowed money; expressed as a percentage.

bonds interest-paying investments; also called securities.

federal funds rate interest rate on loans that banks make to other banks.

Although the federal funds rate is not widely known among the general public, as you will soon see, it is probably the most significant interest rate in terms of the Federal Reserve's monetary policy influence on banks.

Borrowings by banks from the Federal Reserve are called *discount loans* because the Federal Reserve is said to "discount" its loans. To discount a loan means that banks are required to pay the interest on loans from the Fed when the loans are made rather than as they are repaid. The rate of interest charged is termed the **discount rate,** which is set by the Fed. Funds borrowed by banks at the so-called "discount window" at the Fed are typically repaid quite rapidly because banks need these funds to meet a temporary shortfall in the reserve requirement.

discount rate interest rate set by the Fed on loans it makes to banks.

For simplicity, the balance sheet in Table 14-1 ignores *net worth,* which is assets minus liabilities. By definition, the value of the sum of the assets must equal the value of the sum of the liabilities plus net worth for any balance sheet.

In addition to banks, there are other *financial intermediaries,* bank-like institutions that accept funds from savers in order to make loans or investments. With minor exceptions, the discussion of banks in this text also applies to credit unions and savings and loans. Insurance companies, mutual funds, pension funds, and finance companies are examples of nonbank financial intermediaries, because, although they are not banks, they invest the funds they raise.

HOW BANKS CREATE MONEY

When a bank makes a loan, the quantity of money in the economy increases. To see how, suppose you hope to borrow the cost of a new PT Cruiser, $18,000, from your bank, Homestate University National Bank. After you discuss your loan request with loan officer Softheart, the loan is approved.

If you receive the loan as currency, the amount of currency in the hands of the public, which includes you, is greater than before the loan. Recall that this currency, while inside the bank's vault, was not included in the money supply. Once you receive the $18,000, the M1, M2, and M3 money supplies increase by that amount.

You probably received the loan in the form of an $18,000 check deposited in your checking account. Again, the M1, M2, and M3 money supplies increase by $18,000. We can illustrate the effect of a loan on a bank's balance sheet by referring to the changes in Homestate University National Bank's balance sheet, seen below. The bank acquires an asset, your IOU promising to repay the loan. Customer deposits increase on the other side of the balance sheet because the bank increases your account by $18,000 when the loan is made.

HOMESTATE UNIVERSITY NATIONAL BANK: BALANCE SHEET CHANGES WHEN A LOAN IS MADE

ASSETS		LIABILITIES	
Loans	+ $18,000	Customer deposits	+ $18,000

When you pay for your new car, the bank's balance sheet will change again. Customer deposits decrease by $18,000 since you no longer have that money in your account. Bank reserves will also fall by $18,000 since the bank will either lose $18,000 in vault cash, or see its deposits at the Fed reduced by that amount. The balance sheet effects are shown below.

HOMESTATE UNIVERSITY NATIONAL BANK: BALANCE SHEET CHANGES WHEN A LOAN IS SPENT

ASSETS		LIABILITIES	
Reserves	− $18,000	Customer deposits	− $18,000

When borrowers repay bank loans, the quantity of money falls. If a loan is repaid with currency, the money supply decreases because there is less currency in the hands of the public. If a loan is repaid by writing a check, the money supply falls due to fewer demand deposits. Say that you repay your $18,000 loan all at once. That wipes out your IOU and increases the bank's reserves, as shown.

HOMESTATE UNIVERSITY NATIONAL BANK: BALANCE SHEET CHANGES WHEN A LOAN IS REPAID

ASSETS		LIABILITIES
Reserves	+ $18,000	
Loans	− $18,000	

14.3 MEET THE FED

In the United States, it is the Federal Reserve that performs the central banking functions at the heart of the monetary system. The Fed is known to the public for engineering changes in short-term interest rates. However, the Fed does much more.

STRUCTURE AND FUNCTIONS OF THE FEDERAL RESERVE

A central bank is an arm of the government charged with seeing to it that the monetary system functions efficiently. The U.S. central bank is called the Fed, short for **Federal Reserve System.** It was created by the *Federal Reserve Act of 1913* in response to recurring problems of bank failure and the belief that a central bank could contribute to U.S. economic stability. To this end, the Fed does the following:

Federal Reserve System U.S. central bank; conducts monetary policy, holds bank deposits, and performs several other functions.

- **Functions as a banker's bank.** The Fed holds reserves for commercial banks.
- **Functions as a lender of last resort.** The Fed lends reserves to sound banks that are temporarily short of reserves.
- **Supervises banks.** Banks are held accountable for complying with the federal laws and regulations that apply to banks. The Fed is one of several government agencies that is responsible for overseeing compliance.
- **Conducts monetary policy.** Monetary policy involves the Fed in changing short-term interest rates and the quantity of money.
- **Issues currency.** Currency is printed by the U.S. Treasury, but put into circulation by the Fed.
- **Clears checks.** When you write a check, the check must clear, meaning that your bank must reduce your account by the amount of the check. The Fed operates facilities that process and transport checks to the banks upon which they are written so that the banks can clear them.

The Fed is divided into three components:

- **The *Board of Governors,*** which is responsible for the overall direction of the Federal Reserve and its policies.

- The *Federal Open Market Committee (FOMC),* which conducts monetary policy.
- The *Federal Reserve Banks,* which regulate and provide a variety of services for banks.

There are seven members of the Board of Governors. They are appointed to fourteen-year nonrenewable terms by the president, with the advice and consent of the Senate. Terms are staggered so that one term expires every two years, which minimizes political influence over the Fed. One of the seven is named by the president to chair the Board. The chairperson, who serves a four-year renewable term, is the most powerful individual in the Fed and one of the most powerful people in the country. As of mid 2003, Alan Greenspan held the position.

The FOMC consists of twelve members, the seven members of the Board plus four rotating district bank presidents, as well as the president of the New York District Bank. The president of the New York Fed is always a member of the Committee because New York City is the hub of the United States' financial markets. The FOMC usually meets at intervals of approximately four to six weeks, making adjustments in the conduct of monetary policy in accordance with its assessment of economic conditions.

There are twelve regional Federal Reserve Banks, as shown in Figure 14-2. Together with their branches, these Banks perform the routine functions of the Fed. For example, Federal Reserve Banks operate the Fed's check-clearing operations, which allow funds to be expeditiously transferred from check writers' accounts to the accounts of the banks that cash the checks. The regional banks also participate in the supervision of commercial banks in their districts.

INFLUENCING THE MONEY SUPPLY: OPEN MARKET OPERATIONS

open market operations buying and selling of Treasury bonds and Treasury bills by the Fed; tool of monetary policy.

The principal method the Fed uses to influence the money supply is called open market operations. **Open market operations** occur when the Fed enters the financial marketplace to buy or sell government securities, such as Treasury bonds or Treasury bills. The Fed does not itself issue government securities; the U.S. Department of the Treasury issues Treasury bonds and bills. The Fed can only obtain them in the open market, hence the name. Open market operations allow currency, in the form of Federal Reserve Notes, to make its way into circulation.

The bulk of the Fed's open market operations involve banks directly. An open market sale to a bank by the Fed decreases bank reserves. Fewer reserves mean that the bank is able to do less lending. Thus, open market sales tend to reduce the money supply.

An open market purchase by the Fed from a bank increases bank reserves, which in turn tends to increase the money supply because banks have more money to loan. However, whether loans are actually made and the money supply actually increased depends on the willingness of banks to make loans and on the desire of the public to borrow. **Thus, the Fed influences, but does not control, the money supply.**

monetary base sum of currency in circulation plus bank reserves.

However, by conducting open market operations, **the Fed controls the monetary base.** The **monetary base** is the sum of currency held by the public plus bank reserves. **An open market purchase by the Fed always increases the monetary base by the amount of the purchase; an open market sale always decreases the monetary base by the amount of the sale.**

THE MONEY MULTIPLIER AND THE MONETARY BASE

The effects of open market operations do not stop with the initial purchase or sale. Secondary effects magnify changes in the money supply or monetary base. For example, an open market purchase from an individual increases the money supply once when the seller receives the proceeds of the sale. If those funds are deposited in a bank, and then loaned to someone, the money supply increases again. This process can continue over and over.

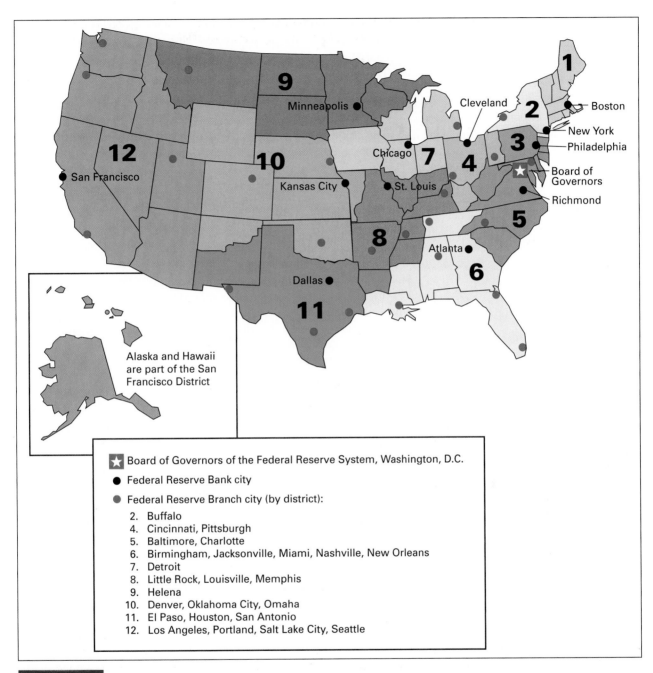

FIGURE 14-2

THE FEDERAL RESERVE SYSTEM The Federal Reserve System is divided into twelve district national banks—those chartered by the federal government—that are automatically members of the Federal Reserve. Banks with state charters may join at their option. Whether or not they are members of the Federal Reserve System, however, all banks have nearly equal access to the Fed's services and are subject to its regulations. Thus, although only about 4,000 banks are formal members, in practical terms all banks fall under Federal Reserve regulation.

Source: http://www.federalreserve.gov/otherfrb.htm.

money multiplier the amount by which a new deposit is multiplied to arrive at the actual increase in the money supply; maximum value is given by the deposit multiplier.

The *money multiplier* shows the total effect on the money supply of each dollar of open market operations. To see how the money multiplier works, consider the sale of a $10,000 bond to the Fed by an individual who deposits the Fed's check in an account at Investor's National Bank.

If we assume for simplicity that Investors' National Bank was just meeting a 10-percent reserve requirement prior to the $10,000 deposit, then the bank will find itself holding excess reserves of $9,000. Actual reserves have increased by $10,000, but the bank is only required to hold 10 percent of that amount, equal to $1,000, as required reserves. The bank is thus able to make loans up to the amount of excess reserves and still meet the reserve requirement.

As it happens, your best friend wishes to borrow $9,000 to finance the purchase of a used Saturn automobile. After your friend speaks with loan officer Pushover at Investors' National Bank, the loan is approved. That loan increases the money supply by $9,000. The auto dealer deposits your friend's check into the dealer's bank. That bank will then have excess reserves to lend. The amount of required reserves equals $900, so excess reserves equal $8,100, the amount that can be loaned.

This lending–depositing–lending sequence could continue. Someone can borrow $8,100. When the loan is spent and someone else deposits the $8,100 in his or her bank, that bank will have excess reserves, which it is able to lend. At each succeeding step in the process, the sum of money loaned, which is new money, grows smaller because each succeeding bank in the sequence must hold a portion as required reserves. Thus the process is eventually exhausted when the last bank in the sequence has essentially nothing left to lend.

What is the total of new money created when the expansion of the money supply is complete? The answer depends on the money multiplier.

$$\text{Money supply} = \text{Money multiplier} \times \text{Monetary base}$$

The money multiplier can vary according to loan prospects and people's behavior, and is thus hard to calculate with precision. However, an upper bound can be found by calculating the *deposit multiplier*—**the maximum possible value of the money multiplier.** The deposit multiplier is calculated by assuming that all money is held as demand deposits and that banks do not hold excess reserves. In practice, the true value of the money multiplier will be less than the deposit multiplier.

deposit multiplier upper bound on the value of the money multiplier; computed as 1 divided by the reserve requirement.

The deposit multiplier is the reciprocal of the percentage reserve requirement, meaning

$$\text{Deposit multiplier} = \frac{1}{\text{Reserve requirement}}$$

For example, if the reserve requirement equals 10 percent, then 1 divided by 10 percent equals 1/0.1, which gives a deposit multiplier of 10. To use this multiplier, multiply the Fed's original open market purchase of $10,000 by the multiplier, 10. The total of new money in that case is $100,000.

You can follow the process of money creation that follows an open market operation by referring to Figure 14-3. The process starts when the seller of the bond deposits the $10,000 received from the Fed in Investors' National Bank, Bank 1 in the figure. Data for the first ten banks in the process are shown. Note that each loan expands the money supply. The process continues through an infinite number of banks. Because the amount of deposits received shrinks with the involvement of each additional bank, there will be a limit on the amount of deposit money that is created. The deposit multiplier formula allows you to compute that amount of money, which is $100,000 in this case.

Bank	Deposits received	Reserves kept	Loans made
Investors' National Bank = 1	$10,000	$1,000	$9,000
2	$9,000	$900	$8,100
3	$8,100	$810	$7,290
4	$7,290	$729	$6,561
5	$6,561	$656	$5,905
6	$5,905	$590	$5,315
7	$5,315	$532	$4,783
8	$4,783	$478	$4,305
9	$4,305	$430	$3,875
10	$3,875	$388	$3,487
Totals: Banks 1 – 10	$65,134	$6,513	$58,621
Totals: Infinite number of banks	$100,000	$10,000	$90,000

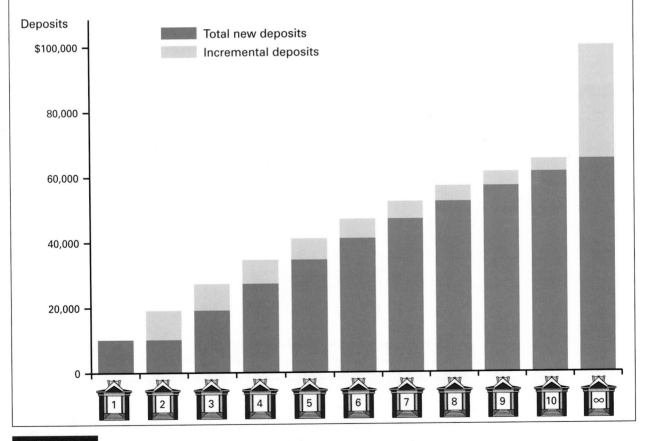

FIGURE 14-3

CREATION OF DEPOSIT MONEY, 10 PERCENT RESERVE REQUIREMENT You can track the expansion in the money supply by following the actions of the banks in the table. The graph presents the same information visually.

The following three factors affect the money multiplier, and thus the actual expansion of the money supply:

- **The reserve requirement:** Changes in the reserve requirement would change the deposit multiplier, and thus the maximum value of the money multiplier. A lower reserve requirement means that banks are able to lend a greater fraction of deposits; a higher reserve requirement has the opposite effect.
- **The public's desire to hold currency instead of deposits:** If people hold more of their money as currency and less as deposits, banks will have fewer dollars to lend. If the $10,000 from the sale of the bond had been received as currency, the multiple expansion of the money supply would not have taken place, thus reducing the multiplier effect.
- **The bank's desire to hold excess reserves:** Excess reserves may be held in order to meet unexpected depositor withdrawals, or because lending opportunities seem poor. Reserves that are not loaned out do not add to the money supply. **Excess reserves reduce the multiplier effect.**

OTHER TOOLS OF THE FED

In response to unexpected customer withdrawals, banks may wish to borrow from the Fed in order to maintain their required reserves. Recall that loans from the Fed to banks are called discount loans, and the rate of interest charged is called the discount rate. An increase in the discount rate makes it more costly for banks to borrow; a decrease makes it less costly.

Increases in the discount rate tend to decrease the quantity of money by prompting banks to borrow less from the Fed. Conversely, a decrease in the discount rate leads banks to borrow more from the Fed, which tends to increase the amount of money in circulation. Thus, **a change in the discount rate tends to cause the money supply to change in the opposite direction.**

Changes in the discount rate are typically front-page news because they are an easily understood signal of the Fed's policy intentions. The Fed may wish to see the money supply grow faster to stimulate growth and employment. An increase in the discount rate signals a tighter policy. Perhaps the Fed would like to slow down monetary growth to fight inflation.

The Fed could change the money supply dramatically by altering the reserve requirement. A decrease in required reserves would increase the money multiplier and spur monetary growth. An increase in the reserve requirement would reduce the money multiplier and thus decrease the money supply. Excess reserves, which banks are able to lend to borrowers, would become required reserves, which cannot be used to make loans.

The Fed is reluctant to increase reserve requirements because banks without sufficient excess reserves would be forced to sell securities or call in loans—actions that could prove disruptive to the bank and its customers. Thus, while potent, changes in reserve requirements

QUICKCHECK

When the Fed lowers the discount rate, why does it become more likely that the money supply will increase?

Answer: A lower discount rate lowers the cost to banks of borrowing reserves from the Fed. Banks that are short of reserves are more likely to borrow reserves from the Fed and less likely to borrow from other banks. Thus, more funds are available in the banking system to lend to the public.

TABLE 14-2	THE FED'S MONETARY POLICY OPTIONS	
TIGHTER MONETARY POLICY	**LOOSER MONETARY POLICY**
Open market sale of securities	Open market purchase of securities
Increase in discount rate	Decrease in discount rate
Increase in reserve requirement	Decrease in reserve requirement

are rarely used as an instrument of monetary policy. Table 14-2 summarizes the Fed's options in setting monetary policy. A *tight monetary policy* is intended to slow the economy down in order to keep inflation in check. A *loose monetary policy* is intended to have an expansionary effect on the economy. Monetary policy is discussed in detail in the next two sections.

14.4 GUIDING MONETARY POLICY

Observers speculate that, in recent years, the Fed has usually followed a **price rule,** by which it conducts monetary policy with the aim of keeping price increases among certain basic commodities, perhaps including gold, within a low target range. The following of a price rule indicates that the Fed's prime concern will often be relative price stability, which means low inflation. We next turn to the equation of exchange, which provides a model to help us understand the cause of inflation and the rationale for monetary policy based on a price rule.

price rule conducting monetary policy in order to keep price increases in basic commodities within a low range.

THE EQUATION OF EXCHANGE—MONEY AND PRICES

The **equation of exchange** was originally proposed in the nineteenth century as a means of explaining the link between money, prices, and output. The equation of exchange reveals that the amount of money people spend must equal the market value of what they purchase, as follows:

$$M \times V = P \times Q$$

equation of exchange $M \times V = P \times Q$; M represents the quantity of money, V is velocity, P is the price level, and Q is aggregate output.

The equation of exchange applies to the aggregate economy. Let's look over the equation one variable at a time.

- M: The quantity of money is indicated by M in the equation. Money is used to purchase goods and services.
- V: The average number of times money changes hands in a year is called the **velocity of money** (V). The dollar you spend today was spent by someone else earlier, and will be spent again later. The typical dollar will change hands more than once as consumers buy the economy's output of goods and services.

velocity of money the number of times a dollar changes hands in a year.

Total spending is calculated by multiplying the money supply by velocity, as shown above in the left side of the previous equation of exchange. On the right side we have:

- P: P is a price index, such as the GDP price index, that shows the level of prices in the economy.
- Q: The aggregate output of goods and services is represented by Q.

When P and Q are multiplied, the result is the dollar value of aggregate purchases. The total amount of purchasing in an economy is equivalent to the economy's nominal GDP. Thus, the **equation of exchange says that aggregate spending, the left side of the equation, equals nominal GDP, the right side. Because the value of what is bought must equal the value of what is sold, the equation of exchange is always true.** Thus, we may expand the equation of exchange to include the interpretation of each side:

$$M \times V \text{ [total spending]} = P \times Q \text{ [nominal GDP]}$$

The equation of exchange forms the basis for the **quantity theory of money.** The quantity theory assumes:

quantity theory of money a theory based upon the equation of exchange; shows that the effect of a change in the money supply is a proportional change in the price level; assumes velocity and aggregate output remain constant.

- The velocity of money (V in the equation of exchange) is independent of the quantity of money in the long run. In other words, V is assumed not to change when the money supply changes, so that we can treat V as a constant value.
- Aggregate output, Q, is also independent of the quantity of money in the long run. Aggregate output depends upon the productive capacity of the economy and is assumed to be at its maximum level. This means that Q can also be treated as a constant.

These two assumptions leave only M and P, money and the price level, to vary. Thus, the effect of a change in the quantity of money must be a proportional change in the price level. An increase in the money supply brings a proportionally higher price level. Conversely, a decrease in the money supply lowers the price level proportionally to the decrease in the money supply. Except for determining the price level, the quantity theory suggests that money does not matter, because the economy will always operate at the full-employment level of real GDP. For this reason, the quantity theory cannot explain recessions.

A numerical example can help you grasp the quantity theory. Suppose that an economy's money supply equals $100 and that the velocity of money is constant and equals 2. Each dollar thus changes hands twice each time period, indicating that total spending in the economy is $200 during that time period. This $200 of total spending is also equal to nominal GDP. Suppose now that the money supply rises to $130, and that in accordance with the quantity theory, velocity remains constant at a value of 2. Total spending must then rise to $260. Because the quantity theory assumes that aggregate output (Q) is always at its maximum level, aggregate output cannot rise. There is only one way for the right side of the equation of exchange to rise to a value of $260—through an increase in the price level (P)!

The link between money and prices can also be clarified by imagining what would happen if, by government decree, we all woke up tomorrow with twice as much money as we have today. One dollar bills would be worth $2 each, five's would be worth $10 each, $100 in a savings account would be transformed into $200, and so forth. Nothing real would have changed, though. Dunkin Doughnuts would still have the same amount of doughnuts for sale as before, the number of new cars for sale at the dealerships would still be the same, and so on down the line for every good and service. Furthermore, if the economy were at full employment, the ability of the economy to produce more goods and services would be no more than before the increase in the quantity of money. What would you expect to happen next? With everyone having twice as much money to spend as the day before, prices would start to rise immediately in response. In fact, if everyone knew that there was exactly twice as much money, prices would immediately double.

The quantity theory can be illustrated with the model of aggregate supply and aggregate demand, as shown in Figure 14-4. An increase in the money supply shifts aggregate demand to the right, because additional money provides greater purchasing power at any given price level. The long-run effect is to move the economy to a new equilibrium at a higher price level. Output remains the same at its full-employment level, as shown in the figure.

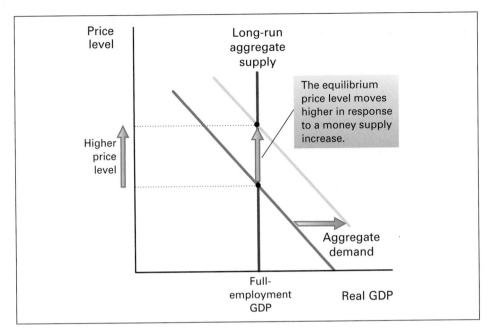

FIGURE 14-4

THE QUANTITY THEORY The quantity theory of money is that, in the long run, an increase in the money supply has no effect except to cause inflation. Aggregate demand shifts out and the economy moves up the long-run aggregate supply curve to a new equilibrium at a higher price level.

SNAPSHOT

TAXATION THROUGH INFLATION—WHAT A MONEY MAKER!

The Fed must keep in mind the equation of exchange when conducting its monetary policy. Otherwise, the temptation might be for the Fed to merely buy back as much government debt as possible. The open market purchases of Treasury bonds and Treasury bills that this would require might seem like a painless way to reduce or even eliminate government debt. But painless it is not, as newly printed money used to buy those Treasury securities would cause inflation that eats away at the value of all of our savings. The effect is much like a tax, and indeed is often referred to as the tax of inflation. ◄

THE MONETARIST PRESCRIPTION

Monetarism is a school of economic thought, associated with Nobel prize-winning economist Milton Friedman (1912–), that offers a modern version of the quantity theory. Monetarists readily agree with one contention of the original quantity theory: Velocity and aggregate output are independent of the quantity of money in the long run. However, unlike the quantity theory, monetarism acknowledges the existence of a short run.

monetarism school of thought that emphasizes the importance of the quantity of money in the economy and a rule for monetary policy; associated with economist Milton Friedman.

QUICKCHECK

If the money supply quadruples, other things being equal, what does the quantity theory predict?

Answer: The quantity theory predicts the price level would quadruple. Prices increase proportionally to the increase in the money supply.

According to the monetarist view, the quantity of money may indeed affect velocity and aggregate output in the short run. Thus, neither V nor Q in the equation of exchange is viewed as constant by monetarists.

■ *Changes in Q.* A reduction in the growth rate of the money supply may cause a reduction in aggregate output, Q. This effect could occur if people cut their purchases of goods and services because there is less money to spend. If that happens, the economy slows down. Hence, monetarism offers an explanation of how too little money can lead to a recession.

■ *Changes in V.* The velocity of money can change because of changes in people's need to hold money. For example, the widespread use of debit cards, ATM machines, and other technologies causes people to economize on their money holdings, and thus causes velocity to increase. Figure 14–5 shows the value of velocity over time, confirming that V increased from the mid-1980s to the mid-1990s. If V were constant, the effects of monetary policy would be more predictable. As seen in the figure, velocity is relatively stable from one year to the next, so that the effects of monetary policy are relatively predictable.

To avoid the recession that could result from too little money, or the inflation that could result from too much money, **the monetarist policy recommendation is for the Fed to increase the money supply at a steady rate, equal to or slightly greater than the long-run growth in aggregate output.** If the long-run growth of output tends to be about 2.5 to 3 percent, a steady annual monetary increase of about 3 percent or slightly higher is called for. The idea is to provide sufficient money so that the economy's additional output could be purchased without setting off significant inflation. Figure 14-6 shows the annual growth rates for the M2 money supply over time. The figure shows that money

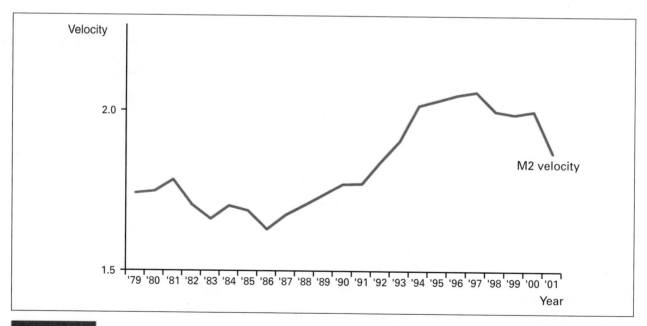

FIGURE 14-5

M2 VELOCITY Changes in velocity complicate monetary policy by making it more difficult for the Fed to achieve its targets. Velocity took an upward turn in the 1980s, as people became more comfortable with financial innovations that allowed them to reduce their money holdings.

Source: Computed by the authors using data from the *2002 Economic Report of the President.* M2 velocity equals nominal GDP divided by M2.

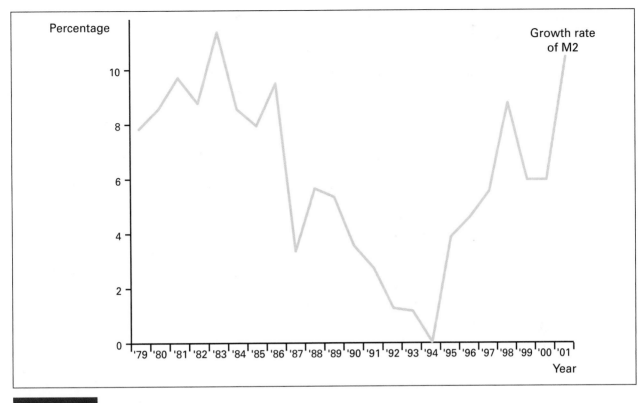

FIGURE 14-6

THE ANNUAL GROWTH RATE OF M2 OVER TIME The M2 money supply has not grown at a steady rate, but has exhibited significant variation over time.

Source: 2002 Economic Report of the President, Table B-69.

growth has varied significantly from year to year, which runs counter to the monetarist recommendation.

Figure 14-7 illustrates a monetarist version of monetary policy. A macro equilibrium is illustrated by the intersection of the long-run aggregate supply curve and the aggregate demand curve. Economic growth is shown by a rightward shift in long-run aggregate supply. If aggregate demand were to remain unchanged after the increase in long-run aggregate supply, the price level would have to fall in order for consumers to be able to purchase the increased production. In contrast, **monetarists recommend growth in the money supply that just matches the growth in long-run aggregate supply,** thereby avoiding the need for price level adjustments. Thus, the new aggregate demand curve in Figure 14-7 intersects the new long-run aggregate supply at the original price level.

The Fed is sometimes accused by monetarists of being too quick to increase or decrease the growth rate of the money supply. Monetarists claim that an activist policy by the Federal Reserve accentuates economic instability. The reason is that changes in the money supply affect the economy with, as Milton Friedman put it, a "long and variable lag." Today's change in monetary policy may not take effect for months or even years, at which time economic conditions may be quite different from what they were at the moment when the policy was implemented. Therefore, the effects of monetary policy are hard to predict. The long and variable lag in the effects of monetary policy is why monetarists call for a steady increase in the supply of money.

FIGURE 14-7

MONETARIST POLICY Monetarists seek to match money-supply growth to growth in the country's productive potential. By doing so, aggregate demand shifts to the right just enough to keep the price level constant.

Price level

Long-run aggregate supply

#1 Economic growth shifts long-run aggregate supply to the right.

#2 Monetarists aim for monetary growth to achieve an equal shift in aggregate demand.

Price level

#3 The result is that the price level stays constant even as the equilibrium changes.

Aggregate demand

Real GDP

Could the Fed ever adopt monetarism as the guiding principle of monetary policy? That is unlikely for there are some practical problems in implementing monetarism. The basic problem is that the Fed does not control the money supply—it only influences the quantity of money. The Fed controls only the monetary base. Growing the monetary base at a slow and steady rate does not mean that the money supply will do likewise. Consumer pessimism or optimism about the economy can greatly affect the money multiplier, which relates the monetary base to the money supply.

14.5 THE FEDERAL FUNDS RATE AND MARKET INTEREST RATES

nominal interest rate the payment from a borrower to a lender, expressed as a percentage.

real interest rate measures an interest rate in terms of its purchasing power.

A **nominal interest rate** is the payment from a borrower to a lender, expressed in percentage terms. A **real interest rate** measures the percentage payment in terms of its purchasing power. To compute a real interest rate it is not necessary to know the value of a price index. Instead, all that is needed is the inflation rate and the nominal interest rate. To obtain the real interest rate, subtract the inflation rate from the nominal interest rate:

Real interest rate = Nominal interest rate − Inflation rate

Consider the case where I borrow $1,000 from you. We agree that I am to repay you $1,050 in one year. The nominal interest rate is 5 percent (the interest payment of $50 divided by the amount borrowed). With an inflation rate of 2 percent, the real interest rate is only 3 percent. You, the lender in this example, will increase your purchasing power by 3 percent when the loan is repaid. The real interest rate in the United States is contrasted to the nominal interest rate in Figure 14-8 on page 336. The real interest rate and the nominal interest rate typically move in the same direction, but the nominal rate is higher than the real rate.

Monetary policy goals can be achieved through changes in interest rates. **A key interest rate is the federal funds rate, the interest rate on reserves banks lend to each other.** The federal funds rate is the price paid by banks that borrow reserves from other banks. For example, suppose Homestate University National Bank borrows reserves from Coastal

Plains National Bank in order to satisfy the reserve requirement that was discussed previously. If the federal funds rate is 5 percent, when Homestate repays the reserves it borrowed, it will have to include an interest payment to Coastal Plains that reflects the 5 percent federal funds rate.

The Fed does not directly set the federal funds rate, but can meet its federal funds rate target by changing the quantity of bank reserves through the conduct of open market operations. Open market sales of bonds by the Fed reduce the quantity of bank reserves because banks that buy bonds from the Fed pay for them by transferring the ownership of reserves to the Fed. When banks have less reserves to lend to each other, the result is an increase in the federal funds rate. The higher price of reserves is likely to be passed along to borrowers in the form of higher interest rates on bank loans. Conversely, open market purchases of bonds by the Fed tend to reduce the federal funds rate, and can thus lead to lower interest rates on consumer and business loans.

The path by which open market operations affect short-term market interest rates is illustrated in Table 14-3. When the federal funds rate changes because of Fed actions that manipulate the quantity of bank reserves, short-term market interest rates tend to adjust in the same direction. Thus, when the federal funds rate increases, short-term market interest rates tend to go up. When the federal funds rate decreases, short-term market interest rates tend to go down. Consumers shopping for loans find their monthly payments increased or decreased accordingly. The higher monthly payments that go along with higher market interest rates tend to discourage consumer borrowing. The lower monthly payments that accompany lower market interest rates tend to encourage such borrowing.

Monetary policy that targets short-term interest rates can be tight (contractionary) or loose (expansionary), just as with monetary policy that works through the money supply. A tight policy causes real interest rates in the economy to rise, with the goal of keeping inflation in check. If successful, then a tight monetary policy would lead to nominal interest rates that are not much higher than the real rates. For example, if tight monetary policy kept the inflation rate down to zero, real interest rates would equal nominal interest rates.

A loose monetary policy causes real short-term interest rates to fall, which leads to more lending by banks to consumers. Such a policy is usually advocated when the economy is weak and inflation is not a problem. Figure 14-8 shows the average yearly federal funds rate since 1979. The nominal federal funds rate is the rate as stated.

Because interest rates are an expense to businesses and many households, some politicians and businesspeople argue that the Fed should aim to keep them low. Although the Fed could try to keep real rates low by expanding the money supply, the long-run result would likely be inflation that might cause nominal interest rates to soar as time passes. The reason is that the Fed's open market purchases that are intended to drive down interest rates will, in the long run, increase the money supply and thus inflation. **Monetary policy cannot**

TABLE 14-3   THE INTEREST RATE EFFECTS OF OPEN MARKET OPERATIONS

FEDERAL RESERVE ACTION	BANK RESERVES	FEDERAL FUNDS RATE	SHORT-TERM MARKET INTEREST RATES
Open market sale of securities to banks	Decrease (reserves go to the Fed to pay for securities)	Increases, as reserves leave the banking system	Increase
Open market purchase of securities from banks	Increase (reserves are received from the Fed in payment for securities)	Decreases, as reserves are pumped into the banking system	Decrease

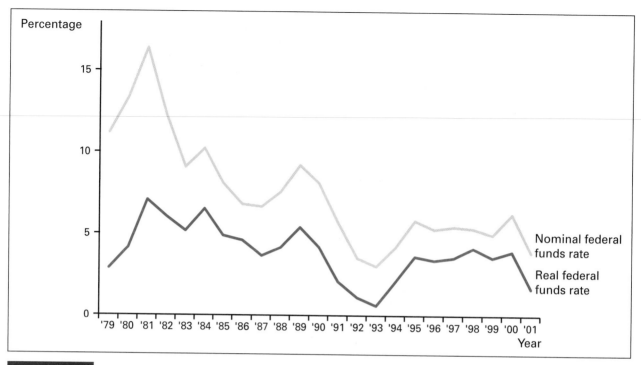

FIGURE 14-8

THE NOMINAL AND REAL FEDERAL FUNDS RATE The real federal funds rate is calculated as the nominal rate minus the change in the GDP implicit price deflator. The real federal funds rate provides a better indicator of the stance of monetary policy than does the nominal rate.

Source: 2002 Economic Report of the President, Tables B-3 and B-73, and National Income and Product Accounts, Table 8.1.

lower interest rates in the long run, except through lower inflation. A Fed policy that ignored this principle is often held responsible for the upsurge of U.S. inflation in the 1970s.

The role of the federal funds rate in monetary policy can be appreciated by referring to Figure 14-9. Part of this figure reproduces an actual Federal Reserve press release intended to inform the public about monetary policy. The wording of this press release suggests that monetary policy was unchanged since the Fed's goal was to keep the federal funds rate unchanged. Press releases like this one are provided to the public on a recurring basis by the Fed. The graph shows the drastic drop in the intended federal funds rate throughout 2001. The goal of a lower federal funds rate was motivated by the Fed's effort to shake off the recession that started in 2001.

SNAPSHOT   **FED WATCHING—FROM WALL STREET TO MAIN STREET**

Because the Fed is so powerful, its actions directly affect people's lives. The stock market, mortgage interest rates, returns on investments in bonds—all these and more are subject to the Fed's influence. The consequence is that Fed watching is something of a national sport. Economists, stock market analysts, and policymakers follow the money supply figures closely. The general public is more likely to have a greater interest in how Fed actions affect interest rates. The monthly payment on that new house or car depends not only on how good a deal the consumer is able to find, but also on monetary policy! Hints as to the future direction of monetary policy can be found when the chair of the Fed testifies before Congress each February and July. In between, the Fed issues press releases that explain monetary policy goals. ◄

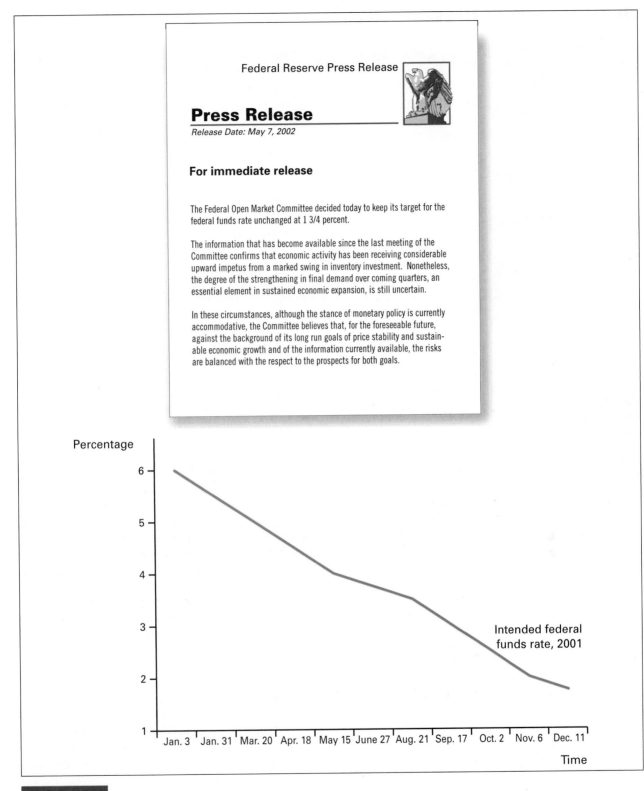

Federal Reserve Press Release

Press Release

Release Date: May 7, 2002

For immediate release

The Federal Open Market Committee decided today to keep its target for the federal funds rate unchanged at 1 3/4 percent.

The information that has become available since the last meeting of the Committee confirms that economic activity has been receiving considerable upward impetus from a marked swing in inventory investment. Nonetheless, the degree of the strengthening in final demand over coming quarters, an essential element in sustained economic expansion, is still uncertain.

In these circumstances, although the stance of monetary policy is currently accommodative, the Committee believes that, for the foreseeable future, against the background of its long run goals of price stability and sustainable economic growth and of the information currently available, the risks are balanced with the respect to the prospects for both goals.

Intended federal funds rate, 2001

FIGURE 14-9

MONETARY POLICY THROUGH THE FEDERAL FUNDS RATE The Federal Reserve press release shows the significance of the federal funds rate. The rate was set at 1.75 percent in December 2001 and not changed again until it was adjusted downward to 1.25 percent in November 2002. As seen in the graph, the intended federal funds rate was lowered numerous times in 2001.

Source: Federal Reserve web site. The press release is dated May 7, 2002.

14.6 HOW INDEPENDENT SHOULD A CENTRAL BANK BE?

The Federal Reserve is unique among government agencies in being subject to relatively few explicit government directives. The Fed has a great deal of independence to conduct monetary policy as it pleases, without interference from Congress, the president, or special-interest groups.

The fear that originally motivated Congress to insulate the Fed from politics is that political pressures could influence the Fed to pursue an expansionary monetary policy at the wrong moment—a policy that would ultimately lead to excessive inflation. Evidence suggests that the inflationary effects of monetary policy do not set in immediately, but appear only after a time lag. Thus, if the Fed were subject to political pressure, decision making could favor short-term popularity at the possible expense of long-term economic goals.

One source of the Fed's independence from political pressure is the structure of the Board of Governors. The president of the United States appoints governors to fourteen-year nonrenewable terms. Governors thus are given the freedom to make policy decisions without the worry of reappointment. Once on the Board, a governor is free to follow the dictates of conscience rather than the decrees of the president or Congress.

Typically, government agencies are funded by Congress. In contrast, the Fed funds itself. By retaining independent control of its own purse strings, the Fed retains independence of action. The Fed's secret of financial independence? The Fed is a banker's bank, and as such earns interest from the discount loans it makes to commercial banks. However, the major source of the Fed's earnings is interest from its holdings of Treasury securities—securities it may have purchased with newly printed Federal Reserve Notes! In recent years the Fed's income has totaled more than a whopping $30 billion each year, much of which it is required to turn over to the U.S. Treasury.

Another source of Federal Reserve independence is found in the financial markets. The Fed's policy actions have the potential to disturb the stock and bond markets, providing substantial gains or inflicting massive losses on the owners of stocks, bonds, and other financial instruments. Financial market participants, called "bond market vigilantes" in the press, stand ready to bail out of investments when they perceive the Fed's actions will threaten the value of those investments. That threat of a sell-off of stocks or bonds influences the Fed to act responsibly in the best long-term interests of the economy.

Even homeowners help keep the Fed independent. Higher expected inflation causes increases in interest rates. The interest rates on adjustable rate home mortgages go up when other interest rates rise. Homeowners with that type of mortgage will see their monthly house payments pushed up by the upward surge in interest rates that accompanies expected inflation. Hence, this segment of the public has a vested interest in seeing that the Fed acts to keep inflation in check.

For the reasons discussed, people have an interest in a stable monetary policy. Thus, the president's appointments to the Board do not go unnoticed. In 1983, for instance, the desire to keep financial markets from losing value influenced Republican President Reagan to reappoint then Board Chairman Paul Volcker even though Volcker had first been appointed to the Board by President Carter, a Democrat. Volcker was perceived by the markets as an experienced policymaker, independent and above politics, and thus a stabilizing influence on the economy. Similarly, President Clinton, a Democrat, was influenced to reappoint Chairman Greenspan, a Republican.

POSSIBLE DRAWBACKS OF THE FED'S ROLE

Critics argue the Fed has too much power, and charge it with decision making that favors its own self-interests and those of special interests, such as bankers. In this view, the Fed is akin to an aristocracy exercising power at the expense of the greater economic welfare.

Ostensibly, however, the Fed operates in the public interest. But what is the public interest? Possible goals include stable prices, stable interest rates, a stable foreign exchange value of the dollar, and stable overall economic activity, at a level sufficient to ensure high employment. Unfortunately, these economic variables fluctuate over time, sometimes severely.

Monetarists view the Fed with suspicion. Many monetarists believe that market economies are inherently stable, and that fluctuations in economic activity occur because of unstable monetary policies. If the monetarist view is true, then the Fed must be reined in, since its exercise of monetary policy is harmful. Thus, monetarists seek to limit Federal Reserve power. Others, especially those on Wall Street with a stake in financial stability, look to the Fed to keep the economy humming. While varying views of the Fed are unlikely to be reconciled, it remains true that Fed watching is a national pastime.

1. Since members of the Federal Reserve Board have so much power, should they be elected directly by the public? Explain.

2. How could the Federal Reserve hurt the economy? Provide some examples of Fed actions that could be harmful and of the damage that could be done. How can the Fed help the economy? Provide examples.

Thinking Critically

Visit **www.prenhall.com/collinge** for updates and web exercises on this Explore & Apply topic.

SUMMARY AND LEARNING OBJECTIVES

1. **Identify the types, functions, and liquidity of various money measures.**
   - Money increases economic efficiency by eliminating the need to barter.
   - Money performs three functions. Money must be a medium of exchange, meaning that it is usable to make purchases. Money also functions as a store of value and a unit of account.
   - Paper currency in the United States is an example of fiat money, which is money because the government says it is money. Commodity money in the form of U.S. silver or gold coins is no longer minted. One shortcoming of commodity money is that it is subject to Gresham's law—bad money drives good money out of circulation.
   - An item has the characteristic of being liquid when it is easily and quickly spendable. Currency is highly liquid.
   - Various parts of the money supply exhibit varying degrees of liquidity, although in general any component of the money supply can be considered liquid in relative terms. The M1, M2, and M3 money supplies are defined according to decreasing liquidity, respectively.
   - M1 is the most liquid measure of the money supply because it contains only currency and coins in circulation; checking account balances, also known as demand deposits; and the value of traveler's checks.

- M2 adds to M1 savings account balances plus small time deposits and money market mutual funds. M2 is considered a less-liquid measure of the money supply because savings account balances are not spendable without first converting them to currency or demand deposits.
- M3 adds to M2 several additional items that are typically less liquid than the items making up M2. Thus, M3 is considered the least liquid measure of the money supply.

2. **Describe key elements of the banking industry.**
   - The U.S. banking system includes 8,500 or so commercial banks that accept deposits and make loans.
   - Bank regulation is designed to provide for a stable banking system.
   - A bank's balance sheet shows its assets and liabilities. The assets include vault cash, deposits held by the Federal Reserve, loans, and securities. Vault cash plus deposits held by the Federal Reserve equals bank reserves. Banks must meet the reserve requirement set by the Federal Reserve. Assets show what a bank does with funds that are deposited with it.
   - Loans and securities, which are government bonds, provide banks with income.
   - The liabilities include customer deposits, federal funds, and discount loans. Federal funds are the

amount of reserves that a bank has borrowed from other banks. Discount loans are funds borrowed from the Federal Reserve.

- The Federal Deposit Insurance Corporation (FDIC) insures deposit accounts up to a maximum of $100,000.

- Key interest rates include the prime rate, the federal funds rate, and the discount rate. The prime rate is also called the bank prime lending rate. This interest rate applies to short-term business loans. The Federal funds rate is the interest rate on funds that banks borrow from other banks. The discount rate is set by the Fed and applies to loans that the Fed makes to banks.

3. Discuss how banks create money.

- Banks create money when they make loans. When loans are repaid, the money supply decreases.

- A borrower is provided with deposit money through the stroke of the banker's pen when the loan is granted.

4. Describe the structure, functions, and policy tools of the Federal Reserve.

- The Fed conducts monetary policy, holds bank deposits, and performs several other functions in its role as the U.S. central bank.

- The Federal Reserve is composed of three primary parts: the Board of Governors, the Federal Open Market Committee, and twelve regional Federal Reserve District Banks.

- The tools of monetary policy are open market operations, changes in the discount rate, and changes in the reserve requirement. Most monetary policy is conducted through open market operations.

- Open market operations occur when the Fed buys or sells securities. Fed purchases of securities tend to increase the money supply. Fed sales of securities tend to cause the money supply to decrease.

- The Fed also influences interest rates, which in turn affect other aspects of the economy.

5. Work through the process of monetary expansion using the deposit multiplier.

- The monetary base is the sum of currency in circulation plus bank reserves. The money supply equals the money multiplier multiplied by the monetary base.

- An initial deposit of new money into a bank results in an expansion of money through the money multiplier effect. The maximum value of the money multiplier is called the deposit multiplier. The value of the deposit

multiplier is computed by taking the reciprocal of the reserve requirement. Thus, when the reserve requirement equals 10 percent, the deposit multiplier equals 1/.10, which is 10.

- With a deposit multiplier of 10, a $10,000 open market purchase by the Fed could conceivably result in an expansion of the money supply by $100,000. This expansion of the money supply would occur as the result of a lending–depositing–lending sequence.

6. Explain the equation of exchange and its role in monetary policy.

- The equation of exchange is $M \times V = P \times Q$. This equation is an identity, meaning that each side of the equation must always equal the other side. The equation says that total spending ($M \times V$) equals the value of production ($P \times Q$). The equation of exchange forms the basis for the quantity theory of money.

- The quantity theory of money makes two assumptions about the variables in the equation of exchange. For one, velocity, V, is assumed to be constant. For the other, aggregate output, Q, is assumed to be at its maximum value, which is achieved when there is full employment in the economy. Thus, the quantity theory states that an increase in the money supply, M, on the left side of the equation of exchange will be accompanied by a proportional increase in the price level, P, on the right side of the equation of exchange.

- The quantity theory of money is illustrated graphically by the model of aggregate demand and aggregate supply. The long-run aggregate supply curve is vertical at full-employment GDP. An increase in aggregate demand occurs when there is an increase in the money supply. The increase in aggregate demand has no effect on output, but increases the price level.

- Monetarists argue that the Fed should target a slow and steady growth path for the money supply, so as to provide enough money for economic growth, but not so much as to cause an unacceptable level of inflation.

7. Address the importance of central banks staying independent of political pressures.

- Central bank independence is thought to insulate central banks from political influences and thus make it more likely that price stability is achieved.

- Independence arises from a number of sources, including the twelve regional Federal Reserve district banks, the Board of Governors' non-renewability of terms of appointment, financial market considerations, and the Fed's interest earnings on Treasury securities.

KEY TERMS

money, 316
barter, 316
medium of exchange, 316
store of value, 316
unit of account, 316
fiat money, 316
Gresham's law, 317
demand deposits, 317
liquidity, 318
M1, 318
M2, 319

M3, 319
bank reserves, 320
required reserves, 321
excess reserves, 321
interest, 321
interest rate, 321
bonds, 321
federal funds rate, 321
discount rate, 322
Federal Reserve System, 323
open market operations, 324

monetary base, 324
money multiplier, 326
deposit multiplier, 326
price rule, 329
equation of exchange, 329
velocity of money, 329
quantity theory of money, 330
monetarism, 331
nominal interest rate, 334
real interest rate, 334

TEST YOURSELF

TRUE OR FALSE

1. In fulfilling its medium of exchange function, money is set aside in savings accounts.
2. M3 includes only currency and checking account balances.
3. Federal funds represent bank reserves that have been borrowed by commercial banks at the discount window at the Fed.
4. The equation of exchange is written as $M \times Q = P \times V$.
5. The Fed conducts monetary policy ignoring the federal funds rate.

MULTIPLE CHOICE

6. Barter is most likely to occur when
   a. money takes the form of commodity money.
   b. M1 is the dominant form of money.
   c. Gresham's law requires people to barter.
   d. there is no money.
7. Which is NOT a function of money?
   a. Standard of measurement.
   b. Unit of account.
   c. Store of value.
   d. Medium of exchange.
8. The liquidity of money refers to its
   a. country of origin.
   b. denomination.
   c. store of value function.
   d. medium of exchange function.
9. Currency held in bank vaults is
   a. part of the M1 money supply.
   b. part of the M2 money supply.
   c. part of the M3 money supply.
   d. not part of the M1, M2, or M3 money supply.

10. The value of stocks is
    a. part of the M1 money supply.
    b. part of the M2 money supply.
    c. part of the M3 money supply.
    d. not part of the M1, M2, or M3 money supply.
11. A bank's total reserves equal
    a. required reserves.
    b. excess reserves.
    c. required reserves + excess reserves.
    d. required reserves − excess reserves.
12. Suppose a bank makes a loan in the amount of $1,000. Which of the following statements is correct about the immediate effect of the loan?
    a. The loan increases the money supply by $1,000.
    b. The loan leaves the money supply the same as it was before the loan.
    c. The loan changes the money supply by some amount that is impossible to determine from the information given.
    d. The loan decreases the money supply by $1,000.
13. Which of the following is NOT a function or activity of the Federal Reserve System?
    a. Lender of last resort.
    b. Accepts deposits from the public.
    c. Supervises banks.
    d. Clears checks.
14. If the money supply equals $100 and the money multiplier equals 10, then the monetary base must equal
    a. $1,000.
    b. $100.
    c. $10.
    d. an amount that cannot be determined from the information given.

15. If the reserve requirement were 20 percent and the Fed purchased $100 of securities in an open market purchase, then the money supply could potentially expand by a maximum of
    a. $5.
    b. $20.
    c. $100.
    d. $500.

16. Which of the following is consistent with a looser monetary policy?
    a. Open market sale of securities.
    b. Closer supervision of banks by the Fed.
    c. Decrease in discount rate.
    d. Increase in reserve requirement.

17. Monetarism recommends that monetary policy
    a. focus on low interest rates.
    b. focus on the stock market, aiming to increase stock prices.
    c. expand the money supply at a steady rate.
    d. be turned over to Congress.

18. A tight monetary policy is associated with
    a. low short-term interest rates.
    b. high short-term interest rates.
    c. alternating increases and decreases in interest rates.
    d. the money supply only, and not interest rates.

19. A monetary policy that aims to keep real interest rates low in the long run by expanding the money supply
    a. is considered the best monetary policy by economists.
    b. could lead to higher interest rates because of higher inflation created by the expansion of the money supply.
    c. would most likely cause deflation.
    d. would violate congressional regulation of the Fed.

20. Operating funds to support the Federal Reserve come mostly from
    a. the budget of the president of the United States.
    b. the Congress.
    c. garage sales, bake sales, and the other charitable fundraisers.
    d. interest earnings.

QUESTIONS AND PROBLEMS

1. *[money]* Suppose it became lawful for anyone to issue money without any government restrictions of any kind. What factors would influence an individual to either accept or reject privately issued money? What institutions might arise in the free market to help a person decide whether to accept or reject a particular private monetary note?

2. *[money]* Although the castaways on *Gilligan's Island* were marooned for several years on an "uncharted desert isle" they apparently had no money and saw fit not to adopt any item to use as money. Speculate on the circumstances under which a group of people stranded without money on an island might see fit to invent money. In your discussion be sure to include answers to the following questions: What form might their money take? Would a smaller or larger group of people be more conducive to the invention of money? Would the length of time they expected to remain on the island be a factor in how useful money would be to them? Would barter be a good alternative to money?

3. *[monetary aggregates]* List the components of M1, M2, and M3. Explain why the additional items in M3 make it a less-liquid measure of the money supply than M1.

4. *[balance sheet]* Are loans an asset or a liability to a commercial bank? Explain.

5. *[bank reserves]* What are the two places that banks can use to keep their reserves? Speculate on the decision process by which a bank decides how much of its reserves to keep in each place.

6. *[bank liabilities]* List and explain three major liabilities of commercial banks. Are a bank's liabilities best described as its sources of funds or its uses of funds? Explain.

7. *[Fed's functions]* Suppose that you are the president of a commercial bank. List the functions of the Federal Reserve System. Then describe how your bank would interact with the Fed in relation to each function.

8. *[Fed's components]* List and briefly describe the three components of the Federal Reserve System.

9. *[open market operations]* What are open market operations? What form would open market operations take if the Fed wished to see an increase in the money supply?

10. *[deposit multiplier]* What is the formula for the deposit multiplier? Compute the value of the deposit multiplier when the reserve requirement equals 25 percent.

11. *[monetary policy]* What Fed actions are consistent with a looser monetary policy? Which are in accord with a tighter policy?

12. *[quantity theory of money]* Write the equation of exchange. Define each variable in the equation and

then explain why the left side of the equation must equal the right.

13. *[quantity theory of money]* Suppose M = the money supply = \$200, V = velocity = 2, and Q = quantity of output = 100 units. What is the price level? According to the quantity theory of money, what happens to the price level if the money supply triples to \$600?

14. *[monetarism]* What is monetarism? How does it relate to the quantity theory of money? What monetary policy would a monetarist recommend?

15. *[interest rates]* What is your bank's current nominal interest rate on savings deposits? What is the real interest rate on savings deposits? If the real rate is negative, would people continue to hold dollars in savings accounts? Why?

16. *[federal funds rate]* What is the federal funds rate? Explain its significance to monetary policy.

17. *[interest rates and monetary policy]* Some people urge the Fed to aim at keeping interest rates in the economy very low, both in the short run and the long run. Yet the policies that keep interest low in the long run might sometimes require high interest rates in the short run. Explain, making reference to the distinction between real and nominal interest rates.

Visit www.prenhall.com/ayers for Exploring the Web exercises and additional self-test quizzes.

CHAPTER 15

FISCAL POLICY

A LOOK AHEAD

Debt is a four-letter word, one that has gotten many people in trouble. It can crimp one's lifestyle and even lead to personal bankruptcy. Many countries have felt the financial straitjacket of debt. In the United States, for example, the federal government has amassed debt of over $6 trillion and a deficit in the federal budget that increases that debt as the years go by. Irresponsible? Perhaps, perhaps not. As we will see in the Explore & Apply section that concludes this chapter, there is cause for both personal and national debt. There are also questions about the effect on the economy of policies that add more.

Government raises revenue through taxation, a topic of this chapter. It often spends more, though, engaging in deficit spending that might be intended to offset economic downturns and reduce economic instability. We will see potential problems with these policy actions, including getting them to take effect at the proper time and providing incentives to keep the economy productive.

LEARNING OBJECTIVES

Understanding Chapter 15 will enable you to:
1. **Explain why wages and prices might be slow to adjust downward, and what significance this can have.**
2. **Discuss how fiscal policy to stabilize the economy is subject to lags, and how the lags can be overcome automatically.**
3. **Explain how balancing the full-employment budget is consistent with a budget deficit.**
4. **List the major sources of revenue for government in the United States.**
5. **Explain the principles of tax equity and how they apply.**
6. **Interpret why the future of Social Security is in doubt.**
7. **Analyze the rationale and limitations of deficit spending.**

At any given point in time, the short-run instabilities of the business cycle often seem more compelling than the long-run tendencies discussed in the previous chapter. Whenever there is an economic downturn, the press and public call upon government to do something about it. People want action!

For example, the economic downturn that started in March of 2001, together with four years of surplus in the federal budget, led President Bush and Congress to authorize refunds of some tax payments in August of that year. Taxpayers received checks for up to $300 per person or $600 per couple. The idea was to energize the economy. In the time period between then and the terrorist shock of September 11, however, there was no discernible increase in consumer spending.

To bring the economy out of what then appeared to be a deepening recession, President Bush requested, and Congress enacted, $100 billion worth of tax cuts and new spending. There was almost no opposition to following this policy action. Elected representatives of the people want to show their constituencies action, not inaction. However, from the perspective of macroeconomic theory, herein lies the great debate. While Keynesians argue for government action, recall that classical economists emphasize that markets are quite capable of doing their own adjusting.

15.1 SHORT-RUN STICKINESS ALONG AGGREGATE DEMAND

The debate over macro policy often comes down to the question of nothing more than whether to wait for a movement along aggregate demand or to take action to *manage aggregate demand,* meaning to shift the aggregate demand curve itself. We proceed by looking at the adjustment process along aggregate demand, and then by looking at some policy options for aggregate demand management.

If a market is not at equilibrium, forces of supply and demand will cause the price to change until the equilibrium comes about. That is the classical analysis: Wage and price adjustments will lead to a long-run macro equilibrium that is characterized by both full employment and its associated full-employment output. Keynesians do not dispute this point, but dispute its relevance when the economy faces immediate macroeconomic problems that call for prompt solutions. Of particular note is the existence of downwardly **sticky wages** and **sticky prices,** where downwardly sticky refers to an inflexibility that makes it difficult for wages and prices to fall. If wages are sticky, the downward movement in wages required to reach a long-run equilibrium could take too long. The downward stickiness could be due to labor contracts between a union and its employees. It could also be due to human psychology—when firms cut wages, their workers resent it.

One reason for wage and price stickiness is that some markets might not move to equilibrium easily. Changes in the demand for outputs make it appropriate for some wages and prices to rise or fall relative to other wages and prices. However, there is resistance to change—*rigidities*—within both labor and output markets. Stores have leases and contracts that are not easily adjusted. In some cases, the contracts are with unions that resist wage cuts.

In principle, wage and price stickiness might occur in either direction—whether for price increases or for price decreases. In practice, **wage and price stickiness is most pronounced in a downward direction,** meaning that there is more stickiness when markets resist lower wages and prices. For example, it is natural for workers to resent a wage cut, no matter what the macroeconomic circumstances might be. Firms that cut wages run the risk of lower productivity and lower quality output from their workers. The problem is often exacerbated by a lack of information and trust. When employers attempt to downsize or close operations, employees balk, which causes adjustments in employment and output to occur slowly.

sticky wages wages that are slow to adjust, usually in a downward direction.

sticky prices prices that are slow to adjust, usually in a downward direction.

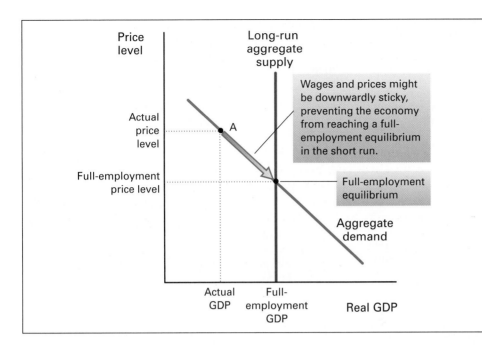

FIGURE 15-1

DOWNWARDLY STICKY WAGES AND PRICES Wages and prices that are downwardly sticky would prevent the economy from moving rapidly to a full-employment equilibrium. For example, the economy might start at point *A*, with a price level that is too high to reach full-employment output. In the long run, that price level will fall, but wage and price stickiness might prevent it from doing so in the short run.

Figure 15-1 sums up the significance of downwardly sticky wages and prices. While wages are not listed explicitly in this figure, wages paid by firms will be a big factor in determining their costs and the prices they charge. In other words, higher wages are associated with a higher price level. When the price level is too high to sustain a full-employment equilibrium, it must adjust downward to reach that equilibrium. Sticky wages and prices can get in the way of that adjustment.

For example, if the actual price level is above the full-employment price level, such as at point *A*, wage and price stickiness would prevent it from dropping fast enough that the full-employment equilibrium can be reached quickly. By delaying movement down the aggregate demand curve to a full-employment equilibrium, wage and price stickiness can mean a prolonged period in which both output and employment are below the economy's potential.

15.2 FISCAL POLICY TO STABILIZE THE BUSINESS CYCLE

Suppose the economy starts at an **unemployment equilibrium,** characterized by a price level that is too high to achieve full-employment GDP, but that refuses to fall because of sticky prices. If the price level cannot fall to correct the unemployment equilibrium, the only solution is to shift aggregate demand rightward by increasing spending power. The shift can be accomplished by monetary policy, as discussed in the previous chapter. Alternatively, aggregate demand can be shifted by **fiscal policy,** which is government policy toward taxation and spending.

unemployment equilibrium a short-run equilibrium GDP that is less than full-employment GDP.

fiscal policy government tax and spending policy.

FISCAL STIMULI AND FISCAL DRAGS

When the economy finds itself stuck at an unemployment equilibrium, Keynesians advocate using **expansionary fiscal policy,** also called **fiscal stimulus,** which is increased government spending or reduced taxation intended to *stimulate* aggregate demand and return the economy to full employment. The Works Progress Administration and other New Deal public works programs of President Franklin Roosevelt are examples of stimulative fiscal

expansionary fiscal policy (fiscal stimulus) occurs when government adds to aggregate expenditures by lowering the amount of tax revenue it collects or increasing the amount of its spending.

FIGURE 15-2

EXPANSIONARY FISCAL POLICY Expansionary fiscal policies shift aggregate demand to the right by adding to government and/or consumer spending, as shown in (a). When the economy starts at an unemployment equilibrium, Keynesians would suggest using expansionary fiscal policy to shift aggregate demand to the right. As shown in (b), the idea is to shift aggregate demand just far enough to reach long-run aggregate supply at full-employment output and achieve a full-employment equilibrium.

policies. Indeed, World War II seemed to prove the validity of Keynesian economics, since the massive amount of government spending it involved paved the way from the Great Depression of the 1930s to the prosperity of the 1950s. With more government spending, aggregate demand shifts to the right, as shown in Figure 15-2(a). The Keynesian idea is to shift it just enough to reach full-employment output, as shown in Figure 15-2(b), thus solving unemployment problems without causing inflation.

Alternatively, when the economy *overheats*—or grows so fast that inflation threatens—government can use **contractionary fiscal policy,** also called **fiscal drag,** to slow it down. Contractionary fiscal policy might involve higher taxes or less government spending. Figure 15-3(a) and (b) illustrate how contractionary fiscal policy can shift aggregate demand to the left to avoid overheating.

contractionary fiscal policy (fiscal drag) occurs when the government reduces aggregate expenditures by increasing the amount of tax revenue it collects or reducing the amount of its spending.

multiplier effect occurs when subsequent rounds of private sector behavior reinforce the initial impact of a fiscal policy change.

Fiscal policy actions are enhanced by the **multiplier effect**, in which subsequent rounds of private sector behavior reinforce the initial impact of a fiscal policy change. For example, if the government increases its spending, people in the private sector will have increased incomes from that spending and in turn spend more themselves. This process generates an ongoing cycle of greater income and greater intended spending. At each stage in the cycle, however, some income is likely to be saved, thus eventually bringing the cycle to a halt.

The multiplier effect is depicted in Figure 15-4. Part (a) shows the multiplier effect for an expansionary fiscal policy, such as for an increase in government spending or a decrease in taxation. Part (b) shows just the opposite, which would occur in response to a contractionary fiscal policy, such as a decrease in government spending or an increase in taxation. Observe that the multiplier effect shifts the aggregate demand curve in its entirety, which could lead to changes in the price level that could partially or fully offset any output changes caused by the multiplier.

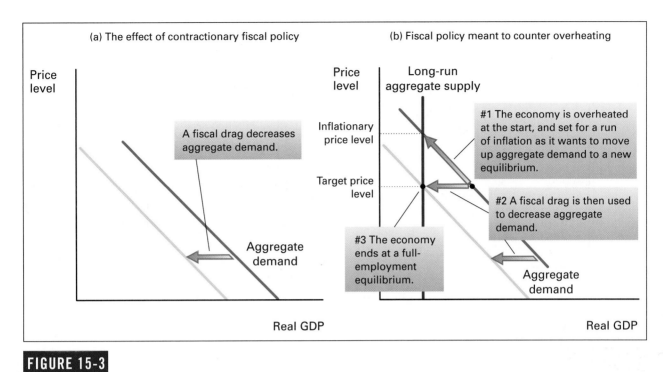

FIGURE 15-3

CONTRACTIONARY FISCAL POLICY Contractionary fiscal policies shift aggregate demand to the left by reducing government and/or consumer spending, as shown in (a). When the economy starts overheating, such that it is likely to cause inflation as it moves up aggregate demand to a long-run equilibrium, contractionary fiscal policy can be used to shift aggregate demand. As shown in (b), the idea is to shift aggregate demand just far enough to the left to reach long-run aggregate supply at the current price level so as to achieve a full-employment equilibrium.

FISCAL POLICY CHOICE: DISCRETIONARY OR AUTOMATIC?

Both expansionary and contractionary fiscal policy are examples of **discretionary policy**— public policy adjusted at the discretion of lawmakers. Unfortunately, even the best intentioned discretionary public policy is unlikely to follow the Keynesian policy prescription of managing aggregate demand in order to counter short-run instability. The reason has to do with the three *fiscal policy lags*:

- The **recognition lag**—It takes time to know that the economy is in a recession. For example, although not an official standard, it usually takes approximately two consecutive quarters of declining GDP before the authoritative National Bureau of Economic Research (NBER) declares a recession. In late November of 2001, the NBER declared that the economy was in a recession that started in March of that year.
- The **action lag**—Tax and spending bills are not passed overnight. The fiscal stimulus aimed at the 2001 recession was not passed until 2002.
- The **implementation lag**—It's great to build a highway, but most people expect to have it planned out before crews are sent to lay asphalt! Once spending is authorized, the details must be planned and the money spent, which takes time. It also takes time before tax changes can take effect.

Because of fiscal policy lags, the business cycle may have turned by the time the money starts flowing from an expansionary fiscal policy. The spending may be more likely to cause inflation than to reduce unemployment. Policy lags make it very difficult, if not impossible, to *fine-tune* the economy to even out the ups and downs of the business

discretionary policy public policy adjusted through explicit changes made by lawmakers.

recognition lag time before policymakers recognize that a problem exists.

action lag time between when the problem is recognized and when policies are enacted.

implementation lag time between when policies are enacted and when they take effect.

FIGURE 15-4

THE MULTIPLIER EFFECT OF FISCAL POLICY The impact of expansionary fiscal policy can be much larger than the amount of increased government spending or decreased taxation. The shift in aggregate demand occurs in multiple rounds, with the direct effect of the policy being only the first round. Indirect effects occur as the spending increases some people's incomes, which lead them to spend more, which increases other people's incomes, causing those people to spend more, and so forth.

The result is that the after-effects of the policy change continue to shift aggregate demand to the right, as shown in graph (a), with the shifts becoming progressively smaller because people don't spend every penny of the income they receive. The same sort of multiplier effect would occur in reverse if the government were to choose a contractionary fiscal policy. Graph (b) depicts this result.

cycle. Fine-tuning would require that contractionary fiscal policy start when the economy pushes above full-employment GDP. Likewise, when the economy sinks to less than full-employment GDP, then finely tuned fiscal policy should be expansionary. Figure 15-5 shows both possibilities.

automatic stabilizers features embedded within existing fiscal policies that act as a stimulant when the economy is sluggish and act as a drag when it is in danger of inflation.

Instead of discretionary policy, lawmakers can rely on **automatic stabilizers.** Automatic stabilizers are components of existing fiscal policies that stimulate the economy when it is sluggish and act as a drag when it overheats. The U.S. economy has automatic stabilizers embedded within its system of taxation and spending.

Consider automatic stabilizers on the tax side. As personal and corporate incomes fall during recession, so too does the amount collected by the federal government in personal and corporate income taxes. The reduced tax burden on individuals and companies helps reduce the severity of that recession. Alternatively, if the economy is booming, income taxes bring in revenue, which is contractionary because it removes some of the excess purchasing power. No policy action is necessary.

On the spending side, payments for welfare, unemployment compensation, and other social programs rise as the economy slows and more people seek these safety-net services. Conversely, this spending falls when the economy heats up, just as Keynesian policy prescribes. Again, the action to stabilize the economy is automatic; no policy adjustments are needed. Taken as a whole, the automatic stabilizers are intended to be expansionary if the economy is below full employment and contractionary when the economy is overheating. **If the economy is at full employment, fiscal policy should be neutral, since there is no need to either stimulate or slow down economic activity.**

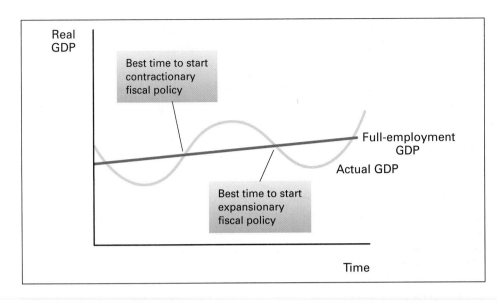

FIGURE 15-5

FISCAL POLICY TIMING The best time for contractionary fiscal policy is when the economy starts to overheat, meaning that it is exceeding full-employment GDP. The best time for expansionary fiscal policy is when the economy has fallen into a recession below the full-employment GDP. Lags make it hard to fine-tune discretionary fiscal policy such that it follows these prescriptions. Automatic stabilizers, in contrast, tend to push down the economy's peaks and push up its troughs without any change in the policies themselves.

QUICKCHECK

(a) Once federal spending is approved, why is there an implementation lag? Use a new highway as an example. (b) Must all fiscal policies have a long implementation lag? Explain.

Answer: (a) Projects must first be planned. A new highway requires a considerable amount of surveying before the specifics of its route and features are established. Land must then be acquired. There continues to be a sequence of employing different types of labor and other inputs for different phases of the construction. The final product may not be completed for several years. (b) Projects that require little planning will have a shorter implementation lag.

BALANCING THE BUDGET

A **balanced budget** occurs when tax revenue inflows just equal government expenditure outflows. Whether fiscal policy is discretionary or is accomplished by automatic stabilizers, economists often suggest that it should be set so that the budget roughly balances over the course of the business cycle. The idea is that, when the economy is overheated and contractionary policy is in order, the government would run a **budget surplus** in which tax revenue exceeds government spending. When economic health is poor and expansionary policy is needed, the government would then choose a **budget deficit** in which government spending exceeds tax revenue. The surpluses could help pay for the deficits.

In practice, however, there is a significant tilt toward the expansionary side, even when the economy is doing well. To assess this tilt, we can look at the **full-employment budget,** which is an estimate of what government revenue and spending would be were there full employment. The full-employment budget has usually been in deficit in recent years. For example, despite being in the vicinity of full employment for much of the past two decades, the U.S. government has run substantial budget deficits in the large majority of those years, as seen in Figure 15-6. The result of the accumulation of past budget deficits and surpluses is, on balance, a U.S. **national debt** of over $6 trillion by the end of 2002. Roughly half of this debt is owed within government (mostly to Social Security), with the other half owed to

balanced budget occurs when government revenue equals government spending.

budget surplus occurs when government collects more revenue than it spends.

budget deficit occurs when government collects less revenue than it spends.

full-employment budget estimate of government revenue and spending were the economy to be at full employment.

national debt how much money the government owes.

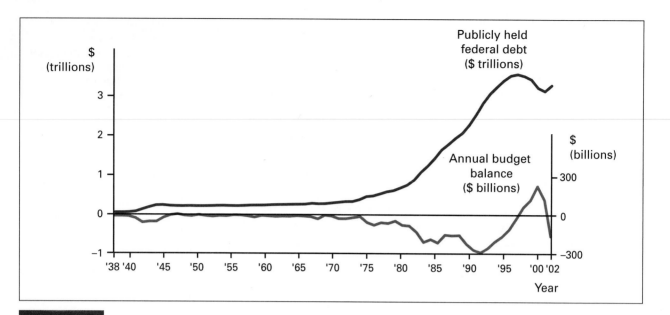

FIGURE 15-6

THE U.S. BUDGET Budget deficits have been the norm in modern U.S. history. These deficits have added to the national debt over time. This figure shows the portion of the debt held by the public. Including debt from one government agency to another (not shown), the national debt totaled over $6 trillion in 2002.

Source: 2002 Economic Report of the President, Table B-78.

the public. The latter portion of debt is shown in Figure 15-6. The national debt increases when there are budget deficits and decreases when there are budget surpluses. This is money owed by the U.S. government, mostly to American citizens. Budget deficits and the national debt will be further discussed in this chapter's Explore & Apply section.

SNAPSHOT   **SQUANDERING THE SURPLUS?**

For four glorious years—from 1998 through 2001—the United States government experienced the luxury of a budget surplus. The national debt got a chance to decline for the first time in three decades. It was more than nice. The declining national debt instilled hope that the country could actually afford its commitments, such as to Social Security for the looming wave of retiring baby boomers. Then reality struck.

First came the stock market slide and later a mild recession, which caused the government to pay out more in unemployment insurance and other assistance. The September 11 terrorist attacks added the need for massive amounts of government spending on national security. All of this combined to create a mentality in Washington, D.C., of spend and spend some more. By the middle of 2002, the economy was expanding, but so too was government spending. With massive new commitments to agriculture, the military, and for homeland security, a return to the days of budget surpluses was no longer in sight. ◀

15.3 POLICY IN PRACTICE

In this world nothing can be said to be certain, except death and taxes.

—*Benjamin Franklin*

Few things are less popular than taxes, since taxes represent money that is taken from us involuntarily by the government. However, we all like to be the recipients of government spending. If we live in the U.S. economy, with its large variety of both taxes and government activities, we are likely to see both.

SPENDING AND TAXATION

Government spending in the United States encompasses a vast array of programs. Some of these programs go toward the purchase of goods and services, such as highways or national defense. Others are regulatory programs, such as those conducted by the Occupational Safety and Health Administration or the Environmental Protection Agency. In addition, a large fraction of government spending goes toward **transfer payments** that redistribute income to the needy. Transfer payments include unemployment compensation, welfare, and other *safety-net programs* that provide economic security. Transfer payments account for approximately 44 percent of total federal spending. Figure 15-7 shows the growth in transfer payments and other components of federal spending over time.

transfer payments the redistribution of income from one group to another.

Because taxes take roughly 30 percent of gross domestic product (GDP), taxpayers are acutely concerned that they not be taken advantage of—in other words, that all pay their fair share. This is the goal of equity. Because taxes can discourage work effort and investment, a second goal in taxation is efficiency. **To achieve efficiency, taxes that are intended to raise revenues should do so in a manner that affects our behavior the least.** Efficiency in taxation gives citizens the greatest possible incentive to be productive.

Figure 15-8 illustrates the relative importance of revenue sources for the U.S. federal government. The personal income tax is the single largest source, providing 50 percent of all revenues. As U.S. citizens accumulate income over the course of the year, the federal personal income tax claims those earnings at incremental rates that increase from 10 percent to 15 percent, to 25 percent, to 28 percent, to 33 percent, and to 35 percent. This incremental tax rate on incremental income is known as the **marginal tax rate,** which equals 25 percent for most American taxpayers.

marginal tax rate tax rate on additional income.

Marginal tax rate = Additional taxes owed as a percentage of additional income

In other words, the average citizen pays twenty-five cents to the IRS on each additional dollar he or she earns. Marginal tax rates are shown in Table 15-1. Note that the marginal tax rate differs from the *average tax rate,* which equals a person's total tax liability divided by total income at the end of the year.

Average tax rate = Total taxes owed as a percentage of total income

The amount of income withheld from your paycheck is based on your projected average tax liability.

As seen in Figure 15-8(a), Social Security taxes, inclusive of the hospitalization portion of *Medicare*—health insurance for the elderly—account for 35 percent of federal revenues, second only to the share of the personal income tax. The Social Security tax is a *payroll tax,* in which the government deducts a flat 7.65 percent from the amount of money the employer pays, plus another 7.65 percent from the amount of money the employee receives. Taken together, the Social Security tax collects 15.3 percent of a worker's payroll income, up to a maximum individual income of $84,900 in 2002, after which only the 2.9 percent Medicare hospitalization tax continues to be collected.

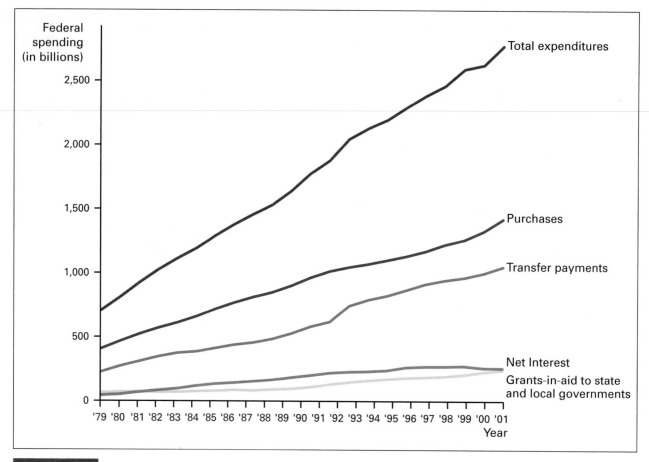

FIGURE 15-7

FEDERAL SPENDING Spending by the federal government has grown rapidly over the last century, especially spending on transfer payments, interest on the national debt, and grants-in-aid from the federal to state and local governments. Slightly more than half of federal purchases are related to national defense.

Source: 2002 Economic Report of the President, Table B-83.

Figure 15-8(b) shows how the taxes collected are spent. The largest category of spending is on transfer payments, especially Social Security. Other federal spending goes to purchase goods and services, pay the interest on the national debt, provide grant monies to state and local governments, and a variety of other government subsidy programs.

The corporation income tax takes in approximately 30 percent of corporate profits, and brought in revenues of $151.1 billion in 2001, equaling about 7.5 percent of total federal revenues. The corporation income tax has proven to be quite controversial over time because, while it may seem fair to tax corporations as though they are people, the **tax incidence** of the corporation income tax—meaning who ultimately winds up paying the tax—is on real people who directly or indirectly own the corporations and who also pay personal income taxes or other taxes relating to that ownership.

tax incidence identifies those who eventually wind up paying a tax.

Figure 15-9(a) shows state and local revenue sources. Most states rely heavily on a combination of individual income taxes, sales taxes, revenue from the federal government, and other charges. Major sources of revenue at the local level include property taxes and sales taxes. Figure 15-9(b) shows how state and local governments spend their

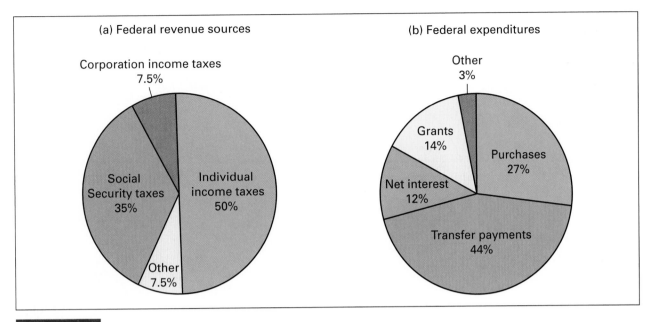

FIGURE 15-8

FEDERAL REVENUE SOURCES AND EXPENDITURES

Source: 2002 Economic Report of the President, Table B–80. The data are for 2001.

Source: National Income and Product Accounts Tables. The data are for 2001.

TABLE 15-1   MARGINAL PERSONAL INCOME TAX RATES FOR SINGLES, 2003

TAX RATE	TAXABLE INCOME
10%	up to $7,000
15%	$7,001–$28,400
25%	$28,401–$68,800
28%	$68,801–$143,500
33%	$143,501–$311,950
35%	$311,951 or more

revenue. The "Other" category is very large because it includes many types of expenditures. Examples include libraries, hospitals, police protection, fire protection, and much more.

States have to be careful not to tax any one source of revenue much more heavily than do other states, or that revenue source will migrate to the less-taxing state. This problem plagued New York in the 1960s and 1970s, as the poor moved in to receive generous welfare benefits, while many of the wealthy moved away to avoid paying the high income taxes that financed those benefits.

When all the revenues received by all units of government are added together, the result is that **government revenues in the United States are over 30 percent of the value of**

FIGURE 15-9

STATE AND LOCAL GOVERNMENT
REVENUE SOURCES AND
EXPENDITURES

*Source: 2002 Economic Report of
the President*, Table B–86. The data
are for 1998–1999.

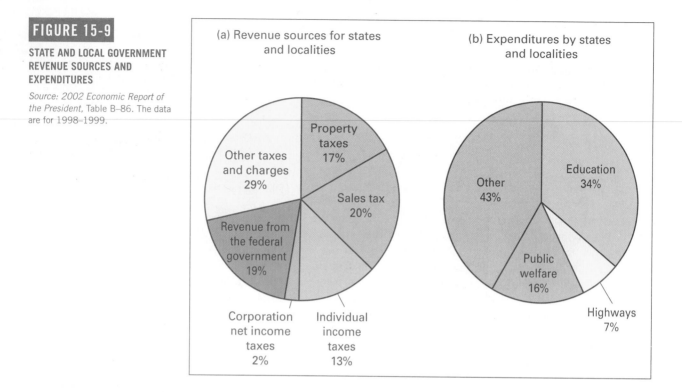

(a) Revenue sources for states and localities

(b) Expenditures by states and localities

production. Another way of looking at this is that the average American must work until "Tax Freedom Day" each year—declared by the Tax Foundation to be April 27 as of 2002—in order to have enough money to pay the government.

SNAPSHOT   **"DON'T TAX YOU, DON'T TAX ME—TAX THAT FELLOW BEHIND THE TREE."**

That was how former U.S. Senator Russell Long of Louisiana put it. In the abstract, taxes sound great. Higher taxes can eliminate the need for government borrowing and can pay for more of the public services we value. There is only one problem. We want to keep our own money and for that reason want those taxes to be paid by people other than ourselves.

Some localities have found a way to do just that through *tax exporting,* which is getting nonresidents to finance government. For example, speed zones on roads through small towns allow those towns to collect revenue from unsuspecting motorists. The payments on their speeding tickets keep property taxes down, while the out-of-towner is never heard from again.

Bigger cities resort to surcharges on rental cars and lodging, since few people will change their travel plans because of such a tax. Although convention planners do pay attention, most tourists and business travelers have probably left town before they know what's hit them. Travelers might grind their teeth and mutter. The locals merely smile as their government pockets the cash. ◄

EVALUATING EQUITY

Taxes are used to redistribute income from the haves to the have-nots, and in the process remedy some of the inequities that arise in a free-market economy. People's views on equity vary widely, however, which means that issues of equity in taxation—*tax equity*—become a matter of hot debate. Some basic principles can help frame this debate. The two most fundamental principles of tax equity are as follows:

- The **benefit principle** states that a fair tax is one that taxes people in proportion to the benefits they receive when government spends the tax revenues.
- The **ability-to-pay principle** states that those who can afford to pay more taxes than others should be required to do so.

The gasoline tax would appear to satisfy the benefit principle of tax equity, because gasoline tax revenues are *earmarked* for—restricted to—highway construction and repair. The more someone drives, the more government-funded highways the person drives on, and the more gasoline tax the person pays. In general, *user fees* are designed to meet the benefit principle of tax equity.

The benefit principle cannot be applied to programs whose purpose is to redistribute income. To see why not, consider food stamps (like money but only spendable on food). According to the benefit principle, food stamp recipients should pay for the cost of those food stamps. However, this would have the effect of defeating the fundamental purpose of the food stamp program, which is to help those in need. Food stamps are of no help if you have to pay for them! Thus, to justify redistributional programs, a different principle of tax equity is invoked—the ability-to-pay principle. The idea of the ability-to-pay principle is that the more a person is able to pay, the more that person should pay.

Many people interpret the ability-to-pay principle to mean that taxes designed for redistributing income should be progressive. A **progressive tax** collects a higher percentage of high incomes than of low incomes. In contrast, a **regressive tax** collects a higher percentage of low incomes than of high incomes. A **proportional tax** collects the same percentage of income, no matter what the income is. A *flat tax* that taxes all income at the same tax rate would be proportional. In practice, proposals for a so-called flat tax almost always provide for some exemptions that make the tax progressive overall.

The key here is percentage. A tax that collects $1,000 from a poor person earning $10,000 and $10,000 from a rich person earning $1 million is regressive, because the poor person pays 10 percent of his or her income, whereas the rich person pays only 1 percent.

Sometimes it is hard to determine whether or not a tax is progressive. For instance, consider the Social Security tax, which is defined broadly to include the Medicare tax. The Social Security tax may be considered either proportional, regressive, or progressive, depending on which aspects of the system are under scrutiny. Up to the 2002 limit of $84,900 of payroll income received, the tax is proportional at 15.3 percent. Because the marginal payroll tax rate beyond that point drops to only 2.9 percent (the Medicare component), the average tax rate declines with income and the overall tax is regressive. However, if Social Security benefits are included along with the taxes, the Social Security system as a whole is highly progressive, as will be discussed in more detail later in this chapter.

benefit principle states that a fair tax is one that taxes people in proportion to the benefits they receive when government spends those tax revenues.

ability-to-pay principle states that those who can afford to pay more taxes than others should be required to do so.

progressive tax a tax that collects a higher percentage of high incomes than of low incomes.

regressive tax a tax that collects a higher percentage of low incomes than of high incomes.

proportional tax a tax that collects the same percentage of high incomes as of low incomes.

QUICKCHECK

If your tax bill rises as your income rises, does that mean the tax is progressive?

Answer: Not necessarily. For the tax to be progressive, it must not only collect more revenue from you as your income rises, but it must also take a higher fraction of your total income.

PROGRESSIVE—WHAT'S IN A WORD?

The terms *progressive* and *regressive* are loaded—they make an implicit normative judgment about what is good and bad. After all, who could argue against progress? Would you prefer to regress? That would be moving backward, not forward. Bear in mind, though, that there is nothing magical about the terms.

The ability-to-pay principle of equity says that, to finance government, the rich should pay more than the poor. It does not specify whether the higher taxes should be less than, more than, or exactly in proportion to the higher income. For instance, it would make life simpler if we had one flat-rate income tax, with no exemptions, deductions, exclusions, and so on. Such a tax would be proportional, but would it be fair? That judgment is entirely up to you. ◄

TRADING OFF EFFICIENCY AND EQUITY

Economic efficiency involves getting the most valuable output from the inputs available. It bakes the biggest economic pie. In general, taxes are efficient to the extent that they do not change our behavior, with the most efficient tax being the one we cannot influence or escape.

To see how taxes cause inefficiency, consider an increase in the income tax. Some workers, especially those who are not heads of households, would cut back their work efforts. Even those who do not cut back would find that getting ahead in the workplace would bring less reward. For this reason, people are less likely to invest their time and money to acquire more human capital. Corporate income taxes mean that businesses also don't invest as much, either, because the corporation income tax cuts down on the return to that investment.

For an efficient tax, we can turn to the *head tax.* In short, if you have a head, you pay the tax! Since head taxes are efficient and require virtually no paperwork, should all of our other taxes be replaced by head taxes? You probably see the problem. While the economic pie would be large, most of us would consider it to be sliced very unfairly. In other words, head taxes would not be equitable.

in-kind benefits a government-provided good or service, as opposed to cash.

Not only are tax laws written with an eye toward equity, but government spending is often targeted toward promoting equity directly through provision of a social safety net. This safety net targets the needy with both cash transfers and **in-kind benefits,** which are any benefits other than money. Social Security is far and away the largest cash transfer program, redirecting a significant amount of current earnings to current retirees. The largest in-kind program is Medicaid, which provides health insurance for the impoverished.

A tradeoff between efficiency and equity pervades our system of tax and spending programs. Ideally, to provide a broad and generous safety net, the government might guarantee good housing, good food, and good health insurance for everyone. The better the guarantees, however, the more the programs will cost and the less the incentives will be to work and invest. There are three reasons for this inefficient reduction in work incentives, as follows:

- There is less need to better yourself to the extent that the government guarantees you a comfortable lifestyle. As the saying goes, necessity is the mother of invention.
- If you choose to forge ahead anyway, your greater ability to take care of yourself causes you to lose eligibility for many welfare-type programs. Over some ranges of income, the loss of benefits from Medicaid, subsidized housing, food stamps, and other welfare programs more than offsets the value of extra income earned.
- Obtaining the money for safety-net programs requires the government to either tax or borrow, which would need to be repaid from future tax revenue. With taxes comes less incentive to work and invest.

We could eliminate the second problem if we offer eligibility to everyone, regardless of income. However, that policy would accentuate the third problem.

There is no ready answer to the dilemma of choosing between a generous safety net and incentives for economic productivity. This is an area of seemingly endless political debate and compromise. We don't want the income tax burden to be so high that our economy stagnates because we have little to gain personally by being productive. However, our economy can afford to provide some degree of economic security for those in need. Choices of this sort are why policymakers face what has been called *the big tradeoff* between efficiency and equity in the design of government tax and spending programs.

15.4 SOCIAL SECURITY

Social Security is far and away the government's largest program, with the Social Security tax alone accounting for more than a third of Federal revenue, as was shown in Figure 15-8. For this reason, we use Social Security as our focus to examine the issues that arise in fiscal policy.

Social Security collects taxes on all payroll income, and allots the proceeds for *OASDI* and *HI*, which stand for old age, survivors, and disability insurance, and hospitalization insurance, respectively. The hospitalization portion is more commonly known as Medicare. The combined employer and employee Social Security tax rate is 15.3 percent of the first $84,900 of that income as of 2002, where the threshold has been adjusted upward over time in response to wage inflation. For income over that threshold, the Social Security tax is eliminated except for the 2.9 percent Medicare component. The rates have risen over time, as shown in Figure 15-10.

Turning to Social Security's impact on wages, consider Figure 15-11, which illustrates the economy's supply and demand for labor. The sellers are the people who offer labor; the buyers are firms. The supply of labor is shown as a vertical line because the quantity of labor supplied depends primarily on the natural rate of unemployment rather than on the specifics of tax policy. The portion of the Social Security tax paid by employers reduces their after-tax demand for labor by the same percentage as the tax, since the value of labor to the firm is reduced by the amount of tax that must be paid for that labor. This reduction is shown in the figure by a downward shift in labor demand, a shift that is just sufficient to cover Social Security taxes.

As seen in Figure 15-11, requiring the firm to pay Social Security taxes causes the equilibrium wage to be lower by exactly the amount of the tax. In effect, the tax burden has been *shifted* from employers to employees. The result is that workers effectively pay the full 15.3 percent Social Security tax. Many employees are unaware of the true magnitude of the Social Security tax, because only half of the combined 15.3 percent rate appears on their pay stubs.

INCOME REDISTRIBUTION—NOT JUST FOR EQUITY

Social Security is primarily **pay-as-you-go,** meaning that current workers pay for people who are currently retired. In this way, **Social Security redistributes income from one generation to another.** This redistribution started off in a small way. When Social Security was first established in 1934–1935, the first pension was not planned to begin until 1942. The tax rate was initially set to reach only 5 percent in total, with 2½ percent levied on the pay of workers and another 2½ percent on the employers doing the paying. In contrast, the current combined tax rate is 15.3 percent.

In 1945, the ratio of workers to retirees was about 50 to 1. It is currently about 3 to 1, and predicted to drop to only about 2 to 1 by 2030. Therefore, the burden on workers rises. To keep benefits constant, the Social Security Administration estimates that, by 2034, the tax rate would need to rise to almost 21 percent (18 percent, excluding Medicare). Without a tax increase, benefits would need to fall to three-fourths of their current amount.

pay-as-you-go referring to Social Security, meaning that current workers pay for current retirees.

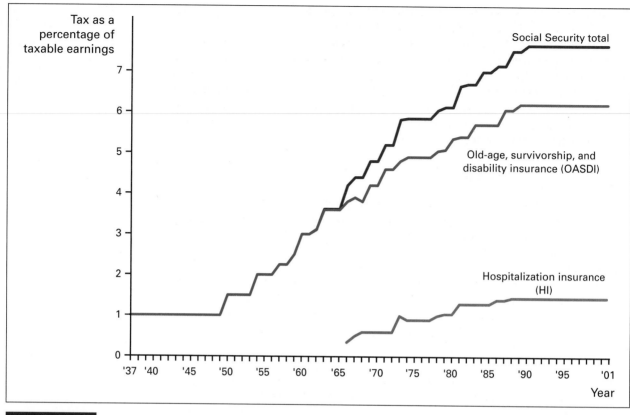

FIGURE 15-10

SOCIAL SECURITY TAX RATES OVER TIME Social Security rates are shown as a percentage of taxable earnings. Rates apply to both employees and employers, so that the total tax rates are double those shown. Hospitalization insurance is more commonly known as Medicare.

Source: U.S. Social Security Administration, data updated March 22, 2001.

FIGURE 15-11

EFFECT OF SOCIAL SECURITY TAX ON WAGES The employer share of the Social Security tax is passed on to workers in the form of lower wages. The market-equilibrium wage rate falls by 7.65% as firms' willingness to pay for workers falls by 7.65% in response to the employers' 7.65% share of the Social Security tax.

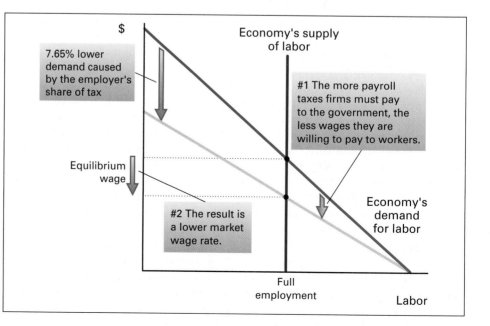

Social Security also redistributes income within generations. The ratio of payments to retirees relative to the amount they contributed in their working years is much higher for the low income than for the high income. Payments are also adjusted on the basis of need, which is determined in part by the number of dependents a person has. Thus, even though the Social Security tax took out the same portion of each person's income when he or she was working, the percentage that Social Security gives back is much higher for the poor.

On an after-tax basis, Social Security may even pay the retired low-income worker more than he or she earned when working. A worker at the maximum income subject to Social Security tax, in contrast, is likely to receive only about 30 percent as much as when employed. The upshot is that, when Social Security taxes and payments are combined, the Social Security system is highly progressive. Low-income workers have money redistributed their way from the tax dollars paid by higher-income workers.

The redistribution from higher-income workers to lower-income workers is one reason participation in Social Security is required by law. If it were optional, workers with above-average incomes would quit, leaving no money to redistribute. Workers would also be deterred from joining voluntarily by intergenerational redistribution, which gives current retirees a much better deal than can be expected by current workers.

If the present structure of Social Security were to be offered by any private business, the owners of that business would be prosecuted for fraud for running an illegal *ponzi scheme,* in which the money from current investors is used to finance paybacks to longer-term investors. Ponzi schemes are very risky; if new investors ever stop coming, the most recent investors lose their money.

Social Security has a significant advantage over the typical ponzi scheme, however. New investors are forced into the system by the government and its power to tax. However, if the government changes its mind down the road, investors who have yet to receive a pay-back could lose out. Even if Social Security were fully financed, though, the low returns it offers would dissuade potential investors. Figure 15-12 illustrates these returns. Note that the return to those born in early years greatly exceeds the return to those born in later years.

A TRUST FUND OF IOUS

There is a **Social Security trust fund,** which is the depository for Social Security tax revenues. The trust fund is currently building up because tax revenues exceed Social Security payouts. However, the size of that trust fund pales in comparison to the expected future demands against it. Moreover, all savings held in the Social Security trust fund take the form of special government bonds. Since a bond is merely a promise to pay in the future, savings within the Social Security trust fund are nothing more than government IOUs.

Social Security trust fund the buildup of Social Security tax revenues above what is paid out in benefits; kept in the form of government bonds.

To pay those IOUs, the government must either create extra money or collect extra tax dollars in the future. Either way, future taxpayers pay. If the government creates new money, taxpayers pay the tax of inflation that eats away the value of their earnings. Otherwise, the trust fund bonds would be redeemed out of general tax revenues, which would require higher personal income taxes or other general taxes. Even if the Social Security trust fund were to stack a warehouse full of its special government bonds, it would still be up to future taxpayers to pay them off. Thus, for the economy as a whole, balances in the Social Security trust fund are not in themselves real savings.

Social Security also reduces private savings to the extent that people expect to receive Social Security checks in the future. Workers substitute the government's promises for their own savings. Moreover, because the Social Security tax reduces take-home pay, current workers have less money that could be saved. The reduction in the national saving rate because of Social Security means there is less money for investment, and thus less economic growth, as will be discussed in the next chapter. The result is that, when current workers

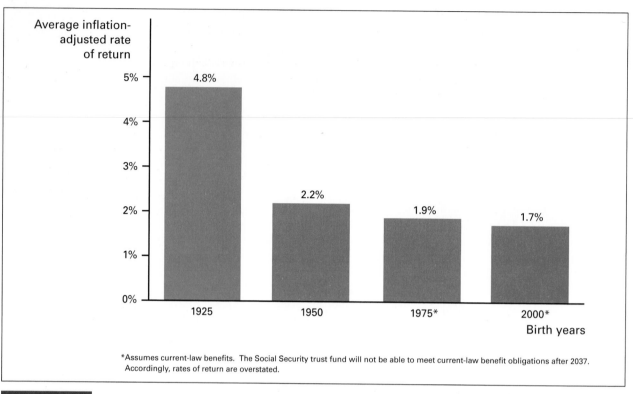

FIGURE 15-12

RETURNS FROM SOCIAL SECURITY The rate of return from Social Security has fallen from generation to generation.

Source: June 2002, http://www.whitehouse.gov/infocus/social-security/.

retire, the economic capacity of the country to support them will be smaller than if Social Security never existed in the first place.

For the Social Security trust fund to represent real savings, it must generate real capital that will increase the country's production possibilities in years to come. This could come about either directly through investment in capital or indirectly through a pay-down in other government debt. If tax inflows into Social Security are greater than the payment outflows, the surplus that is used to buy federal bonds could in turn be used by the Treasury to buy back its other bonds and thereby reduce the national debt. A lower national debt would make room for greater private investment that increases the economy's productive capacity. When Social Security reaches a point where it must cash in its government bonds and draw down its trust fund, the federal government could then increase federal debt once more. In the interim, though, the economy would have grown to be better able to support that debt. That is the ideal situation, but one that is politically difficult to implement. Instead, we are faced with a continuing Social Security budget surplus that is more than used up by other government spending. As a result we see an overall federal deficit that is projected to continue.

Rather than use the trust fund to pay down other government debt, the federal government might directly invest the Social Security trust fund in the production of real capital. It could take one of two routes:

■ **The government could produce the necessary capital itself.** Government production may be justified to the extent that the needed investment applies to the provision of public goods, such as highway infrastructure needed for smoothly flowing traffic. Beyond this, however, direct government investment would lead the economy in the direction of command and control.

- The **government could invest the money in the marketplace, perhaps establishing or designating mutual funds to buy stock in private companies.**

In either case, the danger is that the investments would move the economy toward inefficient central planning and be allocated to firms based on politics rather than economic merit.

The amounts in question are not inconsequential. For the Social Security trust fund to be **fully funded**—able to pay off all its future obligations without recourse to future taxation—it would need to own well over a year's worth of GDP. In other words, the buildup of savings in the Social Security trust fund would need to greatly expand the country's current productive capacity for that savings to be real in a macroeconomic sense. Having the government take over such a large part of the economy's ownership of capital would not be capitalism as we know it in the United States.

fully funded the idea of having enough revenue in the Social Security trust fund to be able to pay off all obligations to current workers without recourse to taxing future workers.

SUPPLEMENTING SOCIAL SECURITY

Individuals do save for their own retirement. **Individual retirement accounts (IRAs)** promote that saving by allowing a limited amount of tax-free or tax-prepaid contributions, the latter termed *Roth IRA*. The contribution limit in 2002 is $3,000, which is scheduled to rise to $4,000 in 2005. The government has been reluctant to increase that limit very much, because any increase in tax-free savings would deplete current tax revenues. The government has also been content to accumulate bonds in the Social Security trust fund, because the special Social Security bonds that the Social Security Trustees buy from the Federal Treasury mean that any extra money collected by Social Security taxes are transferred into general government revenues that can be spent wherever the government chooses.

individual retirement accounts (IRAs) tax-free savings accounts earmarked for retirement income.

If the government wants to promote private saving, its options include:

- Increasing or eliminating the contribution cap on IRAs.
- Eliminating the taxation of income that is saved.
- Requiring that individuals save some fraction of their earnings for their own retirement.

The third option has led to proposals for **Personal Security Accounts,** which would be financed by a payroll tax but be under the individual's own control and ownership. **Personal Security Accounts could only supplement, not replace, Social Security as it now stands,** for three reasons:

Personal Security Accounts savings accounts individuals own, but that they are forced to contribute to by the government.

- **Social Security depends on current workers to support current retirees.** With Personal Security Accounts, workers are saving to support themselves.

QUICKCHECK

Most people consider investing in government bonds to be very secure. Yet, the Social Security trust fund's investment in government bonds is a source of insecurity. Explain.

Answer: At a personal, microeconomic level, government bonds are very secure because they are backed by the full faith and credit of the government. They will be repaid. When it comes to the macroeconomy, however, the bonds do not represent real savings because they are just IOUs that must be repaid by future taxpayers. They do not add to the productive capacity of the economy directly.

- **Social Security redistributes income from wealthier workers to poorer ones.** With Personal Security Accounts, workers keep their own savings.
- **Personal Security Accounts are riskier, with workers making their own investment choices.** They would still need a Social Security fallback in case their personal investment choices lose their value.

While politically contentious, proposals for Personal Security Accounts have been looked on favorably by American presidents of both political parties. President Bill Clinton even included the idea in his 1999 State of the Union address. Workers who get to keep control of their own savings might be more inclined to accept the double tax of paying for current retirees and also building up savings for their own retirement.

EXPLORE & APPLY

15.5 DEFICITS AND DEBT—DO WE SPEND TOO MUCH?

I place economy among the first and most important virtues, and public debt as the greatest of dangers.

—Thomas Jefferson

Why do babies cry? You'd cry, too, if you were born over $21,000 in debt. On average, that is how much debt Uncle Sam has already rung up for each U.S. citizen, babies included. The federal government continues to add to that national debt each year in which it operates with a budget deficit. In 2002, the budget deficit was $106.2 billion and the gross national debt stood at $6.24 trillion. About half of this debt was owed from one government agency to another, with the other half owed to the public.

The national debt can be thought of as the *stock* or inventory of accumulated past budgetary imbalances, and the deficit as a *flow* that adds to that debt. That debt represents almost 60 percent of the $10.4 trillion value of U.S. GDP. Interest payments alone account for about 14 percent of total federal government spending.

Is it fair? Is our government doing the right thing by spending our next generation's money, without them having any voice in the matter? After all, in the 1773 Boston Tea Party, the colonists of Massachusetts rebelled against unjust English taxes. Their rallying cry of "Taxation without representation is tyranny!" provided one more spark to the fire that formed the United States of America. Is our government engaging in tyranny against future American citizens?

To answer these questions, ask yourself when debt is justified. You may run up debt to pay for a college education. If you expect a payback in the form of a better income down the road, some debt while in college seems justifiable. What if you "own" a home? Few people own their homes outright. Yet most homeowners, even those with hefty mortgages to pay off, do not consider themselves debtors. Government statisticians count them as debtors, though.

Most people are willing to take on debt when that debt allows the purchase of assets of greater value. The homeowner who takes on a mortgage and the lender who offers that mortgage figure that the value of the house is more than enough to cover the balance due on the mortgage. Indeed, most homeowners with mortgages view the difference between the value of their homes and what they still owe as a primary source of their savings.

Government statisticians take a different view. When the government measures how much Americans have saved, it subtracts from that savings figure the amount that is owed on mortgages. The value of the homes is left out because it is difficult to measure. Since there are so many homeowners with mortgages in the United States, America's savings rate then appears artificially low when compared with that of other countries.

Likewise, when the government reports its own debt, it does not offset this debt with the value of the assets it owns. After all, how do you value assets of the government? Those assets include such things as parks, highways, military bases, military equipment, a judicial system, and much more. Taken as a whole, we know the value is quite high. We also know that new babies born as U.S. citizens will obtain benefits from these assets for years to come. From this perspective, expecting future citizens to bear some of the costs does not seem so bad.

Would the next generation accept this deal, to be born with both the privileges and obligations of being a U.S. citizen? While we cannot ask them, we can observe their parents answering that question with their actions. It would be most unusual to find an expectant mother seeking to leave the United States so that her baby would be born elsewhere. In contrast, immigrant couples frequently seek entry into the United States so their babies can be born as U.S. citizens.

Just because most people believe that, on balance, there is a positive value to living in the United States does not tell us that the United States has the right amount of debt. If the accumulation of debt exceeds the accumulation of assets, the value of our country diminishes over time. Conversely, if the United States holds down debt by cutting back on public investments, the country runs the risk of missing out on investment opportunities that would look good in hindsight. U.S. opportunities for economic growth would diminish, meaning that long-run aggregate supply would not shift rightward as rapidly as it could.

THE RELATIONSHIP BETWEEN THE BUDGET DEFICIT AND THE TRADE DEFICIT

As a country, we often accuse ourselves of being on a spending binge, one we will have to pay for later. As evidence, we point to both the federal budget deficit and the U.S. *trade deficit*. The trade deficit is the amount by which the value of goods we import exceeds the value of goods we export. Because we spend more of our dollars on foreign goods than foreigners return in exchange for American goods, foreigners have extra dollars left over to invest in the United States. Those investments represent future obligations of this country to other countries. Yet, while it is the collection of our individual actions that leads us to a trade deficit, we don't usually consider ourselves to be personally engaging in irresponsible spending.

The $106 billion budget deficit differs from the amount of the trade deficit, which has been running well over $400 billion in recent years. Still, the two are related, so much so that they have been dubbed the *twin deficits.* By running a budget deficit, the U.S. government leaves more money in the pockets of consumers, some of which they spend on imports. Those U.S. dollars that consumers spend on imports come back to the United States, such as when foreigners buy U.S. exports or invest in the United States.

When the government borrows money to finance the budget deficit, that borrowing tends to draw more investment dollars into the United States in response to the expanded investment opportunities. To obtain dollars to invest in the United States, foreign investors must bid them away from other uses, such as foreign purchases of U.S. products. For this reason, holding all else constant, the higher the federal budget deficit, the higher the trade deficit.

The existence of the twin deficits runs counter to the idea that government fiscal policy can spend the economy out of an unemployment equilibrium. The problem is illustrated in Figure 15-13. If the government attempts to shift aggregate demand to the right through deficit spending, it generates offsetting effects that shift aggregate demand back to the left. Specifically, the higher U.S. trade deficit reflects a reduction in spending on U.S. goods as foreigners substitute purchases of U.S. debt for purchases of U.S. products.

By the same token, the same higher interest rates that cause foreigners to invest in the United States rather than buy U.S. goods will likewise also *crowd out* private sector investment, because the more money investors put into secure government debt, the less there is left over for private sector investments. Together, these effects might offset the

FIGURE 15-13

CAN FISCAL STIMULI WORK? The effectiveness of deficit spending that is intended to shift aggregate demand to the right may in practice be offset by an enlarged trade deficit, together with less consumption and investment spending at home by U.S. residents.

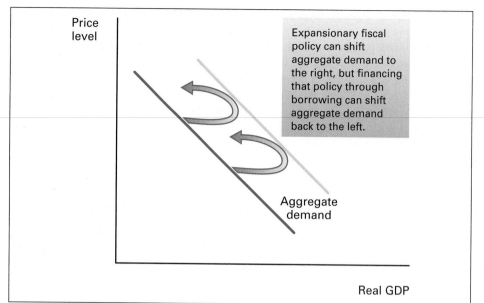

government's expansionary fiscal policy and leave the economy back where it started, as seen in Figure 15-13.

About 80 percent of government debt is owed to itself or to private U.S. investors. Nevertheless, as the federal government adds to its debt, so too do U.S. citizens. Attracting additional foreign investment accumulates obligations to repay that debt in the future. Is that dangerous? After all, Bolivia, Argentina, and many other struggling countries have endured economic crises brought about by foreign debt oligations that they were unable to repay.

When it comes to the United States, the dangers of foreign debt are few. Latin American and other debtor countries ran into problems repaying their debts in large part because their debts were denominated in U.S. dollars, which meant they had to acquire those dollars. To the extent that the United States owes financial debt to citizens of other countries, that debt is also denominated in dollars. The critical difference is that those are our dollars; we control the presses that print the money.

Some people worry over a sudden exodus of foreign investment, possibly as a means to exert political pressure. Such worries are unfounded. If foreigners for some reason wish to stampede out of the United States, they would have to leave behind all but a small fraction of their assets. By investing in the United States, foreigners allow us political and economic control over things of great value to them. In that way, foreigners acquire a strong interest in having our economy perform well and in maintaining good political relations.

We have seen that a budget deficit and consequent increase in the federal debt can be justifiable. We have also seen that this expansionary fiscal policy tends to increase the trade deficit and international debt, but that the consequences of those increases are not as worrisome as many people think. Just how much debt is the right amount, however, remains an open question.

THINKING CRITICALLY

1. Keynesian fiscal policy suggests that deficit spending can be justified to pull the economy out of an unemployment equilibrium. Yet federal budget deficits have characterized most years in recent decades, even when the economy has been at or near full employment. What are some likely explanations for this expansionary fiscal policy?

2. "Our federal government exploits babies by giving them a huge debt upon birth—a debt they did not ask for, but will be forced to repay. Let's care for our children and grand-children. It's time for the government to stop running budget deficits and to start repay-ing our massive public debt!" Evaluate this view, including in your discussion an assessment of the proper role of government debt.

Visit **www.prenhall.com/collinge** for updates and web exercises on this Explore & Apply topic.

SUMMARY AND LEARNING OBJECTIVES

1. **Explain why wages and prices might be slow to adjust downward, and what significance this can have.**

   ■ A short-run unemployment equilibrium occurs when the price level is above the full-employment price level. The economy would operate at a point on the aggregate demand curve that is above the full-employment equilibrium point.

   ■ Keynes suggested that sticky wages and prices might hinder the economy's adjustment to full-employment output, if the economy starts at a short-run unem-ployment equilibrium.

2. **Discuss how fiscal policy to stabilize the economy is subject to lags, and how the lags can be overcome automatically.**

   ■ An expansionary fiscal policy is associated with more government spending and/or tax cuts. Either of these fiscal policy actions would shift the aggregate demand curve to the right.

   ■ A contractionary fiscal policy, which involves either less government spending or tax increases, would shift aggregate demand to the left.

   ■ Discretionary fiscal policy is the term applied to delib-erate changes in fiscal policy that are designed to affect the macroeconomy.

   ■ Discretionary fiscal policy is subject to errors because of the three fiscal policy lags. These lags include the recognition lag, the action lag, and the implementa-tion lag. The recognition lag refers to the length of time before a problem is recognized. The action lag refers to the amount of time it takes to decide on an appropriate policy response and pass the legislation that reflects policy. The implementation lag occurs because policy changes take time to begin to affect the economy.

   ■ Working to counter the problems of an unemploy-ment equilibrium and overheating are the automatic stabilizers that are built into the economy. When the economy slows down, the automatic stabilizers increase government spending. When the economy overheats, government spending tends to decrease. An example of the automatic stabilizers is unemploy-ment benefits.

3. **Explain how balancing the full-employment budget is consistent with a budget deficit.**

   ■ The federal budget records the revenue and spending of the federal government. A balanced budget occurs when the two are equal. A budget surplus is when revenue exceeds spending, and a budget deficit is when spending exceeds revenue. Because the federal budget has mostly been in deficit, the United States has compiled a national debt of over $6 trillion.

   ■ The full-employment budget estimates what federal revenue and spending would be if the economy were at full employment. It's sometimes argued that the government should balance its budget over the course of the business cycle, running surpluses during booms and deficits during recessions. Doing so would help stabilize the economy. It also means that the government could have a budget deficit or a surplus even though the full-employment budget is balanced.

4. **List the major sources of revenue for government in the United States.**

   ■ Taxes are used by government to pay the costs of pro-viding public goods. Taxes also finance income redis-tribution through the provision of transfer payments. Safety-net programs that provide economic security transfer tax dollars to those in need. Welfare and unemployment compensation are examples.

   ■ Two goals for taxes are equity and efficiency. Tax equity is about fairness. The goal of efficiency in taxation is to maintain incentives for people to be productive. To raise revenue efficiently, a tax should be designed to change people's behavior the least.

■ A marginal tax rate is different from an average tax rate. A marginal tax rate states the percent of additional income that is collected in taxes. An average tax rate states the percent of total income that is taken in taxes.

■ Taxes take about 30 percent of GDP. The personal income tax raises the largest share of the federal government's revenue. Federal personal income tax rates start at 10 percent for people with very low taxable incomes and increase to 15 percent, 25 percent, 28 percent, 33 percent, and 35 percent as incomes rise. This series of tax rates provides an example of marginal tax rates, since each of these rates applies to increments of income.

■ The federal government also collects Social Security taxes, including a Medicare hospitalization tax. There is also a corporate income tax that takes about 30 percent of corporate profits.

■ Tax incidence refers to who ultimately pays a tax. In the case of the corporate income tax, the tax ultimately reduces the income of shareholders.

■ State and local governments also collect taxes. States' individual income taxes, sales taxes, and revenues from the federal government make up most of the revenues states receive. Local governments tend to rely on property taxes and sales taxes for their revenues.

5. Explain the principles of tax equity and how they apply.

■ The two fundamental principles of tax equity are the benefit principle and the ability-to-pay principle. The benefit principle provides the justification for earmarked taxes, such as the gasoline tax. It suggests that those who pay a tax should be the same as those who receive benefits from how that tax revenue is spent. The benefit principle cannot apply to redistributional programs, since the point of those programs is to provide assistance from taxpayers to the needy.

■ The ability-to-pay principle states that those with more ability to pay taxes should actually pay more taxes. The federal income tax is modeled according to this principle.

■ A tax may be progressive, regressive, or proportional. A progressive tax collects a larger fraction of income as income increases. The federal income tax is progressive since the marginal tax rate rises as a person's income reaches a threshold level. For example, the income tax starts at 10 percent for low-income indi-

viduals and rises to 38.6 percent for those with relatively high incomes.

■ A regressive tax collects a smaller fraction of income as income increases. For example, a tax that collects $1,000 from a person earning $10,000 and $10,000 from a person earning $1,000,000 is regressive since the first person pays 10 percent of his or her income toward the tax, while the second person pays only 1 percent of income toward the tax.

■ A proportional tax collects the same fraction of income as income changes. If the person earning $1,000,000 in the previous example paid $100,000 in taxes, the same 10 percent as the low-income person, then the tax would be proportional.

■ A flat tax applies a single tax rate to all income. Thus, a flat tax is an example of a proportional tax. While the tax rate is the same for all taxpayers, recognize that people with higher incomes still pay higher taxes. A flat tax, if enacted, would be transparent (meaning easily monitored). In reality, any flat tax likely to be enacted would involve exempting low incomes.

■ It can be difficult to tell whether a tax is progressive, regressive, or proportional. Depending on whether Social Security benefits are included with the tax, Social Security can be viewed as representing a progressive, regressive, or proportional tax.

■ In pursuing the twin goals of equity and efficiency in the tax system, there are tradeoffs. More equity can mean less efficiency, and vice versa. In the pursuit of equity, government programs provide cash and in-kind benefits that can reduce incentives to be productive.

6. Interpret why the future of Social Security is in doubt.

■ The Social Security tax is the second-largest source of federal revenue. Both employees and employers contribute toward Social Security taxes, each paying 7.65 percent of a worker's gross pay to the federal government, for a total of 15.3 percent. The burden of employers' contributions is shifted to workers in the form of lower worker pay. Thus, the ultimate incidence of the Social Security tax is on workers because the market wage rate declines by the amount of the employer's share of the tax.

■ The Social Security system is a pay-as-you-go system, with current workers paying for the benefits received by current retirees. This approach generates no real savings and becomes increasingly difficult to maintain as the population ages. Individual retirement accounts promote saving for retirement. Personal Security Accounts, although politically contentious, might supplement Social Security if enacted into law.

7. Analyze the rationale and limitations of deficit spending.
- An enduring feature of the modern American economy is the presence of a budget deficit, trade deficit, and huge national debt. These features are related, with ongoing budget deficits adding to the national debt and also attracting foreign investment dollars. Because those foreign investment dollars might other-wise have gone to purchase American goods and services, the budget deficit and trade deficit are often called the twin deficits.
- Although people worry a great deal about the large deficits and national debt, at least some of this borrowing is offset by assets. For example, while future taxpayers inherit debt, they also inherit roads, a system of government, and other assets of value.
- If the government attempts to shift aggregate demand to the right through deficit spending, the trade deficit and other offsetting effects might shift aggregate demand back to the left.

KEY TERMS

sticky wages, 346
sticky prices, 346
unemployment equilibrium, 347
fiscal policy, 347
expansionary fiscal policy (fiscal stimulus), 347
contractionary fiscal policy (fiscal drag), 348
multiplier effect, 348
discretionary policy, 349
recognition lag, 349
action lag, 349

implementation lag, 349
automatic stabilizers, 350
balanced budget, 351
budget surplus, 351
budget deficit, 351
full-employment budget, 351
national debt, 351
transfer payments, 353
marginal tax rate, 353
tax incidence, 354
benefit principle, 357
ability-to-pay principle, 357

progressive tax, 357
regressive tax, 357
proportional tax, 357
in-kind benefits, 358
pay-as-you-go, 360
Social Security trust fund, 361
fully funded, 363
individual retirement accounts (IRAs), 363
Personal Security Accounts, 363

TEST YOURSELF

TRUE OR FALSE
1. The implementation lag occurs because it takes time to recognize that a problem exists with the macroeconomy.
2. Aggregate demand will increase in response to a fiscal stimulus.
3. Balancing the budget over the course of the business cycle results in surpluses in some years and deficits in others.
4. The tax rate on incremental income is called the marginal tax rate.
5. A progressive tax is any tax that takes more money from the rich than from the poor.

MULTIPLE CHOICE
6. In Self-Test Figure 15-1, which of the arrows is most likely to be affected by downwardly sticky wages and prices?
   a. *A.*
   b. *B.*
   c. *C.*
   d. *D.*

SELF-TEST FIGURE 15-1

7. An example of an automatic stabilizer is
   a. the U.S. income tax system.
   b. the Internet.
   c. sticky wages.
   d. the full-employment equilibrium.

8. The federal budget deficit
   a. has not existed since 1997.
   b. is the accumulation of all federal debts.
   c. equals the national debt minus the budget surplus.
   d. is the amount by which government spending exceeds its revenue over the course of a year.

9. An average tax rate is
   a. additional taxes owed as a percentage of additional income.
   b. total taxes owed.
   c. total taxes owed as a percentage of total income.
   d. the percentage of income not collected in taxes.

10. The corporate income tax takes about _____ percent of corporate profits.
    a. 10
    b. 20
    c. 30
    d. 50

11. The two most important sources of revenue for local governments are sales taxes and
    a. personal income taxes.
    b. corporate income taxes.
    c. Social Security taxes.
    d. property taxes.

12. The benefit principle and the ability-to-pay principle refer to
    a. whether a tax is progressive or regressive.
    b. principles of tax efficiency.
    c. principles of tax equity.
    d. legal principles that question the constitutionality of Social Security.

13. The gasoline tax
    a. is used to fund various government programs.
    b. is the best example of a progressive tax.
    c. seems to satisfy the ability-to-pay principle.
    d. reflects the benefit principle, since those who pay the tax tend to receive the benefits.

14. If a tax collects $1,000 per person, no matter what a person's income might be, then the tax is
    a. a head tax, which is regressive.
    b. progressive.
    c. a user fee.
    d. proportional.

15. Efficiency in taxation
    a. is less important than equity in taxation.
    b. is best exemplified by the progressivity of the income tax.
    c. is increased when a tax is also more equitable.
    d. often involves a tradeoff with equity.

16. An efficient tax
    a. distorts relative prices.
    b. changes peoples' behaviors.
    c. is paid entirely by employers.
    d. may not be equitable.

17. When added together, the employer share and the employee share of the Social Security tax total just over _____ percent of an individual's wages.
    a. 5
    b. 10
    c. 15
    d. 24

18. Personal security accounts would be financed by
    a. employers.
    b. government.
    c. individuals.
    d. small- to medium-sized firms, but not large corporations.

19. Savings in the Social Security system consist of
    a. IOUs.
    b. shares of stock.
    c. mostly hundred-dollar bills.
    d. gold.

20. The difference between the federal budget deficit and the national debt is that the budget deficit represents the
    a. accumulation of past debts, while the national debt is the amount by which spending exceeds revenues each year.
    b. amount by which spending exceeds revenues each year, while the national debt represents the accumulation of past deficits and surpluses.
    c. amount of money the country owes that it cannot pay back.
    d. amount of money the United States owes foreign countries, while the budget deficit represents the amount of money the United States owes in total.

QUESTIONS AND PROBLEMS

1. *[sticky wages and prices]* Illustrate graphically an unemployment equilibrium and explain how downwardly sticky wages and prices can prevent the economy from reaching the long-run macro equilibrium.

2. *[expansionary fiscal policy]* Show an unemployment equilibrium on a graph and explain how an expansionary fiscal policy can achieve full employment.

3. *[overheated economy]* Explain the appropriate fiscal policy response when the economy overheats.

4. *[fiscal policy lags]* What are the three fiscal policy lags that complicate the task for policymakers of using fiscal policy to manage the economy? Explain each of the lags.

5. *[automatic stabilizers]* Write a brief essay on the contribution that the automatic stabilizers play in creating a stable economy. Provide examples of the automatic stabilizers and use them to illustrate their significance. Why is there an interest in using fiscal policy to stabilize the economy when the automatic stabilizers are available?

6. *[federal budget]* When the economy is at full employment, should the federal government run a budget deficit, surplus, or neither? Explain.

7. *[full-employment budget]* Is the full-employment budget usually balanced? Explain.

8. *[national debt]* How was the U.S. national debt of over $6 trillion created? Who is owed this debt?

9. *[tax revenues]* Without looking at the pie charts in the text, draw a pie chart showing sources of federal revenue. Slice the pie you draw in order to show the relative importance of each source of revenue. After you finish your drawing, compare it to the pie chart in the text and make any corrections needed to your drawing.

10. *[tax revenues]* Repeat the first exercise, but this time show sources of state and local revenue.

11. *[marginal tax rate]* If Sam earns $100,000 a year and pays $10,000 in income taxes, can you determine his marginal tax rate? Explain.

12. *[average tax rate]* If Sue earns $100,000 a year and pays $10,000 in income taxes, can you determine her average tax rate? Explain.

13. *[tax equity]* Most people want taxes to be fair. Yet there are strong disagreements over what constitutes tax equity. Using an example and the concepts of equity discussed in this chapter, explain why such disagreement can reasonably persist.

14. *[tax equity]* Which principle of tax equity, the benefit principle or the ability-to-pay principle, is in closest agreement with your own personal idea of what is fair? Explain.

15. *[taxes and incentives]* Why is it difficult to design aid to the poor that provides work incentives? Explain with reference to cost and the level of the safety net.

16. *[progressive versus regressive]* Suppose that you have been chosen by the president of your college or university to design a tax system that would tax students at your school in order to provide funding for student athletics. You will be allowed to impose a tax on one of the following: tickets to school football games, soft drinks from vending machines on campus, or textbooks sold from your campus book store. Evaluate each alternative within the context of equity, efficiency, and whether the tax you choose would be regressive or progressive.

17. *[flat tax]* On balance, do you think it is a good idea to adopt a flat tax? If such a tax is adopted, how much income should be exempted? Explain your reasoning.

18. *[payroll tax]* Is the term payroll tax another way of referring to the income tax? Explain.

19. *[Social Security tax]* Using a graph and labeling the axes, curves, and all relevant information, demonstrate how employees wind up paying the employer portion of Social Security taxes.

 Visit **www.prenhall.com/collinge** for Exploring the Web exercises and additional self-test quizzes.

CHAPTER

ECONOMIC GROWTH

A LOOK AHEAD

Packets of electronic data surge from your keystrokes or from your voice. Instantly, you and your co-worker can see the results on your computer screen, hear the results with your headset, or both. It does not matter if your colleague is in New Jersey or New Guinea—the computers and networks of today are found all around the globe. It seems that the possibilities for collaborating on business projects have been expanding at light speed. In reality, today's fiber-optic transmission lines really *do* transfer data packets at the speed of light. Along with new possibilities for interacting and sharing comes new productivity and a *new economy*, the topic of this chapter's Explore & Apply section.

The technology and capital for economic growth do not appear by magic, however. Economies produce them, and produce more and better types if the right incentives are in place. Growth like this offers the only means to maintain or improve living standards in the face of an expanding population. In this chapter, we focus on the incentives for economic growth, and ways to adjust public policies to make those incentives stronger.

LEARNING OBJECTIVES

Understanding Chapter 16 will enable you to:
1. **Identify the sources of economic growth.**
2. **Describe the role of saving and investment in the process of capital formation.**
3. **Analyze how taxation affects both saving and investment activity.**
4. **Provide justification for subsidized higher education.**
5. **Summarize new growth theory and supply-side economics.**
6. **Discuss the key role of labor productivity in economic growth.**

economic growth the change in real GDP over time.

In Chapter 15, we saw that government tax and spending policies could change incentives, such as the incentives to work, to save, and to acquire human capital. In turn, these changes affect **economic growth,** which is usually measured by the change in real GDP over time. (Sometimes a real GNP measure is used, instead.)

Economies turn resources into outputs of greater value. The possibilities for doing so expand over time as the economy develops new technologies and acquires new resources. In other words, the economy's possibilities for production increase, which is why Chapter 2 showed economic growth to be an outward shift in the production possibilities frontier. This chapter examines the process more closely to see how the rate of economic growth might be improved. If the growth is in per-capita real GDP, a country can look forward to a better standard of living for its people.

16.1 THE SEEDS OF GROWTH

Economic growth does not just happen. It takes a combination of resources and technology, along with a policy environment, to nurture that combination. These are the matters to which we now turn.

SOURCES OF GROWTH—LABOR, TECHNOLOGY, CAPITAL FORMATION, AND ENTREPRENEURSHIP

The U.S. economy has probably been studied more extensively than the economy of any other country. Evidence from the United States reveals quite a bit about what factors are important to growth, as the United States has a history of increasing real GDP. Table 16-1 summarizes U.S. economic growth according to the terms of office of recent presidents.

From 1947 to 1973, the average real GDP growth rate averaged around 4 percent. Real GDP growth diminished in the 1970s to under 3 percent during the Carter administration. GDP growth picked up steam a couple of years into the Reagan administration to give an annual growth rate average over Reagan's eight years of 3.5 percent. It then stumbled again to less than 2 percent in the following four years under George Bush. Growth was picking up in the final months of the first Bush administration to average a bit under 4 percent in the

TABLE 16-1 ANNUALIZED GROWTH RATES BY PRESIDENCY

PRESIDENCY	YEARS	GROWTH RATE
Kennedy–Johnson	1961–1968	4.9
Nixon–Ford	1969–1976	3.0
Carter	1977–1980	2.7
Reagan	1981–1988	3.5
Bush I	1989–1992	1.7
Clinton	1993–1999	3.7
Bush II	2001–2002(I)	2.5

Source: BEA's NIPA Revision, Released 3–30–2000. Clinton and Bush II growth rates were computed by the authors from NIPA annual growth rates. Bush's rate is current through the first quarter of 2002.

eight years of the Clinton administration. Shortly before Clinton left office, growth slowed and recession took hold in President George W. Bush's first year in office.

While growth was previously stated in terms of presidential administrations, growth is not directed from the top down. It is also sometimes hard to know what the economy's growth rate is at any given point in time, because it takes time to compile the data used to report GDP. This lag can have political repercussions. For example, following the election of President Bill Clinton in 1992, it was widely speculated that President Bush would have instead been re-elected if only voters had recognized the then-occurring economic recovery just a little sooner.

Most U.S. economic growth is attributable to increases in labor and capital, as well as technological change. Both technological change and additional capital increase **labor productivity,** which is output per hour worked. Although there is still some question as to why U.S. economic growth began turning upward in the mid-1990s, many analysts believe that technological change, embodied in the personal computer and the Internet, played a significant role. In turn, technological change increased labor productivity. Increases in labor productivity mean that more GDP is produced for each hour worked by the labor force. Figure 16-1 shows the change in labor productivity in the United States since 1959.

labor productivity output per hour worked.

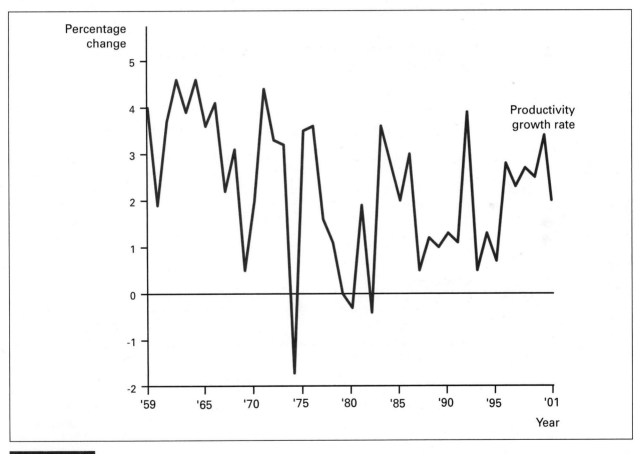

FIGURE 16-1

THE ANNUAL CHANGE IN LABOR PRODUCTIVITY Labor productivity rises and falls as additional capital is made available to workers. Technological change can also contribute to a rise in labor productivity as better equipment on the job makes labor more productive. The business cycle also affects labor productivity, with productivity typically falling in the early part of a recession, and rising as the economy later pulls out of the recession. Government regulations also affect labor productivity.

Source: 2002 Economic Report of the President, Table B-50, and Bureau of Labor Statistics. The data represent output per hour of all persons in the business sector.

The figure makes clear that labor productivity does not necessarily increase each year. Why does the growth rate in productivity decrease in some years, and even fall in others? One important factor is economic slowdowns. When the economy slows down, or enters a recession, labor productivity tends to fall at first because businesses decrease the production of goods and services in response to reduced aggregate demand. However, they also try to retain their workers in order to avoid the costs of recruiting and training new workers when aggregate demand picks back up. Thus, less production, combined with the same amount of labor, must decrease labor productivity. Later, when a recession nears its end, production is at first increased without a corresponding increase in labor employed. Labor productivity rises at that point in the business cycle.

capital formation the creation of new capital.

Labor productivity is associated with how much capital—both physical capital and human capital—labor has at its disposal. The labor productivity statistics suggest correctly that the United States has been quite successful at accumulating capital. The creation of new capital is termed **capital formation.** Capital formation requires initiative, since producing capital requires that people identify what additional outputs need to be produced or technologies should be employed. In market economies, entrepreneurs make these choices based on their best judgments of what is most profitable, meaning of most value to both consumers and producers. The struggle for profit weeds out entrepreneurs who do not make these choices well. Thus, one of the keys to capital formation is allowing this competitive search for profit. Where central planning is practiced, that key is lost. Thus, in Cuba, North Korea, and other economies in which government exercises too heavy a hand, the quantity and quality of capital formation is impaired. Figure 16-2 shows capital formation in the United States over time.

SNAPSHOT   THE ENTREPRENEURIAL ROAD TO RICHES—TAKING THE RISK AND SHARING THE REWARD

The odds of striking it rich as an entrepreneur may not be great—one in two hundred, they say—but the potential payoff does motivate people to try. If successful, the economy wins the products and the entrepreneurs gain a tidy profit.

Entrepreneurial success stories lie behind the companies we take for granted. Former economics major Sam Walton used the concept of one-stop shopping at everyday low prices to smash Wal-Mart's way to success, and in the process propel the Walton family to first place among America's wealthy. Bill Gates amassed his fortune by positioning Microsoft to provide the industry-standard interface for the personal computer. Talk on the phone? Craig McCaw said "take it with you," and took home $11.5 billion from his sale of McCaw Cellular Communications Corporation. Chat over coffee? Howard Schultz earned his fortune by opening Starbucks Coffee Company as a place to hang out over a steaming brew. FedEx your important papers? That was Fred Smith's idea. It was Domino's that delivered for Tom Monaghan, and Motown that recorded Berry Gordy's profit.

The common theme to the success stories of America's modern entrepreneurs is insight into what the public likes to do and how they could do it better or more conveniently. But it takes more. Without the risks inherent in trying to build companies from the ground up, there would be neither entrepreneurial success nor the economic growth that it engenders. ◄

QUICKCHECK

How can entrepreneurship increase labor productivity?

Answer: Entrepreneurship can add to productivity by organizing resources in better ways.

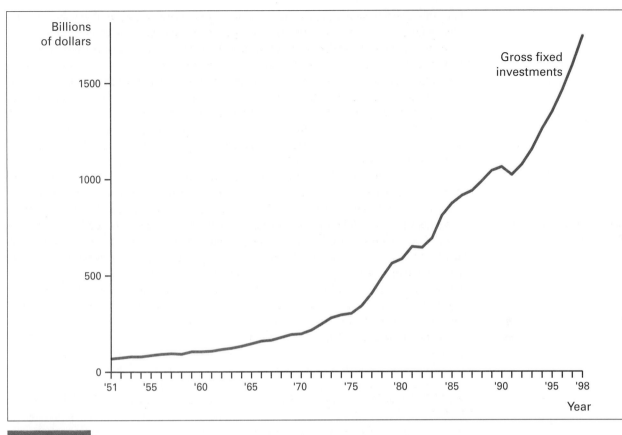

FIGURE 16-2

CAPITAL FORMATION Economic growth is associated with the creation of new capital, termed capital formation. Capital formation usually rises, but has dipped during recessions.

Source: National Income and Product Accounts, Table 5.16. The data are for gross fixed investment, and include both private and government investment.

NURTURING GROWTH—SAVING AND INVESTMENT

Capital formation requires investment, which can be coordinated centrally through government. For example, government ordinarily finances the construction of highways, because it would be very difficult for private investors to acquire rights of way or to charge for highway usage. Indeed, rebuilding highways, especially bridges on the U.S. interstate highway system, is thought to be one of the major investment needs in the United States today.

More typically, investment is a decentralized process that responds to supply and demand in the marketplace. Investors finance the capital formation that is necessary to take advantage of market opportunities. For example, investors who expect to profit from the sale of gum balls, livestock feeders, big-screen televisions, or any other product, must first finance the capital necessary to produce that product. Firms invest when they wish to do any of the following:

- Expand their scale of operations
- Implement better production techniques
- Produce new goods that their old factories are ill-suited to manufacture

To acquire human capital, individuals invest in themselves. This investment includes the time and money it takes to attend college or otherwise acquire new skills.

Private investors have a strong personal incentive to invest wisely. Because their own resources are on the line, private investors can be relied on to investigate closely which products are likely to succeed and which are not. While no one can foresee the future with certainty, investors who judge the best are rewarded in the marketplace with additional funds for further investment.

saving putting aside income for later use.

Saving is when income is put aside for later use. Central to understanding the process of capital formation is the observation that **saving provides the funding for investment.** In general, the more saving, the more investment. Sometimes people invest their savings themselves, such as when they buy houses or stocks. Other times, savers deposit their money into financial intermediaries, such as banks and mutual funds, which then invest that money.

Savers look to investments for good returns without excessive risk. Without aiming to do so, **government reduces private saving and investment.** This reduction happens in two ways. First, **government taxes away income that might be saved.** Second, **government taxes the returns on investments,** thus making them less attractive. In contrast, **government also adds to investment** to the extent that it directly invests the tax revenues it receives. The government investment in highways is an example. So, too, are government investments in schools, the criminal justice system, and elsewhere in the economy. In turn, these investments are used in the private sector. For example, the production of gum balls, restaurant meals, family vacations, and innumerable other goods and services benefit from an efficient transportation system, educated workers, and the system of laws.

Without government, aggregate saving and investment would be equal. This equality would be true because money saved would either be directly invested or would find its way into investment through banks and other financial institutions. With government, the situation is more complicated because tax dollars can be directed toward government investment or government consumption purchases. Thus, the total amount saved plus the total amount taken in taxes must equal the sum of private investment, government investment, and government spending on consumption items. Lumping together private and government investment, and simply calling the sum investment, we have the following equality:

$$\text{Investment} + \text{Government consumption} = \text{Saving} + \text{Taxation}$$

or, equivalently,

$$\text{Investment} = \text{Saving} + \text{Taxation} - \text{Government consumption}$$

Some investment funds also come from abroad and, likewise, some saving becomes investment in other countries.

Investment is a current expense that is made in the expectation of receiving income in the future. When firms borrow to finance new investment, the expected future income must be sufficient to pay off the amount borrowed, plus interest. The amount of interest depends upon the interest rate. **Higher real interest rates raise the cost of investing.** Some investments that would be undertaken at low real interest rates will not be undertaken when those rates are high. This result causes the investment demand curve to slope downward, as shown in Figure 16-3.

The money for investment comes from saving. While people will save some money whether they are paid interest or not, in general the higher the interest rate, the greater the supply of saving. For this reason, the supply of saving curve is shown as upwardly sloping in Figure 16-3. There is only one point of equilibrium, which determines the actual interest rate. The market equilibrium equates the quantity of saving supplied to the quantity of investment demanded, as shown in the figure.

Investment is also affected by other factors, such as business confidence (which encompasses expectations about the future), current economic growth, and opportunities pre-

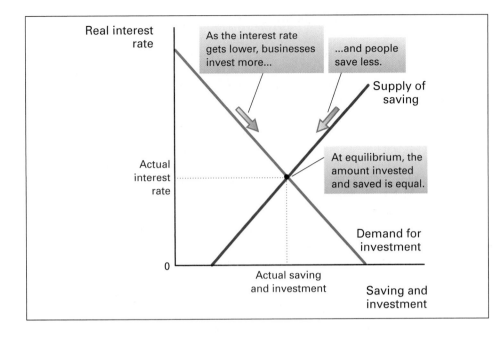

Real interest rate

As the interest rate gets lower, businesses invest more...

...and people save less.

Supply of saving

Actual interest rate

At equilibrium, the amount invested and saved is equal.

Demand for investment

0

Actual saving and investment

Saving and investment

FIGURE 16-3

THE EQUILIBRIUM INTEREST RATE Interest rates are determined in the marketplace by the intersection of investment demand and saving supply. This rate determines the quantity of actual saving and investment. The equilibrium will change if either demand or supply shifts, such as in response to changes in confidence about the future.

sented by technological change. Increases in any of these variables would shift the investment demand curve to the right. Decreases would shift it to the left.

Government fiscal policy can also shift investment demand. An expansionary fiscal policy can stymie the capital formation needed for economic growth. Specifically, when the government increases spending or cuts taxes in order to stimulate the economy, it often finances the difference with borrowing by selling government bonds to investors. However, **government borrowing is in competition with private sector borrowing, and thus can cause higher interest rates.** The resulting reduction in private investment spending is called the **crowding-out effect** of expansionary fiscal policy. In other words, the crowding-out effect represents money that would have gone to private sector investment, but instead goes to finance government borrowing. However, because so much goes on at once in the macroeconomy, it is difficult to interpret from investment data whether, and to what extent, the crowding-out effect actually occurs.

crowding-out effect when government borrowing attracts money that would otherwise have gone to private sector investment.

16.2 INFLUENCING GROWTH THROUGH PUBLIC POLICY

The world's economies represent a mix of markets and government, with government actions holding the potential to either help or hinder economic growth. Understanding the likely effects of public policies requires an understanding of the incentives facing prospective investors. The key elements are risk and return.

THE INVESTMENT DECISION—RISK AND RETURN

Success represents the 1 percent of your work that results from the 99 percent that is called failure.

—Soichiro Honda, founder, Honda Motor Company

Private investors do not know with certainty which products will sell and which will not. They accept some risk of failure, in the hopes of getting a return that compensates for that risk. There is always risk ex ante, meaning before the outcome is known. Investors assess

expected return the value of an investment if successful, multiplied by the probability of success; expressed as a percentage.

actual return the value an investment actually had, judged after the fact; expressed as a percentage.

the **expected return**—the value of the investment if successful, multiplied by the probability of success. The **actual return** can be viewed ex post, meaning after the fact. Ex post, an investment might have turned out fabulously, or it might have failed miserably.

As an example of the difference between expected return and actual return, consider movies. Some movies reap unexpected success at the box office and prove extremely profitable for their investors. In contrast, other movies, some with huge budgets and high expectations, are flops at the box office and lose enormous amounts of money for their investors.

The uncertain return on investment has important implications for public policy toward industry. Consider pharmaceuticals. The production cost of many cutting-edge drugs is very low, although their prices are often quite high. The high prices help pay for the many years of research and testing required to bring a successful drug to market. They also help pay for the many more drugs that failed to make it through the research and testing phase. In November 2002, Vice President Ferdinand Massari of Drugmaker Pharmacia put it this way, "For every new drug you see in the store, there are probably 10,000 that were tested and didn't make it!"

If prices for pharmaceutical drugs are held down by government regulation that aims to make drugs more affordable, less investment would occur in the pharmaceutical industry because there would be less expectation of profit. Investors would be less willing to accept the considerable risk of failure in the hope of only a modest profit from success. The result would be a slower pace of growth in that industry, leading to fewer new drugs. **Thus, the tradeoff is whether to make current drugs more affordable or to allow the quest for profit to lead to new and improved pharmaceuticals down the road.**

THE INCENTIVE EFFECTS OF TAXATION

In addition to regulation, taxes can also affect growth. For example, the United States personal income tax discourages saving behavior by taxing interest income earned on savings, but not taxing the alternative of current consumption. Figure 16-4 shows how a tax on saving increases the market interest rate and discourages investment. Savers face a lower return because of the tax, which makes them unwilling to save as much at each real interest rate. For this reason, taxing the return to saving shifts the supply of saving curve to the left,

FIGURE 16-4

EFFECT OF THE INCOME TAX The personal income tax requires savers to pay a tax on their interest incomes, which reduces people's willingness to save and shifts the supply of saving curve to the left. The result is a higher equilibrium interest rate and less actual saving and investment.

resulting in a higher equilibrium interest rate and less saving and investment. In this way, taxation of the return on saving discourages both saving and investment.

Because saving is so important to economic growth, there is concern over the low *personal saving rate* in the United States in recent years. Figure 16-5 illustrates the fluctuations in the percentage saved out of disposable personal income since 1929. In 2000 and 2001, the personal saving rate plunged to lows not seen since the Great Depression.

Investment is also discouraged by other taxes, such as the tax on capital gains. **Capital gains** represent the difference between the current market value of an investment and its purchase price. The **capital gains tax** takes a percentage of this difference when the investment is sold. Because investors know about the capital gains tax when making investment decisions, it too diminishes capital formation. The reduction in investment demand means that banks pay lower interest rates on savings. Likewise, individuals who invest directly in stocks or anything else subject to capital gains taxation also see their expected returns reduced. The upshot is that the capital gains tax leads to less saving and investment.

capital gains the difference between the current market value of an investment and its purchase price.

capital gains tax a tax on the capital gains from investments that are sold.

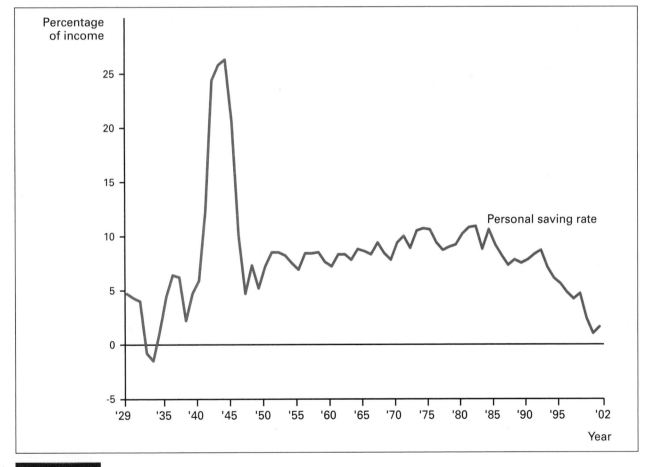

FIGURE 16-5

U.S. PERSONAL SAVING RATE The personal saving rate was low during the Great Depression because incomes were low. The personal saving rate soared during World War II because goods were rationed and people could not spend as much as they wished. In the 1990s, the personal saving rate fell as Americans consumed more and saved less.

Source: National Income and Product Account Tables. The personal saving rate equals personal saving as a percentage of disposable personal income.

QUICKCHECK

Explain why the capital gains tax discourages investment.

Answer: Investors place their money at risk in the hope of seeing their investments grow. By taking a cut out of that expected return, the capital gains tax reduces the expected pay-off and thus makes the investment less attractive.

SUBSIDIZING RESEARCH AND DEVELOPMENT

Even without the inhibiting effects of taxes and regulations, the private sector may not devote an efficient amount of financial capital toward increasing future productivity. This shortfall occurs when there are external benefits from investment in research and development (R&D). An **external benefit** occurs when some benefits are received by third parties who are not directly involved in a decision, such as the decision to research or invest. In effect, these third parties siphon off benefits that would otherwise have gone to the firms undertaking the R&D. The result is a lower expected benefit to investors, which is likely to reduce the amount of resources they devote to R&D.

While often lumped together, there is a significant distinction between research and development. **Research** is aimed at creating new products or otherwise expanding the frontiers of knowledge and technology. **Development** occurs when that technology is embodied into capital or output. For example, research may be aimed at uncovering a superconducting material that allows electricity to flow unimpeded at ordinary temperatures. If the research is successful, many companies could then incorporate the advance in knowledge (research) to design their own products (development), such as transmission lines, electromagnets, or computers.

External benefits are most prominent at the research stage, especially when the research involves the creation of knowledge that can be applied to the production of many different products, as in the example just given. It is difficult for any one investor or group of investors to assert ownership—**property rights**—over the range of applications that can arise from basic advances in knowledge. For this reason, given that the odds of achieving a significant knowledge breakthrough are quite small, private investors usually avoid investments in basic research.

To correct this market failure, and perhaps as a counterweight to the Federal tax code's general distortion against investment, the government subsidizes research. Sometimes the government funds research directly, such as cancer research at the National Institutes of Health. Sometimes subsidies are indirect, such as public support of universities that require faculty to conduct research along with their teaching. There is controversy over how generous these subsidies should be, however, since the diffusion of knowledge throughout the economy makes measuring the value of basic research practically impossible.

Much more controversy exists when government subsidizes development. For example, the U.S. Department of Energy funded a variety of alternative energy demonstration projects after the dramatic rise in world oil prices in 1973. However, most of the investments in windmills, solar energy, shale oil, and other forms of alternative energy were never commercially viable. Even gasoline blended with ethanol (alcohol made from corn) survives in the marketplace only because of ongoing government subsidies.

Such investments are examples of development rather than basic research. Development by one firm does give other firms ideas about what will be successful and what will not, and thus involves external benefits. However, this situation holds true for airline services, fast-food locations, new toys, and a host of other goods and services offered in the marketplace. Competitors learn from each others' successes and mistakes. Such minor external benefits pervade any market economy. It would be inefficient to single out some and not others.

external benefit when some benefits are received by third parties who are not directly involved in the decision.

research aimed at creating new products or otherwise expanding the frontiers of knowledge and technology.

development when technology is embodied into capital.

property rights rights of ownership.

QUICKCHECK

Explain why government subsidies are more likely to be justified in the case of research than for development.

Answer: In the research stage, there is less certainty of having a commercially viable product. Moreover, research can often be applied to many products. The result is external benefits that the researchers themselves might not capture. Thus, without government subsidies, there is likely to be too little research done. In the case of development, in contrast, profit is a much stronger motivation and government subsidies are less needed.

UNIVERSITIES—ADVANCING THE FRONTIERS OF KNOWLEDGE

SNAPSHOT

New ideas and information can confer significant external benefits, particularly if businesses can apply the knowledge to develop more valuable goods and services. The trouble is that the value of new ideas and information is often not known until they are produced, and then the applications could be in a variety of industries. Firms that engage in basic research might be unable to claim property rights to this growth in the knowledge base, since patent laws more effectively protect development than research. Firms that advance the knowledge base might even see competitors use that knowledge as well as, or better than, they do themselves.

So, where are advances in knowledge to come from? Often it is universities that are the sources. Government and academia both recognize the role of universities in engaging in valuable research that companies fear to undertake on their own. Government subsidies or grants often provide the funds that make it possible. ◄

16.3 PROPERTY RIGHTS AND NEW GROWTH THEORY

The prospect for business profits in the future can lead to research and development in the present. While not new in itself, this idea is a cornerstone of what is called **new growth theory.** New growth theory stresses the association between productivity growth over time and technological advances that are embodied in new capital. Since no one can know beforehand which lines of research will prove fruitful and which will fail, economies that handsomely reward productive ideas will grow the fastest. Productive ideas can include all sorts of things, including how to make wireless local computer networks, how to genetically engineer a disease-preventing potato, how to organize a firm, and any number of other thoughts.

new growth theory emphasizes the importance of new ideas in generating economic growth, and of intellectual property rights in providing the profit incentive to generate those ideas.

According to new growth theory, the ideas behind new technologies are promoted most effectively by allowing individuals to claim property rights, and the associated monopoly power, over ideas they have. *Monopoly power* is the idea that others can only imitate, but not duplicate, your product. Profits associated with monopoly power provide the incentive to create even better ways of doing things. The idea that private property is the key to growth, however, is far from new.

New growth theory contrasts with mainstream prescriptions for growth in the decades following the Great Depression of the 1930s and World War II. The viewpoint at that time was that government was the centerpiece of economic development. This view of growth was consistent with the high degree of confidence in government that characterized that period in history. For example, the American public works projects and World War II itself were seen as instrumental in moving the economy from the ravages of depression to decades of peace and prosperity. Aid to Europe under the Marshall plan was also credited with getting that continent back on its feet. Confidence in the ability of government to direct the economy along a pathway of growth rose in the 1930s with the New Deal, and peaked during the period from the 1950s through the early 1970s.

Although new in contrast to the prevailing economic wisdom of that period, new growth theory actually taps into themes that have been central to economic analysis for centuries. For example, private property is central to Adam Smith's idea of the invisible hand of the marketplace, discussed in Chapter 1, which gives entrepreneurs an incentive to invest and grow the economy in their search for profit. Likewise, private property and the unfettered freedom to use it form a central theme of the *Austrian school* of economic thought, which got its start with the writings of Ludwig von Mises (1881–1973) in the early twentieth century. **Austrians emphasize that government rules and regulations that restrict the use of private property impede progress, which in von Mises' words, "is precisely that which the rules and regulations did not foresee."**

16.4 SUPPLY-SIDE POLICY

supply-side economists (supply siders) economists who emphasize incentives for productivity and economic growth, such as lower marginal tax rates and less regulation.

Those economists who particularly emphasize policies aimed at growth are called **supply-side economists,** or **supply siders** for short. Supply siders focus on increasing the value of what the economy can produce in the long run (the supply side), rather than on any desire to change consumers' spending behavior (the demand side). Supply siders figure that the short-run business cycle will sort itself out over time, and will lead to a larger economic pie in the long run if government does not intrude. This long-run, free-market orientation places supply siders squarely within the classical school of economic thought.

The objective of supply-side policy is to ensure that the output associated with full employment is as high as possible. Supply-side policies are designed to increase productivity, such as through increasing capital formation. The intended effect of such policies is to shift long-run aggregate supply to the right, as depicted in Figure 16-6.

FIGURE 16-6

GOAL OF SUPPLY SIDERS Supply-side economists seek to increase productivity, which would cause long-run aggregate supply to shift to the right. This increase would increase long-run per-capita GDP.

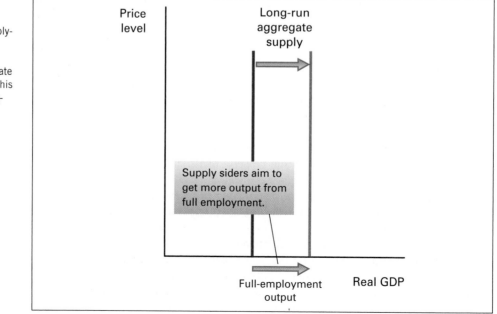

Full-employment output will change in response to changes in *structural features of the economy*, including resources and technology. Structural features also include government policies that change how workers and firms behave. Examples include unemployment compensation, minimum-wage laws, and other public policies that affect the natural rate of unemployment.

Supply siders are concerned with any government policies that might cut productivity or lead to structural unemployment. They look with suspicion at the work disincentives embedded in many safety-net programs, and at regulations that make it more costly for firms to hire and fire employees. They emphasize that regulations should be designed with an eye toward minimizing their impact on productivity.

Supply siders are most known for their focus on tax policies. They recommend keeping marginal tax rates low in order to leave a higher fraction of incremental earnings in the hands of individuals and investors. In this way, there is more incentive to invest and be productive. The result is a higher full-employment output. The reason is partly that there will be more work effort provided at the full-employment equilibrium in response to greater marginal rewards for that effort. Mostly, however, output will be greater because investors will have greater incentives to build up the economy's stock of physical and human capital, and thereby increase the productivity of its labor.

Because the concern of the supply siders is with the long run, they have little use for activist fiscal policies designed for short-run goals. **Supply siders often see an expansionary fiscal policy as an excuse for a greater government presence in the economy, and worry about the increased regulatory and tax burdens that presence may bring.**

Following the election of President Ronald Reagan, the U.S. Congress passed sweeping changes in the tax code. The 1982 tax changes adopted the supply-side agenda of cutting marginal tax rates in order to promote growth. Such growth was intended to provide greater prosperity in the future, as well as a greater tax base over time. Beginning in 1983, after the tax cuts took effect, and lasting through the end of that decade, the economy witnessed real economic growth every year along with an inflation rate that was much lower than in the preceding decade. The average growth rate from 1983 through the end of the Reagan presidency in 1988 was a very respectable 4.1 percent.

Because Congress did not curtail spending in line with its tax cuts, the federal government ran a large budget deficit in the 1980s. The budget deficit exceeded 6 percent of GDP in 1983, although it fell to just under 3 percent by 1989. The Reagan-era budget deficits look like Keynesian fiscal policy run amok, with the fiscal stimulus of a tax cut applied to marginal tax rates at the high end of the income spectrum, rather than to rates paid by those struggling to make a good life for themselves. **Critics thus refer to supply-side policies as *trickle-down economics*.** The term suggests that the policies intend to make the rich richer, so that they might spend a bit more and help the rest of us. **In fact, that is not the process that the supply siders have in mind.** Supply siders aim at productivity, not spending.

The U.S. economy grew in the 1980s after the tax cuts. The rich did indeed get disproportionately richer, at least in terms of the income they reported to the IRS. They also became more productive and paid more taxes. While the tax cuts of the 1980s reduced real federal tax revenues from most groups in the economy, the tax cuts greatly increased tax revenues from the highest income groups. The top 5 percent of income earners increased their share of total income tax payments from 36 percent in 1980 to 43 percent in 1990. Upward mobility also became more commonplace as a result of the lower tax rates. Looking at the lowest fifth of the income distribution in 1980, for example, 86 percent had advanced beyond that by 1988, with 16 percent even making it all the way to the top fifth of the income distribution.

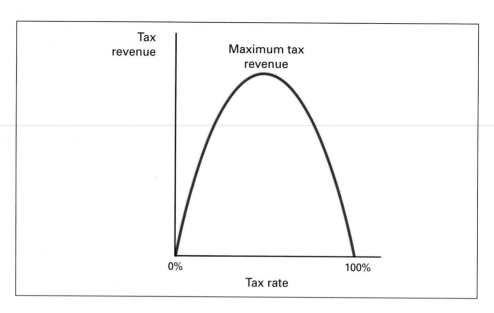

FIGURE 16-7

THE LAFFER CURVE Increasing tax rates will increase tax revenues, but only up to a point. After that point, higher tax rates are self-defeating and actually reduce tax revenues. At a tax rate of 100 percent, there would be no personal incentive to earn any income at all.

SNAPSHOT   **ON THE BACK OF A NAPKIN**

At a tax rate of 0 percent, the government collects no revenue. It can increase revenues by increasing tax rates, but there are limits. After all, a tax rate of 100 percent would also generate no tax revenue—no one would bother to earn money if Uncle Sam took it all. Arthur Laffer, a young UCLA economist, discussed this at lunch one day in the 1970s. He sketched the hump-shaped relationship between tax rates and tax revenues on the back of his napkin. Ever since, as shown in Figure 16-7, that sketch has been called the *Laffer curve.*

Promoted by some of the supply siders, the Laffer curve proved to be a potent idea in the early 1980s. It surely would be nice if government could cut its tax rates and see both the economy and its tax revenues grow. Congress went on to cut tax rates in 1982, and—lo and behold—the economy grew and the rich wound up paying more taxes. They paid more taxes because economic growth meant there were more of them and they had more income.

Unfortunately, although overall federal tax revenues increased by $1.1 trillion in the 1980s, that was not enough to overtake government spending. The Laffer curve became a laughingstock among the I-told-you-so crowd. Yet, no one can dispute its logic. Perhaps, if the right tax is found to cut, the Laffer curve will rise to prominence once more. ◄

*E*XPLORE
&
*A*PPLY

16.5 THE NEW ECONOMY—IS IT REAL?

We have entered a new era in which brains count for more than brawn.

—Royal Bank of Canada Newsletter

American prosperity seemed strong and enduring in the 1990s. The vitality of the economic boom indicated that the economy had changed in some fundamental way. The media needed a catch phrase that would describe what was happening and help define the decade for posterity. In this way, America's economy became the "new economy." That expression was soon on just about everyone's lips, symbolized by the wealth created in California's Silicon Valley. The fast-growing, entrepreneurial firms that dot Silicon Valley were a hallmark of the new economy. Today, the question is whether the new economy is still alive, or ever really was.

You may remember the old economy, with its emphasis on boring old industries, its recurring recessions and high unemployment, its inability to eliminate poverty, and its association with government budget deficits and a host of other ills. Contrast that mental picture to the new economy, which emphasizes the application of technology to raise living standards. The new economy is about high technology and its promise to revolutionize everyday life. From the spectacular special effects in the movie *Twister*, improved treatments for AIDS, and on-line auctions at e-Bay, the range of impacts associated with the new economy is wide.

How much about the new economy is ballyhoo? Consider that new economy centerpiece, the Internet. Over half of U.S. households are currently connected, and that number continues to grow. The Internet provides access to information and entertainment, and allows people to communicate instantly with each other. For buyers and sellers, the Internet provides opportunities to meet in cyberspace to transact business. The problems and failures associated with the Internet are often glossed over, however, when these benefits are raised in conversation. Try as we might to prevent them, problems like crippling new yet-to-be-named viruses threaten millions of computers. Hackers are another problem, able to penetrate allegedly secure web connections and steal millions of dollars. In addition, Internet failures include the liquidation of many Internet businesses that never came close to making a profit. For example, buying groceries on-line from home through Webvan was once touted as a threat to traditional supermarkets. No more!

The Internet bubble, exemplified by Webvan and a host of other failed on-line firms, began to deflate near the end of the longest economic expansion in U.S. history. That upswing in the economy began in the early 1990s and ended with the recession that started in March 2001. Some economists began to question whether the new economy was dead, or even whether it ever existed at all. Let's try to answer such questions, using the framework of macroeconomics.

The three macro goals of high growth, high employment, and low inflation all fell into place for the United States during the presidency of Bill Clinton. Economists will study this era for years to come, seeking to establish with certainty all the factors that accounted for the nation's superior economic performance. Alan Greenspan, chairman of the Federal Reserve at the time, has commented that the economy was revitalized by fundamental changes in the 1990s. Behold technology.

HOW TECHNOLOGY IMPACTS GROWTH

The new economy is characterized by the application of technology to increase business productivity. The growth of computers in the workplace increases the productivity of labor. More productive labor means incomes rise in the long run. Furthermore, increased productivity is the closest thing to a "magic bullet" for the economy. Increased productivity can translate into meeting the three macro goals. Strong productivity growth can keep the economy growing, keep workers employed, and act as a brake on inflation.

Before we discuss how productivity growth can strengthen the economy, let's examine the U.S. productivity data in Table 16-2. This table shows that, when cheaper and easier-to-use technology was provided to workers throughout the economy in the 1990s, workers became more efficient. Output per worker increased. Businesses increased production in response.

Table 16-2 tracks economic performance for three separate time periods: 1979 to 1990, 1990 to 1995, and 1995 to 2000. Row (1) shows the acceleration in the growth rate of labor productivity between 1995 and 2000 relative to the earlier years in the table. In the 1995 to 2000 time period, each year American workers produced 2.7 percent more output per hour worked than in the previous year. Compared to the earlier periods, labor productivity roared ahead in the mid-to-late 1990s.

Rows (2) through (4) explain the sources of growth in labor productivity: increases in capital, labor, and technological change. Note that information technology capital, such as

TABLE 16-2 **SOURCES OF CHANGE IN UNITED STATES LABOR PRODUCTIVITY, 1979–2000**

ITEM	1979 TO 1990	1990 TO 1995	1995 TO 2000
(1) Output per hour (Labor productivity)	1.6	1.5	2.7
(2) Contribution of capital	0.8	0.5	1.1
• Contribution of information technology capital	0.5	0.4	0.9
• Contribution of other capital	0.3	0.1	0.2
(3) Contribution of labor	0.3	0.4	0.3
(4) Contribution of technological change and other factors	0.5	0.6	1.4

Source: Adapted from *Multifactor Productivity Trends,* Bureau of Labor Statistics, USDL 02–128, March 12, 2002. Row (4) shows multifactor productivity, which measures the joint influences of technological change, efficiency improvements, and other influences on economic growth.

computers, fax machines, and so forth, contributed significantly to soaring labor productivity in the 1995 to 2000 period. The same is true of technological change, as shown in row (4). The data in this table allow us to separate the hoopla about the new economy from the substance. What we see is that something fundamental did indeed change in the mid-1990s. Technological change, especially as it related to increases in information technology capital like computers, contributed mightily to the burst in labor productivity, which in turn contributed mightily to the nation's increased prosperity.

The current new economy is not the first time in American economic history that everyone sensed a permanent change for the better because of technology. The Industrial Revolution in the late 1700s was the first. In the United States, that revolution was sparked when Samuel Slater illegally smuggled from England the plans for the textile mill he built in Rhode Island. Throughout history, the economy has been revitalized again and again. The railroad, the automobile, radio, television, and now the computer and the Internet have created new economies in turn.

As in the current new economy, those episodes from history were also filled with hype, speculation, and excess. Life was made better, too, because in spite of the hype, what was new was real. So, the next time you place an order for a music CD at Amazon.com, remember that the new economy is much more. Most fundamentally, it is the building block for economic growth.

*T*HINKING
*C*RITICALLY

1. Until the widespread adoption of personal computers and word processing software in the mid-to-late 1980s, office paperwork was usually typed on an electric typewriter. Describe how the productivity of typists was increased when they shifted to the new technology. Also describe how the human capital that typists needed was changed by the new technology.

2. Should government subsidize Internet access for the poor? Explain, making reference to the benefits and to the problems that could be expected.

Visit **www.prenhall.com/collinge** for updates and web exercises on this Explore & Apply topic.

SUMMARY AND LEARNING OBJECTIVES

1. **Identify the sources of economic growth.**
   - Labor, capital, technological change, and entrepreneurship are important determinants of growth.
   - In the United States, economic growth averaged about 4 percent from 1947 to 1973, but growth fell off after that. From 1992 until the recession that started in 2001, the growth rate in the United States was again in the vicinity of its average during the earlier era.
   - Economies grow through accumulating resources. They have the most control over capital, which in turn improves labor productivity. New capital requires capital formation. Entrepreneurs must identify new products or new technologies and produce new capital according to these opportunities.

2. **Describe the role of saving and investment in the process of capital formation.**
   - Funds for investment come from savings. Together, investment demand and the supply of saving determine the amount of investment.
   - Government both increases and decreases investment. Taxes reduce saving that could be used for investment. However, the government invests some of the taxes it collects, making investments in highways, schools, airports, and elsewhere.
   - The following equation describes the fundamental relationship between investment, saving, and government: Investment = saving + taxation − government consumption. The right-hand side of the equation shows that investment is financed by dollars that are saved and paid in taxes. However, some tax dollars pay for government consumption, and this item must be subtracted.
   - Government fiscal policy can result in a crowding-out effect in which government spending replaces private investment.
   - The interaction of investment demand with the supply of saving creates an interest rate equilibrium. The equilibrium real interest rate makes the actual amount of investment equal to the amount of saving. Graphically, this model of investment shows the investment demand curve to be downward sloping and the supply of saving curve to be upward sloping.

The market equilibrium occurs at the intersection of these two curves.

3. **Analyze how taxation affects both saving and investment activity.**
   - Taxing interest income reduces the supply curve of saving, which leads to a higher equilibrium real interest rate and less investment. A second example is the capital gains tax, which imposes a tax on the rise in value of an investment. Some current regulations also discourage investment.

4. **Provide justification for subsidized higher education.**
   - Government promotes technological advancement through subsidies for basic research, such as is conducted at colleges and universities. Otherwise, the existence of external benefits would lead to too little of such research.

5. **Summarize new growth theory and supply-side economics.**
   - New growth theory recognizes the key role played by research and development in economic growth. This school of thought promotes the idea that property rights to ideas must be protected in order for businesses to have the incentive to engage in research and development.
   - Supply siders seek to minimize structural features of the economy that discourage work effort and capital formation. Reducing regulations and marginal tax rates have been two of their emphases. Supply siders believe that their policies will shift the long-run aggregate supply curve to the right.

6. **Discuss the key role of labor productivity in economic growth.**
   - The new economy is seen as more than just a catch phrase. Information technology capital and technological change both contributed to the rise in productivity that occurred after 1995. This rise in labor productivity has been a key ingredient of economic growth.

KEY TERMS

TEST YOURSELF

TRUE OR FALSE

1. An economy will grow faster when it chooses to produce more consumer goods and fewer capital goods.
2. Saving is used to finance investment.
3. Higher real interest rates shift the investment demand
   curve to the left.
4. A tax on saving shifts the supply curve of saving to the
   left, thus increasing the real interest rate.
5. Supply-side economics favors more government regulation relating to the health and safety of workers.

MULTIPLE CHOICE

6. Technological change and additional capital
   a. increase labor productivity.
   b. decrease labor productivity.
   c. have no effect on labor productivity.
   d. affect labor productivity in unpredictable ways.
7. U.S. economic growth
   a. has generally been characterized by a 5 percent or
      more growth rate since the 1960s.
   b. varied with each president.
   c. was on a downward trend in the 1990s, but has
      recently reversed its course.
   d. is no longer considered an important economic goal.
8. Capital formation is also referred to as
   a. property rights.
   b. technology.
   c. the real interest rate.
   d. investment.
9. Investment equals
   a. saving − taxation.
   b. saving + taxation.
   c. saving + taxation + government consumption.
   d. saving + taxation − government consumption.
10. In Self-Test Figure 16-1, the movement from point A to
    point B is most likely to be caused by
    a. external benefits from research.
    b. external benefits from development.
    c. supply-side policies.
    d. the personal income tax.

11. In Self-Test Figure 16-1, the movement from point A to
    point B is most likely to cause
    a. less capital formation.
    b. more capital formation.
    c. higher capital gains.
    d. more saving.
12. In Self-Test Figure 16-1, axis C should be labeled as
    a. planned investment.
    b. actual investment.
    c. actual saving.
    d. the real interest rate.
13. Higher real interest rates
    a. increase the amount of investment.
    b. decrease the amount of investment.
    c. have no effect on the amount of investment.
    d. have varying and unpredictable effects on invest-
       ment.

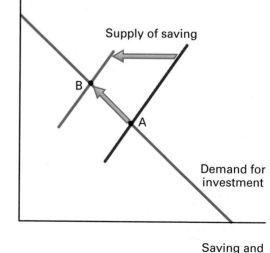

SELF-TEST FIGURE 16-1

14. The crowding-out effect refers to
    a. the crowds of people who attend sports events and rock concerts.
    b. the crowd mentality of investors who rush to buy the latest "hot" stocks.
    c. private sector borrowing that makes it difficult to finance the government.
    d. the reduction in private investment spending when the government borrows.

15. The capital gains tax takes a percentage of
    a. the purchase price of an investment.
    b. the selling price of an investment.
    c. the difference between the purchase price and the selling price of an investment.
    d. the expected return on an investment minus its actual return.

16. External benefits
    a. are most likely during the research phase.
    b. are most likely during the development phase.
    c. are equally likely during the research and development phases.
    d. explain why firms undertake research and development.

17. Research and development are the cornerstones of
    a. supply-side economics.
    b. the Laffer curve.
    c. old growth theory.
    d. new growth theory.

18. Supply siders emphasize
    a. increases in aggregate demand.
    b. higher real interest rates.
    c. a balanced federal budget.
    d. policies that shift the long-run aggregate supply curve to the right.

19. The Laffer curve shows that the effect of increasing taxes too much is
    a. less economic growth.
    b. less tax revenue.
    c. more unemployment.
    d. that only the rich get richer.

20. The new economy is characterized by
    a. the application of technology to increase business productivity.
    b. the need to rebuild bridges and highways to account for today's heavier traffic loads.
    c. widespread goofing off as workers are less accountable for their actions.
    d. the extra pollution it causes.

QUESTIONS AND PROBLEMS

1. *[labor productivity]* What is meant by the term *labor productivity*? What factors most strongly affect your personal labor productivity (or, if you have no job, the labor productivity of your closest family member with a job)? What actions can a person take to increase his or her labor productivity?

2. *[labor productivity]* Explain why the growth rate in labor productivity usually falls during the early part of a recession, but rebounds when the economy begins to improve.

3. *[capital formation]* Does capital formation affect labor productivity? Explain.

4. *[capital formation]* Provide examples of the kinds of capital formation that might have occurred when each of the following entrepreneurs launched his now-famous business:
    a. Bill Gates (Microsoft)
    b. Sam Walton (Wal-Mart)
    c. Howard Schultz (Starbucks Coffee)
    d. Berry Gordy (Motown Records)

5. *[government effect on investment]* Explain how government both reduces and increases investment at the same time. In light of your answer, interpret the following equation from the chapter: Investment = saving + taxation − government consumption.

6. *[saving and investment]* Why does the supply of saving slope upward? Why does investment demand slope downward? Identify the equilibrium in this market.

7. *[saving and investment]* Illustrate graphically and explain the significance of the market equilibrium real interest rate.

8. *[saving and investment]* Illustrate graphically the effect of an increase in the demand for investment on the real interest rate. Could an increase in the supply of saving offset the interest rate effect your graph illustrates? Explain.

9. *[government investment]* List three examples of government spending that might be considered investment. Would the private sector have undertaken these projects if government did not? Explain.

10. *[effect of taxation]* Using a supply and demand graph, explain how taxation of interest earnings reduces the amount of saving and investment.

11. *[crowding-out effect]* An expansionary fiscal policy can reduce private investment spending through the crowding-out effect. Explain how the crowding-out effect could occur.

12. *[personal saving rate]* Figure 16-5 shows that the personal saving rate was very high in the United States during World War II (1942–1945), but is extremely low today. Speculate as to why the war brought about high annual savings rates. Would you expect that the war on terrorism would lead to an upward spurt in the personal saving rate?

13. *[research and development]* What is the difference between research and development? Why is the argu- ment for the government subsidizing research stronger than the argument for subsidies to development?

14. *[theories of growth]* Explain the similarities and dis- similarities between new growth theory and supply- side economics.

15. *[supply-side economics]* Explain why critics of supply- side economics refer to it as "trickle-down economics." Explain why supply siders object to this characteriza- tion. Which president is known for promoting a supply side agenda?

16. *[Laffer curve]* How could the Laffer curve be used by government policymakers? Illustrate your explanation with a graph showing the Laffer curve.

Visit **www.prenhall.com/collinge** for Exploring the Web exercises and additional self-test quizzes.

17

CHAPTER

EXCHANGE RATES AND INTERNATIONAL TRADE

A LOOK AHEAD

We walk in them. We talk on them. We drive them. We wave them in the air and shoot them in the sky on Independence Day. What are they? Imports! It's not that we couldn't make all of our own shoes, phones, cars, flags, and fireworks. It is just not in our interest to always do so. Instead, the price signals of the marketplace lead us to specialize and trade. But what about oil? Do we import so much of it that we are held hostage to oil politics? Are the costs of those imports merely the prices the importers pay, or do those imports add security costs, too? As we will see in this chapter's Explore & Apply section, economic analysis can shed light on such questions.

Countries currently trade with each other more than ever before in history. Yet, no field of economics is more controversial and less understood by the public than international trade. This fact comes as no surprise, since international trade involves all of the elements of the economy within a country's borders—its *domestic* economy. In addition, international trade must also take into account foreign currencies and conflicting interests among countries. Some background information and supply and demand analysis can shed light on this area that at first seems so murky.

LEARNING OBJECTIVES

Understanding Chapter 17 will enable you to:
1. **Identify the balance of payments accounts and their significance.**
2. **Analyze how international trade costs jobs in some industries and creates jobs in others.**
3. **Interpret exchange rates and explain how forces of supply and demand determine their values.**
4. **Discuss the GATT and other trade agreements among countries.**
5. **Distinguish among the various barriers to trade that countries might impose.**
6. **Assess the arguments for and against protectionist policies.**
7. **Examine whether an oil import fee can promote energy security.**

$\mathcal{E}$XPLORE
&
$\mathcal{A}$PPLY

The European Community is breaking down the economic barriers among its member countries. The Chinese have embraced international trade as a key to their economic growth. The United States, Canada, and Mexico are ever more closely intertwined economically because of the North American Free Trade Agreement (NAFTA). The Brazilians have granted foreign investors huge stakes in that country's railroad and telecommunications infrastructure. Chrysler Corporation, once the third largest of the big three U.S. automakers, has combined operations with Daimler-Benz, the huge German automaker, to become DaimlerChrysler. The message is clear. Countries around the world are going global. To see how global, we need only check the balance of payments accounts.

17.1 MEASURING INTERNATIONAL TRANSACTIONS

balance of payments accounts measure of a country's economic interactions with other countries.

Countries trade with one another in order to increase their standards of living. Each country records the details of trade in its **balance of payments accounts.** The balance of payments accounts of the United States measure the economic interactions of the United States with other countries. These interactions include the sale of American-made goods and services to other countries, and the purchase of foreign-made goods and services by Americans.

The balance of payments accounts contain subaccounts that categorize the major types of international economic interactions. The two primary subaccounts are:

- the current account
- the capital and financial account

THE CURRENT ACCOUNT

exports goods and services a country sells to other countries.

imports goods and services a country buys from other countries.

current account account that records the monetary value of imports and exports of goods and services, adjusted for international incomes and transfers.

A country **exports** goods and services when it sells them to another country. A country **imports** goods and services when it purchases them from another country. The **current account** measures the values of

1. **exports of goods and services,** along with income received from abroad.
2. **imports of goods and services,** along with income payments made abroad.
3. **net transfers,** including gifts and foreign aid.

The balance on the current account is the dollar value of exports minus the dollar value of imports, adjusted for international incomes and net transfers. Figure 17-1 shows some leading imports and exports of the United States. Figure 17-2 shows the percentage of total U.S. output accounted for by exports and imports.

balance of trade the monetary value of exported goods minus the monetary value of imported goods.

trade deficit a negative balance on the merchandise trade account, given when the dollar value of imported goods exceeds the dollar value of exported goods.

The current account divides trade into categories of merchandise and services. The **balance of trade** refers to the merchandise portion only, meaning that it is the value of exported merchandise—tangible goods—minus the value of imported merchandise. The balance of trade is currently in deficit—the **trade deficit**—which means that the value of imported merchandise exceeds the value of exported merchandise. In 2001, U.S. merchandise exports equaled $718.8 billion, while merchandise imports equaled $1,145.9 billion. Thus, when the value of those imports is subtracted from the value of those exports, the trade deficit stood at $427.1 billion that year. This amount represented 4.2 percent of the country's gross domestic product (GDP).

When it comes to services—intangible items—the United States exports more than it imports. The result is that the services component of the current account is in *surplus*. Services encompass a diverse array of activities, including the U.S. schooling of foreign citizens, the leasing of rights to broadcast U.S. television shows and movies, and even haircuts for foreign tourists. A wide range of financial and consulting services is also included. Thus,

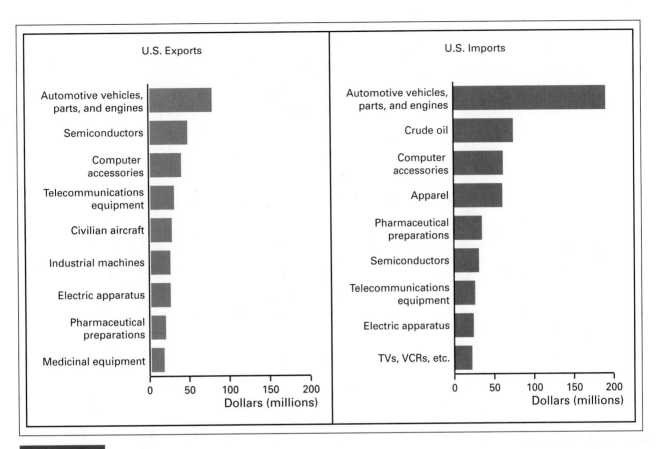

FIGURE 17-1

LEADING U.S. MERCHANDISE EXPORTS AND IMPORTS [BILLIONS OF DOLLARS] Many products, when broadly defined, are both imported and exported. An example is automotive vehicles, parts, and engines. However, the exported goods that fall into this category may exhibit different characteristics than those that are imported. Also, note that some goods, crude oil and apparel for example, are among the leading imports, but are not exported in quantities large enough to be included among the leading exports.

Source: U.S. Department of Commerce, *U.S. International Trade in Goods and Services,* June 20, 2002. Data values are totals for 2001.

if only services were included, the United States would show a surplus in its current account. **Largely because the trade deficit exceeds the services surplus, the current account as a whole is in deficit.**

THE CAPITAL AND FINANCIAL ACCOUNT

The *capital and financial account,* usually referred to as just the **capital account,** looks at flows of investment into and out of the country. Investments counted in the capital account are primarily of two types:

■ **Direct investments:** Examples include foreign investments involving the purchase of tangible income-producing property in the United States such as office buildings, golf courses, and manufacturing plants. Likewise, U.S. investments in similar foreign properties are included in the capital account.

capital account records the monetary value of capital inflows from other countries (foreign investment in the United States), and outflows to other countries (U.S. investment abroad).

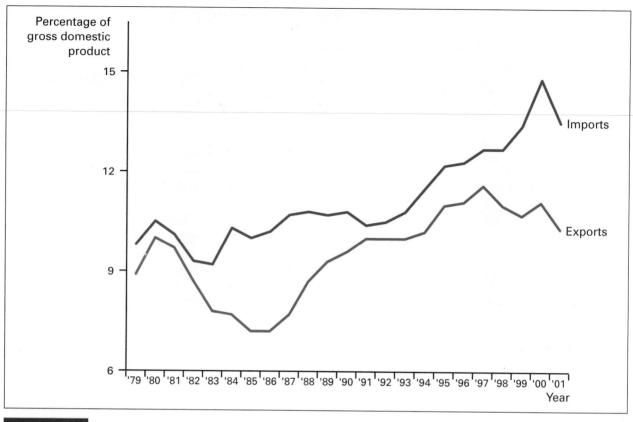

FIGURE 17-2

U.S. EXPORTS AND IMPORTS AS A PERCENTAGE OF GROSS DOMESTIC PRODUCT Whether for imports or exports, the data show an increasingly prominent role for international trade in the U.S. economy.

Source: Calculated from data in the *National Income and Product Accounts Tables,* Table 1.1.

■ **Financial investments:** Financial investments are primarily purchases of stocks and bonds. Examples include foreign purchases of stocks issued by American firms and of U.S. government Treasury bonds. The capital account also includes purchases of foreign stocks and bonds by Americans.

The balance on the U.S. capital account is the dollar value of capital inflows minus the dollar value of capital outflows, with adjustments for government transactions. *Capital inflows* represent dollars that foreigners spend on investments in the United States. *Capital outflows* represent dollars that United States citizens and firms spend on investments abroad. Thus, when looking at the direction of cross-border dollar movements, capital inflows are similar to exports, and capital outflows are similar to imports.

BALANCING PAYMENTS

The balance of payments accounts taken as a whole must have a balance that equals zero. The reason is that, when goods and investments are exchanged among willing buyers and sellers, each buyer and seller must always receive something of equal market value in exchange. For example, consider an export. The recorded worth of both the product sold and dollars received is exactly the same. However, under principles of double-entry bookkeeping, these entries go into different accounts. The result is that, while individual subaccounts

Suppose a country records merchandise exports of $150 billion, merchandise imports of $200 billion, exports of services in the amount of $100 billion, and imports of services of $60 billion. Does this country have a trade deficit? Considering only these transactions, does the current account show a deficit or surplus?

Answer: The trade deficit is $50 billion (computed as: $150 billion minus $200 billion). The services component shows a surplus, in the amount of $40 billion (computed as $100 billion minus $60 billion). The current account deficit would be $10 billion, which is smaller than the trade deficit of $50 billion because of the surplus in services.

can have surpluses and deficits, the overall market value of what is lost and what is gained must be in balance.

Even though the market value of what enters and leaves a country is said to be equal when transactions are voluntary, countries still gain from trade. How can this be? The answer lies in the nature of any kind of trade. Sellers value the goods or investments they sell at less than market value, or they would not care to sell them. Likewise, buyers value the goods and investments they buy at more than market value, or they would not care to buy them. Thus, whenever international transactions occur, both parties gain. These gains are not measured in the balance of payments accounts, because they would be impossible for government statisticians to know.

Even with what is supposed to be measured, the statistical data are imprecise. To force the accounts into balance, it is necessary to include an entry termed *statistical discrepancy*. The statistical discrepancy is often quite large, because data collection is subject to large errors, such as caused by poor recordkeeping, tax evasion, and illegal imports and exports.

Figure 17-3 shows the size of the current account and capital account items in 2001. There is a $393 billion deficit in the current account. When it comes to the capital account, in recent years capital inflows of foreign investments in the United States have exceeded outflows of U.S. investment in other countries, putting the capital account in surplus. The surplus equaled $382 billion in 2001, meaning that $382 billion more investment dollars flowed into the United States than went in the other direction. When the statistical discrepancy is brought in to the balance of payments at the bottom of the table, you can see that the result equals the balance on the current account with the sign reversed. This outcome confirms that the balance of payments accounts as a whole must have a balance of zero, a balance that is forced by the statistical discrepancy. Figure 17-3 also shows in a graph the balance on the current account and capital account since 1982. Figure 17-4 summarizes the balance of payments accounts by presenting them in the form of a flowchart.

BEHIND THE NUMBERS—JOB OPPORTUNITIES LOST AND GAINED

Although international trade increases the aggregate value of a country's consumption, that does not mean that all share in those gains. The reason a country opens its doors to international trade, like the purpose of market trade within countries, is to get more value from the country's resources. However, while the economic pie grows because of trade, some of the slices get smaller. In other words, while there is more to go around, some people will wind up with less.

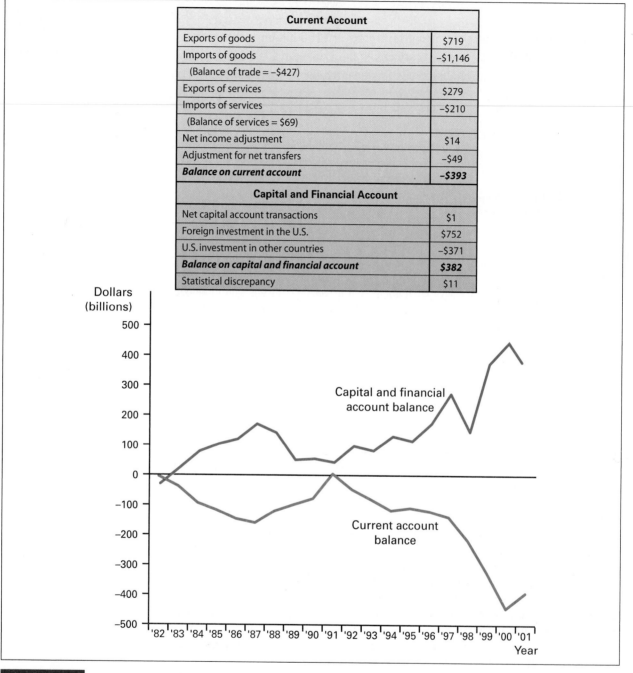

Current Account	
Exports of goods	$719
Imports of goods	–$1,146
(Balance of trade = –$427)	
Exports of services	$279
Imports of services	–$210
(Balance of services = $69)	
Net income adjustment	$14
Adjustment for net transfers	–$49
Balance on current account	*–$393*
Capital and Financial Account	
Net capital account transactions	$1
Foreign investment in the U.S.	$752
U.S. investment in other countries	–$371
Balance on capital and financial account	*$382*
Statistical discrepancy	$11

FIGURE 17-3

THE U.S. BALANCE OF PAYMENTS The table in this figure shows the balance of payments items and their 2001 values in billions of dollars. The graph shows the balance on the current account and capital account over time.

Source: Survey of Current Business, August 2002, Table F.2.

Opportunities in specific industries and types of occupations can change markedly because of international trade. While the manufacturing of goods is still an important part of the U.S. economy, many U.S. manufacturing industries have shrunk in relative importance

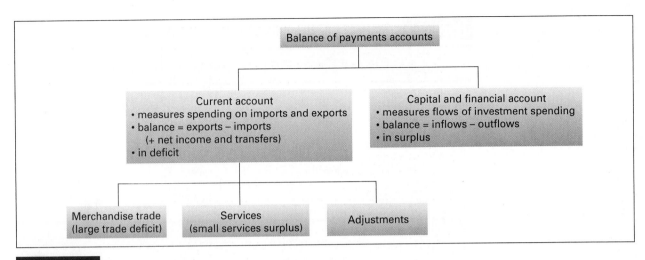

FIGURE 17-4

THE BALANCE OF PAYMENTS ACCOUNTS The U.S. balance of payments accounts record the dollar values of economic interactions between the United States and other countries. The two main subaccounts are the *current account,* which measures goods and services, and the *capital and financial account* (usually just called the *capital account*), which measures investment. The current account is in deficit while the capital account is in surplus. Although not pictured, the poor quality of data used to compute the current account and capital account causes there to be another account called *statistical discrepency* to reconcile the two.

The *balance of trade* refers to the value of exported merchandise minus the value of imported merchandise, which is a portion of the current account. This value is currently quite negative and is called the trade deficit. The services portion of the current account shows a surplus, which reduces the current account deficit to less than the trade deficit.

as imported goods have replaced those made in the United States. For example, a generation ago, consumer electronic goods such as the TVs and radios that were purchased by U.S. consumers were made by American manufacturers in American factories. Today, that is not the case. Even RCA, which stood for Radio Corporation of America, is now owned by the French. While jobs making televisions are hard to find in the United States because of imports, the global economy has created a bounty of jobs in travel services, entertainment industries, and many other industries that produce goods and services popular with foreigners.

The United States has an abundance of both physical and human capital relative to most, but not all, other countries. This means that the United States is likely to specialize in goods that are *capital intensive.* In other words, for the United States to gain from international trade, it exports goods that use a high proportion of capital in their production, such as airplanes, financial services, and movies. Even U.S. farm exports are capital intensive relative to farm products in other countries because U.S. farmers use so much farm equipment relative to labor in growing and harvesting their crops. In return, the United States imports goods that use a high proportion of labor and land, such as textiles and crude oil.

However, there are exceptions. For example, Japan is in some respects more capital intensive than the United States, which explains why Japan exports so many electronic goods to this country. Over all, though, international trade causes the United States to specialize somewhat in capital-intensive goods. Exports thus increase the demand for different kinds of capital in the United States and increase the prices paid for capital. The prices paid for capital represent income to the owners of capital, including human capital.

By increasing the return to human capital in the United States, international trade opens up attractive employment opportunities for those who have acquired skills and abilities. The return to a college education, a significant source of human capital, is higher than it would be without international trade. Conversely, job opportunities for low-skilled labor in

TABLE 17-1   EXAMPLES OF U.S. JOBS GAINED FROM EXPORTS AND LOST TO IMPORTS

EXAMPLES OF U.S. JOBS GAINED	EXAMPLES OF U.S. JOBS LOST
Aircraft workers	Textile workers
Software designers	Shoemakers
Stockbrokers	Electronics assembly line workers
TV and movie castmembers	Steelworkers
Travel agents	Autoworkers

the United States are harmed by international trade, as imports of labor-intensive goods lead to lower wages and fewer job openings in those industries. Table 17-1 shows examples of jobs lost and gained by U.S. workers as a result of trade. The United States can gain jobs when it can export more of a particular good because of trade, or in response to technological changes that are promoted by trade. Workers who lose jobs because of trade are eligible for help from the Federal Trade Adjustment Assistance Program and other government programs.

SNAPSHOT   **YOU CAN'T COMPETE WITH SUNSHINE**

The trade deficit is huge, at over 4 percent of U.S. GDP. In 1992, presidential candidate Ross Perot even claimed to hear "a giant sucking sound" of jobs being pulled to low-wage countries. For centuries, people have needlessly worried about the jobs that are lost, as though there are only a limited number to go around. Some still do worry, but both long-standing economic theory and the last two decades worth of hard factual evidence from the United States tell us to leave those worries behind.

In recent decades, the United States has run a string of trade deficits, several setting new records. At the same time, it has seen some of the lowest unemployment in its history. The reason is simply that people produce in order to earn the income that allows them to consume. They find their comparative advantages. It does not matter if some things are imported cheaply. As French economist Frédéric Bastiat observed a century and a half ago, French candlemakers lost jobs in competition with sunlight, an import that is completely free. But that did not mean France would have been better off boarding up all its windows. Likewise today: We don't make sunlight and few of us even make candles; we make other things. ◄

17.2 EXCHANGE RATES

A world traveler quickly discovers that there are dollars, pesos, yen, the baht, and many more currencies. Even countries that use the same name for their currencies usually do not actually share a common currency. For example, although Canada and the United States both use dollars, Canadian dollars are not the same money as American dollars. However, Ecuador is an exception to the rule. Its currency is the dollar—the same U.S. dollar that Americans use. Other countries may share a currency, as is the case with the euro, the common currency for Germany, France, and many other European nations.

Our world traveler probably will need another country's currency when crossing an international border. How can that new currency be acquired? Different monies can be exchanged for one another in *currency markets,* also known as **foreign exchange markets.** Travelers are familiar with the obvious manifestations of currency markets. Hotels, banks, and airports frequently offer a currency exchange for the convenience of foreign tourists and businesspeople. Even taxi drivers are sometimes willing to offer these services.

The amount of one country's currency that trades for a unit of another country's currency is called an **exchange rate.** In short, an exchange rate is the price of one currency in terms of another. With exchange rate information, cross-border travelers are equipped to compute how much foreign currency they will be able to obtain for their money. Travelers crossing the border between the United States and Canada in mid-2002 who looked up the exchange rate for these currencies found that one U.S. dollar exchanged for about 1.5 Canadian dollars. An American with $10 U.S. in hand would be able to acquire $15 Canadian. While exchange rates are of direct interest to travelers, they affect all of us, as we will see in the following sections. Figure 17-5 shows the currency of various countries.

foreign exchange markets markets in which currencies are bought and sold.

exchange rate price of one currency in terms of another.

MARKET EQUILIBRIUM EXCHANGE RATES— HOW MANY YEN CAN A DOLLAR BUY?

Figure 17-6 illustrates how a currency market operates. The specific example in the figure is for Japanese yen in exchange for U.S. dollars. In this market Americans seek to buy yen (demand) and the Japanese are sellers of yen (supply).

The horseshoe-shaped arrow indicates that, with minor exceptions, U.S. dollars spent on yen never physically make it to Japan. Likewise, virtually none of the yen purchased by

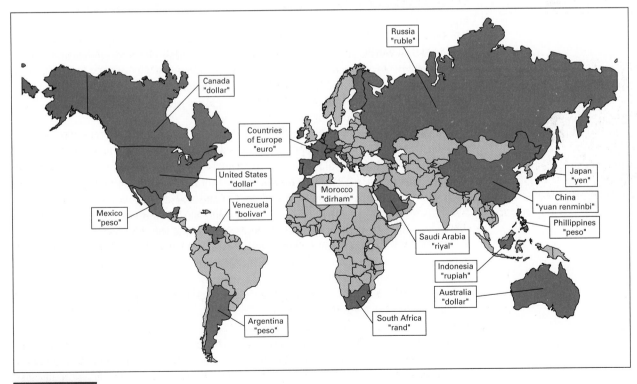

FIGURE 17-5

CURRENCIES OF THE WORLD There is a diversity of currencies in use in the world's many countries. Some countries share a common currency, such as the euro or U.S. dollar, but most countries have their own separate currencies. Thus, the U.S. dollar differs from the Canadian dollar and the Mexican peso differs from the Phillipines peso.

FIGURE 17-6

THE FOREIGN EXCHANGE MARKET—BUYING YEN WITH DOLLARS The equilibrium exchange rate makes sure that all dollars spent on yen are bought by others spending yen for dollars. In essence, the dollars bounce back to be spent in the United States, and the yen bounce back to be spent in Japan.

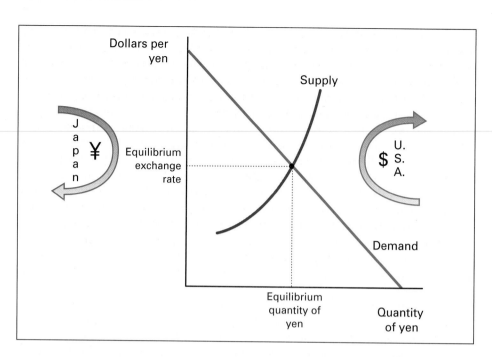

Americans ever makes it to the United States. Rather, currencies are exchanged electronically through banks in major financial centers, such as New York, Tokyo, and London.

Although global in nature, the basic operation of this market is easily understood using supply and demand analysis, as depicted in the center of Figure 17-6. Those on the demand side for yen include U.S. buyers of imported goods and services from Japan. They also include U.S. investors interested in such things as Japanese property, stocks, and bonds. Those supplying yen have the same sort of interests, except now the roles are reversed. They may be wanting U.S. goods or services, or U.S. investments. The exchange of currencies thus represents the exchange of goods, services, and investments—both buyers and sellers have a use for each other's currencies.

As usual with supply and demand analysis, the horizontal axis represents the quantity of a good, and the vertical axis represents its price. Quantity here is the total amount of one currency, and price is its value per unit in terms of the other currency. That price is the exchange rate. In our example, we look at the quantity of yen and see its price in terms of dollars per yen. The market equilibrium exchange rate is associated with the intersection of demand and supply, as shown in Figure 17-6. In mid-2002, that exchange rate was roughly $.0085 per yen, meaning that each Japanese yen cost a little less than one U.S. penny.

At the market equilibrium exchange rate, the total quantity of yen offered for sale is just equal to the total quantity of yen purchased. Moreover, the total number of dollars being spent to obtain yen is just equal to the total number of dollars being received by those selling yen. In other words, all dollars that U.S. residents spend on Japanese imports are received by Japanese sellers of yen. The sellers of yen enter the currency market because they want dollars for some reason.

Exchange rates can greatly affect the prices we see at our local stores. For example, imported products will seem cheaper if the dollar *strengthens*, meaning that it appreciates against many currencies. A stronger dollar buys more of other currencies, although just how much purchasing power is needed to make the dollar strong or how little to make it weak is a normative issue—a matter of subjective opinion. U.S. consumers and U.S. tourists abroad both like a strong dollar. Consider a ceramic vase that costs thirty pesos in Mexico. If the exchange rate is three pesos per dollar, the vase costs the U.S. tourist $10. However, if the exchange rate is six pesos per dollar, the vase costs only $5.

Moreover, not only does a stronger dollar mean that the price of imports is lower to U.S. consumers, it also means that U.S. firms must keep their own prices lower to the extent that their products and imports are good substitutes among consumers. For example, U.S. airlines that fly to Europe must keep their fares competitive with those of Virgin Atlantic, KLM, and other airlines based in Europe even when those airlines' fares decrease in response to a stronger dollar.

Although U.S. consumers benefit from a stronger dollar, U.S. producers of products that compete with imports and foreign tourists in the United States prefer to see the dollar weaken. A weak dollar means that U.S. goods and services seem cheap to foreigners, and foreign goods and services seem expensive to U.S. citizens. For example, the exchange rate between the dollar and the yen in June of 2002 was about 120 yen per dollar. However, it was over twice that (250 yen per dollar) in 1982, two decades earlier. The Japanese tourist in 2002 thus had more than double the spending power in the United States of that same tourist in 1982. Conversely, it seemed to the U.S. tourist visiting Japan in 2002 that everything was twice as expensive as it had been on a previous trip twenty years earlier.

Some have argued that exchange rates will adjust until there is **purchasing power parity,** meaning that prices would be the same around the world for easily tradeable items. If there were purchasing power parity, a dollar should buy you the same amount of rice in New York as it does in New Delhi. In reality, there are often too many costly details of trade for purchasing power parity to be a good guide. The most significant of these details are transportation and storage costs that increase the price of traded goods. Other details involve public policies and even the cost of real estate where the item is sold. For example, the high price of real estate in New York City raises the price of rice in New York City relative to its price not only in New Delhi, but also relative to its price in New Paltz, which is just upstate.

purchasing power parity theory that prices would be the same around the world for easily tradeable items.

SNAPSHOT

BUYING THE BIG MAC

Cashiers ring up Big Mac sales all around the world in all sorts of different currencies. When the Big Mac price is converted to a common denominator of dollars, as seen in Table 17-2, its price varies wildly from place to place. For example, in contrast to the $2.71 it cost in the United States, the Big Mac fetched less than half of that price in Russia. How can this be? There are world prices of oil, grain, ball bearings, and all sorts of other things. Is there no world price of a Big Mac?

The answer is that there is no world price for many items, including perishables such as Big Macs. No one flies from Russia to sell you a burger. If they did cart one along in their luggage, we suggest you not eat it . . . no matter the price! ◄

CURRENCY APPRECIATION AND DEPRECIATION

As we have just seen, exchange rates do not remain constant. Currency **appreciation** occurs when a currency gets stronger. **Depreciation** occurs when the currency becomes weaker. Figure 17-7 illustrates currency appreciation and depreciation.

In Figure 17-7 the demand curve for yen shifts to the right, such as occurred in the 1990s relative to the position of the demand curve in the 1980s. The supply curve of yen is assumed to remain constant. The price of yen in terms of dollars thus rises as shown by the upward pointing arrow on the vertical axis. Since Americans must pay more for yen, we conclude that the dollar has weakened. Since the Japanese receive more per yen, we conclude that the yen has gotten stronger. This scenario illustrates appreciation of the yen and depreciation of the dollar. The dollar depreciation between 1982 and 2002 saw its value drop from 250 yen per dollar to 120 yen per dollar. Instead of getting over 2 yen for a penny, as in 1982, by 2002 a penny would buy closer to one yen.

The depreciation of the dollar against the yen from the early 1980s through the mid-1990s can be traced to an increase in U.S. demand for yen, which drove the dollar price of

appreciation when a currency buys more of other currencies; makes imports cheaper and exports more expensive.

depreciation when a currency buys less of other currencies; makes imports more expensive and exports cheaper.

TABLE 17-2	THE PRICE OF A BIG MAC	
COUNTRY	**IN LOCAL CURRENCY**	**IN U.S. DOLLARS**
Australia	$3.00 (Australian dollars)	$1.80
Canada	$3.20 (Canadian dollars)	$2.17
China	9.90 Yuan	$1.20
Japan	262 Yen	$2.18
Mexico	23 Pesos	$2.14
Russia	41 Rouble	$1.31
South Africa	13.95 Rand	$1.74
Switzerland	6.3 Swiss francs	$4.52

Source: The Economist, 2003.

FIGURE 17-7

DEPRECIATION OF THE DOLLAR AGAINST THE YEN The dollar depreciated and the yen appreciated as U.S. consumers desired more Japanese products in the 1990s than in the 1980s. An increased demand for Japanese products shifts the demand curve for yen to the right. The figure assumes the supply curve of yen does not shift. The combination of an increased demand for yen along with an unchanging supply curve yields a higher price for yen.

those yen higher. A dominant force behind the strong yen during this period was the demand by American importers for yen to buy the Japanese electronics and automobiles that they sold to U.S. consumers.

Depreciation of the U.S. dollar could alternatively be caused by changes in the supply of foreign currency, such as in response to changes in foreign attitudes toward traveling to the United States, investing in the United States, or buying U.S. products. For example, a private lawsuit filed in U.S. courts in August 2002 sought to seize over $1 trillion worth of Saudi Arabian and other Middle Eastern assets in the United States as compensation for terrorist attacks. If foreign investors fear that U.S. courts might seize their assets because of their countries' alleged misdeeds, those investors would have a powerful incentive to invest elsewhere.

Governments sometimes try to influence the market exchange rates. The huge volume of global currency transactions overwhelms the efforts of any individual country. Countries have been slightly more effective when they work in synchrony. The most important of these joint efforts is conducted through a group of eight countries, called *the G8*, whose members include the United States, Great Britain, France, Germany, Japan, Italy, Canada, and Russia. While these countries slightly affect exchange rates through their buying and selling of currencies in the marketplace, their most effective tools involve monetary and fiscal macroeconomic policies that can change the demand for products and investments that underlie supply and demand in the foreign exchange markets. Even so, the currency markets are so huge that governments can hope for little more than to tweak them slightly in one direction or another. For example, **the value of currencies exchanged worldwide in a single week exceeds the value of an entire year's worth of U.S. output.**

This was not always the case. In the period after World War II, governments from around the world adhered to the *Bretton Woods agreement*. The Bretton Woods agreement was a treaty signed in 1944 at Bretton Woods, New Hampshire, by most of the world's major trading countries. This agreement *pegged* the dollar to gold ($35/ounce) and all other currencies to the dollar, thereby implying *fixed exchange rates*. Governments agreed to take whatever actions would be necessary to maintain these rates.

As world commerce grew over the next thirty years, however, the size of currency transactions overwhelmed the ability of governments to follow through on that agreement. The system of fixed exchange rates was modified in stages and was ultimately abandoned as unworkable during a run on the dollar in 1972. This run consisted of dollar selling that overwhelmed the governments' abilities to maintain the agreement, thereby precipitating a financial crisis. American tourists abroad felt this crisis personally, as many tourists were stranded, unable to find anyone willing to risk accepting their rapidly depreciating currency. Since that time, the system has been one of **floating exchange rates,** meaning that exchange rates have been allowed to adjust to whatever level the market dictates. However, **because governments still take actions intended to affect market exchange rates, the system is referred to as a *managed float* or *dirty float.***

floating exchange rates exchange rates that adjust according to the forces of supply and demand; called managed float or dirty float if the government attempts to influence these forces.

Government inability to control exchange rates was highlighted by the precipitous depreciation of Asia's currencies as their values tumbled during the Asian currency crisis of 1998. By late July 1998, for example, the Indonesian rupiah had dropped to 14,000 per dollar from 2,600 per dollar one year earlier. This plunge of the rupiah occurred in spite of efforts by the Indonesian government to prevent it. The depreciation of the rupiah's value in the currency market meant that the 2,600 rupiah that would have exchanged for one dollar in July 1997 would exchange for only about eighteen cents one year later. To put matters another way, U.S. goods imported into Indonesia and paid for with rupiah cost over five times as much in the summer of 1998 than in the summer of 1997.

This abrupt depreciation of the rupiah dramatically increased the purchasing power of dollars in Indonesia and decreased the purchasing power of rupiah in the United States. When the rupiah fell, U.S. investors saw the value of their investments in Indonesia drop. However, many U.S. investors viewed the drop as a buying opportunity, since Indonesian investments seemed available at what looked like bargain-basement prices. However, the precipitous drop also sparked rioting and political unrest, which scared potential foreign investors worried about the security of their investments. These concerns also kept down foreign tourism, even though prices in Indonesia would seem very cheap to those who made the trip.

17.3 TRADE AGREEMENTS

In Chapter 2, we discussed the efficiency of trade. It does not matter if that trade is among individuals, states, or countries—trade can increase our consumption to more than what we can produce ourselves. Yet, over the years, trade has frequently been restricted, and only

QUICKCHECK

Suppose you are planning a trip from your home in the United States to France.

a.   **Would your meals and hotel cost you more if the U.S. dollar depreciated or appreciated against the French franc just as you embarked on your trip?**

b.   **If the reason for your trip was to find customers in France for a product you make in the United States, which event, depreciation or appreciation of the dollar, would benefit your business?**

Answer:

a. Recall that when a currency depreciates it loses value. If the dollar depreciated against the franc, then it would take more dollars to buy the same number of francs. For this reason, as a tourist you would be better off financially if the dollar appreciated. It would take fewer dollars to buy the same number of francs. Thus, U.S. travelers going abroad prefer an appreciating dollar.

b. As a producer of a product, the reasoning is different. An appreciating dollar means that the franc depreciates. As the franc loses value, it means that a citizen of France must spend more francs to get the same number of dollars. As a consequence, U.S. products sold in France carry higher price tags. U.S. producers prefer a depreciating dollar because it makes U.S. goods cheaper when they are sold in other countries.

sometimes for good reason. We start by examining who wins and loses from trade. We then turn to trade agreements . . . and then turn to trade disagreements.

MULTINATIONAL EFFORTS TOWARD FREE TRADE— THE GATT AND THE WORLD TRADE ORGANIZATION

free trade international commerce unhindered by policy obstacles.

Trade agreements promote **free trade,** which occurs when no policies hinder imports or exports. Controversy has been the hallmark of efforts toward free trade. Australians witnessed intense anti-trade sentiments firsthand during the 2000 Olympic Games. Australia, like the United States and some other countries, was the site of violent demonstrations in which protesters rebuked the industrialized nations for purported economic exploitation of less-developed countries. Those protesters neglected to point out the reasons that less-developed countries chose open economies, namely that there are benefits from trade in which both countries gain. Trade policies can reduce or enhance an economy's openness.

Countries design their trade policies with an eye toward their own self-interests. Since governments are by nature political, trade strategies usually contain a mix of political and economic objectives. However, most countries recognize that their interests are usually best served by freeing up trade with other countries. This lesson was learned the hard way during the Great Depression of the 1930s. In a misguided fight against the high unemployment of those days, the United States and other countries engaged in *trade wars,* situations in which countries punish each other and themselves through retaliatory trade restrictions.

General Agreement on Tariffs and Trade (GATT) an agreement signed by most of the major trading countries of the world, which limits the use of protectionist policies; enforced by the World Trade Organization.

Most countries have signed the **General Agreement on Tariffs and Trade (GATT)** that aims to avoid trade wars and promote free trade. The GATT was initially signed in 1947 by the twenty-three major trading countries of the world at that time. Over the intervening years, the agreement has been updated and membership has grown to 110 countries. Since

1995, the GATT has been administered by the **World Trade Organization (WTO),** an arm of the GATT created to settle trade disputes among GATT members and monitor compliance with provisions of the GATT.

The initial impetus for the GATT agreement was the prohibitively high **tariffs**—taxes on imports—imposed by the United States and some other countries in the decade prior to World War II. Most significantly, the **Smoot-Hawley Act** was passed by the U.S. Congress in 1930 as a means to fight the unemployment of the Great Depression. The Act raised import tariffs to an average rate of 52 percent on more than 20,000 products, a level that was so prohibitively high that imports nearly ceased.

Supporters of the Smoot-Hawley Act were surprised by the ultimate outcome. They had expected that high tariffs would protect jobs. But with imports cut back, U.S. exports and foreign investment flows into the country slowed to a trickle because foreigners could not finance their purchase without selling their goods and services to Americans. Rather than lower U.S. unemployment, the Smoot-Hawley Act was followed by even higher unemployment! Such *beggar-thy-neighbor* protectionist policies didn't work for the United States or anybody else. The high tariffs promoted political animosity and isolationism among countries and led to economic tensions that contributed to World War II.

The GATT required significant tariff reductions. It has been strengthened over the years through rounds of trade negotiations that have achieved further reductions in tariffs. The negotiations have also placed restrictions on **quotas,** which limit the quantity of imported products a country allows, and on other **nontariff barriers,** which is a catch-all category for the variety of other actions a country can take to restrict trade. Most recently, the *Uruguay round* of negotiations took eight years of often contentious bargaining before being ratified by the United States and other countries in late 1994. It established the World Trade Organization and dealt with various thorny issues, such as:

- **Tariffs:** Tariffs have been cut by an average of about 40 percent worldwide on thousands of products and eliminated altogether on others, such as beer, toys, and paper. After a phase-in period, the percentage of products that can be imported *duty-free* into industrialized countries will more than double to 44 percent of all imported goods.
- **Agricultural subsidies:** *Subsidies* represent financial assistance to domestic producers. This assistance can lead to inefficient patterns of trade. After particularly heated debate, countries agreed to reduce trade-distorting subsidies to agriculture. Agricultural subsidies have been estimated to cost consumers $160 billion per year.
- **Services:** For the first time, global trade rules will be interpreted to cover services. To reach agreement, many of the details were left vague, especially in regard to banking and other financial services.
- **Intellectual property rights:** New rules were enacted to better protect patents and copyrights, including rights to copy computer software. For example, Malaysia announced in August 2002 that it would begin to crack down on pirated software.

The good intentions of these agreements are not always carried out in reality. For example, the United States and other countries have found it difficult in terms of their own internal politics to make a serious dent in agricultural subsidies. When members violate the GATT agreement, affected countries can turn to the World Trade Organization for recourse. For example, in the late summer of 2002, the World Trade Organization ruled that the United States corporate income tax unfairly subsidized exports. The WTO authorized countries of the European Union to impose up to $4 billion worth of retaliatory tariffs on goods imported from the United States. In response, the United States is considering revising some of its corporate income tax provisions, and might in this way be able to avert many of these penalties.

World Trade Organization (WTO) international organization formed to administer the General Agreement on Tariffs and Trade.

tariff tax on imports.

Smoot-Hawley Act legislation passed by the U.S. Congress in 1930, the Act raised tariffs so high that imports nearly ceased.

quota quantity limit on imports.

nontariff barriers any of a variety of actions other than tariffs that make importing more expensive or difficult.

REGIONAL TRADING BLOCS

trading bloc agreement among a group of countries that provides for lower trade barriers among its members than with the rest of the world.

North American Free Trade Agreement (NAFTA) trading bloc that includes the United States, Canada, and Mexico.

trade creation effect trade that would otherwise not take place; adds to efficiency; caused by lower trade barriers among members of a trading bloc.

trade diversion effect trade among members of a trading bloc that would more efficiently be conducted with other countries outside of the bloc.

The European Union is an example of a regional **trading bloc,** which is an agreement that lowers trade barriers among member countries. The European Union is considered a trading bloc because it has lower trade barriers among its member countries than to the rest of the world. By signing the **North American Free Trade Agreement,** commonly known as **NAFTA,** the United States, Canada, and Mexico also formed a trading bloc. This bloc is envisioned to someday expand southward to include countries of Central and South America, some of which are currently in their own trading bloc called the *Mercosur.*

To the extent that regional trading blocs reduce tariffs and other trade restrictions, the trading blocs promote trade among their members. This trade can come from two sources. First is the **trade creation effect,** which involves an increase in world trade. The trade creation effect is efficient, since it allows countries to specialize according to comparative advantage.

The second is the **trade diversion effect,** which represents trade that would have occurred with countries outside the trading bloc, but that is diverted to countries within a trading bloc solely in response to lower tariff rates within the bloc. An example of trade diversion would be if NAFTA is what induced IBM to assemble its laptop computers in Mexico instead of Taiwan. **Trade diversion is inefficient, since it causes trade to respond to price signals from the government—relative tariff rates—rather than to comparative advantage.**

Economists generally support regional trading blocs as a step toward free trade. However, even supporters of regional agreements have reservations about trade-diversion effects. There are also concerns that regional trading blocs may turn inward and erect higher barriers to the rest of the world. Not only would contentious trading blocs jeopardize gains from trade, they could also be a threat to world peace.

QUICKCHECK

Distinguish the trade diversion effect from the trade creation effect of a regional trading bloc. Why is the trade diversion effect inefficient?

Answer: Both the trade diversion effect and the trade creation effect are associated with the formation of regional trading blocs. Member countries of a trading bloc have lowered barriers to trade among themselves, but have not lowered barriers for trade with countries outside the bloc. Lower trade barriers lead to increased trade, which is efficient and is termed the trade creation effect. Unfortunately, there is also the trade diversion effect, which distorts the pattern of existing trade from what it would otherwise have been. Specifically, the trade diversion effect increases trade within the bloc at the expense of trade that would otherwise have occurred between member countries and other countries outside the bloc.

17.4 TRADE POLICY OPTIONS

Counter to the spirit of the GATT and regional trading blocs, all major countries have some restrictions on trade. For better or worse, countries often seek to protect individual industries or sectors of their economies from foreign competition. Policies that accomplish this goal are termed *protectionist,* even though these policies usually harm rather than protect the economy as a whole. Protectionist policies come in two basic forms: tariffs and nontariff barriers. Nontariff barriers can be either quotas—quantity restrictions on imports—or any of a variety of other actions that make importing more difficult. Consider the tariff.

TARIFFS

A tariff is a tax on an imported product. Demand for an imported product tells the quantities of the product consumers would purchase from foreign sources at each possible price. This demand is sometimes called *residual demand,* since it represents demand that is left over after consumers have bought from domestic suppliers. Because buyers have the ability to substitute domestically made products for foreign-made products, the quantity demanded of imports is typically quite responsive to price, leading to a flatter demand curve than for the market as a whole. Likewise, because suppliers of foreign-made goods can sell their products in many countries, the supply of imports is also relatively flat.

Tariffs increase the cost of selling imported products. This increase in turn increases the prices of those products in the domestic market and, by the law of demand discussed in Chapter 3, reduces the quantity that will be sold. That is how a tariff restricts imports. Figure 17-8 illustrates how a tariff raises the price and decreases the quantity of imports, relative to what would have occurred in the free market. Note that the increase in price is less than the amount of the tariff, indicating that importers are often not able to merely pass along the entire tariff to consumers.

By raising barriers to the entry of foreign products, **tariffs can be viewed as a form of price support for domestic producers.** The higher price of imports causes the demand curve to shift to the right for domestic products that are close substitutes. For example, an import tariff on Toshiba laptop computers increases demand for Dell, Compaq, and IBM laptop computers, which in turn causes a new, higher equilibrium price and quantity for those products. The higher price and quantity sold by domestic producers are why an import tariff is said to protect those producers from foreign competition.

Tariffs are said to be *transparent,* meaning that their effects on prices are clear for all to see. The United States has an extensive array of tariffs, most of which are currently below 6 percent and falling. Most other major trading countries also have similar tariffs. With some exceptions, tariff rates are kept low by the GATT. The decrease in U.S. tariff rates in recent years is seen in Table 17-3.

FIGURE 17-8

EFFECTS OF A TARIFF Import tariffs raise prices paid by consumers and thus cause them to buy fewer imports. A tariff on a good imported into the United States helps American producers who can sell at the higher price, but that help comes at the expense of consumers who must pay the higher price.

TABLE 17-3 EFFECTIVE U.S. TARIFF RATES BY SECTOR, 1992–2000 (IN PERCENT)

SECTOR	1992	1993	1994	1995	1996	1997	1998	1999	2000
Food and live animals	1.99	2.07	1.81	1.42	1.41	1.19	1.34	1.36	1.18
Beverages and tobacco	3.33	3.66	2.71	1.76	1.90	2.04	1.10	1.21	0.95
Crude materials, inedible, except fuels	0.36	0.36	0.32	0.24	0.21	0.20	0.20	0.16	0.16
Mineral fuels, lubricants and related materials	0.47	0.48	0.50	0.42	0.35	0.32	0.42	0.35	0.20
Animal and vegetable oils, fats and waxes	1.05	1.19	0.91	0.64	0.53	0.70	0.84	0.76	1.05
Chemicals and related products, n.e.s.	3.64	3.95	3.81	2.23	1.93	1.73	1.56	1.24	1.03
Manufactured goods classified chiefly by material	3.47	3.31	3.16	2.71	2.56	2.42	2.14	1.91	1.76
Machinery and transport equipment	2.00	2.02	1.86	1.53	1.35	1.14	0.94	0.85	0.73
Miscellaneous manufactured articles	8.41	7.81	7.70	6.86	6.45	6.18	5.88	5.54	5.49
Commodities and transactions not classified elsewhere in the SITC	0.02	0.03	0.03	0.05	0.07	0.06	0.10	0.09	0.03
All sectors	3.15	3.07	2.91	2.43	2.20	2.07	1.95	1.76	1.59

Source: United States International Trade Commission, *The Economic Effects of Significant U.S. Import Restraints,* June 2002, page 146.

QUOTAS

Import quotas are an alternative to import tariffs and can accomplish the same goals as a tariff. Unlike an import tariff, an import quota restricts the quantity of imports directly and thus cuts off supply from abroad at the quota quantity, as shown by the vertical segment of supply in Figure 17-9. The figure illustrates how the truncated supply from abroad under a quota leads to an increase in prices at home.

FIGURE 17-9

EFFECTS OF A QUOTA Like an import tariff, a quota also reduces the quantity of imports and increases price in the domestic market. The quota truncates supply from abroad at the maximum allowable import quantity, thus causing import supply to become vertical at that point.

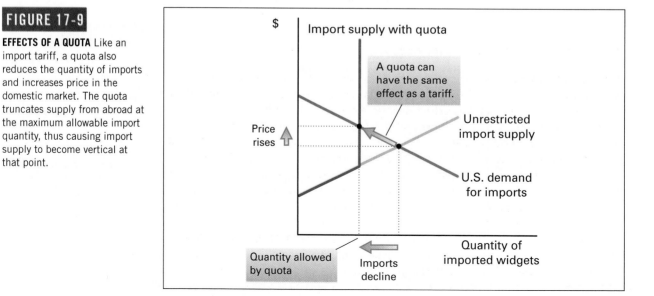

QUICKCHECK

Why are exporting countries better off to agree to a voluntary export restraint than to have the importing country restrict imports with an import quota?

Answer: If the importing country imposes an import quota, exporting countries compete to fill that quota, which drives the prices they receive lower. In contrast, by accepting a voluntary export restraint, the countries are not in competition with one another and can thus receive higher prices for their exports.

GATT limits the extent to which countries can impose import quotas, but does allow quotas for agricultural products and to avoid disruption to countries' domestic economies. While not as widespread as tariffs, most countries have some import quotas.

For example, the United States used to restrict the import of sugar through a set of country-by-country quotas, but has converted them to tariffs with an equivalent effect— *tariff-rate quotas.* These tariff-rate quotas increase the cost of sugar in the United States relative to what it is in the rest of the world. Consumers feel the effects when they buy sugar and sweetened products. Indeed, a primary reason for the use of corn sweetener in U.S. soft drinks has been the high price of sugar in the United States.

As an alternative to tariffs and import quotas, the United States and some other countries have chosen to negotiate **voluntary export restraints,** in which individual exporting countries agree to limit the quantities they export. For example, the *multi-fiber agreement,* currently scheduled for elimination by 2004, sets country-by-country quotas on clothing exports to the United States and some other countries. The alternative would be for the United States or other importing countries to impose import quotas.

The United States offers to forgo quotas in favor of voluntary export restraints in order to maintain good relations with the governments of the other countries involved. Exporting countries know that if they do not agree to the voluntary export restraints, they may face either quotas or some other retaliatory action. Exporting countries can also charge higher prices per unit under a voluntary export restraint than they could if they faced import quotas. Exporting countries charge more because they are not competing against one another— they each have their preassigned export restraints and are not allowed to fill those of other exporting countries.

voluntary export restraints an alternative to import quotas in which exporting countries agree to voluntarily limit their exports to the target country; leads to higher price received by exporting countries.

AN ASSORTMENT OF NONTARIFF BARRIERS TO TRADE

Quotas and voluntary export restraints are examples of nontariff barriers to trade, which include all ways other than tariffs that countries make importing difficult. Most nontariff barriers do not restrict imports explicitly; their effects are less obvious than quotas. For example, paperwork and red tape delays can inhibit trade. Under the administration of President Salinas in the early 1990s, for example, Mexico established a clever system to fight corruption and in the process reduce hidden nontariff barriers. The policy required that any application for a license to import a product into Mexico be automatically approved, if not acted on within ninety days. Prior to that time, unless illegal bribes were paid, applications were often delayed until after the market opportunity to sell the product was gone.

Sometimes, nontariff barriers are incidental to accomplishing other objectives. For example, the United States inspects the manufacturing processes of some products made domestically. It cannot do that for most imports, and so resorts to sampling. For this reason, entire shipments of such products as canned foods from China have been discarded because sampling revealed some to be contaminated, labeled improperly, or otherwise not up to U.S. standards. While sampling does increase the cost of importing and is thus a nontariff barrier, its primary purpose is presumably to protect public safety.

At other times, the effects of nontariff barriers on trade seem intentional, but are hard to prove. For example, Japan made it difficult to sell Louisville Slugger baseball bats in its country for many years, because the bats did not meet Japan's guidelines for use in baseball games. Since the Louisville Slugger was the best-selling bat in the world market, U.S. trade negotiators asserted that the Japanese regulators had set their standards for bats in order to restrict competition from U.S. imports.

Still other times, motives conflict. Europe does not allow the import or sale of beef from cattle fed the bovine growth hormones. While illegal in Europe, use of bovine growth hormones was allowed in the United States. Since the U.S. government would not certify its beef exports as hormone-free, the United States was for a time barred from exporting beef to Europe. That ban was lifted after the U.S. restricted imports of some minor European products and threatened to go much further if the Europeans did not back down. Since buyers in either the United States or Europe could always contract with cattle ranchers for whatever sort of animals they desire, U.S. negotiators argued that no government certification would be necessary.

SNAPSHOT

MADE IN MEXICO, BRICK BY BRICK

Americans need not be told which state is responsible for producing the goods they buy. By law, however, they do have a right to know the country of origin for imports. This information must be labeled on each imported item. The law applies to all products, including bricks from Mexico. No big deal, perhaps, except when you realize that brick kilns in Mexico are rarely high-tech. The cost of imprinting *Mexico* into each brick bound for El Norté is a significant fraction of the entire cost of producing that brick. If that labeling requirement forms a nontariff barrier that reduces Mexican brick exports, U.S. brickmakers don't complain! ◄

17.5 THE FREE TRADE DEBATE

If the arguments for and against free trade were to be counted, the free trade side would come up very short. However, the number of objections is not important. It is their validity that matters. **The objections to free trade commonly have limited applicability or are based on questionable logic.** For example, the previous sections took issue with worries over cheap foreign labor threatening domestic jobs. This section takes a brief look at some additional significant arguments and counterarguments.

NATIONAL DEFENSE—VALID BUT OVERUSED

If imports or exports seriously threaten national defense, it makes sense to restrict them. There is no argument there. However, translating national defense interests into policy requires judgments and debate. For example, the United States restricts the export of certain computers and technology. However, if the United States is an unreliable supplier to other countries, will new technologies evolve elsewhere in places where the government allows producers to reap the profits from exports? Also, how much consideration should be given civilian uses for products that could also be used in war?

The judgments are often difficult and the source of debate. In 1998, for example, President Clinton's decision to allow China to launch U.S. companies' satellites sparked a heated debate in Congress about the role of satellite and satellite launch technology in the production of intercontinental missiles, which the United States naturally does not want the Chinese aiming its way.

TRADE SANCTIONS—DO THEY WORK?

The United States sometimes uses *trade sanctions*, which restrict trade with countries such as Cuba and Iraq that have policies it opposes. Note that Cuba's Fidel Castro and Iraq's Saddam Hussein have had remarkable staying power, even as the trade sanctions contributed to the poverty of their economies. Trade sanctions allowed them to rally their citizens and point the blame outside their borders. **Despite their lack of effectiveness, trade sanctions are often popular with the public.** For example, when a Chinese fighter jet slammed into a U.S. spy plane in April 2001, and the Chinese government refused to let the crew return home, Americans overwhelmingly backed imposing sanctions. Perhaps in response, diplomacy prevailed and the Americans were allowed to return home.

Another question is whether economic sanctions punish the wrong people, including those in the country that imposes them. For example, the United States would be an unreliable source of goods and services if buyers must fear that their governments might do something that would irritate the United States and cause it to impose trade sanctions. Given the multinational nature of business today, buyers may decide to locate new businesses in countries that are more reliable. Thus, U.S. threats of trade sanctions can backfire and cause U.S. companies to be at a competitive disadvantage relative to similar companies located elsewhere in the world.

ENVIRONMENTAL, HEALTH, AND SAFETY STANDARDS— A LEVEL PLAYING FIELD WITHOUT A GAME

Some U.S. industries cannot produce products as cheaply as similar products from abroad, perhaps because foreign producers face weak government regulation of production. For example, they might not need to do as much to protect the environment and the health and safety of their workers. Should the United States attempt to estimate the extra costs of complying with U.S. standards and then add that cost to imports by imposing an appropriate set of tariffs? Some critics of current trade policy suggest that this approach is the only way to achieve a *level playing field*.

For the United States to impose its own standards on other countries, when effects are localized, would benefit neither the United States nor those countries. Such action could easily be interpreted by those countries' citizens as an act of U.S. arrogance or imperialism. For example, environmental costs of production in poor countries are often less than in the United States because of weaker laws or law enforcement. Higher levels of pollution are likely to be efficient for these countries, because environmental quality is a *normal good*—as incomes rise, people demand more. Poor countries value spending extra income on food and shelter more highly than on extra environmental quality. Thus, poor countries have a higher opportunity cost of environmental quality and might efficiently specialize in industries with a higher pollution content. In contrast, by valuing environmental quality highly, U.S. citizens might prefer that heavy polluters go elsewhere.

DUMPING—RARELY STRATEGIC

Dumping is defined as the selling of a good for less than its cost of production. Dumping occurs for many reasons. For example, a company might have overestimated demand for its product and find itself stuck with too much—a clearance sale, so to speak. Alternatively, a company may be selling output at a price that covers wages, materials, and other operating

dumping selling a good to another country for less than its cost of production.

expenses of production, but does not cover the cost of its capital and other costs that it must pay whether it produces or not. Even though the company loses money, it would lose more by not selling. Perhaps it is even able to offset these losses by selling at a higher price in another market where it faces less competition.

Dumping for the above reasons occurs within a country, as well as in international trade. However, dumping is illegal across countries according to the GATT. The United States presumes dumping whenever a foreign company charges less in the United States than it does at home, irrespective of its costs. **The GATT and U.S. law permit anti-dumping tariffs when dumping harms a domestic industry.** However, the world cried foul when, in 2002, the United States slapped anti-dumping tariffs of up to 30 percent on imported steel. Japan immediately retaliated by placing a 100-percent tariff on the token $5 million worth of steel it imports from the United States. Both Europe and Japan took their cases to the World Trade Organization, and have both promised hundreds of millions of dollars worth of additional retaliation if the WTO rules that the United States applied its tariffs inappropriately. At this writing, the WTO has not yet issued its final ruling.

Consumers gain from the low prices that result from dumping. The only strong economic argument in favor of restricting dumping occurs in the special case of strategic dumping. **Strategic dumping** is dumping that aims to drive the competition out of business so that the firms doing the dumping can monopolize output and drive prices up in the future. However, the prospects for successful strategic dumping are highly questionable in most industries. After all, in a world marketplace, there are numerous potential competitors. Even companies that have been driven out of a particular line of business can often reenter it in the future, should an increase in price make it profitable to do so.

strategic dumping dumping with the intention of driving the competition out of business.

INFANT INDUSTRIES—WHERE ARE INVESTORS?

Developing countries often try to nurture new industries they hope will one day become a source of export earnings. These **infant industries** are thought to need protection in the rough world marketplace. The infant industry argument claims that the government must first identify promising industries and then erect import barriers to protect them. When the infants grow strong enough to fend for themselves, the government should remove the barriers.

infant industries startup industries that might be unable to survive the rigors of competition in their formative years.

The infant industry argument is unconvincing if markets function efficiently. In the free marketplace, *venture capitalists* and other private investors will often support firms through many years of losses. They will do so if they expect that the firms will eventually become profitable and reward their patience. If private investors do not foresee profits down the road, they will withhold their funds, and the businesses will fail.

Unfortunately, there is much less assurance that the government will pick industries that are likely to survive on their own. **Governments often use political considerations to select so-called infant industries.** Even if governments do attempt careful economic analysis, such analyses are unlikely to match those of investors with their own money at risk. The

QUICKCHECK

There are more arguments against free trade than there are in favor of it. Even so, economists are for the most part staunchly pro free trade. Why?

Answer: The arguments against free trade constitute exceptions to the rule that free trade promotes prosperity through increased efficiency. Oftentimes, even the purported exceptions to that rule turn out to be invalid.

result is that governments around the world have protected industries that never grew strong enough to withstand foreign competition. By requiring government subsidies to stay afloat, and by charging prices above those in the rest of the world, such industries have proven to be expensive for governments and consumers alike.

17.6 ENERGY SECURITY—A QUESTION OF OIL IMPORTS

*E*XPLORE
&
*A*PPLY

A business scenario can be put together that could have us back on the moon within 10 to 15 years.

—Dr. "Jack" Schmitt, Apollo 17 astronaut and last man on the moon

The business strategy Dr. Schmitt had in mind revolved around that most precious of possessions, energy. As he described it in a speech he gave to the Australian Institute of Physics Biennial Congress, in the summer of 2002, his particular plan involved gathering helium-3 from the moon to use in energy-creating fusion reactions here on earth. The cost? Dr. Schmitt estimated it at 200 billion Australian dollars (110 billion U.S. dollars).

While traveling to the moon to gather fuel might seem an outlandish idea, it is but one of many possibilities for developing *alternative fuels*, so-called because they provide an alternative to the traditional fossil fuels of coal, natural gas, and crude oil. These alternative fuels have one thing in common—they all cost more than the oil and other fossil fuels that they would replace. For that reason, without government assistance, the marketplace has not financed the development and production of such alternative fuels as ethanol, wind power, and solar power. Those fuels could not compete with cheaper oil. But is oil really cheaper?

The price of oil in the world market has fluctuated from under $20 per barrel to over $30 per barrel in the last few years. However, the cost of importing that oil into the United States might be significantly higher. There are costs that the importers do not currently pay that perhaps the country as a whole does pay. These are the costs having to do with energy security.

HOW AN OIL IMPORT FEE AFFECTS OIL PRODUCTION

The U.S. economy consumes tremendous amounts of petroleum, about 777 million gallons per day as of January, 2002. If placed in one-gallon gas cans, they could encircle the globe six times over. That is 18.5 million barrels of oil per year, with a total price tag of over $50 billion. The U.S. imports 55 to 60 percent of the oil it uses, with imports exceeding 50 percent of the total for the first time in 1994. Much of that oil comes from countries of this hemisphere, as seen in Figure 17-10. However, because the oil market is global, a disruption in oil exports from the Middle East would bring Europeans and other countries into competition for oil that would otherwise go to the United States. By the same token, the U.S. presence in the world oil market increases petroleum prices and the wealth of oil exporters. This situation means that:

- **The United States is vulnerable to political instability in the Middle East and in other oil-exporting countries.** The United States has spent a large amount of money and put many lives at risk in its efforts to bring peace to the Middle East. It's impossible to know how much of this effort has been motivated by the U.S. interest in secure energy sources.
- **The United States is a source of income for Middle Eastern countries with interests hostile to those of the United States.** For example, the "axis of evil" identified by President Bush in 2001 includes the governments of Iraq and Iran, two countries with a large amount of oil-related income. Likewise, oil money from the Middle East has been pointed to in Congress as providing funds for terrorist organizations.

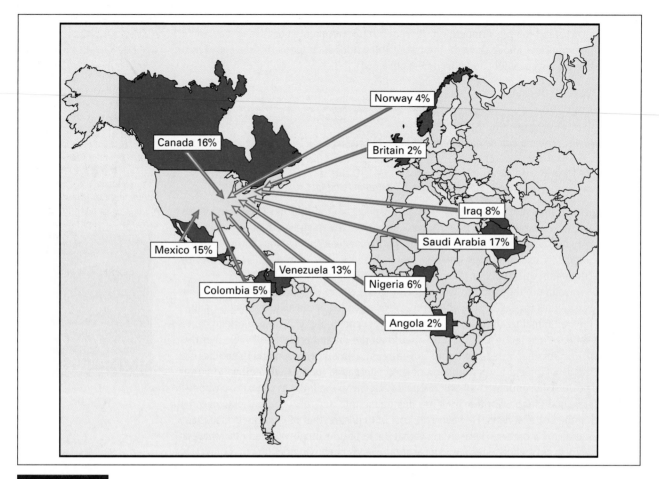

FIGURE 17-10

THE SOURCES OF OIL IMPORTED TO THE UNITED STATES The United States imports oil from many places, with about half coming from the Americas.

Source: Gibson Consulting.

These *external costs* of oil imports are not reflected in the price paid by importers. To "internalize" them, the United States could levy an *oil import fee,* a common name for an import tariff when applied to oil.

An oil import fee would raise the price of imported oil and encourage the development of alternative fuels. U.S. producers would produce more, and consumers consume less, as shown in Figure 17-11. For ease of analysis, the United States is shown in the figure as a price taker in the world oil market.

If the United States raises the price of imported oil, U.S. oil companies will produce more domestic oil, which increases the price of domestic oil relative to oil available on the world market. The higher price would attract resources from elsewhere in the economy to increase production from existing U.S. oilfields, as well as to increase the search for new supplies. Likewise, some existing industries that consume large amounts of oil would shrink or leave the country. For example, a higher oil price in the United States relative to other countries would probably cause petrochemical production to be moved abroad.

Since oil is a nonrenewable resource, opponents of oil import fees argue that such a fee would "drain America first." Down the road, as U.S. wells are pumped dry more quickly, the

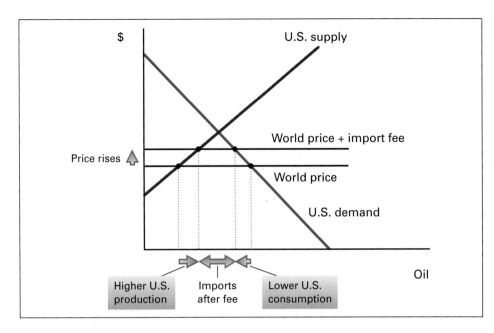

FIGURE 17-11

AN OIL IMPORT FEE An oil import fee would reduce oil imports and increase the U.S. price of oil. Part of the reduction in oil imports would be offset by less oil consumption due to the higher price. The rest would be offset by U.S. oil producers increasing output, also in response to the higher price. The increased U.S. production would deplete U.S. oil reserves more quickly, although the higher price might also prompt additional oil discoveries or development of alternative fuels.

United States might be forced to rely even more heavily on foreign supplies. In that view, oil import fees might help in the present, but would make matters worse over time. The economy would grow faster and stronger with cheaper energy and be better positioned to weather energy disruptions if they ever do materialize.

Also, higher oil prices could prompt the substitution of coal and nuclear power, both of which can harm the environment. Oil production itself can cause significant environmental damage. For example, the General Accounting Office estimated in July 2002 that oil companies pumping oil from Alaska's North Slope oil fields will face about $6 billion worth of environmental cleanup costs when their wells run dry. Since the opening of the Trans-Alaska pipeline in 1977, oil companies have pumped more than 13 billion barrels of oil and provided about 20 percent of the oil produced in the United States. The prospect of additional environmental damages to the Alaska National Wildlife Refuge caused the U.S. Congress to reject President Bush's proposal to allow oil exploration in that area.

The subject of oil import fees is obviously contentious, with the topic discussed off and on for decades. While the United States does not have an oil import fee, it does have another policy that gives it a measure of protection from the uncertainties of oil politics. Specifically, the United States maintains a *Strategic Petroleum Reserve* in the form of a huge quantity of oil that the U.S. government has been stashing away each year, and that President Bush ordered to be filled to capacity in 2002. That reserve was tapped only once when, in the face of oil prices that had doubled to more than $30 per barrel in 2000, President Clinton ordered a limited sale of oil from the reserve. Whether for this reason or other reasons, the price did drop back after President Clinton's action.

1. Would the U.S. military have less to do in the Middle East if the United States did not import so much oil? Should this cost differential be covered by an oil import fee? Explain.

2. Does the Strategic Petroleum Reserve accomplish the objectives of an oil import fee? Explain.

Visit **www.prenhall.com/collinge** for updates and web exercises on this Explore & Apply topic.

*T*HINKING
*C*RITICALLY

SUMMARY AND LEARNING OBJECTIVES

1. Identify the balance of payments accounts and their significance.

- The current account records the value of imports and exports of goods and services, with adjustments for international incomes and transfers. Since U.S. imports exceed U.S. exports, the current account is in deficit.

- The current account includes trade in services and merchandise. The balance on merchandise trade is currently quite negative, and is called the trade deficit. Trade in services shows a surplus, but that surplus is smaller than the trade deficit.

- The capital account measures international investment flows, which currently are characterized by more foreign investment in the United States than U.S. investment abroad, indicating a surplus. Capital inflows involve investment in the United States by foreigners. Capital outflows occur when there is investment in other countries by U.S. firms and citizens. Investments are of two types: direct investments and financial investments.

- The balance of payments' balance must equal zero by definition. Because of errors in measurement in the current account and capital account, the balance is forced to zero by including an item called the statistical discrepancy. When the statistical discrepancy is included with the capital account, the result equals the balance on the current account with the sign reversed.

2. Analyze how international trade costs jobs in some industries and creates jobs in others.

- While trade may eliminate specific jobs, in the aggregate a country's total employment will be unaffected.

- Countries that have abundant capital tend to specialize in the production of capital-intensive goods and export capital-intensive goods to other countries. Likewise, countries that have abundant labor tend to specialize in and export labor-intensive goods.

- The United States is relatively capital abundant, both in terms of physical and human capital. International trade increases the demand for capital, thus increasing its price. The returns to the human capital possessed by U.S. workers are increased by trade, along with the job opportunities in industries that make use of that human capital. Jobs for low-skilled labor decrease because of trade.

3. Interpret exchange rates and explain how forces of supply and demand determine their values.

- The price of a country's currency in terms of another country's currency is an exchange rate. Exchange rates are determined by the demand and supply of currencies.

- Exchange rates vary over time. A currency appreciates (gets stronger) when its value in the foreign exchange market rises. A currency depreciates (weakens) when its value falls in the foreign exchange market.

- As a country's currency appreciates, it is able to buy more of other countries' currencies. Currency appreciation results in lower prices for the country's imports, but higher prices for its exports. As a country's currency depreciates, its exports become cheaper, but the price of its imports rises. This effect occurs because currency depreciation increases the price of other currencies.

4. Discuss the GATT and other trade agreements among countries.

- The General Agreement on Tariffs and Trade (GATT) is a multilateral agreement, meaning that many nations have signed it. The 110 GATT signatories include the United States, Canada, Mexico, and countries of Europe. The GATT agreement is administered by the World Trade Organization, which was created to settle trade disputes among countries.

- Many issues are addressed in the GATT agreement and its updates, such as those made in the Uruguay round of negotiations in 1994. The GATT seeks to cut tariffs, encourage duty-free imports, reduce agricultural subsidies, apply trade rules to services such as banking as well as goods, and protect property rights through the enforcement of rules relating to copyrights and patents.

- Regional trading blocs are an increasingly common feature of the global economy. An example is the North American Free Trade Agreement that includes the United States, Canada, and Mexico.

- Regional trading blocs promote trade among their own members. The trade creation effect is efficient, occurring because member countries can more easily specialize according to the principle of comparative advantage. The trade diversion effect occurs when trade that would have occurred with countries outside the trading bloc if the trading bloc did not exist is instead diverted to countries within the trading bloc. Trade diversion is inefficient because it is a response to differences in tariffs rather than to comparative advantage.

5. **Distinguish among the various barriers to trade that countries might impose.**

   - Tariffs are taxes on imported products. A tariff shifts the supply curve of a product upward by the amount of the tariff. However, the price of the product will usually rise by less than the amount of the tariff because importers are not able to pass on the entire amount of the tariff. Nonetheless, a tariff will decrease the quantity imported of the product it is placed on.

   - Tariffs are a type of price support for domestic producers. Since tariffs increase the price of imported goods, domestic producers experience an increase in the demand for substitutes for the imports, which leads to higher prices in the domestic market.

   - To be transparent means the effects are readily clear to all. Tariffs are an example of a transparent protectionist policy.

   - The United States and most countries have lengthy lists of products that are subject to tariffs. For the most part these tariffs are kept low by the GATT. In the United States, most tariffs are below 6 percent.

   - Quotas impose a numerical limit on imports. A quota cuts off the supply of an imported product once a predetermined number of units of the product have been brought into the country.

   - A country's desire to reduce imports can be achieved by imposing either a tariff or a quota since both tariffs and quotas decrease imports. However, tariffs are more transparent than quotas since consumers usually know little about the existence of quotas or their effect on the price of an import. Quotas on agricultural products are allowed by the GATT, but in general quotas are not as widespread as tariffs.

   - A voluntary export restraint is a quota agreement negotiated between countries. A country would prefer that its exports be subject to a voluntary export restraint rather than a quota. The reason is that a quota induces exporting countries to lower their prices as they compete with each other to fill the quota. In contrast, with a voluntary export restraint in place, each exporting country is allowed to sell only so much and no more to the other country. This means that each exporting country need not lower its price below that of other exporting countries to sell its product.

   - Various other nontariff barriers to trade can be imposed by a country to reduce imports. For example, complicated import rules and regulations in a particular country make it difficult for other countries to sell their goods in that country.

6. **Assess the arguments for and against protectionist policies.**

   - Protectionist trade policies seek to protect a country's industry from foreign competition. Because most countries recognize the benefits that come from more international trade, they have jointly agreed to limit their use of protectionist policies by becoming signatories to the General Agreement on Tariffs and Trade (GATT).

   - There are a number of possible exceptions to the principle of free trade, although application of these exceptions is often subject to debate. These exceptions include the national defense argument. It may be wise for a country to restrict exports of goods that could be used by another country for hostile purposes. Another arguable justification for not trading arises when a trading partner acts in ways that a country disapproves of, and trade sanctions are imposed. A third questionable justification is that a level playing field should be achieved before trade is allowed. For example, a level playing field would require other countries to adopt U.S. environmental policies.

   - Sometimes exporting countries are accused of dumping, which is selling a good for less than the cost of production. The GATT makes dumping illegal and allows a country to impose anti-dumping tariffs in response.

   - The infant industry argument for protectionism argues that a country's new industries need to be protected from foreign competition until they are able to compete effectively against the same industries already existing in other countries. This argument is weak if markets function efficiently, since investors will fund new industries that they expect will eventually be profitable.

7. **Examine whether an oil import fee can promote energy security.**

   - An oil import fee might be used to adjust the price of imported oil upward so as to include costs associated with maintaining energy security. The effect would be to encourage use of alternative energy sources, some of which are likely to be environmentally harmful. The Strategic Petroleum Reserve is intended to accomplish some of the same objectives as would an oil import fee.

KEY TERMS

TEST YOURSELF

TRUE OR FALSE

1. The United States has a deficit in its balance of payments accounts.
2. By increasing the return to human capital in the United States, international trade opens up attractive employment opportunities for those who have acquired skills and abilities.
3. If foreign investors decide that investment opportunities in the United States are better than they used to be and so increase their investments in the United States, the dollar is likely to appreciate.
4. An appreciation in the dollar means that consumers pay less for imports.
5. A tariff raises the price of an import but leaves the quantity imported the same.

MULTIPLE CHOICE

6. In the balance of payments accounts, the current account includes
   a. capital flows and merchandise trade.
   b. trade in goods and services.
   c. immigration and trade.
   d. capital flows and services.
7. The dollars paid by U.S. importers to buy foreign products
   a. circulate abroad until foreigners buy U.S. products.
   b. circulate abroad and do not return.
   c. circulate abroad until Americans buy foreign investments.
   d. usually do not physically leave the country.
8. Suppose that an American import firm purchases some English ironstone dinnerware from an exporter in London. The dinnerware costs £5,000. At the exchange rate of $3 = £1, the dollar price of the dinnerware is
   a. $15,000.
   b. $10,000.

   c. $2,500.
   d. $1,666.67.
9. Currently, currency exchange rates are determined primarily
   a. in the marketplace by demand and supply.
   b. by a computer model developed by the United Nations.
   c. by international gold flows.
   d. in accordance with international agreements negotiated by countries.
10. In Self-Test Figure 17-1, the vertical arrow shows that the dollar
    a. has appreciated.
    b. exhibits purchasing power parity.
    c. exhibits interest-rate parity.
    d. has depreciated.

SELF-TEST FIGURE 17-1

11. If German-made goods have the same price in Germany this year as last year, but the euro depreciated against the dollar during the year, then the dollar price of German goods sold in the United States would _____ and Americans would buy _____ from Germany.
    a. increase; less
    b. increase; more
    c. decrease; less
    d. decrease; more

12. The World Trade Organization
    a. is a trading bloc that consists of the United States and the countries of Japan and China.
    b. has many member countries, but not the United States.
    c. competes with the GATT for members, with about half the world's countries belonging to the GATT and the other half belonging to the World Trade Organization.
    d. is a component of the GATT that administers the GATT agreement.

13. The trade diversion effect is
    a. efficient.
    b. inefficient.
    c. equitable, with no effect on efficiency.
    d. inequitable, with no effect on efficiency.

14. An import tariff shifts the _____ curve of imports upward and _____ the price of the good paid by the consumer.
    a. supply; increases
    b. supply; decreases
    c. demand; decreases
    d. demand; increases

15. The effects of a quota will be to _____ the quantity of imports and _____ the price consumers pay for them.
    a. increase; increase
    b. increase; decrease
    c. decrease; increase
    d. decrease; decrease

16. Nontariff barriers to trade
    a. are illegal under GATT.
    b. are allowed by GATT, but are not currently used by any country.
    c. have the effect of reducing a country's imports.
    d. are a good way to increase a country's exports.

17. Trade sanctions
    a. are generally acknowledged to be one of a country's most effective policy weapons.
    b. have been effective in accomplishing America's goals in regard to Cuba.
    c. were strongly supported by the American public as a means of getting China to release some downed U.S. flyers.
    d. have caused Saddam Hussein of Iraq to lose his grip on power there.

18. Which of the following is NOT offered as a reason to restrict trade?
    a. Infant industries.
    b. Dumping.
    c. Level playing field.
    d. Comparative advantage.

19. Strategic dumping is intended to
    a. result in a cleaner environment.
    b. pollute the environment.
    c. lead countries to seek a mutually beneficial agreement relating to the environment.
    d. drive competitors out of business.

20. In Self-Test Figure 17-2, the effect of the oil import fee shown would be to
    a. decrease price by *A*.
    b. decrease the quantity produced in the United States by *B*.
    c. decrease the quantity produced in the United States by *C*.
    d. decrease the quantity consumed in the United States by *D*.

SELF TEST FIGURE 17-2

QUESTIONS AND PROBLEMS

1. *[balance of payments accounts]* Critique the following statement: "There is usually a deficit in the U.S. balance of payments."

2. *[balance of payments accounts]* "The United States runs a trade deficit." Specifically, what does this statement mean? Briefly distinguish the trade deficit from the current account deficit.

3. *[trade and jobs]* Suppose the United States decides to prohibit all imports and exports. Would this approach reduce unemployment in the United States? Explain.

4. *[exchange rates]* Suppose Middle-Eastern investors decide to sell their U.S. investments. What would be the effect on the exchange rate between the dollar and Middle-Eastern currencies? In what way would that harm Middle-Eastern investors who do not sell their U.S. investments?

5. *[exchange rates]* Paperback novels sold in North America typically have two prices marked on their covers, one in U.S. dollars and another in Canadian dollars. Fifty years ago, there would probably only have been one price. Why?

6. *[currency depreciation]* In terms of demand and supply, what causes a currency to depreciate? How does the depreciation of a currency affect its imports and exports?

7. *[exchange rates]* Suppose the U.S. federal government adopts the policy of "What's good for General Motors is good for the country." To this end, the government decides to prohibit the import of all motor vehicles from other countries. Assuming other countries do not change their own trade policies, what would be the impact on the value of the dollar relative to other currencies? What would be the effect on the quantity of other items imported? What would be the effect on jobs in U.S. industries that did not participate in the making of autos?

8. *[the GATT]* What is the relationship between the World Trade Organization and the GATT?

9. *[NAFTA]* In your opinion, should the membership of NAFTA be expanded to include countries in Central America and South America? Why would other countries want to join NAFTA? What benefits might the United States receive if these countries joined? Why might there be opposition to expanding NAFTA?

10. *[tariffs]* Explain why a tariff can be viewed as a price support for domestic producers.

11. *[tariffs and quotas]* Use a supply and demand graph that illustrates the effects on price and quantity when a tariff is imposed on an imported good. Explain how the effects shown on your graph could alternatively be achieved through the imposition of a quota instead of the tariff.

12. *[voluntary export restraints]* From the perspective of producers in an exporting country, why is a voluntary export restraint preferable to a quota on imports of their product?

13. *[nontariff barriers]* List three examples other than quotas of nontariff barriers to trade discussed in the chapter. Then suppose that the United States wished to create a nontariff barrier to the imports of foreign-made televisions. Provide an example of a nontariff barrier not brought up in the text that could apply to television imports.

14. *[protectionism]* Suppose you are a member of Congress who wishes to protect tomato farmers, who have a lot of political clout in your area. Which of the arguments for protectionism would you apply to make your case to others in Congress? State your argument briefly and in writing, making sure to explicitly relate it to tomatoes.

15. *[national defense argument]* Name three products that might be able to persuasively use the national defense argument for protectionism. Name three other products where you could make a case, but not one you would support.

16. *[level playing field]* Do you think that nations should be put on a level playing field before being allowed to trade? Explain and defend your position.

 Visit **www.prenhall.com/collinge** for Exploring the Web exercises and additional self-test quizzes.

GLOSSARY

A

ability-to-pay principle states that those who can afford to pay more taxes than others should be required to do so.

absolute advantage the ability to produce a good with fewer resources than other producers.

action lag time between when the problem is recognized and when policies are enacted.

actual return the value an investment actually had, judged after the fact; expressed as a percentage.

adaptive expectations when people form expectations as to future prices according to what their experiences have been in the past.

aggregate demand relates how much real GDP consumers, businesses, and government will purchase at each price level; graphically, aggregate demand slopes downward.

allocative efficiency involves choosing the most valuable mix of outputs to produce.

antitrust law public policies designed to limit the abuse of market power by monopolies.

appreciation when a currency buys more of other currencies; makes imports cheaper and exports more expensive.

asymmetric information when one person has access to more information than another on a subject of mutual interest.

automatic stabilizers features embedded within existing fiscal policies that act as a stimulant when the economy is sluggish and act as a drag when it is in danger of inflation.

average cost per-unit cost; total cost divided by the quantity of output; also called average total cost.

average product total quantity of output ÷ total quantity of labor.

average variable cost variable cost per unit; total variable cost divided by the quantity of output.

B

balance of payments accounts measure of a country's economic interactions with other countries.

balance of trade the monetary value of exported goods minus the monetary value of imported goods.

balanced budget occurs when government revenue equals government spending.

bank reserves vault cash plus deposits held by the Fed.

barriers to entry when investors or entrepreneurs find obstacles to joining a profitable industry.

barter the exchange of goods and services directly for one another, without the use of money.

benefit principle states that a fair tax is one that taxes people in proportion to the benefits they receive when government spends those tax revenues.

black market market in which goods are bought and sold illegally; associated with price controls.

block grant a sum of money transferred from the federal government to states that is designated for a particular type of spending, but where the exact programs are not specified.

bond a legally binding promise to repay borrowed funds with interest at a specified future date.

breakeven occurs when economic profit is zero.

budget deficit occurs when government collects less revenue than it spends.

budget surplus occurs when government collects more revenue than it spends.

bundled good in the context of voting, occurs when voters must take the whole package, including elements they don't want; candidates represent bundled goods.

business cycle the uneven sequence of trough, expansion, peak, and recession that the economy follows over time.

C

capital account records the monetary value of capital inflows from other countries (foreign investment in the United States), and outflows to other countries (U.S. investment abroad).

capital anything that is produced in order to increase productivity in the future; includes human capital and physical capital.

capital formation the creation of new capital.

capital gains the difference between the current market value of an investment and its purchase price.

capital gains tax a tax on the capital gains from investments that are sold.

ceteris paribus holding all else constant.

circular flow a model of the economy that depicts how the flow of money facilitates a counterflow of resources, goods, and services in the input and output markets.

classical a macroeconomic school of thought that emphasizes the long run and reliance upon market forces to achieve full employment.

Coase theorem theory that holds parties to an externality would voluntarily negotiate an efficient outcome without government involvement when property rights are clearly defined.

collective bargaining negotiations between an employer and a labor union.

command and control government decrees that direct economic activity.

common property resource a jointly owned resource, such as groundwater; people have little incentive to conserve common property resources, but rather seek to capture them for their own private use.

comparative advantage the ability to produce a good at a lower opportunity cost (other goods forgone) than others could do.

compensating wage differentials additional pay offered by employers to offset undesirable job characteristics.

complements goods or services that go well with each other, such as cream with coffee.

congestion when adding an additional consumer of a public good detracts from its value to other consumers.

consumer price index (CPI) measures prices of a market basket of purchases made by consumers living in urban areas; has a value of 100 in the base period.

consumer surplus consumers' total benefit minus cost; graphically, demand minus market price.

consumption spending purchasing by households; makes up the majority of GDP spending.

contractionary fiscal policy (fiscal drag) occurs when the government reduces aggregate expenditures by increasing the amount of tax revenue it collects or reducing the amount of its spending.

corporation a type of firm that is a legal entity separate from the people who own, manage, and otherwise direct its affairs.

cost-benefit analysis the process of estimating the costs and benefits of alternative policy choices.

crowding-out effect when government borrowing attracts money that would otherwise have gone to private sector investment.

current account account that records the monetary value of imports and exports of goods and services, adjusted for international incomes and transfers.

cyclical unemployment unemployment from a downturn in the business cycle that affects workers simultaneously in many different industries.

cycling when the order of political choices determines the outcome.

D

deadweight loss reduction in social surplus caused by inefficient price; shown graphically as a triangular area.

demand deposits checking account balances at commercial banks.

demand relates the quantity of a good that consumers would purchase at each of various possible prices, over some period of time, *ceteris paribus.*

demand-side deflation occurs when aggregate demand shifts to the left. The result is a movement down the long-run aggregate supply curve to a lower price level, but no change in full-employment output.

demand-side inflation occurs when aggregate demand shifts to the right. The result is a movement up the long-run aggregate supply curve to a higher price level, but no change in full-employment output.

deposit multiplier upper bound on the value of the money multiplier; computed as 1 divided by the reserve requirement.

depreciation when a currency buys less of other currencies; makes imports more expensive and exports cheaper.

development when technology is embodied into capital.

differentiated products products that differ from one producer to another within the same industry.

discount rate interest rate set by the Fed on loans it makes to banks.

discouraged workers people who would like to have a job, but have given up looking; not counted as unemployed because they are not included in the labor force.

discretionary policy public policy adjusted through explicit changes made by lawmakers.

dumping selling a good to another country for less than its cost of production.

E

economic growth the ability of the economy to produce more or better output; the change in real GDP over time.

economic rent earnings in excess of opportunity cost when an input is unique.

economics studies the allocation of limited resources in response to unlimited wants.

efficiency means that resources are used in ways that provide the most value; implies that no one can be made better off without someone else becoming worse off; economic efficiency includes both allocative efficiency and technological efficiency.

elastic demand demand has an elasticity that is greater than 1.

elasticity of demand measures the responsiveness of quantity demanded to changes in price; computed as the percentage change in quantity demanded divided by the percentage change in price; expressed as an absolute value.

entrepreneurship personal initiative to combine resources in productive ways; involves risk.

entry when a firm first opens for business; occurs in the long run.

equation of exchange $M \times V = P \times Q$; M represents the quantity of money, V is velocity, P is the price level, and Q is aggregate output.

equity fairness

excess profit economic profit; the accounting profit in excess of normal profit.

excess reserves the amount of bank reserves that exceed the amount needed to meet the reserve requirement.

exchange rate price of one currency in terms of another.

exit when a firm goes out of business or changes its line of business; occurs in the long run.

expansionary fiscal policy (fiscal stimulus) occurs when government adds to aggregate expenditures by lowering the amount of tax revenue it collects or increasing the amount of its spending.

expected return the value of an investment if successful, multiplied by the probability of success; expressed as a percentage.

explicit costs costs accountants aim to measure.

exports goods and services a country sells to other countries.

external benefits when an externality takes the form of benefits, such as from a neighbor maintaining an attractive yard; when some benefits are received by third parties who are not directly involved in the decision.

external costs when an externality takes the form of costs, such as from pollution.

externality side effect of production or consumption that affects third parties who have no say in the matter.

F

federal funds rate interest rate on loans that banks make to other banks.

Federal Reserve System U.S. central bank; conducts monetary policy, holds bank deposits, and performs several other functions.

fiat money money not backed by a commodity; money by decree of law.

firm a business that employs inputs to produce output.

fiscal federalism the study of the design of a federal system of government from an economic standpoint.

fiscal illusion when voters focus on visible benefits from projects and ignore the less-obvious costs.

fiscal policy government tax and spending policy.

fixed cost a cost that does not vary with changes in output.

floating exchange rates exchange rates that adjust according to the forces of supply and demand; called managed float or dirty float if the government attempts to influence these forces.

foreign exchange markets markets in which currencies are bought and sold.

free markets the collective decisions of individual buyers and sellers that, taken together, determine what outputs are produced, how those outputs are produced, and who receives the outputs; free markets depend on private property and free choice.

free-rider problem the incentive to avoid paying for a public good, because no one person's payment will have any appreciable effect on the quantity of the public good.

free trade international commerce unhindered by policy obstacles.

frictional unemployment unemployment associated with entering the labor market or switching jobs.

full employment 100 percent minus the natural rate of unemployment.

full-employment budget estimate of government revenue and spending were the economy to be at full employment.

full-employment equilibrium the long-run macroeconomic equilibrium that occurs at a full-employment output.

full-employment output the real GDP the economy produces when it fully employs its resources.

fully funded the ideal of having enough revenue in the Social Security trust fund to be able to pay off all obligations to current workers without recourse to taxing future workers.

G

GDP chained price index a price index used to compute real GDP by linking together successive years of data.

General Agreement on Tariffs and Trade (GATT) an agreement signed by most of the major trading countries of the world, which limits the use of protectionist policies; enforced by the World Trade Organization.

general human capital skills such as language and math that are easily transferred from job to job.

government failure the inefficiency of government processes.

Gresham's law states that bad money drives good money out of circulation; applies to commodity monies; means that people seek to spend coins they think might be chipped or otherwise inferior to the ones they keep.

gross domestic product (GDP) the market value of the final goods and services produced in the economy within some time period, usually one quarter or one year.

gross investment the total amount of investment.

H

homogeneous products products that are identical, no matter which firms in the industry produce them; also called commodities.

housing vouchers government grants that recipients can spend only on housing.

human capital acquired skills and abilities embodied within a person.

I

imperfect information occurs when we do not fully understand the choices available to us, or the consequences of those choices.

implementation lag time between when policies are enacted and when they take effect.

implicit opportunity costs (implicit costs) the value that the firm's capital and the entrepreneur's time would have in their best alternative uses.

imports goods and services a country buys from other countries.

income effect the change in the quantity demanded caused by a price change's effect on real income, which measures a consumer's purchasing power; when the wage rate rises, individuals offer to work fewer hours because their higher incomes increase their demands for normal goods, including leisure.

individual retirement accounts (IRAs) tax-free savings accounts earmarked for retirement income.

inelastic demand demand has an elasticity that is less than 1.

infant industries startup industries that might be unable to survive the rigors of competition in their formative years.

inferior goods demand for these goods varies inversely with income.

inflation persistent, widespread increases in the price level.

inflation rate the annual percentage increase in the price level.

inflationary expectations predictions about future inflation that people factor into their current behavior.

in-kind benefits a government-provided good or service, as opposed to cash.

input market the market where resources are bought and sold.

interest payment made by a borrower to compensate a lender for the use of money.

interest rate price of borrowed money, expressed as a percentage.

investment spending now in order to increase output or productivity later; includes spending on capital, new housing, and changes in business inventories.

invisible hand the idea that self-interest and competition promotes economic efficiency without any need for action by government.

K

Keynesian a macroeconomic school of thought that emphasizes the short run and the importance of fiscal policy.

L

labor the human capacity to work.

labor force individuals age 16 and over, excluding those in the military, who are either employed or actively looking for work.

labor productivity output per hour worked.

land natural resources in their natural states.

law of demand as price falls, the quantity demanded increases.

law of diminishing returns states that when additional units of labor or any other variable input are added in the short run, the marginal product of the variable input must eventually decrease.

law of increasing cost the rise in the marginal opportunity cost of producing a good as more of that good is produced.

leading economic indicators statistics that are expected to change direction before the economy at large does, thereby indicating where the economy is headed.

line-item veto power that allows a governor to veto parts of appropriations bills, rather than having to accept or reject the bills in their entireties.

liquidity how easily and quickly an item can be turned into a spendable form.

lobbyists agents who promote a special-interest agenda within the political system.

local public good a public good that affects a particular region, such as a city.

logrolling when politicians trade votes in order to obtain projects of direct benefit to constituents in their districts.

long run in microeconomics, involves underlying economic forces that make themselves felt over time; in macroeconomics, period of time sufficiently long that all inputs are variable.

long-run aggregate supply the idea that, in the long run, the price level does not affect the amount of GDP the economy produces; graphically, long-run aggregate supply is vertical at full-employment GDP.

loss occurs when economic profit is negative.

M

M1 most liquid measure of money; currency plus demand deposits, traveler's checks, and other checkable deposits.

M2 obtained by adding savings deposits, small time deposits, and money market fund balances to M1.

M3 expands M2 by adding large time deposits and several other near monies.

macroeconomics analyzes economic aggregates, such as aggregate employment, output, growth, and inflation.

marginal benefit the incremental value of an additional unit of a good.

marginal cost the change in total cost that occurs when there is a one-unit change in output.

marginal external costs or benefits externalities that cause market outcomes to be inefficient.

marginal product additional output produced by the addition of one more unit of labor; change in output ÷ change in labor.

marginal revenue the change in total revenue that occurs when there is a one-unit change in output.

marginal tax rate tax rate on additional income.

market equilibrium a situation in which there is no tendency for either price or quantity to change.

market failure when markets fail to achieve efficiency, as in the case of public goods, externalities, and common property resources.

market power when individual firms have at least a bit of control over the prices of their outputs; arises from barriers to entry.

market structures models of the way markets work.

marketable permits property rights to a specified amount of an activity, such as groundwater pumping or air pollution, where those property rights can be bought and sold; can efficiently achieve quantity targets set by the government.

median voter model in two-candidate races, the winner will be chosen by the median voter—50 percent of the other voters prefer further to the right and 50 percent prefer further to the left.

medium of exchange the purchasing function of money.

microeconomics analyzes the individual components of the economy, such as the choices made by people, firms, and industries.

minimum wage lowest wage legally allowed to be paid to workers.

mixed economies the mixture of free-market and command-and-control methods of resource allocation that characterize modern economies.

models simplified versions of reality that emphasize features central to answering the questions we ask of them.

monetarism school of thought that emphasizes the importance of the quantity of money in the economy and a rule for monetary policy; associated with economist Milton Friedman.

monetary base sum of currency in circulation plus bank reserves.

money a medium of exchange that removes the need for barter; also a measure of value and a way to store value over time.

money multiplier the amount by which a new deposit is multiplied to arrive at the actual increase in the money supply; maximum value is given by the deposit multiplier.

monopolistic competition a market structure with many firms selling differentiated products and relatively easy entry of new firms; each firm has slight market power.

monopoly a market with only one seller of a good without close substitutes; in the labor market, occurs when there is one seller of labor services (labor union).

monopoly by law (legal monopoly) when legal barriers restrict the supply of a good to one firm, and when there are no close substitutes for that good.

monopoly by possession when a single firm owns a resource needed in the production of a good for which there are no close substitutes.

moral suasion exhortations to do the right thing, as defined by public policymakers.

multiplier effect sequence of spending that takes the economy from one equilibrium to another.

mutually interdependent when actions by one firm influence actions taken by other firms in the market.

N

national debt how much money the government owes.

natural monopoly when one firm can supply the entire market at a lower per-unit cost than could two or more separate firms.

natural rate of unemployment the minimum sustainable level of unemployment; associated with zero cyclical unemployment.

net domestic product (NDP) gross domestic product minus depreciation.

net exports exports minus imports.

net investment gross investment minus depreciation.

new growth theory emphasizes the importance of new ideas in generating economic growth, and of intellectual property rights in providing the profit incentive to generate those ideas.

nominal GDP GDP that is stated without adjusting for inflation.

nominal interest rate the payment from a borrower to a lender, expressed as a percentage.

nominal value a value that is not adjusted for inflation.

nontariff barriers any of a variety of actions other than tariffs that make importing more expensive or difficult.

normal goods demand for these goods varies directly with income.

normal profit the portion of accounting profit that equals implicit opportunity costs.

normative having to do with behavioral norms, which are judgments as to what is good or bad.

North American Free Trade Agreement (NAFTA) trading bloc that includes the United States, Canada, and Mexico.

O

occupational segregation the concentration of women workers in a limited number of occupations.

oligopoly market with multiple firms, at least one of which produces a significant portion of industry output.

open market operations buying and selling of Treasury bonds and Treasury bills by the Fed; tool of monetary policy.

opportunity costs the value of the best alternative opportunity forgone.

output market the market where goods and services are bought and sold.

P

pay-as-you-go referring to Social Security, meaning that current workers pay for current retirees.

Personal Security Accounts savings accounts individuals own, but that they are forced to contribute to by the government.

Phillips curve a graphical representation of data from the 1960s in the United States that shows a curvilinear tradeoff between low unemployment and low inflation.

positive having to do with what is, was, or will be.

poverty line a government-set income threshold that varies by household size and composition.

price ceiling a maximum price that can legally be charged for a good.

price discrimination charging different prices for different units of output, where the differences do not depend on differences in production costs.

price floor (price support) minimum price guaranteed to producers by the government.

price gouging price increases in response to increased demand related to emergencies.

price level prices of goods and services in the aggregate.

price maker a firm that faces a downward-sloping demand curve.

price rule conducting monetary policy in order to keep price increases in basic commodities within a low range.

price signals refers to the allocation of resources through the price system; help consumers decide how much to buy and help producers decide how much to sell.

price taker a firm that sells its output at the market price.

principal–agent problem the difficulty of making agents, such as employees or public servants, act in the interests of principals, such as owners or voters.

private costs or benefits costs or benefits that are borne by the decision maker, such as a buyer or seller.

private goods goods consumed by one person only— excludable and rival; most goods and services are private.

producer surplus producers' revenue minus production cost; graphically, market price minus supply.

production function the relationship between the amounts of inputs and the quantities of output a firm produces.

production possibilities frontier a model that shows the various combinations of two goods the economy is capable of producing.

profit (economic profit) total revenue minus total cost; unlike accounting profit, economic profit defines cost to include implicit opportunity costs.

progressive tax a tax that collects a higher percentage of high incomes than of low incomes.

property rights rights of ownership.

proportional tax a tax that collects the same percentage of high incomes as of low incomes.

public choice the study of economic incentives within government, including those that face voters, politicians, and the administrators of government programs.

public goods goods that are nonexcludable and nonrival, meaning that a person's consumption of the good does not reduce its quantity for others.

purchasing power effect the effect of the price level on consumers' ability to buy goods and services.

purchasing power parity theory that prices would be the same around the world for easily tradeable items.

pure competition a market in which there are numerous firms, all of which are price takers. The product is homogeneous, and there are no barriers to entry.

Q

quantity demanded the quantity that consumers will purchase at a given price.

quantity supplied the quantity that will be offered for sale at a given price.

quantity theory of money a theory based upon the equation of exchange; shows that the effect of a change in the money supply is a proportional change in the price level; assumes velocity and aggregate output remain constant.

quota quantity limit on imports.

R

rate-of-return regulation (average-cost pricing) restricts a monopoly from earning more than a normal profit; shown by the intersection of the average-cost curve and demand.

rational expectations when we base our expectations upon the best information available to us.

rational ignorance when voters make the rational choice to remain uninformed on many public issues.

real business cycle when GDP rises or falls in response to major events that cannot be foreseen.

real interest rate measures an interest rate in terms of its purchasing power.

real GDP the value of GDP after nominal GDP is adjusted for inflation.

real value a value that results from adjusting a nominal value for inflation.

recession a sustained decrease in real GDP.

recognition lag time before policymakers recognize that a problem exists.

regressive tax a tax that collects a higher percentage of low incomes than of high incomes.

regulation occurs whenever the government acts to influence the specifications of goods and services or the manner in which they are produced.

rent controls a price ceiling applied to the price of rental housing.

rent seeking occurs when lobbyists or others expend resources in an effort to come out a winner in the political process.

required reserves bank reserves held to meet the Fed's reserve requirement; expressed as a percentage of deposits.

research aimed at creating new products or otherwise expanding the frontiers of knowledge and technology.

reservation wage the lowest wage offer an individual will accept.

rule of profit maximization produce to the point where marginal revenue equals marginal cost.

S

saving putting aside income for later use.

scarcity a situation in which there are too few resources to meet all human wants.

search costs the costs of finding something; rent controls increase search costs for rental housing.

seasonal unemployment unemployment that can be predicted to recur periodically, according to the time of year.

short run in macroeconomics, a period of time during which the economy transitions to the long run; in microeconomics, a period of time in which at least one input is fixed.

shortage the excess of quantity demanded over quantity supplied, which occurs when price is below equilibrium.

shutdown when a firm produces no output in order to minimize its loss, which equals total fixed cost; occurs in the short run.

signaling the view that education provides information to employers about the characteristics of job applicants.

Smoot-Hawley Act legislation passed by the U.S. Congress in 1930; raised tariffs so high that imports nearly ceased.

social costs or benefits the sum of all costs or all benefits to all members of society; includes both private and external costs and benefits.

Social Security trust fund the buildup of Social Security tax revenues above what is paid out in benefits; kept in the form of government bonds.

social surplus the sum of consumer surplus and producer surplus.

specific human capital human capital that is specific to a particular firm or kind of job.

specificity principle the idea that policies should be targeted as narrowly and directly at a problem as possible.

stagflation the combination of high inflation and unemployment.

sticky prices prices that are slow to adjust, usually in a downward direction.

sticky wages wages that are slow to adjust, usually in a downward direction.

stock shares of ownership in a corporation.

store of value the function of money related to holding wealth.

strategic dumping dumping with the intention of driving the competition out of business.

structural unemployment unemployment caused by a mismatch between a person's human capital and that needed in the workplace.

subsidies payments to promote actions with external benefits or that reduce external costs.

substitutes something that takes the place of something else, such as one brand of cola for another.

substitution effect a lower price of a good causes a person to buy more of that good instead of alternative goods; when the wage rate increases, individuals recognize that the opportunity cost of leisure has risen, choose to substitute labor for leisure, and thus offer to work more hours.

supply relates the quantity of a good that will be offered for sale at each of various possible prices, over some period of time, ceteris paribus.

supply shock an unexpected event that is major enough to affect the overall economy.

supply-side deflation occurs when long-run aggregate supply shifts to the right. The result is a movement down the aggregate demand curve to a lower price level and higher full-employment output.

supply-side economists (supply siders) economists who emphasize incentives for productivity and economic growth, such as lower marginal tax rates and less regulation.

supply-side inflation occurs when long-run aggregate supply shifts to the left. The result is a movement up the aggregate demand curve to a higher price level and lower full-employment output.

surplus the excess of quantity supplied over quantity demanded, which occurs when price is above equilibrium.

T

tariff tax on imports.

tax incidence identifies those who eventually wind up paying a tax.

technological efficiency the greatest quantity of output for given inputs; likewise, for any given output, requires the least-cost production technique.

technology possible techniques of production.

technology mandates government rules that instruct producers as to the exact technology to use in a product or its production.

the margin the cutoff point; decision making at the margin refers to deciding on one more or one less of something.

total cost the sum of the firm's costs.

total product the firm's total quantity of output.

total revenue price × quantity.

trade creation effect trade that would otherwise not take place; adds to efficiency; caused by lower trade barriers among members of a trading bloc.

trade deficit a negative balance on the merchandise trade account, given when the dollar value of imported goods exceeds the dollar value of exported goods.

trade diversion effect trade among members of a trading bloc that would more efficiently be conducted with other countries outside of the bloc.

trading bloc agreement among a group of countries that provides for lower trade barriers among its members than with the rest of the world.

transaction costs the expense of coordinating market exchanges.

transfer payments the redistribution of income from one group to another.

U

underground economy market transactions that go unreported to government.

unemployment equilibrium a short-run equilibrium GDP that is less than full-employment GDP.

unemployment rate the ratio of the number of unemployed persons to the number of persons in the labor force.

unit elastic demand demand has an elasticity that equals 1.

unit of account a use of money that occurs when the value of one item is compared with the value of another in terms of monetary units.

user fees charges for use of a publicly owned good, service, or resource.

V

value added the difference between revenue and the cost of purchased inputs.

variable cost a cost that varies in the same direction as output.

velocity of money the number of times a dollar changes hands in a year.

voluntary export restraints an alternative to import quotas in which exporting countries agree to voluntarily limit their exports to the target country; leads to higher price received by exporting countries.

W

Washington Monument strategy when a government agency offers a bare-bones budget that cuts its most popular functions; intended to increase the chances that a more generous budget will be approved.

wealth effect the change in the fraction of current income spent caused by a price-level change affecting the real value of savings.

World Trade Organization (WTO) international organization formed to administer the General Agreement on Tariffs and Trade.

ANSWERS TO TEST YOURSELF

CHAPTER 1

1. False
2. False
3. True
4. False
5. True
6. b
7. c
8. a
9. a
10. b
11. d
12. c
13. a
14. b
15. c
16. c
17. b
18. d
19. b
20. d

CHAPTER 2

1. True
2. False
3. True
4. False
5. False
6. b
7. c
8. a
9. d
10. c
11. c
12. a
13. a
14. a
15. a
16. c
17. a
18. c
19. b
20. a

CHAPTER 3

1. False
2. False
3. True
4. False
5. False
6. d
7. d
8. a
9. a
10. d
11. c
12. b
13. c
14. c
15. c
16. b
17. c
18. c
19. a
20. c

CHAPTER 4

1. False
2. False
3. True
4. False
5. False
6. c
7. c
8. a
9. c
10. c
11. b
12. c
13. c
14. c
15. d
16. c
17. b
18. b
19. a
20. b
21. d

CHAPTER 5

1. False
2. False
3. False
4. True
5. False
6. d
7. c
8. d
9. b
10. c
11. d
12. a
13. c
14. c
15. c
16. b
17. b
18. c
19. c
20. c

CHAPTER 6

1. False
2. True
3. False
4. False
5. True
6. b
7. b
8. b
9. a
10. c
11. b
12. c
13. a
14. d
15. d
16. e
17. a
18. a
19. d
20. d

CHAPTER 7

1. False
2. True
3. True
4. False
5. False
6. b
7. c
8. a
9. d
10. c
11. b
12. b
13. a
14. d
15. c
16. c
17. a
18. c
19. b
20. b

CHAPTER 8

1. False
2. False
3. False
4. False
5. True
6. b
7. c
8. d
9. d
10. c
11. d
12. c
13. b
14. c
15. b
16. b
17. d
18. b
19. d
20. a

CHAPTER 9

1. False
2. False
3. False
4. True
5. False
6. c
7. c
8. c
9. d
10. b
11. a
12. b
13. d
14. d

15. b
16. a
17. d
18. a
19. d
20. d

CHAPTER 10

1. False
2. False
3. True
4. False
5. False
6. c
7. c
8. c
9. a
10. d
11. c
12. b
13. c
14. c
15. d
16. a
17. b
18. c
19. c
20. c

CHAPTER 11

1. True
2. False
3. False
4. False
5. True
6. b
7. c
8. a
9. b
10. a
11. c
12. d
13. d
14. a
15. d
16. b

17. d
18. c
19. a
20. b

CHAPTER 12

1. True
2. False
3. False
4. True
5. False
6. c
7. b
8. a
9. a
10. b
11. c
12. c
13. d
14. c
15. c
16. b
17. c
18. c
19. d
20. d

CHAPTER 13

1. False
2. True
3. False
4. True
5. False
6. a
7. a
8. b
9. b
10. c
11. d
12. d
13. b
14. b
15. c
16. b
17. c
18. d

19. a
20. c

CHAPTER 14

1. False
2. False
3. False
4. False
5. False
6. d
7. a
8. d
9. d
10. d
11. c
12. a
13. b
14. c
15. d
16. c
17. c
18. b
19. b
20. d

CHAPTER 15

1. False
2. True
3. True
4. True
5. False
6. d
7. a
8. d
9. c
10. c
11. d
12. c
13. d
14. a
15. d
16. d
17. c
18. c
19. a
20. b

CHAPTER 16

1. False
2. True
3. False
4. True
5. False
6. a
7. b
8. d
9. d
10. d
11. a
12. d
13. b
14. d
15. c
16. a
17. d
18. d
19. b
20. a

CHAPTER 17

1. False
2. True
3. True
4. True
5. False
6. b
7. d
8. a
9. a
10. d
11. d
12. d
13. b
14. a
15. c
16. c
17. c
18. d
19. d
20. d

SOLUTIONS TO EVEN-NUMBERED QUESTIONS AND PROBLEMS

CHAPTER 1

2. a. Examples of decisions you might have made at the margin in the last twenty-four hours include when to get out of bed, how much cereal to put in the cereal bowl, how much water or juice to drink, how fast to walk to get to class, and how extensively to take notes in class.

4. a. Macroeconomics, since it pertains to the whole economy.
   b. Microeconomics, since it pertains to a particular industry.
   c. Macroeconomics, since it pertains to the whole economy.
   d. Macroeconomics, to the extent that it pertains to the whole economy.
   e. Microeconomics, since it pertains to a particular industry.

6. The three types of economic systems are free market economies, command-and-control economies, and mixed economies. All modern economies are mixed, including those of Canada, the United States, and Western Europe. In these countries, the mix tends more toward the free market end of the spectrum than toward command and control. In all mixed economies, free markets play a prominent role, but so too does government.

8. The tax system promotes equity to the extent that it redistributes income from the rich to the poor. This increase in equity comes at the cost of reduced efficiency, however, because it means there is less of an incentive to get the education and to do the hard work required for a high income.

10. Farmers grow food in order to sell it. If some of the farmers decide to quit, the result would be higher prices that would prompt the remaining farmers to produce more output. The food appears in the stores because consumers are willing to pay enough for the stores to more than cover expenses, which leads self-interested storeowners to stock the food.

12. Government policy greatly influences what occurs in a mixed economy. Since government policy is strongly influenced by politics, economics is sometimes known as political economy.

14. Saying that movies are too violent is expressing an opinion that is based on normative judgments. How much is too much? The statement about movies would become positive if it was restated as, "Movies are more violent today than they used to be." The statement is positive whether or not it is true. Its accuracy might be determined, however, by defining what kinds of acts involve violence and counting how often those acts of violence occur in a selection of recent movies relative to a selection of older ones of the same general type.

16. a. If classes are spread throughout the day and evening, the same number of students could get by with fewer parking places than if classes are bunched together, such as in the morning.
   b. If there is good bus service to and from campus, students have less need to drive and thus less need for parking places. Bunching classes together would make parking more difficult and increase students' willingness to pay for it.
   c. If students have higher incomes, they're more likely to own cars, which would tend to increase students' willingness to pay for parking places.

CHAPTER 2

2. Management skills can overlap with entrepreneurship, but the two are different. Entrepreneurship involves creativity, putting together resources in new and unique ways. While management might include entrepreneurship, it might also be merely carrying out directions from higher levels of management, or organizing activities according to someone else's direction. Those latter aspects are not entrepreneurship.

4. a. ten baseball bats.
   b. six baseball bats.

6. The graph you draw should have a horizontal axis labeled with one good and a vertical axis labeled with another good. The production possibilities frontier itself should be increasingly downwardly sloping as you travel along it from the vertical axis to the horizontal axis. To show general growth, draw another production possibilities frontier that is everywhere outside the first one you drew. This means that, wherever the economy started on the first production possibilities frontier, it can increase its production of either good without decreasing the production of the other. In the production possibilities frontier in question 4, general growth would occur if each of the numbers in the list were increased.

8. When used as a medium of exchange, money allows goods and services to be traded for one another. Money's use as a medium of exchange means that barter does not need to take place. The flow of money is an integral part of the circular flow model.

10. a. No, consumers in the United States like to make their own choices between California wine and French wine. Those who choose French wine would be worse off if they were not allowed that option. When consumers buy French wine in preference to California wine, they are in effect saying that the opportunity cost of California wine is more than it is worth to them. Therefore, even though Californian winemakers would prefer consumers to buy California wine, the resources producers would need to use to replace the French wine have more value elsewhere in the economy.

b. Either for variety or because they like it better, some French consumers presumably do drink imported U.S. wine.

12. Absolute advantage means being able to produce a good with fewer resources than it would take someone else to produce it. In reality, people specialize according to their comparative advantages, which means that each individual must compare the opportunity cost of the alternative things that particular person could do and choose those for which they have the lowest opportunity costs. Likewise, a country would also specialize according to comparative advantage. It would produce something, but exactly what it produces would depend on its own alternative opportunities. It would choose to produce goods for which its opportunity costs are relatively low.

14. **a.** A country cannot produce outside its current production possibilities frontier unless it acquires new resources or new technology. That's why the production possibilities frontier is called a "frontier."

b. The purpose of trade is to expand consumption possibilities beyond the confines of what the country can produce. For this reason, a country that trades with other countries can be expected to consume at a point outside of its production possibilities frontier. The country would consume at a point on its frontier only if it did not trade.

CHAPTER 3

2. Draw a graph with the horizontal axis labeled "hot dogs" and the vertical axis labeled with "$" or "price." The demand curve that you label "individual's demand" should be a downwardly sloping line. The demand curve that you label "market demand" should start at the same point on the vertical axis as the other demand curve, but should slope downward less steeply, and reach the horizontal axis at the quantity that is twice as much as the quantity at which the first demand curve intersects the horizontal axis.

4. Insurance lowers the cost to you if your house is hit by a hurricane. Because the price is lower, in accordance with the law of demand, you're willing to accept the potential for more hurricanes and are therefore more willing to build a house in hurricane-prone areas. To graph the demand for the new houses in hurricane-prone areas, the horizontal axis would be labeled with "new houses" and the vertical axis would be labeled with "price" or "$". A lower price causes a movement along the demand curve to a greater quantity of new houses demanded.

6. Examples of complementary goods include: pencil and paper, baseball and bat, personal computer and printer, postage stamp and envelope, sugar and cereal, and butter and bread. In each case, if the price of the complement for the good were to increase, the demand for the good itself would decrease. Conversely, if the price of the complement for the good were to decrease, the demand for the good itself would increase.

8. In response to Mr. Johnson's income reduction, his demand for normal goods would decrease and his demand for inferior goods would increase. The following goods are likely to be normal goods for Mr. Johnson: restaurant food, Tommy Hilfiger clothing, fresh vegetables, antique furniture, and tickets to pro football games. The following goods are likely to be inferior goods for Mr. Johnson: generic paper towels, Spam, used cars, and Ramen noodles. Home-brewed coffee would be a normal good for Mr. Johnson if he most prefers the way he makes it himself. Home-brewed coffee would be an inferior good for Mr. Johnson if he prefers coffee from restaurants or coffee shops.

10. There is a difference between a change in demand and change in the quantity demanded. If there is a change in demand, the entire demand curve shifts, showing a new quantity demanded for each possible price. If there is a change in the quantity demanded, the reason is simply that the price has fallen or risen, which would cause the consumer to move from one point to another along the same demand curve. For movements along demand in response to price changes, the demand curve itself does not shift.

12. For each of the following, you would draw a supply curve with the quantity supplied on the horizontal axis and price or $ on the vertical axis. The supply curve would slope upward to the right. If the supply curve increases, that means that the curve itself is shifted to the right. If the supply curve decreases, the curve is shifted to the left.

a. Supply increases.

b. Supply decreases.

c. Supply decreases.

d. Supply increases.

14. When the market clears, the quantity demanded just equals the quantity supplied. There is no surplus or shortage. The situation occurs when the market is in equilibrium. If there is a surplus or shortage, the price tends to change until it reaches that equilibrium. For example, if there is a shortage, there are not enough goods to go around to all of the consumers who want them, and sellers would be inclined to raise their prices. If there is a surplus, sellers have more than they can sell at the current price, and so lower their prices in order to sell more. At equilibrium, when quantity demanded equals quantity supplied, the market clears and price has no tendency to change.

16. A shortage results from a price that is below the equilibrium price. At that low price, consumers want to buy more than producers are willing to sell. In response, producers raise their prices.

18. If the market starts at equilibrium and demand increases, the market would experience a shortage if price does not rise. However, the market forces the price to rise to a new equilibrium.

20. Since total revenue increased when the price decreased, demand is elastic.

CHAPTER 4

2. This answer is likely to vary from person to person. For example, it might have been a new car that you are very happy with, or a really great apartment that you rented at a low price. The difference between what you would have been willing to pay in the abstract and the price that you actually did pay would determine the amount of consumer surplus that you receive.

4. Yes, in the absence of market failures, which will be discussed later in the book, the market-equilibrium output is efficient. For each unit sold, the value to consumers equals or exceeds the price, which in turn equals or exceeds the cost of producing it. For any output above the market equilibrium, the cost of producing it would exceed its value to consumers, and so consumers would not buy it and firms would not choose to produce it.

6. A country will import a good when the world price of that good is less than the country's price would have been without trade. The result will be a lower price within the country after trade, which causes producers in the country to cut back on their output. The lower price moves them down their supply curve, but normally not so far down that they would produce nothing at all. The country as a whole will gain from trade because the trade increases consumer surplus more than it reduces producer surplus. To show this result graphically, label the horizontal axis with the quantity of some good and the vertical axis with its price, or with a $. Draw a downwardly sloping demand curve and an upwardly sloping supply curve to represent the domestic market. Then add a world price that is lower than what would have been the market-equilibrium price in the absence of imports. The quantity actually consumed will be given by the point on the demand curve at the new lower price. The quantity produced in the domestic market will be given by the point on the supply curve at that same lower price. Producer surplus is given by the triangular area below the world price and above the domestic supply curve. Consumer surplus is given by the triangular area above the world price and below the market-demand curve. Note that the sum of these two areas is larger than the sum of the producer and consumer surplus that would occur at the higher price in the absence of trade.

8. For the price ceiling to have an effect, it must be set below the market-equilibrium price. In your first graph, you're instructed to show a ceiling price above the market equilibrium price and interpret the result. The interpretation is that the ceiling price would be ignored. Anyone who tried to sell at that ceiling price would be undercut by other suppliers willing to sell at a lower price. The price would try to drop to the market equilibrium and there would be nothing to keep it from doing so. Therefore, the market would move to the market-equilibrium price. In your second graph, you're instructed to show a ceiling price that is below the market-equilibrium price and interpret that result. The interpretation is that the ceiling price would prevent price from rising to the market equilibrium, and for that reason would lead to a shortage in which the quantity demanded is greater than the quantity supplied.

10. Ticket scalping is efficient in that it makes sure the tickets go to those who are willing to pay the most for them. However, this may seem inequitable to people who get up early to stand in line for good seats, only to find them already gone because tickets for the best seats were purchased in bulk by the ticket scalpers.

12. Some inefficiencies of rent controls are: some people cannot find apartments who are willing to pay more than those who do find them, people waste time looking for apartments, apartments are not properly maintained, and too few apartments are offered for rent.

14. Price floors decrease consumer surplus because they increase the prices consumers pay and decrease the quantities that they purchase.

16. The minimum wage is a price floor, because it sets a lower bound on what wages employers are allowed to pay.

18. A black market is one that is illegal. When prices are held down, there will be some consumers unable to buy at the controlled price. It is in the interest of these consumers and producers to break the law and make a deal at a higher price. Such deals are illegal and therefore would be part of the black market. In the case of price supports, however, producers are normally able to sell as much as they want to at the artificially high price, with the government being the buyer of what would otherwise be a surplus. For this reason, producers have no excess production and thus no incentive to undercut the support price by engaging in black market activities.

CHAPTER 5

2. The four methods of finance are: use personal funds, use retained earnings, borrow, and issue shares of stock. Personal funds have no strings attached to their use, but will generally be limited in amount. Retained earnings also can be used as a firm pleases, but their amount is limited by the profit earned by a firm. Borrowed funds require that a firm find a lender who is satisfied that the firm will be able to repay the funds with interest in the future. Thus, not all firms will be able to borrow. However, borrowed funds can allow a firm to expand beyond its current size. Corporations can obtain funds by issuing stock, but stocks provide only a small fraction of financing for businesses.

4. Internal financing is generated by profits. External financing comes from outside a firm, such as from a bank or the sale of stock. Internal financing is more common.

6. A secondary market is where items are resold after the initial sale. The stock exchanges are secondary markets, meaning that the firms that issued stock originally do not receive monies when the shares are sold on the stock exchanges.

8. Profit equals total revenue minus total cost. Economists usually assume that firms try to maximize profit.

10. Accounting profit = Total revenue − Explicit cost; Economic profit = Total revenue − Explicit cost − Implicit cost. The economic definition of profit recognizes that total revenue must be sufficient to keep resources in their current use.

12. **a.** Opportunity cost associated with depositing the cash in a bank account.

   b. Opportunity cost associated with the income the owner could have earned by holding a job for fifteen hours a week.

   c. Opportunity cost associated with using the automobile for personal purposes.

14. The principal-agent problem recognizes that agents (managers) may have different objectives than principals (business owners). Managers may seek to further their own interests rather than maximize profit for the owners.

16. The long run and the short run differ according to the variability of inputs. In the long run, all inputs are assumed to be variable. In the short run, at least one input is assumed to be fixed, meaning that it is constant. Capital is usually assumed to be the fixed input. The long run is a longer period of time than the short run, and is sometimes referred to as the planning horizon.

18. Marginal product is the increment to total product when the variable input is increased by one unit. Expressed as an equation, we have: Marginal product = Change in total product ÷ Change in the quantity of input. In contrast, Average product = Total product ÷ Total quantity of input. The law of diminishing returns refers to the behavior of marginal product.

20. Your graph should label the horizontal axis as "quantity of input" (labor) and the vertical axis as "quantity of output." Average product rises when marginal product is greater than average product, but falls when marginal product falls below average product. The curves intersect at the maximum point on average product.

CHAPTER 6

2. **a.** The marginal cost of the fourth vehicle would be $40. The marginal cost of a fifth vehicle would be $45.

   b. Marginal cost typically has a J-shape. It also gets its shape from the upside-down J-shape of marginal prod-

uct that in turn is caused by the law of diminishing returns. The numbers for RM Motors are generally consistent with the shape, with marginal cost going in sequence: 50, 25, 30, 40, 45.

4. Going in sequence from 0 to 6, the costs in dollars would be as follows:

Quantity:	0	1	2	3	4	5	6
Total cost:	100,	150,	190,	240,	300,	400,	600
Average fixed cost:	undefined,	100,	50,	33.3,	25,	20,	16.7
Average variable cost:	undefined,	50,	45,	46.7,	50,	60,	83.3
Average cost:	undefined,	150,	95,	80,	75,	80,	100
Marginal cost:	undefined,	50,	40,	50,	60,	100,	200

6. The price taker would like to receive as much as possible for its product, and for this reason charges the market price. If the price taker were to charge a higher price, it would receive nothing because no one would buy its product. If the price taker were to charge a lower price, it would sell all it could produce, but would not be maximizing profit. The price taker maximizes profit by charging the market price, which is the highest price that allows it to sell all that it can produce.

8. The rule of profit maximization is to produce up to the point where marginal cost equals marginal revenue, unless total revenue is insufficient to cover total variable costs (in which case shutdown is preferred). When the firm is a price taker, this rule can be restated as calling for the firm to produce up to the point where marginal cost equals price. Another way of putting this rule is that the firm should keep on producing additional units of output so long as the marginal revenue from those units exceeds the marginal cost of producing them. The firm should not produce any additional units if the marginal cost of producing them would exceed the marginal revenue from selling them.

10. Going in sequence from the quantity of 1 to a quantity of 8, the values are as follows.

Quantity:	1	2	3	4	5	6	7	8
Total variable cost:	$1,	$1.50,	$2.50,	$4.50,	$7.50,	$11.50,	$16.50,	$22.50
Total cost:	$2,	$2.50,	$3.50,	$5.50,	$8.50,	$12.50,	$17.50,	$23.50
Total revenue:	$4.25,	$8.50,	$12.75,	$17,	$21.25,	$25.50,	$29.75,	$34.

The profit maximizing quantity will be 6 units of output, since the marginal cost of the sixth unit is $4, which is less than its marginal revenue of $4.25. The firm would consider producing a seventh unit, but would see that its marginal cost of $5 would exceed the marginal revenue of $4.25. The profit will equal the difference between total revenue and total cost at the quantity 6 units. This computation is $25.50 minus $12.50, which is a profit of $13. At a price of $4.50, the firm would continue to produce 6 units of output, although the profit would be higher. At a price of $5.25, the firm would increase its output to 7 units, since the marginal revenue of $5.25 would exceed the $5 marginal cost of the seventh unit.

12. It may be impossible for a firm to avoid a loss, since the firm will have fixed costs no matter what it does. If it is possible for the firm to generate enough revenue to cover all of its variable costs and have a little left over to cover at least some of its fixed costs, it makes sense for it to remain open for business even if it cannot earn a positive profit. If so, it should produce to the point where marginal cost equals marginal revenue by the same logic as if the firm could earn a profit. In this way, the firm minimizes its loss, which means the same thing as maximizing a negative profit.

14. By producing and selling potatoes, Happy Spud earns total revenue equal to $30,000, and has total costs equal to $35,900. The firm's loss equals $5,900. Since price and marginal cost are equal at $3 and the loss is less than the fixed cost of $6,000, the firm is minimizing its loss. Rather than shut down, the firm should continue to produce.

16. The four forms of market structure are pure competition, monopolistic competition, oligopoly, and monopoly. Numerous price-taking firms that produce a homogeneous product characterize pure competition, such as found in agriculture. In monopolistic competition, such as found among restaurants, there are numerous firms, but each has its own unique variation on the same general product. In oligopoly, such as found in the manufacture of airplanes, there is more than one firm, but at least one of the firms is significant. A single firm that sells an output for which there are no close substitutes characterizes monopoly, such as of local water lines or sewer lines.

18. A homogeneous product is one that is identical among firms, meaning that consumers are unwilling to pay any more for the output of one firm in the industry than they are for the output of another. For example, the bituminous coal produced by one mine is the same as that produced by another. With numerous firms producing a homogeneous product, any single firm is marginal, which means that market supply is not affected by whether that firm exists or does not exist. In other words, no matter what it does, it will not be able to increase or decrease the market price.

20. The graph should be labeled with $ on the vertical axis and the quantity of output on the horizontal axis. The firm's marginal cost should be drawn in the general shape of the letter J. Average variable cost should be drawn as U-shaped and intersected at its minimum point by the marginal cost curve. The portion of the marginal cost curve that lies above average variable cost is the firm's supply curve. The firm seeks to produce where its marginal cost equals its marginal revenue. In other words, for any given price, it offers to sell the quantity of output associated with its supply curve.

22. The market supply would be composed of 5 alternative quantities supplied associated with each of the 5 alternative prices. In particular, at a price of $1, the market quantity supplied would be 10,000. At a price of $2, the market quantity supplied would be 12,000. At a price of $3, the market quantity supplied with the 14,000. At a price of $4, the market quantity supplied would be 16,000. At a price of $5, the market quantity supplied would be 18,000.

CHAPTER 7

2. A firm without market power has a demand curve that is a horizontal line. As market power increases, the demand curve slopes down more and more steeply.

4. A natural monopoly occurs in an industry that has economies of scale throughout the relevant range of output, or at least over a large enough portion of that output that dividing it along two or more firms would lead to higher average costs than just having a single firm produce it. A water company or sewage treatment company is likely to have a natural monopoly, because it is cheaper for only one firm to have a set of pipes below the city streets than to have two or more firms competing and each digging up the streets.

6. A monopolist faces a demand curve that is the same as market demand, which slopes downward and to the right.

8. Just because a firm is a monopoly does not guarantee that the firm will earn economic profit. The monopoly firm will be unable to achieve a profit if its average cost of production is everywhere above its demand curve.

10. Label the horizontal axis of your graph as "quantity" and the vertical axis with a "$." Draw a downward-sloping market demand curve, which is also the demand curve facing the monopoly firm. Draw the monopolist's marginal revenue curve so that it starts at the top point on the demand curve, but then slopes down twice as steeply as the demand curve. Draw a J-shaped marginal cost curve. To ensure that the monopolist incurs a loss, draw an average cost curve that is everywhere above the demand curve. This average cost curve should be U-shaped and its minimum point should be intersected by the marginal cost curve. To minimize loss, the monopoly produces the output for which marginal cost equals marginal revenue, or shuts down if it cannot cover all of its variable costs.

12. Your graph should show that the monopolist produces at the point where marginal revenue equals marginal cost. This amount will be less than the efficient quantity, which is given by the point where demand equals marginal cost. To achieve the efficient quantity, the price would be given by the demand curve at that point.

14. Product differentiation is a means to increase the firm's demand and profit. Society obtains a greater variety of goods because firms practice product differentiation.

16. A firm in monopolistic competition has a highly elastic, but not perfectly elastic, demand. Only a price taker has perfectly elastic demand, and monopolistically competitive firms have some measure of control over their prices.

18. When a firm can segment the market, it is able to charge different prices to the different market segments for the same product. For example, the business might charge a different price to students than it does to others, and

would do so if it thought that students were more responsive to price than were most people. Unless the discrimination is based on race, color, or creed, price discrimination is likely to be legal. An example of price discrimination can be found at many motels, which offer discounts to members of the American Automobile Association.

CHAPTER 8

2. Total labor costs include fringe benefits such as paid vacations and health insurance.

4. Each student will have his or her own reservation wage. Many things can cause a person's reservation wage to change. Examples include education, experience, health, marital status, and access to labor market information.

6. The income effect of a change in the wage rate refers to the change in purchasing power that accompanies a change in the wage rate. An increase in the wage rate will increase purchasing power, which increases the demand for leisure. An increase in the demand for leisure decreases hours of work. Thus, the income effect is associated with the backward-bending part of labor supply. The substitution effect refers to the change in opportunity cost that accompanies a change in the wage rate. An increase in the wage rate increases the opportunity cost of leisure, and increases the quantity of labor supplied. The substitution effect is associated with the upward-sloping portion of labor supply. So long as the substitution effect is stronger than the income effect, the labor supply curve will slope upward.

8. **a.** Nurses: A compensating differential could be associated with exposure to disease and the stress from the death of patients.
   b. Forest rangers: The danger from fire and the stress from policing large areas of forest could provide a rationale for a compensating differential.
   c. Movie and TV actors: People in these jobs often experience long periods of unemployment. That disadvantage would normally be associated with a compensating differential, but in the case of actors the possibility of fame may offset the need for employers to pay a compensating differential.
   d. There may or may not be a significant compensating differential in the occupation you would like to make your life's work. If the occupation is dangerous or unpleasant, a compensating differential will be included in the pay you receive.

10. Each student's answer will vary. Opinions about unions are often based upon emotion as well as logic. Answers should sort out emotional arguments from fact.

12. Signaling provides an alternative to the human capital view that education increases an individual's productivity. Signals that a college diploma sends to an employer include that a person is intelligent, diligent, and trainable. Other positive traits are also signaled.

14. The answer to this question will depend upon a person's values. One person might be highly productive (and highly paid) because his or her parent could afford the best schools. Another person might be relatively unproductive (and poorly paid) because of poor health.

16. Your graph should label the horizontal axis as the "quantity of a resource," and the vertical axis as "$" or "hourly earnings." The resource is in fixed supply, meaning that the supply curve is vertical. It does not start at the horizontal axis, but rather at the resource's opportunity cost, which is given by what it would earn in an alternative occupation. The price of the resource is determined by the intersection of supply and a downward-sloping demand curve. The economic rent would be the rectangular area that is bounded on the top by price, on the bottom by opportunity cost, on the right by the supply curve, and on the left by the vertical axis.

CHAPTER 9

2. A pure public good is nonexcludable and nonrival, meaning that we can't keep anyone from consuming it and that allowing someone else to consume it doesn't affect our own consumption. If the good is impure, then there might be some degree of rivalry or difficulty in excluding people. Most public goods are impure. For example, it might be possible to keep people out of parks or off of highways. If so, those public goods are excludable. Those public goods are also rival if they are subject to congestion when too many people use them at once.

4. **a.** Maybell will consume the good because no one can be excluded from consuming a pure public good.
   b. Marshall and Marsha will consume the same amount.
   c. The value of the good is the sum of its value to Marsha, Marshall, and Maybell, which equals $3 + $7 + $1 = $11.

6. Market failures arise when goods are not purely private. A purely private good does not have external effects on others and is not subject to the free-rider problem. In contrast, there are usually market failures associated with public goods because of the free-rider problem, which limits the revenue available to potential producers of the public good.

8. The free-rider problem arises because it makes little or no difference in the quantity of a public good a person consumes whether or not that person pays anything for the good. Since public goods are not excludable, consumers have the incentive to free ride and to pay nothing. In response, producers in the free market tend to produce nothing. There are exceptions, particularly when the public good is tied into a private good. For example, radio commercials attempt to sway consumers to buy private goods and are paid for by private companies. To get potential consumers to listen to the commercials requires that they be given something in exchange, which in this example would be radio programming, a public good.

10. One intangible that was mentioned is noise, such as from airplanes. This might be used in the cost-benefit analysis of alternative forms of airplane equipment, flight patterns, or landing times. The procedure would be to measure the noise at ground level within affected neighborhoods, and then find other neighborhoods with comparable characteristics but without the noise. The cost of the noise could be estimated as the difference in the property values in these two neighborhoods.

12. Debatable arguments that express somebody's opinions about the homeless and that are related to the specificity principle might include: (1) We should visit homeless shelters and allow the homeless to tell us their specific problems so we can address those issues with them; (2) government should subsidize homeless shelters in order to reduce the problem of homelessness; (3) government should subsidize homeless shelters in order to gather the homeless together in one place where they can be given information about their alternatives, such as about jobs; (4) government should not make safety regulations for the homeless shelters so stringent that the homeless shelters cost more than the homeless can afford; and (5) government should not require employers to pay such high wages to the homeless that the employers do not hire the homeless at all.

14. People are willing to take some risks and weigh the value of extra safety from safety measures against the cost of those measures in terms of money and inconvenience. For this reason, employees might prefer to have higher wages or less hassles rather than have their employers adopt every possible safety precaution. The efficient quantity of safety would have safety devices to protect workers from danger only if their marginal benefit is at least as much as their marginal cost. Many safety devices might fail this test of efficiency.

CHAPTER 10

2. There are many possibilities here, depending upon what you and your family have done. For example, when people admire the outfit that you're wearing, you're bestowing an external benefit on them. If they are admiring your car, that is also conferring an external benefit. Some external benefits are less obvious. For example, taking action to stay disease-free so that you are not contagious to anyone else also provides external benefits. In turn, you might have been the recipient of any of these external benefits from others, or additional ones such when you find yourself admiring a nice-looking yard.

4. Perhaps your neighbors play loud music or have a loud dog. If you are disturbed or awakened by their dog or their music, you have been the victim of an external cost. Most times, people just put up with these external costs and hope they go away over time. Sometimes, the cops are called to enforce noise ordinances.

6. That statement is false, with only a few exceptions for especially toxic substances. In most cases, there are benefits that go along with the pollution in terms of output that we wouldn't know how to produce as cheaply or at all without pollution. If firms face no cost of polluting, they'll pollute too much. However, if firms face a cost of polluting equal to the marginal external costs of the pollution, they have the incentive to cut back to an efficient amount of pollution.

8. In general, the efficient quantity of a good is that for which the marginal social cost just equals the marginal social benefit. When all costs and benefits are private, the market produces this efficient quantity. When there are external costs or external benefits, however, those external costs or external benefits must be added to private costs or private benefits to arrive at marginal social cost or marginal social benefit. When marginal social cost is equated to marginal social benefit, as before, the quantity of output is efficient.

10. The Coasian solution to this problem would be to have farmers sue the railroad company for the damages to the farmers' crops. In response, the railroad company would either change its practices or accept the cost of compensating farmers as merely a cost of doing business. Government might enter the picture to regulate the railroad's habits, which would save transaction costs in the legal system. While the Coasian solution sees no need for such government intervention, it does see a role for government in enforcing property rights, which provides the basis for lawsuits when those rights are violated.

12. You might argue that it's hard to police littering at City Park, and the park experience is more pleasant when there is not a heavy-handed police presence. You might also note the police enforcement is expensive. As an alternative, you might suggest appealing to people's consciences so that they are less inclined to strew trash around the park. Maybe your slogan would be "Keep City Park Looking Sharp!"

14. Draw a graph with the horizontal axis labeled as "pollution emissions" and the vertical axis labeled with the "$." Draw a downward-sloping demand curve by firms for emission rights. Draw an upward-sloping curve that is labeled "marginal external costs." If there were no market failure, these marginal external costs would be marginal private costs and represent the industry supply curve. The efficient quantity of pollution emissions is given by the intersection of the marginal external cost curve and the firms' demand curve. Since there is no market to achieve this quantity, government can instead impose a tax in the amount that would have been the market price. The amount of the tax is given by the intersection of the marginal external cost and the firms' demand, and has the same effect as would the efficient market price. In this way, government has replaced the missing market and achieved an efficient quantity of pollution.

16. In question 14, you showed how a tax could achieve the efficient quantity of pollution. Using that same figure, it is easy to show that a pollution permit system could achieve the same result. The supply of permits would be set equal

to the efficient quantity of pollution emissions. This would present firms with a vertical supply curve for emission rights—no matter what the price might be, the quantity of emission rights offered to the market would remain constant. The price of an emission right would be determined by the intersection of the supply curve and the firms' demand. This price would be identical to the tax that was used in question 14.

CHAPTER 11

2. A benevolent dictatorship occurs when a government dictator makes all public choices and does so with the best interests of the public in mind. A benevolent dictatorship is more efficient than democracy to the extent that it does not waste resources in competition among candidates or for political favors. However, there is no such thing as a benevolent dictatorship in reality, since it is the process of political competition that chooses leaders who reflect the public interest. Even a well-meaning benevolent dictator could not know what the public truly desires, and the absolute power associated with dictatorship is not generally associated with the most well-meaning of people.

4. The principal-agent problem occurs when elected officials or agency employees do not follow the wishes of the voters. For example, for both selfish and public-spirited reasons, employees of government agencies generally desire to spend more than the public would like. This leads to budgeting strategies designed to fool oversight committees and the public.

6. When we elect a public official, we are allowing that person to make many choices while in office. A voter might choose a candidate without supporting all of that candidate's views, since one basically must take the good with the bad. In the terminology of economics, candidates are bundled goods. However, with ballot propositions, voters make the decisions themselves instead of leaving those decisions to their elected representatives. While it takes more time to make a decision on your own than to leave it to someone else, you might choose to do so if you don't have confidence that your representatives will act in your interests once they are in office.

8. You should place voters along a spectrum in terms of how strongly they favor tax cuts versus the status quo. Your spectrum should show five voters bunched together favoring tax cuts with another five bunched together favoring the status quo. There will also be one in the middle, who is the median voter.
   a. The median voter is the one for which half of the voters are on one side and half of the voters are on the other side.
   b. The undecided voter is the median voter because that voter has half of the voters on one side and half of the voters on the other.

   c. To achieve a majority of voters, a candidate would need to win over this median voter. In a two-candidate race, the median voter holds the keys to victory.

10. Rational ignorance means the voters do not stay fully informed on the issues or on the activities of their elected representatives. The less watchful are voters, the more freedom representatives have to follow personal agendas and do whatever they want.

12. If you can identify a local transportation project, such as a new expressway or mass transit system, it is likely that federal money is involved. Such money is sometimes termed pork. Elected officials frequently point to the money they have brought into their districts from Washington. Local voters tend to like that direction of money flow, rather than just always seeing tax money flowing out of their paychecks and into the federal coffers.

14. You would be following the Washington Monument strategy, using up your budget first on the least essential projects, so that if a budget crunch were to come along, you could point to the great need for additional money for your agency. One danger of always doing the least important jobs first is that the most important projects might not ever get done.

CHAPTER 12

2. The answer to those questions will depend upon the year and *the Economic Report of the President* for that year.

4. The four components of GDP are consumption, investment, government and net exports
   a. Investment is measured in gross terms. If it were measured net of depreciation, the result would be net domestic product rather than gross domestic product.
   b. The government component does not include transfer payments.
   c. Net exports has a negative value (which it has had for the past two decades).

6. The output of the underground economy consists of goods and services that are produced but not reported to government. The usual reason is to avoid taxation or because the activities are illegal. Because the output is not reported, it is not measured in GDP statistics.

8. The base period is the point of reference to which other time periods are compared. The index is set to 100 during the base period. Any particular value of the CPI can be compared to the base period by noting the difference between that value and the base period value of 100.

10. The inflation rate is computed as the change in the CPI divided by the starting CPI, which in this case is a CPI of 123 in year 5. The result of this division is then multiplied by 100 in order to arrive at the inflation rate. In this example, the calculation is 7 divided by 123, then multiplied by 100. The result is an inflation rate of approximately 5.7 percent.

12. Persons under age 16 are minors, discouraged from working because of the desire of society to have them finish

their education. Few of them work, so excluding them from the labor force does not impair the accuracy of the data. Adults over age 65 may or may not be retired, and so many of them will be working. Excluding them from the labor force data would result in inaccuracies.

14. This answer will vary from student to student.

16. Your graph should label the horizontal axis "time" and the vertical axis "real GDP." The curve that shows the business cycle looks like a roller coaster tilted upward. The rising part shows the expansion, the top point shows the peak, the downward-sloping part shows the recession, and the bottom point shows the trough. The upward tilt reflects the upward trend in real GDP.

CHAPTER 13

2. According to the Phillips curve, inflation and unemployment are inversely related. When you draw the Phillips curve, place "unemployment" on the horizontal axis and "inflation" on the vertical axis. Then draw a downward-sloping line that is inwardly bowed. The Phillips curve fit the data nicely in the 1960s. Since then, however, there has been no obvious Phillips curve.

4. Actual GDP and full-employment GDP are not equal unless the economy is at a full-employment equilibrium.

6. The natural rate of unemployment represents a long run tendency. Since there will always be workers switching jobs and since job switching often involves a period of unemployment, the long-run tendency includes some frictional unemployment. It also includes some seasonal unemployment and, since change is a constant in the economy, some structural unemployment as well. The exact unemployment rate toward which the economy tends will depend upon such factors as the age profile of the workforce and the degree to which the unemployed are protected by social safety net programs.

8. Long-run aggregate supply is a vertical line because full-employment output does not depend on the price level in the long run. So, whatever the price level might be, long-run aggregate supply shows where full-employment output lies, which is given by the horizontal intercept of the long-run aggregate supply curve. Long-run aggregate supply would shift to the right if full-employment output were to increase. That increase could occur in response to an increase in full employment or in the output full employment is able to produce.

10. Aggregate demand tells how much real GDP consumers, businesses, and others but will purchase at each price level. On the graph, the vertical axis should be labeled as the price level and the horizontal axis labeled as real GDP. The aggregate demand curve slopes downward in response to the purchasing power effect and the wealth effect. (Some other textbooks also explain the slope of aggregate demand with an "international substitution effect" in which changes in countries' relative price levels

affect net exports and investment. Ayers and Collinge do not include this term because the international substitution effect is countered by changes in exchange rates, which adjust to maintain a zero balance in each country's balance of payments accounts.)

12. On a graph with the price level on the vertical axis and real GDP on the horizontal axis, the aggregate demand curve is drawn with a downward slope and the long-run aggregate supply curve is drawn as a vertical line at full-employment GDP. An economy with unemployment would be producing a point on aggregate demand to the left of long-run aggregate supply. The model explains unemployment as being caused by the price level failing to adjust to equilibrium, such as in response to sticky wages and prices. In the long run, the price level falls until the full-employment equilibrium is reached.

14. The student should draw two separate graphs, each with the vertical axis labeled as the price level and the horizontal axis labeled as real GDP. On both graphs, the student should draw an initial aggregate demand curve that is downwardly sloping and an initial long-run aggregate supply curve that is vertical. On the graph showing demand-side inflation, another aggregate demand curve should be drawn to the right of the first one. The student should indicate that the economy moves up the long-run aggregate supply curve to a new equilibrium at a higher price level and the same output. On the graph showing supply-side inflation, a second long-run aggregate supply curve should be drawn to the left of the first one. The student should indicate that the economy moves up the aggregate demand curve to a new equilibrium at a higher price level and a lower output. Both demand-side inflation and supply-side inflation could occur simultaneously, but the causes would be different.

16. Political liberals are more likely to take Keynesian positions on the economy, because liberals favor government action and Keynesian economics provides support for government to take action to solve economic problems in the short run. For example, Keynesian multiplier analysis yields the result that additional government spending would shift aggregate demand to the right, even if the spending were financed by additional taxes.

CHAPTER 14

2. Once the inefficiencies of barter become apparent we might expect that people will spontaneously decide to adopt some commodity as money. The more people on the island, the more likely the limitations of barter will be obvious because there will be more opportunities for exchange that would be facilitated by money. Barter might work for a group that expects to soon be rescued, but if they expect to remain on the island for a long time, money is likely to be adopted sooner. What form the money will take will depend on what is available. For example, if

coconuts grow on the island, they might be used as money.

4. A bank's loans are one of its assets since they are something of value that the bank owns. Namely, the bank owns the right to receive a stream of repayments (with interest) from borrowers who took out the loans. Note that while loans are an asset to a bank, discount loans are a liability. That is because the discount loans are funds borrowed by the bank from the Fed, which the bank must repay to the Fed.

6. Three significant liabilities for banks include its deposits, its discount loans, and its federal funds. These are sources of funds for banks. The deposits come from its customers, the discounts loans come from the Fed, and federal funds come from other banks.

8. The Board of Governors oversees the operations of the Fed. The Federal Open Market Committee (FOMC) conducts monetary policy. The twelve district banks, scattered across the country, operate as banker's banks, providing services to commercial banks.

10. The deposit multiplier equals 1/reserve requirement. With a 25 percent reserve requirement the deposit multiplier would be computed as: 1/0.25, which equals 4.

12. The equation of exchange is: $M \times V = P \times Q$, where M is the quantity of money, V is its velocity, P is the price level, and Q is aggregate output. The left side of the equation represents total spending while the right is nominal GDP, which are the same thing.

14. Monetarism is a school of thought associated with economist Milton Friedman. Its foundation is the quantity theory of money, which is expressed through the equation of exchange: $M \times V = P \times Q$. A monetary policy that follows monetarism will expand the money supply at a steady rate of about 2 to 3 percent a year. This recommendation follows from the idea that the economy will, over the long run, show an increase in aggregate output of 2 to 3 percent a year, and so the money supply should grow to match the increased output.

16. The federal funds rate is the interest rate on reserves that banks borrow from other banks. The Fed targets the federal funds rate primarily by conducting open market operations that affect the federal funds rate. A lower federal funds rate is associated with a looser monetary policy, while a higher rate is associated with a tighter policy.

CHAPTER 15

2. Label the horizontal axis as "real GDP" and the vertical axis as the "price level". Draw a vertical long-run aggregate supply curve at full-employment GDP. Draw a short-run aggregate supply curve that curves upward across long-run aggregate supply and then becomes nearly vertical just past long-run aggregate supply. Draw a downwardly sloping aggregate demand curve that intersects the short-run aggregate supply curve prior to it intersecting the long-run aggregate supply curve. The intersection of

aggregate demand and short-run aggregate supply is the unemployment equilibrium. An expansionary fiscal policy that shifts aggregate demand to the right can potentially eliminate the unemployment equilibrium. The unemployment equilibrium would be gone if aggregate demand were to intersect short-run aggregate supply at the same point short-run aggregate supply intersects long-run aggregate supply.

4. The three fiscal policy lags are the recognition lag, the action lag, and the implementation lag. The recognition lag is the time it takes for policymakers to recognize that the problem exists. The action lag is the amount of time it takes them to actually make a policy to address the problem. The implementation lag is the time it takes for the policy to be implemented, such as actually hiring the workers and beginning the project.

6. When the economy is at full employment, there is no reason for fiscal policy to be either expansionary or contractionary. For this reason, Keynesian economists suggest that the full-employment budget be balanced.

8. The national debt is the sum of the federal government's past budget deficits and surpluses. The result is a debt because the deficits have far exceeded the surpluses. This debt is mostly owed to the American public.

10. Your pie chart showing sources of revenue for state and local governments should emphasize property taxes, sales taxes, and revenue sharing from the federal government. Many other taxes and charges are also used.

12. The average tax rate is simply the amount paid in taxes divided by the amount earned. In Sue's case, her average tax rate equals $10,000 divided by $100,000, which is 10 percent.

14. The answer is a matter of opinion, but should be based on an understanding of the principles involved. The student should be familiar with the definition of the benefit principle, which is to tax according to the benefits received. Likewise, the student should know the definition of the ability-to-pay principle, which is that those who have a greater ability to pay taxes should in fact be made to pay more taxes.

16. A tax on football tickets would seem to satisfy the benefit principle of taxation, since those who go to football games benefit from the student athletics program. By associating the price of the program with the price of tickets, it might also promote efficient choice. Taxing football tickets would only be progressive, however, if college football attendance increased more than in proportion to increases in income. Taxing textbooks or vending machine drinks would not appear to satisfy any principle of tax equity, although such taxes might be relatively efficient in that they would be hard to escape. While taxing textbooks might be the hardest tax for a student to escape, taxing textbooks is also the most likely to be regressive, particularly if the tax is not covered by financial aid.

18. A payroll tax is a tax on paychecks received by workers for the jobs they do. In contrast, an income tax is levied on all

income, although there are likely to be deductions allowed.

CHAPTER 16

2. When a recession first hits, firms reduce the production of goods, but are slow to lay off workers. The reason is that there are costs associated with layoffs and with rehiring workers when the economy improves. Many firms would prefer to retain their workers until it becomes clear that it is not economic to do so. As a result, with the reduction in output greater than the reduction in labor, output per worker falls. This effect is reversed when the economy begins to improve. Firms will be slow to increase their use of labor until they are sure that the economic rebound will continue. Output rises more than proportionally to the use of labor, and so labor productivity rises.

4. a. When Microsoft was started, the success of the firm would have required capital formation in computers and other office equipment.
   b. When Wal-Mart was started, store buildings, fixtures, and merchandise were examples of the capital formation that occurred.
   c. The start of Starbucks required store space, display cases, and office machines.
   d. When Motown Records started, various pieces of recording equipment, billing equipment, and office equipment would have been needed.

6. The supply of saving slopes upward because its slope represents a positive relationship between the quantity saved and the real interest rate. People save more when they get paid more to do so. Likewise, businesses invest more when it costs them less to obtain loans. For this reason, investment demand shows an inverse relationship between the real interest rate and the amount invested. When the quantity of saving supplied just equals the quantity of investment demanded, this market is at equilibrium.

8. You should label the horizontal axis of your graph as "saving and investment." The vertical axis should be labeled as the "real interest rate." Draw a downward-sloping demand curve and an upward-sloping supply curve. The point of intersection is the initial equilibrium. To show an increase in investment demand, draw a second demand curve that's further out than the first. The new equilibrium will then occur at a higher real interest rate and a greater amount of saving and investment. If the supply of saving were to also shift to the right, it could potentially lower the real interest rate back to what it was originally, or even to below what it was originally.

10. You should label the horizontal axis of your graph as "saving and investment." The vertical axis should be labeled as the "real interest rate." Draw a downward-sloping demand curve and an upward-sloping supply curve. The point of intersection is the initial equilibrium. To show the effect of taxing interest on saving, draw a second supply curve that is above and to the left of the first one. The supply curve has shifted because consumers now require a higher interest rate prior to the tax in order to pay the tax due on that interest. Observe that the equilibrium real interest rate has risen as a result of the tax, causing the equilibrium quantity of saving and investment to fall.

12. During the war, the economy reduced the production of civilian goods in favor of war goods. There were relatively few consumer goods available to purchase. At the same time, employment was high, as were incomes, as war production reduced unemployment. The combination of high incomes and few items to purchase led people to save more. Unless the war on terrorism results in shortages of consumer goods, an increase in the saving rate is unlikely.

14. Both focus on the causes of economic growth, but with different emphases. New growth theory emphasizes the role of technology in promoting growth, while supply-side economics emphasizes lower tax rates and less government regulation as the keys to growth. New growth theory also recognizes that technological improvements are encouraged when property rights (in the form of monopoly power) are granted to developers of new technologies.

16. The Laffer curve shows the dangers of setting tax rates too high. It might be the case that a tax would bring in more revenue if its rate were lower. For example, some argue that reductions in the capital gains tax rate might increase revenue from that tax. To graph this case, place the capital gains tax rate on the horizontal axis and note that it can go from zero to 100 percent. Place the amount of revenue collected on the vertical axis. Your curve should be hump-shaped, starting at zero on the horizontal axis, and then rising to a maximum, before falling back to zero when you reach 100 percent on the horizontal axis. The argument that reducing the capital gains tax rate would lead to more revenue from the tax is equivalent to saying that we are on the downward-sloping portion of that Laffer curve.

CHAPTER 17

2. For the United States to run a trade deficit means that it imports more goods than it exports, where goods are measured in dollars according to their market values. The trade deficit is more limited than the current account deficit, which includes the value of not only goods, but also of services, incomes, and transfers.

4. If Middle Eastern investors decide to sell their U.S. investments and use the proceeds to buy investments in other countries, they would be acquiring dollars from their sales that they would wish to convert to the currencies of other countries so that they could buy assets in those countries. Supposing these other countries are Middle Eastern countries, then the dollar would depreciate relative to the Middle Eastern currencies. Those Middle Easterners who did not sell their American assets would find that the value of those assets in terms of the Middle Eastern currencies would be less after the depreciation of the dollar.

6. Depreciation of a currency occurs when there is less demand for it by holders of other currencies or when the holders of the currency increase the amount they offer for sale in exchange for other currencies. In terms of a supply and demand graph—measuring the quantity of the currency on the horizontal axis and the price of that currency in terms of other currencies on the vertical axis—depreciation would occur if demand were to shift to the left or supply were to shift to the right. If the currency depreciates, it will buy less in terms of foreign goods and services, which causes the quantity of goods and services imported to decrease. Likewise, goods and services that are priced in the country's currency will seem cheaper to holders of other countries' currencies. For this reason, exports would increase.

8. The World Trade Organization administers the GATT.

10. A tariff can be viewed as a price support for domestic producers because it increases the price that consumers would have to pay for imports of the good. Because domestic producers are in competition with foreign producers, the higher price for imports means the domestic producers can also charge a higher price.

12. Producers in exporting countries would like to charge as high of a price as possible, which leads them to prefer the voluntary export restraint that is simultaneously agreed to by many different exporting countries. Otherwise, these exporting countries would be in competition with one another and would drive the price of their exports lower.

14. Students' answers will differ. The student might point out environmental dangers, such as that the tomatoes pose the risk of bringing in a tomato-plant disease. Alternatively, the argument might be that the foreign tomato workers are mistreated or underpaid. Another argument might revolve around compassion for domestic tomato pickers who are thrown out of work. Just because an argument might be made, however, does not mean that it would be convincing.

16. The term "level playing field" is hard to pin down. If it is defined to mean that all producers in all countries must pay the same for all inputs, then there would be no comparative advantage and no basis for trade at all. If it is applied to only labor inputs, it would greatly reduce trade and the gains from trade, including gains to low-paid foreign workers whose opportunity costs involve even lower-paying jobs. It could also be critiqued as foreign meddling in a country's internal affairs.

PHOTO CREDITS